# ESOTERIC ASTROLOGY FOR THE NEW AGE

VOLUME 1

**THE ESOTERIC FOUNDATIONS**

BODO BALSYS

UNIVERSAL DHARMA
PUBLICATIONS
SYDNEY, AUSTRALIA

ISBN 978-0-6487877-3-0



Revised 2026



Cover image and front page image: Aries Tablet of Revelation, watercolour by the author.

## Dedication

Thanks to my students, past, present and future, and in particular to those that have helped in the production of this book.

Oṁ

Obeisance to the Gurus!
To the Buddhas of the three times.
To the Council of Bodhisattvas, *mahāsattvas*.
To them I pledge allegiance.

Oṁ Hūṁ! Hūṁ! Hūṁ!

# Contents


Preface ix

1. The Rays, their Source and Purpose 1
   - Cosmic considerations re the Rays 2
   - Three major energy sources 11
   - The evolutionary journeying 14

2. The Planetary Regents 21
   - The planetary Regents generally considered 21
   - The planetary Regents and the Rāja Lords 23
   - The seven Rays exoterically and esoterically understood 28
   - The planets and the interrelated fixed and mutable crosses 48
   - The effect of first Ray energy 52

3a. The Nature of the Constellations to Scorpio 59
   - Aries the ram 59
   - Taurus the bull 65
   - Gemini the twins 72
   - The spring season 78
   - The mutable cross 78
   - Cancer the crab 80
   - Leo the lion 85
   - Virgo the virgin 92
   - The summer season 99
   - Libra the balance 99

3b. From Scorpio to Pisces 111
   - Scorpio the scorpion 111
   - The tests in Scorpio 118
   - Sagittarius the archer 145
   - The autumn and winter seasons 155
   - Capricorn the goat 156
   - Aquarius the water bearer 165
   - Pisces the fishes 173
   - Pisces and the *eighth sphere* 181

4. The Esoteric Interpretation of a Natal Chart 189
   - General notes related to horoscope interpretation 189
   - The Moon, sun sign and the ascendant 192
   - The Houses in general and their keywords 197
   - The aspects 205
   - The Houses 206

5. History of the Zodiac 233
- The early zodiac 237
- Individualisation 239
- The Lemurian epoch proper 242
- The Tau cross 246
- The movement around the ten-signed zodiac 249
- The Atlantean epoch 256
- The 'strictly human' signs in the zodiac 260
- The zodiac during the Atlantean epoch proper 265
- The downward pointed pentagram 275
- The upward pointed pentad 282
- The ten-signed zodiac of the future 287
- The inverted pentad 292
- The upright pentagram 297

6. Further implications of the future Zodiac 303
- The Hierarchical ten-signed zodiac 307
- The hands and tridents of the Hierarchical zodiac 311
- The Shambhalic zodiac 315

7. The nature of the twelve Creative Hierarchies 324
- General considerations 324
- The five liberated Creative Hierarchies 329
- Numerical interrelationships 334
- The cosmic triangle 343
- Further numerological implications 346
- The glyphs of the liberated Creative Hierarchies 352
- The Womb of *saṃsāra* 371

8. The Tablets of Revelation 375

Appendix 447
- The four spiritual festivals and their seven Ray subdivisions 447
- The Festival of the Arising and the Living Christ 448
- The Wesak festival 450
- The festival of the New Age Temple – of Good Will 453
- The Festival of the Great Mother 456

Bibliography 461

Index 463

About the Author 472

# Figures

Figure 1. The evolutionary spiral 15
Figure 2. Manifestation of the Rays astrologically considered 16
Figure 3. A planetary Chain 22
Figure 4. Varuna's trident 25
Figure 5. The ankh - its higher attributes 49
Figure 6. Aries the ram 60
Figure 7. Aries further exemplified 60
Figure 8. The Taurus glyph 67
Figure 9. The glyph for Gemini 73
Figure 10. The claws of the crab 83
Figure 11. The Virgo glyph 95
Figure 12. Directions in the zodiac 105
Figure 13. Sagittarian points of tension 151
Figure 14. The Aquarius glyph 166
Figure 15. The Pisces glyph 174
Figure 16. The Root Races 234
Figure 17. The eight-signed zodiac 238
Figure 18. The Lemurian eight-armed cross 239
Figure 19. The ten-signed zodiac 244
Figure 20. The upright pentad 245
Figure 21. The inverted pentad 245
Figure 22. The Tau crosses 247
Figure 23. The star of humanity 264
Figure 24. The Atlantean ten-signed zodiac 267
Figure 25. The Atlantean Solar Plexus centre 268
Figure 26. The inverted pentagram 276
Figure 27. The upright pentad 283
Figure 28. The zodiac as it will be seen in the Aquarian age 288
Figure 29. The inverted pentagram 293
Figure 30. The upright pentagram 297
Figure 31. The spiral-cycle of Hierarchical attainment 299
Figure 32. The *maṇipūra chakra* and the *siddhis* 306
Figure 33. The Hierarchical zodiac 308
Figure 34. The Shambhalic zodiac for the New Age 321
Figure 35. Pisces and the Creative Hierarchies 330
Figure 36. The Creative Hierarchies as triads 335
Figure 37. The second Creative Hierarchy 355
Figure 38. The third Creative Hierarchy 356
Figure 39. The fourth Creative Hierarchy 358

Figure 40. The geometry of a Seat of Power 359
Figure 41. The glyph for Cancer 362
Figure 42. The Logoic hexagram 363
Figure 43. The Ram's horns 380
Figure 44. The septenary of manifestation 385
Figure 45. Taurus as a cosmic Egg 386
Figure 46. Aquarius and Thusness 438

# Tables

Table 1. The alternating principles 19
Table 2. The Rāja Lords and the planes 27
Table 3. The exoteric and esoteric planetary rulers 47
Table 4. The transformed attributes of the Hydra 144
Table 5. The planes and the kingdoms of Nature 188
Table 6. The influences of the non-sacred planets 204
Table 7. The five liberated Creative Hierarchies 327
Table 8. The seven manifest Creative Hierarchies 329

# Plates

Plate 1. Aries 376
Plate 2. Taurus 382
Plate 3. Gemini 390
Plate 4. Cancer 398
Plate 5. Leo 405
Plate 6. Virgo 412
Plate 7. Libra 416
Plate 8. Scorpio 421
Plate 9. Sagittarius 427
Plate 10. Capricorn 432
Plate 11. Aquarius 437
Plate 12. Pisces 442

# Preface

The information in these volumes is based upon D.K.'s[1] *Esoteric Astrology* and *A Treatise on Cosmic Fire,* and extends his work with additional esoteric information. This is in line with what I have already published in my former books. Those that are familiar with my writings will comprehend the significance of this statement. New readers should acquaint themselves with some of this information, especially with what is contained in *The Constitution of Shambhala.*

There is a vast amount of esoteric information to further present to the world's disciples. In the field of astrology this is especially needed. Some of the information of the subject of *Cosmological Astrology* (introduced in volume two) may be beyond the ken of the average reader to independently verify. The use of impeccable esoteric logic (the foundation of which is presented in my former books), the intuition, and appropriate meditation is needed. The esoteric axiom: 'as above, so below, that which is within is also without' can also be utilised to help comprehension.

There are many passages in D.K's books that are veiled, only hinted at, or come in the form of an Old Commentary. Part of the purpose of my writings is to unveil as much as is possible of what D.K. chose to hide at his time, that he could not then reveal because of esoteric verities, or that the time for revelation had not yet come. Similarly, the revelations of the Buddhist philosophy in my books dedicated to this study unveil aspects of their philosophy long veiled or hidden in the terminology used by the enlightened ones from the past.

This is the time for the revelation of many esoteric mysteries via the expression of the green Ray of Mathematically Exact Activity, as governed by the Mother

1 His books are penned via his amanuensis, Alice Bailey.

of the World. It is Her epoch (under the guise of the fifth Kumāra) that is now to herald. Volume two will reveal (along with presenting a cosmological vision) much more concerning the nature of this Kumāra than was formerly provided in *The Constitution of Shambhala.* The way of development of cosmic Mind (Mahat) is now the fare for the world's disciples to digest, and the green Ray is the means for its expression. Esoteric astrology is the esoteric science par excellence, and its revelation lies on the tide of this Ray's expression. The first, second, seventh and fourth Rays assist in the revelation, whist the fifth Ray becomes the exoteric veil of expression. For some very high Initiates, the Fires of Mind burn crimson-green, tempered by the indigo blue. For them astrological knowledge is the lore of the universe, and this astrology governs the manifestation of cosmic Law.

The Initiates of the world that are gaining inner perceptions (via re-awakening past life attainments in this era that heralds the New Age) must become knowledgeable of this science. It is not possible to attain the higher Initiations without such awareness.

The evolution of humanity is a progression, and so also the evolutionary attainment of Hierarchy. Hierarchy must move with the times and offer disciples more advanced esoteric lore, and their higher scientific verities, than was possible before. My book *Esoteric Cosmology and Modern Physics,* plus these astrological volumes (backed by the abovementioned books of D.K.), are the foundation for many revelations to come. This progression is the Plan of the lodge of Masters, allowing all of their disciples to move forwards into the new Aquarian Age, once they catch up with the agenda presented for their further education and benefit. All of humanity can then also be taught the meaning of the higher way. The old religious dispensations, plus the world's occult philosophies, must make way for the new world religion, which is now forthcoming.

# 1

# The Rays, their Source and Purpose

The Rays are the ever-present streams of energy emanating from sources outside of our solar system that are causative of all observable phenomena. They condition all that can be known by means of consciousness. The physical eyes see the rays of sunlight, but their subjective correspondences, the Rays of Life, are viewed by means of the awakened inner Eyes *(chakras)* that see. The streams of light manifest via different frequencies or octaves of expression. They can be viewed in physiological terms, or else in terms of their effects, as seen in the manifold patterns and arrangements of all that is. The Rays are the energies that need to be appropriated, interblended and redirected by all causative agents, if these agents are to produce their purpose. After all, it is a fundamental postulate of modern science that energy is all that is, and that energy and matter are but expressions of each other. The Rays concern the way energy interrelates with consciousness: of the way consciousness views energy and works with it to produce activities in the phenomenal realms. Consciousness can be viewed in terms of what a human or angelic kingdom have developed and beyond, right through to the greatest cosmic Logos, within whose Body of manifestation, or Mind, all are a part of and play their respective roles.

As far as our 'corner' of the universe is concerned, the Rays have their ultimate source as the primary energy dispensation of certain galactic groups, and are herded by various constellations of stars. Stars, etc., are thus composed of many sheaths of increasingly subtle substance that are animated by an incarnating Being termed a Logos, an embodied Word. We must look to the stars, constellations and galaxies as the outer sheaths or bodies of manifestation of Logoi (similar to the relation between a human's physical form and their incarnating Soul). The Logoic Word is an emanating mantric Sound that appropriates substance and energy to itself, according to the quality of the associated energy field. Sound and the colours of the Rays and sub-Ray hues are interchangeable. All is imbued into the form by means of the originating Thought, the Creative Impulse of the Logos. The quality of the energy field is viewed by those with Eyes to See as auric fields composed of Rays of Light. These Rays are the substance of what was drawn together by the Logos to manifest His/Her Purpose. This Purpose is to provide the evolutionary milieu of an entire solar or cosmic form. The science of esoteric astrology concerns the impact of this Purpose upon our tiny earth and the solar system within which it is a part.

## Cosmic considerations re the Rays

The seven Rays that affect our solar system are said to emanate from the seven Rishis of the Great Bear (Ursa Major). This and all other constellations are but part of the Body of manifestation of the *One about Whom Naught may be Said.* (THAT Logos – who embodies the 88 constellations visible in the night sky, plus those that are invisible.)[1] When it is said that 'naught' can be said, the reference is to the cypher *zero* and its qualities (as explained in my book *Esoteric Cosmology and Modern Physics*). Naught can be known about this Entity as to His Purpose, for the greatest known enlightened Being resides within the Body of Manifestation of That Being. One can, however, know directly of the nature of the Consciousness

1 Concerning this Entity, D.K. states that it is: "The Life which expresses Itself through seven solar systems. The One About Whom Naught May Be Said." Alice Bailey, *Esoteric Psychology I*, (Lucis Publishing Co., N.Y., 1977), 99. I extend this concept to include the visible stars in the night sky. D.K. further states elsewhere that: 'In parentheses, it is well to note that this Existence is termed "the One about Whom naught may be said", not because of secrecy or mystery, but because all formulation of ideas about His life and purpose are impossible until one has completed the term of evolution in our solar system. Note, I say, our solar system, not just our planetary existence. Speculation about the Existence who, through His life, informs seven solar systems is wasted energy. On our planet, only such great lives as the Buddha, the Kumaras and the planetary Logos, are beginning to sense the dynamic impulse of the greater Whole, and even they are only sensitive to it but are, as yet, utterly unable to conceive of its trend, for it lies beyond mind and love and will." Alice Bailey, *A Treatise on White Magic*, (Lucis Publishing Co., N.Y., 1991), 275.

of some of the Logoi evolving therein, with whom there might be some direct affiliation. Much can thus be said as to what transpires *within* That Body, and such Revelation is the basis of what will be revealed to humanity gradually as the New Era unfolds. As the Kingdom of 'God' (Shambhala) becomes increasingly externalised, so more esoteric Knowledge concerning cosmic verities will become a certainty. One can extrapolate as to what may transpire outside of That Body through the law of analogy, but this is conjecture, as one cannot truly Know. Such enlightened awareness can only be known by Initiates and cannot be comprehended by those that do not have their Eye awakened, hence 'naught can be said'.

All constellations can be viewed as various *chakras* and other organs within the Body of THAT Logos. Various Prāṇas (Ray energies) become integrated therein as the Fiery energy constituting the cosmic lower mental plane. These Fires are appropriated by the Seven Rishis, who function as the Throat centre of THAT Logos. The purpose of this centre is to receive, to process and to channel this Mahatic Fire.[2]

Space is thereby criss-crossed by thousands of lines of energy, the *nāḍīs* that interrelate the petals of the various flowers constituting the Logoic *chakras*. There are other factors to be taken into account when considering the organisation of stars within a constellation. The chief of these factors is the fact that a constellation normally represents the externalisation of a Ray Ashram and its sub-Rays. Orion, for instance, is a Heart centre in the night sky. There you can see four main stars that are the externalised ventricles of a Heart. When the three major stars of His belt are added, a septenary of stars is formed. Other stars will embody the functions of various petal groupings of this *chakra*.

By manifesting as the Throat centre of THAT Logos, the Seven Rishis (and their accompanying stars) project the Causative forces (Mahat) that direct the various Logoi ensconced upon the cosmic astral plane. (These projected Logoic Thoughts ultimately cause effects upon the cosmic dense physical plane). For those ensconced in cosmic dense physical space, these Fires demonstrate as the awesome Logoic Will. They are the Commands, forces that direct all movements in space. The Seven Rishis are thus the primordial sources or prototypes of the first Ray aspects of all the Rays.

*Sirius* is said by D.K. to be the source of the energies of Love and Wisdom to our solar system.[3] The reason for this is that Sirius (and the constellation of Canis

---

2 This energy of Logoic empirical Mind is termed Mahat.

3 See, for instance, Alice Bailey, *Esoteric Astrology,* (Lucis Publishing Co., N.Y. 1982), 416, where D.K. states that the: 'energies coming from the Sun, Sirius, are related to the love-

Major) stands as the Solar Plexus centre of THAT Logos. The Solar Plexus is the centre of the personality will (the seat of the mental-emotions) and is also the synthesising centre for the minor centres. This centre manifests as the abdominal brain. At the present level of cosmic Logoic development, the qualities principally channelled can be equated with Desire or Emotional-Mind. When expressed into systemic space (as experienced by those on earth), Logoic Desire becomes:

1. Mahat (cosmic Mind) –via the plane *ātma*.
2. Love – via the plane *anupādaka*.

The reified integration of these two energies is experienced as Love-Wisdom by human units. The Pleiades wield Mahat in its Creative function, hence they are the embodiments of the seven sub-Ray attributes of this primal Fiery energy. They express Logoic Active Intelligence. Our solar Logos is attuned to the harmonies of the Love attribute from the cosmic Kāma-Manas (Logoic Desire-Mind).

D.K. states:

> *Sirius is the source of logoic manas* in the same sense as the Pleiades are connected with the evolution of mind in the seven Heavenly Men, and Venus is responsible for the coming of mind in the Earth chain.[4]

'Logoic *manas'* is an inappropriate term for the energy directed from Sirius, as in reality it is Mind that wields or conditions the substance of the cosmic Waters (the cosmic astral plane). The combination of the two (Mahat and Love) impact upon the environment of our solar system. Consequently, the impact is upon all that exists on our earth sphere. This quality is then best described as Logoic Kāma-Manas, but because of the exalted status of the Logos concerned, the Kāma (Desire) becomes the highest qualified Love to us. It is the Logoic Desire to cause all Lives in the solar *mahāmanvantara* to move along an evolutionary progression to their ultimate liberation from the thrall of substance. This Desire is a magnetic pull of the all towards a cosmic destination. Logoic Wisdom that evolved through countless aeons of evolutionary striving is then applied to see that the Plan comes to fruition. Love-Wisdom therefore is the overriding energy of this Logoic effort, as experienced by us. Love is an attractive energy that the

---

wisdom aspect or to the attractive power of the solar logos, to the soul of that Great Being'. (Henceforth the title of this book shall be abbreviated E.A.)

4 Alice Bailey, *A Treatise on Cosmic Fire* (Lucis Publishing Co., N.Y. 1967), 347. (Henceforth this title shall be abbreviated T.C.F.)

Logos utilises to drive all beings forward towards a greater cosmic centre (of which our solar Logos is but a minor part).

The Pleiades are focussed on Manas as part of Logoic Purpose. They are Creative agents that build the forms within cosmic dense physical space wherein the Love principle can develop and evolve the capacity to respond to the overtures of Logoic Love-Desire. The Pleiades condition planetary evolution so that Life evolves according to the right cyclic rhythm of the Whole. Venus (closely associated with the Pleiades) embodies the focussed attributes of these Creative Potencies. They are integrated by Sirian Love to produce a harmony with the Lives (Souls) on our planet, facilitating the overriding Purpose of the solar Logos. Venus wields Logoic Manas, coupled with an appropriate quantity of the energy of Love, to produce the right changes in the field of consciousness.

As the Solar Plexus centre of THAT Logos, the importance of Sirius in the cosmic landscape can be deduced. Sirius directs Logoic *Manas* to condition the Cosmic Waters, thus influencing the average Logos (as is our solar Logos), which is polarised in the cosmic astral plane. In a similar way, present humanity are polarised in the systemic astral plane. Other constellations that share the qualities of the petals of the Solar Plexus centre of THAT Logos are Lepus the Hare, and Columba the Dove. (They are also associated with the *piṅgalā nāḍī* stream.)

Within the 'Belly' of the cosmic Dog (the constellation Canis Major) lie seven galaxies. They could be considered Sources, or prototypes of the seven Rays that govern cosmic astral space. These galaxies also assimilate energies streaming from a grouping of twelve galaxies surrounding the Solar Plexus centre. These are absorbing centres for zodiacal potencies coming from other galaxies associated with this cosmic astral level. Canis Major absorbs the sum of these Potencies,[5] as well as those streaming from Orion the hunter (which stands as a cosmic Heart centre). Within Orion, the Belt of the Hunter manifests as a Solar Plexus centre and the dual Splenic centre. Much concerning cosmic vitalisation emanates from this Belt, hence the three major Pyramids in the Giza plateau are the earthly representatives of these stars, thereby being energised by them.[6] The associated nebulae veil the cosmic *eighth sphere*.[7]

---

5 Other constellations and stars, such as Canopus (a major second Ray Source in the Heavens), also play their part.

6 This relationship was aptly explained in Robert Bauval and Adrian Gilbert's book *The Orion Mystery* (Heinemann, London, 1994).

7 As usual, it is not my intention to simply repeat some of the vast amount of information

Note that when such things as 'Dogs' or other animals or objects are mentioned cosmically, these great Logoi that are referred to have long passed the human stage of evolution. They now exist many orders of magnitude higher (of transcendent levels of transmuted correspondence) than most can conceive of. Consequently, they are seen at the cosmic stage of evolution as an animal, e.g., 'Dog', with respect to others near their respective Reality level. They are therefore still evolving to the next stage for them, to be a cosmic 'Human'. Thus, they are gathering the experiences needed to Individualise at Their exalted level. Our solar Logos, for instance, would be quite a diminutive Entity compared to such a Being. All Lives evolve together, spiralling within spirals of increasingly vaster universal atoms of evolutionary Being. The smaller is seen in the greater and the greater is seen in the smaller. There is much esoteric wisdom hidden in the mythological lore associated with the night sky, given originally by Hierarchy to the incarnated Initiates that could See. Later, such lore for the southern sky was also seeded into the minds of the European explorers who had been ordained to map the night sky.

Orion the Hunter faces the constellation Taurus the bull, whose famed 0.9 magnitude star, Aldebaran, stands as the third Eye, the organ of direction. This Eye helps channel energies from the seven Rishis to Sirius and the Pleiades. The seven Sisters are the 'Wives', or feminine polarity, to the Rishis of the Great Bear. The Pleiades demonstrate the qualities of a Sacral centre, which is naturally aligned to the Throat centre (the Rishis).

The Sacral centre is responsible for the distribution of the major *prāṇas* vitalising the form and the petals of the seven major *chakras*. It stands as the physical sun. Its main focus is consequently upon the *nāḍīs* that exist in the ethers. For our planet, these ethers are the four higher systemic planes: *ādi, anupādaka, ātma* and *buddhi*. For this reason the Pleiades are of paramount importance to all beings still confined to the sub-planes of the cosmic dense physical. Therein we find our evolutionary journeying. Via these planes causation occurs, precipitating effects upon the physical plane. Causation is literally a *Sacral centre* activity.

The Rays condition the substance of manifest space via the agency of the twelve Creative Hierarchies, who form the Womb of time and space. This Womb takes

---

given by the Master D.K. in his monumental *Treatise on the Seven Rays,* but rather, to extend what has been given. Therefore, considerably more cosmological information shall be provided in my books than was possible for D.K. to reveal at his time. See chapter 3b and elsewhere for a detailed discussion of the eighth sphere--of containment of dark *prāṇas* and associated entities.

the form of the twelve signs of the zodiac, which manifest as a reversed wheel for those conditioned by formed space. The twelve Creative Hierarchies are thus the agents for the conveyance of the signs of the zodiac into manifestation. There are five liberated and seven non-liberated Hierarchies.[8] The four Creative Hierarchies that embody cosmic etheric space, and the five liberated ones upon the cosmic astral plane, empower the symbolic nine months of the gestation period for the forms embodied in cosmic dense physical space. (Our mental, astral and dense physical planes.)

Those that periodically incarnate into that space (humanity) manifest as the foetal child within the Womb. The *deva* substance of the forms they take when incarnating is being developed and transformed so that all will eventually be freed from that Womb. The *devas* and human kingdoms thus together form the Christ-Child. They manifest a symbiotic interrelationship, for this entire process concerns the eventual marriage between the *deva* and human kingdoms. There is a betrothal at the second Initiation, a marriage at the fourth Initiation and complete consummation at the sixth. The Chohans (sixth degree Initiates) that thus evolve can then freely travel out of the Womb and into cosmic space as *nirvāṇees*. The 'Womb' here incorporates nine 'planes' that must be mastered in order to escape into cosmic space. These are the dense physical, the etheric domain, the astral plane, the higher and lower mental planes, *buddhi,* the higher and lower *ātmic* plane, and *anupādaka* whereon the Chohan exists, from which he leaves the planetary domain through the gates in Shambhala.

Three Creative Hierarchies constitute the Lives embodied as the substance of the three worlds of human evolution (ruled by Sagittarius, Capricorn and Aquarius)[9]. They encompass what must be transformed and liberated in the process. Capricorn signifies the concretion of Mind that produces the manifestation of form. Sagittarius projects the thought-forms, causing the crystallisation of substance. Aquarius then represents the ocean of sensation and the forms of activity that eventually produce the development of consciousness. Humanity are the bearers of that consciousness, becoming the crucible for transformation, transfiguration and transmutation of the imprisoned substance. Once human consciousness has been developed, Capricorn then represents the mount of materialism governed

---

8 They will be explained in a later chapter. Foundational information can also be found in the first two volumes of my book *The Astrological and Numerological Keys to the Secret Doctrine,* and in Alice Bailey's *Esoteric Astrology.*

9 They are 'the Crocodiles' (Makara), the 'Lunar Lords' and 'the Elemental Lives'

by mind. Consciousness must climb and master this mountain if the mind is to be converted into its enlightened correspondence (Mind). Sagittarius governs the driving will that allows mastery over selfish ambition in the material domain, whilst Aquarius signifies the freedom gained by consciousness at the top of the mount. Sagittarius the archer embodies the will to shoot arrows of aspiration through the Gates of Shambhala. Capricorn embodies the Initiation process that allows the candidate to master the mountain of substance, and Aquarius signifies the freedom to travel the Waters of cosmic astral space.

In this brief resume of some of the cosmic Sources of the Rays and the work of the Creative Hierarchies, it should be understood that one is considering energies that are within a Master's ken, and which must be directed into the worlds of form. The Master acts as a mediator between great cosmic Beings (Whose energies must be toned down before the Master can use them) and humanity. In a similar sense, the potencies from the Master must be toned down before the disciple can receive them. Everything must be viewed in terms of relativity. It should be noted that when dealing with such esoteric matters, the language used fails to do justice to the subject at hand.

A solar or planetary Logos would observe Ray sources from a far different perspective than the way that we (who are presently entombed upon our little globe) do. For them, the Rays would take on a transmogrified aspect (in contradistinction with that seen from our perspective). Nevertheless, the Rays always persist at higher or lower levels of correspondence for all that exists. Therefore, to truly understand the nature of Being (the ordering and patterning of the sum of all that is, and of the forces needing to be appropriated by all Causative agents), then a consideration of the seven Ray qualities is essential. Everything comes into existence as an emanation of the one primordial Ray, which differentiates into seven subsidiary emanations (e.g., the Elohim in the Bible). These emanations continuously reproduce themselves into/as the sum of manifested Life. The One manifests as Three, and the Three are reflected as the Seven, via the illusory Fourth. The abstracted Three is the Heart of the Life of all, and finds its reflection in all Hearts, wherever there is manifest being. All bow to the Three in One, and the One in Three graces those who raise their Eyes, and who must in time emulate His victorious evolutionary Paean. To do so they must travel the way of the Heart. The Rays are but emanations from the Logoic Heart in the Head that endeavours to infuse all dark and diseased spaces with the Love of Life. The method that Life utilises to overcome arenas of darkness evokes the qualities of the five *vayūs,*[10] and this is translated in terms of Light when consciousness evolves (or is evoked).

Light can be viewed as the embodied streams of conscious Life projected by Deity, in order to stimulate the Hearts of embodied forms in such a way that *consciousness* (at first sentient and then intelligent response to external stimulus) is evoked. Wherever there is a positive response to Light there is evolutionary growth. This evolutionary tendency is clearly shown in the vegetable kingdom, whose positive response to light is self-evident. When viewed cosmically, human Monads are but 'man-plants'. All Masters of Wisdom are consequently students of cosmic Botany.

Light can also be viewed in terms of the modes of the resistance of darkness to the Love of the Life. A negative response to Light leads to the way of the dark brotherhood. Therefore, the seven Ray Paths (or colourings of differing gradations and intensities that light differentiates into) project the spiral arcs for the resolution of the darkness into Light. To evolving beings, the appearance of Light necessitates the development of a mechanism that allows cognisance and registration of its phenomena. 'Man-plants' are thus evolved, and the entire Path opens before them.

*Darkness* can be considered to be *chaos* – non-ordered space, the primordial substance. This substance must be organised and rightly directed toward a specific (Logoic) Purpose. The means thereto is Light. Each photon, or unit of Light, emanates its own characteristic sound or note, and the two (sound and colour) interrelate to embody the plenitude of all evolving forms. Sound, colour, line and form determine the progress of the moving arc of consciousness evolving through time and space. As this 'moving arc' intensifies its vibratory frequency, so then the quality of the Light becomes more brilliant. The dark spaces begin to be lit up in conscious response and things are then seen for what they are. This necessitates understanding, the first step on the path of the evolution of Wisdom.

Light differentiates into the seven Ray Paths (or colourings of different gradations and intensities) for the resolution of darkness into an all-embracive state of absorption into Love. Love is what draws all separative forms (chaos) together into a unity, a synthesis. Light therefore is the vehicle of Love. The seven Rays condition the seven planes and floral offerings *(chakras)* before the Altar of

---

10 The *vayūs* are *prāṇic* winds. They are explained in chapter 9 of the revised edition of my book *The Revelation*.

'God'. The Rays are thus directed by the planetary Logoi (for they are *chakras* in the body of the solar Logos). The solar Logos is the 'God' embodying a solar system. Each *chakra* is primarily responsive to a particular Ray whose energy is directed to the other Logoi. The *chakras* are the means whereby Life can be disseminated into the formed realms, so that form can be properly organised and interrelated into a unity and thus directed into the arenas of Sight.

The arenas of Sight bring to light the entire subject of the *Eye,* and of its evolution as a mechanism for the reception, interpretation, and projection of Light according to the Purpose of the directed Will. The Monad is essentially a mechanism of Logoic Sight. The Monadic kingdom manifests so that a great cosmic entity can peer into formed or darkened space – our systemic planes. The kingdom of Souls similarly allows the Lords of Shambhala to peer into the substance of the cosmic dense realms. This is done by means of the appearance of the personalities that become our physical plane lives. All of this eventuates so that physical substance (the concreted chaos of space) is redeemed and converted into a vehicle of sentient (and then conscious) response. This is because of the conversion process of the Light that has been moulded into it. Light is constituted of *deva* Lives. That *deva* substance is inevitably converted into human consciousness by means of the process of Monadic Vision and its great Sacrifice. (Having incarnated into manifestation for the duration of a solar *mahāmanvantara*, a great evolutionary cycle.)

The subject of the nature of the Eye is most esoteric, and many hints have already been given in my previous books. All *chakras* are but versions of the Eye. They represent stages in the unfoldment of the qualities of the Logoic Mind within the realms of form. The Eye seeded the evolutionary bed with germs of the Light of consciousness through the evolution of the petals of the various flowers: from the four petals of the Base *chakra* to the symbolic 1,000 of the Head Lotus. Note how the petals of a flower grow and unfold in relation to a plant's response to the stimuli of light, coupled with the nutrition gained from watery substance. The plants grow in earthy fields.

Each *chakra* is a manifestation of one of the planetary rulers conditioning the formed world. One can look to the human *chakra* system, or to that of the Logos for the influence of these rulers. The esoteric science of astrology is concerned with ascertaining the energies that manifest through the *nāḍī* system, within which the *chakras* are energy vortices.

## Three major energy sources

The energies in the solar system come from three main sources:

1. The *physical sun,* the heart of the solar system from which comes physical light and vitality. It corresponds to the Sacral centre, which is the centre of physical life and vitality for the average person. This *chakra* is related to the Pleiades in the constellation Taurus. The solar system is said to esoterically revolve around the Pleiade Alcyone. The Pleiades are responsible for the Causation of our material world and its innate intelligence. In Greek mythology they were the daughters of Atlas, the Titan who bore the weight of the earth and the universe upon his shoulders. He was brother to Prometheus, who was the progenitor to the human race (and therefore of human intelligence).

   In the Bible, the Pleiades are mentioned in *Job 38:31:* 'canst thou bind the sweet influences of the Pleiades or loose the bands of Orion'. We also have:

   > Seek him that maketh the seven stars and Orion, and turneth the shadow of death into the morning, and maketh the day dark with night: that calleth for the waters of the sea, and poureth them out upon the face of the earth: The LORD is his name.[11]

   These quotations indicate the profound effect that these stars had upon the ancient seers. They also indicate that the emanating source of all being upon this earth is 'him that maketh', who thus embodies the 'seven stars' (Pleiades) and Orion. 'The shadow of death' causes the descent into incarnation of a human, solar, or planetary Entity, for 'death' in the esoteric sense means entering a cycle of incarnation.

   The word 'morning' symbolises that which allows the light of day (of the spiritual nature) to manifest in the early evolutionary period. The pouring of the 'waters of the sea....upon the face of the earth' refers to the creation of the astral plane and related conditionings. The 'one that maketh' is one who uses the Intellect (Mahat) to create with, whilst the action of making and 'pouring' are expressions of the third Ray. The 'Lord' embodies the Creative Word, here the *Aūṁ*. He is the Jehovah of the Bible that projects the qualities of the 'I AM THAT I AM'[12] (His Throne or seat of Power) into manifestation.

---

11 *Amos 5:8.*

12 *Exodus 3:14.* See chapter 10 of my revised *The Revelation* for detail concerning this statement.

2. The *Heart of the Sun* corresponds to the human Soul, and therefore is found on the cosmic higher mental plane. The energy from this centre is said to come from the sun *Sirius,* from which emanates the progenitor of the energy known as Love-Wisdom. This is the characteristic that our solar Logos presently embodies, and which the 'sons of Mind' constituting His Body are actively evolving.[13] The demonstration of Love-Wisdom is therefore the current Purpose. Sirian Love directly vivifies the Spiritual Hierarchy on earth, who are the Heart centre of the planetary Logos. Their work is to enlighten humanity with Love-Wisdom. They work directly via human Soul-groups, as well as incarnating amongst humanity to foster this energy.[14]
3. The *Central Spiritual Sun,* corresponding to the Monad. This Deity is esoterically known as 'The One About Whom Naught May Be Said' (THAT Logos), of which (according to D.K.) the Seven Rishis of the Great Bear (the Husbands of the Seven Sisters) form the Throat centre. The Rishis are the Source of the energy of Will and of the Life principle animating our Logos. Each of these Rishis beam a Ray of energy that is absorbed by the Head Centres of the corresponding Heavenly Men (Planetary Logoi) of our solar system. They thereby energise the Monads of the threefold human units. These Rays convey the basic characteristics of the Heavenly Men (the planetary Regents). After colouring the Logoi with characteristics (or Personality qualities), the Ray energies are transmitted into the various organs within their bodies of manifestation. Similary, each kingdom in Nature embodies aspects of these Rays (or of their sub-Rays) and colours them with their own particular quality before retransmitting them to the lesser groups with whom they are associated. Very potent cosmic forces are thus stepped down until they can be used, for instance, by the human Soul and then the personality. They also colour our mental, astral and physical bodies.

From the above perspective, the Seven Rishis may be viewed as the facial orifices of That Logos.

The expressed qualities of every entity in the knowable universe can be

---

13 The solar Logos had already developed the cosmic Intelligence in a former Incarnation, thus this principle is latent throughout manifestation.

14 It is interesting to note that the entire course of Egyptian mythology and the annual flooding of the Nile (around which much of their religious system was centred) was timed from when Sirius rose from the horizon to it becoming observable in their night sky.

considered the result of interactions between the Rays. The understanding of these interrelationships forms the esoteric basis to astrology, psychology and philosophy.

When considering the Rays of energy, they can ultimately be resolved into the three aspects of Deity:

- *The Father* (first aspect) – Ray one, represents the Will-to-Be. This energy originally emanated from the Seven Rishis of the Great Bear.
- *The Son* (second aspect) – Ray two, represents the objective of this creation (Love-Wisdom). This energy emanates from Sirius.
- *The Mother* (third aspect) – Ray three, represents the 'Womb of matter'. It concerns the Intelligent embodiment of the Will of Deity as ceaseless Activity, which produces the Son. This energy originally emanated from the Pleiades.

The Will-to-Create is the third aspect of the first Ray of Power, an expression of the Thought behind the directive Eye that sets the Wheel of motion into activity. It is Mind imbuing primal matter with a spark of Life. This Father (or Spirit aspect) represents perfection in all its completeness, that from its plane of abstraction sacrifices an aspect of itself in order to elevate those lesser than it.

The Spirit is that principle that remains immutable, inclusive, unchanging, indestructible, 'uninvolved' in the Creative process, yet it is the cause and result of evolution. It is the firm Base[15] that supports the existence of all else. The Father says allegorically to the Lords of Wisdom during the evolutionary paean: 'Be patient! Love the all. Resurrect the entombed ones. Empower them. They must overcome all obscurations on the Way (to Bliss). Receive my Benediction. Light must conquer darkness. Love must transmute evil. The One only can Be.'

These words inadequately portray the first Ray quality. Its nature will perhaps be better understood if the relationship between the Monad and the personality (or between humanity and the mineral kingdom) is meditated upon.

This Benediction is a descent of first Ray energy. It can be likened to a steadfast, potent impulse, whose effect is to cause the radiatory activity that signifies the ending of the journeying of all evolutionary forms. Yet it is also causative of the beginning of the new journeying *(manvantara).*

---

15 In Sanskrit, *upādhi*. What is essentially inferred here is the diamond Throne of a 'thus gone' Buddha.

## The evolutionary journeying

Once that journeying has begun, then the cohorts of the perfected Sons of 'God' (Buddhas) utilise the Father's Will energy and add their own of Love-Wisdom. These two energies are focussed upon the primal matrix, which is now to flower upon its long spiral of evolution. This matrix consists of the Elemental Lives that are nascently intelligent, for intelligence is the eventual result of motion. The method of manifestation and its achievement are but changes in states of awareness that continually evolve from the conditioned (the atomic, the empirical) to the unconditioned (the universal, the ineffable). The energy of the collective Intelligent Activity manifested by Hierarchies of Servers, the subordinate Sons to 'God', forms the third Ray of Mathematically Exact Activity.

The Rays are the qualities embodying certain great Lives *(devas)* as they cycle in and out of manifestation. Accordingly, they affect (or colour) lesser entities that form part of their constitution. The progress of manifestation is cyclic. The esoteric basis to this lies in the in and out breathings of these Rays of Lives, be they planetary or extra-systemic Beings. A Ray Life that is now registering its energy is, for instance, that of the seventh Ray of Ceremonial Magic. (The primary conditioning energy of the Aquarian age.) It is a wave of motion, a force field that carries with it a number of seventh Ray Souls, who will incarnate to manifest the qualities that will flower in the new era.

At the same time, the sixth Ray of Devotion (which has been conditioning humanity for the past 2,000 years) will ebb and pass out of manifestation, and with it the disincarnate sixth Ray Souls. In this way, the forces engendered by the various Rays are the subjective causes for the objective history of the earth.[16]

There are many cycles of these Ray Lives affecting our globe at any one time. Ultimately, the Lives that affect our solar system have their originating sources from the constellations of the Great Bear, Sirius, or the Pleiades. In their turn, they are unfolding the Will of a great unknowable cosmic Entity (THAT Logos).

Viewed in terms of the planetary regents, the following Figure endeavours to portray the nature of the spiral of evolution.

Saturn, the Lord of *karma* (ruling the third Ray), governs the circumference of a Logoic sphere of attainment. He incorporates the substance of what is to be, in accordance with the *karma* that was generated in the past.

---

16 This has been explained in *The Destiny of the Nations*, and other works by Alice Bailey.

The central point (the Logoic Seat of Power) is governed by Jupiter, the Lord of the second Ray. He establishes the general tone for that *manvantara*. Mars (the sixth Ray of Devotion/Aspiration) governs the spiral motion of the evolutionary path. Finally, Venus (the fifth Ray of the Scientific Mode) governs the manifestation of the substance (the *devas)* that embodies all of the forms that will come into incarnate expression.

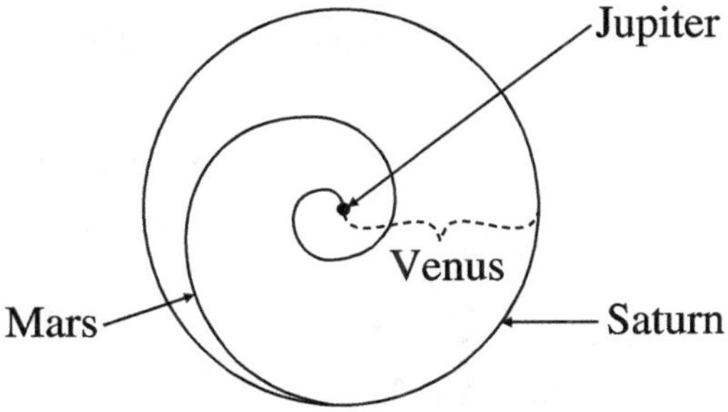


**Figure 1. The evolutionary spiral**

The above is but a generalised statement that can be expanded upon to show the quality of manifestation in relation to the nature of the expression of consciousness (as indicated in Figure 2 below). Jupiter, Mercury and Mars are shown to have a special relationship to each other. They are all along the second Ray line of evolution. Ray six (Mars) is the reflection of Ray two (Jupiter), whilst Ray four (Mercury) is the mirror between them. Rays one, three, five and seven are all along the first Ray line of evolution.[17] Rays one and seven have a similar mirrored relationship to Rays three and five, with Ray four as the mirror for both pairs of reflections. Ray five (Venus) is a reflection of Ray three (Saturn), and Ray seven (Uranus) of Ray one (Vulcan).

When considering Figure 2 astrologically, the Sun is the centre from which manifestation is emanated. It represents the totality, the ring-pass-not of the solar system. However, the symbol of the solar disc but veils the triune expression of Deity, as previously inferred. The solar Logos, as the 'Grand Man of the Heavens', can be equated with the Ishvara (*Īśvara*) of the Hindu theology.[18] He is the eternal

17 Though stated as the first Ray line, it is perhaps better to say that they are on the line of the Rays of Mind, headed by the first Ray.

18 Note that it is Surya that embodies the observable characteristics of the sun as an entity in the Hindu pantheon.

Man, the emanatory cause that embodies and yet is beyond the play of Creation. He therefore represents the Logoic Personality, the Mind that directs and moulds the *ākāśa* (cosmic *prāṇa)* within *saṃsāra.*[19] *Īśvara* manifests as a triune force, anthropomorphised by the functions of the three Deities:

Shiva (Śiva) – the Father, Ray I of Will or Power.
Vishnu (Viṣṇu) – the Son, Ray II of Love-Wisdom.
Brahmā – the Mother, Ray III of Mathematically Exact Activity.

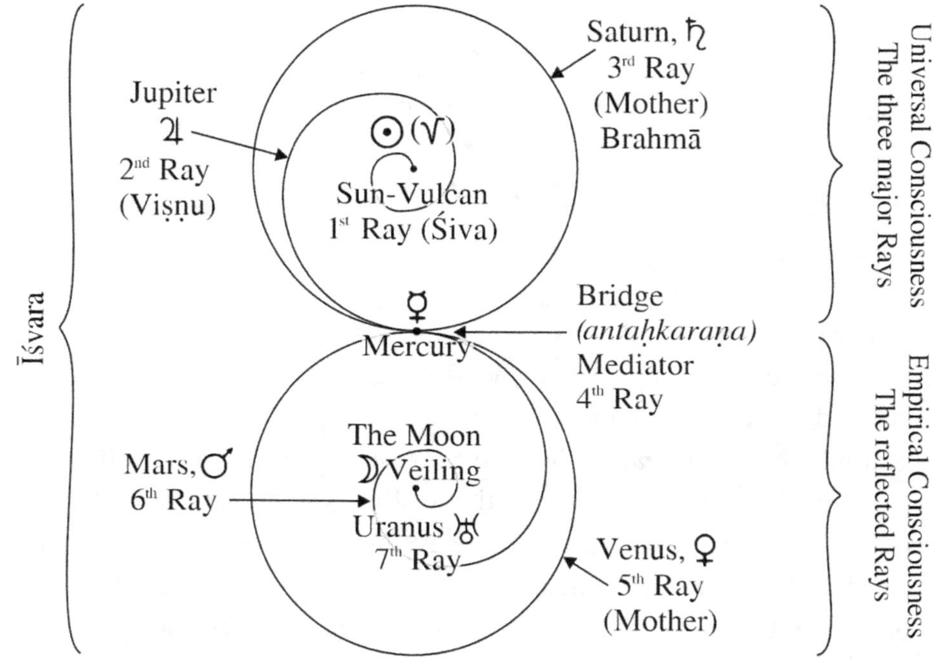


**Figure 2. Manifestation of the Rays astrologically considered**

In Grecian mythology, the sun's attributes are symbolised by Helios, Apollo and Hephaestus (Vulcan).

*Helios* is the solar disk, the giver of light, and as such is the externalised form of the solar Logos. (His physical Fiery nature.)

*Apollo* is the 'spirit' that moves the Fiery chariot, circumscribing the heavens and illuminating both heaven and earth. Apollo demonstrates the subjective

19 See my book *The Astrological and Numerological Keys to the Secret Doctrine, Vol. 1,* 37-8 for detail concerning *Īśvara.* He is an expression of Puruṣa, which can be considered the Logoic Soul that overshadows the personality aspect.

side of the solar Logos, the Body of energy *(prāṇa)* giving vitality, health and rejuvenation to all incarnate.

*Vulcan,* on the other hand, is the hidden force, the God of the transmutative Fire *(kuṇḍalinī).* He is hidden deep in the bowels of the earth, in volcanoes, the central aspect of creation. *Vulcan* can be considered to have an equal footing with Zeus, as he wields or forges the powers of the Gods. The energy He wields is representative of the nuclear energy deep in the sun.

Here, we see an analogy with Śiva in unison with His Shakti.[20] Śiva represents the power, the force or Will, the destroyer/regenerator aspect of Creation. Thus He is the God of the *yogin,* who through his own determined will utilises this force, or the forces latent within his own being, to transmute his base nature and thus gain liberation through the transformation of his personal self. As such, Śiva and the sun (Vulcan) embody the Will or first Ray aspect of Deity. They are placed in the centre (the seed point) of the higher Causative sphere. (See Figure 2.)

*Saturn* is Chronus (Father time) the lawgiver, the adjudicator, the agent of *karma.* Through the cyclic action of time, the Waters of space are stirred and condense into manifested objectivity. Thus Saturn (or rather His feminine aspect)[21] also represents the 'Womb of matter', the Mother aspect of Deity. He is the golden Egg (the world Soul, space manifested as form) from which all the powers and existences of this solar system are derived. These existences are actively intelligent. As such, Saturn is analogous to the Hindu concept of Brahmā (the Creator) who is born out of the naval of Viṣṇu. (The Deity incarnated as the solar system and therefore is manifest Love-Wisdom.) Thus Brahmā is drawn as the circumference of the sphere in Figure 2. He symbolises the manifested aspect of universal Consciousness and embodies the third Ray of Active Intelligence.

Time always limits and conditions. Wisdom, however, overrules time in terms of consciousness, for wisdom is not conditioned by cycles of reason, form, or space. Therefore, wisdom can be said to be eternal, unconditioned, universal and stemming from the highest sources. When directed downwards into the concrete planes (applied in action) as illumination, wisdom manifests as the Truth that knows all. Truth can only be born in the Womb of Love. (For characteristics other than Love would mar or twist Truth into untruth.)

*Jupiter* dethroned his father, Saturn (who conditions the cycles of time). Jupiter consequently embodies the second Ray of Love-Wisdom. As Zeus, he rules the

---

20 *Śakti* – female force.

21 He was originally represented as a male-female figure in early Grecian mythology.

highest heaven, the kingdom of the Gods - Mt. Olympus (the Head centre and seat of the Soul in the human being). In the Hindu theology, his correspondence is Viṣṇu the preserver. When wisdom is united with Love, it preserves or sustains all manifest space.

All forces or Deities in the solar system are but personified aspects of the solar Logos and embody His principles. The Heavenly Men, the 'Seven Spirits before the Throne of God',[22] are His direct subordinates. They are the Regents of the seven Rays for our earth system.

These expressions do not remain abstract concepts; they are vitally dynamic, living principles, inherent in every atom of the manifested cosmos. Thus the first Ray of Sacrifice or Will is not only concerned with primal Causation, but also the ever-present expression of the Will of Deity. This Ray of Sacrifice animates every conscious being that limits itself in some way to perform the duty stemming from its innermost being, to help those that have not yet realised the appropriate degree of attainment. This necessitates a basic grounding in Love-Wisdom, self-control, and directional purpose, for Love is the leitmotiv and functional purpose behind any stream of manifesting Life.

The first Ray is the emanating source, the 'Will that Initiates'. On the ascending circle of evolution, it is also the aspect of Deity that destroys old forms that have accomplished their purpose. The inherent Life (or the developed consciousness within) is thus set free. Therefore, Śiva (the personification of the first Ray) is generally typified as the 'destroyer'.

The Love-Wisdom principle sustains the entire evolutionary process, thus Viṣṇu is styled the 'preserver'. The Creator, Brahmā, causes the cycles of manifestation to come into being and embodies the basic substance of all evolving forms.

All things have an objective reality only to those on their own plane of perception. Therefore, the relationship between animate and inanimate objects shifts in accordance with changes in a thinker's consciousness. For example, the Monad on the plane *anupādaka* (acting as the first Ray aspect of Deity) sacrifices or limits its freedom by sending down a Ray of itself into the material world. The result of that limitation is the Soul (the Monad's 'Son', or Thought-Form). The Soul thereby takes the attribute of the second aspect of Deity. The Soul then Rays down a fragment or spark of itself to form the personality, which thereby expresses the third aspect of Deity. However, the personality can also express the second aspect of Deity when thought-forms are compassionately created. The

22 See *Rev. 4:5.*

resultant action on the physical plane becomes the third aspect, in which case the Soul, the 'Father in Heaven', becomes the first aspect.

Similarly, when separated from its higher Self, the personality represents the first aspect. Its thought-forms then constitute the second aspect. The Elementary Lives or atoms that embody the thought-form are the third aspect. Such a system of interrelationships can understandably lead to confusion, until it is realised that the view to be taken should always be the highest possible in relation to humanity. These alternating principles are tabulated as shown below.

| 1st Aspect | 2nd Aspect | 3rd Aspect |
|---|---|---|
| Will | Love-Wisdom | Activity |
| Sattva (rhythm) | Rajas (activity) | Tamas (inertia) |
| Spirit | Soul | Body |
| Father | Son | Mother |
| Śiva | Viṣṇu | Brahmā |
| Solar Logos | Planetary Logos | Monad |
| Monad | Soul | Personality |
| Kingdom of 'God' | Hierarchy | Kingdom of Souls |
| Kingdom of Souls | Humanity | Animal kingdom |
| Animal kingdom | Vegetable kingdom | Mineral kingdom |
| Ādi | Anupādaka | Ātma |
| Ātma | Buddhi | Manas |
| Manas | Astral plane | Physical plane |
| The Absolute | Intuition | Illumination |
| Illumination | Intellect | Brain |
| Brain | Body (nerves) | Sense reactions |
| Sense reactions | External objects | Energy |

**Table 1. The alternating principles**

The Rays are reflected into the outer form causing the events of all phenomenal life. It can be seen that the first Ray of Will is not only an expression of the

Heavenly Man embodying the planet called Vulcan, for this planetary Deity also subjectively influences those beings of whom Vulcan is the ruler of the house they are born in.

Presently, no personality can directly wield the first Ray effectively. The destroyer aspect of this Ray is too potent with respect to the form nature. This energy thus mainly works through group purpose.[23] It will always be modified, therefore, by the second Ray energy associated with the sun. Even the Soul can only inadequately wield this energy (despite the fact that its intrinsic nature is Love-Wisdom). In fact, the inevitable consequence of the Soul's contact with this first Ray energy is to produce a supernova-like death when the fourth Initiation is attained. Therefore, higher Initiations concern the Initiate's increasing receptivity to this Will energy.

---

23 Here we see one reason why ordinary astrologers rarely recognise Vulcan in their calculations. They are almost purely concerned with personalities and personality reactions to planetary forces.

# 2

# The Planetary Regents

## The planetary Regents generally considered

The Heavenly Men (planetary Logoi) are said to have interrelationships analogous to human beings. They too are observably evolving and seeking to be released from the form that imprisons them. Their actions have a solar and cosmic significance as they respond to a purpose hidden in the mysteries of cosmic Karma. They demonstrate an aspect of cosmic Love, for Love-Wisdom is the keynote to our solar system. They are also bonded to the limitation of their dense incarnate sheaths until every cell in their bodies have attained liberation. (This relates to a process of dying, of cessation from incarnation, *pralaya.)* The type of energies a Logos distributes to Nature's kingdoms depends upon the quality of the evolutionary attainment (character) that the Heavenly Man embodies, the present cyclic purpose, and interrelationships with the other Logoi.

According to their ability to absorb and be modified by the energies, the various Lives constituting the body of manifestation of a planetary Logos respond to His emitted Ray characteristics. Each Life absorbs what is possible, colouring it according to its own qualities, before re-emitting it. As the energy wave progresses on to the lower kingdoms, it gets increasingly modified (or deflected) from its original purity of intent by the emanatory qualities of those that retransmit it.

As a person is a composite entity with many cells and organs in his/her body, so also a planetary or solar Logos is a composite entity with many cells and organs. Thus a planetary Logos consists of many human Soul groups and *deva*

Lives. Correspondingly, the solar Logos then constitutes a cell in the Body of a far greater cosmic Entity, and so forth. There are energy fields, *chakras,* and *nāḍīs* that relate the expression of one to the other, which are the symbolic Body and Blood of the cosmic Christ. Some of these forces originate from other 'cells' within the Body of the planetary Logos. Other energies emanate from the central Life (the sun), or from cosmic sources (the stars and constellations with which our planetary Logos is karmically associated).

Astrologically, the earth is considered the central planet because here the human kingdom plays out its karmic role. The energies from the various planetary Logoi must act through the earth's electromagnetic aura before they can affect conditionings within. This only happens via the general influence of a Soul-group (of humanity) or group-Soul (of the lesser kingdoms in Nature) to which any entity belongs. The exact time and place of birth (expressed in terms of longitude and latitude) is of importance in natal astrology because:

a. The earth has its own indigenous force fields *(chakras)* that greatly modify local conditionings in the biosphere. They project subtle impulses that are built into a person's constitution at the time of birth.

b. The planetary Regents pursue various paths in the heavens, thus their interrelated energies are constantly modified or changed as events progress through time. These energies are received differently at different places, depending upon the nature of the receptive centres *(chakras)* upon the earth.

There are seven sheaths within the Body of manifestation of a Logos. (Just as there are seven sheaths constituting the incarnate form of a person.) The earth is the densest of such sheaths for our planetary Logos. It is the fourth globe of a series of seven, together constituting one planetary Chain, thus:

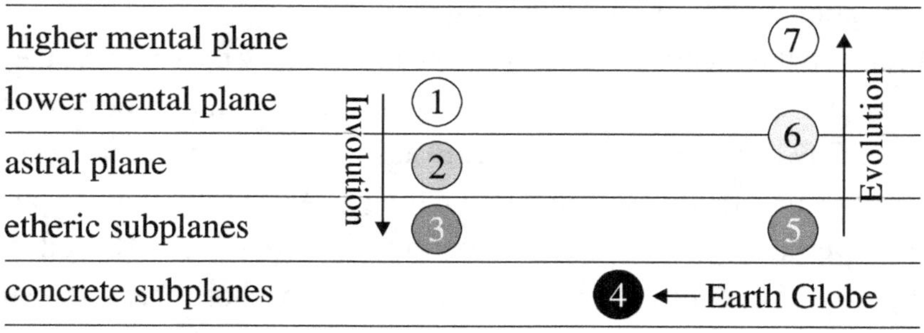


**Figure 3. A planetary Chain**[1]

1 Compare this to H.P. Blavatsky's rendering of the globes in *The Secret Doctrine,* (Theosophical Publishing Co., Adyar, 1888), Vol. 1, 153.

Within the duration of a solar Incarnation there are seven Chains associated with a series of planetary Incarnations (referred to as a planetary Scheme). The seven are synthesised by an esoteric three, making the sacred number 10. There are seven plus three such Heavenly Men undergoing evolutionary experience within the confines of our solar Logos, each forming a *chakra* or centre of force therein. These seven planetary Regents are the Lords of the seven Rays within the solar system.

The lines of interrelationship between the Heavenly Men produce planetary *karma,* affecting conditionings in the kingdom of Souls via *deva* adjudicators, and in all kingdoms in Nature. The science of astrology endeavours to understand the nature of the effect of such energetic interplay. Each of the planes of perception and kingdoms in Nature are directly qualified by the energies from one or other of the planetary Regents.

## The planetary Regents and the Rāja Lords

The information provided in Part B of *The Constitution of Shambhala* concerning the *deva* (Rāja) Lords (who embody the substance of the planes of perception[2]) shall be extended here, so as to integrate them with the planetary rulers. These planetary rulers utilise the substance of the planes in order to project their Ray purpose into manifestation. The Rāja Lords shall be listed from the highest to the lowest planes of perception.

*Ariel* (meaning 'lion of God'), whose colour is silver-red, governs the plane *ādi.* This Lion roars out the third Outpouring of the energies of manifest Being. It produces the Purpose that directs the manifestation of substance to be incorporated in the planes of perception (being the consequence of the first Outpouring). The third Outpouring also produces Initiation and liberation for the worthy candidates.[3] It is therefore the energy of abstraction, producing the death of the incarnate form. The rulership of the highest three sub-planes of *ādi* is Vulcan (the first Ray of Will or Power). For the lower four sub-planes, the rulership is Uranus (the seventh Ray of Ceremonial Activity, Manifesting Power). Ariel reflects the energies from the seventh cosmic astral plane into manifestation, and the *ākāśa* (the prāṇic energy manifesting upon the liberated planes of perception)[4] that it bears is Aetheric.

2 See pages 39-41.

3 The three Outpourings are explained in my book *Meditation and the Initiation Process,* 277-84.

4 For a detailed explanation of *ākāśa,* see the two volumes of my book *The Astrological and Numerological Keys to the Secret Doctrine.*

*Uriel* (meaning 'light of God'), whose colour is indigo blue, governs the plane *anupādaka*. The light emanated here is of the Love-Wisdom that governs the purpose of the present solar incarnation. The planetary ruler is Neptune (the sixth Ray of Devotion-Aspiration). Uriel reflects the energies from the sixth cosmic astral sub-plane into manifestation. The *ākāśa* that it bears is Airy. This energy energises our Monadic Life. The second Outpouring manifests from this plane. It is the Consciousness stream that bears the twelve Creative Hierarchies.

*Ezekiel* (meaning 'God is strong', or 'makes strong'), whose colour is emerald green, governs the plane *ātma*. The first Outpouring manifests via *ātma*. The substance of the planes of perception via this Outpouring is thereby strengthened by the activity of this Rāja Lord. The planetary ruler is Saturn, the slowest moving of all the observable planets. The *ātmic* plane is dual, hence for the highest three sub-planes the rulership is Jupiter (the second Ray). Saturn (the third Ray of Mathematically Exact Activity) governs *karma* and the lower four sub-planes. Directing the manifestation of *karma* necessitates far-reaching visioning and patience in order to rightly mete out the intricacies of this law. Judicial qualities arise from this ability. Jupiter ensures that all karmic rectification is founded in Love and Wisdom. From the *ātmic* plane manifests the qualities of the creative potency of the threefold Word (Aūṁ). Ezekiel reflects the energies from the fifth cosmic astral sub-plane into manifestation, and the *ākāśa* that it bears is Fiery.

*Michael* (meaning 'who is like God'), whose colour is golden yellow, rules the plane *buddhi*. Michael's physical embodiment is generally inferred to be the sun, where the sun's symbol is that of the ineffable creative Deity. Thus Michael is the ruler of the solar domain, the seat of Power of the 'Brain' of the Heavenly Man that is the solar system. Michael's energies also find their reflection upon the higher mental plane via the kingdom of Souls residing thereon. Michael therefore has a specific affinity to the evolution of humanity. The planetary rulership is Mercury and the fourth Ray of Beautifying Harmony Overcoming Strife. Michael reflects the energies from the fourth cosmic astral sub-plane into manifestation. The *ākāśa* that it bears is Watery. Astrologically, Michael is the embodiment of radiant splendour and intuitive awareness. Being an expression of Mercury, Michael is 'the messenger of the Gods'. As Mercury, his symbol is the Caduceus, showing the straight and narrow path to the Gods through the sinewy coils of matter. Also veiled here are the attributes of the *iḍā, piṇgalā* and *suṣumṇā nāḍīs*. Mercury also represents the *antaḥkaraṇa* between the kingdoms of Nature and Deity. Mercury is the nearest of the visible planets to the sun (the Logos) and therefore is 'the servant of the scribe', the emissary of Light, Life and Love to the rest of the system.

*Raphael* (meaning 'God heals', or 'has healed'), whose colour is yellow-orange, governs the mental plane and its discriminative creative abilities. The planetary ruler is Venus, the morning star, who rules the fifth Ray of the Scientific Mode. Raphael reflects the energies from the third cosmic astral sub-plane into manifestation, thus he also wields the *karma* manifesting through the three worlds of human livingness. Raphael bears the Earthy *ākāśa* as an extension of the 'middle Finger' of the planetary Logos.

Astrologically, the symbolism of Venus denotes the resurrection of a Soul newly born into spiritual life. It produces a life of beauty and harmony, manifesting through the type of Love that only a well-directed mental principle can produce. Raphael reflects the karmic purpose of Ezekiel into manifestation. Whatever manifests on the mental plane is normally projected into the physical via the principle of desire (the substance of the astral plane – Gabriel). The astral body is a Watery modifying principle that often sways the mind. The mind must in time dominate the Watery emotional world. Inevitably also, via the meditative process, the empirical mind must be controlled by the archetypal, abstract Mind, which reflects directives from *ātma* via *buddhi*.

Ezekiel, Michael and Raphael embody the three prongs of Varuna's trident.[5]

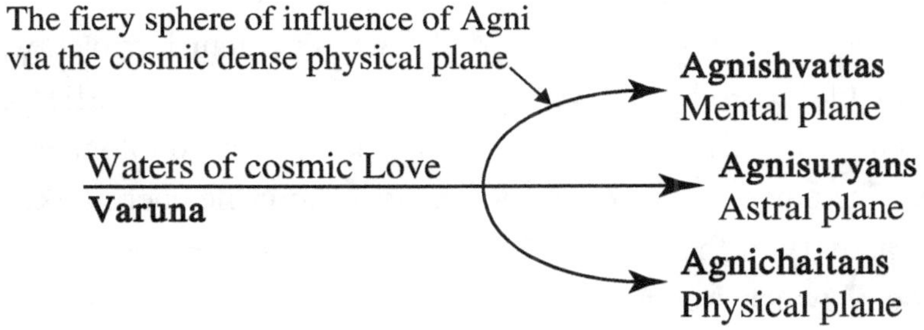


**Figure 4. Varuna's trident**

This means that the *ākāśa* that they convey vitalises the three lowest planes of perception, reflected into the three orders of *devas* that embody the substance of these planes: the Agnichaitans, Agnisuryans and the Agnishvattas. Ezekiel's Fiery aspect of the cosmic Waters vitalises the mental plane (the cosmic dense physical) via *ātma*. Michael's Watery aspect vitalises the astral plane and the *lunar pitris* via *buddhi*. Raphael's Earthy quality from the mental plane crystallises the

5 See Figure 1 from *The Constitution of Shambhala*, Part B, page 5, for a detailed explanation of this trident.

mineral kingdom (the Elemental Lives). The fifth Creative Hierarchy (Makara, the Agnishvattas) is thereby empowered to act by them to rule the manifestation of form. Raphael also manifests the energies of the Son of Mind. This means that part of Raphael's dispensation is the emanation of the general energies that vitalise the kingdom of Souls. Under Raphael, two other *deva* Lords also play roles: Galadriel, who empowers the abstract Mind (here governed by the energies of the sun), and Rivendiel (who vitalises the empirical mind, whose emanation is governed by the functions of Pluto, the Lord of death).

*Gabriel* (meaning 'God is powerful'), whose colour is rose, governs the astral plane. Gabriel manifests the directive potency that controls the creative Watery principle that dominates solar evolution. The planetary rulership is Mars (the sixth Ray of Devotion/Aspiration). Gabriel reflects the reified energies from the second cosmic astral sub-plane into manifestation as an extension of the central prong of the trident wielded by Varuna. Gabriel was the angel sent to Mary in St. Luke's Gospel who announced that she would give birth to a child called Jesus.

Astrologically, Gabriel embodies the forces of materiality and its regeneration through the sexual impulse via Mars, the planet symbolising activity and strife. Mars also expresses the virility and dynamic energy that motivates manifestation. Upon the path of discipleship, his energy works to overcome the allurements that hinder a person's quest for liberation from form.

*Samuel* (meaning 'his divine name is El'), whose colour is violet, works via the etheric double, ruled by the Moon.[6] Samuel expresses the reified energies from the seventh cosmic astral sub-plane, which are projected into manifestation via Michael. The etheric plane distributes *prāṇa,* the virile energy that sustains all forms of activity in the realm of manifestation. The *chakras* reside within the etheric body, which are in general ruled by the seventh Ray of Ritual, Cyclic Activity and Materialising Power. Consciousness evolves and manifests its field of activity within the field of activities of the *chakras.*

Astrologically, Samuel expresses the qualities of victory and passion. They are qualities attributed to the Moon, which governs the human psychic constitution. Exoterically, this is concerned with tides and menstrual periods, thus with fertility and propagation. Esoterically, one looks to the positive and negative forces in

---

6 Note that when referring to the astrological planets, of which the Moon, the Sun, and the Earth are considered such, I shall capitalise them, but when referring to them as the physical moon, the sun and earth, then lower case shall apply. Throughout my books the earth was also put in lower case in order to distinguish it from the Element Earth, which is capitalised, as are all of the other Elements. This rule shall still apply.

manifestation as aspects of the externalised liquid constitution of our planetary system. The Romans symbolised the Moon's functions by the attributes of the goddess Diana, who in later medieval times was also the goddess of sorcery and witchcraft. Such attributes manifest because of her association with the astral plane and the control of Nature's forces via lower psychism. (The Moon therefore also expresses the more maligned aspects of the Waters, whereby the reflected light of the person manifests as left hand magical activities.)

For the physical plane, governed by *the Earth,* another archangel can be added: *Zachariel.* His keynotes are mercy and greatness. He is the mediator between Mars (the god of war – the virile energy underlying manifestation) and Saturn (who is *karma*). Zachariel is thus the great stabiliser, as an embodiment of the wisdom that is expressed as compassion. He is the scribe who fulfils the book of the law (the book of *karma)* as dictated by Saturn and desired by the Logos (or, from a different perspective, desired by the Soul) who is Love. He also empowers the second Ray energies of Jupiter on earth. Jupiter governs the way of the Heart and its wisdom that manifests on the physical plane when all other principles are working in perfect accord. The dense physical realm is a complete reflection of the higher mental plane (Venus). Via it, *karma* (directed by Ezekiel from the ātmic plane) must play out its role. For *karma* to be properly expressed, it must be assisted by the wisdom that Jupiter brings.

| Name | Plane | Element | Colour |
|---|---|---|---|
| Ariel | Ādi | | Silver-Red |
| Uriel | Anupādaka | | Silvery Indigo-Blue |
| Ezekiel | Ātma | Aether | Green |
| Michael | Buddhi | Air | Golden |
| Galadriel | Mental - Abstract Mind | Fire | Opalescent White |
| Raphael | Mental - Son of Mind (Soul) | Fire | Golden Yellow-Orange |
| Rivendiel | Mental - Concrete Mind | Fire | Orange |
| Gabriel | Astral | Water | Rose/Sky Blue |
| Samuel | Etheric | Earth | Violet |
| Zachariel | Dense | Earth | |

**Table 2. The Rāja Lords and the planes**

All of these forces play upon and produce the sum of the manifestation seen upon our earth globe. The activities of the five non-sacred planets come under the general direction of Venus, as all things conditioning *saṃsāra* come under the dominion of the mind/Mind. These planets are: the Sun (veiling other planets), the Moon (also veiling other planets), the Earth, Mars, and Pluto. The non-sacred planets are those wherein pain and strife still rule the Lives (subjective or objective) found upon them. On the non-sacred planets evolutionary purpose has not yet been gained. The seven sacred planets are those that have already gained relative evolutionary perfection.

## The seven Rays exoterically and esoterically understood

The forthcoming summary of the various Rays will principally concern the esoteric portent associated with astrological forces influencing the totality of human conditionings. Planetary conditionings shall also be briefly touched upon. An exoteric account as to the nature of astrological effects will also be given because:

a. Many people are still governed by them.
b. This will tend to show how the thought-forms concerning the qualities given to the planets and signs by astrologers came about.
c. It will also tend to create a harmony by relating the esoteric to the exoteric.

The term *exoteric* refers to the empirical or mundane, the personality and its attributes, which pertains to the world of illusion *(saṃsāra)*. The term thus concerns the 'eye doctrine', based upon what the physical eyes can see and deduce by means of the intellect.

The term *esoteric* refers to the inner universe and subjective planes of perception, such as the activities associated with the Soul, Monad, Hierarchy, or what comes via Shambhala. The esoteric concerns the wisdom teachings known by those Initiated into the Mysteries of the Kingdom of 'God'. This is an expression of the revelations accorded to an enlightened being. The esoteric interpretation is necessary for the proper study of all divine texts (such as the *Revelation of St. John)* which are inundated with astrological implications.

### *Summary of Ray 1 of Will or Power*

The basic quality of a first Ray personality is seen as a strong driving will or energy towards the satisfaction of a set goal. This can be a will towards illumination (in which case the person will sacrifice all towards that end), or a selfishly motivated will that brings one into positions of power, or towards the centre of attention.

The microcosm reflects the macrocosm, subjectively and objectively. The human personality therefore tends to possess reflected and highly reified attributes of the Heavenly Men (the planetary rulers). Though there is no real analogue to the first Ray from an *exoteric* astrological viewpoint, this Ray can be viewed in terms of being *the Sun.* The sun is the centre of the solar system and thus the ruler of all the other planets.

Our sun is said to emit rays of a predominantly yellow-orange hue. This colour stimulates intellectual tendencies. Because the sun is the symbolic king, the ruler, the central factor in the solar system, so the main exoteric characteristics of those influenced by the Sun are said to be pride, vanity, ambition, lordship, desire for self-assertion, using the intellect for personal gain. Such a person would tend to be a leader, the centre of his/her little group, whatever it may be.

These tendencies are somewhat softened when they are blended with the beams of life-giving force, the vitality *(prāṇa)* that emanates from the majesty of the Heart. First Ray personalities thus emanate good health, a radiant vitality that allows them to achieve, conquer, make and do things with a forceful passion. As rulers, they blend firmness with kindness, producing a healthy protective stimulus, and are fond of the wellbeing of their subjects. They can be harsh, stern, and yet be magnanimous, determined, noble, hating all petty dispositions. In short, this emission of vitality is via harmonious, often forceful, and sometimes magnanimous interrelationships. This is coupled with being the centre of their universe. By wielding a strong will, characteristics are produced that are generally given by popular astrologers to those influenced by the Sun. For detailed exoteric information on the nature of the various planetary rulers, one can refer to their accounts.

Esoterically, *Vulcan* rules the first Ray of Will or Power. It is an etheric planet and is situated closer to the sun than any other planet. The colour of this Ray is red (red is for blood, for Blood is Life). This Ray is the giver and taker of Life. The first Ray expresses the Life and Power of the incarnate Deity. In humanity, the first Ray works through governments, politics and through military conquerors such as Napoleon and Caesar. They wielded the powerful forces of their wills to change the course of civilisation, or to shape the political map of their time. (As such they were agents of Shambhala.) The Will also needs to be developed upon the path of Initiation, if one is to overcome the vicissitudes of *saṁsāra*. Initiates therefore spiritually become 'world conquerors'.

*Pluto,* the Lord of death and of the underworld, also governs the first Ray. In this case, the first Ray produces the transition from one state or dimension of perception to the next. Pluto therefore helps produce the transformations of consciousness.

A first and second Ray combination produces the magnetic attraction seen in the mineral kingdom, and also in the drawing of all Life towards a Central Spiritual Sun. When harnessed by humanity, this Ray combination has produced (via the fifth Ray) the comprehension of the nature of the manifestation of electricity. Electrical energy is an active effect of the first Ray. We therefore have developed all of the wondrous technology and electrical appliances that are the mainstay of our present civilisation. The first Ray energy produces the organised activity of our armies, and in our political organisations, as well as the amalgamation of companies empowered by a military-like efficiency to rape resources from the common person.

The first Ray person is a natural ruler, exoterically or esoterically. Those of this Ray are aspects of the 'Brain' of the Heavenly Man. The first Ray Soul is involved with the adaptation of form to Life in a progressive manner, so that it will eventually release the indwelling Spirit. To allow for the emergence of new Life, this force is also the cause for the disappearance of whole kingdoms of Nature, and of human races. The evolutionary pageant is a matrix wherein the Will can work to release the inherent Life embodied in any form. Such release happens as the Lives progressively aspire to higher dimensions of perception or levels of realisation. Esoterically, this adaptation of form to Life produces the evolutionary process.

The influence of the first Ray in humanity is hinted at in the Bible by the story of Noah, which is concerned with the preservation from destruction, and then evolution, of the present fifth (Aryan) Root Race humanity. This history began when the seeds for the fifth Race were selected from the Atlantean stock, from those who were developing mind. This was in preparation for the coming catastrophic events associated with the great 'flood'. All was sequenced as part of the evolutionary Plan. After the destruction the Atlantean (fourth Root Race) civilisation by the application of the Logoic Will, Noah carried the seeds of the new Race in the Lotus of his Ship. These seeds were the most advanced of the Atlanteans, who possessed Aryan (intellectual) characteristics. The Aryans thus developed the attributes of the mind. Mental Fires needed to be evoked for first Ray qualities to be developed.

Evolution is cyclic. Much of the ancient *karma* due to the misuse of the will via black magical practices (which necessitated the destruction of Atlantis) has not yet been annulled. Vast are the effects of first Ray energy that has been perverted by people. This has been seen in the abuse of political power producing a tendency towards totalitarianism. Mass social injustice, iniquitous laws and wars have been the result. There has also been financial rapacity by the billionaire class. (Those displaying such attitudes are often the reincarnation of black magicians of former eras.) Widespread are the general massed, one-pointedly materialistic, selfish or fanatical tendencies of people. These qualities (in their present sixth Ray modifications) are the reverberating excreta of that ancient karmic pattern.[7]

The first Ray department is headed by the progenitor of the fifth (Aryan) Root Race, Vaivisvata Manu (and his lieutenants). He is the Father (the Noah) of what evolved into this present science based civilisation. His 'ark' is a lotus flower *(chakra),* in which each of its petals exemplifies a divine principle governed by an aspect of the energy of the Will. This lotus is an open doorway for the transference of Life through multidimensional space. When it is time for a new Ray governing a larger or smaller cycle to appear, a Manu wielding an aspect of the first Ray force comes with a 'shipload' of Lives to forge the new dispensation. He projects the Souls that can adequately respond to the new heightened energies, to take the next step forward in planetary evolution. All of Nature's kingdoms are consequently affected.

The effects of first Ray energies presently work through the seventh Ray, via Uranus, the exoteric ruler of Aquarius. The first Ray always works towards liberation from form. On the physical plane this liberation signifies cataclysms and the hastened, transmutative work of the Fire *devas.* Among its grosser effects, such work may be witnessed in the rapid unfoldment of earthquakes, humanity releasing the power of the atom via nuclear bombs, as well as the world wars of the past century, and what is to come. Our civilisation is presently in a stage of constant turmoil and flux, subjectively preparing for the forthcoming New Era.

Cyclic cataclysms and destruction often follow war, for change is endemic within *saṃsāra.* All major changes utilise the first Ray potency to accomplish their task. When the old form is too restrictive, or limited, it must give way for the new. Many forms of the animal kingdom, for instance, are presently gaining their liberation. They are preparing for the opportunity to enter the human kingdom in the new globe that is now forming.

---

7 The subject of the effects of the first Ray energy will be further developed later in this chapter.

To meet the above ends, and also for the incarnation of sixth Race humanity that is concomitant with the New Age, an Avatar of Power shall incarnate with (or as) the Christ. As Jesus stated:

> (N)evertheless I say unto you, Hereafter shall ye see the son of man sitting on the right hand of power, and coming in the clouds of heaven.[8]

An Avatar is an embodiment of the Law of Sacrifice (another first Ray attribute). This represents a descent from Divinity to assist, progress, or liberate the Lives such a One appears for, or incarnates into. All true Avatars embody the first Ray or its sub-Rays, as far as the formed realms are concerned. They therefore represent Power, to whom even the Christ (who sits at His 'right hand' of such a One), is subservient to.

An Avatar is the wielder of the sword or Rod of Power that can swiftly bring sweeping changes to a civilisation, or a world sphere. The forthcoming Manu shall build His ark in the domain of Fire and of Air. Those to enter this ark will seek higher Revelations than hitherto have been broadcast. They will seek and be found, bringing with them a new dispensation along the first Ray line that the Christ will empower with His second Ray purpose. This is an important note, as the first Ray always works in conjunction with the second Ray. (If an emanation of the white Brotherhood and not of the dark brotherhood is demonstrated.)

Phenomena manifests as the effect of Law that is Life, sustained by the Blood of Deity. 'God is Love', yet the Lover appears to be separated from the beloved. The rapture of the Desire of the Lover for the beloved must pierce and burn away all confining walls (a first Ray aspect). This is to the degree that the beloved can respond to the Divine Embrace. Such an Embrace expresses itself as the 'Sword' and 'Fire' that the Christ said He would bring.[9]

All events should be looked at from the angle of meditative unfoldment. From this viewpoint, we can say that the various lotuses that constitute the force plexus *(chakras)* of the planetary Logos are constantly altered as the aeons slip by, according to the rate of His meditative unfoldment. The entities embodying these *chakras* are consequently brought into activity or swept into obscurity. The activity of the Throat centre (fifth Root Race humanity) of the Planetary Logos is His present focus. The Heart centre is presently receiving a rapidly increasing stimulation, causing the seeds of the new sixth Root Race to incarnate amongst

---

8 *Matt. 26:64.* See also *Mark 9:1.*

9 *Matt. 10:34* and *Luke 12:49.*

humanity. They shall produce the new civilisation together with the sixth sub-Race of the fifth Root Race (which are the children of the New Age). This civilisation will be one of harmony and intuition and will respond to a fluid all-embracing creativity, manifesting the garden city of the planet earth, termed 'the New Jerusalem' in the *Revelation of St. John.*[10]

## *Summary of Ray 2 of Love-Wisdom*

The second Ray of Love-Wisdom expresses the Desire-to-Unify of a Logos, to produce coherence or fusion. The Ocean of Quietude is a key expression of this Ray. From this Quietude streams radiatory activity that is magnetic in its effect. The second Ray is the cosmic Magnet that draws all unto it. A relationship to the first Ray is seen here, in that the first Ray expresses the electric field that produces the magnet flux. This supports the teaching dispensation generated through the second Ray's magnetic attraction. The tendency of disciples influenced by this Ray is to lovingly convey the Will (of 'the Father') as service or duty, to integrate all disharmonious teachings with the universality of the *dharma*. They work to heal the sicknesses and diseases of the psyche and to bring all beings into a harmonious integration with the greater Plan of Deity.

The second Ray is the basis of the teaching dispensation of the world's foremost spiritual teachers and sages. A notable example is the Christ who personifies the Son aspect of Deity. (Christianity, however, is a sixth Ray religion, expressing the Ray quality of the Master Jesus rather than the Christ. The sixth Ray is the vehicle of the second Ray.) The actions of the Christ-Jesus unfolded the second Ray purpose, wherein the Christ principle is expressed as active dynamic Love, the ability to sanctify and to save. The sixth Ray added the devotional dynamism and aspiration that brings the second Ray purpose to fruition. The sixth Ray produced the crucifixion experience of Jesus, whilst the second Ray was the emanation of His Teaching for the good of the whole. After Jesus' resurrection, Love-Wisdom was seen as a potent force for the world's salvation to overcome the stranglehold of ignorance and selfishness. In the crucifixion experience, the Blood of the Christ was mingled with the substance of the earth, to infuse the soil of the planet with dynamic Love.

The nature and purpose of one embodying the second Ray is best expressed in the words of Jesus in chapter 17 in *St. John's Gospel,* such as:

---

10 *Rev. 21:2.*

> And now, O Father, glorify thou me with thine own self with the glory which I had with thee before the world was. I have manifested thy name unto the men which thou gavest me out of the world: thine they were, and thou gavest them me; and they have kept thy word. Now they have known that all things whatsoever thou has given me are of thee.[11]

Here the relation of the first Ray ('the Father') to the second Ray (Christ-Jesus) is presented. The emanating force of the second Ray (as far as humanity is concerned) is from the Monad (the Father) on the plane *anupādaka* and thence to *buddhi,* the plane of at-onement.

When reflected into the world of the personality it is found that disciples on the second Ray tend to be wise, religious (in the esoteric sense), judicious, philosophic and intuitive. They are generally engaged in a service arena to humanity, according to the degree they are susceptible to *buddhic* illumination. They generally have an intuitive and comprehensive grasp of the entire panorama of life, instinctively knowing human nature and how to deal with it.

Astrologically, the second Ray of Love-Wisdom manifests through the agency of *Jupiter. Exoterically,* a Jupiter native is the happy medium between the 'coldness' of Saturn and the fiery tempo of Mars. Therefore, those born under Jupiter's influence tend to be jovial, warm, good natured, friendly, compassionate and judicial. They fuse the best elements of the sensual, active qualities of Mars with the taciturn, demanding, methodical nature of Saturn.

The colour generally assigned to this planetary deity (Jupiter) is *blue,* the colour of spirituality and of loving-kindness. The Jupiter native is therefore benevolent, giving hope to all that comes his/her way. Jupiterians tend to be full of religious aspiration, with a high sense of law and order. They are said to generally be possessors of wealth, or one to whom wealth (spiritual or otherwise) falls easily upon.

Due to the above qualities, Jupiter is known as the greater fortunate in astrological texts. (Venus is known as the lesser fortunate.) Being good-natured, the second Ray person may fall victim to the caprices of others. There is a mixture of nobility coupled with kindness that should be inherent in the natures of the ideal parent or dedicated clergyman.

The second Ray is pre-eminently the Ray of the teacher, the scholar of life, who often has a clear, comprehensive grasp of the principles involved in the

---

11 *John, 17:5-7.*

chosen subject. This is often engendered to the point that the person becomes over-absorbed in his/her study in the quest for Truth. This can happen to a degree that borders on contempt towards the mental limitations of others. Self-pity, or a Messiah complex can also be found in second Ray types.[12]

The *esoteric colour* of the second Ray is indigo blue, the colour of the vast sky in the very early dawn. This colour therefore indicates the immutable, ineffable, unifying path of the vast cosmic evolution. It is the colour of the doorway to the meditation-Mind, leading to the Soul or to the abstracted planes of perception. In our solar system all of the other Rays are sub-Rays of this fundamental Ray, and therein lies the progression of human destiny. Indigo-blue is the colour of the solar Logos and of Kṛṣṇa (an incarnation of Viṣṇu). All Lives in the solar system therefore find that receptivity to Love-Wisdom is the way of progress along their evolutionary paths.

The second Ray is the 'Word of God' that 'in the beginning was....and the Word was with God and the Word was God'.[13] This Word is spoken from the Heart, the Soul or sun of all manifested Life. The sages of the world testify to (and radiate the potency of) this force through their works and deeds. When united with the Will, it produces a magnetic attraction that draws all unto it. This Ray is 'the way, the truth, and the life',[14]that the Christ so aptly embodied. The second Ray makes the work of the Builders of the form possible.

### *Summary of Ray 3 of Mathematically Exact Activity*

The third Ray manifests as a will to evolve. It expresses the wisdom of Deity as an evolutionary capacity. It is the ever-present result of the progressive cyclic action of great angelic Lives that stimulate lesser evolved entities to experience and evolve through intelligent cognition. Active intelligence is therefore the keynote

---

12 See Alice Bailey's *Glamour, A World Problem,* 120-123, for a general list of the personal afflictions possessed by people along the various Ray types. That entire book could also be used as an esoteric supplement to understanding the nature of these afflictions amongst humanity if thought out in astrological terms.

13 *John 1:1.*

14 *John 14:6.* Note that when analysing such esoteric statements, one must be careful to properly consider the structural content. The entire phrase is a second Ray statement, but within this the three major Rays are also implied. 'The way' as a third Ray function is the path that one takes to find the Truth. 'The truth' as a second Ray function is an emanation of the Love principle that is the sustaining motivation behind following the path to Life. 'The life' is a first Ray function. Life being the underlying Purpose behind the Way and the Truth.

of the third Ray. It is the combined result of the activities of the intelligences that coherently build what is to be. It manifests in a mathematically certain way when expressed via a higher Mind.

Experience is, and results in, the emergence of the mind, which must eventually give birth to the Christ-consciousness (the second Ray). Because rightly ordered active intelligence gives birth to the Christ or Son aspect, so the third Ray is known as the Mother aspect of Deity. The third Ray synthesises the minor four Rays (called the Rays of Attribute), whilst it eventually merges into or becomes the second aspect. The seven become the three primary (Rays of Aspect), the three become the two and the two are eventually abstracted back into the One Ineffable Light.

The third Ray corresponds to the organisational aspect, the 'thinking part', or brain of man or Heavenly Man. It could be said to represent the managerial position of a company or government, whereas the other (lesser) Rays represent the staff, the members or organs of a body whose function is to supply the information, the labour, and to manifest the various permutations of the will of the management.

In the Hierarchy of Enlightened Being, the Mahāchohan governs the manifestation of this Ray (and the four lesser ones). Together, the Manu, the Christ and the Mahāchohan form the triune executive council of that Hierarchy (the Heart centre in the body of Deity).

Astrologically, the third Ray is ruled by *Saturn.* As Saturn is the bearer of *karma exoterically*, so Saturnians are depicted as being very unfortunate in their undertakings, causing woes and ills to those around. Saturn's influence is thus the most maligned of all the planets and is traditionally known as the greater maleficent. (Mars is known as the lesser maleficent.) Because this planet appears to travel on an orbit further away from the sun than any other traditional planet, astrologers typified the personalities ruled by Saturn as somewhat cold, stern, icy or overbearing in disposition. The long time taken to complete this orbit makes those who are born under its influence apt to be meditative, solemn, cautious, taking much time to make up their minds. The Saturnian is, however, normally industrious and active in world or social affairs.

The *exoteric* colour assigned to Saturn is green. This hue has a wide range of meanings, and indicates that a 'Saturnian' subject could be a teacher, the prototype scholarly professor, or stern didactic schoolmaster. Saturnians are involved with anything concerning learning, meditativeness, organisational abilities and business acumen. Despite the activity associated with the third Ray, those governed by this sign tend to be against most forms of change, of anything new and vital. This reflects the slow movement of this planet in the heavens.

Green can also correspond to selfishness and adaptability. Thus the actions of third Ray personalities often have a selfish undertone. They are generally hard working, active and industrious, the natural bank clerk or miser, for they are said to be fond of money. Green is also the colour of compassion and of healing. The third Ray personality can also be imaginative, intellectual, and tend towards selfishness, critical assertiveness and pride. The above tendencies are, however, modified by the activity aspects of the third Ray and its associated wisdom.

*Esoterically,* the colour assigned to this Ray is emerald green. This is the general colouring of the vegetable kingdom, which is embodied by this activity Ray. The third Ray is a direct effect of the activity of the third Creative Hierarchy via *ātma* (the third plane of perception) and governs the *devas* that actively embody the forms of all Lives. This Ray is the head of the emanation of the fivefold Brahmā aspect.

Emerald green is said to be the colour that governed the previous solar system. It is the overall colour of healing and of compassion. The colour is found predominantly manifest in spring, the beginning of Nature's cycles, when the activities of the various Creative Intelligences are at their height. Green later gives way to the autumn reds and yellows, spelling the death of the previous cycle of activity. These colours indicate periods of cyclic breath productive of meditation. (Yellow is a colour attributed to *buddhi.*) The explanation of the true nature of the esoteric colours is too abstruse to be provided here. Colours veil the Real.[15] They are radiations, the effect of sound, of force that is moving and affecting substance of some kind. Everything depends, as always, upon the angle of vision, the polarisation of the observer, and the nature of clairvoyance. All of these can colour the vision. The exoteric colours seen by the personality are part of the great illusion.

Mathematically Exact Activity describes the nature of the enlightened Mind that can view vast panoramas of the domains of manifestation, and so quickly discern the correct path of action. Third Ray disciples therefore have the ability to rightly rationalise the correct path of action in any field of endeavour. They are natural executives in any business enterprise, in the field of science, or service arena. Active Intelligence best describes the expression of this Ray amongst humanity in general.

15 See Alice Bailey's *Letters on Occult Meditation* for a more detailed exposé of this subject.

The attributes of Saturn find their densest expression in the element lead. Jupiter relates to tin, Venus to copper, and the Sun to gold.

### *Summary of Ray 4 of Beautifying Harmony overcoming Conflict*

This Ray, governing the fourth plane *(buddhi),* stands as the middle between extremes (the higher and lower three of the septenary). It produces the tendencies of the higher Mind to imitate qualities of Deity, harmonising evolutionary progression amidst the natural disharmony of human civilisations. It finds its outlet as an inclusive, loving inspiration, an evoked rhythm of spontaneous beauty often found by overcoming conflict. Conflict is a natural property of the mental plane, wherein is found the war of ideas, concepts and thought-forms. These are ever-changing, evolving and adapting to new emotio-mental climates and attitudes. All eventually becomes resolved when the person strikes a golden mean that equilibrates all opposing factors; thus the capacity to appreciate beauty and peace is evolved. This is an expression of the intuition that is fostered when a person treads the narrow razor edged path. (The middle way that leads to enlightenment.)

Conflict and intellectual resolution, producing illumination and harmony, are keywords of the Mercurian fourth Ray individual. He/she becomes the apt mediator, quick to see the cause of trouble and its resolution. Mercury here signifies the wise person, the sage giving good advice in all intellectual matters.

Mercury corresponds to the yellow band of the spectrum, where yellow implies fluid, abstract thought capabilities. The fourth Ray individual thereby becomes the ideal teacher, linguist and abstract thinker. Because of Mercury's nearness to the sun, the Mercurian person is greatly influenced by that orb, possessing many of its astrological characteristics. In general, there is however a lack of the emotional thinking, pride and desire to outshine others possessed by those ruled by the Sun in Leo. Mercury revolves rapidly around the sun, thus those ruled by this planet are said to be quick, active, extremely inventive, loving all forms of speed. All these qualities allow the sensitivity to subtle impression that makes a poet, artist or musician, the philosopher and certain types of medical practitioners and business people. As well as the arts, the fleet-footed messenger of the Gods rules transport, shipping, and thus the entrepreneur involved in such activities. This concerns all enterprises that are quick and active, enabling the person to efficiently do what needs to be accomplished. The Mercurian is normally keenly in tune with all higher intellectual or intuitional faculties and thus is fond of all the enterprises that involve the intellect, wit and intuition. He/she is well balanced and adjusts harmoniously to all the laws of Life. Thus Mercury also rules the tongue and the art of speech.

*Esoterically,* the colour of the fourth Ray is golden yellow. It is a combination of the abstracting principle of the Air that brightens the Fires of the mind and the orange of the fifth Ray, which consumes the green of activity. Yellow vivifies the Heart *chakra,* which sustains all Life. It is also the colour of the crown, which the enlightened King wears. He has conquered all of the cycles of activity in his domain, possibly with the sword (the first Ray energy conveyed via *buddhi*), but must rule his subjects with a loving Heart and hand (the second Ray). A wise general disposition must manifest if he is to retain his crown.

Mercury governs the actions of humanity, as the qualities of the fourth Ray embody the keynotes of human aspirations and their evolutionary method. The purpose of humanity is to become a mediator between the universal and the particular, between substance and energy, 'God' and His Creation. Humanity esoterically is to embody the Heart centre of the planetary Logos. As they evolve the capacity to think with the Heart (the central sun in the system) so they awaken the organ of Vision (the Ājñā centre, the Mercurial Eye), as enlightened Seers. This eventuation is an esoteric reason behind the pageant of human evolutionary progress and suffering. Mercury governs the path of the *antaḥkaraṇa*, the bridge that leads from one kingdom to another in all levels of expression.

Mercury is quicksilver, the great solvent in the metallic world. Its physical properties suggest the above-mentioned mercurial qualities. The colours of its ores are red, yellow and black, and are very poisonous. (As are also the very potent energies that *buddhi* conveys when distorted by the astral vehicle.) The life and trials of Mercury (in the form of its oxide) is what the alchemists used as the starting point in their endeavour to evolve the philosopher's stone. With it the alchemical, transmutative process is thus produced. Consequently, Mercury aptly expresses the spiritual qualities of the aspiring person.

### *Summary of Ray 5 of the Scientific Mode*

The Active Intelligence of the third Ray is reflected into corporeal expression as the *fifth Ray* of the *Scientific Mode.* When reflected into physical expression, the archetypal Mind *(ātma)* becomes the empirical mind, the classifier, the segregator. The abstraction of the third Ray thereby becomes circumscribed by empirical considerations.

The *deva* Hierarchy that embody the mental plane ('Makara the Mystery'—the Agnishvattas) modify what is conveyed from the plane *ātma* to suit their creative needs. They scientifically, mechanically and with exactitude, utilise inherent intelligence to fashion or make the formed universe. This necessitates a geometric and mathematical encoding that reflects as far as possible. In this way, Mother Nature has produced the most marvellous designs and patterns in the mineral, plant and animal worlds. Every expression of Nature's kingdom (be it a leaf, flower, atom, or person) conveys the very evident geometrisation of the fifth Ray Builders. We see perfections in harmony and creativity all around. Humanity but feebly imitates this through their achievements in science and technology, united with art.

Venus (who governs the fifth Ray) gives birth to the physical laws of Nature, whilst all that are polarised in their mental body are products of Her 'Womb'. This Ray is an emanation of the Element Fire. It is with such Fiery forces that humanity and *devas* build and create. In Fire, the metals and the implements of destruction or creation are forged. Heat and light are aspects of Fire. Heat warms, it is the result of embodied Life, and light illumines, shows the way to understanding. Yet Fire is also destructive. Through utilising it we destroy the old in order to build the new. The fifth Ray therefore rules the creative and destructive forces in Nature, of which the harnessing of atomic energy is the symbol. (The 'splitting of the atom', for instance, was the direct result of human beings developing the ability to think to conclusion with regard to the laws of the dense physical plane. We have yet to do this in the other departments of Life.)

*Exoterically,* Venus is the closest planet to the earth (apart from the Moon). She is the morning star, the personification of serene beauty, thus she sends warm, beneficial, loving rays to the earth. The colour attributed to the fifth Ray is *orange*, the colour of the intellect, and also of Fire. This is the colour of illumination, towards which the Venusian will always strive with the highest ideals and aspiration. They are generally warm and sociable. They cling to their own sense of form, yet yield to the laws of Nature and of the beauty of the universe around them. They are fond of the dictates of life and are easily attracted to the selfish side of their nature, for social and national prestige. They are changeable and are generally found in jobs where their hands and intellect are jointly used as tools to make or fashion what they desire, such as carpentry, art or mathematics. This is especially so for the scientist and technologist.

*Esoterically,* the fifth Ray colour is also orange. It is the principal hue that qualifies the knowledge petals of the Soul, therefore is also the colour of the mental plane. The *yogins* of the East wear saffron coloured robes, signifying the importance for them to master the mind. Only therein, through its right control and use, can the path of liberation be sought. Orange blends with the three primary colours – red, yellow and blue, as well as with white – to make the colours of the mineral kingdom of the earth, which are a direct reflection of the mental plane.

The metal copper is the dense concretisation of this Ray energy. Its salts are orange-red when amorphous, and blue-green when united with water (e.g., copper sulphate). The blue-green colour also symbolises the astral plane.

### *Summary of Ray 6 of Devotion or Aspiration*

The sixth Ray is expressed via the substance of the astral plane. The potency of the effect of astral substance, and of this Ray upon humanity, is partly due to the fact that the path of least resistance for buddhic energy is to bypass the empirical mind (that segregates as it classifies and thus restricts the free flow of the energy of Love), to find a receptive vehicle of expression in the astral plane. This is the field of people's emotions, desires and attachments. Thus the Solar Plexus centre becomes the receptive centre for astral energy. Love-Wisdom then translates as devotion. Water, when calmed, will reflect the image of the surrounding scenery. Similarly, the astral body, when calmed and freed from emotions and desire, will reflect the images of at-onement and universality emanated from *buddhi,* the fourth cosmic ether. The complete intensity of what emanates via *buddhi* can, however, only be experienced at the fourth Initiation, and the attainment of *śūnyatā.*

The sixth Ray of Devotion or Aspiration, embodied by Mars, represents the force of desire on all planes of perception. It is the potent Logoic force that causes manifestation, as well as our physical actions. Thus Mars is the exoteric ruler of desire, virile vigour, and assertiveness in all its expressions. Desire is eventually transmuted into devotion – to noble ideas, thoughts and works. It is the first stage of the means whereby the lover can unite or fuse with the beloved. (The beloved here is the force of beauty and harmony that represents the higher Self.)

This is the Ray, therefore, that rules the devotional religions, such as Christianity and Islam. It governs the common person and also the soldier, be he of fortune or of light. Rightly used by the aspirant (when desire is transmuted into Love), this force allows the person to unite with what has been desired throughout the ages, producing the ecstasy of the mystic.

This Ray has governed the western world via its religion for the past 2,000 years (as seen by the many wars fought 'in the name of God'). Its influence is now waning as humanity takes a more mental attitude to religious doctrines. The age old desires and aspirations of the mystic are being replaced by the exact knowledge and positive energy direction of the scientist and esotericist. The desire is now to not only 'love God' but to have intelligible knowledge concerning Deity. The time has come when what has previously only been 'spoken in darkness' shall be 'proclaimed upon the housetops'[16] for all to know of.

The ruler of the sixth Ray conveys the concreting emanations of the Logos. They express the limits of His expression as a force in *saṃsāra*. (The etheric plane is the medium of transmission for these forces into dense substance.) All manifestation is but an expression of the concretion of energy. Mars directs this energy. A creative magician consciously utilises energy dynamics to produce the materialisation of phenomena. Such a one also works directly with Nature's creative agencies (the *devas*). Conversely, the materialistic scientist works but blindly with the same agents, hence the marvels of our present scientific age will be largely superseded by the esoteric sciences that will flourish in the New Age.

Exoterically, the colour attributed to Mars is red (or deep pink), which is also the visible colour of this planet. This is the largest wavelength of the visible portion of the electromagnetic spectrum and is akin to heat, the effect of mechanical or frictional energy.

Aurically, red is the colour of passion or anger in the personality. It conveys the sensual, creative and destructive energies (of humanity or 'God'). Therefore, Mars is said to be the god of war. Mars clutches the universe in his powerful grasp, bereft of either fear or timidity. The Martian personality can be fiery and fierce, relentlessly pursuing his/her prey (both in *saṃsāra* and also in the realms of meaning). The unevolved personality ruled by this sign is said to be full of animal passion and vigour, thus it is aggressively selfish with a tendency to pick fights, and to boast.

Red is also the colour of the blood stream and the *prāṇa* therein, which Mars also rules.

Though the goddess Venus was the wife of Vulcan in classical myths, she very often couples with Mars, thus indicating the union of mind with desire *(kāma-manas)* that dominates most personalities. Martians are extremely enterprising (with mechanical things), involved in any activity where there is a sense of personal vigour and will. However, a person under its influence can be malicious and untrustworthy, especially if martial energy helps to foster schemes for personal aggrandisement. It can thus be gathered that the sixth Ray person has much energy

---

16 *Luke 12:2.*

that is often misdirected and lost in self-made glamour. (There is a tendency to assert these upon others.) When this energy is rightly used, it can make the person a very effective receptor and transmitter of Love (transmuted desire). Of this, pink is the exoteric colour and indicator. (Red transforms into pink.) Due to the above qualities, Mars is said to be malefic in its effects.

The esoteric colour of the sixth Ray is rose or turquoise (the blue-green of the great oceans and Watery sphere of this earth). This energy governs the astral plane that is the great Womb of Nature. From it, our terrestrial Life came, and its energies sustain all of our lives. The sixth Ray is the lowest tonality of the second Ray line (2, 4, 6) in the world of forms.

The metal iron embodies this Ray energy, and much could be gained if we meditate upon its qualities. There are, for instance, the red-brown and greenish hues of its ores, and the fact that iron colours the haemoglobin in the blood (making it red). Thus it is the oxygen carrier, the conveyer of *prāṇa,* the vitality empowering the cells in our bodies.

### *Summary of Ray 7 of Ceremonial Magic, Materialising Power*

The seventh Ray of Ceremonial Magic is ruled by *Uranus.* This Ray is basically the reflection of all the Rays, but principally the first Ray line (via the third and fifth Rays). This makes the physical plane an automatic externalisation of the mental.

'As a man thinketh in this heart, so is he', is an occult platitude of very ancient standing. It has profound practical significance to humanity. In many ways, it denotes the means whereby the magician engenders his work – through the powers of thought directed by the Heart, the vehicle of the Soul. To think means the power to visualise, and this implies the right use of the eye,[17] whilst to be creative the thought process must produce phenomenal results. This creativity generally also necessitates the use of the hands. The Eye, the Heart, and the hands are the prime tools of the white magician. All meditation work, the intonation of mantras, or even wishful thinking, therefore, must be ruled by the above adage.

Ceremony is understood as rhythm and ritual that have the ability to bring down and fix in place certain spiritual forces. Ritual is seen in the external world within the cycles of nature, such as the happenings of day and night, the advent of the seasons, the procession of the equinoxes, the phases of the moon, the comings

---

17 The right and left eyes, as well as the third Eye are specifically indicated here, but all of the *chakras* can also be considered 'Eyes'. The right eye is said to be the eye of wisdom, and the left the eye of the intellect, of *manas*.

and goings of the weeks. These external happenings are the result of conditionings within the body of Deity. When a person has a true sensitivity and ability to tap the psychic and subtle forces within (such as the flow of *prāṇa),* then the outward life becomes increasingly simplified and automatic, as a ritual governed by the radiatory activity of the Spirit within. The ceremonial activities of many of the world's religions are simply the outward form or symbolism that indicate certain spiritual cycles, events or evolutionary tendencies (past, present or future) within Nature, or of 'God's' Kingdom. Many *devas* can be contacted through the evocative effect of mass or group rituals, especially the violet *devas* of the ethers.

The *esoteric colour* of this Ray is violet, which colours the etheric plane, via which much magical work of the future will be conducted.

*Exoterically,* Uranus is regarded as the planet of occultism, affecting the higher centres of the brain. It influences those who have a tendency toward the occult way of life with strong spiritual leanings. Uranus influences the world's great mystics, seers, revolutionaries, and all whose works effect far-reaching changes upon humanity. It is also said to influence those that are regarded to be eccentrics, geniuses, or reformers. They are far-sighted people who (because of their nature, their insightful eccentricity) can arouse active hostility, producing many enemies. (For example, as did Copernicus, Galileo, Paracelsus, Goethe, etc.). Their unusually strong, dauntless characteristics and extraordinary abilities generally allowed them to be independent amidst the regimented, concise ideals and indoctrinations of the people of their time. The Uranian subject often travels upon the face of the earth endeavouring to impart a vision of utopia, demonstrating great inventiveness to all around.

Because it takes seven years for Uranus to pass through a single sign of the zodiac, its influence generally affects the wider community rather than the individual (except those that are strong willed). These influences depict whole cycles of events, as well as concepts such as the 'universal brotherhood of man', international peace movements, and revolutionary changes of all types that are concerned with the advancement of humanity (or of the subhuman kingdoms).

The outer planets (Uranus, Neptune and Pluto) are said to have a greater intensity of vibratory emanation than those of the other planets (thereby acting through our higher principles). Thus, only those that have a measure of Soul contact can respond to their subtle forces. This only becomes possible when people are engaged in humanitarian services to the group with which they are involved. A true Uranian personality, therefore, was quite rare in the past, but will be found with greater frequency in the Aquarian age. Such people will work to spread Light, Love and Peace amongst humanity.

The qualities of the less evolved type of Uranian are often greatly modified by the energies of the Moon, which esoterically veils Uranus. Uranus governs the etheric body. Because forces from the astral realm largely control etheric effects, so astrologically, the Moon greatly modifies the energies of Uranus and can be said to take its place for average humanity. This will be the case until people dissipate the fogs and mists of glamour and *māyā* in the world, and they become intuitive and illumined (Mercurial). This will increasingly eventuate during the New Age.

The *exoteric* colour of the Moon is said to be silver (or white) and therefore is an excellent reflector of the light of the sun and of psychic or spiritual forces. The fourth Ray governs the Moon, which is the bridge between the mind and the physical body. (Mercury, as was seen, is also qualified by the fourth Ray and is the mediator between the higher and lower minds.) The higher Mind governs the subjective world and the lower mind governs the objective (the world of *māyā).* The Moon here is but the 'shadow' of Mercury, thus veiling the substance of the astral plane, the various psychic forms therein, and their interrelationships.

The relationship between the Moon and Uranus can be intuited by progressively conceptualising that the Moon governs many of the cycles associated with the dense physical plane, and Uranus governs the etheric planes. The moon revolves around the earth once every twenty-eight days and has different phases that greatly affect the earth, causing among other things atmospheric and oceanic tides. She rules anything concerning Water. Astrologers therefore say that those born under the lunar influence tend to be fishermen, sailors, etc., people that are very apt to roam about, born wanderers. The moon also symbolises the female principle, such as the menstrual periods (which normally occur every 28 days, the number of days that it takes the moon to revolve around the earth) and the period of gestation (that takes exactly ten lunar months). This shows the close relationship of the moon to the 'Mother of all forms'. This maternal quality in the personality that is ruled by the Moon expresses itself as affinity to domestic abilities. When the 'womb of matter' has given birth to a 'Son of Wisdom', then Uranus takes over the rulership of the individual.

Our lunar orb is said to be disintegrating, a dead shell, for the lives that had embodied it left in waves aeons ago to animate the earth. Thus, the moon is said to be the earth's Mother.[18] The earth continually leeches powerful emanations

18 As somewhat explained in the works of Blavatsky, Bailey, and my volumes on *The*

of a disintegrating and disruptive type from it, whilst the moon itself (as a dead body) is also a vampire to the earth, helping to cause the lower forms of psychism. From this idea, the word lunacy derives its factual basis. Therefore, lunar energy aids the work of the lower type of medium. They often similarly 'leech out' *prāṇa* from others and themselves in order to produce their materialisations. Also, because of the above, witches are said to traditionally hold their Sabbath rites during full moon periods.

We see here why those born under the Moon's influence may be said to be semi-intellectual, lacking in decision-making, following the example of others. They become inactive and dreamy, indifferent, submissive and sometimes offensive. The lunar orb also governs the physical senses (to an extent), animal passions, and in conjunction with Mars, it controls the deeply subconscious and instinctive abilities in humanity. Its ascending node is considered as fortunate or helpful, while its descending node is considered unfortunate. They differ because of the difference in distance away from the earth.

It can be clearly seen from the above how the exoteric account of the nature of planets as they affect the personality is based on the observable (visual) relationships of those planets to the earth. The influences of the planetary regents are in the nature of an immense thought form (an illusion) built by humanity throughout the ages that completely conditions the unevolved personality. A person is born into the rulership of the planets as governed by their prototypes that exist within the ring-pass-not of thought-forms existing on the astral plane. Humanity created them aeons ago, and because of their extreme potency they now rule those polarised upon the astral plane.

A property of the astral plane is to reverse the images from the world of meaning, the realms of Light, often distorting that reflection. For this reason, humanity retrogresses (travelling clockwise) through the zodiac as they cyclically reincarnate during their evolutionary journey through *saṃsāra*. However, once someone aspires to the higher Self and can tap the forces from the domains of Light, then their path reorients, to progress from Aries to Pisces via Taurus (instead of from Pisces to Aries via Aquarius). Eventually the 'great illusion' is negated. (This is because in this reversal process one 'fights' or works off the illusions that were created during past incarnations.)

This 'turning about' in the seat of consciousness is a great crisis in an aspirant's life, enabling the disciple to eventually contact new, more subtle and potent forces

---

*Constitution of Shambhala.*

from the subjective (esoteric) planetary Rulers. Such a person has entered the path of discipleship and of Initiation. Old thought-forms then no longer condition the disciple, thus the charts and predictions of the average astrologer are no longer viable. The disciple has started on the journey to complete self-mastery of the entire personality world (including his/her planetary conditionings). When the disciple enters the realm of causes and not the world of effects, an Initiate has then appeared that has accrued mastery over the world of forms. The exoteric planetary effects are then ineffective and the esoteric planetary rulers influence the Initiate. They project energies from the domain of the Soul, or from the abstracted planes of perception. For the period between the first three Initiations, disciples generally waver between being influenced by the exoteric and esoteric rulers.

| Constellation | Exoteric Ruler | Esoteric Ruler |
|---|---|---|
| 1. Aries | Mars (Ray 6) | **Mercury (Ray 4)** |
| 2. Taurus | **Venus (Ray 5)** | **Vulcan (Ray 1)** |
| 3. Gemini | **Mercury (Ray 4)** | **Venus (Ray 5)** |
| 4. Cancer | The Moon (Ray 4) | The Sun (Ray 2) |
| 5. Leo | The Sun (Ray 2) | The Sun (Ray 2) |
| 6. Virgo | **Mercury (Ray 4)** | The Moon (Ray 4) |
| 7. Libra | **Venus (Ray 5)** | **Uranus (Ray 7)** |
| 8. Scorpio | Mars (Ray 6) | Mars (Ray 6) |
| 9. Sagittarius | **Jupiter (Ray 2)** | The Earth (Ray 3) |
| 10. Capricorn | **Saturn (Ray 3)** | **Saturn (Ray 3)** |
| 11. Aquarius | **Uranus (Ray 7)** | **Jupiter (Ray 2)** |
| 12. Pisces | **Jupiter (Ray 2)** | Pluto (Ray 1) |

**Table 3. The exoteric and esoteric planetary rulers**

Table 3 shows a list of the exoteric planetary rulers governing the ordinary person, and the esoteric ones governing disciples and Initiates.[19] The planets in bold are sacred planets. They symbolise the planetary Logoi that are no longer influenced by the matter of the past solar system, thus whose humanity

19 The list is taken from Alice Bailey's *Esoteric Astrology*, 68.

have mastered the physical domain. Such planetary Logoi can be considered as 'Initiates', whereas the non-sacred planets are thus considered as 'Personalities'. The sacred group relate principally to the energies above the diaphragm of the solar Logos, whereas the non-sacred planets relate principally to the energies of the Inner Round, as synthesised by the Solar Plexus centre. This group thus principally concern themselves with the great transmutative battles (such as found on our earth). The Logoi of the sacred planets are repositories of Wisdom for the training of Initiates (above the third degree) and whose true focus is upon cosmic shores.

## The planets and the interrelated fixed and mutable crosses

Information concerning the interrelationship between the esoteric planetary regents can be obtained from a study of the interrelated fixed and mutable crosses summarised in Figure 5 below. This figure can be considered an extension of the information presented in Figure 44 of my book *Esoteric Cosmology and Modern Physics.* This is part of the section of Appendix 1, entitled 'The Heart is the Mind'.[20] Consequently, I will not explain the meaning of the eight directions in space here other than providing their names, for such information is provided there plus in various other books of mine.

The circles radiating out from the centre of Figure 5 represent wheels, or spheres of activity of the triune Logos, of the trinities of all manifested Life. The eight directions have astrological signs assigned to them, which will assist the reader to gain much further esoteric understanding. The signs utilised here are of the planetary Regents that embody the qualities of the seven Rays, plus those of the three Synthesising Schemes (Uranus I, Neptune II, and Saturn III). Though Earth and Mars are non-sacred planets, they take the role of the seventh and sixth Ray Regents respectively. (These are the southeast and southwest directions of *expression* and *understanding.*) They represent the 'feet' through which the other Ray lines must be grounded. Note that the Earth is governed exoterically by the third Ray and esoterically by the seventh. Ceremonial ordering thus flavours all Life upon this convulsing sphere of mutable activity. The seventh Ray grounds all other Ray lines, as the Earth must also be able to do, if the corporeal forms of humanity are to evolve through all possible Ray combinations.

---

20 See Appendix one, pages 505-20 of *Esoteric Cosmology and Modern Physics,* and page 516 for Figure 44. Parts of the communication on page 506 are also quoted here.

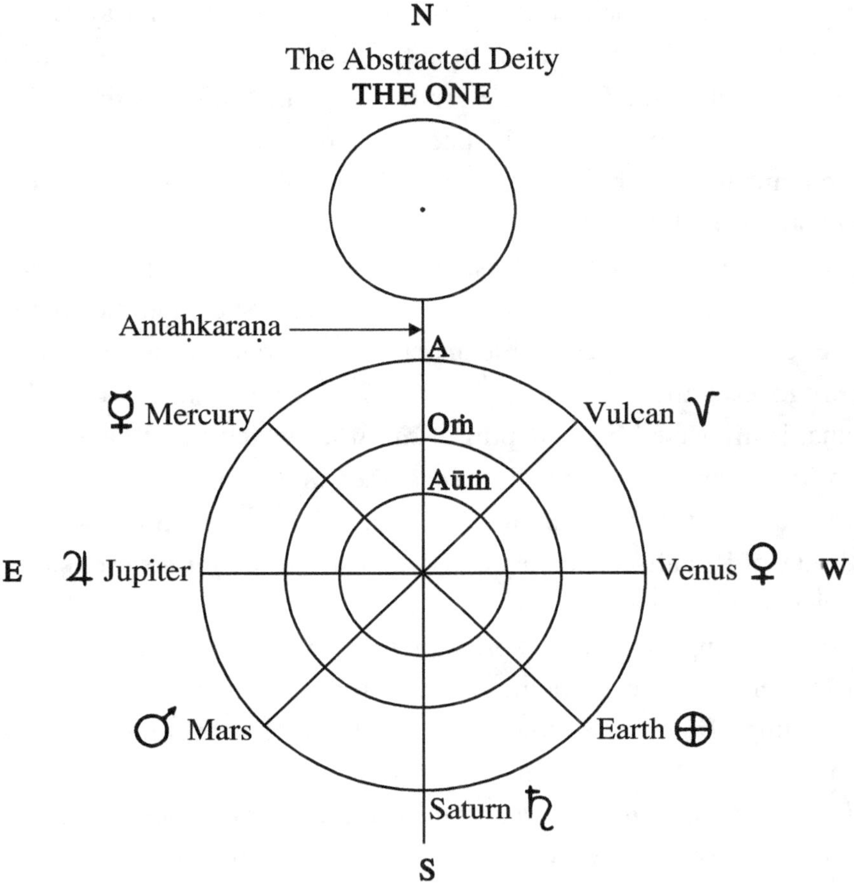


**Figure 5. The ankh - its higher attributes**

*Mercury* governs the *northeast,* the direction of *unity*, which integrates all of the forces and energies that must be brought to bear to produce any purpose. It listens to its Brothers so that the Plan can be effectively accomplished. The needed energy to accomplish such purpose is the fourth Ray of Beautifying Harmony Overcoming Conflict. This Ray works to harmonise any new zone of created activity amidst the chaos of discordant energies. Being the messenger of the Gods, Mercury is the mediator, or mirror that reflects the archetype (the formulated Plan) into manifest space. At first this is to produce the appearing phenomena. Later, the energies work to overcome the vicissitudes of *saṃsāra.*

*Mars* governs the *southeast,* the direction of *expression.* Mars listens to the directives from the northeast direction, but may not acknowledge them, thus producing distortions of the Plan. This is the effect of the Watery sixth Ray energy that Mars governs. Alternatively, the devotional and martial sixth Ray can facilitate the outward expression of energies from the directive Eye to project its Purpose into the realm of form. This is the driving force that sustains the activities of all atomic units, interrelating their spheres of endeavour. (Either in a positive or negative manner.) Conflict, battle, the clash of forces, the symbolism of blood, blood relations, and its spilling into the deserts of Life are all implicated here. The astral plane, governed by Mars, necessarily colours the originating seeded mental impulse according to its own conditionings. Such qualities manifest as desires of the causative agent while undergoing its transformative expression.

*Earth* governs the *southwest,* the direction of *understanding.* At first, the individual is immersed in the depths of *saṃsara,* which 'slays the Real'. As the personality battles with its conditionings, then understanding gradually comes as to the nature of its allurements. The quest for liberation then ensues. The seventh Ray of Ritualised Activity and demonstrable Power governs such a path. The cycles (the seasons of aeonic involvement) come and go on the sphere of the earth, allowing the initial expression to be moulded by all Ray colourings and mental-emotional conditionings. This produces beneficence, or the gain in understanding of the originating Causative Impulse within the human unit or group, which thereby matures in cyclic resolve.

*Vulcan* governs the *northwest* arm (of *good will)* of the mutable cross. It thus sounds out the note of the accomplished gain of all former activity. It 'repeats what it knows' to all that have the capacity to hear. The energy of the first Ray of Will or Power is utilised here to terminate all past causative cycles and to project the gain into new fields of abstraction and Revelation.

The four cardinal positions manifest the fixed cross of the crucified Christ. They represent the major directions of force that condition the causative agent when formulating the plan to create, to accomplish any field of action.

*Jupiter* governs the *eastern* arm (of *inwards* to the Heart of Life), hence the second Ray of Love-Wisdom that manifests the heartbeat pulsating the rhythms of Love. Attunement to this heartbeat accords the Sound of Revelation, thus producing a synthetic understanding of the purpose for the Causative impulse. The past, present and the future can be envisioned in a moment of timelessness. The Plan (Idea) to be projected into objectivity is instantaneously seen and adapted so that beneficent Purpose for the whole is achieved. All the obstacles that may mar the Plan are seen at a glance, as well as what facilitates the projected Idea, so that success eventuates.

*Saturn* the Lord of *karma* governs the *southern* arm, of *downward* into the realm of the little ones. The third Ray of Mathematically Exact Activity comes into expression here. This Ray causes the projection of the Idea downwards via the field of *karma* into the morass of seeded Ideas governing the multitudinous atomic unities swimming together in the ocean of sensation. The karmic implications and interrelations in the fields of activity must be comprehended by the causative agent if the Idea is to succeed. The synthetic overview from the eastern direction is now particularised into the minutiae of energy interactions and associations. Saturn projects the Logoic Will, to form the domains of illusion, which 'perverts' the Real.

*Venus* governs the *western* direction of *outwards* into the field of service. The fifth Ray of the Scientific Mode rules via the domain of the mind. Here the service arena of the Idea is brought to fruition within that sphere or class of entities of which that Idea is a part. The relation between the major classes or groupings of seeded Ideas is now scientifically unfolded, so that the whole is benefited rightly. All will thereby move on to the next major cycle of evolutionary activity.

*The Sun* governs the *northern* direction of upwards to the domains of Divinity. (The One from which the entire originating Causative gesture emanated. This One is here symbolised by the circle that projects the *maṇḍala* of the eight-armed cross.) To this One the lesser causative agents (thinkers) aspire, for which purpose the Logoic Idea was seeded and projected into objectivity. The evolution of mind into Mind by the forms that evolved to bear the mind is the objective of the Causative process.

From the central point radiates the triune circle of expansive embraciveness that is the Heart of Life. It beats out the dynamism of the Word (the seeded Idea) in its multifarious intonations (versions, forms or types) to the Hearts of all Being. This concerns the expression or *essence* of the Idea, its essentiality as part of the great whole. It therefore manifests as a trinity, a reflection of the triune Deity (or Word) – signified by the solar disc. This trinity is therefore veiled by the Sun, producing the perfect number ten. This is the energy that drives the inherent structural ordering of the Idea onwards and outwards to perfected fulfilment. It is the Soul (or Heart) of the Logoic Idea. As such, it is an aspect of the Soul of all Life (the *anima mundi)* that manifests the Idea of the Triune Word.

The A – the first Logos – the Father. (Uranus I Synthesising Scheme.)
The Oṁ – the second Logos – the Son. (Neptune II Synthesising Scheme.)
The Aūṁ – the third Logos – the Mother. (Saturn III Synthesising Scheme.)[21]

21 These Synthesising Schemes are explained in Alice Bailey's *A Treatise on Cosmic Fire.*

The *antaḥkaraṇa* is the line of relationship that holds all together. It is singular and yet continuously moves in the eight directions, repeating 'what it knows' to the 'drum of the heartbeat'. As this dynamo of mutability projects the Aūṁ throughout time and space, the *antaḥkaraṇa* brings the Idea into fruition and also becomes the path of its resolution. It is the sight of the Eye (its line of direction) that allows the Causative agent to project his purpose.

## The effect of first Ray energy

Humanity has for ages been protected from the direct potency of the first Ray by Hierarchy, who tone down this Shambhalic energy. In the twentieth century, however, this force from Shambhala has been directly projected upon humanity. The effect has been such that it intensified human self will, thus enhancing separateness and nationalistic determination, as well as the potency of dark brotherhood activities. Two world wars resulted, demonstrating some of the effects of first Ray (Will) energy.

The first Ray has also produced intensified scientific activity and research. This has been especially related to the application of all forms of energy to control matter and the harnessing of nuclear power by means of nuclear fission and fusion. There has also been an increased radiatory and radioactive effect within all kingdoms in Nature. Meanwhile, in the field of human relations, there have been large-scale demonstrations of the Will-to-Good by many all over the world. The forces of materialism and evil incentive also ride on the waves of the first Ray fiat. This has produced an increased frenzied activity by the members of the dark brotherhood to control all aspects of human society in order to counteract the increasing possibility of human progress.

This first Ray fiat is again booming directly upon humanity, who are responding with massed selfish and separative militaristic attitudes, so as to make a third world war well-nigh inevitable. For example, the arms race, conflicts in trouble spots such as Ukraine, the Spratley islands and Taiwan, Israel and other regions in the Middle East, and frequent acts of international terrorism are all intensifying.

The approach of a third world war should not be necessary for humanity. They could avoid it, and the types of lessons that they must properly learn as a consequence of such mass imposed destructiveness and pain. Specifically, the lessons of active goodwill, brotherly love, sharing of world resources, and cooperativeness in all endeavours upon an international scale should have been well assimilated as a consequence of past wars. Instead, we have had an almost immediate continuation of an arms race, first between the Communistic powers and NATO, and later between Russia, China and Iran (amongst others) verses the Western nations. This has rendered impotent what should have become the basis of a true world government (the United Nations Organisation). Such acts as the inclusion of totalitarian and Western imperialistic powers within the UN's essential governing body was truly a disastrous move. How can nations that fervently suppress basic human freedoms and manifest an aggressive stance for world supremacy be put in a position of power in such an organisation, without destroying any framework for building world peace? The break up of the Soviet Union in recent times has not done much to improve the efficacy of the United Nations, especially as 'the big five' still have veto power in the Security Council. There are also the all-pervasive evil effects projected by the world's banking-military-industrial Hegemonic superpower, with over 900 military bases all over the world to police its spheres of dominance.

There has thus been an intensification of the attitudes of selfishness and materialistic might, as seen predominantly in the West, and impressed upon all the nations of the earth. Note specifically the burden these attitudes have had upon the masses in the 'third world' countries: sowing the seeds for insurrection, Fascist indoctrination, and the imposition of dictatorial regimes by means of violent uprisings and subversive coups.

Some of the major reasons for this coming war were explained and prophesised as far back as 1948-9 by the Tibetan Master D.K. in the book *Externalisation of the Hierarchy* (and elsewhere, which need not further distract us here).

There may be intense, immensely destructive exchanges of tactical nuclear weapons in the battlefield and conflict surpassing the worst of the past war. Nonetheless, the world will not be destroyed in a mass nuclear exchange, as the many well-intentioned, but narrow visioned, peace activists would like us to believe. The earth IS the Personality-vehicle of 'God' (the planetary Logos), and it is not His Intent to allow humanity's demise as a consequence of uncontrolled factors therein. His Purpose or Plan for Incarnation will not be frustrated by the wilful intent of a relative few in His Body of Manifestation. The law of *karma,* however, is inviolate. All nations have much negative *karma* to cleanse from their plates before they can truly sup upon the providence of 'God' and the Body and Blood of the Christ in the Aquarian Age.

The war will be a truly global conflict, but those which will specifically be affected are Europe, Japan, Israel, Russia, the Middle Eastern countries, China, the USA and its four English speaking subordinates–England, Australia, New Zealand, and Canada.

This war is seen by esotericists as the recapitulation of the Atlantean *karma.* It is a higher (Aryan) spiral of what was fought between the Lords of the dark Face (the forces of evil) and the Lords of Shining Countenance (the Brotherhood of Light). The result was that the then Kingdom of 'God' set loose the Watery forces that sank the last portion of the Atlantean continent (known as Poseidonis). All totalitarian regimes are a present major power base for the 'Dark Face' on the earth, but the main power base for the forces of evil on this planet is the USA and its subordinates. Vast financial manipulation of the world's resources, the indoctrinational power of the mass media, as well as technologically potent military forces are at the disposal of the USA. This empire of evil must be defeated (and it will be) for true peace (and all the freedoms of the human spirit it entails) to reign.

The physical plane war will effectively be the precipitation of a cosmic, systemic and planetary war on the inner realms. This concerns the way of removal of the forces of evil from the high places where they presently sit, and their imprisonment within the *eighth sphere* at the appointed time. (Fulfilling an aspect of the prophecy given in *Rev. 20:1-5* about Satan being bound for 1,000 years.) This Evil represents an extended version of the Hydra that Hercules battled within his twelve labours. The nature of the 'psychic' war cannot be explained here, other than to mention that much that conditions the outer world of seeming has its causes upon subjective levels.[22] Evil everywhere must be largely vanquished if the planetary Christ is to rule supreme on earth.

All has been foreseen and planned down to the smallest detail. Nothing can escape the All-seeing Eye of the enlightened Ones. The Masters have worked out well in advance how humanity may best be cleansed of all aspects of evil *karma,* thus facilitating the dawning of the New Age of peace and Love. Thenceforth the resurrected Christ (the Hierarchy of Light) can once again walk openly amongst humanity. Hierarchy has remained largely on subjective levels since the sinking of Atlantis. However, members of Hierarchy are periodically sent out according to world need, to become great reformers, artists, scientists, prophets, sages, etc.

The emergence of the golden New Age is now a certainty. Much information of a Revelatory nature will then be possible to demonstrate to humanity. The

---

22 See my revised book *The Revelation* for more details concerning the nature of evil.

externalisation of the Hierarchy is proceeding according to Plan, and its existence will soon be a demonstrable fact. The Christ will come, the Avatar of Synthesis will demonstrate His Power, and 'the Rider will issue forth from the secret place'.[23]

The reasons for the endowment of first Ray energies upon humanity are (briefly speaking) threefold:

**First**. A sufficient number of people have evolved the intellect to adequately allow a collective (though unconscious) ability to channel this first Ray energy. (The release of this and all other Rays is governed by cyclic law.) This is because the mind/Mind is the natural vehicle for the first Ray (being of the 1.3.5.7. Ray line), though great problems arise when this energy finds its outlet via the Solar Plexus centre, thus fomenting aspects of the desire-mind and the intensification of self-will.

It is obvious, therefore, that Love-Wisdom must be the dominant factor in evolution if the abuse of the Will is to be countered and the full weight of the first Ray can pour forth into humanity. The first and second Rays must always work as a unit. (As stated, all Rays are sub-Rays of the second Ray in this solar system.)

The awakening of the qualities of Love-Wisdom via the developed mind has indeed been the major concern of the Hierarchy since the advent of the Christ. The endeavour to seed active Love into humanity is intensifying on all fronts, so as to produce the major second Ray cycle upon the earth. (Thus, to supersede the third Ray cycle of intelligent, materialistic activity that has governed us for so long.) This is the cycle of the Son, the living Christ that will demonstrate as a fully illumined sun (the externalised Hierarchy of Light) on the earth.

When the Christ outwardly manifests amongst us, He will give out new Revelations concerning the nature of 'His Father'—the Lords of Shambhala and the energy of the Will They embody. The distortions of the Will (producing war-like activity) afford the first necessary lessons as to its effects (the fields of war, strife and suffering). This is preparatory to the greater Revelations that will follow when humanity will desire to seriously ask why the cycle of suffering happened, and be willing to listen to the wise.

Reaction to the factor of pain and frustrated self-will is the greatest teacher humanity possesses. Whilst people are totally self indulgent in their repetitious forms of pleasure-seeking activities, comforting securities of everyday pursuits

---

23 See my book *The Constitution of Shambhala,* Part A, for information on the Avatar of Synthesis, and pages 171-54, 187, 401-05 for detail concerning this Rider.

and habits, they have little or no true impetus for evolutionary change. (To become enlightened beings.) To incite them to progress, they must be brought to points of crises, so that the crises can be resolved through right understanding and right action. This is to ensure that past mistakes are not perpetuated through ignorance. The process is much like the education of a mischievous child, only listening to his/her parents after some discipline, as a consequence of wilful disobedience to necessary rules.

People are thus gradually brought through cycles of activity whereby their attitudes to life change. They progress from self-centred, pleasure-seeking, wish-fulfilling enterprises, to activities that focus upon the good of the whole, or the community of which they are a part. Thus the reason for the projection of first Ray energy at a juncture when the intellect is dominant in humanity is to produce points of crises. Consequently, people may understand through applied reason what the true causes for suffering and happiness are. (Along the lines of the Buddha's Four Noble Truths and Eightfold Path.[24]) This then awakens the Love within, apart from the relative few who will entrench themselves in attitudes of self-will and materialistic aggrandisement on the path of evil, of the dark brotherhood. They will consequently need further hard-learnt lessons.

**Secondly**. The emergence of what is known as the New Group of World Servers.[25] This group is composed of thousands from all nations, faiths, walks of life and occupations who are actively serving through an innate Love for humanity. They can (as a unit) thereby directly bear the energies from Shambhala, and convey them in a form that general humanity can utilise. (Before the twentieth century, only the Hierarchy of Light working principally from subjective levels could manifest this function.)

The individuals composing this group are rarely aware of their subjective links to each other, the existence of Hierarchy, or esoteric teachings such as those presented here. Nevertheless, their outward response to world and community need, and contemplative mode of thinking, produces in them a lifestyle that is fruitful of 'good works'. This unites them subjectively with a strong bond via their service interrelationships. (The subjective and objective bonds between them are actually stronger than those between racial, social and national groups, or 'tribal ties', because their bond remains unaffected by external events or death.)

---

24 Details concerning them are expounded in my book *Maṇḍalas, their Nature and Expression.*

25 See *The Rays and Initiations,* by Alice Bailey.

This group generally instinctively recognise each other as kindred spirits. They identify with similar attitudes of mind when they perchance meet. This assists them to network together to start the various enterprises that will be the mainstay (or indications of the eventual trend) of the coming new world order. They are visionaries of one type or other, trying to make the world a better place to live in. They can thus act as direct mediators between the Kingdom of 'God' (the 'Father') and humanity. This group, when expanded, will become the true Christ-Child of this era. Their work, in time, will externalise that Kingdom on earth so that all will see and know the expansive vistas and power thereof. Mass Initiation for humanity will be the outcome.

Their emanatory energy is one of general Love and good will for their fellow beings. This good will is but a lower reflection of the Will-to-Good emanating from Shambhala. These groups are subjectively being trained to assist the Avatar, or the Christ, when He appears. Thus they must necessarily have the ability to share in the expression of the power of the first Ray that will herald the epoch of this coming. This is one of the interpretations of the phrase presented by Christ-Jesus where He stated that He would come again 'sitting at the right hand of Power'.[26]

**Thirdly**. The fact that our Logos is undergoing the process of Initiation into a higher level of cosmic Being. As a consequence, the earth is being transformed from a non-sacred to a sacred planet. The planetary Logos moves from being a cosmic Aspirant to taking a high Initiation, through passing the needed testings. The quality and degree of refinement of substance and the ability to handle intensified energies are far greater for the Initiate than the aspirant. The aspirant can only handle such energies rightly if they are toned down. Working from the Heart, the Initiate has the ability to receive impressions and awareness from the higher realms without any possibility of personality distortion.

There is always the possibility of negative reactions (fear, glamour, pride, emotionality, etc.) amongst humanity from interference by the dark brotherhood, which may cause the entirety of planned events to go astray. This also signifies the difference between a sacred and non-sacred planet. For Sanat Kumāra, the Personality Incarnation of the planetary Logos, this will allow Him to finally relinquish his long vigil on earth as the 'Great Sacrifice, the Silent Watcher' and finally leave the planet.

The 'cellular constitution' of the planet – human Souls and the angelic Triads – is thus being greatly stimulated through a consequent downpour of

26 See *Matthew 26:4* and *Mark 9:1.*

intensified energies into the realms of the human personality. This produces the abovementioned effects regarding the energy of the Will.

As the Logos prepares His incarnate Form for Initiation to manifest throughout the sum of the Body of manifestation, so all hindrances to this Great Awakening must be overcome. These hindrances constitute the *karma* amassed by humanity throughout the ages, which will come to a head in the forthcoming war and the cataclysms that will follow later. Ancient debts must be paid off and the slate wiped clean of adverse qualities so that a new cycle can commence.

This new cycle will be based upon higher, more aesthetic and wholesome values. This is the reason why world events have 'quickened' in the past few centuries, why there are so many people incarnate, and also why mass emotional-mental turmoil underlies the external happenings of our time. These periods of crisis for humanity will eventually result in 'points of tension' – a heightened and concentrated focus of (unconscious) evocative appeal that will bring down and anchor the needed energies.

The world disciple is thus on the verge of a mass Initiation into the Mysteries of Being. Part of the restitution process after the coming war will concern the building of the new schools and community structures that will cater to humanity's needs. This will be an effect of the flowering of a new world religion that will be based upon the best that can be extracted from the religions and philosophies of the past. This is part of the momentous changes the coming Avatar is to bring.[27]

---

27 Further information concerning the nature of this Avatar and associated events can be found in my books *The Constitution of Shambhala* and the revised *The Revelation*.

# 3a

# The Nature of the Constellations to Scorpio

The zodiac is an imaginary path (or belt of constellations) in the heavens. It is about seventeen degrees in width, through which the sun is said to travel. There are twelve constellations, from which the names of the twelve signs are taken. (Astrologers have divided the zodiac into twelve portions of thirty degrees each, which roughly correspond to the twelve constellations.) The greater zodiac is a cycle of over 25,000 years. This is the apparent result of the motion of the sun through space, taking approximately 2,160 years to traverse each sign. The lesser zodiac is the result of the motion of the earth around the sun each year, taking one month to complete each sign of the zodiac, and it is upon this path that astrologers normally base their computations. The signs of the zodiac are part of the great illusion of the astral universe that is created by the desire-minds of humanity, and which conditions their personalities as they evolve.

The twelve signs of the zodiac depict the phenomenal appearance of the Heart centre of the Grand Heavenly Man in the cosmos (THAT Logos). These twelve qualities are also reflected in the internal constitution of the solar Logos.

What is presented below is derived from, and a commentary of, what is provided in Alice Bailey's *Esoteric Astrology.*

### Aries the ram

*Aries the ram* (♈) embodies the Head and Brain of the Grand Heavenly Man, His thinking and directive capabilities. Aries represents the point of power of the circle of abstract Being from whence emanated the Divine Ideation, the Will-to-Be. Aries also directs what the all-that-is will eventually be resolved into. The head and brain subjectively incorporates the Head centre. Aries governs the functions of the second Creative Hierarchy (the 'Divine Builders').

Aries connotes the first differentiation of manifestation, the Divine Ideation that was the cause of the creative process of the Logos. Aries thus concerns the development of the Will, the projection of first Ray energies. Seen in this symbol is the perfected achievement of a former spiral of evolution that becomes the seed germ (the Father aspect) for a new field of expression.

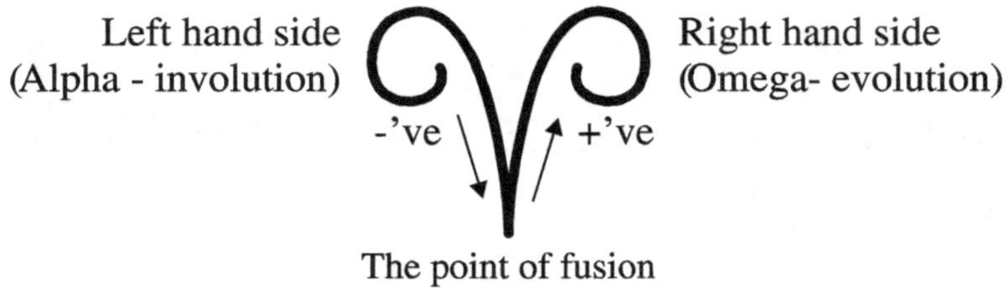


**Figure 6. Aries the ram**

The downturned horns of the Ram signify the descent into incarnation of primordial causative energy (signifying the 'death' of the spiritual). This causes the appearance of manifestation, *saṃsāra* in its entirety. At the point of fusion the achieved balance produces a Ray of dynamic, qualified energy. It reaches the lowest aspect of manifestation (in the form of the *sūtrātma)*, and then on the path of return it reaches the highest (as the *antaḥkaraṇa)*. Once human units have begun their weary march upwards along the Initiation path, at the attainment of the fourth Initiation, the projection of the Monadic Will causes the death of the Soul form. This allows the human unit to spiral into the omega of attainment.

The above symbol can be elaborated thus:

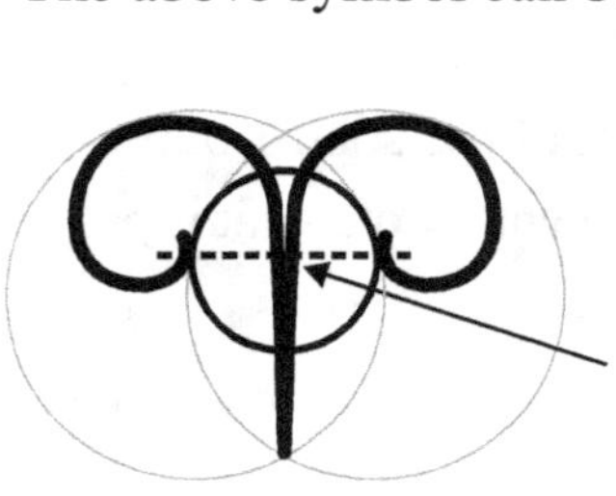

Mergence of two oppositely polarised spheres of influence, forming a new sphere into which the Divine can manifest - the cardinal cross that impels Logoic Purpose into the four directions in space.


**Figure 7. Aries further exemplified**

Aries empowers the Thought of the Divine Thinker that originally caused the concretion of matter. This is reflected or expressed as the process of intelligent thinking. Arian energies are used to express the Will of the reasoning ability of humanity (or of 'God') to project thoughts.

It is easy to see, therefore, how the Arian personality is considered to be the innovator and originator of mental beginnings, especially when ruled exoterically by Mars, the god of war. Mars governs personal vigour, *prāṇa* and psychic energy, all of which condition the manifest world (the outer form).

The use of the head of the Ram to batter and buck also comes to the fore, so the Arian subject is said to be headstrong, determined and impatient. The Ram is ruled by his head and lives on the grassy plains, and sometimes upon the rocky slopes of the earth. There, the nourishment for everyday living is easily obtained, and the activities of his herd are also easily regulated. The herd can also be viewed in terms of someone's internal (emotional) constitution, outer responsibilities and associations, as well as group living conditionings and affiliations.

The major activities of the Ram concern the manifestation of a dominant personality, or with maintaining, controlling, and developing the coherency of the group's activity and social harmony. The Arian battles or strives towards unity.

Directed personality effort, primeval beginnings, activity, strife, and manifestation, the will and synthesis, are all keywords of the Arian disposition. Instinctual reactions govern the undeveloped person.

*Esoterically,* Aries is ruled by *Mercury,* for the path of return (the *antaḥkaraṇa)* is closely related to the development of the Will (the Arian disposition). The higher Mind (which Aries dominates) is the medium of the 'messenger of the Gods' (Mercury). The empirical mind, with its conflicting opinions and critical attitudes, is however ruled by Mars. The Arian martial energy and warlike activities govern the desires of the undeveloped person (Mars). These are eventually transmuted. The person then becomes an agent of focussed will, capable of traveling the narrow razor edged path (Mercury) leading to liberation. In relation to the energies of the Ram, both Mars and Mercury embody the principles of conflict that help engender points of crises in one's life.

Mars helps produce the strife, struggle and war that are the result of people's ambitions, fanaticism, or desires. However, under the influence of Mercury such attitudes are karmically cleansing and ultimately enable one to vision the Real. The major part of this struggle is undertaken in Scorpio (ruled both exoterically and esoterically by Mars, and therefore related to Aries), where the various tests in life and of discipleship are undertaken. The cleansing process ultimately produces the death of the personality (in Scorpio) and liberation (in Capricorn).

D.K. calls this process 'the crises of the battlefield', which happens upon the path of aspiration. The result of the final battle in Scorpio allows the rectification of the reversed wheel in Libra. (It is upon the clockwise wheel, which the aspirant and humanity in general travel. The reorientation process to counter clockwise directionality will be explained in the sign Scorpio.) This crisis involves the ability of the aspirant to perceive the nature of the great illusion.

Mercury rules the fourth Ray of Harmony Overcoming Strife and mediates between the higher and lower mind, the Soul and personality, the pairs of opposites, and also the conflict associated with the resolution of these forces. Such resolution is a primary objective of the life of the aspirant. When this happens, illumination takes place and the light of the sun can give birth to the Christ in Capricorn, via the womb of Virgo (of which Mercury is the exoteric ruler). Such crises concern the probationary disciple and eventually produce the attainment of the first Initiation. D.K. calls this 'the crises of the birth place in Virgo'.

The next crises, 'of the burning ground', instigated via Uranus, the Hierarchical ruler of Aries, concerns the attainment of the fourth Initiation and of the Initiate's decision to walk the higher way leading to any of the seven cosmic Paths that must later be chosen. Via Uranus, Aries is the major purveyor of the Fire Element to the solar system, for it is the first of the Fire signs: Aries-Leo-Sagittarius. From Aries emanates cosmic Fire, relating to the Spirit (or Monadic aspect). From Leo emanates solar Fire, as it relates to the Soul (the consciousness-aspect), and from Sagittarius emanates planetary Fire, that relates to the personality (the embodied form).

Fire is the substance of the mind and is the major purificatory and transmutative agency for this age. It 'clears the way by burning' the dross left after the action of Water has taken its toll and has prepared the person to take the first two Initiations.

Of the three Fire signs, Sagittarius is one of the conditioning signs of the mutable cross, the cross of repeated incarnations and constantly changing attitudes and experiences of the personality. At first in the Sagittarian, this Fire produces self-will. Later is produced the one-pointed determination, fixed upon the way of Love, that characterises the disciple.

Leo is one of the conditioning signs of the fixed cross. It is the dominant Fire sign in the solar system at this time, for the solar Logos is said to be crucified on this cross, causing the second aspect of Deity to dominate all of our activities via the Leonine dispensation of mind – the I AM principle. Leonine energies facilitate the development of self-consciousness in humanity, the ability to clearly think and reason things out, to determine what is right and what is wrong to do. One can consequently tread the 'burning ground' to gain illumination, to produce complete freedom from the dominance of form. Leo's energies are therefore of supreme importance to the life of the aspirant and disciple. Leo draws upon Aries to fulfil these functions.

The significance of Aries as the purveyor of Fire becomes clear in the life of the Initiate; for Aries is one of the conditioning signs of the cardinal cross, the cross of the Spirit, of electric Fire, which predominantly conditions the Initiate of higher degrees. Aries thereby fuses all cycles, from the beginning to the end, into a consummating unity. It Initiates one into the higher Mysteries, whereby time and space no longer veil. Aries is the alpha and omega, the conditioning force of the 'wrath of God',[1] and is also the 'Lamb of God'.[2] (All phrases from the *Revelation of St. John* have much esoteric meaning.) This Fire produces the enlightened Will of the Initiate, becoming effective after the third Initiation.

The polar opposite of Aries is Libra the balance. The initial beginnings, desires and schemes of the Arian find their point of equilibrium or Judgement day in Libra, and consummation in Capricorn. There the ram becomes the scapegoat, and takes upon itself the sins *(karma)* of the group (or herd) in its endeavours to relieve their sufferings and to help them achieve their liberation, and so scale the mountainside of Initiation. In the transformation of the ram into the goat lies the esoteric basis to the concept of the *atonement* (so misunderstood by Christian Theologians).

In Libra, the desire to manifest Arian qualities (which causes the myriad personality incarnations) achieves a point of balance and equilibrium. The resultant mental integration allows one 'to aspire to be' and tread the path of active return.

Aries is part of the cardinal cross (with Capricorn, Libra and Cancer). This cross relates to Shambhala, the Monad, the Father aspect of Deity. It governs the path of Initiation and of beginnings. Three of the signs of this cross are concerned with *birth,* the beginning of new cyclic undertakings and of effort. Libra is the point of balance, the focal point of the Wheel of Life that governs the various Laws that condition the associated Lives.

*1. Aries.* 'The birthplace of Divine Ideas.' This signifies the start of every new cycle and constitutes an open door into the Life of Shambhala when the Initiate has fulfilled his/her tasks and has undergone the necessary training within Hierarchy.

---

1 *Rev. 14:19, 15:1-7,* etc.

2 *John 1:29, Rev: 5:6 ff.*

2. *Cancer.* 'The birthplace into the life of the form.' It is an open door to incarnation into the human kingdom, as well as to the mass awareness associated with the lesser kingdoms.
3. *Capricorn.* 'The birthplace of the Christ.' Here, the second birth eventuates and it constitutes an open door to the life of Hierarchy. (Taurus is the door for the first two Initiations.)

Together, these three signs focus their energies through Leo, which becomes 'the birthplace of the individual', of self-consciousness in humanity. It is the birthplace of the mind, the medium of eventual immortality, and the foundation of the journey to the central Spiritual Sun (situated on the cardinal cross). In this manner, the fixed cross is also related to the cardinal cross via Leo.

The understanding of the nature of the relationship between the three crosses (cardinal, fixed and mutable) is of paramount significance in esoteric astrology.

As D.K. states:

> The theme of all three crosses is fusion and integration. The fusion of the personality into the one functioning whole; the fusion of soul and personality consciously; the fusion of the threefold expression of Divinity – Monad, Ego and personality – so that there is an appearance of blended energies.[3]

The cardinal cross is the 'cross of the risen Christ' whereon the Spirit that governs the evolutionary progress of the Soul is crucified.

Being the sign of mental beginnings (of the originating thought form) Spirit and matter are brought together in Aries through a relationship that can produce tangible results. The Thought construct is precipitated into incarnation (the dense form) in Cancer, the sign of mass consciousness, mass life. In Libra, a point of equilibrium in evolution is reached between involutionary and evolutionary forces. Then there is an eventual turning upwards in the arc of evolution, until in Capricorn, the heights of any cycle (either of the personality or of the spiritual) are reached. A new cycle is initiated in Aries on a higher turn of the spiral, and thus the wheel ever turns.

The secret of Life itself, the energy that motivates the entire evolutionary process, and that causes its final demise, is veiled by the cardinal cross. The secret of the Soul, which governs the psychic mechanism of response, is veiled by the fixed cross. The mutable cross veils the mystery of the form and its central cohesive Fires.

---

3 *Esoteric Astrology,* 563.

***Summary:***

- *Keynote:* Aries turns towards Capricorn.
- Aries is the Head and Brain of the grand Heavenly Man.
- The *exoteric ruler* is Mars, Ray six of Devotion.
- The *esoteric ruler* is Mercury, Ray four of Harmony through Conflict.
- The *Hierarchical ruler* is Uranus, Ray seven of Ceremonial Magic.
- The *Element* is Fire. (As also for Leo and Sagittarius.)
- The *polar opposite* is Libra the balances (an Air sign).
- *Cross:* cardinal.
- The Sun is exalted in Aries, the power of Venus is lessened, and Saturn falls.
- The *Decanates* given for Aries are – exoterically: Mars, Sun and Jupiter, esoterically: Mars, Sun and Venus.

The *keywords* that D.K. gives for this sign are:[4]

> In the world of form: 'And the Word said: Let form again be sought'.
> On the path of active return: 'I come forth and from the plane of mind, I rule'.

## Taurus the bull

*Taurus the bull* (♉) embodies the Neck and Throat of the Grand Heavenly Man. This supports the Head and is the foundation or sustaining principle underlying the entire cycle of Being. Taurus manifests the substance that is the embodiment of the divine Word, the second or Son aspect of Deity. The neck symbolises the constructed *antaḥkaraṇa* that relates the personal will to the created form (the body), and later to what one must build if eternal residence in the uppermost (Head) centre is to be achieved. Taurus is therefore the sign of illumination, of the power of the directive Eye. These qualities correspond to those of the third Creative Hierarchy ('the Elements') that constitutes the Eye of the five liberated Hierarchies.

The Taurean subject must learn to control speech and endeavour to explain the nature and meaning of the Word of 'God' in such a way that the self-willed, blind, onrushing stampede of the bull is transformed into the path of the ageless wisdom. The Taurean must thereby become a vehicle of the Divine. The Taurean is said to be fond of good living, luxuriating in the comforts and security of 'the grassy fields' and of his house, and is hard working.

---

4 These keywords and the summary below, for this and all of the other signs are taken from Alice Bailey's *Esoteric Astrology,* to which the reader must turn for detail.

Both Aries and Taurus have similar characteristics and are often found living and working together on the fertile and grassy plains of the earth. Both are headstrong, dominating, ambitious and wilful. One is said to be ram headed and the other bull headed. Both manifest aspects of the first Ray of Will or Power. Taurus clothes this Ray with astral substance and Aries projects mental substance into objectivity. Taurus represents the energy that brings to fulfilment the initial impulse engendered by Aries. Taurus is the expression of the Desire of the Logos, sustaining His Plan of action. Desire is found in every field of application. In the gross, sensual man, desire drives physical urges to fulfilment. Desire eventually morphs into the aspiration of the disciple, and then transmutes into the illumined Will of the Initiate.

Taurus gives substance to the divine Thought Form, and thus provides life to the varying images found on the astral plane, cosmically or systemically considered. Thus it gives rise on earth to the glamour of the many images created by people's desire bodies that constitute their astral heaven and hell. Taurus is thus identified with the great Mother and the world Egg depicted in many creation myths and assists in the formation of the Christ-Child in the Womb of Virgo. Taurus then helps to propel that Child's birth in Capricorn, the ninth sign after Virgo (including Virgo), when the Child comes out of the Womb and begins the ascent up the mount of Initiation. (The number nine signifies the months of gestation in the womb of the mother.) Taurus, Capricorn and Virgo are strongly related, for all three are Earth signs.

The Earth signifies the dense physical plane, of what is incarnate, the dense forms through which humanity must work. The effect of the energies of the Earthy triplicity (and of those born under its influence) are of immense importance on our planet today. This is because humanity is presently oriented towards the physical form, and our materialists acknowledge no plane of perception other than what is associated with the five senses. Humanity's response to the Earth, of the dominance of the mineral kingdom in their lives, is the foundation of this present civilisation, for science and technology utilises the forces of the mineral kingdom in most of its accomplishments. We see it in the bricks and mortar, the concrete, plastics and metals that form the substance of our buildings and appliances. The Earth-quality is also found in the coal, Uranium and oil that drive our turbines and generators, producing the electricity that feeds our energy hungry societies. We wage war with metal implements and mineral explosives, whilst gold and silver are the precursors to our monetary system.

The Desire and Will of the Logos and of all the subjective energies that motivate the action of humanity and 'God' find their dense physical expression through the medium of the Earthy triplicity.

*Capricorn* (ruling the arid, rocky mountain wastelands) marks the point of greatest immersion and concretion in the world of form, of substance and its effects. Capricorn symbolises the point of greatest materiality and crystalline hardness that imprisons the Life of the spiritual person.

In *Virgo,* Life's imprisoned splendour first makes its notice felt and prompts a reaction from the outward focused form. Thus, by the time the Taurean cycle is reached, desire for outward expression becomes so strong that the subject rushes blindly onward with ever-increasing bursts of vigour. He/she hearkens at one moment to inner aspirations and at another to the outer urges. One thus progresses on one's way, painfully conscious of duality and at first often manifesting destructive actions. Even though the Taurean finds it difficult to practically apply the knowledge gained, the evolutionary path is however eventually completed. Then the person finds him/herself atop the great heights of Capricorn and can truly view things in perspective.

Once all of the effects of desire expressed through the form are played out until exhaustion, the labour begins in Virgo. This enables the great reversal on the wheel of Life and in the seat of consciousness to then take place (in Libra). This will enable the disciple to scale the mountainside in Capricorn to take Initiation, to be freed from the control or pull of matter. The Christ-Child is effectively born in a manger set in a rocky cave (symbolic of the Earthy triplicity) surrounded by the beasts of the field. It is within the concrete caves of our present civilisation that He will thus reappear.

The relation of Taurus to the Moon (which is exalted in Taurus), whose symbol is the horn (or the crescent), can be seen in the horns of the Bull (the Taurean native). The moon is the Mother of forms, and Taurus embodies the desire of the Mother. This is clearly depicted in the symbol for this sign:

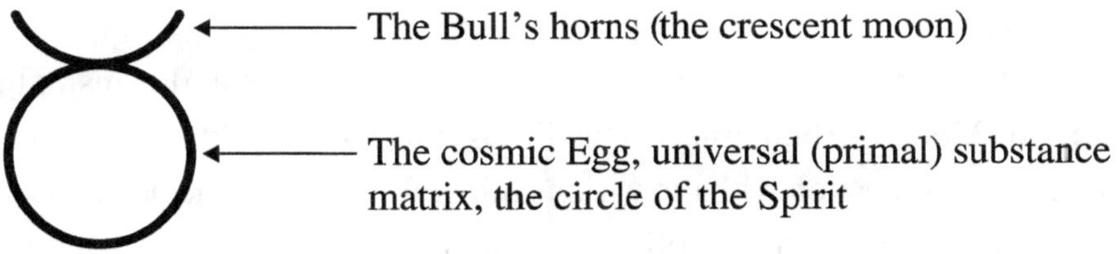


**Figure 8. The Taurus glyph**

The Bull's horns symbolise duality emerging from unity: the psychic nature and the mental-emotional forces that sustain the form. The arc of the horns is an incomplete circle, thus implying limitation: the emotional or psychic projections of a self-enclosed personality into the external domain. Here the personality attributes subjugate the spiritual. Later, upon the rectified wheel, it symbolises the Soul rising out of the confining cycles of the form and the material nature.

In the early stages of its career, the Bull is both destructive and blind (for instance, to the goodwill of those around). He is quick to temper and often found on a path of rampage because of self-will and self-centredness. The pointed horns symbolise this strife, and also desire, the ability to pierce and project. They are the dual points through which the strength and power of the Bull are focussed. Also in the Bull is seen the ability to trample and destroy the life associated with the form.

The Moon veils the potency of Vulcan, the esoteric and Hierarchical ruler of Taurus. Vulcan is the hard working fashioner of all beautiful, psychic, as well as material things, for he is (as previously stated) the God of the Fire found at the heart of every atom. He works at the transmutation of all base metals into spiritual gold, and empowers the forces of creation – the powers of the Gods – by forging the necessary weapons in his underground furnace.

Vulcan, ruled by the first Ray, is the bringer of death (as also does a Volcano, which Vulcan rules exoterically) and aids the destructiveness of the Bull. He helps destroy the form so that the Life and Light of the Soul can be set free. Vulcan works in darkness so that therein may be engendered Light, which manifests through the Eye of the Bull, producing the illumination of the path to be trodden, and also of the Plan of 'God'. Vulcan descends into the depths to fashion what is most beautiful and useful to the evolving Life. Vulcan therefore stands for the Soul and embodies its evolutionary purpose in the realms of form. Vulcan also governs the activity of the mineral kingdom and strongly relates Taurus to Capricorn. Thus he virtually fuses the life of the aspiring disciple to the 'ritual of the magician' imposed by the Will of Deity residing on the summit of the mount in Capricorn.

Vulcan embodies the flux that allows the various trials and transmutations in the life of Mercury (humanity). This life is then sublimated in the crucible of experience, in conjunction with the various minerals (the salts and acids) that come from the earth. Thus, as it establishes a relation between the two (the mineral and the human kingdoms), Vulcan is causative of the powers of the Philosopher's

Stone. Vulcan is thereby also related to the attainment of the fourth Initiation. (The crucifixion of the Initiate upon the fixed cross of the heavens.) Upon this cross both the highest and the lowest become known and interrelated, yet the Initiate stands detached from both.

It is said that Taurus 'rushes blindly' (because of his innate desire for material things) to darkness and death in the world of sensation. Eventually, under the direction of the one-pointed aspiration of Sagittarius, the Taurean evolves the ability to see in the realms of death (for by then Vulcan also rules the native). Then he/she aspires to the source of Light, finally becoming a perfected vehicle of that Light. The Initiate is then able to illumine others, as did the Buddha, who gained His *parinirvāṇa* in the sign Taurus. His life exemplified the nature of this sign. Illumination, and on the lower arc of evolution, desire, are therefore the keywords of Taurus.

Light, desire, creation (fertility), illumination and the All-seeing Eye have always been the properties of the divine cow Goddesses and Gods, such as Mithras, Hathor and Isis. This also indicates why the sacred cow is still worshipped in India.

It is interesting to note that the Eye of the Bull, cosmically considered, is the star *Aldebaran* (the central point of the Hyades cluster that forms the horns of the Bull). This Eye is also the Eye of Shiva, the third Eye, the Eye mentioned by the Christ that 'fills the whole body with light'.[5] The Eye can also be depicted in the form of the *ankh-tie*, another form of the symbol of Taurus:

It 'is a Cross on which all the human passions have to be crucified before the Yogi passes through the "strait gate", the narrow circle that widens into an infinite one, as soon as the *inner* man has passed the threshold'.[6] It is also an early form of the Ankh: ♀ and thus of Venus (♀), the exoteric ruler of Taurus.

*Venus* signifies intelligent (and also sensual) love via the energies of the mental plane when expressed upon the earth. Seen here is the cause for much of the exoteric Taurian's preoccupation with sex, sex magic, and also with the mystic's desire to fuse or be married with the Divine. Upon the reversed wheel the final sublimation of the sex expression into the higher creativity is seen. Venus also embodies the Light of the mind/Mind. Thus from every angle it may be seen that the theme of illumination runs through the story of Taurus:

---

5 *Mathew 6:22.*

6 Blavatsky, *The Secret Doctrine,* Volume 2, 549.

a. The Eye of the Bull (Ray three), the Eye of Shiva, focussing Mahat from the central spiritual Light and coordinating the personality light.
b. The Light of the Soul in Vulcan (Ray one), hidden in the depths of matter (darkness) wherein it reveals the higher secrets.
c. The searchlight of the mind/Mind in Venus (Ray five), which becomes illumined and then illuminates others.

In the above is seen the difficulty of the Taurean subject, in that all of the controlling Rays are along the first Ray line of endeavour, which greatly enhances the Taurean self-will, determination, and destructiveness. The Taurean must learn to offset and transmute these attributes. Thus, for instance, self-will must be changed into the Will-to-Good and the results of destructive aspects on the personality life moulded into a necessary constructiveness. Thereby are fashioned the tools and vehicles needed for enlightenment. The Eye of Wisdom must be developed instead of critical assertiveness. Knowledge (the 'eye doctrine') must be transmuted into Wisdom (the Heart's awareness). Therein lie the challenges for the Taurean subject, yet his/her ability to penetrate and perceive the causes and results of any line of action and of the Plan or Will of 'God' is also great. The potential benefit of the aspirant's constructive manifestation of information is vast, to both mankind and the lesser kingdoms. From many angles, therefore, Taurus is one of the most important signs of the zodiac affecting humanity today.

The polar opposite of Taurus is Scorpio. At first in Taurus the lower nature triumphs because of the overpowering desire to satiate the senses, leading eventually to the depths of *māyā* in Scorpio. Eventually, through the trials of the disciple in the desert (Scorpio), desire gives way to aspiration, and the disciple moves from death-like attitudes to liberation. The disciple moves from darkness to Light and finally stands illumined and liberated in Taurus.

Taurus is one of the arms of *the fixed cross.*

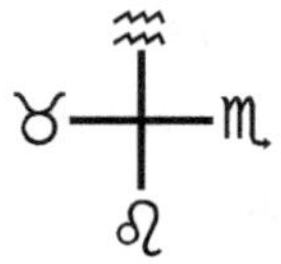


This is the cross of the crucified Christ. It concerns the path of discipleship that leads to the Heart of the Sun. It implies the ability to stand steadfast and with fixed intent upon this self-made cross, in the field of service to help others to gain salvation. It concerns the ability to bring into manifestation the light of the Soul.

At first, this path concerns gross desire (Taurus), reinforced by self-centredness (Leo), leading to the many personality tribulations and frustrations on the battlefield of life (Scorpio), as one selfishly hoards the fruits of pillage and ravages in the world for personal benefit (in Aquarius). Eventually, desire for material and sensual pursuits no longer attract the Bull, so desire is transmuted into aspiration. The Ājñā centre begins to awaken and reveals the path to the Heart of Life. The individual is increasingly dominated by the Soul (the Lion that is the glorified Sun), and now spiritually provides for the group of which he/she is a part. The Leonine native becomes the ruler of the kingdoms in Nature, enabling the undertaking of the many tests of leadership under the sign Scorpio. Eventually Initiation is undertaken so that the Waters of Life can be dispensed in Aquarius. A completely selfless world server thereby arises.

This cross is the major transformative agent (for it stands between the cardinal and mutable crosses) in the life of the disciple working to serve the kingdoms in Nature. The four Elements: Earth (Taurus), Fire (Leo), Water (Scorpio) and Air (Aquarius) are here brought together and fused. The Earthy material nature of the Taurean must at first be washed and cleansed by the purifying Waters of Scorpio if the Baptism (second) Initiation is to be undertaken. The 'midway point, which is neither dry nor wet' must be sought and stood upon, if the disciple is to mould the Earthy light (Taurus) with solar Fire (Leo), and thus produce a form that will be able to receive the Spirit (or Dove) of Peace (Air, Aquarius). This is the objective of every disciple and is the result of the work of the magician and his crucible. This process is guided by four needed tools: the manipulative hand (Scorpio), the well-endowed Heart (Leo), the creative Word (Aquarius) and the focussed Eye (Taurus). They must all work in cooperative harmony upon the field of service.

The brilliant white Light envisioned by 'the Eye of the Bull' is distributed in a fourfold direction by the one on the fixed cross. Leo (the major Fire sign in the zodiac) wields that Fiery Light for all group undertakings. Scorpio uses this energy to overcome the hindrances in the field of battle within human civilisation. Aquarius pours what the Bull directs so that all Lives can be nourished and transformed by its enlightening embrace.

***Summary:***

- *Keynote:* Taurus rushes blindly until Sagittarius directs.
- Taurus is the Neck and Throat of the grand Heavenly Man.
- The *exoteric ruler* is Venus, Ray five of the Scientific Mode.

- The *esoteric ruler* is Vulcan, Ray one of Will or Power.
- The *Hierarchical ruler* is Vulcan, Ray one of Will or Power.
- The *Element* is Earth (as is also for Virgo and Capricorn).
- The *polar opposite* is Scorpio the scorpion (a Water sign).
- *Cross:* fixed.
- The Moon is exalted in Taurus, Mars is in detriment and Uranus falls.
- The *Decanates* given for Taurus are: exoterically: The Moon (or Venus), Mercury and Saturn. Esoterically: not given.

The *keywords* that D.K. gives for this sign are:

> The Word of the form is 'to take, grasp and go courageously after that which is desired' – 'Let struggle be undismayed'.
>
> The Word of the Soul is: 'I see and when the Eye is opened all is light'.

## Gemini the twins

Gemini rules the Arms and Hands of the grand Heavenly Man and thus the work of the accomplished magician, who is the builder that moulds the energies of the Lord. For this reason also, Gemini interiorly rules the lungs, the organ through which the (divine) breath is absorbed and distributed throughout the rest of the body. Exoterically, this produces the oxygenation of the blood, and thus the vitalisation of the principle of Life, which is directed to all of the cells and organs within the body.

Here is seen the strong relation between Gemini and Aquarius (both are Air signs), for Gemini embodies the vital body, and Aquarius is concerned with the distribution of vitality (the Waters of Life). In the other Airy sign, Libra, there is a necessary balancing of the energies that will allow right distribution of this vitality, to produce a perfectly healthy body. Air is the exoteric symbol of *buddhi,* thus of enlightenment consciousness. These three signs are therefore focussed upon helping to stimulate and develop the intuitive faculties of a person.

Taurus represents that stage in evolution connoted by the term 'hermaphrodite', whilst in Gemini the latent male and female forces, Soul and form, become separated though remain interrelated. This is symbolised by the nature of the twins, Castor and Pollux, pursuing their lives together through their course in the zodiac. One brother is mortal and the other is immortal, one is waning and the other (the immortal one), waxing. This basic duality, symbolised by Gemini, and the resolution of that duality forms the basis of all evolutionary growth.

Gemini governs all of the pairs of opposites in the zodiac and thus in the life of the evolving person. It subtly relates all of the signs together, keeping their interplay in a fluid mutual response to one another to help produce fusion. Here is seen the importance of Mercury (the orthodox ruler of Gemini) who helps the interplay of all categories of relationships, be they zodiacal or planetary. Mercury is the divine intermediary on all levels of perception. It relates the higher and lower minds, the Soul and personality, as well as the Soul and Monad. Mercury produces the mental agility and fluidity so often found in the Gemini subject, helping to foster his/her latent sense of duality. Exoterically, Mercury makes the Gemini native fluid, analytical, able to reason well in all types of situations and circumstances. The native is versatile, apt to wander through many fields of expression, is constantly active, sensitive and quick to react to his/her own or to other's needs.

The esoteric ruler of Gemini is Venus (♀), who rules the fifth Ray of Science and the energies of the mind. She also relates Gemini to Taurus, Libra and Capricorn (all of whom have Venus as one of their planetary rulers). The manifestation of desire in Taurus results in the full interplay and pull of the sex forces in Gemini, wherein the primal cause of the suffering associated with the sex relationship of the animal and humanity is hidden. Through a wise use of the developed fluid Mercury-Venus Mind, the sexual and otherwise spiritual struggles of a person find a point of balance in Libra, to be finally resolved in Capricorn.

The Gemini subject is said to 'move towards Libra', for in Libra the interplay of the pairs of opposites becomes evenly balanced, being the platform from which the climb to the mount of Initiation can be earnestly begun. In the fusion of the energies of Mercury and Venus, an objective of evolution is seen, in which the solar Angel (Venus) and its messenger – the enlightened person (Mercury) – are united and function in perfect accord. The higher correspondence is found in the 'marriage song of the Heavens' and the subsequent union of the fourth and fifth Creative Hierarchies. Also related to this eventual union is the fact that the Earth is said to be the Hierarchical ruler of Gemini.

The glyph of this sign speaks for itself:

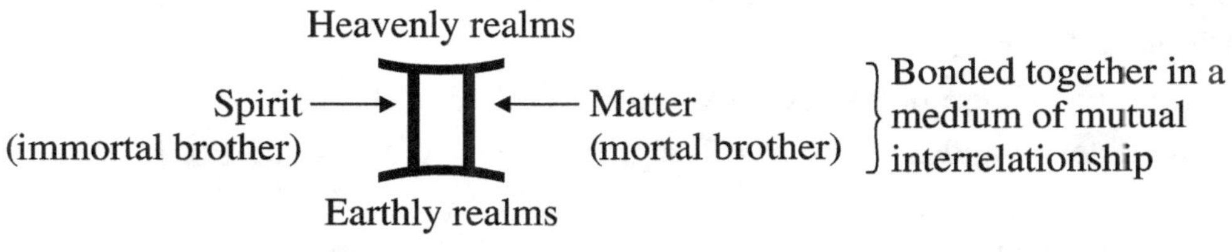


**Figure 9. The glyph for Gemini**

This glyph is a shorthand form of the temple of Initiation (symbolic of Hierarchical endeavour) where the two uprights bear the qualities of the Ray Ashrams of Mind. The fourth and sixth Ray Ashrams represent the right hand *nāḍī* or pillar, and the fifth and seventh Ray Ashrams, represent the left hand *nāḍī* or pillar. In the Bible they are the pillars supporting Solomon's temple, named Jachin and Boaz, and are an integral part of modern Masonic philosophy. The obvious importance of this sign is therefore seen in that it underlies the foundational energies of the Temple of the Lord, be it of the Soul or of the personality. The two brothers can also be interpreted in terms of the relation between the qualities of the *iḍā* and *piṇgalā nāḍīs.*

Gemini is related to and controls the functioning of the etheric body, the internal vital Life of the person, the transmitter of psychic energy. The *iḍā* and *piṇgalā nāḍīs* are the central coordinating channels for the distribution of the related energies. The seven major *chakras* that allow the Soul to control the personality are found within the etheric form. They are the personality's subjective mechanism of response, the organs of relationship between the various planes of perception and the person. Similarly, the hands are a principal organ of contact between the personality and the rest of the environment. They embody the gesture of giving, of feeling, the sense of touch that is extended by means of the *chakras* to all levels of perception. The hands also indicate the service that the immortal and mortal brother must render to each other, if the separative relationship between them is to be annulled. Service is a major theme of the relationship between the brothers in the latter stages of their development. For many ages the Gemini subject serves only himself, until finally he comes to know of the needs of his brother and serves him. When the brothers have banded together in service (as all must eventually unite), then their service is to undertake the Will of 'God'. All of Nature is benefited by such salutary action.

Gemini's deep relation to the attributes of the fourth Creative Hierarchy (humanity) is seen in the function of embodying the vitality that sustains the form. This Hierarchy is esoterically externalised upon the fourth cosmic ether, *buddhi,* whose energies they convey into manifestation via the *bodhicitta* that drives the Bodhisattva path.[7]

Gemini's governorship over the etheric body and the *chakras* allows much of the potency and mystery of this sign to be brought to light. For instance, it

---

7 This function is esoterically celebrated in the festival of the New Age Temple – of Good Will, which is explained in Appendix 1.

governs the properties and functions of the cosmic etheric sub-planes, therefore ruling over the entire field of activity for the Spirit-Soul-personality in the present period of incarnation of our solar Logos. Gemini also governs all the fields of energy interplay that the science of Astrology deals with, thereby subtly relating all of the signs together. These forces are dual: either the light of the mortal (the personality) or immortal brother (the Soul) is dominant at a given time and therefore is the focus of all activity. Once the energies are fused, then a goal of evolution has been consummated. For long ages, however, there is a fluid, mutual, yet also conflicting interplay between the brothers. At first this produces much strife and friction, and then harmony and heights of revelation supersede when the attributes of the immortal brother prevail.

This relation eventually awakens the Christ aspect of all manifested Life. Gemini (who rules the cosmic ethers) can be seen to be uniquely the sign of the cosmic Christ. This is similar to the way that the fourth cosmic etheric plane *(buddhi)* reflects the energies of the planetary Christ. (This Christ being an embodiment of the immortal Brother.) In this capacity it is said to transmit energy from Sirius to the earth. From this perspective, Sirius also embodies the attributes of the immortal Brother, whilst the Pleiades (who build the forms via the cosmic ethers) signify the attributes of the mortal Sister. The Sisters embody the substance of *manvantara,* whereas Sirius governs the attribute of Love-Wisdom, whose development works to liberate from form.

The festival of the New Age Temple, of Good Will, is in Gemini (the first full Moon in June). This indicates that this sign was influential when Jesus died on the cross. At his death, he told the disciple whom he loved (symbolising the spiritual world) that Mary was his mother[8] (the symbol of matter), and vice versa—again relating to Gemini. Finally, he died at the 'place of the skull'[9] and ascended to the Kingdom of 'God'. (The relationship between Golgotha and this Kingdom exemplifies the nature of Gemini.) As the moment of death determines the moment of the next birth (for a person is said to die and be reborn in the same sign), it seems possible that in his next appearance Christ-Jesus could have a Gemini disposition, with Aquarius being his field of Service (or rising sign). Here also the mortal brother signifies humanity, and the immortal one represents Hierarchy, headed by the Christ. The externalisation process of the Hierarchy that will usher in the Aquarian age will indicate the successful linking of the

8 *John 19: 26-7.*

9 *John 19:17.* Golgotha symbolises the material world.

hands of the Brothers on a planetary scale, allowing the Light and Love of the cosmic Christ to inundate all.

For the past incarnation of Christ-Jesus, Capricorn is the sign wherein later Christian assertion made him to have been born, whilst he helped usher in the Piscean age. Hence, he said: 'Follow me, and I will make you fishers of men'.[10] The early Christians used the symbol of the fish as a determinative for their faith. Capricorn is the sign of the Initiate, indicating the planetary Initiation that will eventuate as a consequence of the work that will be done by the coming Avatar to help usher in the new era. The etheric body of the world will then be significantly vitalised and the *prāṇic* flow rearranged by the energy of *buddhi* to produce the coming world order. Part of the work of the Avatar will draw upon the energies of Gemini via the cosmic Christ.[11] *Buddhi* will become the medium of expression for the incoming energy of Will that will precipitate catastrophic changes in all fields of expression of Life on the earth. This will allow the appearance of sixth Root Race Humanity, who will be born out from the Fiery ashes of the fifth.

A person's etheric framework exemplifies the nature of Gemini. The centres below the diaphragm (the Solar Plexus, Sacral and Base of Spine centres) constitute the mortal brother. They govern the sensual person. They are principally fed by emotional and physical energies. When the person becomes more mentally and spiritually polarised, the centres above the diaphragm (the immortal brother) are increasingly vivified by energies from the higher planes of perception, and the energies from the lower *chakras* become refined. This makes the Gemini subject responsive to the dominant subjective forces that energise and crystallise all actions. That Gemini governs the etheric body and the *nāḍī* system means that it also governs the nervous and blood systems, which are the dense externalisations

---

10 *Matt. 4:19.*

11 This process will happen in two stages: first the 'stage of the forerunner', manifested by the new Mahāchohan, followed by the advent of Jesus. (See my two volumes: *The Constitution of Shambhala,* for detail concerning this.) They represent the pillars of the Temple to be established. Similarly, the overshadowing principle will also be in two stages. First will be the incoming energies of the Mother of the World to herald the new feminine dispensation. This stage represents the anchoring of the seventh Ray function of the Aquarian age. Next will be the energies of the cosmic Christ in order to fully flower the second Ray dispensation on earth. Two planetary Avatars will therefore manifest to produce the necessary changes, which will herald the manifestation of a third one –the reappearance of the Christ.

of the *nāḍīs*. Gemini therefore governs the sensitivity of the person's reaction to external stimuli and the development of consciousness so that fluid interactions and exchanges of information between all may manifest.

The centres above the diaphragm (the Heart, Throat, Ājñā, and Head centres) represent the immortal brother. They convey energies from the planes of reality, wherein divinity can be contacted and experienced. Receptivity to these energies concerns the process leading one to the Heart of Life and the consequent liberation from the realms of form and all forms of bondage.

The dualism of Gemini also facilitates its ability to integrate all pairs of opposites in the zodiac. It helps to build the house of the form by integrating the *iḍā* and *piṇgalā* streams of interrelationships through the *chakras* that come into existence via its agency.

The polar opposite of Gemini is Sagittarius. The fluid interplay and instability of the Gemini subject, plus the one-pointedness of the personality focus of the Sagittarian, eventually produce a balancing of the pairs of opposites in Gemini. The directive Soul effort of the disciple in Sagittarius can then manifest. The power of the Soul waxes greatly in glory, whilst the self-willed personality no longer shines.

***Summary:***

- *Keynote:* Gemini moves towards Libra.
- Gemini is the Arms and Hands of the Grand Heavenly Man.
- The *exoteric ruler* is Mercury, Ray four of Harmony through Conflict.
- The *esoteric ruler* is Venus, Ray five of the Scientific Mode.
- The *Hierarchical ruler* is the Earth, Ray three of Mathematically Exact Activity.
- The *Element* is Air (as are Libra and Aquarius).
- The *polar opposite* is Sagittarius (a Fire sign).
- *Cross*: Mutable.
- No planet falls or is exalted in this sign.
- The *Decanates* (given by D.K.) are exoterically: Mercury, Venus, and Saturn. Esoterically: Jupiter, Mars and the Sun.

The *keywords* for this sign are:

> For the ordinary man the Word goes forth: "Let instability do its work".
>
> For the disciple the Word is uttered by the Soul itself: "I recognise my other self and in the waning of that Self, I grow and glow".

## The spring season

The energies from the three signs Aries, Taurus and Gemini embody the qualities associated with *spring:* initial beginnings, the awakening of the Heavenly Man from the rigours of winter, abstracted meditation, or deep sleep. They result in the vitalisation of all Life, renewed benevolence and joy. It concerns the subjective world and the creative Thought-Form that cause the emergence of the vital Life, rejuvenating and bringing prosperity to all forms. The fertile bed thereby manifests that allows the distribution of the Waters of Life by the embodiment of divinity in Aquarius.

Aries relates to the mental plane, to the third Initiation, and to what D.K. calls 'the secret of beginnings of cycles and of emerging opportunity'.[12] After the third Initiation the secret to be revealed concerns the Higher Way that leads from the Soul to Monadic Identification, and the secret of Life. Aries manifests the Element Fire, which melts the winter's ice and rejuvenates the hibernating forms. Aries also expresses the Uranian energies of the first Christ (the Buddha).

Taurus relates to the astral plane, to the second Initiation, and to the 'secret of the revealing Light that results in the ending of glamour'. With Taurus comes the release of the floodgates of desire (Water) and the sustaining nourishment. Taurus releases the Neptunian qualities of the second (blue) Christ.

Gemini relates to the etheric plane, to the first Initiation, and the secret of relationships, which will eventually allow the birth of the Christ-Child. Gemini allows the form to assimilate and digest the life-giving vital potencies emanating from the higher spheres. Gemini veils the potency of the third Christ (the new Mahāchohan[13]), the Life of the spiritual Sun.

These energies find their outward expression through the open gate of Cancer. They are consolidated and directed in Leo, to find their most concrete (or else their highest) expression in Capricorn. The next nine signs (from Cancer to Pisces) are more strictly associated with human evolution from birth and instinctual glimmerings in Cancer, to the full development of the World Saviour in Pisces.

## The mutable cross

Gemini is one of the signs of *the mutable cross* (along with Sagittarius, Pisces and Virgo). This is the cross of repeated incarnations, of constantly changing

12 *Esoteric Astrology,* 387.

13 Explained in *The Constitution of Shambhala,* Part A.

and mutable experiences. This cross is associated with humanity and the material world.

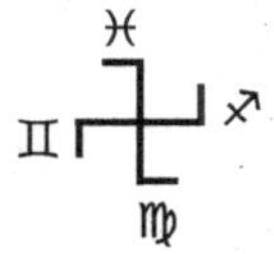


The experiences upon this cross last for by far the greater part of the evolutionary period, for the lessons to be learned are basic and fundamentally related to the evolution of the sentience of the form, the development of the mind and of its response to the Soul.

After entering the cycle of incarnation, an average person is inevitably found in Pisces, where fluidic relationships manifest. He/she is psychically sensitive to the impact of other's feeling perceptions and yet is still completely submerged in the formed realms, groping for experiences and blind to the objectivity of sense perception (for the intellect has not yet awakened).

In Sagittarius, the normal person projects desires with one-pointed selfish attitudes. In Virgo, the embryonic intellect begins to be developed and the Soul Light appears for the first time, which develops until it has produced an innate sense of duality by the time the person enters Gemini. This sense continues to grow, becoming ever more complex and defined until eventually the mystical vision is awakened when re-entering Pisces. Here the fish symbolically emerges from the sea and enters dry land. The person has begun to stabilise his/her tenuous and flickering thoughts, to control desires somewhat, and has started thereby to control the Watery domain.

In Sagittarius, the person's self-will and selfish ambition begin to be translated into a will to serve the common good. In Virgo the mental principle becomes developed, increasingly analytical and critical, that in Gemini becomes fluid and therefore directed in a widespread and more expansive, inclusive manner. The energies of the immortal brother begin to dominate, which allows the development of the Intuition. Symbolically, the fish in Pisces can then learn to fly in the Air. The energy that will spell the death of life in the Waters of sensation is first expressed, thus ensuring the reversal of the wheel in Libra.

The one-pointed disciple emerges in Sagittarius, firing the arrows of the mind unhesitatingly towards a visioned goal in Capricorn. In Pisces, a person's instinctual drives and urges finally die, allowing the brother who lives in the light (of the Intuition in Gemini) to aptly serve all in the fields of Life. The result is a well-prepared and fertilised womb in Virgo that will inevitability produce the Christ-consciousness via undertaking Initiation in Capricorn.

Thus is the journey upon the mutable cross, which all of humanity are undertaking and some are presently consummating. (They will then be impaled upon the fixed cross of the heavens.) The mutable cross is consequently concerned with mass consciousness and is the cross that the orthodox astrologer knows much about, for here the orthodox planets predominantly rule. It is related to the third aspect of Deity (Active Intelligence) and the development of the personality. The fixed cross is related to the second aspect (Love-Wisdom) and the experiences productive of the downpour of Light from the Soul. The cardinal cross is related to the first aspect (the Will) and reception to the energies from the Monad, to eventually produce Monadic Identification.

## Cancer the crab

Cancer the crab rules the chest and stomach of the grand Heavenly Man, which in humans are identified as the sources of deep-seated emotions. The function of the chest is to guard and protect the heart and lungs, to shield the central animating Life. In a similar manner, the crab carries its outer protective casing (its house) with all its possessions and earthly desires wherever it goes. Therein (in the case of the hermit crab) it is able to retreat in the face of danger. It would rather lose a claw than let go of something it desires. It lives both on the land (the physical plane) and in the sea (the astral plane). The 'shell' provides a form and protects the energies that sustain the emerging highly sensitive and emotive personality that symbolically scampers from rock (a 'safe' space) to rock within the depths of the ocean's tides, and the turbulence of the pounding shores. The individual thus moves from one transient anchorage of emotional (in)stability to another in order to find sustenance.

The Cancerian is extremely sensitive to all forms of impressions that continually inundate him/her, imaginarily or in actual fact. To them Cancerians almost immediately react, or else hide in their shells.

The stomach is related to the principle of desire, for we desire what we eat. This greatly conditions the habit of the Cancerian, for he/she desires nearly all that glitters, glistens, has glamour, or forms part of the collective mass desires of society. The crab can be likened to a walking stomach. The Solar Plexus centre energises the stomach and governs the emotions. This centre is subjectively conditioned by the massed emotional or desire currents of humanity. A cumulative Solar Plexus outpouring of emotions, moods, and feelings greatly colours the entire tonality of both the individual and collective human auras.

Within the chest there are twelve pairs of ribs. Seven of these are called true pairs and are related to the seven sacred planets. The other five are termed 'false pairs' and are related to the five non-sacred planets. There are twenty-four ribs in all, the number of the Elders that 'sit round the Throne of God'.[14] In this number can be seen the relationship between the twelve Creative Hierarchies (the seven and the five) and the twelve signs of the zodiac. The significance of the ribs in relation to Cancer, therefore, is that they allow or help facilitate the condensation and assimilation of external energies (of the zodiac, Creative Hierarchies or from the planetary Regents) by the internal person. The ribs help the lungs to precipitate external energies into the form, yet they form the outer boundary (the ring-pass-not) of the central reservoir of Life and Light (the Heart), protecting it from harmful, extraneous influences.

*Esoterically*, the objective of Cancer is to eventually emerge from the waves and to vision life on dry land. There, it is transformed, becoming the scorpion after the lessons learned in the sign Leo have been acquired. Cancer, it is said, 'visions the life in Leo', and does so because the Leonine subject offers a sense of emotional stability and security without the need to carry protective armouring. Leo fears no one; he/she is strong, independent and self-reliant. This is quite unlike the hypersensitive, ever-fearful crab that scampers from hiding place to hiding place. Cancer is the sign of the mass, instinctual consciousness that must eventually give way to the dominant self-consciousness of Leo.

Implicated here is the triad of the mass consciousness of Cancer, the self-consciousness of Leo, and the group or universal consciousness of Aquarius. The Cancer-Leo-Aquarius triangle is therefore one of the most important triangles affecting humanity today. People are now beginning to evolve out of the mass instinctual type of awareness that characterised the late Lemurian and early Atlantean period (which was ruled by Cancer). Though most are still ensconced in the emotional Cancerian Atlanteanism, our present materialistic civilisation is governed by the self-awareness characterised by the sign Leo. The most advanced of humanity are now awakening to higher perceptions, as associated with the Airy characteristics of the Aquarian disposition, whose epoch is now coming to the fore. Many are developing meditative pursuits, and thereby acclimatising to the attributes of the higher Mind, helping to produce the group consciousness expressed by the Hierarchy of enlightened being. As the 'new group of world

14 *Rev.* 4:4.

servers'[15] become increasingly active in world affairs, they will help to bring the Aquarian dispensation into manifestation.

Cancer represents the fourth stage in evolution that produces the concretion or externalisation of the energies and qualities associated with Aries, Taurus and Gemini. It denotes what is implied by the phrase 'the fall of the three into the four', and 'the completion of the square or quaternary'. Cancer is the sign of mass consciousness and of mass incarnation because all entities first physically manifest through this sign, carrying their formerly developed attributes with them. It expands the great Womb of Nature. The Laws that govern the incarnation process – the in and out-breathing of Life, governed entirely by the cardinal cross, by group and cyclic Law – find their expression through the open gate of Cancer. This development is veiled by the symbolism of the yin-yang (of which Cancer's glyph is but a modified version).

In this disguise Cancer conditions the manifestation of the energies of the four Mahārājas, and the Lipikas (the Scribes), who embody and circumscribe the boundaries of a Logoic Head centre. This allows the establishment of the Throne of 'God', the 'tabernacle of the Lord', via which manifestation of the material domain is possible. The path of Initiation allows one to control one's destiny, causing freedom from mass (emotional) psychic receptivity, the Cancerian energies that afflict and completely dominate unevolved humanity. Upon the rectified wheel, Cancer stands as the open gate into cosmic astral space, after the Initiate has mastered the Capricornian mountainside. (The polar opposite of Cancer.)

The Cancerian subject lives either in the shell of emotions and moods that he/she has built or else as a disciple, in a body of light, which is needed to dispel the glamour (darkness) of humanity's emotional world. Humanity has collectively built a shell or 'house' of such darkness that must be dispelled by the combined actions of the light bearers, the world-disciples. This darkness has become the planetary dweller on the threshold, which is ruled by Cancer/Capricorn. This darkness must be overcome for planetary Initiation to happen, allowing the earth to become a sacred planet in the Aquarian age. The Avatar must appear for this purpose, to coordinate the battle and the related events.

Capricorn is the 'gateway to eternal Life', whereas Cancer is the gateway to birth in the physical world, thus towards perpetual death. Capricorn signifies the door that looms ahead of the person working to undertake the Initiation process. The continual rounds of experience and its emotional conditionings (Cancer) lead

15 See Bailey's *The Externalisation of the Hierarchy* for detail.

eventually to crystallisation and extensive materialism, symbolised by the jagged rocks and boulders that the goat must eventually climb. When the person does so and has attained lofty heights in Capricorn, then he/she is able to enter both gates at will and choose to serve in the realms of death for the salvation of the world.

Cancer also governs the fifth liberated Creative Hierarchy, which precipitates into objectivity the Desire currents of the planetary or solar Logos, allowing the manifestation of the 'Sons of Desire' (the seven lesser Hierarchies).

Cancer is a dual sign:

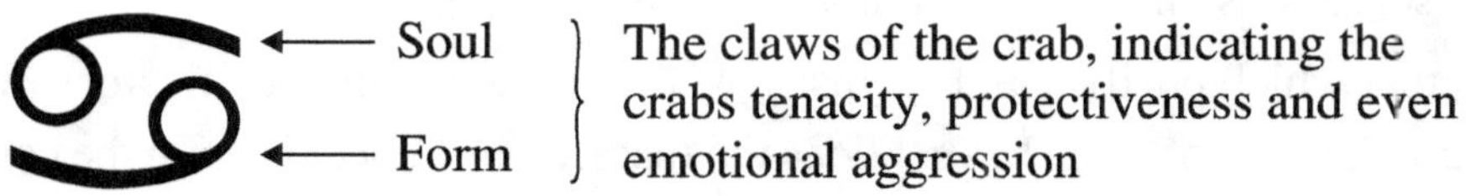


**Figure 10. The claws of the crab**

The emotional, fluid, embryonic Cancerian consciousness (best described as Atlantean) is exemplified by the properties of its ruling planets: exoterically the Moon, esoterically and Hierarchically Neptune.

The Moon (☽) highlights the Cancerian psychic receptivity, emotional awareness, sensitivity to mass reactions and impacts from all sides of the form nature, for the Moon is the mother of forms.

Neptune (♆) is the God of the Waters. Esoterically, Neptune assists the Cancerian to control desire (the Waters) if the light of the Soul is to shine, which enables the wielding of the triple pronged trident of spiritual Energy. Neptune governs the manifestation of the second Initiation. During the Atlantean era it symbolised the incarnate Christ. Together, the Moon and Neptune make Cancerians the most mediumistic of the natives of all the signs (except maybe a Piscean with Cancer rising).

In the Greek myths, Neptune also ruled herds of horses, implying mass movements of the animal nature (human base appetites), which would later be controlled and directed by the thinking person.

Cancer is part of the Watery triplicity (together with Scorpio and Pisces) which is the cause of humanity's mass emotional conditionings and perpetual misery in *saṃsāra*. One can look at the effect of this triplicity from two angles:

a. Regarding the world of sensation. The person enters incarnation in the sign Cancer and is completely immersed in the Waters of mass instinctual currents and emotional receptivity. He/she is buffeted this way and that, according to the mood of the currents. In Pisces, the Soul is firmly yoked to the personality and the Fish learns to swim wherever it wills within the confines of its conditioning environment, until eventually it attains individualised character traits and self-reliance is obtained. In Scorpio, the person has learnt to sting, hurt and bring death. He/she has emerged from the Waters, but has yet to master the experiences on the land and therefore suffers much, causes much suffering, and undergoes many trials through the sense of isolation and enmity to all around. Thus is the Will developed, signifying the ability to break free from the sensations and conditionings of the mass of people.

b. As that which purifies and cleanses, where in Cancer the purificatory Waters begin their action, which conditions the masses (for Cancer is upon the cardinal cross). This causes radical changes in the environment and habitat of the crab: the periodical, cyclic, racial and seasonal changes that affect the kingdoms of Nature as a whole. The cleansing of the attributes or aspects of their evolutionary development are thereby changed towards perfection.

In Pisces (upon the mutable cross), the individual is karmically purified through the actions of words and deeds via the incarnation process. The fish now swims free and in company with its fellows, and by developing its life it finds sustenance in the Waters of enlightened Being. What was formerly developed and later found unnecessary or hindering in the life of the person has been eliminated, or purified and transmuted. When the necessary purification of the grossest aspects of Life have been accomplished, then one can mount the fixed cross and undertake the many tests related to taking the Baptism Initiation, so to emerge free from the control of the Waters.

By then the reversal of the wheel has taken place and the person stands again in Cancer in a body of Light, being able to help disperse and dispel the emotional ailments and glamour of those in the world. Inevitably, after many turnings, the Wheel will place him/her in Pisces to become a world Saviour. That One will then have learnt to esoterically direct and educate the masses. The Saviour is the embodied repository of the energies that condition whole kingdoms of Nature and planetary evolution. In Pisces manifests the transmuted correspondence of the type of mass instinctual consciousness that developed when animal-man first incarnated in Cancer and Individualised in Leo. For most Initiates, however, the turning of the Wheel leads them to become the Bodhisattva in Aquarius, and through its gate they find the way of escape to cosmic sources.

- Cancer therefore relates to experiences in the human kingdom.
- Scorpio relates to the experiences of the disciple in the spiritual Hierarchy.
- Pisces relates to what is developed by those in Shambhala (the Kingdom of 'God').

***Summary:***

- *Keynote*: Cancer visions the life in Leo.
- Cancer is the Chest and Stomach of the grand Heavenly Man.
- The *exoteric ruler* is the Moon, Ray four of Harmony overcoming Conflict.
- The *esoteric* and *Hierarchical ruler* is Neptune, Ray six of Devotion and Aspiration.
- The *Element* is Water, as also Scorpio and Pisces.
- The *polar opposite* is Capricorn.
- *Cross:* cardinal.
- Both Jupiter and Neptune are exalted in Cancer. Saturn is in detriment.
- The *Decanates* (given by D.K.) are exoterically: the Moon, Mars and Jupiter. Esoterically: Venus, Mercury and the Moon.

The *keywords* that D.K. gives for this sign are:

> 'I build a lighted house and therein dwell', which is the 'objective of the Cancer experience and the purpose for which incarnation has been taken... The temporary method of the personality is also clearly given when we are told that the Word proclaimed by the Soul as it takes incarnation is 'Let isolation be the rule and yet - the crowd exists.'

## Leo the lion

Evolution proceeds from the instinctual stage of mass-rule to an intensely individualistic, self-aware stage of consciousness. The outer contacts and psychic sensitivity of people coarsen and crystallise, until eventually they are completely immersed in a world of their own making. Thereby they become personalities. This self-conscious stage is signified by the sign Leo the lion. The acute sensitivity to the impacts of the surrounding environment associated with the Cancerian is further developed in Leo, to produce one that is completely aware of the source of those impacts. The task of Leonine subjects is to first relate their own sensitivities to those of the other personalities in any group to which they may belong. Such individuals eventually become the centre of a group because their developed qualities allow them to draw all to them by means of personal magnetism, self-glorifying intelligence.

Upon the path to light, the intelligent Leonine can eventually sensitively incorporate the energies of the conditioning Soul, and later of Monadic impressions. This will then produce liberation from all types of self-identification in relation to the formed realms. Nevertheless, spiritual Identity (which distinguishes one liberated being from another) perpetually remains.

The symbol of Leo is simply the Lion's tail, a shorthand notation exemplifying the qualities of the lion in terms of energy expression.

♌

The tail signifies the stabilising element that allows the lion to pursue its prey with effectiveness. It is the only symbol in the zodiac (apart from Sagittarius) that is not dual or triune. Therefore, it also implies the innate separateness of the self-aware individual.

Leo is the fifth sign in the zodiac, and for the individual the attributes of the pentagram are exemplified in this sign via the prowess of the five senses. (Capricorn, the tenth sign, embodies the pentagram in a psychic, magical, or more universal application.) These attributes can make the Leonine subject very materially and personally selfish, with a strong lust for power, the ideal dictator or manipulator of human emotional ideals. On the reversed wheel Leo is the eighth sign, showing that here the Christ energy can be eventually perfected as Leo looks towards its polar opposite—Aquarius, the sign of universal consciousness. The self-centred Leonine subject then becomes group conscious, aware of other people's needs (not just his/her own) and learns the art of sacrifice upon the path to liberation.

In many ways Leo is the dominant Fire sign in the zodiac, especially in this materialistic Aryan epoch where people are taught to develop their intellect and worship selfish, materialistic incentives. Leo brings and stabilises on the earth (through the self-conscious individual) the creative and transmutative ability of Fire, originally projected in Aries and finding its major direction or focus in Sagittarius. Fire is the Element governing the mental plane, and so its incandescence becomes the means of the purification of the mental-emotions and the entire threefold body on the path of return. Though Hercules battled through his labours in the sign Scorpio, he is exemplified as a sun-Initiate or world-server for having symbolically worked his way through the zodiac wearing the skin of the lion that he slew when he was eighteen. This indicates that he was master of the Leonine characteristics as he undertook his labours.

Leo directs solar Fire (symbolised by the Sun) and represents the energies of the Soul, which is 'the lion that seeks out his prey'. In the latter evolutionary stages, the 'prey' is the lower quaternary, the animal nature and the mental-emotional personality. The solar Lion takes the remnants of the prey to its lair after it has metaphorically caused its death. The radiant Sun (or Soul) transforms and engulfs the (lunar) light of the personality. For the major part of the evolutionary period, however, the lion is identified with the 'beastly' passion of the personality. The Sun is the source of *prāṇa* (being the strength and vitality of the lion) to cause progressive evolutionary growth. Forms of *prāṇa* (or *ākāśa)* find their direct correspondence and importance on all three major levels of awareness. For this reason the Sun rules Leo exoterically, esoterically and Hierarchically.

The major theme of the Leonine subject is the development of self-awareness. For the Initiate, self-awareness becomes the illumined group consciousness of the Soul, its sensitivity to the energies of the twelve Creative Hierarchies, and the many planetary and zodiacal impacts. Wherever solar Light manifests, it indicates that self-consciousness has been gained. The individual has then evolved from instinctual awareness and the feeling-perceptions that condition the masses. The process of the evolution of consciousness is the major objective of the physical manifestation of a sun, a process ruled by Leo.

An Initiate develops sensitivity to impressions from the Heart of the Sun, the central reservoir of Light and Love in the solar system. The self-aware personality, the Soul and the Initiate, all act as powerhouses of Love and Light, becoming sources of energy, radiant suns to all beings. The personality expresses the light from the physical sun (solar light). The Soul expresses Hierarchical Light (from the Heart of the Sun), and the Initiate of the higher degrees begins to express the Light from the central Spiritual Sun. In each case the person acts as a powerhouse of Love, Light and vitality, becoming a source of the energy of a radiant sun to all those around. This happens from an increasingly vaster perspective as progress is made from intelligentsia to Initiate status. The Sun can therefore be found governing the life of the Leonine subject from all angles.

The physical sun (governing the mutable cross) stimulates the life of the personality and his/her body nature. Under the general stimulus of this sun, complete self-awareness is evolved. This is focussed through Jupiter (the second Ray) and Mercury (the fourth Ray), the orthodox rulers of the mutable cross.

The Heart of the Sun governs the fixed cross and stimulates the Life of the Soul, producing the mystical vision in the personality – the ability to respond to group law and Love. This energy is focussed through Neptune, which esoterically is veiled by the Sun. Neptune governs the Waters of Life and rules the astral plane. It is the regent of the sixth Ray and facilitates the development of the second Initiation. Neptune gives a Leo subject the ability to rule the emotional world that dominates his subjects. It is an embodiment of the energy of the Christ and allows the transmutation of emotion-desire into love-aspiration. Neptune also relates Leo to Cancer, for it is the esoteric, Hierarchical and exoteric ruler of Cancer (though veiled by the Moon).

When the transmutative energy from the Heart of the Sun is brought to bear upon the form (ruled by the Moon) via the mediatory effect of Neptune in Leo, then base emotional substance is transformed into the subtle, and the form is sublimated to become the essence of the Divine. (This then manifests as the perfume that the 'heavenly censors' seek.[16]) The energies of the Sun, the Moon and Neptune are a combination of the second, fourth and sixth Rays. This is a most important relationship, for they are all along the second Ray path and therefore must produce that which leads to the Heart of the central animating Life. The relationship of the Moon to Mercury is important in this light, for both are ruled by the fourth Ray – the central factor in the alchemical process, and that is the process that concerns this path.

The central Spiritual Sun that governs the cardinal cross, stimulates an esoteric aptitude of the Initiate's abilities to consciously express divine energies through the use of the enlightened Mind. The planet Uranus (the seventh Ray of Ceremonial Magic and Organisational Aptitude) now completely controls and directs the energies of the mental and physical plane. It provides the enlightened Leonine subject a great depth of Vision: to become an innovator and a magnetic, dynamic leader with great inner resources and vitality.

Leo is said to rule the upper part of the back and the power associated with the clenched fist and wrist, thus of the dominant and sometimes aggressive personality, or ruler. The wrist enables great manoeuvrability and flexibility of the hands (Gemini) and thus of the ability to rightly direct and control all of the energies associated with the personality. In Leo the 'I am' principle dominates. The upper part of the back supports and aids the functioning of the head, neck and chest. It particularly allows the development of the mind, relating it to the emotional

---

16 *Rev. 8:3-6.*

body. In this is seen an important function of the sixth and seventh Creative Hierarchies, in that they support the energies of the five liberated Hierarchies (the Mind aspect of the solar Logos) and direct those energies towards the development of the Logoic Personality. (His body of Desire, in the form of the seven manifest Creative Hierarchies.)

Leo rules the Heart, the central reservoir of Life. Much has been written concerning the Heart centre elsewhere, needing no reiteration here.

Exoterically, Leo is the source of the factor of pride of the beast (when united with Solar Plexus energies and directed by the mind). In Leo, all of the diverse energies associated with the personality are regulated so that the light of the personal sun shines before humanity, allowing the Leonine subject to attract them to his/her purpose. The personality thus shines supreme and is dominant in this sign. Thus the Leo subject generally possesses an individuality that outshines all his peers. Leonines are leaders in all spheres of Life and are motivated by a strong tendency towards intellectual superiority, to dominate and rule. Thus they are often boastful, assertive and proud. They are also capable of real magnanimity and generosity in all their undertakings. (As is the sun through the *prāṇic* vitality it releases.)

One of the major characteristics often seen in the Leonine is that he/she finds it hard to accept advice from others, especially in matters of discipline. Therefore, self-discipline is what the average Leonine must learn. Overconfidence in their own powers and abilities is another of the Leo subject's major faults. They often procrastinate, allowing things simply to be and then finding it is too late to act. Like the lion who spends many days basking in the sun, and when forced to obtain food, it discovers that game is difficult to catch. Also, if things do not turn out the way that Leonine subjects expect, they are apt to retreat into their 'lair' and stay there.

Leo is part of the *sphinx,* where Virgo is the head of the sphinx and Leo is its body. The sphinx relates to Atlantean times when the two signs were united as one, and proper self-consciousness was still an evolutionary objective. This interrelation is part of the answer to questions concerning the mystery of the sphinx. The Lion and the Virgin together stand for the entire person; the relation between the Womb of Life (manifesting as the Virgin) and Leo is the form, the self-conscious individual evolving therein, and to whom the 'Virgin' gives birth. The sphinx therefore symbolises the path to be taken to evolve out from the Womb and into the domain of eternal Life. This then concerns the work needed to be done to relate Spirit and matter, which brings to light the process of Individualisation (the birthing of mind in an animal form).

The emergence of animal-man comes about by the sacrifice of what is possessed by a liberated Hierarchy (carrying the spark of mind) needed to aid a lower Hierarchy bound to the animal body. This is seen in the relationship between the fourth and fifth Creative Hierarchies (the human and *deva* kingdoms) and the coming of the Lords of Flame at the time when humanity were ready to Individualise. From this perspective Leo becomes the human group Soul, the 'tawny lions' that establish themselves upon the higher mental plane. Virgo manifests the attributes of the third and fifth Creative Hierarchies (the lesser Builders and Makara) that establish and incarnate into the Causal form per se, wherein the human Spark (the Monad) can reside.

Hidden also within the symbolism of the sphinx is the relationship of Leo to Aquarius the water bearer (the sign of the man bearing a pitcher of water), for they are polar opposites. Leo-Aquarius is the vertical arm of the fixed cross. It relates Spirit to matter, divinity to the lesser fields of evolution in terms of consciousness. It is consequently one of the most important relationships in the zodiac, particularly in this age, for Aquarius is on the ascendancy. This is now producing a strong tendency towards fusion, the banding together of intelligent thinkers into coherent groups that share a common purpose. The self-conscious or self-willed types that are influenced by Leo (be they individuals or nations) will thereby become awakened, part of the collective Awareness of Hierarchy. This interrelation is therefore, incidentally, a major cause for much of the clash of ideologies that is everywhere prevalent. The coming Aquarian age will produce the emergence of world servers everywhere. However, the resistance to the emerging cooperativeness by the entrenched egoists, who fear loss of control of their power bases over people's minds, will be fierce.

The New Age will be the era of humanity singularly striving towards world unity, the cooperative enterprise of humanity as a unity. This significance cannot be overestimated, for in the present era humanity have achieved self-awareness. They are beginning the path of aspiration towards the Mysteries of enlightened Being – the Soul, the Sun, the Christ-aspect (of which Leo is the guarantor). Leo is the open gate to Hierarchical involvement, the Heart of Life upon our planetary sphere. It is the vital Life of the externalising Hierarchy roaring out its note of rulership over the sum of the planetary domain, of the material world where selfishness and aggressive separateness once held sway.

The Waters of cosmic Love are poured forth via the Heart of the Lion (Regulus) to our planetary sphere. There is thus an important triangle of energies between Sirius, Leo, and Varuna (Neptune) to convey this energy to the Hierarchy of Enlightened Being on our planet.

At first, regarding personality attainment, a person's awareness of things is only superficial and fleeting (in Aquarius). This awareness however grows and deepens until eventually the individual can utilise the environment for purely selfish reasons and dominate his/her fellows (in Leo). This personality dominance grows and expands until one is eventually able to direct the activities of one's group or field of activity (in Aquarius). There is a constant mutual interplay between Leo and Aquarius at this stage (interrelated by Gemini, the sign of the subjective Christ). As the Sun (the Christ) can increasingly illumine the form, so the personality interests become submerged for the good of the whole (in Aquarius), and later (in Leo) one can shine as a world leader. Finally in Aquarius one becomes a world server.

***Summary:***

- *Keynote:* Leo seeks release in Scorpio.
- Leo rules the upper part of the Back, Clenched Fist, Wrist and Heart of the grand Heavenly Man.
- The *exoteric ruler* is the Sun (veiling Jupiter), Ray two of Love-Wisdom.
- The *esoteric ruler* is the Sun (veiling Neptune), Ray six of Devotion and Aspiration.
- The *Hierarchical ruler* is the Sun (veiling Uranus), Ray seven of Ceremonial Magic, Cyclic Activity and Materialising Power.
- The *Element* is Fire (as also for Sagittarius and Aries).
- The *polar opposite* is Aquarius.
- *Cross*: fixed.
- No planet falls, nor is any planet exalted in this sign, however, the power of both Uranus and Saturn are somewhat lessened.
- The *Decanates* (given by D.K.) are exoterically: Saturn, Jupiter, and Mars. Esoterically: the Sun, Jupiter and Mars.

The *keywords* that D.K. gives for this sign are:

> 'And the Word said: Let other forms exist. I rule because I am'.
> 'I am That and That am I'.

The 'I am' is the Word of the self-conscious, selfish individual. The 'I am That' is the Word of the Leo subject who is rapidly gaining the higher consciousness and preparing for fresh and universal expression in Aquarius, working to evolve the 'That am I'.

## Virgo the virgin

Virgo the virgin rules the Abdomen, Womb and Breasts of the grand Heavenly (Wo)Man, ensuring that the ideal conditions are obtained for the birth of the Christ-Child (enlightenment-consciousness), and the later nurturing and growth during its infancy. This is the natural extension of the development of self-awareness, as governed by the sign Leo, and constitutes the major goal of the evolutionary process in the solar system.

The abdomen holds the intestines, which are responsible for the latter stages of the digestive process, and thus of the assimilation of the right categories of knowledge and experience that will enable the person to set foot upon the path of probation. Upon the Initiation path it concerns the alchemical transmutation of the process of everyday living.

The various mother Goddesses (such as Isis, Ishtar, Ceres, Hecate and Lilith, leading to Mary the mother of Christ-Jesus) epitomise the qualities of this sign. Virgo typifies the various powers and forces constituting Mother Nature, who embodies the substance from which all forms are wrought. The qualities of this sign have been depicted in many ways by the ancients because of the magnitude of the evolutionary process in the Womb of Nature. Some of these ways to be considered are:

a. To imply the depth (or bowels) of the earth, of the caves from which the various forces are to be born (as also was Jesus at Bethlehem). Here we find the 'darkness, quiet and warmth; it is the valley of deep experience wherein secrets are discovered and "brought to light"',[17] to quote D.K. In this sign the powers of the personality are seen to be strongest. Here Jesus is symbolically overshadowed by the Holy Ghost (Hierarchy).
b. The picture of Ceres, the goddess of the harvest holding the ear of wheat. This signifies material prosperity and abundance, the gaining of the efforts of life's long toil.

---

17 *Esoteric Astrology*, 260.

c. The various qualities of woman and motherhood (with the emphasis of childbearing and fertility) are the most obvious characteristics of this sign. The Virgin symbolises the primal, undifferentiated, universal substance matter, which offers promise of the evolution of the Christ aspect and of its resurrection in the far distant future.

d. When the form and the psychic nature were unduly emphasised, then the Virgin was also identified with the magicians of the left hand path, and the witch (e.g., as Lilith and Hecate) ruling the elemental forces of Nature, who has the ability to lure one to a life of degradation and psychic sodomy. Virgo effectively oversees everyone that worships telluric forces, the etheric energies associated with the formed realms, the ley lines, dolmens, sacred healing spots, stone temples and circles of the ancients. These are concerned with earth magic, elementary psychism; the clairvoyance that allows one to communicate with the nature spirits, fairies, pixies and other *deva* forces that embody substance. Virgo and the Mother of the World are virtually synonymous terms, but all too often Her worship has degenerated into sex-magic and other forms of circumscription and debasement of psychic abilities.

Ritualised sex-magic necessarily focussed upon the evocation of the powers of the *chakras* below the diaphragm (and often by using drugs) does not lead to the earth Mother. Such magic does produce illusions of psychic power and heightened emotive sensations, but also leads to being controlled by elemental psychic forces and dark entities. (The Elementaries, the demons of darkness, the vampires and beasts of the night, the frenzied and Bacchanalian denizens of Pan's domain.) Let the curious novice in magic, the dilettante and those desirous of elemental psychic power beware. Through purity of motive and method lies safety and the way of true union with the Divine Mother.

Virgo relates to the type of matriarchies that were prevalent in Atlantean times, when the Brahmā, the third (Mother) aspect of Deity, was the dominant factor in evolution.

Virgo is the Womb within which time evolves. It is one of the most ancient of the signs (with Cancer and Capricorn), as it embodies the sum of countless cycles of material evolution of past aeons and Incarnations of solar Logoi. This concerns how the third aspect of Deity gains its ascendancy, which eventually allows the birth of self-consciousness. In this sign, therefore, the third Ray of Mathematically Exact Activity can find its greatest scope for right evolutionary expression. Virgo governs the period when the evolving personality is blind and completely lost in a world of mass psychic receptivity, until the time when humanity can perceive the clear Light of the spiritual Day on the event horizon. Virgo veils the Christ Light that must evolve from the earth (the material world). Here the evolved Christ must raise in Light the essential Life of the earth to the Throne of His Father.

Pisces represents the entire Watery sphere upon which the 'Spirit of God moved',[18] and Virgo is the Earthy world that evolved from it. Virgo therefore represents the negative receptive pole to the positive Father aspect of Deity. Virgo is the sign in which the duality associated with Gemini is blended and fashioned into the unity represented by Her Son. She forms an ideal matrix wherein the Christ within us, 'the hope of glory', the hidden spiritual reality, can grow and mature.

Virgo is the sixth sign in the zodiac (the seventh on the reversed wheel). Thus here is veiled the qualities associated with the hexagram, which blends the qualities of Spirit and matter. From every angle of vision, the hexagram governs the evolution of all aspects of the form, as embodied by the feminine, receptive, *deva* hierarchies. Along with Scorpio, Virgo is a triune sign where Spirit-Soul-matter are interrelated. The task of Virgo, therefore, is to build the forms allowing such interrelation, that become the medium whereby Spirit can utilise matter as a vehicle of expression, and to set about the task of its transmutation and elevation into the realms of mind/Mind.

Virgo consequently embodies the substance of the three tiers of petals within the Sambhogakāya Flower (the Soul, which is evenly balanced between Spirit and matter), for this form is embodied by the Solar *devas,* who wield its karmic affiliations.[19] The inherent attributes of this Soul form must be mastered during the evolutionary process, which will be productive of gaining the third Initiation. Leo embodies the sum of the gained qualities of these petals in terms of the unfolding consciousness and the quality of Light demonstrated. In this idea is resolved part of the mystery of the sphinx with its woman's head and lion's torso. Leo is the solar Light and Virgo represents the light of intelligent substance. They must interrelate in such a way that their blended lights produce the vehicle that will allow the Heart of the One (the Spirit manifesting as the Jewel in the Heart of the Lotus) to irradiate the form with vital Life and thus elevate it to become the seat of Power of the All-encompassing Lord.

As the person gains many experiences by means of incarnation into the substance of the Earthly domain ruled by Virgo, so the qualities stored in the petals of the

---

18 *Genesis 1:2.*

19 Information concerning the formation of the kingdom of Souls is provided in Alice Bailey's *A Treatise on Cosmic Fire.*

Causal form grow. Eventually in Scorpio the spiritual person can demonstrate control over matter. This happens as the disciple (symbolically taking the attributes of Hercules) undergoes the major tests associated with Scorpio and effectively lifts the nine headed Hydra of desire triumphantly over his/her head. The serpent of time has grown into a Hydra in Scorpio, with its nine heads embodying the attributes of the carnal person. The potency of the Hydra is summed up in the qualities of the lowly scorpion, a creature possessing a most venomous sting, who is fond of dark and damp places, but can also be found in the desert. The sting can produce the end of the cycles of time (by the time Pisces is reached) if death of the form nature allows the spiritual life to be trod. However, the sting can also perpetuate the cycles, if the poisons it carries are that of lust, conceit, desire, avarice, etc. The story of Virgo is consummated in the process of overcoming this Hydra and climbing the mount of Initiation in Capricorn.

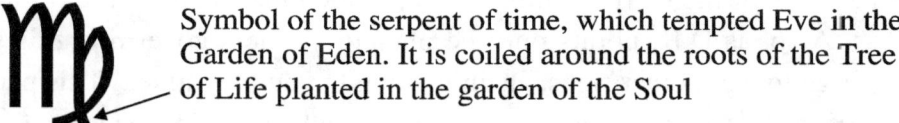

**Symbol of the serpent of time, which tempted Eve in the Garden of Eden. It is coiled around the roots of the Tree of Life planted in the garden of the Soul**

**Figure 11. The Virgo glyph**

Virgo's rulers help exemplify her qualities. First there is the intuitive Mind of its *exoteric ruler,* Mercury, the messenger or mediator of the Gods, and who in many ways stands for the Sun. Mercury makes Virgoan natives fluid, quick, exact and meticulous in all undertakings. They are often fond of detail and embellishment, are finicky, and possess keen intellects. Mercury governs the fourth Ray of Beautifying Harmony overcoming Conflict that rules humanity. In the form of the Soul or sun, Mercury is therefore ideally placed to reveal the hidden reality in Virgo that the form veils, and to facilitate the development of the intuition that will allow the disciple to tread the path to Light.

The Moon, which veils the energy of Vulcan in Virgo's case, is her *esoteric ruler.* Vulcan is the Deity hid deep inside the caves and depths of matter, and in the forms that the Moon embodies. The relationship between the Moon and Mercury (both ruled by the fourth Ray) is important here, for it allows the revealing light of the Soul (Mercury) and the developing intellect of the Virgoan to wisely utilise the energies of form (the moon) for his/her own purposes. Within that form the fiery hammer of Vulcan will produce havoc and destruction, or else reveal the Light of Life. D.K. states:

> Virgo is related to Taurus through Vulcan which brings in what might be called the *endurance* aspect of the will-to-be which carries the incarnated Son of God through the experiences of the dark time wherein the personality becomes the Mother in the stage of gestation, through the period of infancy upon the physical plane and through the stage of adolescence until the initiate attains full maturity.[20]

The ability to develop the spiritual Will (as exemplified by Vulcan, ruled by the first Ray) first emerges in Virgo and gives the person the incentive to tread the path of discipleship. This path will eventually result in the attainment of Initiation in Capricorn, and the revelation of the meaning of Light in Taurus (ruled by Vulcan esoterically). As explained previously, Virgo, Capricorn and Taurus constitute the Earthy triplicity.

On the reversed wheel there are nine signs from Virgo to Capricorn (including Virgo) that relate to the nine months of the gestation period. This results in the effectual birth of the Christ-Child, or else, to the nine stages of the Initiation process. Also, as D.K. points out, the planetary rulers governing this sign relate Virgo to eight other signs, again making the number nine.[21] This plainly demonstrates the fact that from every angle the symbolism of Virgo is associated with gestation, birth, the prenatal life of the developing planetary Christ, and the process of evolution.

| Path | Sign | Keynote | Exoteric Ruler | Esoteric Ruler |
|---|---|---|---|---|
| 1. Right Understanding | Aries | Beginnings | Mars | Mercury |
| 2. Right Aspiration | Taurus | Desire | Venus | Vulcan |
| 3. Right Speech | Gemini | Relationship | Mercury | Venus |
| 4. Right Action | Cancer | Movement | Moon | Neptune |
| 5. Right Livelihood | Scorpio | Test-trial | Mars | Mars |
| 6. Right Effort | Sagittarius | Direction | Jupiter | Earth |
| 7. Right Mindfulness | Aquarius | Service | Uranus | Jupiter |
| 8. Right Absorption | Pisces | Salvation | Jupiter | Pluto |

**Table 3. The Eightfold Path**

20 Ibid., 274.

21 *Esoteric Astrology,* 264-5 and 271.

These nine signs are given in the list on page 278 of *Esoteric Astrology.* They are related to the Buddha's Eightfold Path, which are explained in my book *Maṇḍalas: Their Nature and Development.*

They all exist within Virgo, in the form of the Womb *(saṃsāra* or the material domain) of the Mother. This Womb conditions the process that sets the stage for undertaking the Buddha's Eightfold Path. This Path represents the stages of the process that will allow one to be born out of that Womb and into the realm of enlightened Being.

The Moon also veils Neptune, the God of the Waters, again relating Virgo to Cancer and the early evolutionary period when mass consciousness and the Waters governed all that was.

Hierarchically, Jupiter rules this sign. This must necessarily be so, for the Initiate born in this sign must inevitably develop the second Ray of Love-Wisdom. The Initiate is the Christ-Child whose birth was the objective of the Virgin-Mother and the third Ray of Activity to bring to light.

The polar opposite of Virgo is Pisces the fishes. Their relationship can best be viewed in terms of the evolutionary process. On the involutionary arc, virgin matter dominated. For untold ages it developed and expanded, producing increasingly diversified and complex forms of Life, until eventually animal-man came into being possessing a Soul. The Mother aspect was dominant for this entire period, whilst the light of the Soul (the masculine principle) was hidden in Her Womb. (The Womb here being the mental plane, from which all forms in the physical plane are derived, for the physical is but the reflection of the mental.) After the human kingdom was born it grew and matured as it travelled round the zodiac from epoch to epoch, to finally produce a World-Saviour in the sign Pisces. This Saviour will then rightly nurture and reveal the nature of the Souls (hidden in the caves and depths of matter in Virgo) upon a new arc of evolution. The inner radiance of the buried Lives (humanity) will then shine forth. Pisces consummates the work begun in Virgo.

The symbol of the mermaid, with a woman's torso and the tail of a fish, exemplifies the relation between Virgo and Pisces. This symbol implicates a purely material evolution when the various processes of Life were feminine, during the early Atlantean era. The Soul completely identified with the form and swimming in the waters of sensation, was for the first time able to climb on to dry land (the Earth) and breathe the Air. This signified becoming receptive to *buddhic* stimulation, which in those days related to clairvoyant perception without any development or input from the mind *(manas)* whatsoever.

Virgo it is said 'hides the light which irradiates the field in Aquarius',[22] for therein the Christ-Light is nurtured, which the disciple must develop and then utilise to 'irradiate with light the sons of men and their entire field of activity'. They must produce the garden city on the earth. Here Virgoan energy (of the *devas*) must be rightly appropriated to fertilise and nurture the earth to produce its greenery and salutary beneficence in abundance, thus countering the present well-nigh disastrous widespread rape of the earth Mother. Humanity has amassed much evil-doing to atone for before the light hidden in Virgo can properly serve them. Despite this, the Mother cares for Her callous and unthinking delinquent children. She must necessarily educate them through processes of tribulation and repetitive denial of what they greedily desire, if they are to learn from their folly. Inevitably they will grow in light and mature as loving adults. Cataclysms, famines, pestilence upon the face of the earth thus continuously come as the Mother convulses and reacts to Her rapine.

***Summary:***

- *Keynote:* Virgo hides the light, which irradiates the field in Aquarius.
- Virgo rules the Abdomen, Womb and Breasts of the grand Heavenly Man.
- The *exoteric ruler* is Mercury, Ray four of Harmony overcoming Conflict.
- The *esoteric ruler* is the Moon, Ray four (veiling Vulcan, the first Ray).
- The *Hierarchical ruler* is Jupiter, Ray two of Love-Wisdom.
- The *Element* is Earth (as also for Taurus and Capricorn).
- The *polar opposite* is Pisces.
- *Cross*: mutable.
- Mercury is exalted in Virgo, Venus falls into generation. The power of both Neptune and Jupiter is lessened (despite the fact that Jupiter is one of the ruling planets of this sign).
- The *Decanates* given for Virgo are, exoterically: the Sun, Venus and Mercury. Esoterically: Mercury, Saturn and Venus.

The *keywords* given for this sign are:

> On the ordinary wheel the command goes forth in the following words which institute the activity of Virgo 'And the Word said, let Matter reign'.
>
> On the wheel of the disciple the voice emerges from the Virgin Herself and she says: 'I am the mother and the child. I, God, I, matter am'.

22 Ibid., 332.

## The summer season

The energies from Cancer, Leo and Virgo produce the *summer season* in the northern hemisphere. The Sun (being exalted in Leo) causes the yellowing and reaping of the harvest of Life. If the energies of Leo (the personality) become too dominant and overbearing, then there are the famines and droughts that often characterise summer. The destroyer aspect of the Sun overpowers to bring hardship, death and the extended difficulty for all in the domain of the Leonine subject. The Sun can stimulate the outbursts of the various Fires of the (critical, proud and separative) minds of people that burn and ravage the many forests, towns and beneficent works of humanity. This is the produce of the (evolutionary) harvest, threatening the unborn child in Virgo to issue forth as stillborn.

On the other hand, if Cancerian activities are not rightly regulated by the Lion's roar, then Leo's domain can give way to the flood of incessant desires, glamour and emotions. The land of reason can thereby be submerged by the ravages of the Watery sphere. This also makes it difficult for the child to be born.

When the beneficence of the Sun is rightly invoked to ripen the fruits of the sower (Taurus), and the light of reason causes the recession of the Waters of desire, then the golden grains of prosperity can be plucked from fertile fields (Virgo). This will enable the person to nurture the child (the hopes of the future) throughout the winter's darkest nights. The ability to wisely balance desire and reason evokes within the person the qualities of Libra and the autumn season, explained later.

## Libra the balance

Libra the balance rules the lower part of the Back of the Grand Heavenly Man. Apart from the central spinal column (governed by Capricorn) this part of the back is characterised by an absence of bones. In a similar fashion there are no major discernible characteristics qualifying the Libran, for it is the sign in which the various pairs of opposites are brought together and blended. Libra is said to 'relate the two in Gemini', though the early part of a person's career often seesaws from one to the other. Libra is the sign wherein latent duality and all the issues that concern the separative twins are brought into a field of resolution, of equilibrium. It thus allows the Law of the Good to dominate all their relationships and activities.

The lower back allows for greater flexibility of movement for the entire torso: to bend downwards, upwards, sideways and backwards. This flexibility and extension in all directions of the consciousness principle, and its ability to view a thing from all angles, is a major quality of the judge. He needs to be able to see things from all points of view and to uphold great flexibility of thought before pronouncing his judgement. Libra is consequently the sign of legislation, the upholder of the Law from every angle. In relation to the world of the personality, there were thus at first the great religious codes of ethics, such as the Ten Commandments, imposed from above, via the mediating priests, prophets and priest kings. Next were the laws formulated by humanity, which govern every aspect of our family and social life.

The various Laws and potent energies from the Creative Hierarchies govern the subjective world and the life of the disciple. The Laws of Life that sustain the entire manifested universe are expressed during the creative process. Science is just beginning to comprehend the A.B.C.'s of the subjective Laws that the disciple who is mounting the cardinal cross is increasingly subjected to.

The legislative field has rapidly come to the fore in the modern world and is becoming ever more crucial towards maintaining world economic and political stability and prosperity. Much has yet to be achieved by the exponents of our judicial systems to rightly and judiciously govern human affairs, especially in the fields of international legislation of all aspects of human livingness and right human relationships. Nations that commit wholesale atrocities against those in their sphere of influence must be held accountable by international law. Even the USA lives under certain constraints of public opinion and of the international legal documents that it has signed. That nation's internal and external activities have increasingly come under public scrutiny by the leaders of other nations in the world. International codes of ethics formulated amongst the nations, however, are normally flawed. This includes those concerning the proliferation of nuclear weapons, the laws regulating the environment, international monetary policies, and the principle of economic sharing. The power of the Hegemon (the USA) unfortunately has undue sway over the outcome of most international legal contracts. Also, the international body that should hold sway in world governance (the U.N.) has become corrupted from within. It thus barely serves the good intentions of its charter. This organisation has become very flawed and is now ruled mainly by the power of Veto of the major players, and of the surreptitious influence of the Hegemon to bribe or to coerce the other nations. The U.N. no longer has the capacity to settle wars, which is one of the things it was originally set up to do. Countries are economically dependent upon others for their stability and survival. Thus war in any country today affects every country in the world, and also most people, via the medium of T.V., the Internet, newspapers and world economics. Though there is much left to be changed, the development of international legislation has nevertheless contributed somewhat towards birthing the conditions associated with the Aquarian age.

Libra largely governs the interim period between the Piscean and the Aquarian age. In this lies the guarantee of future success in bringing forth the New Age. From one point of view, Libra will be a sign that will condition the Avatar, for He brings in a new cycle of expression, and also a time for the rectification of much world *karma*. In this statement lies a hint as to the purpose of some of His work, for He will come to rectify all aspects of distortion of the good Law on earth. Here also lies a basis for comprehending much of His esoteric work to help negate the efforts of the Lords of the Dark Face (the masters of evil). The main purpose of the Lords of evil is to try to project power over the world's legislative and governing bodies, to write and promulgate the laws governing humanity. People little realise how much the forces of evil dominate every sphere of their lives, for they think shallowly, and have not learnt to put cause to effect, neither have they been taught to think in terms of universals before particularising the specifics of any thing. They should look closely at how virtually in every respect the legislative system serves best those who are selfishly or materialistically motivated, and who possess the bulk of the world's monetary resources.

The suppression of the rights for true individual freedom of action is everywhere evident, increasingly so in Western 'Democracies', which are now relying heavily on censorship of truthful information that governments find too revealing of their malfeasance. The mendacious mainstream press are good at presenting lying propaganda to seduce the masses at the behest of the governments concerned. We now, for instance, have tyrannical vaccination laws totally depriving people's freedom of expression. Witness also how the drug laws of every nation deprive people of their basic freedom of independent action to experience aspects of the subjective and phenomenal worlds in relation to themselves. No matter what the excuses for their existence, these laws denigrate the essential capacity of an individual to choose how he/she wishes to live, as long as it harms no other being. As a consequence, the laws have caused an enormous amount of human misery. They have bred extreme violence, both by 'law enforcement' officers, and the organised crime that has capitalised upon human misery to obtain enormous profits. These laws have artificially put a caustically high premium upon what by rights should not have such an associated cost. This is because the plants (from which these substances are derived) are naturally and abundantly found in Nature. The ancients have always known of them and have used them for healing and religious purposes. The related hallucinations are but experiences associated with the lower psyche, which humanity shall one day properly understand and outgrow.

Imagine what would happen to government coffers and the self-interest of many wealthy entrepreneurs, if such an easily obtainable form of intoxication and amusement could be simply grown by all who wish to, and thus is not taxable or controlled by a cartel of companies. Thus alcohol and tobacco (which need much processing and packaging before they are consumed) are advocated instead. People are not yet aware of how the Wheel of the Law (Libra) works on a national or international scale regarding massed *karma* making. Individuals must pay for the karmic consequences of their actions, and similarly so for nations. The cycle for the payment of old debts inevitably comes as the Lords of *karma* project a most exacting toll. This is not to say that all man-made drugs should be condoned, or that people should take hallucinogens. A case can be made for certain harmful effects also, and they are certainly antithetical to the awakening of higher perceptions leading to enlightenment. Many are the negative effects of psychotropics upon the psychic and physiological systems of the individual that need later healing.

Nevertheless, if people were left in a completely free environment in this respect, with every effort of governments concerned to rightly educate those in their care, our jail population, for instance, would be greatly reduced. Many so-called criminals are but the victims of abhorrent legislation. Imagine what would happen if crime was seriously interpreted in terms of those who perpetuate acts that work against the common good, against the well being of humanity as a whole through acts of gross selfishness, separateness, avarice and legalistic violence. (To be viewed not just against human beings, but to all kingdoms of Nature and our biosphere as a whole.) Many of those that are presently our wealthiest, most powerful, and often most respected individuals, will then be labelled 'criminals'.

Astonishingly, our legislators have masked many of the attributes that are fundamentally evil (such as the amassing of fortunes at the expense of the welfare of all others) as something respectable, even as virtuous. Much that they deem 'criminal' is in effect the result of people fighting for individual freedoms, or because of the curse of the poverty that they have been born into. Yet poverty exists because the world's resources have been cornered by the ruthless and wealthy few, for whom such legislation largely serves. Those who thus legislate are nearly always in the category of basically self-serving individuals. Truly, 'It is easier for a camel to go through the eye of a needle, than for a rich man to enter into the kingdom of God'.[23]

The lower part of the back and its extension into the abdomen is literally an extendable muscle that protects the viscera, and yet is able to greatly expand so as to be able to hold the developing foetus. The major part of the work of this part of the back (and therefore also of the judge) is to maintain a protective environment in which the divine child must be nurtured and protected from the ravages of the beast (Leo); the tenacity, desires, and emotionality of the crab (Cancer); and from the deathlike sting (vengeful and separative in quality) of the Scorpion in the deserts of Life. The judge must do this not through the attitude of imposed fear and penalty imposition, but by the gradual improvement of social inequalities and the wise utilisation of esoteric psychology and astrology. (Based on the understanding of the law of *karma* and of reincarnation.)

The family unit, wherein the crucial years of the child's development are nurtured, must be protected. Also, the environmental and economic conditions wherein people live must be greatly improved by distributing national wealth more equably, thus causing the disappearance of urban slums. An educational system must also be introduced based on sound spiritual values. Children must be taught selflessness, the brotherhood of humanity, the love for all of Nature and each other, and about the awakening of their spiritual faculties and meditative insights into the nature of reality. Promoting the amassing of wealth by selfish and avowed materialistic tendencies should be eliminated from any such curriculum. All forms of competitiveness (that breeder of foul disposition, war-like ambition, aggressiveness and separative tendencies) must go. These qualities must be replaced with the spirit of oneness, of sharing resources, of altruistic and cooperative endeavour in all undertakings. This would greatly help in preventing what is now known as 'crime'.

The judiciary and legislators must truly build a shield of protection against all forms of evil (specifically of selfishness and separative empire building) for those in their care. They must work for the dignity of humanity, safeguarding all hard wrought human freedoms, allowing beings to act and enquire as to the nature of Life as they will, so long as it does not intrude upon the rights of others to act similarly.

---

23 *Matt. 19:24.*

The capitalist incentive system that presently governs all human action in Western countries, based on avarice and ruthless competitive striving for material wealth, ever increasing wages, profits and financial prosperity (if one does well) should be replaced by another system altogether. Here the incentive should be the joy obtained through developed meditative insights and from the wellbeing and prosperity of whole communities and nations. Then the individual part played in cooperative endeavour becomes well known, where the incentive becomes a type of honour system (where one gains respect through what is done for others). Incentive thus becomes aspiration to serve 'God' and humanity. In time, money as the major medium of exchange will largely disappear when barter and free exchange of goods and services will become the norm. Good will and community sharing will become more important than greed and possession of material things.

Libra governs the hub of the wheel of Life, of the Law, thus of the various cycles of Being. It conditions the moment when one can mount the fixed cross and so rectify the wheel – to travel from Aries to Pisces via Taurus – and so to no longer retrogress through the zodiac. One is then upon the path to enlightenment and of Initiation, and thus largely breaking free from the conditionings of the great illusion.

The hub of the wheel is vitalised by the energies of the Jewel in the Heart of the Lotus. This demonstrates in the case of Libra as first Ray energy in its third sub-Ray connotation. The hub is a place of dynamic peace, yet embodies the potential of all Logoic mutable activity.

In the twelve-signed zodiac, which governs our present evolutionary epoch, the clockwise direction concerns the present process of the march of the equinoxes through the zodiac. It turns from Pisces to Aquarius, the opposite of the way that the zodiac is drawn. The direction appropriate for the evolutionary development of humanity, however, is from left to right. In this manner, the qualities pertaining to *śūnyatā* (of the nature of enlightened being) are developed. This is the motion signified by the twelve aspects of Dependent Origination,[24] relating to *saṃsāric* involvement and eventual release from it.

When the reversal of the Wheel happens upon the Initiation path, then the path may be viewed as counter-clockwise, with the direction of travel being from left to right. This is the way of the generation of the higher *prāṇas*. The motion of the equinoxes do not change for humanity, rather they are changed internally for the Initiate concerned, who is now aligned with the cosmic Wheels that are not

24 In Buddhism, the twelve links of causal connection. See Vol. 5A of *A Treatise on Mind*, 163-9.

conditioned by the great illusion *(saṃsāra)*. The right to left motion is that of the dark brotherhood, who work to counter the evolutionary trend of the turning of the Wheel. They remain trapped within the great illusion, but are also trying to counter the progression of the Wheel.

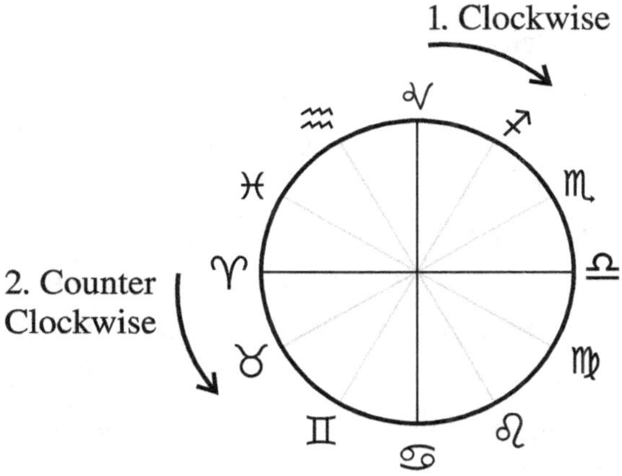


**Figure 12. Directions in the zodiac**

The reversal of the Wheel also means that new astrological conditions come into play, for the esoteric and Hierarchical rulers now dominate. Also, the Initiate inevitably moves from the twelve signs of human (emotional) interplay of *saṃsāric* formations, to the ten signs that concern the rule of Mind, enlightened consciousness.

On the ordinary wheel the person emerges out of the sign Scorpio (after having undergone many trials in the field of desire) to then face the drastic trials of Initiation, allowing what will eventually produce enlightenment. Normally a lifetime of quiet activity and reflection is then spent in Libra. Once the experiences are assimilated and digested (where the Soul extracts what is needed for the next life), the result can be the manifestation of the activities that will birth the divine Child. (The rectification of the wheel.) The alternative is to produce an intensification of the material, selfish attitudes within the Womb of the Mother (Virgo).

Libra rules the narrow razor-edged path that leads to liberation, for here the agile and analytical mental faculty has complete reign, being at the height of its powers. The Libran can therefore wisely balance and rightly judge the difference between the right and wrong, between the elements composing the path to liberation and those that lead to illusion and glamour in the vales of experience. In Libra, therefore, the intuition is first sensed and made to manifest, enabling one to make the choice that will tip the balances towards travelling along the road to liberation.

Libra is another dual sign, and its glyph is a shorthand notation of the upright scales with its pans:

♎

These scales are effectively found in the hands of the 'judge of the living and the dead'. In Egyptian Mythology the scales are in front of Osiris in the judgement hall, where the deceased's heart is weighed against the feather of Ma'at (signifying truth, the natural order or balance in the universe). The judge weighs the good and bad actions, thoughts and deeds, and the overall worthiness of the candidate's entry into the heaven (or hell) of the various religions. Libra is the sign of the Judgement Day when the 'sheep will be divided from the goats.[25] (This phrase can also be in terms of signifying the separation between the adherents of the left hand and right hand paths.) This Judgement confronts the person on the rectified wheel. Until one has attained the third Initiation it is still possible to travel the way of the left, and possibly embrace the activities of the black magician. Libra governs the final separating of these two paths. When the world disciple is at the stage of attaining its second Initiation, and is preparing for the third, then there will be a clearly defined demarcation between these two paths on the world stage. The advent of the Avatar of the New Age will help to bring about the epoch of planetary Initiation, wherein the nature of the dark brotherhood will be clearly elucidated so that the separation process can properly begin upon a planetary scale.

Libra governs the diaphragm, which effectively divides the upper part of the person (the head and the heart) from the lower, or animal nature. The four higher *chakras* associated with the divine person are thus divided from the three lower ones associated with the carnal person. Here quite clearly is seen Libra's ability to 'relate the two in Gemini' (the keywords of this sign). This is especially seen in the fact that the diaphragm is one of the major organs needed in the meditation process. Its movement helps regulate the breath, thus allowing the maintenance of the quietude needed for contemplation upon the needs of Humanity's spiritual education, as well as of the nature of the realm of enlightened Being, of the laws governing Life.

This period of equilibrium in the Soul's life, and also of the personality, signifies a necessary period of quiet that allows the manifestation of illumination. The Soul-infused personality can then act on the plains of the earth, with the rectified wheel turning towards Taurus to Pisces. This natural contemplative affinity allows

---

25 *Matthew 25:32.*

the Libran to rightly judge and fulfil a role as the arbitrator between warring and opposing sides. Also (in relation to the equilibration of the pairs of opposites), one must therefore come to grips with the entire problem of sex, and to achieve a balanced solution thereof, both in one's own life and in the world around. This is especially evident when it is seen that Venus is the exoteric ruler of this sign. As stated, Venus embodies the intelligent mind, at first united with desire (as *kāma-manas),* though later desire is transmuted into Love, producing a world of ordered beauty and harmony. Venus governs the fifth Ray governing scientific reason, enterprise and productivity.

In Taurus, Venus produces knowledge of things, thus bringing illumination. Here the mind is related to desire, therefore the person's sexual expression perpetuates incarnation in the formed realms, where lower creativity dominates. In Gemini, Venus (the esoteric ruler of Gemini) relates the pairs of opposites, often producing conflicting and warring ideas and ideals. In Libra, these opposing qualities (and indeed, all of the forces of the material world) become balanced and resolved. Finally, in Capricorn, which is ruled by Venus Hierarchically, the lower sexual creativity becomes translated into the higher mental form governed by the Throat centre. Desire then becomes Love for all aspects of Being. In the above, the story of Venus and her part in the zodiac is briefly depicted for us.

The above four signs that are linked by Venus (Libra, Gemini, Taurus and Capricorn) are also intimately connected with the appearance of the Avatar. This is because the Logos of the Venus Scheme is the Soul aspect to our earth, and thus stands as the medium of transmission for the cosmic energy of Love to our planet from Sirius. Venus is also the originating home of the Lords of Flame that established Shambhala at the time of the Individualisation of humanity of this earth. The Venusian connection will allow the lesser planetary Avatar to stand as a mediator between the greater cosmic Avatar (who can descend no further than the mental plane) and humanity. Venus facilitates the needed development of humanity to awaken higher mental perceptions, a response to the energies from the *dharmakāya* that will allow the new Aquarian era to properly manifest. The advent of this new era will therefore manifest as a higher correspondence of the approach of Individualisation. (The kingdom of the Soul was then formed, producing the consequential incarnation process.) This new era represents the reverse of the process, the true beginning of the ending of the rebirthing process, and eventually the death of the Soul form at the attainment of the fourth Initiation for those who pass the needed testings.

These signs will allow the Avatar to work via the medium of the three crosses: the cardinal cross (Libra and Capricorn), the fixed cross (Taurus) and the mutable cross (Gemini). Capricorn becomes the Mount of the Lord, the place from whence the new planetary dispensation and Covenant with 'God' can be issued. (The projection of the higher correspondence of the Ten Commandments given to Moses upon Mount Sinai, though for this new era in relation to the sixth Root Race humanity.)

In Libra, the entire question of material evolution and its Laws (of the third or Mother aspect of Deity) is brought to justice and tried in the realm of consciousness. Here, therefore, the evolutionary process associated with the third Ray finds its Judgement Day, and the process is begun that will eventually allow the Soul (the sun or second Ray aspect of Deity) to rule the form. It is fitting, therefore, that Saturn, the Lord of *karma* (ruling the third Ray of Mathematically Exact Activity) is the Hierarchical ruler of Libra, for it brings to light a major function of the tenth (or third) Creative Hierarchy (Makara the mystery, ruled by Capricorn) and of their relation to the fourth Creative Hierarchy (humanity, the 'Lords of Sacrifice'). This concerns the uplifting and transformation of the substance that is the residue of the past solar system. The third Creative Hierarchy are *devas* that build the three planes of perception wherein the human personality resides. Via them therefore manifest the various Laws and *karma* that condition human actions, and the manifestation of Life in the terrestrial world.

Under the auspices of Libra manifests the wise organisation and direction of the massed *karma* of the three worlds to produce the maximum beneficence for the greater whole, in accordance with the Shambhalic Plan. Obviously, the manifestation of all of the laws of Life governing Nature needs the active, enlightened, contemplative guidance of the divine adjudicator. This Judge (Libra) needs to be so steeped in Divinity and abstracted from the realms of form to be able to see the entire view from the great height of the mountaintop (Capricorn). Thus the Will is projected to initiate new beginnings (Aries) into the realms of form. The massed Lives therein (Cancer) can thereby be conditioned. This Judge thus embodies the wheel of the Law *(dharmachakra),* the karmic fount of the *dharma* for all lesser lives. Here is expressed another definition of divinity. Depicted also here is the nature of the expression of the cardinal cross.

The esoteric ruler of Libra is Uranus, who governs the seventh Ray of Ceremonial Magic. This energy relates Spirit to matter, causing the precipitation of divine energies into the material world. This materialising energy can also be thought of in terms of the concretion of *prāṇa,* seen as the manipulation of money in the physical world. The manipulation of material resources can be related to the movement of the diaphragm (ruled by Libra) through the control of the breath in order to produce tangible results in the world of form. Here another function of the Libran personality is brought to light. Such a one is often an apt financier, responsible for the control of the monetary systems of the world, and who can also be the arbitrator of the world's commerce and trade. One can also see here the potential for misuse of the contemplative function of the Libran, when such contemplation is solely used for self-aggrandisement, the cornering of huge monetary reserves for avaricious and often malign power-seeking activities. Much *karma* is thereby created that will later need rectification.

Libra is one of the major signs that must of necessity govern the occultist. The practical occultist must be grounded in wise contemplation, and magical activity must be serenely balanced within a circle of protection, if all related energies and forces are not to produce danger of possession by the evoked entities and forces.

As the planetary rulers of Libra are all along the Rays of Mind, so Librans are generally very effective in all physical undertakings and affairs with humanity, for they can draw upon strong inner resources and power. The Libran will be able to command attention and produce the desired results in all judgements and decisions. People will tend to listen and successfully act upon the good practical advice.

Libra is said to govern the kidneys of the grand Heavenly Man, the functions of which are to secrete urine and maintain the blood pressure. The ability to wisely judge between what is useful, harmful or evil (and therefore to be eliminated in the body) is an important function of the Libran. Here the relation of the eighth Creative Hierarchy (the Lesser Builders) to Libra emerges, in that this Hierarchy deals with the expression into our system of the Waters that are the residue of the past solar system and which manifest as the base *karma* governing all Life on earth. This Hierarchy thereby helps cause the dense phenomenal world, but is aloof from incarnation. The next Creative Hierarchy (the human, ruled by Scorpio) incarnates into this 'residue', which is then the substance embodied by the tenth Creative Hierarchy (ruled by Capricorn), the mental plane *devas* known as the Agnishvattas. They objectivise the subjective causes. The ninth Creative Hierarchy (humanity) incarnates into the *māyavirūpa* (illusional forms) in order to gain their evolutionary experiences.

***Summary:***

- *Keynote*: 'Libra relates the two in Gemini'.
- Libra rules the lower part of the back, diaphragm, and the kidneys of the Grand Heavenly Man.
- The *exoteric ruler* is Venus, Ray five of Concrete Science.
- The *esoteric ruler* is Uranus, Ray seven of Ceremonial Magic, Cyclic Activity and Materialising Power.
- The *Hierarchical ruler* is Saturn, Ray three of Mathematically Exact Activity.
- The *Element* is Air (as also for Aquarius and Gemini).
- The *polar opposite* is Aries.
- *Cross*: Cardinal.
- Saturn is exalted in Libra, the power of Mars is lessened and the Sun falls.
- The *Decanates* (given by D.K.) are exoterically: Venus, Saturn and Mercury. Esoterically: Jupiter, Saturn and Mercury.

The *keywords* given for this sign are:

> To the average man: And the Word said: 'Let choice be made'.
> The response from the Soul is: 'I choose the way which leads between the two great lines of force.'

# 3b

# From Scorpio to Pisces

## Scorpio the scorpion

*Scorpio the scorpion* rules the Pelvis and Reproductive system of the Grand Heavenly Man. This system is concerned with humanity's descent into incarnation. It is consequently a sign of death, which incarnation into the realms of form and limitation signifies to the spiritually disposed. Being a Water sign, and because of the nature of the testings associated with Scorpio, so one can 'die by drowning' in this sign. Here the normal person is immersed fully in the Waters of sensation and mutable experience, staying there for many lives. On the rectified wheel, the personality however dies in this sign, for it is the sign of the triumphant disciple. The other major sign of death in the zodiac is Pisces. There, as will be seen, the Soul eventually dies through the effect of Pluto (the esoteric ruler of Pisces) and a completely new cycle of evolution begins.

The objective of the reproductive system is the birth of a son, symbolically the Soul or second aspect of Deity. The vision of the nature of the divine Child first manifests in Taurus, but the desire for its birthing reaches its greatest intensity in Scorpio (the polar opposite of Taurus). Scorpio keeps the spiritual being bound to the form, for it governs the emotionally drastic, intoxicated and sensuous experiences of the average person. Scorpio constantly projects the desire for sensation, the motivating mechanism that makes the descent into the realms of experience a recurrent happening. After much initial testing, tribulation and then decision-making (in Libra), the divine Child (the appearance of a disciple amongst humanity) is finally conceived in Virgo. It grows and expands in the Womb (of Nature). There it is subject to many tests concerning its worthiness or readiness for birth in the liberated domains as it grows cycle by cycle and adapts to ever-increasing environmental demands. (The 'environment' here relates to the sphere of consciousness.) Finally (in Capricorn) nine months or signs later from Virgo (on the reversed wheel), the birth ensues. By then the last major test associated with parturition has been successfully undertaken in Cancer, the polar opposite of Capricorn. This entire period of growth of the Child in the Womb of Virgo is ruled by the *karma* of the moment of conception.

Taurus generally governs the desire principle, but Scorpionic energy is what projects sexual desire, whereby the seed is symbolically planted in the womb of Virgo. What is born represents the sum of human conditionings. This indicates why humanity must undergo the major tests undertaken in Scorpio. They condition the entire field of evolution of the fourth Creative Hierarchy (humanity, 'The Initiates'). The objective of the tests is to produce the appearance of the second aspect of Deity from the remaindered substance (material *karma* from the past solar Incarnation). Humanity is therefore situated in the central (fourth) position in the tabulation of the Creative Hierarchies.

The fourth Creative Hierarchy relates Spirit and matter. They are 'Lords of Sacrifice', always incarnating into the realms of form and of death in order to elevate the Elemental Lives that embody dense substance. Pain, suffering, tests and tribulation must then be mastered, producing a triumphant resultant enlightenment. These are consequently keywords for humanity.

The Hierarchical Ruler of Scorpio is Mercury, which exemplifies the position of the fourth Creative Hierarchy (humanity) as the divine intermediary between the lesser and higher kingdoms in Nature. In relation to the seven incarnate Hierarchies, humanity forms the function of the Ājñā centre of Deity, but in relation to the twelve they manifest the attributes of the Reproductive system. This function is also held by the Lunar Lords (governed by Sagittarius), the sixth of the seven manifest Creative Hierarchies. This indicates a strong alignment between these two Hierarchies, who are respectively termed 'the Lords of Sacrifice' and 'the Sacrificial Fires'.[1] One (the Lords of Sacrifice) represents the All-seeing Eye and the other (the Sacrificial Fires) what this Eye must direct and control. Both are concerned with the process of birth. The Lunar Lords with the birth of the form (via which the Christ-Child must incarnate), and the human Initiates

1 An alternative name for the Lunar Lords.

with the actual birth of the Child. The Lunar Lords form the substance of our emotional and desire bodies, which for most humans represents the great nemesis of their spiritual lives. They must battle and overcome the allure of these Watery Lives on the upward way to liberation, and it is their potency that sets most of the testings in Scorpio.

On the ordinary wheel, a person emerges out of the sign Sagittarius with generally one pointed attitudes and desires. In Scorpio, the next sign, they are put to the test. The objective of the proverbial sting of the scorpion is here directed to acquire the object of people's desires, and also to overcome all of the various hardships associated with life in *samsāra*. Scorpios often become one pointed towards the satiation of desires. Extremely selfish and bestial attitudes can be developed, that always lead to strife and pain. The person is found in the desert of materiality, with its metaphoric adders, vipers, scorpions, burning heat, thirst and vultures, whilst pockets of nourishing water are few and far between. People are hopelessly lost in this desert, which drives them mad with its image-forming tendencies (mirages). The above symbolism provides an apt description of the nature of the attitudes that compose much of our present Aryan civilisation.

Mars, the god of war, rules Scorpio exoterically and esoterically. This martial quality in its lowest aspects is what torments the person: war, death, strife, desire for possessions, cruelty, greed, deception, and all the endless debacle that keeps one tied upon the wheel of birth and death. Mars effectively energises the entire form nature, its various interactions, clashes, juxtapositions and instinctual reactions. In Aries (ruled exoterically by Mars) the various pursuits that arise from the person's greedy, warlike and material desires are first initiated, finding their satiation in Scorpio. Here one must develop that strength of character and determination that will allow gain from those experiences, to recapitulate what is needed on one's path in life. This will either foster further selfishness (in Virgo), or else it will produce the re-orientation of one's entire life process, resulting (after the balance has been achieved in Libra) in the firing of the arrows of aspiration towards the mountaintop in Capricorn.

Mars governs the physical senses, and therefore the entire attitude of people's sex life, replete with the knowledge of life and the meaning of the related experiences. This is especially so in Scorpio. Experiences of turmoil and conflict associated with sex and the battle of the sexes are brought to the fore and given special emphasis: the question of imposed celibacy as opposed to widespread promiscuity, and the various arguments and pursuits associated with the sex relationship. This is necessary if the sex question is finally to be resolved in the sign Libra.

Mars rules the bloodstream (hence the distribution of *prāṇa).* Literally, much blood has been spilt in human history over the question of sex, as well over blood relationships (family, tribal and religious blood ties). Similar conflicts have arisen regarding the various pursuits of the desires of the Scorpio subject. The activity of Mars (especially when wedded to Venus) forms the desire-mind *(kāma-manas)* and has produced the height of humanity's empirical attainment and present technological innovations.

Esoterically, Mars helps engender the many tests that condition the aspiring disciple in this sign. In relation to this, the three tests of Jesus when he fasted for forty days in the desert can be noted.[2] The *first test* concerned His body nature: 'that stones be made of bread', which he resisted. The *second test* concerned his desire nature: doubt as to whether or not he was the Christ was presented to him. To this test he answered: 'It is written again, thou shalt not tempt the Lord thy God'. The *third test,* or temptation, concerned his mental body. The nature of power and the conscious understanding of his value or purpose to the world were being tested. Thus he was offered all the kingdoms of the world 'and the glory of them'.

Each of these tests is really triune. Together they constitute the *nine-headed Hydra* that Hercules (who personifies the disciple in this sign) had to battle. One of the Hydra's heads was immortal, for it symbolises that aspect of life's manifold experiences that is of value to the Soul, and which is absorbed into its constitution.[3] For the other heads, it was said that if one were destroyed then two more would take its place.

Hercules needed deep humility, much discrimination, patience, effort and labour to overcome the Hydra. He was eventually brought to his knees and in that position of humility, he lifted the Hydra up in the air and thus away from contact with its lair, the darkness and murky filth of the swamp, which he realised was the source of its strength. He realised that he could not battle the monster on its own ground and hope to win. Thus it is with all disciples in this sign, if they continue to intoxicate their senses and cloud their vision with the pursuits and habits that have always kept them tied down in the mud of *saṃsāra*. This battle, therefore, constitutes their particular problems or torments.

---

2 *Matt. Ch. 4.*

3 See *The Labours of Hercules,* 142, by Alice Bailey for a discussion relating to this head, which was said to be 'buried under a rock'. It represents that aspect of all this *karma* that will be recycled, so as to be transformed in a later life, upon a higher cycle of the Initiation path.

Chapters 9:5-11 of *St. John's Revelation* astrologically describe the nature of the nine heads of the Hydra, or tests that disciples (as well as humanity in general) must undergo in Scorpio. The 'five month' period of torment mentioned in chapter 9:5 (and later in another form in chapter 9:10)[4] firstly refers to the five zodiacal months. There humanity first takes form and birth in the sign Cancer. They tread the wheel (Libra) until the development of the mental principle has been obtained in Leo, to produce birthing of new ideas in Virgo. Self-analysis in Libra eventually results in battles with the desire-mind by the time that humanity had reached the sign Scorpio. Other aspects of the symbolism of the number five is that it refers to the five sense perceptions and the attributes of mind developed by humanity. The 'five month' torment therefore relates to the Aryan period of human development wherein the mental-emotions reign supreme, which must be battled upon the path to enlightenment in order to transform mind into Mind.

Upon the reversed wheel are created the thought-form and glamour-engendering principles by the mass of humanity, which reach their greatest intensity in Scorpio. They are developed via the five great epochs in the history of humanity, from the first to the fifth Root Race. There are five signs from Cancer (including Cancer), the sign of birthing, to Scorpio the sign of testing for Initiation, wherein humanity struggles with the effects of these testings. These five signs can therefore specifically represent the signs of 'torment'. First, there is a Watery birthing into the material world in Cancer to suffer the trials and tribulations of being in a physical body. In Leo, humanity undergo the processes associated with the development of the empirical mind, with its pain engendering forms of mental-emotions that everyone knows so much about. Virgo signifies experiencing the depths of materialism, which the individual struggles to overcome, until eventually the first glimmerings of higher reasoning enters consciousness. (Symbolised by the birthing of the Christ-Child.) Libra signifies the incessant turning of the wheel of *karma,* of the laws of Life that afflict the reincarnating individual. Eventually a meditating one arises who can rationalise all of life's activities, such as the sex experiences that produce the rebirthing process. In Scorpio, either the intensity

4 This concerns those who had 'not the seal of God on their foreheads' (that is, average humanity): 'And to them it was given that they shall not kill them but that they shall be tormented five months: and their torment was as the torment of a scorpion, when he striketh a man. And in those days shall men seek death, and shall not find it; and shall desire to die and death shall flee from them. And the shapes of the locusts were like unto horses prepared unto battle...and they had tails like unto scorpions, and there were stings in their tails: and their power was to hurt men five months'.

of the passions associated with one's desires, selfishness and materialism rule, or else the testings finally manifest that allow the higher gains of the ratiocination in Libra to be accomplished. They produce hope for eventual escape from the trammels of the form. The testings inevitably produce a toll of suffering, as former negative *karma* is cleansed upon the Initiation path.

As stated, Scorpio governs the evolution of humanity. This is especially so in this period at the end of the fifth Root Race, for the world disciple has emerged and many can now be found battling in a manner similar to Hercules. They are found in every nation, cultural grouping, and field of life. The vicissitudes of the desire-mind of the world disciple must be mastered as people try to overcome some of the fundamental causes for the present turmoil, unrest and distress found throughout the world.

Another rendering of the phrase 'five months' refers to the five months or signs that the disciple travels after emerging triumphant from the tests in Scorpio. They then set their new targets high in Sagittarius, to climb the lofty mount of achievement in Capricorn and so take Initiation. They then become a world-server in Aquarius, finally dying to all remaining attachments to aspects of *saṃsāra* in Pisces. (For some the complete death of the Soul-form happens here.) Eventually a new beginning on a higher cycle or arc of the spiral of liberating activity manifests in the sign Aries. This is the sign of mental beginnings, of the initial impulses of the abstract Mind. (The number five relates to the powers of the mind/Mind in its totality.)

Similar to Virgo, Scorpio is a triune sign:

♏

The three legs of the glyph represent the interrelationship between the three aspects of Deity: Spirit, Soul, and personality. One can also look to the three planes of human livingness (the realms of *saṃsāra*—the mental, astral and physical domains). First, there are the interrelationships between the three attributes of the personality, producing the inevitable sufferings and 'stings' upon the path of life. As a consequential response, the individual desires to be freed from suffering and eventually finds the methodology of escape depicted in Buddhism as the Eightfold Path. This effectively produces the testings that allow the person to eventually integrate with the Soul (the Sambhogakāya Flower) at the third Initiation.

Firstly, the relationship between body and Soul produces the inevitable death of the personality traits. Later, an intensified interrelation between Soul and Spirit will produce the death of the Soul form. (In both cases, the symbolism of the Scorpion's ability to sting to death is implicated.) The symbol that indicated the cycle of time in Virgo has been changed into the glyph representing the scorpion's sting. (Or else the aspirational zeal of Mars.) This indicates that time no longer continues at a slow and leisurely pace, for the rapid rate of change in the disciple's consciousness quickens the perception of time. The *kuṇḍalinī* serpent is also no longer coiled in potential (as in Virgo), but is ready to spring into space to kill the limiting cycles that have for so long caused death-like activities.

The picture of the *serpent* in the desert of materiality and its ability to poison and cause death, as well as of the *eagle* (or even the vulture) in the skies looking for prey, are also ancient symbols of Scorpio.

Esoterically, a serpent eventually evolves into a Fiery Dragon of Wisdom. This transformation symbolises the gradual rising of *kuṇḍalinī* along the course of consciously applied evolution, from the appearance of an aspirant to the awakening of a Master of Wisdom. This transformation necessitates the progression of compassionate undertakings, until eventually the serpent has released its grip on the cycle of time and can fly free (as the Dragon) into multidimensional Space, breathing out the Fires of applied Wisdom to all encompassed within its sphere of influence. (Technically, the Ashram of a Master, esoterically considered, or the body of manifestation of a Logos.)

If Leo is the sign wherein the qualities of the Heart evolve and make their appearance within the personality, then Scorpio is the sign wherein the Heart grows wings and flies free from the limitations of the imprisoning form. This is the product of the twelve labours of the Herculean disciple. In this sign, the powers of the twelve petals of the Heart within the Head are unfolded as the tests associated with each of the petals are successfully mastered.

The symbolism of the winged Heart (compassionate awareness moving in space) morphs into that of an eagle soaring free from the earthy domain, that can vision the vast panorama below and the forms of activity of all the animals (beastly passions) found therein. The focussed gaze from the eagle's Eye (Ājñā centre) is used to do so. This is synonymous with the powers of the awakened Heart that can vision the vast duration of space-time in a moment of timelessness. Thereby, it spots with pinpoint accuracy what is desired by the vision (the symbolic animal prey) to further the plan of evolution. The eagle thus symbolises the accomplishment of the Initiate, specifically one of the fourth degree who can soar free in the spiritual sky (the Airy Element) that is *buddhi (śūnyatā)*.

The esoteric import of the testings in Scorpio are also veiled here, for they relate to the awakening of the powers of the petals of the various *chakras*. These petals can be symbolised in the form of 'wings'—hence the eagle also implicates the level of the awakening of internal perceptions governed by the nature of the 'wings' that have been unfolded.

***Summary:***

- *Keynote:* Scorpio stages the release of Leo.
- Scorpio rules the Pelvis and Reproductive system of the Grand Heavenly Man.
- The *exoteric* and *esoteric ruler* is Mars, Ray six of Devotion, Aspiration.
- The *Hierarchical Ruler* is Mercury, Ray four of Beautifying Harmony overcoming Conflict.
- The *Element* is Water (as also for Cancer and Pisces).
- The *polar opposite* is Taurus.
- *Cross:* fixed.
- Uranus is exalted in Scorpio, the power of Venus is lessened and the Moon falls.
- The *Decanates* for this sign are not given, for D.K. states that a new planet is rising in this sign which humanity must discover and 'rightly place it within the circumference of the Great Wheel'.

The *keywords* that D.K. gives for this sign are:

> Upon the ordinary wheel, whereon is found an individual 'blind and apparently helpless', then: *'And the Word said, Let Maya flourish and let deception rule'.*
>
> On the reversed wheel, 'the Soul chants or sings the words: - *"Warrior I am and from the battle I emerge triumphant'.*

## The tests in Scorpio

D.K. groups the tests in Scorpio under three categories, governed by three signs:

1. **Pisces**, the tests concerning the mental processes.

   a. Leo. *Pride*—which is intellectual satisfaction with personality methods, thus making the mind the barrier to soul control.
   b. Virgo. *Separativeness*—which is the isolated attitude and which makes the mind the barrier to right group relations.
   c. Capricorn. *Cruelty*—which is satisfaction with self-gratifying personality methods and which makes the mind the instrument of the sense of power.

2. **Taurus**, the tests concerning the desire element.

    a. Cancer. *Fear* —which conditions activity today.
    b. Aries. *Hate*—which is a factor in conditioning relationships.
    c. Sagittarius. *Ambition*—conditioning objectives.

3. **Scorpio**, the tests concerning the dense form.

    a. Scorpio. *Sex*—The relation of the pairs of opposites. These can be selfishly utilised or divinely blended.
    b. Taurus. *Physical comfort*—Life conditions, selfishly appropriated.
    c. Aquarius. *Money*—selfishly cornered (if I may use such a phrase).[5]

All of these tests can be integrated into one broad category, which forms the body of the Hydra, and that is *ignorance*. Ignorance can be equated with the substance of the darkness, wielded by the forces of evil. Ignorance is the great deceiver and exemplifies their mode of activity, which is to work to keep all beings bound to the darkness of non-comprehension of the true nature of things and of the way of reality. This is mainly done by fostering half-truths, omitting pertinent information in a propaganda stream, distortions of truth, and straight lies. All forms of lying propaganda, anything that serves to confuse and cloud people's minds as to the true nature of Love and Light, are projected by the dark brotherhood.

The significance of the nine heads of the Hydra shall be explained from two perspectives. First in terms of the way that the dark brotherhood develop and embody the attributes of the heads. This comes as a consequence of members of humanity manifesting wilful volitions over a significant number of lives that counter evolutionary law so as to empower the attributes of these heads. Next the focus shall be on the heads of the Hydra as fields of testings for disciples to master as they walk the path to Initiation.

### *a. The dark path.*

The main body of the Hydra, plus its nine heads, forms the *Dweller on the Threshold* (the sum of the personality *saṃskāras* that prevent the attainment of enlightenment) that battles in its entirety with Hercules, the disciple. The disciple must lift this entity up to the Angel of the Presence (the Soul), the bearer of Light

---

5 *Esoteric Astrology,* 206. I have rearranged his statements here and have added the associated governing signs.

that will consume the ungainly *saṃskāras* upon the testing ground. Within that Light the disciple will see what is needed, and consequently act rightly.

Those that are converted to the path of darkness gradually walk up the Hydra's back through fostered ignorance, delusion, blindness and the expression of the base qualities of its heads, until they finally stand as one of the heads with the ability to project its venom. They are then members of the left hand path, and will brook no opposition, having become adepts of evil, of vile temperament, cunning avarice and base disposition. The continuous, repetitious perpetuation of the great illusion is the leitmotif for their existence. The focus of the wrath of their dark ire is then consequently vented upon the activities of the forces of Light, the white brotherhood. The potency of their one-focussed and separative psychic powers are utilised for this aim, according to the attributes of the particular head they will embody.

The dark brotherhood work in *duality*, manifesting the qualities of the *iḍā* and *piṇgalā nāḍīs*. (The white brotherhood fuses these qualities into a unity, in terms of *suṣumṇā prāṇas*.) Each of the nine heads of the Hydra are consequently dual. We have, for instance, the self-centred pride (associated with the mental plane) that is purely material (utilising the Fires of matter), specifically manifesting a sense of personal power, hence of the *iḍā nāḍī* stream. Then there is the type of pride that draws upon group (coven) energy; using that energy is a function of a dominating group centre or Sorcerer for separative purposes. (This concerns the evocation of *piṇgalā prāṇas*.)

This idea can be extended to the entire nine heads of the Hydra, making three groups of six (thus 18 altogether, or the number 666), the number of 'the beast' explained in chapter 13 of the *Revelation of St. John*. The number 18 signifies that the second Initiation is possible for the black brother, for it simply means that all aspects associated with astral plane phenomena (the mire of the swamp in which the Hydra resides) can be conquered by the dark one. He works within its illusions for his own separative ends.

Below is a list of the qualities of the Hydra, as associated with what is developed by the dark brotherhood. Bear in mind that each member of this brotherhood can be seen to be specialists in the projection of the *prāṇas* of one or other of the heads, the qualities of which they embody. The mysteries associated with these heads represent the way of aspiration for them. It should also be noted that each of these dualities are related to the powers of a *minor* psychic centre *(chakra)*. They are in turn synthesised by the qualities of the major centre through which the dark ones work.

Of these minor centres, the left Hand centre relates to the qualities of the *iḍā nāḍī* stream and the right Hand centre relates to the qualities of the *piṅgalā nāḍī* stream in relation to their activity. The Splenic centre is also important here; it empowers the two Hand centres and is dual in nature, consisting of two superimposed *chakras* that veil the mode of manifestation of the *eighth sphere,* which is but the Gorgon Medusa's head. This sphere can be considered the store of dark *prāṇas* in the body, the point of expulsion of all the reject (dark) *prāṇas* of the four Elements out of the system altogether. For this reason Medusa's head could 'turn to stone' (produce gross materialistic incentives) all who looked upon it. She had hair composed of hissing serpents, each spitting out the vile poisons of the qualities of the Hydra.

1. *Physical plane appetites,* ruled by Scorpio in general, and synthesised by the functions of the integrated Sacral/Base of Spine centres.

a. *Physical Comfort.* This head of the Hydra is embodied by the members of the dark brotherhood that specialise in the manipulation of commodities and resources of the three planes and the kingdoms associated with the cosmic physical plane, for their benefit. They ensure that the world's commodities (and other material resources) remain in the powerful hands of the relatively few, who they dominate by means of thought suggestion, as well as by other coercive means. They are organised in their dual capacity by the functions of the left and right Foot centres. The symbol is the Sea Monster.[6]

b. *Money.* This head of the Hydra is embodied by the members of the dark brotherhood specialising in the cornering and redistribution of all grey, selfish *prāṇas* of the cosmic ethers. These energies are then projected into the well-placed avaricious ones that possess financial empires and great materialistic power. Their energies can then manipulate the masses of greedy people that similarly desire financial empires for the power that such accumulated, crystallised energy brings. They embody the general energy body of the Hydra, vitalised by the left and right Knee centres. The symbols are the Hydra and the River.

c. *Sex.* This grouping of the dark brotherhood are concerned with dominating the principle of desire, thus with the relation of all pairs of opposites in the formed realms. They work through the integration of coven activity, sexual

---

6 The symbols I present have cosmological inferences, which shall not be explained here, but may be delved into in a later book.

licentiousness and pornography. The energies are derived from the more beastly passions of humanity and related sexual urges. Their object is to keep people so absorbed in transient sensual allurements and related issues that they have no desire for lofty concepts of divinity or of compassionate activity. They work with suppression, as well as overt expression of sexuality. Through their activities, for example, the sex-concept in most religious streams became forms of enforced suppression of natural sexuality, of rigid codes and narrow-minded ethics, or of the complete dominance of one sex over another, as in the Muslim world. The consequence of the human misery derived from such bigoted attitudes, and also of licentiousness, is everywhere evident.

The manifestation of sexual rites to try to force *kuṇḍalinī* and the *siddhis* (psychic power) concerning control of astral substance is a well known adjunct of sex magic. Thought-suggestion and the power to project images to control others (even via the mass media) is part of their modus operandi. The present forceful projection of the 'woke agenda' and Western governments facilitating the desire to mutilate children's sexual organs, are good examples of the power of this Hydra.

These members of the forces of evil obtain their manipulative power from the left and right Hand centres, thus they wield the sense of touch. Sex is more than just a gonadial activity. The symbol is the ruddy coloured Winged Horse.

2. *Astral plane (emotional) appetites,* ruled by Taurus in general, and synthesised by the functions of the Solar Plexus centre.

a. *Fear.* This dark brotherhood grouping is concerned with the manipulation of Solar Plexus energy in the production of fearsome thought-forms of all types. They stimulate the factor of fear in humanity, mainly through the projection of lying propaganda via the world's political, religious, social and philosophic spheres. Here the factor of the creative imagination of people is especially worked upon, where they are induced to imagine possibilities and scenarios that are basically not true or are distortions of the truth.

There are a myriad of fears that can be worked upon, though all relate to the life of the personality. Basically, these fears concern loss of aspects of the personality, of death or material possessions that the person wishes to possess and hang on to no matter what. These may be in the fields of sex relations, valuable possessions, material comforts, political or theological indoctrinations. The spectre of fear in the world is like a huge malign cancerous growth that with increasing rapidity is consuming the vital Life of the host organism (humanity). For fear of insecurity, etc., people (cells within the organism) selfishly hang on to amassed material wealth that is not shared and is thus detrimental to general growth. The cancer grows in networks with major hubs of such selfish concern. National, religious and racial fears all help to cause the many forms of warfare, terror, strife and arenas of sickness upon our planet, thus preventing goodwill and right human relations from manifesting to any beneficent degree.

Mantric sounds (or lying propaganda) causing the emanation of fear are an almost continuous product of the dark brotherhood, being particularly active via the mass media outlets. The streams of lying propaganda negatively stimulate people's astral bodies to be fearful in almost any arena of human livingness. They are taught to fear other groups (in societies, religious organisations, nations, etc.) so as to go to war with them, or to acquiesce to rapine of other's resources. People little realise how much they are influenced by the massed forms of fearsome thoughts that universally exist on the lower strata of the astral plane. This is truly the outer darkness that covers out planet. Recently many people have awakened to the nature of mass conditioned fear through the indoctrination concerning the Plandemic (Covid-19), whose real harmful effects were totally overblown by our governments. They worked for the benefit of big Pharmaceutical companies that made humongous profits by selling dangerous vaccinations.

The centres activated here are the Stomach (left hand) and Liver (right hand) *chakras*. Their symbols are the Centaur and the Seated Lady.

b. *Ambition.* This concerns the prostitution of creative energies for personal gain. It implies a ruthless grasp and conquest of things desired for the personal self (or a separative group), no matter the consequences upon those around. It arises from the competitive spirit. The effects are self evident of those that build personal material empires by rapaciously denuding the earth of its resources (mineral, plant and animal) and who cunningly manipulate massed human psychology for selfish purposes.

This ambitious quality of one-focussed, determined, pyramid climbing is one of the main driving forces of the dark brotherhood; this is not just in terms of building of material empires, but psychic ones as well. The lust for power (the misuse of first Ray energies) is the foundation for the types of magical endeavour they embark upon. For this reason, the left and right Gonad centres rule this activity, for these centres are concerned with creativity as it relates to the formed realms. (The use of sexual energies directed upwards to achieve mental-emotional purposes.) Psychically, this facilitates the wilful manipulation of the five *prāṇas* associated with the *nāḍī* system. The symbols of these centres are the Chained Woman and the Charioteer.

Without such a driving ambition, the dark brotherhood could not hope to counter the forces of Love guiding the entire evolutionary process. To climb their ladder of ascent they must completely dominate and hold on a leash the ambitious grasping of those below them. The greater the ability to manipulate and direct the rapacious pursuits of their underlings so as to serve their own plans, the greater the position in the hierarchy of darkness the dark brother assumes. Eventually they become a sorcerer, an adept of the way of darkness (symbolised by the number 666).

c. *Hatred.* The third of the heads of the Hydra associated with the desire-mind concerns the total debasement of the energies from the Heart of Life. All energies, planetary and zodiacal, are used to attack and counter the activities of the workers of Light and Love. These sorcerers can utilise the five petals of their Heart centres associated with intelligence (the five sense-consciousnesses). They generally work via group endeavour. These *prāṇas* are directed through the most material aspect of *kuṇḍalinī,* to concretise or encapsulate in dense substance whatever is of the good and beneficent within humanity. That which has the potential for good becomes distorted – mutated into a seed of destructiveness, disease and disruption in the world. They thereby produce *chaos* in all organised forms of group endeavour that may serve humanity. They ferociously oppose open-mindedness, equanimity, cooperative attitudes and positive lifestyles within humanity.

Wherever there is loving activity they will endeavour to sow seeds of hatred, to produce a consequent disruption in the expression of the good. The first step in this direction is to produce irritability, then the spirit of criticism among co-workers. This is fed all the way with dark *prāṇas* until disruption of group endeavour occurs. There are many other modes of activity of the dark ones in this field.

The minor centres associated with the activities of the dark brotherhood are the left and right Lung centres. They allow the control of the inward and outward breathing of the above-mentioned energies. The symbols are the Seated Lady's Consort and the Dolphin.

3. *Mental plane aspects.* These are generally ruled by the sign Pisces and synthesised by the Throat centre. Pluto (the esoteric and Hierarchical ruler of Pisces) is the sign of death, which is exemplified here by means of dark brotherhood activity.

a. *Cruelty.* Some people get pleasure from observing those they perceive to be weaker than them going through pain and suffering. They may attempt to destroy the work of others out of sheer malice or spite. These cruel ones revel in the power they have over others and foster situations hindering those who are struggling to achieve. Those embodying the qualities of this head of the Hydra specialise in the evocation of malicious mantric sounds, the Words of Power designated to inflict pain, or to destroy all organised forms working to benefit the whole. Mantric sounds may psychically manifest in the form of sharp razor-edged projectiles or of sound that produces or exacerbates wounds and arenas of sickness already evident in those victims who are being attacked. These sounds aggravate weaknesses (areas of grey, disharmony or discord) existing in an organised structure that works for the common good. The dark ones focus their forces to intensify the disparagement, thus causing chaos or destruction of the purpose of the group or organisation. Clairvoyantly, one can then see the arenas of grey from any of the heads of the Hydra appearing within the auras of groups that are under attack. Whenever individuals within these groups fall prey to their lower base natures (begin to be self-seeking, separative, critical, deluded, lazy or selfish) then the dark ones that constantly monitor these groups pounce like vultures or flies over carrion. These sickness-producing tendencies within the individuals are exacerbated with further grey or black *prāṇas* and mantric sound, hence the term 'cruelty'.

The associated psychic centres are the Mouth and the Splenic centres, specifically via utilising the effects of the Gorgon Medusa's head. The *mouth* is the vehicle of power and therefore of direction, for this power must be directed to all points of the compass (the moving arms of the swastika). What is uttered from the mouth (lying gossip, slander, vituperation and deceit) is what causes most pain to others. The symbols are the Compass and Medusa's head. (Note that a sailor depends upon his compass to get him over rough and stormy seas.)

b. *Pride.* This is a major emanatory quality of all members of the dark brotherhood, in their various organised groupings and chain of ascent up their ranks. It concerns hearing incoming mantras (from all subservient directions of the black camps) by those that specialise in this quality, and the consequent redirection of these mantras in a prideful, forceful manner upon various target arenas.

Hearing is the sense associated with the (cosmic) dense physical plane. The objective here is to try to dominate the sum of evolution within manifest space through constantly bathing these beings in discordant, syncopated, abrasive and sonorous sounds. These mantras become the emanatory pride of the dark ones, producing the conditions for disease and sicknesses to manifest everywhere. To be noted here is the base quality of the *deva* lives that are forced to do the bidding of the dark ones. By means of various sounds, the most direct form of manipulation of dense substance is made possible.

The centres concerned are the left and right Ear centres, and the symbols are the rapacious Wolf, and the Lyre.

c. *Separateness.* Those that specialise in this quality work to foster all attitudes of differentiation associated with the unfolding lower critical mind of humanity. They work to aggravate everything that is mutually contradictory or can be made to clash in all religions, philosophies, political situations and social systems. They then project energies and thought-forms designed to divide, segregate and to produce conflict within all people, groups and nations on earth.

They endeavour to produce constant turmoil, warfare, strife and the clash of ideologies, making impossible the peaceful conditions and social contentment that allow the flowering of meditative attitudes, charitable activities and pursuit of enlightenment. People become devitalised, fearful and aggressively competitive so that arenas of good will and mutual sharing become virtually impossible. The conditions of *saṃsāra* (the Hydra's swamp) within which the dark brotherhood reside and are nourished by, are indefinitely perpetuated.

The associated *chakras* are the left and right Eye centres, whose symbols are the Serpent of illusion and the Phoenix (here bearing dark colourations).

The main body of the Hydra is *ignorance (avidya),* governed by a group of beings that embody the functions of the Alta major and Base of Spine centres within the dark camp. (The symbols are the Bear and the Dragon.) They project the Fiery *kuṇḍalinī* to the sum of the dark Hierarchy and thereby wield the Rods of Power that control all the others. These Rods manifest the powers that harness the energies from the rulers of the various heads of the Hydra and keep their ambitions on leash (by means of black *antaḥkaraṇas),* as they will do whatever they can to take higher positions in the dark domain.

Every aspect of the dark camp is ruled by coercion, manipulation and ruthless domination. The various heads thus work to control the incarnate masses and all kingdoms of Nature by aggravating the basic instincts and primary forces and urges within them. This activity is ruled by the sign Cancer, and concerns control of the feminine characteristics of the dark brotherhood.

The right and left hand *nāḍī* streams terminate in the right and left lobes of the Ājñā centre (the third Eye) and are then distributed to the Head centre. The energies can also be directed to any direction the Eye wishes to see. This Eye is the most separative of all the other centres in the body, in that all of the forces of the personality are concentrated there. Wherever the Eye is focussed there is energy directed, be it towards the left or the right hand attributes of the *chakras* of the body. The power is projected via the Eye – from the one to all others in the chain of command, to control them all. Taurus, the Bull of (cosmic) desire, rules this Eye of one-pointedness and directed vision.

Within the various aspects of the Head centre much that can be considered cosmic evil finds its place. It is not yet time for a detailed exposition of this subject. The above suffices to indicate to the reader how widespread and powerful the forces are that adamantly work to oppose the Law of the Good (embodied by the white Brotherhood). Capricorn rules the activity from the Mind of THAT Logos (Mahat). The symbol is the Altar, upon which the ritual implements and sacrificial victims of the dark camp are placed. This concerns the control of the generally masculine forces of the dark brotherhood. Cosmic aspects concerning the mystery of *Makara* the Crocodile are found here.

### *b. The field of testing.*

The nine tests undergone by disciples to overcome the base attributes described above (and which counter the machinations of the dark brotherhood) are depicted in *St. John's Revelation* as follows:

1. Sagittarius *(Chapter 9:7): 'And the shapes of the locusts were like unto horses prepared unto battle'*. The symbol of Sagittarius is the Rider on the white horse armed with bow and arrow, hence is prepared for battle. This fight concerns the tests of *ambition* – to dominate, for material power, or for the many forms of wealth. The Sagittarian may battle with the forces of Life, but inevitably the battling must be transmuted into the aspiration that must motivate an aspirant. This then evokes the tests in Scorpio.

In Sagittarius the aspirant reorients towards the mountaintop, with the aspiration of becoming a world-server, and so to learn to fight for the Lord. This reorientation process causes constant trials and struggles, reaffirmations of faith to overcome personality hindrances. Through Sagittarian persistence this will produce eventual triumph.

Ambition is deep-seated personality will, whilst aspiration is the endeavour by the aspirant to subordinate personal will into divine Will. The various tests concern the process of the conversion of ambition into aspiration and then to steadfast service.

Ambition produces the competitive spirit that is so prevalent in our societies. It is espoused as a virtue in our schools (such as to produce competitiveness in sports and to achieve high grades) so as to later make one successful in life. This often translates as competitiveness in the business world for material gain, for the individual, the company, nation, or multinational organisation. Such competitiveness fosters greed, the building of material empires at the expense of all else. Everyone thereby suffers one way or other, especially the poor that have lost out in the high stakes competitive activities of the world.

The world's natural resources are thereby cornered and its wealth amassed by the most ruthlessly ambitious, who direct it towards separative and selfish aims. These self-focussed predatory 'beasts' of avaricious desire consequently rob the planet of its life-sustaining ecosphere. This activity produces pollution, industrial and consumer wastes, environmental catastrophes, and the suffering of the masses whose resources are thereby stolen. Most people are deprived of their rightful share of the wealth of the nations when the ambitious, greedy ones collude with those in government, enriching the few at the expense of the many.

Instead of competitiveness, a saner approach to life would be cooperativeness and communal sharing, collectively utilising labour (in whatever field this may be) for the common good. Such then is the focus of the world's disciples that are mastering the testings in this sign. Only true widespread, cooperative service to all will prevent the destructive blight that ambitious competitiveness has ravaged upon our planet.

2. Capricorn *(Chapter 9:7): 'And on their heads were as it were crowns like gold'.* The phrase 'crowns like gold' esoterically indicates those who are rulers of the domain of the mind (ruled by Capricorn), who have awakened the powers of the Head centre. The crown makes a king, one who rules all aspects of the material

domain, and also the realm of enlightened Being, once the 'king' has evolved into an adept. The crown is situated on the head, the symbolic mountaintop, which the goat-man must climb. The awakening of this centre relates to the taking of the third Initiation, which is ruled by Capricorn. This Initiation necessitates the complete mastery of the material domain and all aspects of the empirical mind. Such a mind can be very hard and unyielding in its attitudes, unable to bend to accept broader views, and as such can manifest many cruel attitudes. All of the intellectual attributes that are focussed upon the material world, and its qualities alone, are symbolised by the hard, rocky mountainside that is the terrain of the goat. This the aspirant must master completely as he/she moves symbolically from crag to crag seeking sustenance. On top of the mountain, in the clear air and light of the sun, the goat is symbolically illumined and transfigured, and so can fly into the spiritual sky in the form of a symbolic Unicorn that possesses a single horn of divine Reason. (The cornucopia, the 'horn of plenty' replete with vast stores of knowledge.)

The tests here are concerned with *cruelty* (which finds its hardest, deepest expression in the Capricornian). This trait must be converted into its opposite virtue, *harmlessness.* Cruelty is one of the first major offshoots of ambition, for the ambitious person must often of necessity be cruel to obtain the objectives of his/her ambition. This is especially so if such a one wishes to be a 'king' or ruler of any portion of the material domain, to have power in any sphere of human activity, or in the psychic realms. Such people constantly take from and dominate all aspects of the world around them. The king must often utilise his power ruthlessly and with effectiveness, if he is to remain king in a world full of intrigue and deception. Forms of 'cruelty' can be some of the first attributes that emerge in the life of a highly devotional and idealistic aspirant. Militant and fanatical attitudes are often seen in the religious, who assert their beliefs of the rightness of their views of the nature of the 'Word of God' upon others. (Witness the Inquisitional period in Europe for instance, or fanatical Muslims conquering in the name of Allah.)

Those wanting to climb the mount to enlightenment must therefore develop the humbleness to listen to and accept the views of others, and so to temper speech so that what is spoken only serves the greater whole. When analysing all of the methods of cruelty, especially those imposed by the extension of the mind through the use of the mouth, then we see that there is good reason that Capricorn is depicted as the sign of the black magician. People produce far more pain and harm through use of the mouth (by vituperation, slander, cynical, deceitful and lying utterances) than by purely physical means. Add to this the effects of base mantric sounds of the black magician and his forms of lying propaganda. Such 'lying propaganda' is also fostered as the disinformation continuously manifesting via the main stream media parroting an agenda fostering the purpose of corporate bosses and politicians, rather than for the true needs of the audience.

The transference from cruelty to true harmlessness is therefore a difficult accomplishment for most of the world's aspirants. They often possess firm and entrenched attitudes as to their interpretations of religious scriptures or general crystallised attitudes of mind (concerning the rightness of their personal philosophies). When they can be truly harmless, then the 'golden crown' of Initiation is theirs.

*Harmlessness* is well worth meditating upon. It does not simply mean the non-harming or non-killing of animal life, but also that harmlessness in thought, word and deed, or in implied gesticulation that always produces a closer cooperation between all people. Esoterically, it necessitates developing the ability to read the minds and touch the hearts of those one seeks to serve, so as to know how best they can be helped. Constant meditation upon the cause and result of every action is the only way that true harmlessness can be engendered.

When one is fully imbued with this virtue then the transfiguration experience upon the mountaintop (the third Initiation) can be undertaken. The tests, trials and struggles of the disciple in this sign are therefore concerned with overcoming tendencies towards cruelty (which arise from ambition and insensitivity to the nature of others' suffering) to develop the harmlessness that must replace it.

3. Aquarius *(Chapter 9:7):* the phrase *'And their faces were as faces of men',* symbolises this sign, which is the 'sign of a man'. The tests here concern *the right handling of money.* They bring into focus the extreme selfishness that people evidence in their desire to hoard, or to squander money to satiate their sensual appetites. All aspects of selfishness must be overcome in this testing ground. The evils associated with those who control and misuse the handling of large sums of money are obvious to everyone. Selfishness is a universal human trait, and great is the desire of most people to gather material wealth.

A subtler aspect relates to the aspirant working to obtain religious gleanings via a focussed self-centredness, thinking more or less only of what he/she can gain personally to attain salvation or *nirvāṇa*. There is little real regard for the needs of others, of how they can be best served.

Acquisition of all types of possessions (physical, emotional and mental) is one of the most obvious hindrances in the life of the aspirant, needing to be eliminated upon the path to Initiation. The right handling of money is, however, what most find difficult to do. They often avoid the responsibility altogether. How to rightly utilise resources thus constitutes the major test in this sign. Aspirants learn to rightly appropriate and utilise this form of energy so that it benefits the whole, the society or nation in which they are a part (and not just the individual, or their religious sect).

Unselfishness is consequently the virtue developed, allowing the Water Bearer to dispense the spiritual nourishment (the Waters of Life) freely. (Rather than symbolically hoarding all goods in his/her pot.) Humanity will inevitably accomplish such communal sharing and generosity during the Aquarian age. The ramifications of this testing for inherently selfish humanity is everywhere manifest, producing much general conflict in our society.

Money is materialised energy, thus the tests concerning the handling of money and the rectification of human greed serve disciples well for when they need to handle the far more potent subjective energies associated with Initiation into the higher domains.

The problem regarding the world disciple and the direction of world finances has been explained in the consideration of the sign Libra. The right handling of money invokes Libra's judicial qualities, thus determining the moment of the rectification of the reversed wheel and the emergence of the disciple in the scenario of liberated Life. The timing of the reversal of the wheel is however undertaken in Leo (the polar opposite of Aquarius) with Libra rising. This is because in Leo the qualities of the Soul (the sun) begin to dominate the personality, which in turn governs the process of the reversal of the wheel. In Libra, the process is stabilised and brought forward to higher cycles of expression. The Soul-infused disciple then travels around the zodiac from Aries to Pisces via Taurus, and not in the mode of the great illusion.

The tests in Aquarius, Capricorn and Sagittarius (the signs prior to Scorpio) concern primarily the life of the aspirant, whilst those from Virgo to Aries primarily concern the problem of the probationary disciple. The disciple becomes so when his/her motives are unselfish, becoming harmless in all actions and undertakings. The fourth sign (Cancer) is concerned with the development of the fearlessness needing to be developed if the disciple is to undertake Initiation. The tests in the sign Scorpio are concerned with the general problem of the transformation of grosser energies into more refined ones within the bodies of Initiates and disciples alike.

4. Virgo *(Chapter 9:8): 'And they had hair as the hair of women'.* This phrase refers to the development of Virgo's keen, sharp, analytical mind and the consequent attitude of separateness that it produces amongst most people. This is symbolised by the phrase 'the hair of women', for hair is composed of an innumerable number of separate strands, though unified by the head from which they derive. Here a major attribute is vanity, signified by the many different shades and hairstyles of women, each vying to outdo the other.

   Separateness or segregation means limitation, pain, suffering, disharmony and friction. It is the sense of separateness in people's minds that is perhaps the greatest evil on this earth today, for it fosters the blindness of sectarianism and leads to imprisonment, hatred and war. Love (magnetic attraction) is a blending together and fusion of all separative units into a cooperative unity or harmony, producing prosperity, freedom and joy. It produces an all-embracive open mindedness and far-reaching inquiry and understanding of all things. Separateness is a function of the material domain, of the third or Mother aspect of deity, symbolised by the women's hair. This form of materialistic and separative pursuit in the world is what the disciple battles through the testings in Virgo. These tests consequently concern developing the countering virtue (the sense of the oneness and livingness of Deity) and to express that realisation as cooperative endeavour and unity of purpose in all of one's relationships. One begins to work as part of an enlightened group, unfolding the Plan worked out by the senior Initiates embodying the Hierarchy of Light. As the tests are passed, so the nature of Deity is increasingly revealed.

   The Heart centre becomes quite vivified as the person becomes responsive to group energies. First, these energies come from a loving interaction with the general world, the spiritual group (Ashram) to which one's Soul belongs and to Hierarchy in general. Energies finally come down from the Kingdom of 'God' (thus interplanetary and cosmic sources).

This emerging internal life increasingly becomes a more potent factor in the disciple's life, as the meaning of the phrase 'the Light of the Christ' becomes revelatory, progressively enlightening. The Christ-Child has now been born in the cave of the Heart, for the Mother has completed her labour. This Light reveals the Truth, enabling one to see into arenas of involvement that were formerly in darkness. All further testing and progress on the path depends upon the ability to receive and hold in consciousness the potency of the intensified Light that comes after the attitude of separateness (in its various categories) is transmuted into the expression of unity, of Oneness. The disciple wishes to shout this feeling of Oneness from the rooftops to make it known to everyone. The strife and division in all categories of human livingness throughout the world are seen and the disciple must utilise the keen Mercurial mind that Virgo has bestowed to eliminate the divisions seen around – but how? These are the nature of the testings in this sign.

5. Leo *(Chapter 9:8): 'And their teeth were as the teeth of lions'.* This phrase refers to Leo the lion, and the sense of *pride,* of intellectual satisfaction—the 'teeth' that bite and the mouth that snarls. By now a newfound sense of power has had time to take effect in the disciple's constitution. New energies vitalise and the disciple begins to gain high revelations from fragments of ancient truths. Elated in the sense of well being and importance, the disciple often visions him/herself as a Messiah, a leader in one sense or other, little realising that this sense of dominance is a major weakness at this stage of the path. The tests thus concern overcoming pride and the need to dominate (others) in one way or another. The importance of one's position or status must be transmuted into that *humbleness* that knows the immensity of space and of the embodying Deity, therefore elucidating one's own place in the scheme of things. The disciple must symbolically stand with his/her back to the immense vastness of Being, with hands outstretched in loving service to those that follow.

   The Christ washing the feet of His apostles is an example of the humbleness that the disciple must similarly develop. Humbleness has nought to do concerning nurturing an inferiority complex or of false meekness, but comes from the knowledge and realisations that emanate from the deepest recesses of the Heart.

   The tests in this sign concern overcoming the state of mind that tends to produce glamour of one's own self-importance and which tends to cloud people's minds to the true state of things. Such deception is ever the effect of pride, producing the distortions and glamour that make the person to be the centre of attention, or to have power over the action of others.

The testings in Scorpio are said to 'stage the release of Leo', for these tests add another dimension of perception to the empirical thoughts that have for so long bound the Leo subject to the form, and to personality. After passing them, one obtains the 'freedom of the skies', being able to project thoughts to include many dimensions of perception in all directions of time and space.

The mental principle that has until now (in Leo) been the purpose of evolutionary development has become the disciple's most cherished possession. It must now however step down from its lofty position to allow the energies from the Heart and the Soul to take control. Such transference of consciousness is the objective of the tests undertaken in this sign, but is difficult to accomplish. This is because pride in one's accomplishment is the central edifice of the developed personality, and humbleness cannot be obtained by simply desiring or working to be humble, for that in itself feeds pride. Thus, one is tested.

6. Taurus *(Chapter 9:9): 'And they had breastplates'.* Breastplates refer to the sign Taurus the bull, being that to which the bull or ox is harnessed so as to plough the field to produce the things needed for the security and comfort of one's home life. The tests here thus concern *the desire for material comforts* that the average Taurian is infatuated with, as is also our present society.

   Much of the working person's time and energy are devoted to buying a large amount of consumer items, which are later discarded as waste. This drains much of humanity's resources, leisure time and creative abilities. This is the evil that can be defined as: 'that state of mind that ever tends to drive people and their sense of values away from the realm of causes and into the world of effects'. The tests undertaken in this sign therefore concern the endeavour to eliminate this evil in oneself, and in one's social and national climate.

   Subjectively, however, the major danger to disciples in this sign is that after battling through the many tests concerning the sense of pride and having developed some true humbleness, they are then often content to settle down and rest upon the laurels of this achievement. They reside in a comfortable environment and simply allow things to happen as they may. They have had sufficient experiences to bolster and affirm their religious or spiritual convictions, and with these they are content. They become generally apathetic or indifferent to further progress, or even to the true needs of humanity. They have symbolically built their house and have chosen to reside therein. They may be involved in temporal or even spiritual work that may be of benefit to the world at large, but are content with that and wish to go no further. Therein the danger lies, and thus the significance of the tests of this sign.

The tests concern a developing sense of desirelessness. The disciple must learn to consecrate all actions to benefit others without projecting personal desires and needs, so to allow the forces of Life and the meditative processes to carry him/her on in such a way that future glory and a wealthy harvest for all are produced (in Virgo). Disciples must allow the force of *karma* to manifest and carry them onwards to fulfil their spiritual destiny without offering personality hindrance or divergence. Neither must that *karma* be prevented from manifesting by nurtured apathy.

The problem here necessitates right contemplation and meditation, to allow the meditation Mind to influence every action, so that true serenity conditions the desire body. (Instead of that body ruling.) This is difficult to accomplish, for it is easy to blame *karma* for this or that, or to use it (or something else) as a scapegoat for inaction. What needs to be developed, therefore, is true desirelessness through the power to vision the cause and effect of any line of action, and so to work steadfast to make the vision a reality. One strives to be a desireless instrument of the subjective Plan of 'God' so that the vision is objectivised. Only thus can the good manifest in the dense physical world.

7. Aries *(Chapter 9:9): 'As it were breastplates of iron'.* Iron is the metal that Mars the god of war rules, who wears 'breastplates of iron'. Mars is the orthodox ruler of Aries the ram, and of the hatreds, the emotio-mental impulses and rash actions that produce the divisions and cleavages among us. The results of hatred are plainly evident to all, needing little further comment.

   The major problem, however, that concerns the disciple in this sign is not so much hatred in the personality sense, for that has long gone as a conditioning factor. What manifests instead is the development of strong critical attitudes, for instance, to other philosophies and ideologies, to the mistakes, lack of judgement and errors of the various leaders in the world around. The disciple is prompted by a strong sense of righteousness, of responsibility, idealism and devotion. So much is seen to be wrong in the world (and great is the desire to rectify those wrongs) that the methodology chosen is usually one of direct confrontation and attack, or zealous and even fanatical application of what is felt to be right. Forms of emotional extremism have crept into the disciple's judgement. They have to be discovered and eliminated, so that a truly compassionately logical gaze manifests, wherein the remedy for the ailments are properly comprehended and a wise plan of action then implemented.

There is, for instance, the preacher at the pulpit, eulogising on the nature of Satan and his influence in our lives. Or there can be the example of the demonstrator, political or environmental activist, orator, or faddist – those that condemn this or that aspect of society with equally earnest motives, but without a truly all-encompassing and far-reaching logical insight of the nature of the problems concerned. The subject has not been broadmindedly thought out to conclusion; errors of perception have consequently resulted. Much shallow thinking, prompted by desire of one form or other, has caused such hatred, or the various forms of *irritation* that are aspects of it. Control of the tendency to irritability is important here. It is not without cause that Master Morya calls irritation 'imperil' in the book *Agni Yoga*, for irritation of any type is what imperils the spiritual life of the aspirant. It destroys the foundation for the expression of Love. Irritation is really an effect of frustrated personality will (Solar Plexus based), which is the lower correspondence of the divine Will that is associated with the sign Aries.

The tests here therefore concern the tendency of the disciple to be critically assertive, producing the consequent cleavages that criticisms of every kind engender. What is needed, therefore, is to develop *loving kindness and patience* in all relationships with others. The tendency to criticise, to try to impose one's point of view upon others, has no place in the heart of the disciple who wishes to follow in the footsteps of the Christ, and so become so uniquely compassionate as to become the 'servant of all'.

Criticism produces retaliation. One must develop the perception to see aspects of the good in all human relations, in people's methods, modes of conduct, and in every ideology. All have their place in the scheme of things and are part of the Plan of 'God'. If there are things wrong with them according to the perception of the disciple, then discrimination should be wisely used to rectify the wrongs. Direct confrontation to try to assert or impose one's views upon another is not the method to be used. The plan is not served, nor is a Christ made thus. The mind must be quietened and much contemplation upon the problem at hand made. Effort should be applied to find logical pathways to overcome any perceived flaws, injustices or problems seen in the world or in others.

The aspirant must learn to work from a zone of quietude, from the stillness of a controlled Solar Plexus activity whose energies are directed via the Heart centre. Working at all times from the poised, controlled, contemplative and cool stillness of the Heart is one of the most difficult things for the Arian aspirant to do. A profound patience must be developed to wait for the right time and opportunity to talk and act to produce the desired beneficent results in the face of all adversity. A great sensitivity to inner energies and outer environmental conditionings will have been attained, and an unwavering urge to help. The conversion from Solar Plexus to Heart centre activity becomes the unique agony of a disciple, wherein lies his/her testings.

The problem of *irritation* comes from the agony of the testings. Most often instead of drawing from the Heart centre the aspirant draws Fire from the Throat centre. The aspirant has a highly developed mental apparatus, and so is sensitively perceptive in many areas. When problems arise, especially in dealing with others, their faults or lack of perception are seen, then a mental-emotional impatience arises, stimulating the critical mind. The disciple must curb the tendency to criticise by developing the wisdom of foresight, forbearance and the patience to analyse the right approach by using the Heart's input. The manifestation of compassionate understanding is therefore the key to the overcoming of critical attitudes, to know when to step back and to not be involved in areas of little spiritual importance. The disciple learns to curb his/her tongue and to direct thoughts to loftier heights, and so the testing proceeds. The problem of *irritation* confronts the disciple right up to the time the third Initiation is being gained.

A large portion of the world's spiritual and reactionary literature has its roots in misapplied Solar Plexus energy (the abdominal brain), ranging from astrally based visions to heightened emotive sensations and related feeling-perceptions. These the disciple or zealot mistakes as coming from the highest sources, or from the Heart, thus viewing them as infallibly correct, of profound revelatory import, etc. Many of these visions are the results of high aspiration stemming from seeds of truth, but interpreted by those that have little or no esoteric understanding. They are not grounded in a contemplative lifestyle, and have not yet mastered their emotions or the chatter from their empirical minds. (Though many think they have.)

There is a place for criticism, if constructively based upon reason – an explanation of things as they really are, based upon insights, truths emanating from the domain of the Heart. Such will consequently produce beneficent results, though sometimes such truths may produce a seeming negative impact upon those engrossed in personality pursuits. The more enlightened one is, the greater the perception of truth, the more profound the critical insight, thus producing long lasting, beneficent and pervasive effects of the 'two-edged sword' of truth.[7] (This may however mean radical changes and destruction of the mental conditionings, customs, habits and social attitudes of those thus taught.) An example of one who could use this 'sword' well (with its martial implications) was Jesus, whose statements were bewildering to the orthodox exponents of the Jewish religion of his time. They are similarly mostly misunderstood by the fundamentalists of today.

When such a truth bearer manifests, the aim is to change the concepts and modes of activity no longer conducive for the spiritual development of those to be taught. These ones are generally deeply entrenched in rigid attitudes and belief systems, thus rarely react wisely to concepts of change. Nevertheless change is needed, hence the two-edged sword of truth is utilised to produce the changes. In this way a new world religion or aspect of civilisation may appear to further the trends towards human betterment. Rarely is this seen for what it is at the time by those being taught the truth.

A major problem manifests when true evil (the emissaries of the dark brotherhood, using any of the methodologies of the nine heads of the Hydra) confronts the disciple. Logical reasoning, straight talking, or compassionate action will not work with them. They will twist and distort everything said into untruths and will plainly lie if need be. The dark ones will brook no other agenda or ideology but their own. They are not interested in truth, logic or reason, unless aspects thereof somehow fulfil their agenda. Such beings are best avoided, and group activity collectively worked out regarding how to mitigate the effects of their lying propaganda and invectives. There are also esoteric means, such as the projection of the energy of light, discovered upon the second Initiation path.

The major attributes of the tests in Aries thus concern a disciple's first tentative aptitude in the handling of first Ray energies, of which 'hatred'

---

7 See *Rev. 1:16, 2:16* and *19:21.*

is the most distorted expression. Rightly handling the intensity of first Ray energies is generally difficult and thus often misdirected or perverted by the disciple being tested. The tendency to manifest the critical mind negatively is therefore strong. The disciple's motives consequently need to be demonstrably correct, and the mouth must produce only beneficent and harmless statements. Such testings are necessary for the path of Initiation, especially from the third Initiation onwards. These testings are almost entirely concerned with the Initiate's increasing capability to utilise first Ray energies.

Critical attitudes stage the testings concerning irritation and the mastery of related Solar Plexus energies. If the Solar Plexus is not controlled then the effects of the first Ray could be to produce explosive reactions that greatly intensify aspects of the self-will, especially in relation to the forceful projection of thought-forms. Such can quickly lead one onto the path that produces a black magician. (They manifest a one-pointed evil and selfish subjective or objective intent in their undertakings.) What is incarnate through the black magician is 'the father of lies',[8] which always twists the truth to suit the purpose of the dark one. The aura of such a being will always reveal his/her presence.

8. Cancer: *'And the sound of their wings was as the sound of chariots of many horses running into battle'.* The phrase 'chariots of many horses running' refers to *Neptune,* the esoteric ruler of Cancer. Neptune (veiled by the Moon) is the God of the sea, and (as the Greek myths testify) of herds of horses. The horses imply mass movements of the animal nature, thus of the desire body. This refers to the various forms of *fear* that considerably condition humanity. Nowadays these fears are verbalised and carried through the air by means of the mass media: the Internet, newspapers, T.V. and the radio. Such activity is symbolised by the phrase 'the sound of their wings'. These sounds now fly long distances through the air from a transmitter to the various appliances people possess. The fears cause myriad major and minor battles and squabbles amongst humanity. Their mass projections via the media machines are a prime means of control and indoctrination by governments and the powerful wealthy 'elite'. The term 'wings' also refers to people's thought-form making tendencies, which are often of a fearful nature.

   Here, therefore, the disciple battles with the evil that is the state of mind that ever perpetuates the doctrine of fear. There are five types of fears (explained

8 *John. 8:44.*

in my book *The Revelation*) which are the distorted stimulations of the five types of instincts. An objective of the tests in Cancer is therefore to gain the transmuted qualities of these instincts.

The fears explained in that book are:

- Fear of death and the unknown.
- Fear of old age, sickness and senility.
- Fear of isolation and of loneliness.
- Fear of not being noticed, being left behind, or failure.
- These fears produce the fear of the pains engendered by humanity itself.[9]

Once all fears have been properly conquered then the obstacles preventing one from gaining revelatory understanding of the Mysteries of Being have been mastered. The door to the Initiation experience then looms. There are many levels of testings concerning the subjective fears that must be mastered (transmuted) as one passes from Initiation to Initiation.

If the tests in Aries are successful then a major cycle of evolution is consummated. The disciple is effectively reborn in the sign Cancer, where the last major test is necessary for the disciple to appropriately serve humanity and also to overcome entities that may assail the disciple from the inner realms. Many problematic karmic situations from past lives will have to be cleansed upon this path. Similar difficulties to what Jesus went through may be faced, or the more psychic types of temptations, such as the hordes of Māra faced by the Buddha before his enlightenment. The disciple must rise triumphant and yet be able to use the testings as a means to enlighten those around.

Second Initiation testings also concern the ability to rightly counter grey and black emanations from the dark brotherhood with the energies of Light. The emanations from these entities will always try to instate any of the categories of fear into the aspiring disciple, so as to dissuade further progress upon the way of Light, or to try to convert him/her to the ways of darkness. Subtle and cunning are the modes of conversion.

In Cancer, the disciple experiences the sum total of the subjective Watery personality life that manifests as remnant *karma* from past lives of activity. The various ancient personality characteristics and traits, glamour, instincts and tendencies; many subconscious thoughts and fears are brought to light.

---

9 See my revised *The Revelation,* 320-330, for an explanation of these fears.

The deep recesses of hidden feeling perceptions or adverse tendencies in the psyche that can come to the surface may prevent or hinder future work from being accomplished. The *'chariots of many horses'* thus symbolise the thought-forms of various hidden desires, phobias and ambitions that are revealed. They can be terrible things that must be faced, and consequently battled with. The latent unsubdued and unconquered characteristics form the sum total of the personality nature, and constitute what is known as 'the Dweller on the Threshold'. This is literally the 'shell' that the Cancerian carries around everywhere. It constitutes the sum of the character traits and fears incorporated into the Cancerian's constitution during the many cycles of incarnation through the spheres of material activity and Watery existence (the astral plane).

The Cancerian carries this karmic shell wherever he/she goes, and retreats into it at times of seeming danger to the habitual thought pattern and activities thus engendered. This is the comfort zone of the individual, their ego or personality sphere, which will fight to its very last drop of energy to prevent its environment from collapsing all around. This collapse must however happen if the Christ-Light is to be engendered. These thought-forms and habit patterns are the substance of the darkness of the past. (Which the dark brotherhood are always ready to perpetuate, for that is the environment in which they reside.) It is the Watery material aspect with which the disciple must battle until it has been victoriously dissipated and converted into a sphere of Light (the transformed 'shell').

The Angel of the Presence (the Soul) and the Dweller stand face to face upon the Initiation path, until the Dweller's light is eventually consumed by the Light of the Soul. The disciple has by then symbolically entered Scorpio and undertaken the associated self-initiated trials and tests, is triumphant and mounts the fixed cross of the Heavens. The arrows of aspiration are ridden in Sagittarius until a well-deserved Initiation in Capricorn is attained. The Initiate becomes a world server in Aquarius, recapitulating (on a higher cycle) the types of tests previously undertaken in the various signs.

The *future* represents the arenas of Light into which the disciple must travel, but of which he/she is uncertain, because unknown, new causes for the arousal of fears and other hindrances may arise upon the Path. This is the stage (on the threshold of entering the Light) when disciples are most susceptible to the subtle whisperings from the forces of evil[10] that do everything possible with grey energies to exaggerate the fears, and to prevent the onset of Love.

Disciples must be wary of all forms of fear, which should have no place in their life. They must look only to what is productive of Light. There is nothing to fear but fear itself. (An oft repeated but necessary statement of fact.) Fears come as the result of the Cancerian sensitivities to the various forms of feeling-perceptions. They are Solar Plexus based anticipations of things that have no basis in fact. They only appear to be real because they are caused by the creative imagination of the person concerned. If there is a factual basis, it is normally distorted by the fearful being.

It is easy to observe gross fears and emotions, but the subtler ones are far more dangerous to the person. They are more intrinsic, built deep into the psyche, are often difficult to detect and they often pose as virtues. Virtues of days gone past become the evil of the present, if they hinder progress to Love and Light.

It is fitting that the personality shell is finally karmically dismantled through the tests undergone in Cancer. The Angel of the Presence can then reveal the Temple of the Lord, so that the personality can become a fit vehicle for the complete incarnation of the Soul into it. (This effectively happens in the sign Leo.)

Both Cancer and Scorpio have a strong relationship to the desire body via the sixth Ray of Devotion. (Cancer is ruled by Neptune both exoterically and esoterically, and Scorpio by Mars.) The desire of the Soul in Cancer for experiences binds it to the form, whilst in Scorpio the tests of the disciple stage the release of the Soul. Scorpio is the sign of sex and of regeneration whilst Cancer is the sign of generation. Each lays the condition for the success of the activities of the other. This activity is carried right through the tests undertaken by the Scorpio disciple in the sign Cancer.

The strong relation between Mars and Neptune can also be seen in the fact that Mars is said to be 'objective and full of blood' and Neptune is 'subjective and full of life'. Together they condition the sum total of the energies that manifest through the physical equipment of the disciple, producing the ability to control every aspect of that body after the tests in Cancer have been completed. They

10 The teachings concerning the activities of the Anubis provided in my book *The Constitution of Shambhala,* Part A, must be understood here. Cancerians are particularly prone to such whisperings.

relate the disciple to Sagittarius (who rules Mars Hierarchically), producing a closer contact with the Lunar Lords (the second Creative Hierarchy) that govern the Watery Element, thereby facilitating control of the entire emotional vehicle.

9. Scorpio. Finally, in *Rev. 9:10* are the words: *'And they had tails like unto scorpions, and there were stings on their tails',* symbolising the qualities of Scorpio and of the various tests ('stings') undertaken therein. The nature and extent of these tests are conditioned by the experiences of the aspirant in the various signs previously explained, though they are collectively undertaken (or recapitulated) in Scorpio.

   These tests overtly concern the problem of *sex* and the pains, petty squabbles and nastiness that many people evidence in their lives based on sexual interrelationships. Many of the unpleasantness associated with maladjusted sex urges need to be dealt with. The problem of sex and the consequent overpopulation of the world, resultant mass diseases, urban violence and associated legalities, are major problems facing humanity today.

   In Scorpio, the disciple learns to handle all innate urges and energies, and also the external ones arising from the relationship to the environment and society in general. The tests are consequently applied in this sign, for whatever may have been internalised in the former signs now becomes externalised and 'full of blood, or passion' in Scorpio. This focuses on the problem of right human relationships, which is fundamental to the wellbeing and survival of humanity. Trying to solve this problem within their social and national groups is what eventually initiates aspirants into the mysteries of enlightenment. This happens as they manifest these relationships rightly by learning to serve all beings. There can be no true awakening to the Light without developing the need to serve. Jesus said: 'He that is greatest among you shall be your servant. And whosoever shall exalt himself shall be abased; and he that shall humble himself shall be exalted'.[11]

   The tests in Scorpio thus concern the developing sense of the need for service to humanity and to all manifest Life. They constitute a scientific mode of release of the aspirant from the tyranny of the personality and desire nature. (Which keeps the aspirant tied to the wheel of birth and death and of suffering by means of concepts of I, me, mine, and other self-glorifying and self-serving pursuits.)

---

11 *Matt. 23:11-12.*

The qualities developed by these tests are needed upon the compassionate path whereby the disciple finds his/her placing in one of the Ray departments in the Hierarchy of Light, working therein in an ever-increasingly enlightened manner. In this way an Initiate moves increasingly closer to the Heart of Life. The main qualities developed are:

| | |
|---|---|
| Aspiration | Sagittarius |
| Harmlessness | Capricorn |
| Unselfishness | Aquarius |
| The Sense of Oneness | Virgo |
| Humbleness | Leo |
| Desirelessness | Taurus |
| Lovingkindness | Aries |
| Fearlessness | Cancer |
| Compassionate undertakings | Scorpio |

**Table 4. The transformed attributes of the Hydra**

Subjectively, however, the testings concern the relation of the pairs of opposites and the transference of the energies from the centres below the diaphragm to those above it. This involves the appropriate vivification of the Throat, Heart, Head and Ājñā centres. This gradual transference is expressed throughout the course of actively moving through all of the signs. The implication is of an ever-growing capacity to act as a medium in the transmission of the energies from Hierarchy, and later from the Kingdom of 'God' to humanity. It thus also concerns the right direction of *prāṇa* and *kuṇḍalinī* (esoterically, the sting in Scorpio's tail) that is awakened upon the path to enlightenment. Transformation of the base elements of consciousness and the transmutation of the grosser energies into enlightenment vectors is the nature of this path.

Compassionate service becomes the disciple's keynote for all kingdoms of Nature and from all angles of vision in time and space. Disciples become examples for others to emulate. Nevertheless, often their actions (what is said and done) are scrutinised and criticised by others, because they represent the unknown and incomprehensible to self-focussed individuals. Sometimes disciples are applauded and given the highest praise. Disciples can become saints or martyr in the public's eyes, or be condemned as heretics or demons.

No matter what, the disciple always works to 'sting' (or to cause death to) all forms of evil, misconstrued and aberrant doctrines and dogmas. The focus of the service arena is upon whatever limits or denigrates human freedom and traps the Spirit within, regardless of what people or those in power think. As disciples become Initiates, the capacity to produce positive changes in the world thereby grows accordingly.

Three of the signs do not have any particular testings associated with them. They are Gemini, Libra and Pisces. Pisces is the sign of death, and its general influence produces the consummation of the experience associated with the tests. Libra is the hub of the wheel of Life and governs the period of contemplation when all the various antagonistic forces associated with the tests are evenly balanced, giving the person time to reflect upon their influence. The influence of Gemini is all-pervasive and is subtly found throughout them all, relating all of the pairs of opposites.

## Sagittarius the archer

Sagittarius governs the thighs of the Grand Heavenly Man. The hip bones are the major supportive bones in the physical body, as the entire torso rests upon them, giving balance and the ability to hold ourselves upright. They consequently help to produce physical power and protective strength, the fulcrum from which most of the other bones and appendages, and thus organs of the body, centre their leverage. They thus support their inherent powers. The Sagittarian governs or directs the activities of the other signs of the zodiac because of this position in human anatomy (and thus of 'God'). Sagittarius occupies the central position concerning one's strength to make and to accomplish goals. Right (or wrong) direction in fact is one of the keynotes of this sign, for the activities of the Sagittarian first direct the unevolved person towards Scorpio. There, ambition for material power leads to deepening sensuality and to death, as well as to heightened materiality and selfishness in Virgo.

When ambition transforms into aspiration, then an aspirant enters Scorpio to undergo the many tests therein. Sagittarius governs the driving or motivating force, the focussed consciousness that propels one from victory to defeat and thence to victory again. From battle to battle the disciple goes, until finally the struggle is over and the triumphant disciple arises out of the sign Scorpio. Sagittarius then directs that one to the mountaintop of Initiation in Capricorn. The person's aspirational zeal and personality ambition thus all find their central source of power in Sagittarius.

The consciousness of humanity has gradually evolved from mass instinctual activities, as symbolised by the sign Cancer, to that of the self-conscious individual in Leo. By the time one reaches Scorpio, the mind has been sufficiently developed to comprehend the problems of the environment it resides in. It is rational, highly perceptive, analytical, and is becoming susceptible to the influence of the Soul. This causes the various tests associated with Scorpio as the personality light and the Soul light battle. Eventually the Soul light is triumphant and the illumined disciple emerges and enters into the sign Sagittarius. There the intuition is developed and the disciple receives the flashes of light that allow visioning the attainment that will be accomplished in Capricorn. The disciple knows the past well and has learnt to live fully, utilising all his/her faculties to serve the present, but now gains the added faculty to vision the future and to shoot the arrows of the mind from 'point to point on the way'. The disciple can figuratively 'dismount constantly from his white horse and find where the arrows of intuitional aspiration will take him'.[12] The 'white horse' here is the developed mind, purified and rightly oriented.

The hips and thighs (and the muscles attached to them) are of vital moment in the latter stages of the gestation period (from the symbolic sixth month onwards), for then the child is a definitely formed entity, where the aspects of form and those of the Soul are interrelated and blended. These aspects of the body will eventually bear the responsibility of the weight of the child to help bring about its right orientation, facilitating the speed and safety of its evolution. After the birth, the hips help the mother (Virgo) to carry the child from place to place in the environment (the zodiac). Later, the hips enable the legs and feet (Pisces) to travel the great Wheel (the rounds of the zodiac), thus the path to liberation. This path leads eventually to the second death, the death of the Soul form in Pisces, thus to be resurrected to Life eternal in the realms of enlightened Being. The disciple in Sagittarius thereby becomes the saviour in Pisces.

In early Atlantean times, Sagittarius was symbolised by the centaur who was half man and half horse. The selfish thought-form making tendencies (the desires, various ambitions, incentives and lofty aspirations of the person) were united to the animal aspect, which impels one this way and that over the plains of the earth.

The control of the material form and animal nature were the tasks that confronted the centaur, but for a long time he was swayed by the instinctual

12 *Esoteric Astrology,* 181.

reactions of the group or herd (the masses and their passions). In such a form the indwelling Soul struggled to work and evolve. Later, in Aryan times, the mind was sufficiently developed to be in control of the animal nature. The mind was separated from its instrument, which in turn was becoming a purified and highly refined vehicle. The person and beast were separated, symbolically becoming the *Rider on the white horse*, who (with the bow and arrows of the thought-form making process) was able to fire them in whatever direction wished. The goal was consequently consummated. The person was able to find sustenance and adequately nourish the form nature thereby, as well as feeding his/her aspirations.

Nowadays, the Archer, horse and centaur have been eliminated from the symbol and we have only a fragment of the bow and arrow to remind us of the major incentive of the Sagittarian: aspiration, and its direction by the intuition.

The symbol is depicted thus:

♐

This arrow is a straight and one-pointed line that leads to liberation. It is able to pierce all the veils and cloaks of illusion and glamour as an attribute of the directive thought of the Archer. The arrow is quick, direct to the point and piercing. (Qualities associated with the intuition.) The Archer can quickly penetrate the heart of any matter. He/she can thus receive an understanding of the related properties or qualities of any subject or meditation being pursued long before the information becomes evident in the world of form.

One must also look to the symbolism of the bow and arrow –poised in tension and ready to be fired in a given direction towards a target. The word *tension* is of significance when related to meditative attainment. Here can be found the clue to the true purpose and mode of operation of the Sagittarian, esoterically considered. Tension can be defined as the point in the circle—a storehouse of power, of focussed immovable Will, a state of dynamic poise. Where a point of tension exists, energy is being generated, held in potential and focussed in such a manner for future use so that its force can be directed for whatever purpose needed. Tension has a direct relation to the energy of the Will, and thus governs the way to Shambhala. Tension is the heart or foundation of all manifestation, the energy that coheres all into a unity. Without tension no form could exist, all would be chaos.

Tension exists where there is no subject-object duality, where there is perfect understanding, when one is standing directly under some principle or concept and allowing the light of that principle to pour vertically downwards into consciousness. Tension originates outside the realms of concern of temporal reality. The highest expression is the Will of 'God' just before the Word of Creation was Uttered, because the greatest potential is the All-Being/Non-Being lying beyond the bounds of time. Tension is an intensity of purpose involving an inner orientation and organisation of energies directed towards service and sacrifice. It is an inner constant cyclic attitude of determined and planned abstraction.

The concept of tension underlies the seventh of the Buddha's Eightfold Path: *right or perfect concentration.* If all the other precepts of this path are followed,[13] then everything preventing one from obtaining lasting release from suffering (and thus from the wheel of birth and death) falls away. One is left with concentrated energies (physical, emotional and mental) that are assimilated and projected towards the goal. This produces perfect mindfulness of all things. Such concentration implies that the only elements that remain are those that allow meditative development and the demonstration of the *dharma.* All aspects that relate to the Divine are concentrated upon, after the types of *karma* that tie one to material existence have been eliminated. This produces a specific effortless tension: a state of being where naught can distract from the application of the meditation Mind. It is a point of focussed receptivity where the Mind is held steady, unwavering in Light. The ability to do this necessitates the application of the will, the positive, dynamic fruition of the person's long drive to liberation. (This is also the impetus sustaining that drive.) When focussed upon a form or an idea, it becomes the seed or germ that effectively explodes into the empowerment and complete unfoldment of any stream of realisation. It can also direct one to realms beyond all thought. Such concentration is effortless through being the outcome of long periods of meditative unfoldment that have become a spontaneous state of transcendence. There remains naught in the meditator to resist the realisation of the most potent energies or associated revelations. This then produces the last step of the the Eightfold Paths: perfect meditative bliss or absorption.

It should be obvious here that the aspirational zeal that allows one to tread this entire Eightfold Path is governed by the Archer's focussed direction and application of the will. Symbolically, however, the path is trod in the Womb of

13 These precepts are: 1. Right or perfect understanding. 2. Right or perfect aspiration or attitude of mind. 3. Right or perfect speech. 4. Right or perfect action. 5. Right or perfect livelihood. 6. Right or perfect effort. 7. Right or perfect concentration or mindfulness. 8. Right or perfect meditative bliss or absorption.

Virgo, where the 'divine Child' in her Womb is born as the liberated, enlightened one. The result of this perfected concentration (or mindfulness) of energies is the service work that is the leitmotiv of the Aquarian.

The production of a point of tension allows the building of the bridge that connects Spirit to matter (the arrow of the *antaḥkaraṇa).* The three main components of the resultant 'tensed sphere' are: *the Will* to reach beyond, *the Love* to extend outwards and magnetically draw all into a unified sphere, and *the skill* to rightly direct the two upon the battlefield of Life.

Tension comes from eternal vigilance, implying watchfulness when another would normally be asleep. It is produced through an intensity of striving and salutary toil, through adaptability to the cycles of change producing an ability to handle incoming forces. Such forces constantly change through differing points of focus upon the lower sheaths. Focussed tension allows us to project the potency of the Spirit within. Tension is The Jewel in the Heart of the Lotus of each *chakra* that manifests as a point of tensed receptivity.

From the mundane perspective, tension is viewed as being 'stressed out' to the point of producing crises. For esotericists, points of tension and points of crises are virtually synonymous, for tension shatters the boundaries of present possibilities because they limit what must be, and that is the crisis. The effect of tension produces a rapid expansion and explosion of the potential of the auric qualities of an individual, throwing off what is negative and which hinders the true expression of the Divine. This produces the points of crises. Tension empowers and reveals the good from what was formerly imperfect, evolving. When mastered, points of crises produce amazing revelatory expansions of consciousness. These are in the nature of the tests to be passed if Initiation is to be undertaken. Sagittarius fires the arrows of tensed activity to proceed from one Initiation goal to another.

Tension is an expression of Bliss (universality of consciousness). Its effects are like a nuclear explosion in the realm of consciousness. It produces the building of the *antaḥkaraṇa* to the Monad, producing the effects of Monadic Identification upon consciousness. To sustain such a point of tension, the form needs to be consubstantiated with the Christ-force in order to receive this downpour from the Father. The way of Bliss, of one-pointed service work, inevitably results in the destruction of the Causal form when the fourth Initiation is attained.

Like a compressed spring, tension powerfully drives forward spiral-cyclic motion when its potential is released. In a state of complacency of inactive torpor, its potency is however destroyed. Complacency is an undue focus upon the vicissitudes of the ever-changing desires of the personality (thus lacking the action of Love in service), and is the enemy of tension. This prevents the Archer from rightly firing arrows of directed purpose. A form of spiritual 'ambition' is needed to produce the required point of tension to project the *antaḥkaraṇa* to the higher domains.

Sagittarius is part of the cross of constant mutation and mutable activity. It shares this cross with Gemini, Virgo and Pisces. Through manifesting points of tension, the Archer can fire the arrows of aspiration that will allow the aspirant to eventually mount the *cardinal cross.* (The cross of synthesis, dynamic resolve and spiritual power.) Finding its mark upon the cardinal cross allows the Archer to return to the Source of all Being. Forever the arrows are fired to this Source because the Heart is ever expanding, and it is the Will of the Heart that keeps this arrow steady upon its trajectory. This expanding Heart of consciousness is true *samādhi,* in which there is no sense of self, no duality. Group consciousness is the consciousness of the common good. Group evolution becomes the ever-growing target as the Archer moves far into the domains of cosmos. From star system to star system can the moving dynamics of the arrows of Mind lead the accomplished One that has mastered this process.

The collective focussed purpose of a group of beings produces the bow that sustains the point of tension of a greater (Logoic) One. Each individual thought structure becomes the arrows or 'sparks of tension' fired by that One. Such a One can also be viewed as the *Avatar of Synthesis,* who directs His energy through the principle of directed Purpose. The arrows fired by Him become the manifesting Plan, which those with tensed, focussed intention receive (being but the targets of this One), and they re-release the potency thereof in their service to all, according to their capacity to direct the energies. An emissary of such a One is the Rider on the white horse.

A group of such beings (as is the Hierarchy) manifest an aura that can be viewed clairvoyantly in terms of a multi-tiered ringed structure that becomes the target for the arrows. The point of tension is represented by the central point of this structure of the various Ashrams of the Masters of Wisdom. Each Ashram is constituted of the sum of all the individual points of tension and are focussed at the centre by means of the potency of the Master. Those on the periphery of the aura (the aspirants and probationers) possess but little tension, but as their auric pull becomes increasingly tense, so they come closer to the centre (thus evolving in Initiatory status). The interrelated *antaḥkaraṇas* are drawn to produce the 'bow and arrows' of Ashramic purpose. An Ashram can thus be considered fully formed when it produces a unified spiritual point of tension with a Master at the centre pulling the 'bowstring' to fire arrows of purposeful resolve. Those 'arrows' become the service arenas of the disciples constituting that Ashram.

The principle of directed purpose finds the target of the Ashrams and lights a Fire in all, which helps all to tense their bowstrings and fire the arrows of blissful joy to others so that their internal Fires are also lit up. The junction of the descending energy of Spirit with the horizontal life of service of the disciple forms a cross. The extension of this cross in the eight directions produces the sphere of endeavour of the 'tensed' disciple. Each spoke of the eight-armed cross of Life (the interrelated mutable and fixed crosses) can thus be seen as arrows fired outward to all spheres of Life, producing effects according to the direction fired. All such individual crosses together form the intricate patterning of the 'spider's web' that is the *nāḍī* system of the Logos. This indicates the true Sagittarius-Gemini relationship, in that one embodies the qualities of the *nāḍīs* (Gemini), and the other (Sagittarius) helps project the direction of the related energies.

The figure below depicts the bow and arrow of the Archer. In the tensed bow there are effectively three 'points of tension' (relating to the three aspects of the first Ray of Will or Power) that together manifest as purposeful direction. The Good (the Father or Spirit aspect), the True (the Son or consciousness aspect) and the Beauty (the activity or Mother aspect).

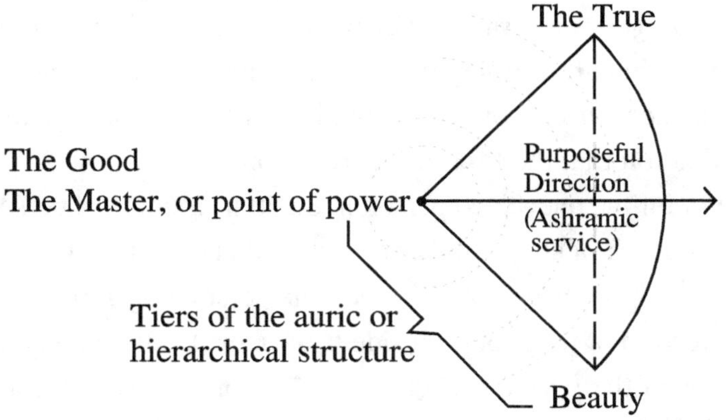


**Figure 13. Sagittarian points of tension**

The *Good* is the fundamental goodness in the sum of manifestation. It represents the Heart of Life, the point of power from which all emanates and into which all is resolved. It is the essence of all things in its uttermost simplicity and purity. The *True* is that point in the equilibrium of the tension that projects the aspects of the Good necessary for the great service, embellishing those aspects or 'arrows' with the imagery that allows the purpose to be sought. This embellishment is of the Archer's thoughts that seek the target, and the focus allowing him to hit the bullseye. The True becomes the truth that emanates as the wisdom associated with the Law of 'God' that is Good. The *Beauty* is the effect of the arrows of the True purposeful direction once they hit the target. Beauty can be viewed as the resonance of the arrows of Love in the field of sensation, producing the harmonies and patterns of accomplished service.

The arrows (or 'sparks of tension') can also be called Flames of Love, literally *antaḥkaraṇas* projected to encompass the All. These 'sparks of tension' are moving points of crisis. They create the destruction that must come before the building of the new forms, civilisations, or aspects thereof. They can also be viewed as flashes of illumination or intuition (directed from Hierarchical levels) that pierce the Heart, making it bleed in Love for all. This produces the consequent actions of service and sacrifice that distinguish the illumined One, the saint or seer.

In the human body the diaphragm can be viewed as a bow, firing arrows of aspiration from the centres below the diaphragm to those above it. Later the orientation alters, when arrows of Light are fired from above the diaphragm to the centres below. Such arrows control the functions of the petals of all the target centres, directing their purpose. Here the Good becomes the controlled Solar Plexus centre. True purposeful direction relates to appropriately projecting the *prāṇas* within the *iḍā, piṅgalā* or *suṣumṇā nāḍīs* to the centres above the diaphragm.

The disciple is inspired in Sagittarius, carrying out a practical intent. This is the result of former periods of contemplation as symbolised by the sign Libra, and the illumination that the tests in Scorpio confer.

The *keynotes* for the unevolved person in Sagittarius concern personality desire, ambition – the pursuit of some goal or objective that arises out of the desire-mind and its activities. Upon the reversed wheel, the personality moves away from the harsh, barren terrain of the mountainside (Capricorn), wherein some of the more negative aspects of the *karma* associated with a former cycle of incarnation had to be cleansed. In Capricorn, a glimpse was obtained of many things in life that are needed which would make life more worthwhile. Upon entering Sagittarius (in the form of the centaur, the man-beast), desired things are sought with intent, upon the green and adequate pastures of the plains below. This is done with such determination and effectiveness that eventually the person's environment is ravaged and becomes a desert wherein the Scorpion finds its home. To overcome the desert conditions, the testings of discipleship then begin.

Jupiter (the second Ray of Love-Wisdom) is the *orthodox ruler* of Sagittarius. It governs the entire activity of the mutable cross with Mercury (the only other planetary Regent governing this cross). As stated, Sagittarius is one of the rulers of this cross and its will directs the myriad experiences of the personality's journey upon it. The reaction to conflict, dissidence, warfare and active turmoil eventually produces harmony – the settling of human desires through the logical activities of the mind. Jupiter's influence allows the manifestation of clear logical thinking. A period of quiet or peace manifests before the elements of desire and attachment are reorganised and redirected towards the engendering of a better scheme, or ambition.

On the *rectified wheel*, the triumphant disciple emerges from Scorpio into Sagittarius, then finds that his/her activities are also qualified by the second Ray of Jupiter, for Love-Wisdom is the quality the disciple has for so long striven to obtain. The second Ray facilitates giving a form to formerly vague desires and feelings. This allows the formulation of a vision, plan or a goal to which one's ambition or aspiration may strive, and so the distant goal is seen on the mountaintop in Capricorn.

*Esoterically, the Earth* (Ray three of Mathematically Exact Activity) rules Sagittarius, for the disciple must strive towards liberation upon the earth whilst incarnate in the personality vehicle. Here must be undergone the many enterprises and activities. From them the developed Sagittarian's aspirational zeal will in time clear whatever obstacles exist that prevent the needed testings to be undertaken in Scorpio. The third Ray mathematical Mind facilitates passing the testings. If successfully passed, then the goal to liberation in Capricorn will be clearly seen. The Sagittarian can also cleanse the *karma* of attachment to the material world with facility. Such tests are engendered upon the earthy sphere. The goal visualised in Capricorn (an Earth sign) will then embody the highest point of achievement that the earth can offer.

Capricorn's esoteric ruler, Saturn (here ruling the abstracted essence of the Fires of the Mind), completes or absorbs the cycle of material activity begun upon the earth (the great Mother or Womb thereof) in Sagittarius. This activity happens subjectively in Gemini (the polar opposite of Sagittarius), which is ruled Hierarchically by the Earth. Sagittarius (from this angle of vision) consequently started the turning of the great wheel of the zodiac in Lemurian days, when there were only eight signs to the zodiac.[14]

Saturn allows the Soul to utilise the earth and its substance in order to produce a pre-determined result. Herein also lies the cause of the pain and sorrow that is the result of the battle of the pairs of opposites in our Earthy material bodies. In this battle, the pull of the spiritual is resisted by the inertia of the material on the earth and the resultant constant mutable experiences by the person evolving thereon. This relationship, however, guarantees eventual immortality for the fourth (human) Creative Hierarchy (Scorpio), allowing its fusion with the fifth *(deva)* Creative Hierarchy (Capricorn). The process of this fusion, the marriage ceremony of the Heavens, is presently a mystery to humanity.

The relationship between Capricorn and Sagittarius is exemplified when it is seen that Capricorn is also ruled by the third Ray (via Saturn, its exoteric and esoteric ruler). Therefore, the Lord of *karma* sets the field of activity whereby the one pointed disciple can finally become the Initiate and work to become *karmaless* (as far as life on the material world, the earth, is concerned). Third Ray and Saturnian activity also sets the field of activity for the life of the average person.

Gemini is the only other sign in the zodiac that is ruled by the Earth. Great is the significance in this unique relationship, and in the fact that they are polar opposites. This relationship governs the entire field of energy interplay that gives life to the form nature (the earth). It allows the fluid, dual, temperamental, mercurial mind in Gemini (which wavers from this to that and from one to the other) to eventually find the path that lies between the two. (Through the one-pointed aspiration in Sagittarius towards the lofty heights in Capricorn.) Sagittarius propels Divine Causative energies through the pillars of the etheric domain in Gemini, thereby helping to manifest the objective appearance of the original Thought-construct.

Psychically, Sagittarius governs the Sacral centre. This is the major centre for the distribution of all the energies that govern the personality, which the person must use in all creative pursuits. This is a predominant function of the eleventh Creative Hierarchy, the Lunar Lords (or the 'Sacrificial Fires'). In the scheme of things, Sagittarius is the sign that governs the evolution of these Elemental Lives that embody people's emotional and desire bodies.

Hierarchically, the ruler of Sagittarius is Mars (the sixth Ray of Devotion), which also rules the Lunar Lords.

---

14 See chapter five, as well as *Esoteric Astrology,* 159-60, for detail.

***Summary:***

- *Keynote:* Sagittarius, the disciple becomes the Saviour in Pisces.
- *Sagittarius* governs the Thighs and Sacral area of the Grand Heavenly Man.
- The *exoteric ruler* is Jupiter, Ray two of Love-Wisdom.
- The *esoteric ruler* is the Earth, Ray three of Mathematically Exact Activity.
- The *Hierarchical ruler* is Mars, Ray six of Devotion and Aspiration.
- The *Element* is Fire (as also for Leo and Aries).
- The *polar opposite* is Gemini.
- *Cross:* mutable.
- No planet is exalted or falls in Sagittarius, however the power of Mercury is lessened.
- The *Decanates* given for Sagittarius are *exoterically*: Mercury, the Moon, and the Sun. *Esoterically*: Jupiter, Mars, and the Sun.

The *keywords* given by D.K. for this sign are:

> In the world of form: 'And the Word said: Let food be sought'.
> On the reversed wheel: 'I see the goal. I reach that goal and then I see another'.

## The autumn and winter seasons

The signs Libra, Scorpio and Sagittarius empower the *autumn season*. Libra is the judgement, the turning of the wheel and the movement of the balance – from the heights of Life, to the rigours of age and the looming death that comes with the autumn of one's life. Scorpio, under the dominance of Mars, reddens the landscape with the forbearance of a seasonal death (the sting of the nocturnal scorpion) and of the sleep that the setting sun brings. The determined arrows of the Archer take with them the fruits and vitality of the summer harvest from those who have not found shelter in a hearth, house or cave. This allows the grim reaper (Capricorn) under the dominance of *karma* (Saturn) to follow with death and icy coldness for all that remain.

Capricorn (the Lord of the mountain), with Aquarius and Pisces, therefore embodies the winter season, with its hard, barren, stone-like grip. Capricorn enforces meditativeness upon the denizens of the field while they wait in silence through the rigours of the cold. This eventually allows the release of the inspired Life (Aquarius), for in Capricorn the person has time to think of how, why and of the effects of what has been done. He/she stands on the mountaintop of achievement, has looked back and now anticipates what was envisioned. Aquarius brings thoughts of the approaching spring, of the future and possibly prosperous new year.

Pisces means final death of the old, a period of calm before the new spring begins. The free thinking man (Aquarius) must again come to the plains of the earth, or the realms of the Waters from the symbolic mountain, and be bonded or yoked (as the Fishes) to the new cycle of work that must be accomplished. The person must also respond adequately to the new life that is now seen.

## Capricorn the goat

Capricorn rules the Knees of the Grand Heavenly Man, for it is only on the knees, in gratitude and humble servitude to one's Soul and to all members of 'God's kingdoms', that one can gain Initiation. Only when one has thus learnt to kneel in all humility on the mountaintop of accomplishment can the Mysteries of the Kingdom (Shambhala) and of enlightenment be revealed. One then gains the harvest of the many eventful lives that one has lived through the various signs of the zodiac. If one stands boastful and arrogant, then the true implications and reality of the vision from the heights will be clouded and blurred, consequently staging the setting for a rapid fall from the mountain. One must thus learn to humble oneself and symbolically climb the mount of accomplishment on one's knees, in respect to those that have gone before and who are the teachers who guide and help with the pitfalls on the way. Humbleness destroys the stumbling block of the empirical (concrete) mind, which is the greatest load or weight that one can carry on the path. One must also humble oneself for those that must follow, for unless one can speak words of wisdom aimed at their hearts, they will never be rightly guided upon the Way.

No person can successfully climb the mount heavily burdened by the heavy weight of arrogance, of convoluted reasoning concerning the nature of this and that. Assertive pedagogy, self-focussed mindfulness, and the rocks of materialised thought-forms as to the ways things ought to be, will not be helpful. The Greek god Atlas (who bore the weight of the world) also succumbed to the weight of such material strain.

Capricorn also rules the bony structure and spinal column in the body. All of the organs, muscles and functions of the body are hinged to and supported by the bony structure. Similarly, the entire milieu of being is hinged to the Initiation process. Our bones hold the body together and provide a person's rigid appearance. Rigid empiricism is also an exoteric effect of the energies of Capricorn in the material world, for Capricorn is ruled by the third and fifth Rays. (Saturn, orthodoxically and esoterically, Venus Hierarchically.) These Rays exemplify all forms of the activity of the mind. The mind/Mind is symbolised by the mountain, being the point of greatest materiality or crystalline hardness achieved by the evolutionary process in all the kingdoms of Nature. This is the function of the intellect – to materialise, crystallise thought. However, eventually the empirical mind can awaken to the far expanses of the enlightened Mind once the mountaintop is scaled.

Capricorn is the polar opposite of Cancer, the gateway of birth from whence the evolutionary process had its material beginnings. In the personality life, the exoteric effect of these planets is seen in terms of the materialising, rigid, material attitudes of an unyielding mind. The Capricornian personality can be hard (to the point of cold, calculating cruelty) in dealings with others, as well as in the effects of his/her actions upon all aspects of the general environment.

Capricorn is the most Earthy of the Earth signs. It is the point of densest concretion to which the Soul is capable of projecting itself, thus is consequently the sign of the Sorcerer (symbolised by the inverted pentagram). Here the person's intellect completely dominates and rules the activities of the Mother, the third Ray, and the form-building tendencies of evolution. Scorpio is the sign of the black magician (who is manipulated by the Sorcerer) that controls the material and psychic evolution by means of sex magic. As the Capricornian can be the most cruel, greedy and rapacious of beings, desirous to build vast material empires as his/her power base, so upon the path of evil nought will stand in the way towards satisfying his/her ambition and material incentive. The surest, straightest path to the way of the Sorcerer is the development of intelligence *per se,* directed towards the projection of materialistic incentives, with scant regard for the true awakening of compassionate insight. This is the road that leads to hell states.

Capricorn thus rules the worst in a person and also the best, via the intellect, which governs all of one's feelings (when united with the desire principle, producing *kāma-manas)* and thought processes. The intellect rules until one is on the path of aspiration, when the Heart increasingly comes to the fore. Then the two paths: the *iḍā* path, the way of the Head (the mind), and the *piṅgalā* path, the way of the Heart (compassionate insight), are fused and blended on the path to Initiation, the *suṣumṇā* path.

Capricorn rules this present period of Aryan evolution where the energies obtained from the mineral kingdom (mechanical tools, physical implements such as cars, computers, airplanes and mineral drugs) are the mainstay of our civilisation. Its influence upon intelligence is clearly evidenced in the attitudes of our scientific, technological and medical professionals. Every aspect of our lives is conditioned by technological advancement. Witness also the completely empirical and circumscribed materialistic philosophy advocated by the scientific wizards and philosophic leaders of the immediate past, and which is fed to all students of our educational and university systems. Scientific materialism has become the backbone for the work ethic needed in this civilisation, if one is to survive financially and support a decent lifestyle in our cities.

There comes a point of time in the evolution of the form when it becomes most crystalline and hard, but correspondingly fragile and therefore easily shattered, as is the bony structure of the aged. Capricorn is consequently a sign of conclusion, of termination of a cycle of evolution. It is the highest (or lowest) point in the evolutionary process for that particular entity, as far as the material domain is concerned. From the mountainous heights of any such achievement, people must descend again to the valleys of experience to seek new pathways of accomplishment. They must undergo another cycle of evolution (of struggle, pain, strife and strenuous effort) to fight with all the forces of the material world and of those that live and lurk on the plains, in the caves and depths of the earth. They must undertake the many tests associated with Scorpio before again attempting to scale the mountainside of ambition or achievement.

Capricorn is said to 'consummate the work of Scorpio'. It is the tenth sign of the zodiac. As previously explained, ten is the number of perfection and of completion, which verifies Capricorn's significance as the end point of evolution in the material world, as far as the development of the empirical mind is concerned. This evolution finds its full consummation on the higher mental plane in the sign Pisces. This becomes increasingly evident when the significance of Saturn being both the exoteric and esoteric ruler of Capricorn is understood. Saturn is the Lord of the *karma* that governs the three worlds of human livingness: mental, astral and physical (denoted as 'body, speech and mind' in Buddhism). The focus here is physical plane livingness as conditioned by mind, to master the many material conditionings that a person is found in. Saturn is the deity that utilises the activities of the past to wield the future, and He is said to be stern, melancholy and disciplinarian.

Upon the rectified wheel, the activities of the disciple and the results of the tests in Scorpio produce the termination of *karma* in the form that personalities understand it. It terminates what restricts us to the limitations of the form nature and which bind us to cycles of birth and death. In Capricorn, the person on the mountaintop is given the 'freedom of the planet' by having mastered the material domain. Symbolically, all of the kingdoms of the earth are offered to the Initiate, over which he/she can effectively rule in Saturn's place.

The manifestation of *karma* produces the individual as well as the planetary Dweller on the threshold. (Conceived of as the sum of the mental-emotional thoughts and proclivities, the astral heavens and hells, as well as the physical plane forms of hell states that many find themselves in.) The Dweller is effectively the mountain of opposition that the disciple, as the Angel of the Presence, has to battle in the last major test of Scorpio. This happens under the influence of Cancer, the polar opposite of Capricorn. The Dweller is fully objectivised in Capricorn, but the battle that finally frees the person from all karmic impositions (from the Dweller) is waged in Cancer, providing free reign to scale the mountainside of achievement once the Dweller has been overcome. Cancer is the sign of the thought-form making proclivities of the human (which becomes the 'shell' carried by the Cancerian native). The sum of these desire-thought constructs throughout the many rebirths of the individual is what had created the Dweller, hence the rebirthing process eventually produces a life, or series of lives, wherein what was created must be vanquished.

The spinal column houses the threefold cord (the *iḍā, piṅgalā* and *suṣumṇā nāḍīs)* and is the symbol of the mountain that a person must climb when the Initiation process to liberation is undertaken. This threefold cord embodies the totality of the energies that govern an individual and which are channelled through the *nāḍī* system. It relates to both the path of matter (the *iḍā nāḍī)* and to evolution in the field of consciousness (the *piṅgalā nāḍī),* as well as to the direct line that is the path of the Spirit (the *suṣumṇā nāḍī)* that relates the two. It relates the highest to the lowest, thus the Base of Spine centre (wherein the *kuṇḍalinī* forces are stored) to the Head centre. This is the path of illumination that eventually results in undertaking the third Initiation—the transfiguration of the third (material) aspect of Deity—and its elevation to the Throne of 'God'. (For this reason, Saturn and the third Ray of Intelligent Activity rule Capricorn.) Capricorn is the mount of transfiguration upon which the Christ stood, and on which His disciples were illumined. It is consequently the open door to Hierarchical experience.

Capricorn is thus a significantly mysterious sign, in many ways ruling the Mysteries of Being, as seen in the fact that it governs the activities of both the black and white magician, as well as the sum of material evolution. It therefore governs the activity of the goddess *kuṇḍalinī.* (The feminine or procreative forces that sustain the sum of the activities of the formed realms.) Many of the esoteric reasons why so much pain and suffering are evidenced on the earth is veiled by this sign. This concerns the cause and resolution of the *karma* in the three worlds, and of all material cycles in the Body of THAT Logos.

The true nature of this sign can only be properly understood by advanced Initiates. D.K. has thus stated that this sign has never been correctly delineated, that its symbol is 'undecipherable and intentionally so', and has sometimes been called the 'signature of God'.[15]

The symbol is generally depicted thus: ♑ or similar, but the proper esoteric version is:

This glyph can cursorily be interpreted to be a combination of the glyph for Vulcan with the addition of the goat's tail. This indicates the deep relation between Taurus and Capricorn (both are Earth signs), and of the downward plunge of the spiritual into the material world, as well as the eventual ascent of the goat-man to the Fiery realms (ruled by Aries). The glyph depicts the nature of descent of cosmic Mind through the spiral of creation (symbolised by the ankh-tie, indicative of the function of Taurus) into the depth of matter. There is thus the descent of one spiral of activity *(manvantara)* to its lowest, most material level and then the climb up again to great spiritual heights. The ankh-tie also veils the sphere of the Monad, from which the descent into matter is instigated.

There is a reason why D.K. stated that:

> I must not attempt to interpret it for you, partly because it has never yet been correctly drawn and partly because its correct delineation and the ability of the initiate to depict it produces an inflow of force which would not be desirable, except after due preparation and understanding. It is far more potent than the pentagon and leaves the initiate "unprotected."[16]

This is because the glyph can be seen as a shorthand notation of the mode of projection of energies of a sorcerer. It was not advisable to present this image for the minds of esotericists in D.K.'s time because sufficient background knowledge was not then laid for disciples to obtain a proper understanding. The dark brotherhood

---

15 *Esoteric Astrology,* 155.

16 Ibid.

could use this symbol as an ancient paradigm to project images into a disciple's mind. This is still the case, however, nowadays the background knowledge is presented in my works and the pathway is now existent for disciples to be trained in how to resist psychic predation. Proper knowledge concerning the forces of evil and how they work *must* now be instated for disciples in the esoteric schools that will arise, to train them how to climb the new Initiation Tree. All disciples must pass the testing upon this path, by zapping away dark brotherhood predations (thus the disciple's own psychic *karma)* with streams of light, if they are to attain the second Initiation. No more should this Initiation be relegated to a later life to properly master. The epoch of Mind that confronts us during the forthcoming dispensation of the Mother of the World demands such training.

The tail of the goat can be interpreted to indicate the rise of *kuṇḍalinī* energy, the unfoldment of the serpent of time. The V shape also has a similarity to the symbol for Aries (the horns of the ram or goat). All of these factors unite the three horned signs of the zodiac in one glyph. These three signs have an interesting relationship.

1. **Aries** – related to the first aspect of Deity: the Father, Shambhala, Will, the primal creative urge, the Will to manifest that emanates from the higher mental plane. The downturned horns of the ram signify the projection downwards of divine energies.
2. **Taurus** – related to the second aspect of Deity, the Son (Love-Wisdom), Hierarchy, the 'homestead' of the desire-propensity that builds the thought constructs within the created form impelled by Aries. Taurus therefore governs the evolution of consciousness from the astral light. The Soul thereby emerges from the realms of form by manifesting the salvaging light that awakens the All-seeing Eye.
3. **Capricorn** – related to the third aspect of Deity, the Mother, human activity in the material domains. Capricorn signifies eventual resolution of and liberation from the form nature, through climbing the mountainous heights of consciousness to the high peaks of attainment.

Makara, the fifth Creative Hierarchy, embody the energies of this sign, for they are the angelic Kingdom existing on the mental plane that are the builders of the dense form. (The symbolic bony structure of the world.) Note that the physical plane is a direct reflection of the mental. This Hierarchy are the Agnishvattas that are the divine mediators that project into the realms of form the energies from the other Creative Hierarchies, thereby causing the concretisation of substance and the manifestation of the material world. The entire field of activity and interplay in the three worlds of human expression (the dominion of *karma)* thereby comes into expression. This action is paralleled in humanity by the activity of the spinal column and the threefold cord that resides within it.

Venus (governing the fifth Ray that rules the mind/Mind) rules Capricorn Hierarchically, for this form-building activity must be accomplished through scientific methodology, with mathematical exactitude, and with Love.

When the higher and lower mental planes are eventually interrelated by the *antaḥkaraṇa,* and the powers of the Soul are fully developed and dominating, then one consciously enters into a relationship with the fifth Creative Hierarchy. (They wield the energies and laws of the mental plane, which empower the kingdom of Souls. The Causal forms of this kingdom they also embody, for this Hierarchy is dual.) When one stands on the mountaintop, upon the higher mental plane, and enters the open door into Hierarchical activity, then the power of Saturn is weakened. The person then comes under the domination of Venus, the fifth Ray of the scientific mode, of beauty, ordered purpose, and divine revelation. The powers of the Mind are awakened, with which one can control one's own destiny, for a working relationship with the fifth Creative Hierarchy that rules *karma* in the three worlds is now possible.

The principle of mind/Mind is innate within the sum of the field of evolution in the material world. It is what was developed in the former solar system. Through gaining complete dominance over the substance of that evolution, one then works directly with the fifth Creative Hierarchy – for they embody the substance of the past that has been moulded into the present. They are a sister Hierarchy to humanity, who are masculinely polarised in relation to them. The mental principle is the key linking the two Hierarchies. As Capricorn embodies activities upon the mental plane and their externalisation upon the dense material world, therefore Venus must rule Capricorn Hierarchically. The dense material world is an expression of what transpires on the mental plane; the *karma* (Saturn) that regulates the activity of that world exoterically and esoterically is the effect, or externalisation, of the group-minds of the thinkers of the world. The Lords of Life that have created the phenomenal conditions that we all reside in work with this *karma* via their control of the sum of the substance of the mental plane.

The Initiation process is concerned with the ability to control and direct *karma* so that it will cleanse the matter that is qualified by the vibratory emanations (the residue) of the past solar system. This residue concerns the matter of the three planes of human livingness: the dense physical, astral and mental planes. These planes correspond to the dense, liquid and gaseous sheaths of the dense form of the planetary Logos. (They are not, however, considered to be principles by that Deity). A major objective of the work of the Initiate and the evolutionary process thus concerns the etherealisation of this substance so that it no longer offers resistance to the divine energies. The impact of the various Rays of Light upon dense substance (enlightenment) produces the etherealisation via the appropriate transforming agents (humanity). In this idea lies hid the esoteric interpretation of such phrases given by Jesus, as 'I am the light of the world'.[17]

The entire process of evolution can be spoken of in terms of the manifestation of the different degrees of Light, or in terms of the various signs of the zodiac.[18] The mystery of the relationship between the fourth and fifth Creative Hierarchies (humanity and Makara, ruled by Scorpio and Capricorn) is of significance here. They represent the doorway between the realms of Light and those of darkness – between the mountain (the abode of the planetary entities ruled by Makara) and the Sun (the doorway to the abode of the Gods, ruled by human meditative activity). The entire story of divine alchemy is hid in this relationship, as well as the esoteric history of all religious texts.

Divine alchemy and transmutation upon a massive scale is the method of the manifestation of Light in the empirical domain. This concerns an immense period of time, incorporating the collective undertaking of countless self-conscious beings. The mountaintop in Capricorn is the mountain load of *karma* that the Initiate must overcome and transmute by the wise use of the mind, wedded to the principle of will *(ātma)* and the intuition (*buddhi),* then regulated by the Heart centre so that brilliant Light manifests as a result.

The history of the symbolism of Capricorn is interesting. It was originally symbolised by the *goat-fish, Makara*. This is reminiscent of the time when there were only ten signs to the zodiac, when the qualities of Pisces-Aquarius and Capricorn were united in the one sign. The symbol of the *crocodile* (Sebec of the Egyptians) has a similar meaning to that of Makara in that it is a greedy, determined, voracious and sometimes vicious animal that is able to take refuge both in the Waters (of sensation) and on the Earth. Eventually the goat can free itself from its Watery counterpart and so began to seek sustenance in the most rocky, barren and

17 *John 8:12*.

18 See here *Esoteric Astrology,* 328-31.

inhospitable terrain. It is able to eat almost anything (symbolic of the thought-form making activities of the mind) and thereby its evolving ambition, strength and struggle to aspire upwards will inevitably produce the mountaintop experience.

The ten-signed zodiac was dominant when the *deva* kingdom was prevalent in creating the material world, wherein animal life, then human, could take form and evolve. Once human consciousness was developed, then the two missing signs of the zodiac were added, to accommodate the elements of consciousness that were evolved. Thus the twelve-signed zodiac, which presently rules us, came into effect. In the future, when consciousness begins to totally master the formed realms, then attachment to those realms disappears and another ten-signed zodiac will manifest. Virgo (the material domain) will then merge with Libra, governing the manifestation of *karma* and the cycles of Life. Pisces will also merge with Aries. (The beginning and ending of cycles then become merged in consciousness into the experience of timelessness.)

Rocks are the symbol of the cleavages, fractures, friction and hardness of the material world (where the mental plane is the cosmic dense physical plane). Over this the goat can travel with sure-footedness and determination. He can progress to higher, dizzier heights than any of his competitors. From pinnacle to pinnacle he can jump and finally, when reaching the top, he is effectively transfigured into the unicorn. This stately and courageous animal is sometimes represented with wings (of the Soul), with which it can fly to wherever it wills. Its one horn (the symbol of the third Eye), straight and spear-like (the *antaḥkaraṇa),* allows it to pierce and conquer the various 'beasts' and illusions of the world. As depicted by an old English folk myth, the lion, the king of beasts, is inevitably killed by him. In medieval times the unicorn has been likened to the Christ who 'raised up a horn of salvation' for mankind. This horn was reputed to have wondrous properties, including the ability to cure the various sickness and poisons that beset humanity. Note the relation of this to the cornucopia: the horn of plenty (which is a goat's horn), an attribute of the Greek god Pan, the lord of Nature. There are also a few scanty references to the unicorn in the Bible, such as in *Psalm 92:10.*[19]

### *Summary:*

- *Keynote:* Capricorn consummates the work of Scorpio.
- *Capricorn* rules the Knees, Bony Structure and Spinal Column of the Grand Heavenly Man.

---

19 'But my horn shalt thou exalt like *the horn* of a unicorn: shall be anointed with fresh oil.'

- The *exoteric and esoteric ruler* is Saturn, Ray three of Mathematically Exact Activity.
- The *Hierarchical ruler* is Venus, Ray five of the Scientific Mode.
- The *Element* is Earth (as also Taurus and Virgo).
- The *polar opposite* is Cancer.
- *Cross:* cardinal.
- Mars is exalted in Capricorn, the power of the Moon is lessened and Jupiter and Neptune both fall.
- The *Decanates* given for Capricorn are *exoterically:* Jupiter, Mars, and the Sun. *Esoterically:* Saturn, Venus, and the Sun (veiling a hidden planet).

The keywords given by D.K. for this sign are:

> In the material domain: 'And the Word said: Let ambition rule and let the door stand wide'.
>
> Upon the path: 'Lost am I in light supernal, yet on that light I turn my back'.

D.K. continues: 'For him there remain now no goal but service. He therefore passes back through the gate of Cancer, but with his consciousness held steadily in the sign Aquarius. From being the world Initiate in Capricorn he becomes an incarnated world server in Aquarius, and later a world saviour in Pisces.'[20]

## Aquarius the water bearer

Aquarius governs the general appearance of a person (of the Grand Heavenly Man). It is the sign of the man who bears a pitcher of water, symbolising the totality of human energies and capabilities when integrated and aligned. This is after having gained the visions and awareness that the mountain top experience affords. It expresses all human capabilities, latent or real and objectivised.

As is well known, this sign is now on the ascendant, and its energies are beginning to influence humanity. Its influence is presently subjectively pervasive, but only beginning to manifest the awakening of a broadminded universality of thought. This progress is being heartily countered by the dark brotherhood, who wish to continue imposing the worst of the Piscean epoch upon humanity. The Water Bearer is the bringer of Life, quenching the thirst for knowledge, wisdom, Love, the Divine or transcendental (or else of sensuality, materiality and the

20 *Esoteric Astrology,* 174.

transitory). The symbol of this sign is dual, denoting the mutual embrace of two parallel streams of energy:

← Soul - (Anima mundi or world Soul)

← Matter - (Corporeality, personal forces)

**Figure 14. The Aquarius glyph**

The upper band represents the higher Self, the Soul that is the source of inspiration, high ideals and creative aspirations. It is the storehouse of all knowledge gathered through many aeons of evolutionary growth and experience. When viewed in its universal aspect, the upper line symbolises the Purusha of the Hindu philosophy, the Heavenly Man that far outlasts the birth and death of the solar system, which is His physical Incarnation. This band also symbolises the *anima mundi,* the world Soul of the Greeks, and Alaya Avalokiteśvara of the Mahāyāna Buddhists. He is the Lord, who with immense compassion looks down upon the manifested realms and has vowed to never rest until all sentient beings have been saved from suffering. They will have thus obtained enlightenment: 'gone to the other shore' of *saṃsāra.*

These higher aesthetic qualities are embraced or paralleled by those of the sensual, corporeal material world (symbolised by the lower zigzag line). There is a vibratory mutual interplay, a balance of forces between Soul and matter that has the ability to evoke the highest in us: the most visionary, constructive, artistic or creative amplitude that one is capable of. Otherwise, one will be fully involved in the vicissitudes of the *māyā,* the phenomenal world. In both cases the personality will however be responsive to the Aquarian influences through participation in group activities, for the wavy lines indicate an openness to the polarised influences from all that embrace him/her. On a higher cycle, the two wavy lines symbolise the relation between spirit and matter.

The symbol indicates that Aquarius is a fluid sign, one of constant movement, periodic cyclic activities and recurrent mutations. (Aquarius is the sign where the various cycles of Life are consequently acknowledged and worked with.) This is seen nowadays in humanity's intensely active and sometimes chaotic mass transportation systems, communications, and rapid efflux and interchange of ideas.

Undeveloped Aquarians will be swayed by the glamour, emotions, idle chatter and opinions of their particular social group; they will tend to be selfish, serving only themselves, where their water pot is full of self-esteem. Their thoughts will often be airy, wandering this way and that, sometimes superficially brilliant and intuitive, but rarely prolonged or practical and well conceived. They are dilettantes and fond of the various aspects of human society that are glamorous and offer scope to display their wares. These wares: emotional, intellectual, monetary wealth, and goods are brought forth for all to see, but there is rarely anything of real value backing up the showy exterior. Much of the average Aquarian's life is a wavering motion between two extremes: of what they wish or imagine idealistically and the reality of their superficiality.

The superficiality, selfish attitudes and the various facades of appearance crystallise into stern and unapproachable selfishness, rock hard attitudes, and oft deep-seated cruelty, by the time the unevolved person reaches Capricorn. (The next sign on the reversed wheel.)

Disciples in Aquarius, on the other hand, have effectively put all of their spiritual and intellectual goods into their water pots. The activities of their entire lives are stored there and offered up for service to humanity. They give this freely to the needy, distressed and the sick and ask for nothing in return. They are truly universal in their embrace, are sensitive to the needs of the group that they serve with all their hearts. Superficiality has transformed into deep-seated realisation and intention. Selfishness has become selflessness, and personal service has become selfless service to all beings. Their hands, minds and Hearts are open and outstretched to those served; their good thoughts and energies are universally propagated thereby through the 'wind' of discursive speech.

Aquarius is the polar opposite of Leo. The intensely self-aware self-consciousness of the Leo subject is translated in Aquarius into the awareness of the group. Here group-consciousness and service to the group emerge to the fore in the life of the disciple, who endeavours to express this relationship in all activities.

The Element attributed to this sign is Air, corresponding to *buddhi*, the plane of liberation. To be emphasised is that humanity's impending spiritual, or subjective conquest and receptivity to impressions from the *buddhic* plane (allowing them to be 'born anew' to the 'measure of the stature of the fullness of Christ'[21]), are symbolised by humanity's relatively recent conquest of the air by means of the aeroplane.

Indications are evident of a forthcoming mass human awakening, producing the attainment of the first Initiation by humanity that will inevitably break

21 *Eph. 4:13.*

the veils between physical and etheric (Airy) vision. (Especially amongst the alternative lifestyle and subculture groups, those who oppose the mainstream media indoctrination, as well as in the more radical members of the scientific community eulogising such things as 'the new physics'.) The webs between the three dense physical sub-planes and the fourth ether will inevitably be ruptured via the new visioning.

Humanity has even developed a timetable of space exploration, and has sent probes to Venus, Mars and the outer planets. This activity is an outer manifestation of the *buddhic* consciousness (interplanetary awareness in a subjective or directly perceptive sense) that the enlightened Seer has evolved. Considerably later, a touch of cosmic Consciousness will be obtained by the world disciple, all signified by the implications of the first steps towards space exploration. In the future, however, this fervent race to space by means of prohibitively costly physical plane instruments and rockets will be superseded by the direct use of the enlightened Mind. The power inherent within the Mind and the human psyche, as rightly directed by the trained Seer using group energies and working out the divine Plan, will allow travel in space by means of the speed of thought.

Humanity's landing on the moon symbolises the awakened energies of the personality – fully integrated and controlled, reaching out into the higher dimensions of space. Reaching to the moon and beyond implicates the achievements to be obtained in consciousness by the world disciple in the Aquarian age. Up to the last century, humanity has been busy conquering the seas and exploring the continents of the earth. This activity symbolises the progress towards controlling the energies of the Watery (astral) and physical sheaths of the personality, which were the development of human consciousness in the Piscean era (a Water sign).

A clue to help in the understanding of Aquarius is via the preceding sign, Pisces the fishes. In Pisces, the symbol of the two fishes denote limitation, Soul and personality are yoked by a common bond and immersed in the waters of sensation. Freedom, on the other hand, is the keynote of the Aquarian disposition. The bond is separated, though interrelated and recognised so by the spiritual person. Therefore, in Aquarius there will be a widespread rebellion against the old Piscean authoritarian, socio-political and religious systems. Many of these bonds tied people to regimented and concise ideas concerning family and cultural ties. Victorian ethics, race customs, etc., will be broken by a new permissiveness, a new exploration of human livingness. (Even beyond the confines of our earth sphere.) There will be an amazingly rapid expansion of consciousness, eventually producing a revelatory understanding of the nature of the cosmos and of the Life in it.

In Aquarius, the Solar Angel can fully embrace the material world, fecundating it with the seeds of the divine, the aesthetic. The lotus bud (the vibrant Womb of enlightenment-consciousness, out of which the foetal Christ will be born) shall be nourished. Aquarius is said to 'release Virgo from her load'.

When humanity as a whole develop the needed sensitivity and warm-hearted conscious responsiveness to the force of Love and universal enlightenment (as indicated by this sign) of which the Christ is the custodian, then He will reappear among us. He indicated the eventuation of this when he told His disciples to go out in the street where they would meet a man bearing a pitcher of water (the symbol of Aquarius), and there they will partake in the last supper, the Passover, in the upper room of his house.[22] The 'Body and Blood' of the Christ would then be symbolically consumed.

Aquarius governs the blood system and its circulation. It distributes the Waters of Life, the energy of *buddhi* (the Blood of the Christ) to all of the various cells in the Body of the planetary Logos. Their health is thus sustained and the elimination of toxic substances is aided.

Aquarius also rules the lowest of the Creative Hierarchies, the twelfth. This Creative Hierarchy are established upon the etheric domain, and via them the dense physical world manifests. They govern the substance of the physical plane that reflects the attributes of all the other planes of perception. This is the first link in the food chain that sustains the Lives of the higher kingdoms. Esoterically, blood is *prāṇa,* and the etheric substratum of the physical plane is what transmits solar *prāṇa* to all Lives incarnate in dense forms within the solar system. This twelfth Hierarchy are consequently called the 'Baskets of Nourishment'. The general appearance of a human form is thus the consequence of the amalgamation of various units of this Hierarchy. The Christ principle must manifest through such a form if it is to effectively liberate the imprisoned beings on the earth. The major work of the Aquarian (the world server) is therefore concerned with such an act of sacrifice and salvage.

That which nourishes must be utilised with radiant Light, so that the embodied form can be etherealised. The 'prisoners of the planet' (all Life forms) must be liberated if the earth is to become truly sacred. This is a long term goal of the Aquarian dispensation. It will allow the planetary Christ to awaken, with millions possessing the ability to command *devas* to convert the 'loaves and fishes', as Jesus did to feed the multitudes with revelations of great glory and of Life eternal.

---

22 *Luke 22:10.*

The importance in the relationship between Leo (the Heart) and Aquarius (the Blood stream) cannot be overemphasised, for together they embody the vertical life of the disciple upon the fixed cross of the heavens. Here also is seen the relationship between Soul and form, and between the first and seventh (incarnate) Creative Hierarchies in the cosmic physical plane. Leo is the Heart that pumps Life into the various cells (or atoms of substance) throughout the Logoic Body according to the rhythm of their cyclic activity. This brings into focus the functioning activity of the energies of Uranus (Ray seven), the exoteric ruler of Aquarius, which naturally governs the movement of the Blood flow. Uranus interrelates the first and seventh planes of perception and all the associated conditionings, allowing the Blinded Lives (or elemental substance of the seventh Creative Hierarchy) to be manipulated by the will of the thinker.[23]

Regarding Leo, Uranus is said to be its esoteric ruler (though veiled by the Sun), allowing the energies of the central Spiritual Sun to manipulate the form nature of the Soul. (The 'elemental substance' in the realm of enlightened Being.) This is the cause for the Heartbeat of all manifested Life.

The rulers of Aquarius are of significance. They are:

- Uranus, the seventh Ray, the *exoteric* ruler.
- Jupiter, the second Ray, the *esoteric* ruler.
- The Moon, the fourth Ray, the *Hierarchical* ruler.

Together they produce the conditionings whereby the form nature can manifest, to be vivified and generally stimulated throughout its long evolutionary journey. Uranus incorporates a ceremonial or ritualised activity to relate the highest to the lowest, prompting the evolutionary urge according to the vicissitudes of the law of cycles. Jupiter encourages the evolution of consciousness (Love-Wisdom), whilst the Moon (also ruling the lowest Creative Hierarchy) constitutes the basic substance through which, and with which, evolution must be accomplished.

The objective of this twelfth Creative Hierarchy is to manifest those conditions that will allow instinct to eventually be transformed into intellect. Jupiter then produces the fusion and blending that relates the various forms together. This produces conditions that will eventually allow the Soul to be born and so to

---

23 There are a number of ways of counting the Creative Hierarchies. In this case, only the seven that are incarnated into the cosmic dense physical plane are counted. Hence (when including the five liberated Creative Hierarchies) the seventh Creative Hierarchy are also the abovementioned twelfth Creative Hierarchy, and the Blinded Lives are another name for the Baskets of Nourishment.

manifest through a physical vehicle. Uranus can then take control, bringing into relation the great pairs of opposites. It is the transforming agent in Nature, allowing the unfoldment and expression of the intellect and its later translation into the intuition. Jupiter and Uranus will then have worked together to produce a beneficent organisation of the totality of the energies found in the person's equipment. This allows freedom from the limitations of the form, to which the person has for so long been bound. Esoterically, one's atomic substance becomes radioactive upon the approach of enlightenment.

This activity between Uranus and Jupiter consequently occurs at a particularly late period of evolution. (In the latter stages of the Initiation process.) This leads to the influence of the Moon that in this case veils the activities of the fourth Creative Hierarchy (also ruled by the fourth Ray). Therein the Initiated disciple becomes a fully conscious member. He/she is thereby able to relate the energies of the fourth to the seventh Creative Hierarchies, and thus play a part in regulating the laws of the world and its gifts to the various kingdoms of Nature (via the bloodstream). Thus a world server comes into existence.

Generally speaking, the disciple influenced by Uranus in Aquarius is primarily concerned with the establishing of the Kingdom of 'God' on the physical plane, by advocating brotherly love, natural harmonious living styles, and receptivity to the laws of Nature. Uranus stimulates the organisational trend in humanity towards amalgamation and the formation of communal units. Much of humanity's activities in the future will be organised towards a more receptive approach to the world's needs to produce cooperativeness between its various groupings.

The influence of Uranus will also produce changes in the earth's topological sphere (heralding the cataclysms to come) and will engender the discovery and understanding of the four ethers, the vehicle of *prāṇa*. This will involve many radical changes in human understanding of the nature of Life, especially in relation to medicine. That there is a life after death will be a demonstrable fact, for many will then see this clearly (or rather vision) by means of the subtle etheric body and the forms of *devas* that reside in it, as well as the vital body of the departing person.

Particularly the violet *devas* of the shadows[24] and those of healing (the transmitters of *prāṇa* to all forms) will be noted. Humanity will eventually enter into a new relationship with that angelic order. (As, for instance, was earlier demonstrated by the Findhorn community in Scotland.) The influence of Jupiter, the esoteric ruler of Aquarius, is also prevalent here. It helps Uranus in its task

24 They are the *devas* embodying etheric substance.

of amalgamating people into various (New Age) groups, giving them a sense of world goodwill and brotherly love, and thus a tendency to fusion, which nothing can arrest.

Uranus also governs the etheric body, hence the activities of the occultist, alchemist and *yogin*. Through ritualised endeavour, they can directly work with this seventh Ray energy and consciously utilise all energies manifesting through the etheric body.

The effect of Uranus in the Aquarian age will produce a revolutionary change in the mode of scientific investigation. The way of thinking of the esotericist will be increasingly taught and practiced in our universities, partly replacing (and complementing) the techniques associated with scientific materialism. Experimentation to ascertain the nature of phenomena and the laws of Life, based on the use of the critical assumptions of the analytical mind and utilising incredibly expensive instruments, will gradually become superseded by the powers of the meditative Mind. (That produces transcendental awareness.) This will allow direct perceptive insights into the nature of things. Proper comprehension of the laws that govern the manifestation of phenomena will then no longer be obscured by the parameters set by the concrete minds of our scientists and philosophers. (Though they have given us much knowledge thereby to be thankful of.) The age of scientific materialism and related 'technological miracles' of the mind will (and must) pass. Then will come an era whereby 'miracles' engendered by active Love-Wisdom and the Will (of subjective visioning and 'gifts of healing') will become prevalent. The power of applied ritualised loving thought and its ability to seemingly transcend the bounds of physical plane laws will be aptly demonstrated and explained.

Such power will fall into the hands of the world's disciples working in interrelated groups for the common good of all on earth. They will thus take power from the hands of the oligarchy of entrenched evil that dominate our present civilisation. Such evil is embodied by those that are the most ruthless in their drive for materialistic power, using all means: monetary, psychological, psychic or political, to impose their will and types of attitudes upon all. They can be found in all walks of life that offer scope for such activity, from the financier, politician, lawyer, businessman and soldier, to the more accepted evil types, such as the Mafia boss. The dark ones generally work behind the scenes, behind the glare of public life, for too much publicity greatly hampers their freedom of activity and increases the prospects of accountability. They feed off the fostered greed, or projected need, for such things as unnecessary consumer items, pleasure palaces of all types, ever 'more wondrous' scientific marvels, gadgets and the related war-machines of every nation. All of which are a direct product of scientific materialism.

***Summary:***

- *Keynote:* Aquarius releases Virgo from her load.
- Aquarius governs the *Bloodstream and the general appearance* of the Grand Heavenly Man.
- The *exoteric ruler* is Uranus, Ray seven of Ceremonial Magic.
- The *esoteric ruler* is Jupiter, Ray two of Love-Wisdom.
- The *Hierarchical Ruler* is the Moon, Ray four of Beautifying Harmony overcoming Conflict.
- The *Element* is Air (as also for Gemini and Libra).
- The *polar opposite* is Leo.
- *Cross:* fixed.
- No planet is exalted and no planet falls, the power of the Sun, however, is lessened.
- The *Decanates* given for Aquarius are *exoterically:* Venus, Mercury and the Moon. *Esoterically:* Saturn, Mercury and Venus.

The *keywords* D.K. gives for Aquarius are:

> In the material domain: 'And the Word said, Let desire in form be the ruler.'
> On the path of active return: 'Water of life am I, poured forth for thirsty men.'

## Pisces the fishes

*Pisces the fishes* rules the Feet, and thus the ability of the Grand Heavenly Man to progress in time and space, to undertake His cosmic journey through the universe. The feet are directed by the eyes, hence of the entire cognitive faculties of the person. This implies the ability to think of where to go and what to do in the journey, which concerns the ability to think out to conclusion one's entire path or progress in life from beginning to end. Here the entire Thought-Form making ability in the cosmological process comes to view, and the circumscription and projection of that Idea throughout the Logoic Body of Manifestation.

Pisces is the last sign of the zodiac and is therefore the sign of conclusion of the entire gamut of the evolutionary process. It thus incorporates the deep sleep or *pralaya* state before the commencement of a new cycle of evolution. The first (highest) Creative Hierarchy directs the entire *manvantara* of being from out of *pralaya,* hence takes on the attributes of the Piscean function.

As previously stated, Pisces is the sign of sacrifice and death, not specifically of the personality nature, but rather that of the Soul, and of its entire evolution. This process can be viewed from two angles.

At first the Soul detaches itself from identification with the Spirit (Monad) and descends into the ocean of sensation: form and matter. It becomes bonded or yoked to the life of the personality by means of the *sūtrātma* and undergoes what mutable incarnation has to offer. The personality thereby comes under the beneficence of the planetary Christ, for Love-Wisdom is what must be evolved. Jupiter, governing the second Ray, is thus the exoteric ruler of this sign.

As Pisces is the first sign on the reversed wheel after Aries, so here the personality undergoes the beginning stages of its evolution and thus will be in its most unevolved, negative and fluidly psychically sensitive state. At this stage, instinctive receptivity to the mass emotive life and its psychic currents and attitudes will abound. The mind is dormant, and the germ of the Christ-consciousness is unawakened and hidden deep within the activity of this psychic receptivity. The Soul is bonded to the form and held captive to the experiences and sensations accrued by the person in the ocean of antagonistic, as well as beneficent forces, in *saṃsāra.* Deep within the turbulence of the ocean of these forces, the fish, the Christ nature, swims.

Mediumship, personality inhibition and receptivity to (massed) emotional agitations and moods, are some of the major qualities of the unevolved personality in Pisces. The influence of Jupiter, however, ever pulls one towards one's evolutionary goal by bringing the Soul and form together in a functioning relationship. The symbol of this sign indicates this:

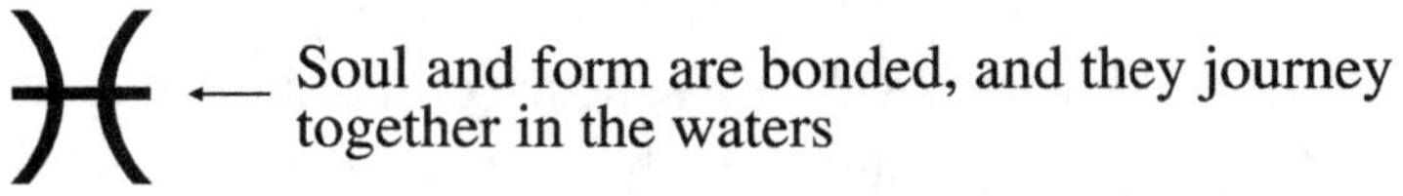

Soul and form are bonded, and they journey together in the waters


**Figure 15. The Pisces glyph**

Jupiter always brings the Soul into new and fresh relationships with all aspects of the form, from which the Soul-personality can gain the needed qualities. Cataclysms, civilisations and many cycles of racial evolution come and go, yet this bond always exists. The objective of the experiences in this sign under the general stimulus of its exoteric ruler will therefore allow the imprisoned Soul and the personality to enter upon that process which will transmute:

1. The lower nature into the higher manifestation.
2. The lower psychical powers into the higher spiritual faculties, i.e.
    a. Negativity into positive soul control.
    b. Mediumship into mediatorship.
    c. Clairvoyance into spiritual perception.
    d. Clairaudience into mental telepathy and finally inspiration.
    e. Instinct into intellect.
    f. Selfishness into divine selflessness.
    g. Acquisitiveness into renunciation.
    h. Self-preservation into selfless world service.
    i. Self pity into compassion, sympathy and divine understanding.
3. Spiritual and mental inhibition into Soul expression and mental sensitivity.
4. Devotion to the needs of the self into developed devotion and response to the needs of humanity.
5. Attachment to environment and to personality conditions (identification with form) into detachment from form and ability to identify with the Soul.[25]

The second mode of sacrifice by the Soul is seen due to attaining the above conversions. The Soul can then detach itself from the personality and re-identify with the Monad, the Life aspect, producing the final death of the Causal form at the fourth Initiation. The bond now becomes the higher one of the developed *antaḥkaraṇa* between Spirit and form, and is composed of living conscious Light. All lesser attachments and unions have been severed. Such action is produced through the agency of Pluto, the esoteric and Hierarchical ruler of Pisces.

Pluto, the regent of death, is the Lord of the underworld. He rules the first Ray of Will or Power that produces the various detachments, renunciations and deaths throughout the lives of the personality. Pluto produces the death of all attachments associated with desire, and the material possessions that the personality finds so hard to let go. Similarly for the detachments that disciples must undertake upon the road of compassionate service and renunciation, that inevitably result in the death of the Soul form. This final death allows the Soul to focus its attention on its 'Father in Heaven', and so to manifest the Will of 'God' on a planetary scale.

25 *Esoteric Astrology,* 123-4.

Very few Initiates, however, terminate their cycles of experience in Pisces to become Shambhalic recipients, to which Pluto is the open door. Most consummate their work in the sign Aquarius, after being servers of the world. They then enter into a *nirvāṇa* or *pralaya* within the earth Scheme and find their mode of approach on other world systems, or out of the solar system upon one of the cosmic Paths. Those who remain in the sign Pisces have chosen the path of earth Service[26] and remain with the Planetary Hierarchy. They become Avatars that sacrifice themselves so that all kingdoms of Nature can benefit. They wield the magnetic potency of the first Ray coupled with the second, that allows them to draw all men up to the Throne of 'God'. Their effect is all pervasive, amalgamative and transmutative, which destroys the aspects of the form that prevent the hidden Life from being released. The energy of Pluto always brings this about. Thus is born a world Saviour. This process is regulated by Law, and by the activity of the World-Soul (the Christ aspect) as it travels through the zodiac.

The history of the Bible can be analysed in this light, showing the evolution of the Christ-Light through the various signs. For instance, from when it hovered above a 'burning bush' in front of Moses, until the time it was personified in the body of Jesus as the 'Word made flesh'. This Word is the Christ who became the world Saviour and took the Rod of office of the Bodhisattva governing Hierarchy at the beginning of the Piscean era.

One could write a treatise to explain the significance of the signs of the zodiac as they appear in the context of ancient Jewish history. There is, for instance, the obvious reference to the sign Gemini in the pillars of Solomon's temple, named Jachin and Boaz.[27]

The sign of Taurus the bull appears in *Exodus* chapter 32 when the Israelites in the desert built a golden calf and worshipped it. Moses appeared at the time when the sun was transiting into the sign Aries the ram. The sin of the Israelites (the worship of the golden calf) referred to the recourse of the religion of the time of Taurus the bull, which was to be superseded by the new Covenant given by 'the Lord' to Moses. They contravened this Covenant, thus evoking the wrath of 'the Lord' that manifested upon those dancing in front of the calf when Moses came

---

26 See *A Treatise on Cosmic Fire* and *Rays and Initiations* by Alice Bailey for a detailed account of the cosmic Paths undertaken by Initiates (of the sixth degree) when they are ready to leave the earth altogether as *nirvāṇees,* no longer finding a field of service on earth.

27 *II Chronicles 3:17.*

down from mount Sinai. Those that were destroyed were the die-hard adherents of the old worship of the bull (or the Cow-Goddess).[28] This was the predominant religious dispensation of the theisms of the world at the time when the sun was astronomically in the sign Taurus the bull.[29] The Israelites forgot, or had at that time not fully realised, the import of the new Mosaic teachings that manifested when the sun was in Aries the ram.

The symbol of the ram or scapegoat underlies the entire Jewish religion, and the Martian aspect of strife and conflict has ever followed the Jewish people. Some of the keynotes of the Arian individual are characteristics of the Jewish people. (Being headstrong, impulsive, fixed in determination, inventive and taking the initiative.) There is also the picture of the 'wandering Jew' journeying over the face of the earth always looking for pasture, the Promised Land. The ram was the principal offering that Aaron was told to sacrifice to the tabernacle of God.[30]

Jesus, as the Jewish Messiah, came at the beginning of the next age (Pisces the fishes) to reform their religion, thus bring an end to the Jewish Arian dispensation. They have rejected this, thus are effectively still in the age of Aries. This is the principal reason why they have suffered conflict and strife (via the activities of Mars, the orthodox ruler of Aries) ever since. Though Jesus failed in this objective, he did however impulse the Piscean era, and has taken the attributes of a World Saviour, the symbolism of which abounds in the New Testament in such phrases as:

> I am come a light into the world, that whosoever believeth on me should not abide in darkness. And if any man hear my words, and believe not, I judge him not: for I came not to judge the world, but to save the world.[31]

The theme of the Christ as the means to salvation is common to all Christian doctrines. That He was the dispenser of Piscean energies is seen in the constant recurrence of the symbology of the fish in the New Testament. For example, when

---

28 One can also look to the recourse to sex magic centred around the desire principle associated with Taurus the bull, as hinted at in the statement: 'And when Moses saw that the people were naked' *(Exodus, 32:25).*

29 Some of these are Hathor and the Bull Apis in Egypt, the Minotaur in Crete, and the sacred cow in India. The later Mithraic cult in the Roman Empire transplanted from Persia, which sacrificed the bull, signified the transition from the age of Taurus, amongst other things.

30 *Exodus 29:15.*

31 See *John 12: 46-47.*

Jesus called Simon and Andrew, who were fishermen, to: 'come ye after me and I will make you to become fishers of men'.[32] Note also the feeding of the 5,000 with fish and bread. The sign of the fish was even the principal symbol that the early Christians identified themselves with, adapted from the Greek of the first two letters of the name Jesus Christ, I, X, i.e., ><>. Later Christianity contains many examples of the continuance of this symbol, such as the bishop's mitre, the custom of eating fish on Friday, the day dedicated to Venus (the planet exalted in Pisces) and the Piscina or receptacle of holy water.

The fact that Jesus came not to 'send peace on earth...but a sword'[33] implies the first Ray energy of Pluto, which governs this sign, and of its effects that the aspirant finds difficult to understand. The Christ's imminent reappearance in the Aquarian age as a world Server in which He would dispense the Waters of Life (effectively his compassionate Blood) was explained in the treatment of the sign Aquarius.

It should be obvious from the above that the period of Jewish history (as covered in Genesis, Exodus and later texts) is more ancient than is suspected by our Biblical historians and Archaeologists. This history was properly codified much later, when symbolism related to the then contemporary times was overlaid upon that more or less unwritten lore and sanctified myth that was passed on from one generation to the next. This was the onus of the priestly class (the Levites) to memorise. Thus we get the symbolism of the Arian age incorporated into the personages of the then contemporary rulers. The time of Isaac and Joseph, for instance, as the period for the genesis of the Israelites as a tribe, would herald from the time of Gemini the twins. Here, the 'twins' manifest in the form where the God of the Jewish nation represented the 'immortal brother', whilst the twelve tribes (or infant Hierarchy) represented the 'mortal brother'. The tribes therefore manifested in the form of a Heart centre (each tribe being ruled by one of the signs of the zodiac), which reflected the attributes of the Kingdom of 'God' (the Head centre).

The plagues, etc., that fell upon the hapless subjects of the Pharaoh and which finally convinced him to let the people of Israel go, as well as the parting of the Red Sea, refer to an aspect of first Initiation testings (here for the Egyptians and Israelites as a whole). This occurred with the cleansing of the hydra of material comforts (Taurus the bull) that was to be enacted upon those in Egypt. Under

---

32 *Mark 1:17.*

33 *Matt. 10:34.*

this symbolism there was also the forty years of wandering by the Israelites in the desert. In addition, the intricate temple symbolism associated with the arc of the covenant and the sacrificial ram given to Aaron and the priestly clan was distinctly under the auspices of Aries.

The red sea symbolises the *suṣumṇā* channel at an early stage of development (filled with the red-orange *kuṇḍalinī* energy). The pillar of fire that protected the Israelites from Pharaoh's hosts (the Taurian dispensation) represented the energies of the Head centre situated above the central spinal column. (The symbolism of Aries, for instance, is an expression of the Fiery Element of initial mental beginnings.) The mount of the Law (Mt. Sinai), from whence the Ten Commandments emanated, is a symbol of Capricorn, as well the Fiery Element, which was part of the Jewish dispensation to bring to the world.

The main energy of Pisces is that of the first Ray (Pluto), which must of necessity utilise the second Ray (Jupiter) as a vehicle in the realms of form. As indicated, this Ray combination has a profound effect upon the life of the aspirant, producing the lure that leads to the path to Initiation (as well as that of evolution itself). This is followed by the consequent transmutative process and 'eventual escape through death'. (To quote D.K.) The piercing and magnetic potency of this Ray combination liberates the evolving Life, abstracting it back to its originating Source. The combination also produces the psychic sensitivity and mediumistic capacities of the unevolved, for its penetrating and attractive qualities enable them to contact the emanations from the kingdoms of Nature (or entities from the emotive world around them) without being aware that such contact is happening. The effects of unconscious psychic receptivity to the subjective world within which they live often bewilder people.

Humanity's acute susceptibility to such impression is one of the major problems today, for it enables people to be sensitively influenced by mischievous disincarnate entities, thought-forms, and currents of feeling-perceptions of all types from the astral plane. They are also susceptible to planned streams of manipulative thought-forms and lying propaganda from news organisations, world leaders, and other sources that are now taken over by the dark brotherhood.

In reference to the *anima mundi* (world Soul) and the psychic emanations from the kingdoms of Nature, one can look to Neptune (taking the place of Jupiter) as the ruler of Pisces. Neptune is the God of the Waters and the Initiator for the first two Initiations. It gives Pisces the sixth Ray flavour that is so noticeable when speaking of this sign esoterically, and through which the first Ray can manipulate the movement of the Waters and the fishes therein. Jupiter affects the individual person. Neptune relates Pisces to the sign Cancer, and when the two are found together, it indicates mediumship in the life of the individual, or mediatorship in the life of the Initiate.

As well as the feet, Pisces is said to rule the liver and the lymphatic system. This system is one of the physical body's major mechanisms of protection against diseases and exemplifies the relationship of Pisces to the concept of an Avatar or world Saviour. The liver produces bile and plays an essential role in the metabolism of carbohydrates, proteins and fats, as well as helping to ward off antagonistic entities.

The Logoic significance of the Feet presents an idea as to the mode of manifestation of Logoic energies from the first Creative Hierarchy (ruled by Pisces) to the seventh, the Greater Builders (that are also ruled by Pisces, and Virgo). They are the seventh of the Hierarchies, and manifest upon the plane *Anupādaka.* Via them is built the sum of the cosmic dense physical plane. They direct the main energies and purpose governing the evolutionary progress of the seven incarnate Creative Hierarchies. Being the seventh, they signify the Feet of a Logoic Being, a Grand Heavenly Man. This Hierarchy commands the energies (Words of Power) that mould the cosmic dense physical plane (our mental plane) according to Logoic Purpose. The substance of this plane is that upon which Logoic Feet stand (from a Logoic perspective). For them the mental plane is the equivalent to what the dense physical plane is for humans. The concept of 'walking' here relates to the turning of the zodiacal wheel at various levels of such cycling. (Be they 25,000 year cycles, 250,000 year cycles, etc.) Each step, as governed by Pisces, signifies the accomplishment of another great Year of evolutionary journeying.

The feet enable one to travel where one wills in order to find and select right foods (energies needed for the maintenance of all bodily functions). They are also used to escape from the many types of dangers that lurk in the jungle or on the stony desert paths that one may have to travel upon. This role of Pisces, affecting the sum of the body of manifestation, is also characteristic of the work of the world Saviour when seen from the cosmic perspective. With the advent of every major cycle, a cosmic Avatar appears to impel the beginning of another step of the Logoic journeying in *manvantara.*

Pisces is said to 'take from all the signs', for the results of the experiences in those signs are needed before the final death of the Soul form can be eventuated.

This allows the mediator between 'the one and the other' to manifest. A world Saviour must have undergone every possible experience and test in all the signs in the realms of Being, and have surpassed them, before being able to salvage and save the related Lives.

***Summary:***

- *Keynote:* Pisces takes from all the signs.
- Pisces rules the *Feet, Liver,* and the *Lymphatic system* of the Grand Heavenly Man.
- The *exoteric ruler* is Jupiter, the second Ray of Love-Wisdom.
- The *esoteric* and *Hierarchical ruler* is Pluto, the first Ray of Will or Power.
- The *Element* is Water (as also Cancer and Scorpio.)
- The *polar opposite* is Virgo.
- *Cross:* mutable.
- The *Decanates* given for Pisces are *exoterically*: Saturn, Jupiter and Mars. *Esoterically:* Jupiter, Vulcan and Mars.
- Venus is exulted in Pisces and the power of Mars is lessened.

The *keywords* that D.K. gives for this sign are:

> In the world of form: *'And the Word said, go forth into matter'.*
> On the path of active return: *'I leave the Father's home and turning back, I save'.*

## Pisces and the *eighth sphere*

The substance of this solar system is the recycled energy (rejected substance) of the previous solar system. What is recycled comes from an *eighth sphere* zone from the past. Our Monads have incarnated into the rejected substance of the past solar system in order to redeem it, therefore to transform the solar *eighth sphere*. The Regents of sacred planets and the solar Logos do not have as part of their Minds the physical, astral and mental bio-spheres known to us on earth, hence no longer need to convert an *eighth sphere* zone. The Logoi of non-sacred planets, however, do have an *eighth sphere* zone to transform. The non-sacred planets are the Sun and Moon (veiling planets), Mars, Earth and Pluto.

Note that people must overcome their ideas concerning life, of thinking only in terms of terrestrial lives, as appearing on earth, but should also think in terms of astral and mental spheres of attainment. There is also a time sequence concerning the appearance and disappearance of terrestrial life upon planets not understood by our modern scientists.

The *eighth sphere* is a bounded zone of containment of conscious Lives, sentience and of substance, that have not passed the requirements of any former evolutionary cycle or present sub-cycle. They can be considered the failures of an evolutionary system (a *manvantara)* that need to be recycled in a later evolutionary space so as to be given another chance for progress. For our solar evolution such zones of containment contain what has not achieved the goal relating to the expression of the energy of Love. The sacred planets have achieved that goal; the non-sacred planets have not. They are therefore zones of transformation wherein the evolutionary battles proceed within multi-dimensional space.

The *eighth sphere* is relative. On our planet, we see the externalisation of the *eighth sphere* on the physical plane. Mars concerns the astral 'locality' and Pluto the mental 'locality'. Pollution, war, plagues, etc., are the externalisation of the *karma* of the effects of the desire-minds of humanity, and this manifests as a prison of sorts, the *eighth sphere.* Everything below the diaphragm relates to attributes of the *eighth sphere*, but the interrelation between the two Splenic centres signifies the *eighth sphere* zone. All *chakras* of the Inner Round, of which the Solar Plexus centre is the synthesising centre, process the *prāṇas* of this sphere.

Pisces is a sign of the cosmic Christ. It is also the sign of the dead Christ and His salvage from the realms of death. Pisces rules the opening and closing of the Door of the cosmic *eighth sphere,* but Aries manifests the Will that either directs the entities into their prison for the appointed cycle, or else opens the Door of release. It is the sign that prepares for the three Spiritual Festivals in Aries, Taurus and Gemini. Preceding these signs, Pisces therefore projects their way the types of energies that the Festivals will try to overcome or to capitalise upon through their ritualistic purpose.

The key mechanism of the Doors to the *eighth sphere* for us on earth is however determined by the interrelationship between Leo and Cancer. The Sun and Moon (being their planetary rulers) bring to the fore the relationships between the lunar and solar cycles upon the earth, specifically the earth-moon relationship to sun. As the lunar cycles come and go, so they rhythmically open and close the *eighth sphere* Doors. Much concerning the ancient happenings upon the moon Chain needs to be rectified this way. The two twins of Gemini are also related, for the Doorways are of an etheric construct.

The mystery of the Sphinx is intimately related to the mystery of the *eighth sphere.* Glamour, *māyā* and the planes of illusion (the physical, astral and mental) compose this sphere. The Sphinx is Leo-Virgo. They are part of what is veiled in the ten-sided zodiac of the past epoch.[34] The evolving form of the interrelationship of the sun and moon is the Mind of the Sphinx, and that interrelationship is carried on the back of Cancer. Wherever there are reject *prāṇas* of mental-emotional interrelationships, there is the *eighth sphere.*

Pisces is the sign of the World Saviour. The glyph (♓) is revealing. It is composed of two wheels, cups or cogs that also manifest as Doors, though the symbol should be turned around (when the cups are oriented in a north-south direction) to better depict Piscean purpose. The lower Door is oriented to systemic space and the higher Door is to the Monad and cosmic space. The glyph of Aquarius has a similar significance: one line signifies the cosmic ethers and the other signifies the terrestrial ethers. One Door of Pisces is also to the cosmic *eighth sphere;* the other is the world situation. The cosmic *eighth sphere* bears the rejected cosmic *prāṇas* from former evolutionary cycles of expression, hence the *karma* from the past. Each epoch of creativity, from the smallest to the greatest, must facilitate the salvage of past *karma* and its projection into the future. The world Saviour must thus work with the *eighth sphere* in His great creative sweep. Past *karma* is utilised to create the future.

The exoteric ruler of Pisces is Jupiter, thus signalling that Love is the force that permits all evolutionary development in this system. The esoteric ruler is Pluto, so indicating that the purpose of creation concerns the purification of evil, whether in terms of what is contained in the microcosmic or macrocosmic *eighth spheres.* The forces wielded by Pluto are major tools of the Manu's Department. The Lord of Life brings death thereby to all of the vicissitudes of the form.

This sign is a unique opportunity for the dark brotherhood. The release of entities from the *eighth sphere* for the rectification of *karma* provides the dark brotherhood the chance to bend *karma* to their own ends. These entities are to be educated and directed for evolutionary purposes. The energy released in Pisces usually takes nine months to gestate via Virgo (the polar opposite of Pisces), to be earthed in Capricorn (during the turning of the reversed wheel). This corresponds with the downpour of the energies of cosmic Mind, facilitated by Capricorn, in its most Earthy form. This also facilitates the purposes of the dark brotherhood.

Pisces is directly related to mediumship, which draws upon *eighth sphere* energies. Mediumistic qualities are heightened and massed autosuggestion is activated. All subconscious forces affecting large masses of humanity are under

34 There is a veiled relationship here between the numbers 5 and 6, between the pentagram and the hexagon, upon which the *maṇḍala* of the *nāḍī* system is built.

the influence of this sign (and by Cancer). In Cancer these tendencies are witnessed as crowd hysteria, mass psychosis, mass religious fervour etc. This energy quality manifests principally via the sixth and seventh Rays.

Pisces also works via a higher level of expression, in relation to the purposes of the Avatars. Avatars work through a direct application of the Will. Will is a potent quality to produce planetary change. The two fishes represent two present planetary Avatars. Here the greater Avatar can be seen via the sixth Ray (1/6 Ray purpose) of Master Jesus. The lesser Avatar is the New Mahāchohan (2/1 Ray purpose).[35] The band that connects them is the Mahāchohan ℛ (using 1/7 Ray purpose). The first Ray is here exemplified because what is implicated is the cosmic energy of the Will. To the 1/6 potency of Jesus must be added the direct second Ray potency of the cosmic Christ. The number 6 draws from the sixth cosmic astral sub-plane and the number 7 from the seventh cosmic astral sub-plane.

The 2/1 Ray of the new Mahāchohan also draws the Will of the Mind from the fifth cosmic astral sub-plane, but fuses this Mind with the second Ray purpose of Sanat Kumāra. The cosmic Christ embodies this second Ray Purpose, and draws His fundamental Impression from the fourth cosmic astral sub-plane. Christ-Jesus therefore embodies the potency of the fourth and sixth cosmic astral sub-planes via the Will, whilst the new Mahāchohan and the Mahāchohan ℛ draw upon the fifth and seventh cosmic astral sub-planes, modified by the energy of the Love of our Logos. These are the energies that will pour through at the ending of the Piscean epoch. They produce the stages of the Forerunner (the function of the New Mahāchohan) and the Reappearance of the Christ that will externalise the Hierarchy and so cause the appearance of the Aquarian epoch.

The potency of these Avatars will thus manifest in a way to try to offset the effects of the *eighth sphere* influences manifesting via Pisces, and of the way that the dark brotherhood can utilise them. The energies pouring through Pisces thus have great geopolitical and cosmological implications. This is especially seen in the present epoch at the ending of this age, where the Capricornian influx of dark brotherhood potencies can strongly influence the Piscean potency. The Lives on earth that cannot free themselves from these dark influences are consequently being prepared to be abstracted into the zone of containment (the *eighth sphere),* preparatory for recycling in a new dispensation.

---

35 See the two volumes of *The Constitution of Shambhala* for detail concerning the New Mahāchohan and His purpose. The 2/1 Ray is His special dispensation.

The Pisces glyph can also be considered as three eyes. The left eye of the past is the lower cup, the right eye of the future is the higher cup, and the eternal Now (the All-seeing Eye) is the band that unites the two. Pisces similarly integrates the Base of Spine and the Sacral centre into a unity. The higher cup representing the Sacral centre and the lower cup the Base of Spine centre, with the uniting band integrating the two signs. This is significant if one considers the Base of Spine centre from a higher perspective—to convey the energies of *saṁsāra,* the three planes of human evolution. From this perspective, the Sacral centre conveys the energies of the four cosmic ethers.

Energy can go down to the Base of Spine centre, which is awakened when incarnation into the dense form is needed. Cancer comes into perspective here to accomplish this incarnation. Its glyph (♋) signifies the interrelation between these two *chakras,* the yin-yang process that binds the entities of the *eighth sphere* into the incarnating expression of their manifest forms. Life and form are thus bound into a mutable unity. When the energies go up to the Sacral centre to vitalise the form, then the potency of Gemini comes into perspective to empower the *iḍā* and *piṇgalā nāḍīs* (the two pillars of the temple of the body that Gemini embodies) so the *prāṇas* can be distributed. In this analogy, Sagittarius fires the arrows (the direction of distribution) for the energies. Cancer is the opened gate and Pisces governs the cycles of each opening gate that conditions the manifest form. Thus the influences of the twelve signs of the zodiac come into manifestation.

Gemini, Sagittarius and Pisces are linked via the earth. In this analogy the earth is the *eighth sphere* and the glyph for the earth ⊕ represents the four ventricles (gates) of the Heart (the fixed cross). Pisces embodies the functions of the gates, Sagittarius opens and closes the gates, and Gemini represents what passes through the gates. Note that the Hierarchical ruler of Gemini is the Earth, while the Earth is the esoteric ruler of Sagittarius (the polar opposite sign). Pisces, on the other hand, has Pluto ruling both the esoteric and Hierarchical rulers. There is no direct rulership of the Earth, nevertheless, there is an indirect relationship where (through Pluto) Pisces is the reaper of the karmic consequences of what transpires on earth.

From one point of view, the Earth is signified by Virgo. The circle that surrounds the earth symbol is Cancer, the 'shell' that it carries on its back. (Cancer signifies the mode of incarnation into the earth sphere.) The cross symbolising the earth is here depicted as the fixed cross whereon the consciousness-principle is crucified. This is the orthodox rendering, however, the mutable cross can just as easily be placed there, for this cross more specifically relates to the process of repeated and mutable incarnations on the earth sphere. Of the mutable cross, the Pisces-Virgo arm represents the *iḍā nāḍī* stream. The Sagittarius-Gemini arm represents the *piṇgalā nāḍī.* Cancer (the southern direction of the cardinal cross) signifies the *suṣumṇā nāḍī.* Cancer is the mouth from which proceeds the Sound of creation. Later, it signifies the upward way that leads to the Door of liberation via Capricorn (its polar opposite).

The energies that will allow one to battle the attributes of the dark brotherhood that primarily lurk on the astral plane manifest via Taurus and Scorpio (who are on the fixed cross). Taurus embodies the attributes of the cosmic astral, and Scorpio is the battlefield upon systemic astral space. Cancer and Capricorn (upon the cardinal cross) wield the energies of mental plane sorcery directed from cosmic sources (Capricorn) into every aspect of material plane livingness (Cancer). This produces the fear-ridden attributes of the scurrying crab. All of these signs relate to the opening and closing Doors of the *eighth sphere.*

The role of the Manu (the Lord of the first Ray department in Hierarchy and who directs all streams of Life towards their karmic fruition) is connected with Pisces. The Manu astrologically works with cosmic animals. Fomalhaut, the mouth of the sign of the fish (Piscis Austrinus) governs the entities that have been stored in the cosmic *eighth sphere.* They can be directed to earth via the Manu's department by the agency of Pluto in Pisces.[36] This happens via the *ātmic* plane to impact upon the mental plane, thence to affect the physical. The entities of the fifth Creative Hierarchy (Makara the Mystery, the Agnishvattas) are consequently activated to build into the physical domain the consequences of materialised thought-constructs. The type of energy projected, cosmically, is animal by nature, conditioning the human animal form (the personality and its world) via the Watery astral body. The astral plane is a human creation, hence the animal kingdom does not directly imbibe in it, other than to the extent that humans may influence them.

Pisces thus directs animal-like energies cosmically and systemically. It is concerned with the concept of death of the old forms, absorbing the gain of their evolution before recycling via a new cycle of expression (in Aries). Dying solar systems are dying Beasts.[37] There is therefore a certain psychic energy

36 This theme shall be elaborated in a later chapter.

37 Note also that the great Beings that surround the Throne of God are called 'beasts' in *Rev.*

streaming from such animal forms that the Manu (in conjunction with the Lords of Shambhala) must shield humanity from—anything that is not the *karma* of the human kingdom to handle. Being an evolving animal form, the human body has receptivity to such cosmological influences. Such evolution is generally along the *īḍa nāḍī* line of development.

The dark brotherhood work directly with the Beastly energies streaming from the dying cosmic forms in order to control and manipulate those animal-like aspects of humanity. (The sum of the forces that constitute the three-fold animal bodies of the human kingdom. This incorporates the substance of the mental, astral and physical planes, the domains constituting the manifestation of our *karma*.)

This brings to perspective the role of the three Watery signs, seen from a vaster cosmic perspective:

- Pisces—the reject cosmic Waters that impact upon the mental plane shores of our planetary system, to help precipitate the substance that sustains *saṃsāra*. The mental plane acts as a fluidic liquid Fire. The substance of this plane is moulded by the agency of Pluto.
- Cancer—the emergence of the Life forms on earth, to produce their massed Watery interplay and interrelationships. Consciousness thereby eventually evolves. This work is produced via the influence of Neptune, the esoteric and Hierarchical ruler of Cancer.
- Scorpio—the emergence of a human kingdom that causes the appearance of the Earthy astral murk of the world's heavens and hells. The Watery astral plane here is Earthy in nature because humanity precipitate therein their most materialised thought-forms that create zones of habitation for them in their after death life. This astral domain comes into existence under the influence of Mars, hence through the principle of desire.

The astral plane manifests in an *īḍa nāḍī* function when mind is coupled with emotions *(kāma-manas)*. Humanity's Solar Angels (Sambhogakāya Flowers) are expressions of *buddhi* clothed in mental substance. Human Love has its origin in *buddhi*. This manifests as a *piṇgalā nāḍī* function.

The scale of existence can be typified as given below.

---

*4:6* ('In the midst of the throne and, round about the throne, were four beasts full of eyes before and behind.') This has reference to their spiritual stature in cosmos.

| Plane | Kingdom | Sign |
|---|---|---|
| Physical | Mineral | - |
| Etheric | Plant | Aquarius |
| Astral-mental | Animal | Sagittarius |
| Mental | Angelic | Capricorn |
| Buddhi | Human | Scorpio |

**Table 5. The planes and the kingdoms of Nature**

Note that the astral-mental zone here is freed from human massed desire conditionings, hence it is a zone of energies whereby the animal kingdom is broadly stimulated with *manasic* energies, to assist them to evolve mind over a vast period of time. This is part of the work of the angelic kingdom (the *devas)* to accomplish. Eventually, the conditionings manifest whereby the animal sentience can Individualise into a humanity.

# 4

# The Esoteric Interpretation of a Natal Chart

## General notes related to horoscope interpretation

An understanding of the Houses is necessary for the proper interpretation of natal charts and for the way of the manifestation of *karma*. Astrologers have presented much information, and some have tried to present esoteric indications, but little is truly understood concerning the nature of this subject. With esoteric astrology, it is a necessity to have a well-developed comprehension of the subjective nature of the human psyche and of the way of the manifestation of the Soul. The information herein should help the modern astrologer to more accurately interpret the natal chart of mystics, disciples and Initiates. One can overlay esoteric factors upon the exoteric, according to the degree of enlightenment of the disciple concerned. The questions to be asked will concern how awakened the client is, how much the Soul is in control, and what the intrinsic Initiation status is. The main concern is to what extent the inner Initiation status reflects outwards into the personality life. For the most part, both exoteric and esoteric factors need be considered, until the disciple is fully awakened.

It should be noted that if it is said that a person's ruling planet is Venus, for instance, then Venusian energies were dominant at the time of his/her birth, and thus had a greater effect upon the forming of his/her subtle constitution than the other planetary forces. This builds into the person's subtle bodies (at the moment of first breath when the *chakras* are vivified) a type of vibration that is in empathy with the Venusian qualities. Thus, the substance of the child's constitution will be susceptible to that frequency of vibration throughout his/her life. This produces a tendency to manifest the various qualities attributed to Venus. This force will however be greatly modified according to the strength, polarisation and aspects of the other planets at the time of birth, as well as by the earth's influence at the place of birth.

Such influences manifest as tendencies towards the generation of certain qualities, thus they will not always manifest as actualities. The qualities assigned by astrologers to the various planets are in the nature of huge thought-forms built by the potent creative minds of people throughout the ages. They have a potency of their own that affects the actions and qualities of personalities immersed in the great illusion. This potency lessens as people begin to master their personalities. Much depends upon the strength of the will, or of the emotional control of the personality concerned. The exoteric planetary attributes will have very little influence upon a person on the Initiation path. It is important to note, therefore, that when speaking of the astrological forces that affect and condition the personality, the concern is with the nature of a mind-conditioned illusion, which nevertheless does have real effects upon the unevolved.

A different set of planetary energies that have nothing to do with the desire or thought-form making images of humanity condition those who are spiritually evolved. These are the *esoteric* planetary (Ray) energies. Consideration of them will therefore, by necessity, differ from exoteric interpretations generally given in popular astrological texts.

Concerning the Sun and Moon, and other planets generally, D.K. states:

> It is only in the present cycle that the Sun and Moon "veil" and are exoteric symbols for certain esoteric forces. As evolution proceeds, the planets will not be veiled. Their influences will not be so remote. At present the mechanism of the majority of the human family is not tuned to the reception of the rays from Vulcan, Uranus or Neptune whilst Pluto only evokes response from groups or from those disciples who are enough evolved rightly to respond. The three veiled planets—Vulcan, Uranus and Neptune are all sacred, embodying first, seventh and sixth ray energies. Vulcan is never an exoteric ruler and only comes to real activity when a man is on the Path, whilst Uranus and Neptune are rulers of the eleventh and twelfth houses, and govern Aquarius and Pisces.[1]

---

1 *Esoteric Astrology,* 509.

He further states:

> (T)here is a relation between Mars and Pluto analogous to that of Venus and the Earth. Esoterically speaking, Mars is the *alter ego* of Pluto; the activity of Pluto at this time and in this lesser world cycle is very important on account of its esoteric approach to the Earth, impelled thereto by the vivification of its life by a display of Martian energy. The Earth, Mars and Pluto form an interesting triangle with Venus behind the scene acting as the impelling soul acts towards a rapidly integrating personality. This triangle should not be forgotten when casting a horoscope, because it indicates a relation and possibility which can be (though it often is not) a major determining factor, prior to the passing on to the Probationary Path. The four houses, governed by the four non-sacred planets (not counting the Sun) are "houses of the personality mundanely orientated" and the reason is not far to seek. The seven remaining houses, governed by the seven sacred planets are not so purely material nor are they so exoterically orientated, yet all the twelve indicate limitation or that which withholds the Dweller in the mansion from expanding his consciousness, if he permits himself to be imprisoned by them. On the other hand, they offer opportunity if he is orientated towards the higher life.[2]

The statement: 'The Earth, Mars and Pluto form an interesting triangle with Venus behind the scene acting as the impelling soul acts towards a rapidly integrating personality' is significant because these non-sacred planets[3] manifest the function of the triune *eighth sphere* in our solar system. The *eighth sphere* contains the repository of the rejected *prāṇas* of the system. Such *prāṇas* constitute the rejected Lives (members of the dark brotherhood, and the Lives waiting to be transferred to another planetary system). They represent *saṃskāras:* units of *karma* that can no longer be expressed (transformed in the present body of manifestation). Hence they must wait for a later cycle before the energies and qualities they possess have a chance of further evolutionary progression.

The earth represents the physical plane arena of this sphere. It is the battleground wherein such *saṃskāric* qualifications are sorted out. This involves the ancient

---

2 Ibid., 507-08.

3 D.K. states that: The effect of the influences of a non-sacred planet or a sacred one are very different, for one will affect primarily the life in the three worlds whilst a sacred planet will aid in the process of affecting the fusion of soul and body, of consciousness and form; it will also produce the quickening of the intuition (the spiritual soul) which is the lower aspect of the Monad. *(Esoteric Astrology,* 506.)

'war' between the white Brotherhood and the Lords of Dark Face. The field of this 'sorting out' process therefore constitutes the *eighth sphere* zone on earth. Consequently, it is not a specific locality, but rather zones of conflict, of determined adherence to non-loving attitudes that are detrimental to the evolution of all. Whilst this battleground ensues, where there is no clear victor, then the rulership of the non-sacred planets dominates and the great illusion, where the sun signs retrograde through the zodiac, persists. In the forthcoming Aquarian age (the New Era) this battle will have been won by the forces of Light, thus the great reversal of the wheel will take place and the earth will become a sacred planet. This is the hoped for eventuation that the entire Hierarchy are presently working towards.

Mars represents the astral zone of the *eighth sphere,* thus is the prison house for the dark brother miscreants upon the astral plane. Therein will be fought the final battles of transformation of the hell states of the Watery *prāṇas* in our solar system. During the Aquarian epoch on earth, many units and groupings of human life will be transferred to Mars so that they can work to cleanse *kāma-manasic* (desire-mind) *saṃskāras.* Conditionings on earth will then no longer allow this low level of karmic interrelationships. Mars indeed, in many ways, is a sister planet to earth. The significance of the rulership of Scorpio by Mars, as the foundation for the testing ground in this sign, is also veiled here. Esoterically, Mars will move closer to the earth during the New Age. Its influence will loom bright in the night sky.

Pluto represents the *eighth sphere* zone of the mental plane *saṃskāras* in the solar system. It will house the most recalcitrant of the members of the dark brotherhood, preparatory to their eventual release in the new solar system. They will then again have opportunity for karmic transformation toward the arenas of Light. This is a major reason why Pluto is the esoteric and Hierarchical ruler of Pisces, the last sign in the zodiac. Pisces represents the place of containment (in *pralaya)* for all lives at the ending of any cycle, prior to the start of a new zodiacal cycle. The twelfth House therefore is exoterically the House of confinement and of the imprisoned Soul. Pluto's influence, therefore, is generally distant and looming. It is concerned mainly with the *manasic* decision making of humanity, hence conditioning the *karma* of unfortunate self-focussed, selfish thinking.

## The Moon, sun sign and the ascendant

The significance of the Moon, the sun sign and the ascendant in a person's chart can now be analysed.

The place of the *Moon* indicates past life expression *(saṃskāras)* brought into the natal chart, thus what normally limits or hinders the personality. The focus is specifically upon the physical form. An intuitive astrologer should carefully meditate here for any flashes of insight indicative of a person's past life expression. The *Moon's nodes* refer to the psyche of the personality, specifically the emotions, astralism, as well as to the psychism of the average spiritually orientated being. The *karma* of such attributes is thus indicated. The *ascending node* (north node) refers to future qualities being developed that the personality is headed towards. These can be positive with respect to qualities that help discipleship, or else negative with respect to intensification of wrongly focussed (left hand) psychism. The *descending node* (south node) refers to past qualities (from whence the innate psychism or astralism has come), thus past life *saṃskāras.*

D.K. states that:

> (T)he influence of the moon is purely symbolic in nature and in effect and is simply the result of ancient thought and teaching (descended to us from Lemurian times) and is not based on any true radiation or influence.... The moon, from the angle of the esoteric knower, is simply an obstruction in space—an undesirable form which must some day disappear. In esoteric astrology, the effect of the moon is noted as a thought effect and as the result of a powerful and most ancient thoughtform; nevertheless, the moon has no quality of her own and can transmit nothing to the Earth.... astrologers would do well to experiment with this suggestion I have made anent the moon and (instead of working with the moon) *let them work with Vulcan* when dealing with the undeveloped or average man *and with Uranus* when considering the highly developed man. They would find some interesting and convincing results eventuate.[4]

Concerning these substitute planets for the Moon, it should be noted that Vulcan introduces first Ray energies that force drastic changes in an individual's life, wherein the *karma* for past mistakes can be cleansed. Vulcan can intensify the native's inherent self-focussed will. Uranus facilitates seventh Ray ritualistic attitudes re the Divine, to foster spiritual power in arenas of the chosen service work. This planet also stimulates occult practices and esoteric thought.

The *sun sign* governs the exoteric background to the *present* personality equipment, the personality Ray and the responsiveness (or lack thereof) to the energies and impressions from the Soul. It indicates whether any personality-Soul

4 Ibid., 13.

integration has been achieved. Also analysed are the possibilities of present group interrelations, or how the personality is handling the external environment. One looks for what the purpose of a particular incarnation may be – the quality of the life tendencies. (The signature of the native's consciousness to respond to presented opportunity in life.) While exoteric planets suffice for determining the chart of the average person, the esoteric planetary rulers need to be used for the natal chart of the disciple or Initiate.

D.K. states:

> The Sun sign, governed by the *esoteric* planets and the rising sign governed by the esoteric planets, can both be used in casting the horoscope of the Initiate; when superimposed upon each other, the outer life of the Initiate in the three worlds and the inner life of subjective realisation will appear. This mode of super-imposition will be a feature of the new astrology.
>
> When the Sun sign with the *exoteric* rulers is worked out in a chart, the rising sign with the *esoteric* rulers is also worked out and the two are superimposed upon each other, the problem of the disciple in any one incarnation will appear.[5]

The *ascendant* (rising sign) indicates the future direction or destiny (the Soul purpose, or spiritual opportunity) for the personality. This is determined in relation to which of the three crosses the ascendant's House is found in, and the aspects to the esoteric planets. If the hints in the chart are properly followed, they indicate the pathway to Soul-personality integration for the disciple, and the service work of the Initiate. There will also be hints as to the work to be done, or attributes that may flow though to the next life, and which may need to be mastered. Esoteric astrologers must think of more than one life in their analysis. The *saṁskāras* flow from a past life (the Moon's determinant), to be experienced and worked out in the present life's circumstances (the sun sign), and then the remainder will flow on to the next life or lives in order to be further refined or corrected (the ascendant). Such a flow of events (karmic expression) needs to be very carefully pondered upon in order to gain meditative impressions (or if possible, past or future life images).

D.K. states:

> The *rising sign* indicates the remoter possibilities, and the spiritual goal and purpose of the immediate incarnation and of the immediate succeeding incarnations. This sign concerns itself with the struggle of the spiritual man "to carry on" from the point achieved so that when the life energy is temporarily

---

5 Ibid., 514.

> exhausted and the "death" of the personality" takes place, the man finds himself "nearer the centre of life, closer to the centre of his group and approaching the centre of divine life".[6]

It should also be noted that *Saturn* and its aspects must be observed to view the position or placing of the *karma* of the individual. *Capricorn* indicates the Initiation process in general, specifically the third Initiation. Any left hand tendencies can also be noted. *Neptune* and its aspects indicate the possibility of being tested for the second Initiation. *Virgo* is the house associated with the first Initiation.

Significant aspects to *Scorpio* can indicate the real possibility that tests for Initiation are to occur in that life. There are five minor tests preceding any major Initiation, and each Initiation necessitates overcoming significant periods of crises for the individual that concern attributes to be mastered. Particular tests are governed by the signs attributed to any of the various heads of the Hydra. Such attributes can be indicated by the aspects of particular planets in a House ruled by Scorpio. (These aspects will be conditioned by the influences of the esoteric planets.) Initiation testings are always a major theme in the life of disciples, and the esoteric astrologer needs to study with care the pertinent information provided by D.K. in the books by Alice Bailey in order to properly analyse natal charts of disciples and Initiates.

Many astrologers are often a little too finicky in their interpretations, giving us such aspects as Septiles (360°/7 = 51°26'), Noviles (360°/9 = 40°), Sesqui-quadrants (135°), etc. On the whole, it is best to ignore such fine-tuning and to concentrate upon the major characteristics. One needs to consider that *karma* indicates probabilities only, and that a person, having *free will,* may develop differently than the way that the *karma* intended. In a similar manner, the erratic emotional behaviour of many people mitigates against fine-tuning possibilities.

D.K. states:

> The effort on Earth today (as seen by the planetary Logos) is to bring about a transformation of the web of the planet and thus change the existing squares into triangles. This is done by the creation of division, by the application of the Law of separation, but also by the recognition, in consciousness, of duality, the application of directed motion and the appearance of two triangles in the place of one square...It is for this reason that the astrologers of the future will emphasis

6 Ibid., 17. D.K. presents useful information concerning the sun and rising signs, etc., in *A Treatise on White Magic*, 434-43.

> the relation and inter-relation of triangles. The new astrologer will, as I have hinted before, lay the emphasis upon:
>
> 1. The Science of Triangles, as the result of the growth of the initiate understanding.
> 2. The rising sign, as it indicates the way of the soul.
> 3. The place of the three Crosses (the Cardinal Cross, the Fixed Cross and the Mutable Cross) in the life of the soul. This will eventually supersede the houses in the horoscope and the 12 arms of the three crosses will take the place of the 12 houses when casting the horoscope of the soul.
>
> I would reiterate again the fact that the new astrology will be occupied with charting the life of the soul. The 12 constellates, as they play their part in the life of the disciple through the medium of their distributing agents, the ruling esoteric planets, will gradually transform the exoteric form of the chart of the individual. This will be due to the focussing of the various energies in man, consciously and through intent, and will not concern his negative reaction to the conditioning energies.[7]

D.K. makes an interesting point[8] in relation to the new astrology, which I shall paraphrase. Virgo and Scorpio are both triple signs, thus signifying the scientific interrelation between Spirit-Soul-form. When disciples grasp the meaning behind this triplicity they will be able to properly work with this most ancient science of esoteric astrology. Virgo and Scorpio are concerned with the growth of the Christ-consciousness, and so mark crucial points in the Soul's experience. They are points of integration wherein the Soul is at-oneing itself with both the form and the Monad at the same time. (This relates to the Soul's experience and not that of the person upon the physical plane.)

D.K. states:

> When the experience undergone in Virgo is consummated in Pisces, and the tests of Scorpio have led to illumination in Taurus, then the effect of these four energies (Virgo, Pisces, Scorpio, Taurus) will make man the true triangle, expressing the three divine energies as they come from the three major conditioning constellations: the Great Bear, the Pleiades and Sirius.[9]

Virgo and Pisces are polar opposites, as are Taurus and Scorpio. Virgo and Taurus bear the energies of the Pleiades, whereas Scorpio bears Sirian energy. At

---

7 Ibid., 479-80.

8 See *Esoteric Astrology*, 480.

9 Ibid., 481.

times Pisces can be a conduit for the energies of the Great Bear, to bring death to all cycles of expression. The Great Bear integrates these polarities via Aries and Libra. The meditative focus of Libra therefore balances all of these energies, whilst Aries produces the driving Will to accomplish the appearance of the triangles from the squares.[10] The energies of the Pleiades are found in the left pan of the scales, those of Sirius in the right pan, and the body of the scales and fulcrum (held in the mouth of a dragon of Wisdom) wields the potency of the Great Bear via Aries and Libra. Therefore, the arms of the three crosses are found in these three pairs of signs: the mutable cross (the Virgo-Pisces interrelation), the fixed cross (the Taurus-Scorpio interrelation) and cardinal cross (the Aries-Libra interrelation).

One can also consider Virgo to govern the zodiac of the womb (the struggles of the personality in *saṃsāra).* Scorpio governs the zodiac of the centres below the diaphragm, producing the struggles of the disciple working to overcome attachments to saṃsāric allurements. Leo governs the zodiac of the chest, thus of general Hierarchical interrelationships. Capricorn governs the zodiac of the Head centre, thus of the Way of the Initiate.

## The Houses in general and their keywords

The Houses are the mansions that imprison the freedom of the human Soul. They therefore manifest limitations that must be overcome as far as the life of the aspiring disciple is concerned. D.K. suggests the following (which I have paraphrased).[11] First one should substitute esoteric planets for other exoteric planets, for much instructive information can be gained. Next, one should distinguish between the effects of the sacred and non-sacred planets. The sacred planets help to make the personality an instrument of the Soul. The non-sacred planets influence the form nature. In comparing the two forms of influence, comprehension concerning the pull between the pairs of opposites may then manifest. Through studying the 'fluid area' where the planets veiled by the Sun and the Moon come into play, one must decide (from a study of the chart, and other esoteric knowledge possessed) at what point of evolution the individual is at and which of the three veiled planets rule. Much intuitive understanding can then be obtained. Significant light can be thrown on the problems aspirants

---

10 This relates to the reversal of the process of the 'fall of the three into the four' (explained in my book *Esoteric Cosmology and Modern Physics)* that caused the manifestation process.

11 See *Esoteric Astrology,* 510.

and probationary disciples undergo when considering *exoteric* rulers and the problems of disciples when dealing with *esoteric* rulers.

Before delving into the houses proper I shall summarise the houses, the astrological signs, planetary rulers, the key phrase, the associated cross and Element. The Hierarchical rulers do not affect the average disciple, and only come into consideration for the high Initiates (of the third Initiation or above), who deal with planetary conditions as a whole. The Hierarchical rulers are effectively the concern of Shambhala, the members of which also deal with interplanetary and cosmic interrelationships. In the consideration of the Houses, therefore, only the exoteric and esoteric rulers shall be discussed. After the zodiacal sign thus two planetary rulers will be shown; the first presented being the exoteric ruler, the next the esoteric.

I will only present an elementary account of the exoteric astrological considerations. Readers can consult various astrological texts for detail. The Houses shall be organised in accordance with their placing upon the three crosses. They are: the mutable cross of repeated incarnations and constant activity in *saṃsāra,* the fixed cross of steadfast focus and service work upon the path of discipleship, and the cardinal cross that rules the higher Initiate. The cardinal cross concerns the application of Shambhalic Will to cause the liberation of the all. Because the qualities of these crosses have been dealt with in detail in my earlier books, I shall simply refer to them here in relation to the Houses that come under their influence.[12]

The *Mutable cross* (where the Christ principle is hidden, veiled within the confines of the form) is represented by the third (Gemini), sixth (Virgo), ninth (Sagittarius) and twelfth (Pisces) Houses. These Houses condition the Soul's expression in *saṃsāra* to gain the foundational experiences of Life that will later serve the basis for the development of Love-Wisdom.

The keyword for the *third House* is the *environment.*[13] The associated sign is Gemini the twins upon the southeast arm of 'expression' of the mutable cross. This House builds the environmental 'prison' of the Soul (the 'immortal brother')

---

12 D.K. provides an astrological accounting of these three crosses (of the hidden, crucified and risen Christs) in his book *Esoteric Astrology,* pages 553-75, and elsewhere therein.

13 The keywords have been taken from the book by Marc Edmund Jones, *Astrology, How and Why it Works* (Penguin Books, New York, 1975). I have used this book as the standard reference for the exoteric form of astrology, coupled with Alan Oken's book: *Alan Oken's Complete Astrology* (Revised edition, Bantam Books, N.Y. 1988). Many other books could have been used, such as those by Dane Rudyar, Alan Leo, and Charles Carter.

via the conditionings of the *chakras*. Here the *saṁskāras* that empower the *chakras* at first manifest via the centres below the diaphragm, which become the 'mortal brother'. The Solar Plexus centre and the Inner Round inevitably dominate the personality activities for many millennia. Gemini is governed by Mercury exoterically and Venus esoterically. Gemini is an Air sign and is said to 'move towards Libra'.[14] The key phrase for the average person is 'fluidic often unstable relationships', for the disciple we have 'the temple builder', and for the awakened Initiate the phrase is 'the Divine intermediary'. These key phrases represent the stages of the evolution of consciousness in the various signs.[15]

The *sixth House* keyword is *duty*. The associated sign is Virgo the virgin and is upon the southwest arm of the mutable cross, signifying 'understanding'. In Virgo the personality attributes are firmly established and the Soul enters into the depths of its activities in the realms of form. The *saṁskāras* developed here are therefore the most materialistic, Earthy, where at first the 'duty' expressed is to the material needs of the personality and to the immediate family relationships.

Virgo is an Earth sign and the planetary rulers are Mercury and the Moon. Virgo is said to 'hide the light which irradiates the field in Gemini'. The key phrase for the average person is 'the activity in the Womb of Nature'. For the disciple we have 'the mother of the divine child', and for the awakened Initiate the phrase is 'the sower for the Harvest'.

The keyword for the *ninth House* is *understanding*. The associated sign is Sagittarius the archer upon the mutable cross, signifying 'good will'. Sagittarius at first drives the Soul's ambition to increasingly experience the vicissitudes of life in *saṃsāra*. The experiences gained for the personalities concerned produce incremental understanding of what causes pain and suffering, thus they learn what is right to do to overcome this. The planetary rulers are Jupiter and the Earth. Sagittarius is a Fire sign, where the disciple will eventually 'become the saviour in Pisces'. The key phrase for the average person is 'one-pointed ambition'. For the disciple we have 'the directed arrow of aspiration' and for the awakened Initiate the phrase is 'the Avatar on the white horse'.

The *twelfth House's* keyword is *confinement* and the associated sign is Pisces the fishes. Pisces signifies one complete round or cycle of experience ('confinement') for gaining any major attribute by the Soul. The consequence produces the start of a new cycle in Aries so that something else can be learnt and mastered. Pisces is

---

14 See *Esoteric Astrology,* pages 332-33 for the keynote statements.

15 These key phrases are derived from *Esoteric Astrology.*

upon the northeast direction of the mutable cross, denoted 'unity'. This concerns gathering the consequences of the past cycle, so that the *saṁskāras* for the new can be projected.

The planetary rulers of Pisces are Jupiter and Pluto. It is a Water sign and is said to 'take from all signs'. The key phrase for the average person is 'the imprisoned Soul, bonded activity, mediumship'. For the disciple the phrase is 'the sacrifice of the one for the other', and for the awakened Initiate we have 'the World Saviour'.

The *fixed cross* of 'the crucified Christ' is that of the disciple whose consciousness is crucified upon the field of compassionate service work (the western arm of this cross). The other directions are upwards towards Divinity (liberation), inwards to the Heart of Life (the eastern direction), and downwards to the suffering little ones. The disciples are fixed upon this cross of sacrificial service until the time comes when they are removed from it by having passed high Initiation testings. The arms of this cross are represented by the second (Taurus), fifth (Leo), eighth (Scorpio) and eleventh (Aquarius) Houses. Upon this cross, the Soul works towards its own crucifixion and thus the death of its form at the fourth Initiation. This is accomplished by its ability to bear increasingly more intense Monadic energies via the *antaḥkaraṇa* between the Jewel in the Heart of the Lotus of the Soul and the Monad. In doing so, the Soul gains ever more experience concerning the nature of Life in cosmos.

For the *second House* the keyword is *possessions*. The associated sign is Taurus the bull, an Earth sign governing the eastern arm of the fixed cross. The planetary rulers are Venus and Vulcan. Through Taurean conditionings, the Soul builds the 'house' of its own form: all of the exemplary attributes that produce and express its pulsating luminosity to such an extent that the energies can no longer be contained. A supernova explosion then happens on the higher mental plane, signifying its death and transcendence into a higher form. Taurus is said to rush blindly until Sagittarius directs. The key phrase for the average person is 'blind onrushing desire'. For the disciple we have 'the clother of the divine thought', and for the awakened Initiate the phrase is 'the all-seeing Eye'.

The keyword for the *fifth House* is *offspring*. The associated sign is Leo the lion. In Leo, the Soul develops the consciousness attributes of the Ray characteristics (its 'possessions') on its own domain. This happens through the process of the repeated incarnations of the personalities ('selves') that Leo projects into manifestation. (The southern direction of the fixed cross.) The Soul gleans the best *manasic* characteristics they have developed while adding what has been experienced through the collective awareness of the other Souls residing upon the higher mental plane (especially those manifesting its own Ray colouring). Such Souls become the constituency of a Master's Ashram. The planetary rulers are the Sun (exoteric) and the Sun (esoteric). (In each case veiling certain planets.) Leo is a Fire sign and is said to 'seek release in Scorpio'. The key phrase for the average person is 'the self-conscious individual'. For the disciple we have 'the lord of the earthly domain', and for the awakened Initiate the phase is 'the Soul of all Life'.

The *eighth House* keyword is *regeneration.* The associated sign is Scorpio the scorpion and the planetary rulers are Mars (exoteric) and Mars (esoteric). During this period (Scorpio ruling the western arm of the fixed cross) the Soul mainly completes the empowerment of the Love-Wisdom triad of petals and increasingly brings into activity the Will or Sacrifice triad of petals. Under the auspices of the potency of the Will the incarnate personalities are stimulated. They undergo the trials and testings in their spiritual struggle to overcome the nine-headed Hydra and so attain Initiation, doing so via their service arenas amongst humanity. Scorpio is a Water sign and is said to 'stage the release of Leo'. The key phrase for the average person is 'the battlefield of desire'. For the disciple we have 'the triumphant disciple', and for the awakened Initiate the phrase is 'the sword bearer of the Lord of Life'.

The *eleventh House* keyword is *friendship* and the associated sign is Aquarius the water bearer. In Aquarius, the northern arm of the fixed cross, the Soul develops the complete expression of the attributes of Love-Wisdom. Its incarnate personalities become fully accepted disciples and then enter the ranks of Hierarchy. This happens during the last period of 70 lives of the symbolic 777 incarnations of the Soul. The Soul is then oriented upwards so as to become a Monadic emissary, whose energies then feed the remaining arms of the fixed cross. The planetary rulers are Uranus and Jupiter. Aquarius is an Air sign and is said to 'release Virgo from her load'. The key phrase for the average person is 'superficial and selfish activity'. For the disciple we have 'the group-conscious disciple', and for the awakened Initiate the phrase is 'the world-server'.

The *cardinal cross* relates to the path of Initiation for the Soul that increasingly stages its release from the confines of the limitations of its own form. Sacrifice and continuous cycles of death to various personality attributes are therefore the consequential result, as the Soul enters the final phases of the last seven lives of its symbolic 777 incarnations.

For the *first House* the keyword is *identity* and the associated sign is Aries the ram, situated on the eastern direction of the cardinal cross. Aries provides the will to undertake the Initiation path by way of the awakening Heart and the stimulus of the manifestation of the Mind that liberates. It facilitates the downpour of energies from the Monad to the rest of the signs of the zodiac. The planetary rulers are Mars and Mercury. Aries is a Fire sign and is said to turn towards Capricorn. The key phrase for the average person is 'the fiery warrior'. For the disciple we have 'the lamb of God', and for the awakened Initiate the phrase is 'the Divine Will'.

The keyword for the *fourth House* is *home,* the home here being the shell of the personality vehicle. The associated sign is Cancer the crab, focussed upon the southern direction of the cardinal cross. Cancer brings the first Ray energies to bear upon the reincarnating personalities that work to transform the manifesting *saṁskāras* into enlightenment vectors. The Soul works to overcome the fears of the scurrying crab through awakening transformative *(kuṇḍalinī)* energies in such a way that the Watery 'home' that has been carried for so long becomes a body of Light.

The planetary rulers of Cancer are the Moon and Neptune. It is a Water sign and is said to vision life in Leo. The key phrase for the average person is 'biased psychic sensitivity and reaction'. For the disciple it is 'the dispeller of the Waters', and for the awakened Initiate we have the phrase 'the Light of the Watery Lives'.

The keyword for the *seventh House* is *partnership.* The associated sign is Libra the balances and the planetary rulers are Venus and Uranus. Libra, in the western direction of the cardinal cross, facilitates the meditative absorption of the personalities concerned that have been consecutively incarnated to fulfil various educational arenas in the field of Life. This means that their consciousness is steadily drawn to the abstracted domains of the Mind, hence forms of service work related to the third Initiation. The 'partnership' here thus concerns that between Soul and personality, and then between the awakened Initiate and Hierarchy, so that congruent, harmonised service work is attained.

Libra is an Air sign and is said to relate the two in Gemini. The key phrase for the average person is 'the balance between opposing desires'. For the disciple we have 'the interlude in the breath of God', and for the awakened Initiate the phrase is 'the adjudicator of the Law'.

The *tenth House* keyword is *honour* and the associated sign is Capricorn the goat. Capricorn, on the northern position of the cardinal cross, signifies the attainment of the various Initiations that will eventually lead through the open

Door of Shambhala to cosmic vistas. It is an honour indeed to be able to travel thus. The planetary rulers are Saturn and Saturn. They consequently deal with the rectification of *karma* on various levels of perception via the mathematical and methodical activity wielded by the third Ray. Capricorn is an Earth sign and is said to 'consummate the work of Scorpio'. The key phrase for the average person is 'the hard and oft cruel material man'. For the disciple we have 'the mountaintop of attainment', and for the awakened Initiate the phrase is 'the unicorn of God'.

D.K. states that:

> It is interesting to note that the non-sacred planets rule the first, the fourth, the fifth and the eighth houses in the lesser zodiac. Our Earth is also a non-sacred planet. You have, therefore, four non-sacred planets, ruling a fifth non-sacred planet—a correspondence to the four aspects of the lower man...From a larger and more synthetic attitude, you have the four kingdoms in nature and the veiled fifth kingdom, the kingdom of God.
>
> From another angle you have:
> Aries—ruled by Mars.
> Cancer—ruled by the Moon, veiling a sacred planet.
> Leo—ruled by the Sun, veiling a sacred planet.
> Scorpio—ruled by Pluto.
>
> You will note that Pluto and not Mars is here mentioned by me as a non-sacred Planet, ruling Scorpio. The reason for this is that there is a relation between Mars and Pluto analogous to that between Venus and the Earth. Esoterically speaking, Mars is the alter ego of Pluto; the activity of Pluto at this time and in this lesser world cycle is very important on account of its esoteric approach to the Earth, impelled thereto by the vivification of its life by a display of Martian energy. The Earth, Mars and Pluto form an interesting triangle with Venus behind the scene acting as the impelling soul acts towards a rapidly integrating personality. This triangle should not be forgotten when casting the horoscope, because it indicates a relation and a possibility which can be (though it often is not) a major determining factor, prior to passing on to the Probationary Path. The four houses, governed by the four non-sacred planets (not counting the Sun) are "houses of the personality, mundanely oriented" and the reason is not far to seek. The seven remaining houses, governed by the seven sacred planets are not so purely material nor are they so exoterically oriented, yet all the twelve indicate limitation or that which withholds the Dweller in the mansion from expanding his consciousness, if he permits himself to be imprisoned by them. On the other hand, they offer opportunity if he is oriented towards the higher life.[16]

---

16 Ibid., 507-8.

Earth, Mars and Pluto are the *eighth sphere* zones in our solar system. Here the fact of the influence of these negative forces upon the natal chart via the aspects of the Houses wherein they appear should be noted in the interpretation. They indicate *saṃskāras* and *kleśas* (defilements) that a disciple needs to master.

It is interesting that D.K. states that 'Pluto and not Mars is here mentioned by me as a non-sacred Planet, ruling Scorpio'. Pluto is the lord of death and adds a first Ray impetus to the battles of discipleship to overcome the nine-headed Hydra. The attributes assigned to these heads must be mastered and transformed into their positive characteristics through right comprehension and the use of the will, if the tests of Initiation are to be passed. Mars, in contradistinction, embodies the desire-attachment that generated the attributes of these heads. Upon the path of discipleship, desire is converted to aspiration. The forces of Pluto are then evoked to put to death all negative aspects that prevent the attainment of the spiritual goal.

Taking the above into account, the equipment into which a person incarnates will be conditioned by:

| | | | | |
|---|---|---|---|---|
| The physical shell | Earth | 3rd Ray | 9th House | Sagittarius |
| Etheric (vital) body | The Moon | 4th Ray | 4th House | Cancer |
| Astral body | Mars | 6th Ray | 1st House | Aries |
| Mental body | Pluto | 1st Ray | 8th House | Scorpio |
| The personality | The Sun | 2nd Ray | 5th House | Leo |

**Table 6. The influences of the non-sacred planets**

In the ninth House, the one-pointed driving impetus of Sagittarius works to master the physical environment wherein the individual is found. This can later extend to include the domain of one's spiritual group. The clear, multifaceted thinking of those influenced by the third Ray assists in this task. The materialistic personality, on the other hand, works to manipulate the physical environment to suit his/her own needs.

In the fourth House, the fourth Ray works to integrate the internal forces with the external manifestation, so that the individual can properly incarnate in the personality vehicle. Control of his/her own capabilities is then possible.

In the first House, the desire principle is projected in order to set the stage for all that consequently follows in the life of the individual. Later upon the evolutionary path, aspiration rules in order to lead the native to gain high achievement in any field in Life, or towards enlightenment.

In the eighth House, the mind must learn to control the principle of desire, thus the will must be exerted to overcome the proclivities that lead to perpetual incarnation.

In the fifth House, Love-Wisdom must inevitably be developed to overcome the attributes of the prideful lion. This produces the striving towards becoming a Soul infused personality.

## The aspects

The aspects to the natal chart are also sometimes viewed somewhat differently esoterically than via the exoteric interpretation. Below is a listing of their esoteric qualities with the effective orb (the area of influence in which the associated planets can influence each other) indicated. The intuition should be used as to the effectiveness of the area of influence of the orbs, according to the importance of the associated planetary ruler in the chart.

- *Conjunction* (0 degrees), the orb is normally about six to eight degrees.
  *Meaning:* where two or more planets lie in close proximity and so enhance each other's power. This depends upon the attributes of the planets so interrelated. Congenial interrelationships are produced.

- *Opposition* (180 degrees apart), the orb is normally six to eight degrees.
  *Meaning:* aspects that are in opposition and influence each other with respect as to whether they are pulling away or towards each other. This can be good or bad (acting cooperatively or non-cooperatively) according to the way the characteristics of the respective planets interrelate, for the opposition allows energies to flow from one to the other.

- *Square* (ninety degrees apart), the orb is six to eight degrees.
  *Meaning:* that which challenges, conflicting energies from the angle of physical plane involvement. Here energies and related qualities are blocked and prevented from interrelating. The associated problems may need to be solved. The reason for this can usually be found from a study of the complete chart.

- *Trine* (120 degrees apart), the orb is six to eight degrees.
  *Meaning:* that which is harmonious, especially to the development of the emotional and physical bodies. This can be problematic on the path of discipleship, but positive for normal interrelationships. The energies and

qualities flow freely from one planet to the other. One therefore interprets the planetary interrelationships accordingly. If Saturn, for instance, is one of the members of the trine, then the mode of the expression of the *karma* indicated by the planetary rulers is facilitated.

- *Sextile* (60 degrees), the orb is four to six degrees.
  *Meaning:* similar to trine, cooperative unfoldment, especially in relation to the development or expression of emotional interrelationships, desires or aspiration for spiritual or inspiring goals.

***The minor aspects.***

They have smaller orbs because the influence of these aspects is relatively weak.

- *Inconjunction (Quincunx* – 150 degrees), the orb is two to four degrees.
  *Meaning:* here to be analysed is the relation of mind to form (the emotions), regarding the evolution of consciousness and what facilitates that relation. This produces the challenges or conflicts that are associated with controlling the mental-emotions *(kāma-manas).* These are problematic for most of humanity.
- *Semi-square* (45 degrees), the orb is two degrees.
  *Meaning:* conflicting energies in the realm of consciousness. Possible tests in relation to Initiation must also be sought. This depends upon the associated planetary rulers and the Houses they are in.
- *Semi-sextile* (30 degrees), the orb is two degrees.
  *Meaning:* what is sympathetic to emotional (energy) interrelationships, or which facilitates the exchange of pleasant ideas. This depends on the nature of the planetary rulers concerned.
- *Quintile* (72 degrees), the orb is two to four degrees.
  *Meaning:* that directly associated with the evolution of consciousness, of the mind *per se,* and which facilitates that development. The possible influence of the Soul upon the vehicles should be looked for.

## The Houses

When interpreting a natal chart, consideration of the astrological Houses is needed. Their influence conditions the interpretation of the attributes of the planets and their aspects that fall within them. This is needed in addition to the esoteric interpretation of the twelve signs of the zodiac wherein the major conditioning factors for the life of the disciple or Initiate are found.

As stated, the intention of this chapter is to give the basic framework so that interested people can analyse a natal chart from the esoteric viewpoint. I shall consequently not present a detailed account of the interpretation of charts. The reader can integrate the information presented here with what is given by astrologers that follow Alice Bailey's works (such as Alan Oken or Dane Rudyar).[17]

Concerning the Houses, D.K. states:

> It is not my intention to deal with the houses in detail. Modern astrologers have worked this out relatively satisfactorily, for the houses concern the prison of the soul and its limitations, and with these there is a widespread familiarity. As you know, I am concerned with the astrology of the soul and with the influences of the esoteric planets.
>
> Three suggestions I will however make:
>
> 1. If the investigating astrologer will substitute the esoteric planets for the orthodox exoteric planets (and I have indicated these in connection with the signs of the zodiac) he will get much instructive information, and (if he perseveres) the verification of my ideas.
> 2. If he will distinguish between the effects of the sacred planets and the non-sacred he will find the sacred planets endeavour to fuse the personality and make it the instrument of the soul and the non-sacred planets influence more specifically the form nature; much light on the pull between the pairs of opposites may then pour in.
> 3. If he will study the "fluid area" where the planets, veiled by the Sun and Moon, come into play and will realise that he must decide (from a study of the chart of the subject and any knowledge he may have) what is the point in evolution reached and which of the three veiled planets is the ruler, he will get much intuitive understanding. He will find himself able to throw much light upon the problem of the probationary disciple when considering the *exoteric* rulers and upon the problems of disciples when dealing with the *esoteric* rulers.
>
> If the astrologer will consider these three points and will be willing to experiment with them, a great stride forward into the unveiling of the astrology of the soul will take place. He will find it useful also to work out the higher correspondences to the material realities for which the houses stand.[18]

---

17 In my exoteric accounting here I have used the books by Marc Edward Jones *(Astrology: How and Why it Works)* and Alan Oken *(Alan Oken's Complete Astrology).*

18 Alice Bailey, *Esoteric Astrology,* 509-10.

Alan Oken provides an excellent summary of the exoteric effects of the Houses:

> We can see that the first three Houses are specifically oriented to the expression of oneself, as the First is one's immediate approach to life, the Second constitutes one's personal wealth, and the Third one's personal way of relating to those people in the immediate environment. The next three Houses involve relationships based on the family as signified by the Fourth House. The Fifth House is the fruit of the family or the children as well as the creative ability coming from a firm foundation, while the Sixth House represents those jobs necessary to support a family as well as those social connections directly related to the family such as servants and household pets. The next group of three is based on social interrelationships with its foundation in marriage or business as designated by the Seventh House. The Eighth House shares the fruits of those relationships and reveals the potential for greater gain. The Ninth House reveals one's understanding of the underlying concepts upon which a social structure is based and the future aspirations resulting from that understanding. The last three Houses are the most impersonal of all insofar as they involve the merging of the individual's efforts into the collective of humanity. This is based in the Tenth House which signifies one's social contribution and position, while the Eleventh House represents the fruits of endeavors based on group involvements (as contrasted with the Eighth House which is most concerned with one's immediate partners). The Twelfth House signifies those areas of the personal life which have to be refined so that the energy contained therein may be purified for use by the Forces of Creativity.[19]

## The first House

Governed by Aries, Mars and Mercury (the sixth and fourth Rays).

### *The exoteric consideration*

The first House rules the general focus of the personalities' consciousness and life's activities in the immediate environment, in simple action or reaction responses. The key attribute[20] is identity and its persistence. It specifically rules the bodily organism and its general appearance. This physical type is modified in correspondence with the divisions of the zodiac through which the rising sign (eastern horizon) passes. This House also rules the early mental-emotional

19 *Alan Oken's Complete Astrology,* 319.

20 The key attribute is the expression through which the native in that House is revealed, either to themselves, or to others, in any given situation or issue.

environment, factualised in specific new phases of experience, thus the general self-revelations of the personality. This produces a dominion over physical plane life, when focussed upon the immediate states of things. There is a wholly natural and unconditioned contact with experience at the point of maximum self-focus and minimum social involvement.

Concerning this House, Alan Oken states:

> First House: Ascendant. The Ascendant-or, as it is also called, the First House cusp or Rising Sign-is the 'projected image, the door through which we express and activate our inner motivations and psychological needs in the immediate environment. It characterizes our body types as well as the way other people receive their first impressions of us.[21]

### *The esoteric consideration*

Taking the cues from D.K.'s statement concerning the Houses, it can therefore be said esoterically that this House governs the physical (bodily) shell and the three-fold personality in general. It governs the Soul Ray expression on its own realm and how its Rays influence the personality. One can consider the emergence of the Soul's energies in the form, producing its creative unfoldment in the life of the personality, thus a possible dominance of the form by the Soul. The esoteric ruler of Aries is Mercury (governing the fourth Ray of Beautifying Harmony overcoming Conflict), hence its influences in the life of a disciple must be taken into account. Mercury facilitates the manifestation of intuitive perceptions, which in this House would signify receptivity to the beginning stages of the path of discipleship.

This is one of the houses that D.K. provides an explanation for. He states:

> Mars is the transmitter of sixth Ray force and this makes the first House of action in the physical body that of the devotee who fights for that which he desires or for that to which he aspires. The warrior, devoted to a cause, comes into being upon the field of action, the Earth, which is itself an expression of the third Ray of Intelligent Activity. Aries, the first house, and Mars and the Earth Initiate conflict, focussed in a form.[22]

---

21 *Alan Oken's Complete Astrology,* 313.

22 Alice Bailey, *Esoteric Astrology,* 508. Interestingly, D.K. also here considers 'the Earth' in his description of this House, whereas for the disciple the ruler is Mercury. D.K. may be considering 'the Earth' here because this House is concerned with the physical plane field of action.

He further states in relation to this House:

Physical body or form.—The causal body of the Soul.
Appearance or manifestation.—The emergence of the Soul.
The head Brain.—The head centre.
Personal activity.—Soul expression.
Mannerisms, etc.—Ray types and qualities.[23]

## The second House

Governed by Taurus, Venus (the fifth Ray) and Vulcan (the first Ray).

### *The exoteric consideration*

This house governs possessions: the material goods that are accumulated in one's physical abode as the normal consequence of existence. They relate to financial and fluid resources, the property, etc., possessed. This house may even indicate the lack of such—poverty as something to overcome. Money and the way that it is utilised is an important consideration. Money provides an individual the greatest possible facility in life to fulfilling social responsibilities. It produces a comforting lifestyle, allowing assistance to others (or to receive such). This produces the potential for advantageous social relationships and the personal liberty that comes from possessing financial assets. The desire to hoard possessions can often be seen. There is a definite conscious cushioning of self to establish what will hopefully ensure a favourable outcome in action. An ability develops to order what is convenient for the moment through right communication and the establishment of fixed procedures. This House shows the common habits and mores of the individual and the various groups to which s/he belongs. There can be a tendency to order purely transient things through propaganda, advertising and salesmanship to respond to immediate impressions and prejudices.

Concerning this House, Alan Oken states:

> The Second House deals with rewards coming from personal efforts as indicated by the First House. The Second is also affiliated with property and individual financial security in general.[24]

### *The esoteric consideration*

Spiritually, 'possessions' can relate to the wisdom that has been developed

23 Ibid., 511.

24 *Alan Oken's Complete Astrology*, 317.

to help control the form, or the entire personality. Emotional-mental attributes are one's possession carried through as a result of the incarnation process from former lives. This brings into question the intrinsic spiritual age of the native, for the production of illumination is an esoteric keynote of this House.

The second is a House of choice between left and right (hence there is a possible involvement in left hand practices). The building forces needed to master the spiritual Life come to the fore. Areas of self-interest, yogic practices, dietary considerations, alternative healing practices, thought-form building and mantra work can all be considered. The general propaganda of any society or group to which the disciple belongs is also seeded here.

D.K. states concerning the second House:

> Finances. Monetary interchange.—Prana.
> Expenditures.—Use of energy.
> Possessions.—control of the form.
> Losses.—Withdrawal from matter.
> Gains.—Acquisition of spiritual powers.

> ...Taurus, the mother of illumination, and Venus the endower of mind plus the embodied soul, are related and active in this house. The light of matter and the light of the soul are both involved in the use of energy and in the problem of what is desired, what is regarded as loss, and what shall be the gained objective. It is therefore the house of values—material or spiritual.[25]

*Prāṇa* relates to the type or quality of the energy (qualitatively or quantitatively) that manifests through the personality vehicle. 'Money' is also a form of *prāṇa,* and can also be viewed as *karmic* reward or karmic opportunity, seen here in terms of producing freedom, rather than limitation. Such freedom necessitates dissipating past *karma,* or to produce actions leading to liberation, the ability to rightly build for the afterlife. 'Possessions' esoterically concern the ability to draw upon Ashramic resources by gaining the experiences and qualities (newly emerging light) wherein Ashramic involvement becomes possible. The native learns to rightly utilise *prāṇa* and psychic resources to awaken the illumined Mind. (Thus explaining the *yogin's* concern for breathing exercises.) Much affected by the various energies and impressions continuously manifesting through the lower psychic centres ('atlanteanism') can come to the fore. The general attitudes of the devotee may be seen.

---

25 *Esoteric Astrology,* 511.

## The third House

Governed by Gemini, Mercury (the fourth Ray) and Venus (the fifth Ray).

### *The exoteric consideration*

The keyword is the environment: the ordinary environment or conveniences through which someone achieves a perspective upon his/her own existence. This House concerns the personal ties manifesting as blood relations of all family connections (brothers and sisters, relatives), except maybe parents or children. The concern is with the fundamental outward rather than inward impulses, producing all possible casual relationships such as the people one works with, commuters, etc. It also includes all immediate and practical conveniences or communications of normal life (the run-of-the-mill possessions that are taken for granted). This House governs short journeys or activities where no adjustment in consciousness or current routine is involved, needing only the simple perception of things.

Concerning this House, Alan Oken states:

> The Third House concerns short-distance travel (those lasting one day or less, or a series of such short journeys which may collectively last longer). Its primary function is to describe the nature of *relationship* to the immediate environment (as opposed to the First House, which shows self-projection upon the immediate environment). A study of the Third House is often instrumental in determining the general mental structure of a given individual. It is also the "House of Immediate Family" (excluding parents and including neighbors and fraternal-type friends) and the sphere of the horoscope devoted to high school.[26]

### *The esoteric consideration*

*Mercury*, the illumined mind, and *Gemini* the twins are the intermediaries between all positive and negative forces. They produce the fluid, analytical Gemini native that is able to reason well in all types of situations and circumstances. Versatility, constant mutable activity and a quick sensitive reaction to his/her own and other's needs are the keywords of the Gemini aspirant. There is much struggle between the divine (the immortal brother) and the sensual (the mortal brother) aspects of the Gemini subject. The brothers must learn to hold hands in service to humanity. Such struggle can be reflected in this House.

The general etheric framework of the body and its relation to the impact of external energies must also be noted. (There can be a constant agitation of *prāṇic*

---

26 *Alan Oken's Complete Astrology*, 317-18.

and auric energies via the *chakras.)* The concern is thus with developing psychic awareness (the powers associated with the *chakras,* right auric qualities, etc.).

General concerns with lower psychic achievements and general *prāṇic* energies throughout the body can manifest – thus short journeys of mental reveries and emotions, growing into light and the higher awareness via intuitive perceptions. The fourth Ray wielded by Mercury governs humanity in general, hence right human relations come to the fore here. There can be a general affiliation with esoteric groups (the esoteric concept of 'family') wherein service work is accomplished, producing much involvement with the environment wherein resides general humanity.

## The fourth house

Governed by Cancer and the Moon (fourth Ray), veiling Vulcan (for the undeveloped or average person – the first Ray) and Neptune (the sixth Ray) for the highly developed person.

### *The exoteric consideration*

The keyword is the *home environment,* the true place of residence of the mental-emotions, thus the place wherein experiences of the personality life are gained. The personal self's own special positiveness.

This House reveals the nature of the personality as an abstraction, or else it charts that point in life where all external forces merge to produce the totality of self-existence. This House concerns the characteristic activity of the personality's relatively unchanging being, rather than the momentary or transient dependence upon exterior events. Seen are those qualities substantiating one's inner creativeness that may be relied upon. The 'home' here is the truly self-sufficient and personal milieu of experience (what one builds for oneself, thus the establishment of one's private reality), specifically in relation to family life. The native's degree of conformity to the ultimate expectation in life is seen – what is kept on in perpetuity for that life, rather than its later termination. What is perpetuated is the bondage to what was established early in life.

This is the House of responsibility, the father who creates and preserves the family name or its reputation. ('The father' here is the ambassador for the inner child fascinated by the world beyond the confines of daily routines and physical limitations.)

Concerning this House, Alan Oken states:

> The Fourth House is the foundation of life insofar as it reveals the nature of one's domestic situation. It is also a contributing factor which reveals the way events in life often terminate.[27]

***The esoteric consideration***

D.K. states:

> The Moon is the ruler of Cancer and is related to the fourth ray, and rules the fourth house. Here you have the idea of form being the custodian of a living spiritual essence, of the home, whether the home is the fourth or lowest aspect of the personality or the fourth kingdom in nature, but all ruled by the fourth Ray of Harmony through Conflict—a harmony to be wrought out within the form on Earth.[28]

The Moon is a non-sacred planet and therefore is one of the planets that primarily affects personality life in the three worlds. The 'home' therefore is whatever Ray (mental, emotional, or physical quality) dominates the disciple's environment. It is specifically concerned with what has been built from the substance of the past and which is established as 'the home' of the present activities. This relates to the mental or emotional habitat that produces the native's long-term observable characteristics, rather than the vicissitudes of fleeting, fickle thoughts and emotions.

Indications must be sought here for the ability of the aspirant to seek out and mould into his/her personality equipment what is needed for future Ashramic activity or service work. The establishment of a specialised field through which one may serve (and by which one will become known, such as a scientist or doctor) might be seen. The *bodhicitta* Mind manifested in accordance with the native's esoteric Ray line then dominates the personality life. This is directed by the sixth Ray Neptunian potency.

Here a 'home' concerns one's ability to refine and stabilise one's auric qualities (the Cancerian 'shell'), thus to eliminate undesirable qualities. The priority is an establishment of the fundamental spiritual goal or ideal that expresses the Ray type, and to harmonise this in relation to the group or society wherein one forms a part. Indicated also is what is needed to produce an adequate mental 'permanent' spiritual home – a job future, career or field or service. 'The Father' refers to what produces complete Soul expression (enlightenment) by mastering *saṃsāra*.

27 Ibid., 316.

28 *Esoteric Astrology,* 508.

## The fifth House

Governed by Leo, the Sun (exoterically) and the Sun (esoterically), which veils Uranus (the planet of occultism, group relations and organisations). Uranus also relates Leo to the eleventh House.

### *The exoteric consideration*

The keywords for this House are offspring plus the unlimited potentialities for self-discovery and real adventure. This 'offspring' represents the outreaching, relatively instinctive activity of the personality learning through experimental trial and error. It is the gain of direct experience through non-inhibitive self-observation.

Here manifests self-expression of the personality, which incorporates all forms of pleasurable experience and the places (outlets of amusement) whereby they can be experienced. These include temperamental or emotional outbursts, courtship rituals, casual sexual relationships, pregnancy and children. (Courtship leads to marriage in the seventh House.) This House shows the degree of generally persistent self-expression, thus the strength of the personality in decision making, as how to act or react in any given circumstance. All forms of self-discovery in childhood are embraced. The rulership persists through the creative dynamics (artistry, etc.) of one's identity though a relatively dilettante interest. When such effort manipulates creativity for purposes other than intrinsic pleasure, then the rulership shifts to the third House. Despite the artistic, rhythmic and creative effort of the native, the activity here remains solipsistic. The creativity becomes the experience through which the self is momentarily sufficiently aware to act freely and without inhibition. A negative outcome can be the wastage of resources through speculative gambling.

Alan Oken states:

> The Fifth House is concerned with family resources, in the form of children, and the expression of personal creative ability in the arts which come about as the result of a firm establishment of oneself as an individual as expressed through the Fourth House. The Fifth House is also extremely important in regard to one's romantic life to the extent that one's love nature is very much an expression of the state of emotional development (Fourth House).[29]

### *The esoteric consideration*

Here the energies of the Soul project many facets of *illumination* into the

29 *Alan Oken's Complete Astrology*, 317.

aspiring personality, its 'offspring'. This produces unlimited potentialities for the creative expression of that personality.

D.K. states:

> The Sun, the transmitter of the energy of the second ray, rules the fifth house or mansion of the soul, the causal body in this case; the force of Leo is also involved, the force of the self-conscious soul. The spiritual man, aware of his identity says in this house: "I am the eternal cause of all relation. I am and I exist." The dualism of the second Ray is first realised in the fifth house by man, the embodied fifth principle.[30]

In many ways, this is the House of the illumined Soul, ruled by the Sun. The Sun is a non-sacred planet that primarily affects the life of the mental body and consequently the illumined Mind of aspirants and their various ideas. Trials and errors here concern the field of service, the thought-forms and impressions that can be likened to 'children and pleasurable sexual relationships'.

In this House, the Ashramic experiences of the Soul-infused disciple come to the fore, plus the disciple's involvement in groups and in society in general. The awakening Mind of the meditating aspirant or disciple allows it to be a spectator of the appearing images and upon its reflection of *saṃsāra*. The ability to thus visualise is prominent here, for the Soul projects into the personality the qualities or illumination needed to meet aspirational thinking, lofty ideas and service work. In this way, the Soul becomes definitely involved with its 'child', or 'children' (if a series of seven incarnations are taken into account). Hints concerning these incarnations may be gleaned in this House. The quintiles (72 degree angles) in the natal chart are important in relation to the possibility of such discovery. The qualities to be gained by the personality to become illumined may thus be gleaned. This process includes various experiments, trials and errors in many fields of expression, for one must be master of all aspects of phenomena in order to become enlightened. The mind must be fully developed if the aspirant is to become an Initiate. Specifically, hints that concern taking the third Initiation might be gleaned. After knowledge has been fully gained by the personality, and thus imprinted into the petals of the Soul, it then becomes a quality of expression in the ninth House. Possible hindrances to illumination or impressions from the Soul (or the misapplication of its energies) should also be looked for in the aspects to this House.

---

30 *Esoteric Astrology*, 508-09.

## The sixth House

Governed by Virgo, Mercury (the fourth Ray) and the Moon (the fourth Ray).

***The exoteric consideration***

The key concept here concerns duty, where one's social responsibilities determine one's place in the world. This House governs work that people do not particularly enjoy. For example, what is inconvenient or distasteful, difficult or unsuited occupations in decidedly unfavourable situations that must be accomplished. The labour may result in climbing up a social ladder via activity that may affect a whole organisation. A mutual benefit may be produced and useful skills gained, though often in an impersonal manner.

The sixth House also governs sicknesses, fatigue, aches, pains and dissatisfaction in life. One can either learn from such experiences or succumb to them emotionally. Thus various physiological and psychological aspects of the psyche must be analysed. Inner strengths can come to the fore, or else various frustrations in life.

Group living, social responsibility and sense (what can be learnt from such relationships), plus communal activities, care for domesticated or farm animals, working in factories, being involved in the military, etc., must also be analysed. This House rules all professional activities and whatever offers values and rewards for an individual, as well as conscious sharing of personal relationships with others. There is a movement from subjective to objective realms of experience to produce beneficial practical realities. Here momentary caprices must give way to serious disciplined activity needed to fulfil one's obligations. The native must generally learn to adjust to all forms of situations, to help or rightly act, or else there is an inability to do so through lack of capacity to control what is happening.

Alan Oken states:

> The Sixth House controls various jobs which may or may not constitute separate facets of one's career. The Sixth House is concerned with the general state of health and with those individuals who are employees. It is also concerned with small animals, especially household pets.[31]

***The esoteric consideration***

Virgo holds the foetal Christ consciousness in her womb. It is for this reason that the sixth house governs the service work that will definitely bring that consciousness into fruition. Here also the powers of the personality can be seen

---

31 *Alan Oken's Complete Astrology*, 318.

to be the strongest. Virgo governs that point in time wherein the angelic kingdom (Nature, governed by this sixth, feminine sign) and humanity are first able to interrelate and work at a common goal. The fluid, intuitive, analytical mind of Mercury allows the native in this House much scope in any of the chosen various fields of service work.

Virgo and Scorpio mark the crucial points of integration of body, speech and mind, where the personality is consciously working to become Soul infused. The process starts in Leo and by the time Scorpio is reached there is the crisis of the testings for Initiation in that sign. Virgo produces the forms of activities that signify the lowest point of descent of Spirit into matter. Virgo is consequently the bearer of the Christ-child. The signs of the birthing of that 'child' must thus be sought.

Virgo rules the manifestation of time. This House thus governs the entire background of the external service work for humanity and for animals. Much experimental trial and error, with consequential misdirected zeal and attachments to erroneous and distorted viewpoints and philosophies, is a distinct possibility. Sought for is everything that might seed the undertaking of the first and second Initiations. The concept of impersonality within the context of the spiritual group one belongs to is first developed (a difficult thing to do). This happens as the Heart centre is increasingly awakened. Thus is produced a developing capacity to respond to and consciously translate inner Hierarchical impressions into an outer field of service. One can also seek the possibility of the native to clairvoyantly contact and work with *devas.*

The concept of 'sickness' (to which natives of this sign are prone) can also be thought of in terms of frequent relapses into worldly affairs and mundane consciousness *(saṁsāra).* The battle between divine and personality forces often produce physiological and psychosomatic effects. The inability to meditate and the engendering of undesirable thought-forms may thus come to the fore. Such tendencies must here be overcome and the consequent gains utilised as a springboard towards enlightenment. This House may chart the aspirant's ability to thus strive.

'Sickness' also concerns problems associated with refining the energies from the lower centres (as centred upon the Solar Plexus) and directing them to the Heart centre. Causes for emotional distress and turmoil may be seen as a consequence of the stimulus of incoming energies from the Soul and contact with Hierarchy. Such stimulus conflicts with personality activities, producing the testings in Scorpio in the eighth House.

The rewards of organisational activity to discipline the physical body and its addictions to sensuality and various attachments need to be sought out. There may be attraction to *hatha yoga* techniques that involve correct eating, breathing, postures, the control of the emotions and thoughts. (The things related to attaining the first Initiation.) Note that generally Virgo governs the precepts of the Eightfold Path of the Buddha.

## The seventh House

Governed by Libra, Venus (fifth Ray) and Uranus (the seventh Ray).

### *The exoteric consideration*

The keywords for this House are partnership and long-term relationships. Partnerships can be seen as business endeavours or as in marriage. Such partnerships are genuine, whether transient or life-long. They may however lack personal satisfaction unless there is a proper change in oneself, such as is found in the eighth House. Here one continually rediscovers oneself in relationships with other selves where there may be joint interests. Bonds are seen to develop between people that share similar social conventions or activities. These bonds are viewed as between equals and not between superior and inferior. (They are not the taken-for-granted experiences seen in the third House.) The seventh House also rules the broad interrelationships between people in all forms of human affairs, especially all professional relationships where exchange of money is involved. (The attributes of their clients and patients are shown in the sixth House.)

Both friendly and unfriendly relations and affairs are indicated in the seventh House. Thus, tendencies towards conflict, animosity and war may emerge. Such can often be the case when exchange of money is involved. Various alternatives and opportunities that partnerships may produce in any given situation can thus also manifest. All special involvement in public activity, such as in the field of music or in any of the other arts, can also be looked for in this House.

Alan Oken states:

> The nature of the First House can be characterized as the "House of Self." The Seventh House, its polarity, can be called the "House of Others." It concerns itself with marriage and the marriage partner as well as with business partnerships. It is the House of open enemies and opponents as well as of those circumstances in which one has to develop a sense of cooperation in order to successfully achieve one's goals.[32]

---

32 *Alan Oken's Complete Astrology*, 316.

***The esoteric consideration***

Libra governs lasting relationships because it is the sign of the balance between all extremes, allowing all beings to settle and equilibrate their differences. The judicial attitude, or equanimity, of the Libran allows contemplation between right and wrong, especially where sex, partnership and money matters are concerned. Venus embodies the intelligent mind that is at first united with desire and later is transmuted into Love, producing an ordered world of beauty and harmony. The fifth Ray (Venus) is that of scientific adaptation and productivity in all of life's activities.

The esoteric ruler, Uranus, the planet of occultism, assists the practical ritualistic awareness for the aspirant here. Uranus facilitates work in an Ashram or exoteric organisation, the ability to relate to group energies and pressures. 'Marriage' can relate to the union between various energies *(prāṇa)* in the body, the complete integration of personality and Soul forces. This produces the proper work of the Initiate or disciple in the world, and their relationships with other disciples and people in general. Here the Ray qualities of the general field of service or environment in which one labours can come to the fore.

One can look towards karmic qualifications needed for future life's activities, hence the esoteric or karmic gain (or loss) of one's social work. The social or karmic effect of the work done is seen, whether immediately sensational or having long-term effectiveness. (It may be truly beneficial or useful only for the immediate present). The *karma* can produce warring attitudes. Such 'war' is seen esoterically in the oft fanatical antipathy possessed by those entrenched in limited ideas, philosophies and viewpoints. They are generally materialistic or associated with the left hand path. These attitudes clash with those presented by the Initiate or disciple. The Initiate's views will always seem radical and new to those that resist change. There will thus often be a clash or warring of opinions.

D.K. states that:

> The seventh Ray of Ceremonial Order or Organisation is felt in the house of relationships, of organisations and of mutual effort and of aspiration (either towards good or evil). The forces of this ray work out in the seventh or physical plane—the plane whereon major changes in all forms are made and on which the disciple must firmly stand as he takes initiation.[33]

---

33 *Esoteric Astrology,* 540.

The seventh House also indicates spiritual opportunity and alternatives, such as opportunity for intense meditative activity, or teaching service via presenting a definite organisation through which to work. Opportunity can be afforded by money, travel (physically, or to the higher domains), or spiritual partnerships. Alternatives regarding vocations (such as a scientific trend, be this materialistic, esoteric or occultly speculative) might be seen. There could also be a visionary or psychic opportunity associated with awakening psychic powers. Possible inner revelations of the occultist might thus be gleaned. Indications of the coming testings for Initiation (in the next house ruled by Scorpio) might also be found.

## The eighth House

Governed by Scorpio, Mars (the sixth Ray) and Pluto (the first Ray).

### *The exoteric consideration*

The keyword is regeneration of oneself (or resources) through harnessing one's inner potential. This produces self-discovery, psychological rebirth, and production of new or higher forms of experience. Regeneration means the death of former attitudes and attachments. The native of this House accepts the new values or attitudes in society after psychologically surrendering the old. The new cycles and relationships may be challenging after the death of the old limitations have been achieved. This is therefore the place or House of death, of sudden changes, which may be anarchistic, but the response may be in order to please others, an outreaching in hope for a reward, to live in the context of the ideals of others. Sexual attractiveness or romance can thus also strongly manifest in this House. The native can pander to the whims of the self or produce sacrificial activity in order to meet the challenges ahead.

There can be significant fretting over past concerns, or else there is the production of emotional exhilaration, or its violent corollary. Obtaining money through legacies, wills, or coming through other avenues (rather than one's own hard work), can also be indicated. Religious matters or intellectual pursuits can be exemplified, hence the manifestation of a significant conscience, internal morality, being intuitive, or possessing sustained rational thought.

Alan Oken states:

> The Eighth is the House of other people's resources insofar as the Eighth House signifies the ability or inability to regenerate one's Self and material possessions through a harnessing of the energies available to the individual through partners

> and general social relationships. This is especially true in regard to legacies and other benefits brought either through marriage, business, and partnerships or in ways in which money is not directly earned by the individual. It is the "House of Death" because this is the phase of human existence wherein the individual passes through a state of complete transformation and joins with the collective energies of the human race. It is also the "House of Sex" (as opposed to the Fifth, the "House of Romance"), since sex is another transforming principle at work in human existence.[34]

***The esoteric consideration***

The concept of death, dissolution and detachment are concerned with the changeover from empirical to spiritual or abstract thinking upon the path of discipleship. Mars is a non-sacred planet, its energies therefore primarily affect life in the three worlds – particularly concerning the astral body (the emotions) and the planetary astral shell.

D.K. states:

> Pluto, transmitting first ray energy, rules Scorpio, the sign of discipleship, of the man ready for the fusion brought about through the influence of the sacred planets, and governs the house of major separations and of death. "The arrow of God pierces the heart and death takes place." But in this connection it must be remembered that death is definitely brought about by the soul. It is the soul which shoots the arrow of death. (The upward pointing arrow is the esoteric symbol of Pluto.)[35]

This is the House of birth from one state of consciousness to the next. Here the 'turning about in the seat of consciousness' that first eventuated in the seventh House (the house of contemplation and of relationships) redirects the aspirant's vision to new and challenging cycles of relationships. The eighth House is that of trials and tests of every kind concerned with emotional cleansing which leads to regeneration. Regeneration here signifies the ability to comprehend the past and to envision the future, to work towards a long-time goal where new attributes to awaken and master will develop. Possible traits carried through into the next life may need to be sought out. The astral form is completely interwoven with that of the society or group to which the aspirant belongs, thus this cleansing process necessitates coming to grips with the various realities of human society. It may

34 *Alan Oken's Complete Astrology,* 317.

35 *Esoteric Astrology,* 509. See also page 538.

incur a reclusive existence or direct pragmatic involvement with human affairs. In any case, these activities are the result of the new awareness that emotional cleansing affords, producing a second birth. Always seek here the possibility of trauma or a set of traumatic experiences, points of crises that lead to revelations and new perspectives on life.

Death can be considered as:

- Physical death wherein people vacate their shells to enter the astral or mental realms.
- The death of undesirable qualities (such as emotional and personality traits) leading eventually to the death of the personality at the third initiation. This concerns the yogic death associated with overcoming *saṃsāra* – the fleeting, phenomenal world of illusion and the emotion-filled activities that obscure people's spiritual vision.
- Death of the Soul at the fourth Initiation.

The tendency is to conform to the attitudes of the spiritual group, by following the guru or teaching by imitating the example. Via the influence of Mars, there can be a (fanatical) demonstration of faith in 'God', the afterlife, the guru figure, the development of the creative imagination, or complete identification with group activities. There is thus the religious devotee of all types. The emerging theme of world service (rather than self-service) can lead to extremes: celibacy, fanaticism, or if the emotions are completely controlled – the Initiate. In this House thus, self-sacrifice and service (the zealous devotion to a chosen path, profession or service) is greatest.

Violence (often internalised) may result from the emotional tests succumbed to (of the associated karmic cleansing), for there may be resistance to the rhythms of the new cycle and the ending of glamour. The aspirant must defeat the normal sluggishness of consciousness. The resultant problems of a disciple's illumination in the society to which he/she was formerly attached (which may clash with the new outlook) must be looked for. Implied are *karma* producing crises and the qualities possessed to deal with them.

Legacies, wills, etc., signify *karma* that may fruit, reaping the rewards of good actions from past lives. Sudden 'wealth' esoterically concerns having to deal with increased energisation and spiritual realisations concurrent with emotional control. This produces attendant problems and also exaltations for the disciple.

Truly loving attitudes may manifest once the emotions are properly controlled as a result of the first Ray activity of Pluto. Major tests in this House will concern thought-form building, which the disciple must learn to rightly express, and then to dissipate. Ideas, ideals and aspirations of all types must be checked in relation to aspects with this House. The religion or philosophy to which the disciple adheres and advocates will become esoteric in nature. Receptivity to the inner *dharma,* the ability to respond to the Intuition and what facilitates or hinders this, should be sought for. 'Long journeys' relate to the ability to grasp comprehensive abstract formulations and mould them into the service work in any of the directions of the eight-armed cross.

## The ninth House

Governed by Sagittarius, Jupiter (the second Ray) and the earth (the third Ray).

### *The exoteric consideration*

The key term for this House is understanding, which comes as a consequence of passing through the death process of the eighth House and of the testings to establish the new. Understanding is the expression of the gain of former experiences. This is the House, therefore, of consciousness – of all forms of thinking, people's memories or imagination that build the attributes of the personality, of self-identity. All aspects of one's consciousness including dreams, memory, the thinking processes, inspiration, general knowledge and imagination. (Everything, therefore, except the immediate focus of self-identity, which is handled by the first House and the ascendant.) Scientific thinking, gleaning facts, producing publications, expressions of wisdom and social mores all come to the fore. This is also the House of religious outpouring, the manifestation of fame, the sense of justice, thinking and travel in relation to remote things and places.

This is the House of long journeys, of looking towards remote places, of explorations of the mind, which produce freedom of thought, to revel in attitudes and ideas away from simple everyday experiences. There can be an attraction to others who are similarly deep thinkers.

Alan Oken states:

> The Ninth House has special regard to long-distance travel, higher education, and the personal understanding of social mores and those concepts from which national law is derived. It is also the House of one's religious aspirations and associations. Since it is the Third House from the Seventh, it relates to a partner's relatives, just as the Third House from the First signifies kin.[36]

---

36 *Alan Oken's Complete Astrology*, 318.

***The esoteric consideration***

Sagittarius governs the thighs, the central position as far as the strength to do, make and accomplish things goes. Its keynote is direction in consciousness, time and space. The archer with his bow of aspiration fires arrows to any envisioned goal, and to the mountaintop of Initiation.

Here Jupiter (the lord of Love-Wisdom) rightly directs the activity of the mutable cross. The myriad experiences of the personality thereon (where wisdom is inevitably the outcome) are thereby brought to a final conclusion. Jupiter expands the aspects of the mind to produce comprehensive understanding in a far-seeing, compassionate manner. The awakening Mind helps direct the aspirant to the vision of the work to be done in Aquarius (to become a world server). Having passed the testing ground in Scorpio, disciples then naturally find their service arenas on earth via the Sagittarian one-pointed focus. (The esoteric ruler of Sagittarius, the Earth, focuses activity upon the terrestrial sphere.) The objectives of the manifestation of spiritual will and directives towards enlightenment are to be sought. The aspirant's intuition thus comes to fruition in this House. The Soul and personality become at-oned (for periods of time at least) and work to the visioned goal. Mental integration in the arena of the chosen profession or in service work produces a clear-headed grasp on the problems at hand and the ability to solve them. (Depending upon the aspects.) The higher spiritual Way of being directed through receptivity to impressions from Hierarchy becomes a definite possibility.

Law, fame, justice, publications and lectures, scientific work, the compendium of a large storehouse of knowledge, the ability to tap the 'rain cloud of knowable things', are all aspects of the aspirant on any of the Ray paths. The particular Ray path the native is on may become evident here. The innate hindrances, or what facilitates work in the chosen field of action (the strength of the mental capacity to achieve) may also be determined.

If one substitutes the words Initiate or disciple for the personality (in the exoteric consideration), then the general background of consciousness, which preserves the Initiate's self fidelity, identity, etc., will also be seen.

## The tenth House

Governed by Capricorn and Saturn (third Ray), both esoterically and exoterically.

### *The exoteric consideration*

This house governs the focus of a person's external situation in society, their honour or place in life as determined by considerations of normal or ethical human values. Here is seen the status or recognition by others of their professional capacity, which manifests as a set of socially accepted, dignified skills that are normally moralistic and honourable. Socially conditioned concepts of steadfastness of self-worth, superiority and personal integrity, professionalism and authority, are seen. Spiritual relationships also come to the fore, and sensitivity to group activities. This house thus also connects to the nature of the relationship to one's employer (or superior in business, etc.), or else one's competency in business or other activities. Demonstrative prestige or power naturally comes to the fore as a consequence of the ambition that continues from the former Sagittarian disposition. With this comes the enjoyment of one's success and consequent security in life. Highlighted is the mother, or a parent one is closely linked to, for such family life provides a sense of security and integration into social structures.

Alan Oken states:

> This domicile is extremely involved with one's social position and the career through which one makes one's social contribution. It is the House of the most dominant parent in one's life while the Fourth House represents the other, less influential parent.[37]

### *The esoteric consideration*

Capricorn is the tenth sign (the number of perfection and of completion). It rules the mountaintop of Initiation and also the most material depths of being (the hard, rocky earth). This relates to the consummation of the mind and the power it can wield for good or for evil. Hints of significant materialistic attitudes and strong intellectual characteristics can thus be sought in this House. The surefooted, determined goat eventually becomes transfigured into the unicorn with the single horn of high perception and prosperity. Prosperity may be material or spiritual, for great heights in either may be seen. There can be a demonstration of authority over others once the needed learning process associated with a chosen field has been completed.

Saturn (the third Ray) is the Lord of *karma* that governs the three worlds of human livingness. In this House, therefore, people reap the benefits of their earthly

---

37 *Alan Oken's Complete Astrology*, 316.

*karma*. The disciple's concern in this House is the nature of the manifestation of *karma* and what needs to be done to work it off. Inevitably, the Initiate must be able to control his/her own manifestation of destiny.

Concerning Saturn, D.K. states:

> An understanding of these hindering or stimulating effects can easily be grasped by those who can comprehend the nature of the activities of Saturn. This is the planet that conditions primarily the point in evolution where choice definitely becomes possible, where rejection of opportunity or its acceptance can consciously be undertaken, and the shouldering of personal responsibility becomes a recognised fact in a planned and ordered life.[38]

The third Ray of Mathematically Exact Activity rules this House, honouring the special skills needed to govern all aspects of material life. 'Honour' relates to the Initiation level undertaken, or a disciple's high point of revelation.

Forms of *rāja yoga* practices to awaken the Head or Throat centre are exemplified here. The objective is complete control over the physical form – its appetites, desires and activities in the world. Complete mental equilibrium and general freedom from illusion thus comes to the fore.

Capricorn also rules the central spinal column, the liberation of the goddess *kuṇḍalinī* and her destructive or creative potency. Right awakening of this energy signifies the open door into Hierarchical experience. Possibilities of left hand tendencies (materialistic or psychic ambition) in the native can, however, also be sought for. Many spiritually ignorant people desirous of psychic power try to awaken *kuṇḍalinī* prematurely, producing problematic effects in their psyche. Such tendencies are exemplified in this House. Also, most disciples upon the spiritual path have significant residual *karma* from past lives with black magical practices. The nature of the manifesting *karma* is thus always a significant theme of this House. For the Initiate, ambition is completely transformed into subservience to the Plan that produces the needed expansions of consciousness. The mode of travel up the mountaintop for them is symbolically on the knees, via humbleness.

The disciple's relation to their spiritual teacher (Master) or group (the symbolic 'mother') and related service arena (according to Ray type) can also be sought. This House thus indicates the nature of the flowering of the Mind in a service arena as a consequence of contact with them. The environment of the related Ray service activity may thus be indicated. The 'mother' also concerns the entire

38 *Esoteric Astrology*, 19-20.

material world (Nature), and the angelic kingdom. In this House, attraction to the magical arts is highlighted, thus indications of a disciple's possible working with *devas* can be sought. (Similarly for the sixth House.)

## The eleventh House

Governed by Aquarius, Uranus (the seventh Ray) and Jupiter (the sixth Ray).

### *The exoteric consideration*

Friendship is a major attribute of this House, where the hopes or wishes of one to one relationships are exemplified. This may produce preferential treatment. From this evolves counselling and the advice presented, or the way that this may be framed by legislation or enacted by law. (Rather than what comes through direct experience, a ninth House expression.) Conscientious favouritism through personal choice or through other means may also manifest. The general momentum of the way a person's life evolves is indicated, to produce increasingly expansive experiences. (The opposite to the inferences of the fifth House.) Such momentum is generally ruled by the objectives, hopes and wishes of a person, especially through socialising and cooperating with others. Thus there is the enjoyment that comes from communal sharing or working together to produce common objectives. (This is contrasted with the self-opinionated solipsism of the native of the fifth House.) Success then is obtained through such friendship, group experience, partiality to ideas, and social coherence. This produces a collective flow of events, optimism, visioning, idealism, hopes of success. The potentialities of the group whole are thereby strengthened and often materialised in the form of legislation or codes of conduct. The dynamism of such interrelationships strengthen the power of the individual to cope or succeed in life, to visualise a bright future.

Alan Oken states:

> The Eleventh House concerns social connections obtained through one's career or position. This is the sphere of activity where personal ideas for self-expression become broadened through the assimilation of new data and the application of intellectual growth toward the larger collective of humanity.
>
> The Eleventh, the "House of Friends and Associates," is the natural domicile of Aquarius and its rulers, Uranus and Saturn.[39]

### *The esoteric consideration*

Aquarius indicates the totality of one's energies and capabilities (latent, real,

39 *Alan Oken's Complete Astrology*, 317.

or objectivised) when integrated and aligned. This happens after having gained the visions and awareness that the mountaintop experience affords. In this House the thirst for higher knowledge, wisdom, love, the divine, the transcendental, etc., is quenched. Otherwise the personality motivated native pursues the sensual, the material or the transitory. Aquarius stimulates the highest, most visionary, constructive, artistic or creative amplitude that a person is capable of. An Aquarian leitmotif concerns group activities, group sharing, thus opportunity for group focused activity must be sought in this House. The wavy lines of this sign indicate a free-flowing openness to all influences that embrace the person, as Aquarius is an Air sign. The downpour of *buddhi,* the 'Blood' that vitalises groups (as coherent organisms), signifies this fact. What may be seen is the extent that this energy can manifest without glamour (emotional distortions) manifesting. This House thus signifies the ability to express Love to all beings.

The energy of Uranus (ruling the seventh Ray of Ceremonial Magic, of Materialising Power) encourages the formation of beneficent organisations that will govern the interrelationships in our society. It also governs the mineral kingdom, wherein lies the esoteric work (the alchemical processes) to transmute base metals (base psychological attributes) into spiritual gold (enlightenment attributes). Uranus stimulates the trends towards the ideals and idealism, of cooperation and the community spirit, which need to be sought in the native of this House. Such attitudes will be the mainstay of the forthcoming Aquarian age.

Here friendships, interrelationships between disciples in their spiritual group (or Ashram), must be sought. There may be positive and negative aspects in such relationships, such as during discussions and formulations of plans of the best course of action. The mode of how the New Age organisations and structures will be built, developed and rightly financed, will be on the mind of those influenced by this House. The visioned plan or goal regarding the field of service and the ability to galvanise those with whom one must serve is actualised. Such activity establishes a (spiritual) code of ethics or rules of conduct that the members of the group can follow. The ability to council other's esoteric needs may come to the fore. The various factors (esoteric or exoteric) concerning group involvement are thus indicated here. The Ray qualifications of the group (seen as a unit and possessing a life of its own), or the interrelation between various Rays may be discovered. They are the needed potentialities that will strengthen the group's effectiveness in the world.

This House thus determines the ability of the group or individual to respond to new Aquarian impulses, or whether they are still in the throttlehold of Piscean ideas and methods.

## The twelfth House

Governed by Pisces, Jupiter (the second Ray) and Pluto (the first Ray).

***The exoteric consideration***

The key concept is that of confinement, an inward compulsion to institutionalise all relationships and experiences. Things are put within artificial bounds or social limitations of mind, thus potentially manifesting in a disciplined lifestyle (as seen working in a business regime, or within a hospital). Good or bad can come from such limitations. Confinement can relate to the creation of imaginary devils, evils or enemies. Psychological problems thus can result, and outward reactions of violent action, malice or crime. This may result in incarceration, or mental-emotional self-isolation. Problematic *karma* thus often surfaces.

This House may also produce fortunate circumstances, significant wealth, or valuable human interrelationships. The native discovers the relation of his/ her little place in the vaster universe to awaken hidden reservoirs of knowledge. This allows true independence from limiting social constraints, to be able to consciously shine in that society.

There is therefore the possibility of a two-faced consequence. In the subjective life, flights of fancy may appear where the native may feel persecuted and misunderstood. Conversely, they may experience a positive response to intuitions that produce self-confidence in handling the problems of life. Thus, all things that either stimulate or conflict with consciousness may manifest. Once understood, it allows the native to galvanise all resources to overcome imaginative foibles, the confining beasts of fear, etc. The native can then awaken to the mastery of all social possibilities.

Alan Oken states:

> The Twelfth House affects clandestine relationships and hidden enemies. In this respect the Twelfth House may also indicate those internal factors which can contribute to one's undoing. The Twelfth is called the "House of Karma" and for good reason. The situations described through a study of this domicile, its ruler in a given nativity (as opposed to its natural rulers), and those planetary bodies located within its boundaries describe the circumstances an individual must overcome in order to be free of firm bindings and destructive restrictions as well as negative patterns of recurrent relationships. Such institutions as prisons, asylums, and monasteries and other forms of secluded places of residence or confinement are also associated with the Twelfth.[40]

---

40 *Alan Oken's Complete Astrology*, 318-19.

***The esoteric consideration***

Pisces is the sign of bondage, mediumship, sacrifice and death. The objective of the experience in Pisces (under the stimulus of Jupiter) is to allow the imprisoned Soul within the personality to begin the process of transmuting the lower negative aspects of the human psyche into positive, liberating virtues. A real problem to the native of this House concerns the mediumistic tendency of being receptive to collective thought-forms, or of powerful vitalised ideas and ideals, but not having the capacity to properly discern truth from untruth. There can be much wrongly emphasised Piscean zeal and attachment to devotional *(bhakti)* organisations. The pros and cons of such possible attachment need careful study in the natal chart.

The statement by D.K. in relation to Pisces has some bearing upon its significance in the twelfth House:

> It would be of interest to find out two things scientifically:
>
> 1. Whether the majority of the lowest kind of medium (trance mediums in particular) have Pisces dominant in some powerful manner in their charts.
> 2. Whether those mediums who are becoming more positive and more *self*-controlled and who are beginning to get a glimpse of the higher correspondence in their work – mediatorship and interpretative activity—have not got Virgo appearing somewhere with real potency and activity. This might indicate the awakening of the mind, in the first instance, and eventually that there was a shift in the influence controlling them, from the orthodox planetary rulership to that of the more esoteric planets.[41]

Pisces governs the final death of the Soul form. The possibility of lesser forms of death of personality aspects (such as of emotional attributes) and of the karmic situations that might bring these about will thus be found in this House. There will be a tendency to institutionalise or to create completely self-enclosed thought-forms (concerning the next sphere or phase of the needed creative work) and to actualise them in the material world. Pisces signifies a general preparation of a Soul's need to return to incarnation, which reflects in the disciple as a downward focussed meditation to consciously project energies into the form. (The service arena of the disciple.)

Here one must look for the possibility of the lower psychism within a person. If unable to adequately express the full potential of the divine (the impulses of the Soul), then the consciousness can be considered to exist in a prison. The

41 *Esoteric Astrology,* 124-25.

possibility of such imprisonment, and the mechanism of release, needs to be scrutinised via the aspects to this House.

This House can provide the ability to discipline attitudes towards internal realisations, thus producing death to all outer attachments and contacts (the yogic attitude to life). One may then receive unanticipated help, the gift or 'grace wave from the guru', or meeting the Master or Teacher who shows the way out of the imprisoned form. (An effect of the esoteric ruler, Pluto, the lord of death.) Modes of discovering Hierarchy or impressions from them may be sought here, thus special karmic situations that might facilitate this (coming from unexpected directions).

This House signifies the possibility of complete death of the personality nature, to consciously reside in the domains of the Soul, or of Hierarchy. For Initiates, Shambhala may become the focus. There is a possibility of visioning the broad overall perspective of world events in any field, to act to rectify imbalances, and yet be independent in that action. The first Ray (Pluto) provides a 'stand aloof' attitude, and yet the second Ray's compassionate understanding from Jupiter can also manifest.

This House can chart the esoteric problems associated with gaining the resources needed for the task of world salvation: whether purely subjective (as in terms of thought-form projection), or with more mundane organisational practicalities and activities. There is thus a consequent possibility of handling large numbers of people and rightly directing their common realisations (their collective unconsciousness). If viewed yogically, then the elements composing the body and its consciousness as a whole must be dealt with.

# 5

# History of the Zodiac

Comprehension of the nature of the history of the zodiac necessitates understanding somewhat the esoteric doctrine concerning the evolution of the Root Races of humanity. For those who are not familiar with this subject, a summary is provided in Appendix two of my book *Esoteric Cosmology and Modern Physics.* Detail is given in Volume two (entitled 'Anthropogenesis') of H.P. Blavatsky's *The Secret Doctrine.* The reader can also peruse through the many comments made by D.K. in his books.

The Lemurians were the Root Race wherein what passed for human consciousness then (being nearly void of mind *per se,* and the emotions were non-existent) first incarnated into dense (animal) forms many millions of years ago. Subsequently, the Atlanteans developed the emotions and consequently built the desire forms that became the heaven and hell states now known as the astral plane. The Aryans (our present human civilisation) developed the intellectual capabilities of the mind. The next Root Race will become vastly more intuitive and adept in abstract thought than what people presently are.

Below is a figure taken from *Esoteric Cosmology and Modern Physics* (Figure 45 therein), summarising the evolution of both the subhuman (the numbers 1-10) and human kingdoms (1a-10a). This is provided as a quick reference for those with little or no knowledge of the subject. I shall only give the description taken from that book that concerns the evolution of humanity here. (Omitting therefore the earlier cycles of evolutionary expression, numbered 1-10.)

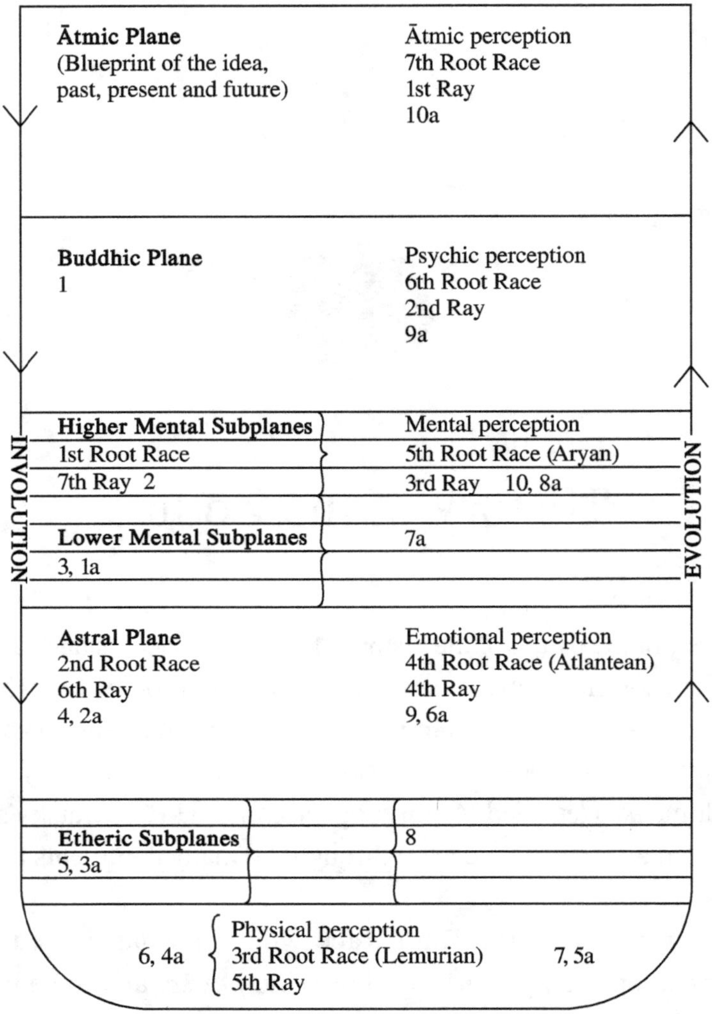


**Figure 16. The Root Races**

## *The interpretation of Figure 16*

The first two Root Races are symbolised by the story of Adam and Eve in chapters 2-3 of *Genesis* and their ousting from the 'garden of Eden'.[1] This garden symbolised the mental-astral planes of perception as they existed then. This happened as a consequence of the eating of the 'forbidden fruit' from the tree of 'knowing good and evil'.[2] This early subjective development really represented the precursors of

1 *Gen. 2:8.*

2 Explained in Genesis chapter 3.

what developed into humanity proper, for the human Soul had not yet appeared. This was to happen later in the third, Lemurian Root Race, when the human progenitors could incarnate into dense forms. This is symbolised by the phrase 'coats of skins',[3] by means of which Adam and Eve were consequently clothed. The process of the formation of the human Soul upon a mass scale, via which the human psyche could inhabit animal forms that had developed the capacity to bear mind, is known as Individualisation.

1a. Upon the lower mental plane Adam exists blissfully in the 'garden of Eden'. The first Root Race *Adamic humanity* symbolises humanity as a whole. Hearing is the sense developed, the sense of sight is awakened. They develop mineral-like mental consciousness, governed by the seventh Ray of Ceremonial Activity.

2a. Upon the astral plane Eve is formed out of the 'rib' of Adam. Adam-Eve, the hermaphrodite second Root Race *Hyperborean humanity*, now exist in blissful union and duality eventually finds its expression as desire. For a long period they know no wrong, nor each other's 'nakedness'. (As the mind was still nascent.) They are governed by the second Ray of Devotion and develop a vegetable type of mental consciousness. The sense developed is touch.

3a. Upon the higher ethers (literally the astral at this stage of evolution) *Eve*, via the contrivance of the serpent (of time, desire, *karma,* etc.), eats the forbidden fruit from the tree of knowledge. This allows the complete expression of desire to manifest. Adam and Eve are now separated into two distinct sexes.

4a. Upon the dense physical plane *Adam* and *Eve* are expelled to the earth. There, through cycles of sense contact and experience, they reap the benefit from the 'tree of knowledge'.

5a. The third Root Race *Lemurian humanity* is born, established by the formation of an overshadowing Soul (the Sambhogakāya Flower), hence is the first truly human Race. At first human consciousness is psychic, instinctual, and physically orientated. Gross sexuality and violent forms of activity are needed to properly incarnate their higher Selves into the animal form. The instincts dominate, focussed upon the instinct towards knowledge. The governing Ray is the fifth of the Scientific Mode. Here, this simply means that this Root Race had to learn much about the physical plane, its dangers,

3 *Gen. 3:21*—'Unto Adam also and to his wife did the LORD God make coats of skins and clothed them'.

and its usefulness. The rudimentary mind had to develop and grow by this means. The sense of sight is fully developed within the context of mastering the Element Earth, via which their Race came to an end (by geological upheavals and volcanism).

6a. By the time of the evolution of the fourth Root Race, *Atlantean humanity* have developed an astrally conditioned consciousness. This was first largely dominated by emotions and desire, and later by devotion and love. Desire-mind is eventually developed, causing many problems for this Race. (Especially related to the onset of widespread black magic.) The fourth Ray of Harmony overcoming Strife governs the Atlantean evolutionary development. The sense developed is taste and the Element Water was to be mastered, via which their Race came to an end by the 'great flood' mentioned in all ancient myths.

7a. Appropriately developing the substance of the lower mental plane, humanity now enters into the present fifth Root Race *Aryan* era. The emphasis for evolution is now the development of abstract thought. Intellect rather than emotion rules, thus the many trials concerned with the battle of the mind versus emotions are undertaken. Much suffering eventuates. The governing Ray is the third of Mathematically Exact Activity. The sense to be developed is smell (hence the mental reflection of *ātmic* perception). The ruling Element is Fire, by means of which it has been prophesised (in *The Secret Doctrine)* this Race shall be destroyed. One can look to the eventual fulfilment of this prophesy via the development of modern warfare and the nuclear bomb.

8a. Upon the higher mental plane, the abstract Mind and the Sambhogakāya Flower eventually dominate consciousness. Humanity thus emerges as a liberated Soul. This happens as a consequence of the development of meditative practices and passing the respective Initiation testings. Esoterically, the Word is now consciously uttered as part of the process of humanity becoming a Deity. The formation and evolution of the Hierarchy of Light out of the present humanity occurs.

9a. The sixth (Neptunian) Root Race comes into existence when a significant number of human units develop higher perceptions. (The enlightenment derived via the buddhic plane.) Hierarchy have moved from the higher mental to this plane as a place of residence at the time of the formation of the sixth Root Race. The entire process concerning the externalisation of Hierarchy occurs, to produce the New Age civilisation. Humanity begin to consciously work with the laws of group evolution and the second Ray of Love-Wisdom dominates human affairs. Then the esoteric senses manifest as the fundamental consciousness. The sense perfected is taste and the governing Element is Air. Eventually, the densest sheath will be of etheric matter.

10a. The seventh Root Race. The prodigal Sons return home to their 'Father', as *nirvānees* that undergo their cosmic journey. Ray one of Will or Power rules, producing abstraction into the higher domains of all that is material. The sense perfected is smell, *ātmic* perception. The Element is *Aether.* Eventually, the densest sheath will be of mental substance.

## The early zodiac

D.K. states:

> In ancient days, as you may perchance have heard, there were only ten signs, and—at that time—Capricorn marked the end of the zodiacal wheel, and not Pisces as is at this time the case. The two signs of Aquarius and Pisces were not incorporated in the signs for the simple and sufficient reason that humanity could not respond to their peculiar influences; the vehicles of contact and the mechanisms for responses were not adequately developed. Originally, there were eight signs; then there were ten and now twelve.
>
> In *Lemurian* days, during the early period of animal man and before humanity appeared on earth, in the interim period of development, eight signs influenced the planet and the kingdoms of nature found upon it. There was not response to the influences of *Leo* and *Virgo.* The mystery of the Sphinx did not exist and these two signs were not then part of the zodiacal wheel. Then individualisation took place and the seed of Christ-hood was planted in man and these two signs began to influence humanity, and gradually that influence was recognised and the zodiac was then known to have ten signs. The Mutable Cross dominated, but it was then the Tau, for Pisces was lacking and only Gemini, Virgo and Sagittarius was evidenced. Aries to Capricorn marked the circle of experience.[4]

During the time *prior* to Individualisation, therefore, the eight-signed zodiac can be visualised (as below) where only the cardinal cross was functioning. The cardinal cross manifests as the *sūtrātma,* the Life link. It is the cross of the Spirit aspect.

---

4 Alice Bailey, *Esoteric Astrology,* (Lucis Press Ltd., London, 1982), 159-60.

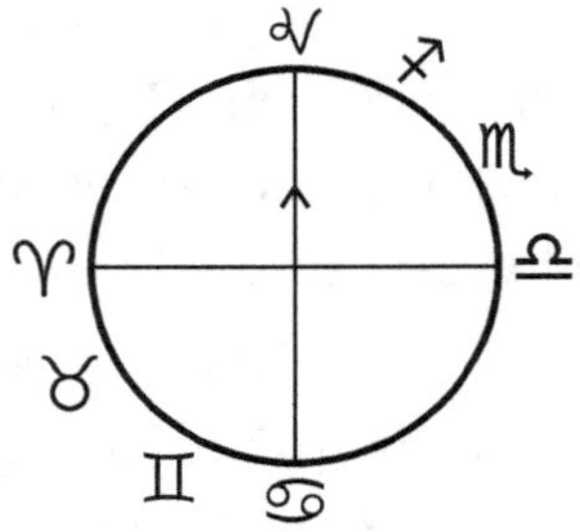

**Figure 17. The eight-signed zodiac**

Note that this eight-signed zodiac relates to *human evolution only,* which governs the process of the precession of the equinoxes. For Nature as a whole, the rectified Wheel manifested. There, for instance, Virgo (governing the activities of the *devas)* would have been active in order to produce the evolution of the species, etc.

The cardinal cross initiates and regulates (Aries) the cycles of the turning of the wheel of the zodiac (Libra), the mass incarnation of the Lives (Cancer) and the mount of materiality (Capricorn) that governs the sum of *saṁsāra*. The focus of animal-man (early Lemurians) was consequently a Capricornian struggle with the material forces of Nature, which the door to incarnation (Cancer) provided access to. The Capricorn-Cancer interrelation also represented the mode of expression of the *devas* that worked mainly to implant the Fires of nascent mind into the animal forms being prepared to bear them. Gemini and Cancer were also virtually synonymous because no Watery astral plane was yet developed by humanity. The forces that poured through from the higher domains bathed them etherically, which gave etheric vision to the fledgling humanity.

The focus of this etheric development and mode of visioning was the arm of the mutable cross (Gemini and Sagittarius) that then existed. This stage in evolution can be symbolised thus:

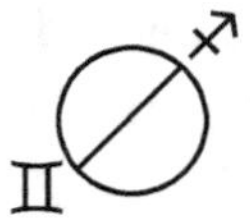

This Gemini-Sagittarius interrelation helped to manifest a primordial form of the intuition, reinforcing the instinct for survival, which helped animal-man to evade predators and to develop defensive tools. Elementary intuition was seeded into their receptive, forming minds by the angelic kingdom.

Gemini fostered an inherent sense of duality between what the Lemurians perceived inwardly *(devas,* manifestations of divinity) and the material domain they were ensconced in, and its dangers. The will energies from Sagittarius assisted the animal-man in the struggle for survival in the then physical landscape (over 18,000,000 years ago), when there were many dangerous predators in existence. Primarily, however, Sagittarius signified an avenue of approach for manifesting Divinity to seed animal-man with the attributes of mind. D.K. states that the Rider on the White Horse (Sagittarius) hearkens to a period: 'remote in the night time, when the greater world cycle started in the sign Sagittarius, the Archer', though '(in the early part of the cycle) as a centaur'.[5]

## Individualisation

If the eight-signed zodiac, manifesting as the eight-armed cross (*aṣṭadiśas*), is viewed in terms of Sagittarius starting the cycles of the turning of the zodiacal wheel, then Sagittarius will be found in the northern direction (upwards to the 'kingdom of God'). The appellation 'the Rider on the White Horse' then concerns the approach of the members of this Kingdom (Shambhala) to the earth at the time of the formation (Individualisation) of the kingdom of Souls. At this time, the members of Shambhala consisted of the Lords of Flame and Sanat Kumāra.[6] This event is said by D.K. to have taken about 5,000 years to accomplish, when the sun was in Gemini (detailed below).[7] With respect to this, Gemini manifests the southern position of downwards into the material domain.

Capricorn here takes the northeast direction of 'unity', for it gathers together the Logoic Thought-Constructs of what must be and the Commands needed to direct the Builders, the *devas* that are to incarnate as the substance of the forms of the new kingdom in Nature.

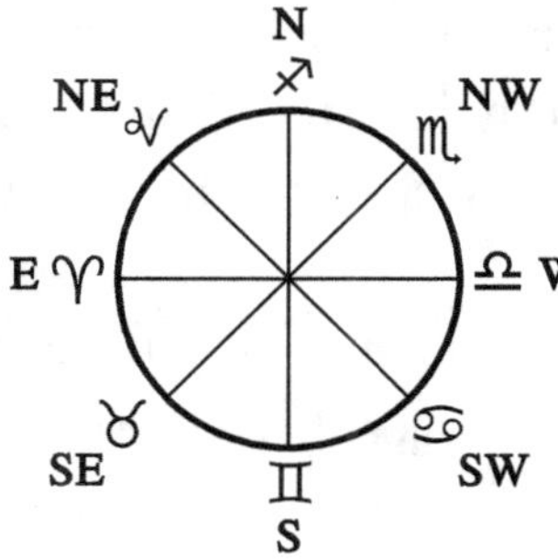


**Figure 18. The Lemurian eight-armed cross**

5 *The Externalisation of the Hierarchy,* 269.

6 See my book *The Constitution of Shambhala,* Part A for detail concerning Shambhala.

7 There are 2,160 years for each sign from Aries to Gemini, and taking the cusps into account, produces the symbolic 5,000 year period for the Individualisation process.

The eastern direction of 'inwards to the Heart' is here taken by Aries, who helps to bring into manifestation the Fiery energies impacting upon the higher mental plane that will vitalise the newly forming Causal forms. This was also the direction that the Lords of Flame (bearing this energy) swept into the planetary manifestation. (The greater Shambhalic Lords came to the earth via Sagittarius.) This produced the Initiation process by means of their combined energies and the 'sacrificial act' of the Solar Angels.[8]

Taurus rules the southeast direction of 'expression'. Taurus is the sign of the homestead, the building of the terrain of the Logoic Desire of what is to be. Pleiadian forces were thereby also brought to bear to help mould the new field of expression wherein the Causal forms would reside upon the higher mental plane. This work was in conjunction with the Venusian energies borne by the Lords of Flame, to build the needed forms for the accommodation of the *manasic* principle.

After the completion of the Causal forms in Gemini, this eight-armed zodiac moved to Cancer, the southwest arm of 'understanding'. The mass consciousness of the early Lemurians that came into incarnation was thereby produced. The Cancerian reactions (the fearful scurrying crab) to the dangerous environment they resided in helped them to begin to properly ground onto the dense physical plane. For the most part, however, during this period the Gemini influence of etheric perception ruled. The energy field that governed the manifestation of things was easily seen, along with the accompanying *devas*.

The western direction of the field of 'outward service to humanity' is occupied by Libra, which simply signifies the turning of the zodiacal wheel that slowly allows the new humanity to evolve empirical thoughts. Many were the great cycles of zodiacal turning needed for what could be considered the 'consciousness' of the early Lemurians to properly incarnate into the physical forms provided for them. This needed to happen in such a way that they were fully cognisant of their physical environment.

Finally, the northwest direction of 'expanding experience', ruled by Scorpio, signifies the development of the major characteristics of this third Root Race. This was the entire field of sexuality and the field of desire that came into play. Through developing bestial activity and forceful forms of sexuality this Root Race began to master the physical domain they resided in. Later came responsiveness to group

---

8 See *A Treatise on Cosmic Fire,* 707-21 and 807-38 for detail on the subject of Individualisation and of the Solar Angels.

and family interrelations. (This was a major objective of their then evolutionary attainment.) As a whole, humanity is ruled by Scorpio, which conditions their main field of testings as they undergo their evolutionary journeying.

The awakening of the ten-signed zodiac for the Lemurians happened by developing concepts of individuality (of a determined ego, demonstrated via Leonine impulse), then a proper response to and involvement with all of Nature (the Virgoan domain).

Concerning the time of Individualisation, D.K. states:

> [T]he "Great Approach" of the Hierarchy[9] to our planetary manifestation when individualisation took place and the fourth kingdom in nature appeared. I placed that stupendous event as happening 21,688,345 years ago. At that time the Sun was in *Leo*. The process then initiated upon the physical plane and producing outer events took approximately 5,000 years to mature and the Sun was *in Gemini* when the final crisis of individualisation took place and the door was then closed upon the animal kingdom.
>
> It has been stated that Sagittarius governs human evolution, as the Sun was in that sign when the Hierarchy began its Approach in order to stimulate the forms of life upon our planet. *Sagittarius, however, governed the period of the subjective approach.*
>
> The Sun was *in Leo* when physical plane individualisation took place as a result of the applied stimulation.[10]
>
> The Sun was *in Gemini* when this Approach was consummated by the founding of the Hierarchy upon the Earth.[11]

Note that Blavatsky gives a figure of 18,618,727 years ago, when the Sun was in Leo, for the founding of Shambhala on the earth.[12]

---

9 At that time they were members of Shambhala, as what is now known as Hierarchy did not exist.

10 This evolution was therefore governed by the sign Leo.

11 *Esoteric Astrology,* 64. The time mentioned by D.K. was therefore calculated when this book was written.

12 H.P. Blavatsky, *The Secret Doctrine,* (The Theosophical Publishing Company, 1888), Vol. I, 150. Blavatsky states: 'The Occultists, having most perfect faith in their own exact records, astronomical and mathematical, calculate the age of Humanity, and assert that the latter (as separate sexes) has existed in this Round just 18,618,727 years, as the Brahmanical teachings and even some Hindu calendars declare.'

## The Lemurian epoch proper

In continuing with the significance of Gemini in early Lemurian times, a quote from *Esoteric Astrology* is of importance:

> Attraction and repulsion are therefore conditioning factors in our solar life, and this conditioning reaches us through Gemini. It is the effect of a cosmic energy at present unknown to humanity. The waxing and the waning light which distinguishes soul experience from the first faint move towards incarnation and Earth experience, the rise and fall of civilisations and the growth and unfoldment of all cyclic manifestations are produced by the "interplay between the two brothers," as it is called. In that far-off time when the greater round of the zodiac was started in Gemini, as it now is in Pisces, there was a relation between the waxing and waning Moon, due to the pulsating power of Gemini. This is now greatly lessened, owing to the removal of the responsive life from the Moon, but the rhythm then set up still remains, producing the same basic illusion.[13]

As there was no conscious response then, evolution was purely material and therefore the mutable cross was dominant. However, this was simply a straight line (the matter aspect).

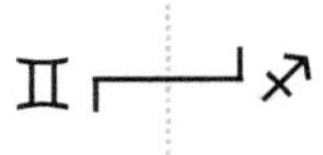

This shows that the nascent duality and the etheric form were progressing on one path to Virgo to begin the completion of the mutable cross. This was needed if humanity were to begin the process of the cycles of activity that would allow them to eventually master the physical domain. Virgo carries the incarnation process in her Womb and adds the Earth Element. This the Lemurians were in the process of dominating as they moved from etheric perception to full incarnation in the physical form. Concerning the Gemini-Sagittarius interrelationship, in relation to the fact that the Earth is the Hierarchical ruler of Gemini and the esoteric ruler of Sagittarius, D.K. states:

> These are the only two constellations ruled by the Earth, and this fact is of major significance, creating an unusual situation in the solar system and a unique

13 *Esoteric Astrology,* 352. See pages 301, 446 for references concerning the ending of evolution on the moon via a triangle of energies manifesting under Leonine influence, consisting of the energies from the sun, the Jupiter and the Mercury Schemes.

> relation. The cosmic line of force from Gemini to Sagittarius and the reverse is subjectively and esoterically related to our Earth, thus guaranteeing its soul development, the unfoldment of form as an expression of that soul, and leading our sorrowful humanity upon this woeful planet inevitably to the very gate of Initiation in Capricorn.
>
> In this statement and in the fact of the pain and sorrow which are the distinguishing qualities of our planetary life lies hid a secret mystery.[14]

This mystery is related to the Individualisation process, the happenings on the moon, and the mystery of the Sphinx (whose significance was a consequence of an early Virgo-Leo integration). As the Lemurians became more integrated with the dense physical, they developed a working relationship with the violet *devas* of the shadows and also a concept of self-identity (Leo). Their developing awareness, coupled with the ability to visualise *devas,* allowed them to begin to utter the words of command (which they heard and retransmitted without understanding) associated with Earthy *siddhis*. The Sphinx therefore came into being in human consciousness.

The kingdom of Souls (governed by Leo) incarnated into the material domain (governed by Virgo), however, there was very little to tie the two together except the etheric body. (Which is effectively but a field of energies.) The Souls consequently overshadowed their incarnate forms without being able to properly utilise them. For a long period of human evolutionary time, therefore, Leo and Virgo were linked etherically. Planetary energies impacted directly upon the etheric form, conditioning Lemurian activity as a whole (or in groups) rather than individually. Virgo still had to give birth to the Fiery Element – the Leonine gift to the human forms that were then more etheric than dense physical.

When the Watery Atlantean emotional attributes began to be developed, then Leo and Virgo separated into two distinct signs. This produced the ten-sided zodiac. For millions of years the attributes of the Sphinx and the developing Watery dispensation existed concurrently. As stated, the symbolism for this stage of development was the Tau cross. This cross signified the Lemurian civilisation, but more correctly the expression was Lemurio-Atlantean.

The *ten-signed zodiac* that was dominant at this stage of evolution is shown below:

---

14 Ibid., 356.

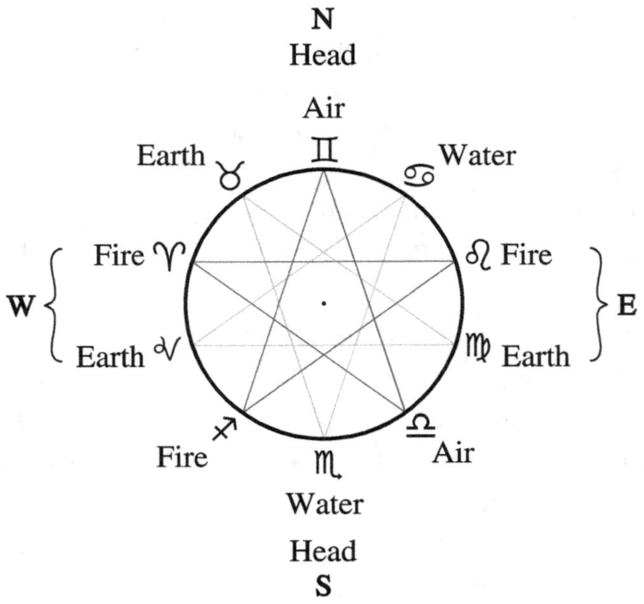


**Figure 19. The ten-signed zodiac**

There are two main pentagrams indicated here, one with Gemini (the head of this pentagram) facing the northern direction, and the other with the head (Scorpio) pointed downwards in the southern direction. Each pentagram possesses two hands and two feet. The left hands and feet bear *iḍā prāṇas* and the right ones bear *piṇgalā prāṇas.* All of the feet and hands in the eastern direction wield mainly *piṇgalā prāṇas* and those of the western direction wield mainly *iḍā prāṇas.*[15] Note that the eastern and western directions are reversed in this zodiac compared to that earlier given of the eight-armed cross. This is because the ten-armed zodiac is concerned with the reversed wheel that governs the great illusion, whereas the eight-armed zodiac is conditioned in the correct, primeval wheel. (Because human consciousness had not yet developed.)

Gemini starts the turning of the zodiacal wheel in the ten-armed zodiac. It reflects into manifestation the energies from the fourth cosmic ether *(buddhi),* which energised the Lemurian *nāḍī* system. This facilitated the development of the *siddhis* concerning the etheric domain developed by them. These *siddhis* allowed control of the telluric forces, thus the accomplishment of such things as the levitation of large blocks of stone. It was consequently far easier for them to build with cyclopean blocks weighing many tens of tons than with small bricks, such as we presently use.

---

15 In such a case one would see the mix of *iḍā-piṇgalā prāṇas,* or *piṇgalā-iḍā prāṇas.*

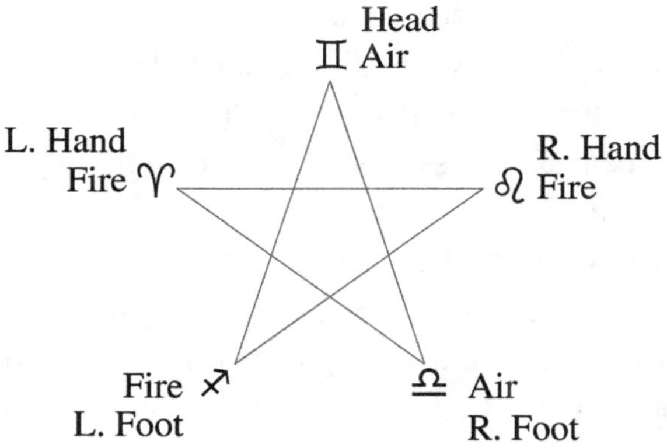


**Figure 20. The upright pentad**

The upright pentad predominantly conveys Fiery energies, assisted by those of the Air. Shown here are three Fire signs: Aries, the left hand, Sagittarius, the left foot and Leo, the right hand. The two Air signs are Gemini and Libra. The feet are the focus of this pentad. They assisted the Lemurio-Atlanteans to ground themselves on to the physical plane. Sagittarius provided the energy of the will to overcome the hardships of the material environment wherein they lived, in a hunter-gather society that co-existed with many dangerous animals. Rudimentary aspects of the mind were developed (the Fiery Element) in the struggle for survival. The Airy Libran right foot assisted their abilities to ground and master the etheric energies that their consciousness was bathed in (the head being in Gemini). The contemplative attribute of Libra here facilitated their ability to see and direct the etheric forces. The hands (that could gesticulate, grasp and make implements) added the Fiery Element needed to develop rudimentary mind.

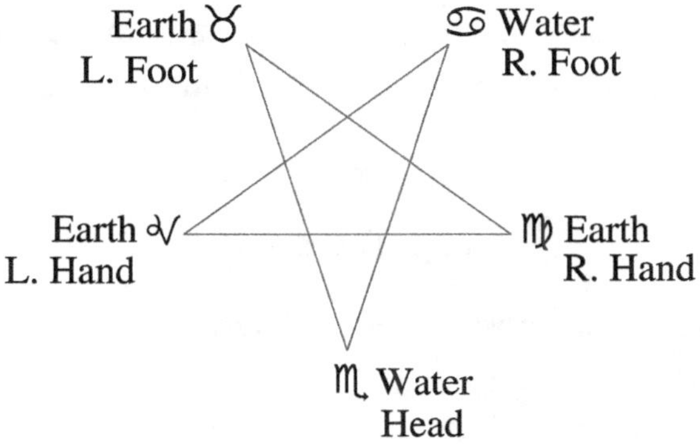


**Figure 21. The inverted pentad**

The inverted pentad consists of three Earth signs: Taurus (the left foot), Capricorn (the left hand) and Virgo (the right hand). They are assisted by two Water signs: Cancer (the right foot) and Scorpio (the head).

The head of the pentad relates to the Scorpionic thinking process, which was downward focussed towards all forms of sexuality, to satisfy primitive desire urges. The objective was to evolve emotional characteristics. The hands convey the expression of the emotions—to do, make and manipulate. They are governed by two Earth signs (Capricorn and Virgo), as they needed to grapple with the many survival tasks in their physical environment. The right and left hands relate to the *iḍā* and *piṇgalā* attributes of such development.

Because the feet walk upon the earth (the way of conduct in the material domain), Taurus (the left foot) thus facilitated grounding in the earthy domain. Its energies assisted the Lemurio-Atlanteans to build shelters and other forms of dwellings there. (Taurus being the sign of the homebuilder.) The Watery attributes of Cancer (the right foot) facilitated the development of family and social ties, specifically via developing emotional interrelations.

Gemini governed the general etheric vision, or perception, of the Lemurio-Atlanteans. (The body of energies coming via the *nāḍīs* and the associated *devas.)* The understanding of what was perceived gradually developed, so the hands were used to try to manipulate and control the types of energies and entities that they saw. Inevitably, the 'feet' dominated the focus of attention, for the then humans became increasingly ensconced in the material form. (The feet got them where they needed to go.) This produced the beginning of the process of their testings upon that domain, associated with the sign Scorpio. Cancerian (governing emotional development) and Taurean influences (governing the principle of desire) led eventually to the development of the intensely emotional, Watery characteristics of the Atlantean dispensation. The inverted pentagram then dominated, whose arms the Atlanteans had to travel up as they began to master the qualities of the associated signs.

## The Tau cross

There are two types of Tau cross established during the Lemurian epoch, shown in the figure below.

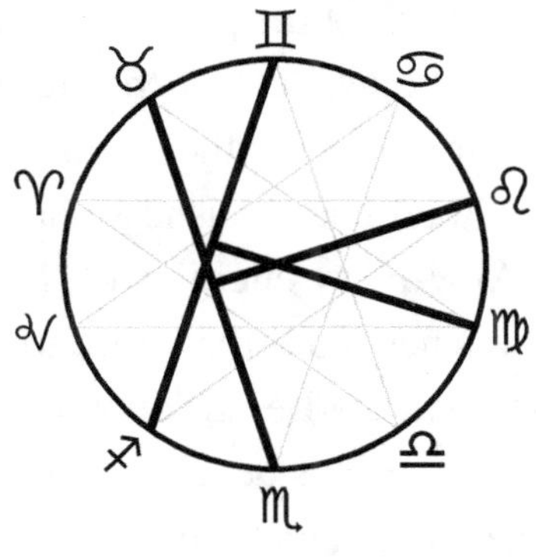

**Figure 22. The Tau crosses**

One of these was more strictly Lemurian in its attributes.

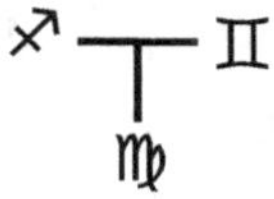

Its horizontal Sagittarius-Gemini arm is part of the upright pentagram of the ten-signed zodiac. This Tau cross firmly anchors the Lemurian on the earth (via its Virgoan base). The horizontal arm draws energies from the attributes of the eight-armed cross. The more masculine energies from the horizontal arm, coupled with the feminine energies from the Virgoan anchor, produced a pronounced sexual dualism. This concerned the separation of the sexes from the earlier hermaphroditic situation that existed in the 'garden of Eden' before Eve ate the forbidden fruit. Virgoan energies therefore helped to oust Adam and Eve from this garden in order to be able to wear the 'coats of skins'[16] needed for the early humanity to survive the rugged conditions on earth. Virgo assisted the development of the sexual function of the Lemurians, allowing Adam to know 'Eve his wife; and she conceived'[17] after they were ousted from heaven.

The Sagittarius-Gemini arm helped 'precipitate' the Lemurian consciousness onto the etheric domain, facilitating the manifestation of the earlier mentioned *siddhis* concerning the transition from etheric to dense conditionings. The Lemurians literally 'knew' of the nature of the manifestation of physical plane

16 *Genesis. 3:21-4.*

17 *Genesis. 4:1.*

phenomena without comprehension of the process involved.[18] Sagittarian energies assisted them to manipulate the aspects of the (feminine) *deva* kingdom, to facilitate the grounding of their awareness there and to control the Earth Element. The Earthy *devas* dominated their consciousness via the awakened Sacral centre that was energised by the Airy-Fiery energies of the Sagittarius-Gemini arm. Sacral centre development was needed if they were to procreate so as to populate the earth. These Fires en-flamed the Lemurian sexuality. Inevitably the strong, often bestial sexuality of the Lemurians developed. This activity was exacerbated by the Scorpionic arm of the ten-signed zodiac.

The extension of the Virgoan point to what would then be considered its polar opposite (Aries) produced the formation of an ankh, when Lemurian aspirants developed the Arian Will to aspire upwards. Aries provided the Fire to liberate the *kuṇḍalinī* that would help them to gain the first Initiation. This was via the methods of Hatha yoga that developed the *siddhis* possessed by the (first degree) Initiates of those times. They had awakened the third Eye, hence were the one-eyed Cyclopes mentioned in the ancient Greek myths. (They were also the 'giants' mentioned in the Bible.) There was therefore a strong connection between the Sacral and Ājñā centres. The two other signs that incorporated the head of the ankh are the Earth signs (Capricorn and Taurus) which energised the two lobes of the Ājñā centre. The three Earth signs were therefore incorporated into a unity by the Fiery Arian Will. This produced mastery of the dense physical terrain that the Lemurians resided in. Being able to levitate huge blocks of stone and the ability to mould them into required shapes (as if they were clay) represented part of their powers.

Leo formed the base of the other Tau, hence was concerned with the development of Atlantean self-conscious individuality.

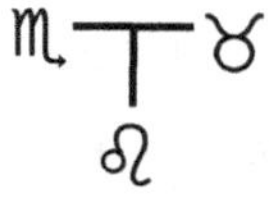

As Leo governs the main attributes of the kingdom of Souls, so this Tau was conditioned to bring some of that kingdom's attributes into incarnation. Leonine pride, and group or family interrelationships and responsibilities became dominant. Because the main arm of this cross incorporates Scorpio (the head of the inverted pentad), it facilitates the development of the Watery emotions, and Taurus with

18 My book *Esoteric Cosmology and Modern Physics* explains the nature of the materialisation of physical plane phenomena from the ethers.

desire-attachment to material goods. Other elements of the practicality and wisdom inherent within Taurus were also awakened. With the Scorpio-Taurus combination, all of the nine heads of the Hydra were developed, plus the murky swamp that it resides in.

Because the extension of the Leonine arm led to Capricorn, so it produced the possibility of scaling the mount of Initiation to take the second Initiation by means of mastery of the attributes developed by the Scorpio-Taurus arm. It was, however, all too easy for self-centred forms of black magic to arise, exemplified by the Fiery egotism of the Leonine individual, and the pronounced materialism and hatred that Capricorn provided. The sharp division between the white and dark brotherhoods that characterised Atlantean development consequently arose and finally dominated. Because of this fostered human selfishness, widespread black magic and witchcraft arose. It eventually necessitated the sinking of the Atlantean continent by the Lords of Life. Sagittarius and Aries, the other two points of the ankh that formed, are the two signs in the zodiac wherein the will is developed and exemplified. Both are Fire signs. This Fiery will, focussed via the Leonine egotism (another Fire sign), assisted the Lemurio-Atlanteans to master the physical domain they lived in through self-focussed activity and incremental intelligence.[19] The will also facilitated the development of the strong pride characteristic of all black magicians. As the Fires of selfish mind increasingly developed amongst humanity, it produced a very dangerous period for the Atlantean civilisation.

The mode of the interrelation and integration between those who followed these two types of crosses also contributed to the symbolism of the mystery of the Sphinx. This is seen in the fact that the vertical arm of the two crosses stems from Virgo or from Leo. There was consequently a symbiotic relationship between the two signs.

## The movement around the ten-signed zodiac

The regular movement through the zodiac in those times started with Gemini and travelled towards the eastern direction of the reversed wheel. The first sign after Gemini is the Watery sign Cancer. At first, Cancer simply signified the massed incarnation of the earliest Lemurians and their conscious awareness of the general environment in which they were thrust. Gemini and Cancer signified

19 Intelligence *per se* was not widespread. Rather, it was the onus of the then Initiates of both the black and white camps.

the primitive, mediumistic type of awareness that then manifested. As the cycles proceeded through time, Watery Cancerian traits were gradually awakened. Thus the Atlanteans of the next sign (Leo) eventually appeared and the attributes of the Tau cross centred upon Leo were consequently developed. Cancer also embodied the functions of the southwest direction of the eight-armed cross.

The next sign (Virgo) assisted the Lemurio-Atlanteans to consciously ground themselves upon the physical plane, and to psychically work with *devas* to produce the magical incantations associated with what can be described as Earth magic. The attributes associated with the Tau cross based on Virgo were therefore established. This ruled a great deal of Lemurian evolution. Leo-Virgo could therefore be considered separately, but were unified in the consciousness of the Initiates of that time to produce the potency of the Sphinx.

Together, Leo-Virgo signified the eastern direction of an eight-armed cross, which constituted the entrance into the Hierarchy of those times. The second Initiation was then the high point of Atlantean civilisation, whilst fourth degree Initiates had a similar function to the Chohans of nowadays. The polar opposite (Aries and Capricorn) of these two signs manifested the attributes of the western direction of this cross. Aries and Capricorn thus signified the direction outwards into the field of service for humanity. They assisted in the production of the will to master the sum of the material domain (via Capricorn, the then polar opposite of Virgo) and the will to master the attributes of the mind (via Aries, the then polar opposite of Leo). This was the focal point of what was the objective of the two Tau crosses to produce. In those days the development of the Fiery will (Aries) to climb up the mountain of experience (Capricorn) produced the appearance of the third degree Initiate. (This was the equivalent then to being a Master of Wisdom.)

Libra, the southeast position of 'expression' (of an eight-armed cross), signifies the experiences gained through the continual turning of the wheel of the zodiac. The law of cycles is governed by Libra and seeds the *karma* to produce the querulous, quarrelling, demanding, dangerous and carnal experiences associated with the next sign, Scorpio the scorpion. Libra may have also produced some calm interludes of experiences (in caves and other locales of consciousness), to allow the humanity of those days 'breathing space' from an otherwise hostile environment. This then facilitated the development to receive internal impressions, thought constructs for what needed to be done. Taking the pentads into account, Libra here is a 'polar opposite' of Gemini. Here, this means that it is a direct conduit for the down flow of etheric impressions from Gemini. Each sign here has two of these 'polar opposites', governed in general by the functions of the two brothers in Gemini.[20]

The next sign is Scorpio (a Water sign), the head of the downward pointing pentagram, composed of Earthy and Watery *praṇās*. As the Earth was the focus of Lemurian development, whilst development of Watery *praṇās* was the focus of the Atlantean dispensation, so the potency of Scorpio was extreme during this epoch. Scorpio is the sign of testing (especially in relation to the sexual function). Its poisonous stings engender any of the aspects of the nine-headed Hydra, producing the negative attributes of the dark brotherhood. All of these attributes eventually need to be mastered upon the wheel of Life. During this time, however, the attributes of the Hydra's heads were still being developed. The base attributes of Scorpio's polar opposites (Taurus and Cancer) were very important in this production. Coupled with this, the southern point of the Tau cross stems from Leo, adding the qualities of the three Fiery heads of the Hydra. The negative effects of Scorpionic influence therefore cannot be overemphasised.

Sagittarius (a Fire sign) in the southwest direction of 'understanding' helps produce the driving will (along with Capricorn and Aries in the western position) for Lemurian humanity to overcome the hardships in their environment. This had to happen in such a way that comprehension was inevitably produced. The needed tools for communication and survival were accordingy developed. Later came the construction of the more complicated and sophisticated elements of the Atlantean civilisation. The Sagittarian will manifested in the form of ambition, personally expressed, to master all the hardships of the material domain.

The next two signs (Capricorn and Aries) that signify the western direction of this zodiac have already been explained. What should be emphasised, however, is that the field of outwards service to humanity did not effectively exist until the latter part of the Atlantean epoch (when a few trod the path of discipleship). The energies from these two signs were directed to intensify the personal prowess of the individual, producing forms of aggression to others. The basic willpower that was generated concerned survival in their terrain, to fight tribal wars, to hunt large animals for food and to defend against predators. Here one needs to consider the existing conditions and the animals that lived well before the last ice age. Present anthropological concepts concerning the evolution of the early human species are erroneous. They are a result of 'knowledge filtration',

20 This is another aspect of this zodiac that could be delved into, once a basic history of that ancient time is provided for us by an enlightened Seer.

explained in Michael Cremo and Richard Thompson's monumental work *Forbidden Archaeology.*[21] Anthropologists are mainly investigating the anthropoid apes that are a consequence of what Blavatsky calls the 'sin of the mindless'.[22]

Blavatsky states:

> How, if the anthropoid and *Homo primigenius* had, *argumenti gratia,* a common ancestor (in the way modern speculation puts it), did the two groups diverge so widely from one another as regards mental capacity? True, the Occultist may be told that in every case Occultism does what Science repeats; it gives a *common* ancestor to ape and man, since it makes the former issue from primeval man. Ay, but that "primeval man" was *man* only in external form. He was *mindless* and *soulless* at the time he begot, with a female animal monster, the forefather of a series of apes. This speculation — if speculation it be — is at least logical, and fills the chasm between the mind of man and animal. Thus it accounts for and explains the hitherto unaccountable and inexplicable. The fact that, in the present stage of evolution, Science is almost certain that no issue can follow from the union of man and animal, is considered and explained elsewhere.[23]

Later she states:

> The anatomical resemblance between Man and the higher Ape, so frequently cited by Darwinists as pointing to some former ancestor common to both, presents an interesting problem, the proper solution of which is to be sought for in the esoteric explanation of the genesis of the pithecoid stocks. We have given it as far as was useful, by stating that the bestiality of the primeval mindless races resulted in the production of huge man-like monsters — the offspring of human and animal parents. As time rolled on, and the still semi-astral forms consolidated into the physical, the descendants of these creatures were modified by external conditions, until the breed, dwindling in size, culminated in the lower apes of the Miocene period. With these the later Atlanteans renewed the sin of the "Mindless" — this time with full responsibility. The resultants of their crime were the species of apes now known as Anthropoid.[24]

---

21 Michael Cremo and Richard Thompson, *Forbidden Archaeology* (Bhaktivedanta Book Publishing, Los Angeles, 1998).

22 H.P. Blavatsky, *The Secret Doctrine* (The Theosophical Publishing Co., 1888), 20. See also my book *Esoteric Cosmology and Modern Physics,* 528-31.

23 Ibid., 189.

24 Ibid., 689.

Finally, there is Taurus, who occupies the northwest direction of 'goodwill'. 'Goodwill' was then of the most primitive level. It was an expression of the group or tribe the individual belonged to, who together built their safe zone, or 'home' so that all could survive.

Taurus (as found on the northern arm of the Atlanteo-Lemurian Tau cross in Figure 22) signified the 'open gate' for instructions from the equivalent of Hierarchy in those days. The corresponding 'goodwill' position of the ten-signed zodiac (that was more strictly Lemurian in its attributes) was the mechanism of reception to those instructions. (From what might be considered the Lemurian 'elders'.) Perhaps the shamans or medicine men of the more primitive tribes on earth are the modern day descendants (upon a much higher level of expression) of these Lemurian instructors. It is difficult for us today to comprehend the nature of such instructions to those who were 'mindless'. (This mode of instruction was more psychic than verbal.)

The northern (Gemini position) played a similar role, but it signified a more visual impact that was directly provided by the appearing Sons of 'God' from Shambhala. They gave many gifts of learning, and then promoted technological advancements. One cannot, however, compare the 'technology' of those times with what we possess now, for then mantric control of matter was the basis of what was achieved.

In later Atlantean times, the Instructors were the feminine Hierophants from the Pleiades and from Venus (the Lords of Flame). This interrelationship is symbolised in the Bible thus:

> There were giants in the earth in those days; and also after that, when the sons of God came in unto the daughters of men, and they bare *children* to them, the same *became* mighty men which *were* of old, men of renown.[25]

The giants were the Lemurians, who were of gigantic stature compared to humanity today. The Sons of 'God' who came to instruct the then infant humanity were the 'younger' members of Shambhala, whose function was to instruct infant humanity. Because of their etheric vision the Lemurians could perceive these Initiates, and see their luminosity, but they had no understanding of what this signified. The spiritually youngest of these instructors still had *karma* with the material domain to cleanse. Some also saw that the best method of instruction

25 *Genesis. 6:4.*

was to incarnate amongst the Lemurians, and so help them develop the needed advances in this way.

The phrase 'the same *became* mighty men which *were* of old, men of renown' implies that those who incarnated became the Initiates – the guides ('men of renown') that helped develop the founding of the then Hierarchy on earth. They were assisted by the 'daughters of men' that responded to the teachings. This Hierarchy was established under the auspices of Gemini in the northern position of this zodiacal wheel. These Initiates gained eventual receptivity to the higher aspect of Taurus (wisdom) and Gemini (the Christ principle) once true service was established in the western direction. This allowed them to extend the reach of the polar opposites of these signs (Leo and Virgo), in the eastern direction towards Aquarius and Pisces. Such activity established the appearance of the twelve-signed zodiac.

The concept of being 'mighty men' related firstly to their huge stature, but more specifically, it referred to those who developed mental faculties. (This was the onus of the 'Lords of Flame' to bequeath to those who were receptive to the *manasic* Fire.)

Concerning this early evolutionary period, D.K. says:

> There was a time when (in the early history of the planet) there was no Hierarchy; there were only two major centres in the expression of the life of the Lord of the World: Shamballa and His embryonic throat centre, Humanity. Shamballa was the head centre. There was no humanity, such as we know it, but only something so primitive that it is well-nigh impossible for you to grasp its significance or factual expression. But the life of God was there, plus an inherent "urge" and a dynamic "pull." These two factors rendered the mass of men (if one may call them so) inchoately invocative, thus drawing from high spiritual centres certain developed and informed Lives Who—in increasing numbers—"walked among men" and led them slowly, very slowly, forward into increasing light. The early history of the Hierarchy falls into two historical eras in the process of its becoming a "mediating Centre":
>
> First: The time when the relating, mediating, enlightening correspondences to Those we now call the Masters trod the earth with men and were not withdrawn and apparently invisible, as is now the case. Their task was to bring the primitive intelligence of humanity to the point where there could be the presentation of the Plan, with eventual cooperation. In occult parlance, Their work was the establishing of a rapport between the unrevealed second aspect (to which They were responsive) and Humanity. In this They succeeded, but the matter aspect and quality—that of active intelligence—was so strong that the second historical phase became essential.

Second: The time when the Hierarchy was created as we know it today; the heart centre of Sanat Kumara came into its own life, formed its own magnetic field, possessed its own ring-pass-not, and became a dynamic mediating centre between Shamballa and Humanity.

It has oft been told in occult and theosophical literature that the Hierarchy withdrew as a penalising measure because of the wickedness of mankind. This is only superficially true and is an instance of a man-made interpretation, giving us the first example of the fear-and-punishment psychology which— from that time on—has conditioned all religious teaching. The withdrawing Masters had Their Paul to distort the truth, just as had the Christ, Their august Head today. The truth was far otherwise.

The time came in those distant aeons when a certain percentage of human beings reached, through their own efforts, the stage (at that time demanded) of preparedness for initiation. This attainment brought surprising results:

a) It became possible for certain of the Masters to "return from whence they came".

b) It became necessary to provide conditions where these men "accepted for unfettered enlightenment" could receive the needed training.

c) The process of creation had reached the evolutionary stage where the centres of the Lord of the World were differentiated; function and radiatory activity were established, and this produced a stronger "pull" and placed the Hierarchy "at the midway point." A station of light and power was formed. All this was made possible because humanity could now produce its own "enlightened ones."

These two historical periods (not events, except in so far that all TIME is a sequence or pattern of events) covered vast cycles; aeon by aeon, the work went on until we have today the three major centres in the planet, demonstrating great activity, much more closely related than ever before, and ready now to enter into a third historical period. In this coming cycle we shall see the first stages of the great spiritual fusion towards which all evolution tends; it will take the form of the externalisation of the Ashram, so that the Hierarchy (or the centre where the *love* of God is known and the purpose of Sanat Kumara is formulated into the Plan) and Humanity will meet on the physical plane and occultly know each other. Two centres then will be "visible in the light"—the Hierarchy and Humanity. When these two centres can work in full cooperation, then Shamballa will take form and will no longer be found existing only in cosmic etheric substance, as is now the case.[26]

26 Alice Bailey, *The Rays and Initiations,* (Lucis Press Ltd., London, 1970), 380-82.

## The Atlantean epoch

From the above we see that there was no smooth transition from the Lemurians to the Atlanteans. Instead, there was a gradual development of some Lemurian types (who developed their emotions) into Atlanteans, who lived concurrently with the great mass of Lemurians. As time progressed through many cycles of such development, the Atlanteans gradually gained the preponderance. Similarly, though we are presently in the Aryan epoch (wherein the empirical mind is dominant), the great mass of humanity are in fact Atlantean-Aryan.

D.K. states:

> In Atlantean days, man had become so responsive to the planetary and solar influence that the door of initiation into hierarchical experience was opened and two more signs were added. These two signs were the higher correspondences of Leo and Virgo and were the polar opposites of these two: Aquarius and Pisces. Their influence became active and effective and thus they formed part of the zodiacal wheel because man began to respond to their potencies. It then became possible for the Fixed Cross to function esoterically in the life of humanity, and the first reversals of the wheel in the life of the advanced men of that period took place. It was this reversal which was the true cause of the great contest or battle between the Lords of the Dark Face (as they are called in *The Secret Doctrine)* and the Lords of Light—a contest which is today persisting. Certain men then reached the stage of discipleship wherein they could consciously mount the Fixed Cross and be prepared for a major initiation. This the forces of Materiality and of Obstruction (as they are sometimes called) fought and the battle was fought out and conditioned in the sign Scorpio.
>
> Today, in Aryan times, a similar conflict on a higher turn of the spiral is taking place. The reason is that certain world disciples and initiates have reached the point in their unfoldment wherein they are ready to mount the Cardinal Cross and take some of the higher Initiations. So the conflict is between humanity (under the control of the Lords of Materiality) and the Hierarchy (under the control of the Forces of Light and Love), and right before our eyes the battle is being waged. The influences of the twelve signs of the zodiac (particularly of seven of the signs) are being engaged, for today all men of all rays are responsive to their influences and are implicated in one way or another in the affair.[27]

The dark brotherhood (the Lords of avaricious materialism and of forceful obstruction) became actively known at the time of the reversal of the zodiacal wheel

27 *Esoteric Astrology,* 160.

because then disciples appeared that could work to attain the second Initiation. Clear divisions then manifested between those vying to obtain liberation from materialism and the vales of illusion, and those who actively schemed to obtain power over everybody and everything. The psychic war was most active upon the astral plane, which the disciples were endeavouring to master. Thereon existed huge contorted beasts of desire and other selfish thought-forms that humanity created, which were the power base of the dark brotherhood. The desire-forms were further contorted ('whipped up') by mantric invocations and directed to fulfil the bidding of the dark ones. The white brotherhood countered with projections of illuminating light. Because the Atlanteans were astrally (psychically) and intensely selfishly focussed, so the fight against the potency of vast clouds of dark desire constructs was very difficult and fraught with many setbacks.

The astral plane is feminine in polarisation and very powerful witches evolved, casting spells of fear and of psychic control over all within their ken. The most powerful ones also battled against each other in order to manifest dominance over the continent. Vast were the battles. Eventually, such activity of the forces of darkness became so overwhelming that the Lords of Life in Shambhala caused the sinking of the Atlantean continent. They drowned the participants with the Watery Element, whose energies the dark ones so aggressively misused.

Scorpio conditioned this battle, because, as well as the potency of Scorpio associated with the nine-headed Hydra, the *left hand* of the inverted pentagram focussed upon Scorpio is Capricorn. This 'hand' projected the hatred and forceful psychic materialism of the black magicians that were ruled by Capricornian impulse.[28] This conditioned the Atlantean consciousness and was thoroughly reinforced by the intensified desire principle of the Taurean influence of the *left foot* of the pentagram. (Another Earth sign.) Scorpio governs the conditionings of the materialistic desert and the swamp wherein the Hydra resides. This represents what the disciple must battle in order to be freed from *saṃsāra.*

After briefly discussing the reasons for the appearance of syphilis as a mass educational tool for the Lemurians, D.K. then delves further into the Atlantean dispensation:

> As the ages passed away, humanity entered into the Atlantean stage of development. The conscious control of the physical body dropped below the threshold of consciousness; the etheric body became consequently more potent (a fact not

28 Capricorn's symbol here is an inverted head of a goat, depicted in the Tablets of Revelation for this sign.

oft considered), and the physical body reacted increasingly like an automaton to the impression and the direction of a steadily developing desire nature. Desire became something more than simply response to animal physical urges and to the primitive instincts, but was directed to objects and objectives extraneous to the body, towards material possessions and towards that which (when seen and coveted) could be appropriated. Just as the major sins of Lemurian times (if they could be called sins in any true sense, because of the low intelligence of the race) were through the misuse of sex, so the major sin of the Atlantean people was theft—widespread and general. The seeds of aggression and of personal acquisitiveness began to show themselves, culminating in the great war (as related in *The Secret Doctrine)* between the Lords of the Shining Countenance and the Lords of the Dark Face. To procure what they coveted and felt they needed, the most highly evolved of that race began to practice magic. It is not possible for me to outline to you the nature and practices of Atlantean magic with its control of elementals and of forms of life which have now been driven back into retreat and are inaccessible to humanity; neither can I indicate to you the particular methods used to acquire what was desired, the Words of Power employed and the carefully planned rituals which were followed by those who sought to enrich themselves and to take what they wanted, no matter what the cost to others. This magical work was the misdirected travesty of the White Magic so openly used in those days, prior to the great war between the Forces of Light and the Forces of Evil. Magic of the right kind was very familiar to the Atlantean people, and was used by those Members of the Hierarchy Who were entrusted with the guidance of the race and Who were combating rampant evil in high places. That same evil is again upon the warpath and is being fought by the men of goodwill, under the direction of the Great White Lodge. Heights of luxury were reached in Atlantis of which we, with all our boasted civilisation, know nothing and have never achieved. Some faint traces of it have come to us from legends and from ancient Egypt, from archaeological discovery and old fairy tales. There was a recurrence of pure Atlantean mischief and wickedness in the decadent days of the Roman Empire. Life became tainted by the miasma of unadulterated selfishness and the very springs of life became polluted. Men only lived and breathed in order to be in possession of the utmost luxury and of a very plethora of things and material goods. They were smothered by desire and plagued by the dream of never dying but of living on and on, acquiring more and more of all that they desired.[29]

Under the heading of *Tuberculosis,* D.K. continues his narrative:

29 Alice Bailey, *Esoteric Healing* (Lucis Press, Ltd., London, 1993), 230-32.

> It is in this situation that we find the origin of tuberculosis. It originated in the organs whereby men breathe and live, and was imposed—as a penalty—by the Great White Lodge; the Masters promulgated a new law for the Atlantean people when Lemurian vice and Atlantean cupidity were at their most ruthless height. This law can be translated into the following terms: "He who lives only for material goods, who sacrifices all virtue in order to gain that which cannot last, will die in life, will find breath failing him, and yet will refuse to think of death until the summons comes".
>
> It is difficult for us in these days to appreciate or to comprehend the Atlantean state of consciousness. There was no mental process whatsoever except among the leaders of the race; there was only rampant, ruthless, insatiable desire. This action of the Great White Lodge forced two issues and confronted the race with two hitherto unrealised problems. The first was that psychological attitudes and states of consciousness can and do bring about physiological conditions, these being both good and bad. Secondly, for the first time the people faced with recognition the phenomenon of death—death which they themselves brought about in a new way and not just by physical means. This had to be dramatised for them as some definitely objective manifestation, for as yet the masses did not respond to verbal teaching but only to visual events. When, therefore, they saw a particularly predatory and rapacious person begin to suffer from a dire disease which seemed to arise from within himself and—whilst suffering—hold on to his love of life (as tubercular people do today), they were faced with another aspect or form of the original law (imposed in Lemurian times) which said: "The soul that sinneth, it shall die." Death had hitherto been accepted without question as the fate of all living things, but now, for the first time, mental relationship between individual action and death was recognised—as yet in a dim and feeble way—and a great step forward was made in the human consciousness. Instinct failed to handle this situation.[30]

In the above, D.K. firstly provided an illustration of general life in Atlantean times when the two Tau crosses conditioned the zodiac, before the full advent of black magic and sorcery. This happened after the Lord of the World (Sanat Kumāra) opened the gates for the downpour of the energies of mind, plus the rapid incarnation on earth of the moon Chain humanity. Rapacious acquisitiveness then manifested upon a vast scale. A slowly developing mental awakening was gained by an increasing number of humanity (coupled with their innate psychicism, forceful mantras of spite). This produced a host of problems on our planet. Myriad

30 Ibid., 232-33.

psychic entities of desire were emanated via invocations of destructive potency. The predominant paradigm was: 'if I cannot have it, neither can you, so I will destroy what you have that I cannot possess'. The entire face of the Atlantean continent was eventually blackened with smoke and also darkened with rapacious psychic malice. This energy was exacerbated by the Plutonian first Ray energy brought into activity, for Pluto is the esoteric and Hierarchical ruler of Pisces, which now started influencing humanity. Pisces is a sign governing the cosmic *eighth sphere* (as shall be explained in a later chapter). Its residents could then be released, because the moon Chain *karma* also had to be cleansed. They incarnated upon earth in a cycle when the psychic conditionings were roughly similar to the moon's before its destruction.

Pisces is the sign of the Avatar, but the converse of this function are the mass of dark brotherhood Riders that then came to the earth. The impact of what poured through this opened cosmic gate contributed greatly to the rampant witchcraft (specifically) and sorcery that manifested during this epoch. When Aquarius began to make its presence felt, this completed the appearance of the twelve signs of the zodiac. Then Uranus (the seventh Ray of ritual magic) also played an important role in fostering the potency of the black magic of those times.

## The 'strictly human' signs in the zodiac

Tabulation V on page 66 of *Esoteric Astrology* provides the esoteric rulers of the signs of the zodiac (which therefore is rectified, going from Aries to Pisces via Taurus). There it is shown that Gemini (fifth Ray) and Libra (seventh Ray) are not related to any other sign. (The other signs are related through their ruling planets having the same Ray.) In relation to this, D.K. states:

> (T)here was a time, as you have heard, when there were only ten signs, and in those ancient days as in the present time, there was a divergence of opinion among the astrological scientists; they differed as to which the ten signs might be and in this connection there were several schools of thought, but mainly two of importance. One group fused or made one sign out of Leo-Virgo and perpetuated their belief in the Sphinx; the other omitted Gemini and Libra altogether. They were of an earlier date than the latter who really had a zodiac of eleven signs. This is a fact of importance to you today. The other point of note and of a relative importance is that Gemini and Libra are the two strictly human signs; they are the signs of the ordinary man. Gemini upon the Mutable Cross stands for man's humanity, whilst Libra upon the Cardinal Cross rules man's subjective and spiritual life.

> The other signs in their consummation carry man beyond the stage of ordinary humanity[31]...The emphasis, however, upon Gemini and Libra *as far as humanity is concerned* is on human attainment and achieving the point of balance before other attainments became possible.[32]

D.K. used the phrase 'strictly human signs' in an earlier passage, when he stated:

> Libra can also be spoken of in terms of the meditation process as taught both in East and West. It can, therefore, be regarded as the "interlude between two activities," which is the explanation given to that stage in meditation which we call contemplation. In the five stages of meditation (as usually taught) you have the following: Concentration, meditation, contemplation, illumination and inspiration. These five stages are paralleled in the five strictly human signs of the zodiac:
>
> 1. Leo—Concentration—Soul life focused in form. Individualisation. Self-consciousness. Undeveloped and average man. Human experience.
> 2. Virgo—Meditation—Soul life, as sensed in man, the gestation period. The stage of the hidden Christ. Intelligent man. Personality, as hiding the Christ life.
> 3. Libra—Contemplation—Life of soul and form is balanced. Neither dominates. Equilibrium. An interlude wherein the soul organises itself for battle and the personality waits. This is the probationary path. Duality known.
> 4. Scorpio—Illumination—The soul triumphs. Experience in Taurus consummated. Astral glamor dissipated. Soul light pours in. The Path of Discipleship. The Disciple.
> 5. Sagittarius—Inspiration—Preparation for initiation. Soul inspires personality life. Soul expresses itself through personality. The Initiate.
>
> I would here remind you that, though initiation is taken in Capricorn, the man is an initiate before he is initiated. This is the true secret of initiation.[33]

When interpreting any of the signs, it is important to emphasise the point of view that one is coming from. For instance, Virgo is in the above list. Generally this sign is considered that of the Mother, governing the activities of the feminine *deva* kingdom. (Thus is a 'non-human' sign from this perspective.) Capricorn and Taurus also have a significant relation to the *devas,* for all three are Earth signs. The function of meditation is usually attributed to Libra, where here D.K. provides

31 Ibid., 242-43.

32 Ibid., 243.

33 Ibid., 228-9.

'contemplation'. Meditation can be viewed as a state of contemplative absorption, whereas here D.K. provides the process that leads to that absorption (as a step progressed from 'concentration'). In D.K.'s list, the point of view relates to the stages of awakening higher perceptions, from the average person to one who is 'preparing for initiation'. For an Initiate, the stages could be considered as: concentration, meditative practice, contemplative absorption, abstraction and revelation.

Gemini is the temple of the body (of the Lord), of the energy field wherein the meditation process ensues. Contact with this field allows the two brothers to hold hands, for the immortal brother to draw the mortal one into the inner sanctum of Life to cause liberation from form. Gemini interrelates all of the pairs of opposites, facilitating the making of choices via the meditative space offered by Libra the balances. Both are dual signs, and the signs between them (Cancer, Leo and Virgo) signify the three worlds of human livingness (Earthy – Virgo, Mental – Leo and Watery – Cancer). Therein the main aspects of the human life experience manifest. After each cycle of these experiences, one then comes to 'the place of judgement'[34] (Libra) wherein the gain of those experiences is judged.

After many cycles of such experiences (of pain, suffering, happiness, etc., through the vicissitudes of *saṁsāra),* one eventually enters the field of testing in Scorpio. The result of the mastery of those testings allows a disciple to enter Libra and undergo the stages of concentration, meditation, contemplation, illumination and inspiration. The manifestation of these activities, as a function of the (Libran) human activity of meditation, is what D.K. refers to in the phrase 'strictly human signs'.

Earlier, from a different perspective, when dealing with the sign Sagittarius, D.K. states:

> This sign is, as you know, a peculiarly human sign and is connected in a definite manner with the appearance of humanity upon our Earth. There are three of the zodiacal signs which are more closely connected with man than are any of the others. These are: Leo, Sagittarius and Aquarius. In one peculiar (but not yet provable) manner, they are related to the three aspects of body, soul and spirit.[35]

He then presents a tabulation[36] as to why they can be considered so. This list, however, is also not quite correct as it mixes the exoteric and esoteric points of

34 Ibid., 229.

35 Ibid., 174.

36 See *Esoteric Astrology,* page 174.

view, which is difficult not to do in such a generalised listing. From the point of view of the evolution of the zodiac, the one-pointedness and struggle of Sagittarius is that of the animal-man (the Centaur), governing Lemurian development. He works to master the material domain, to produce the rider upon the horse. The self-consciousness, egotism, pride and intellectual aspects of Leo are attributes developed by the Atlanteans near the ending of the epoch in the transition to the Aryan epoch. The Airy, Aquarian attributes will now be developed by Aryan humanity as they move into the New Age. (Which will govern the sixth Root Race evolution.) Later, the Leonine qualities of the Soul are 'grounded', as the aspirant struggles up the mountaintop of Initiation. The illumination to be gained there is Leonine. Sagittarius governs the manifesting will of the Initiate to overcome obstacles, and then to conquer all aspects of *saṁsāra,* including the limitations of the Soul form.

At all stages Aquarius will govern the needed service arena – of the developing group consciousness (Leo) and then universal consciousness (Aquarius) that makes the Bodhisattva. One should note here that Leo and Aquarius are polar opposites, whilst Gemini, the 'strictly human sign' mentioned above, is the polar opposite of Sagittarius. These four signs produce an interrelation between the fixed and mutable crosses, that are integrated by Libra into the cardinal cross via the process of: concentration (Leo), meditation (Virgo), contemplation (Libra), illumination (Scorpio) and inspiration (Sagittarius). This integration, in the 'interlude between breaths', then produces liberation from form, and inevitably from the human kingdom altogether. (At the attainment of the sixth Initiation.)

One can also consider D.K.'s statement:

> It is interesting, in this connection, to trace the unfolding of the human consciousness through the influence of the energies let loose through the various zodiacal signs:
>
> 1. Instinct, governing desire—Cancer. Mass unevolved consciousness.
>    I desire.
> 2. Intellect, governing ambition—Leo. Individual consciousness.
>    I know.
> 3. Intuition, governing aspiration—Sagittarius. Soul consciousness in early stages. Initiation 1 and 2.
>    I vision.
> 4. Illumination, governing intuition—Capricorn. Soul consciousness in later stages.
>    I realise.

5. Inspiration, governing service—Aquarius. Group consciousness.
   I go forth.
6. Identification, governing liberation—Pisces. Divine consciousness.
   I and the Father are one.

> In these signs—Cancer, Leo, Sagittarius, Capricorn, Aquarius, and Pisces—you have the six signs which constitute the six pointed star of the human or fourth Creative Hierarchy; Cancer and Pisces marking the two extremes. The Crab symbolises imprisonment (the hard shell and the rocks under which the Crab ever takes shelter), and the Fish signifies freedom. In between—in Leo, Sagittarius, Capricorn and Aquarius—come the four stages of personality development, struggle with the pairs of opposites, and finally release into full spiritual service.[37]

The cross that is formed can be called 'the star of humanity' and is illustrated in the figure below. A seventh sign, Scorpio, has been placed in the centre because Scorpio governs the evolution of the fourth Creative Hierarchy in general.

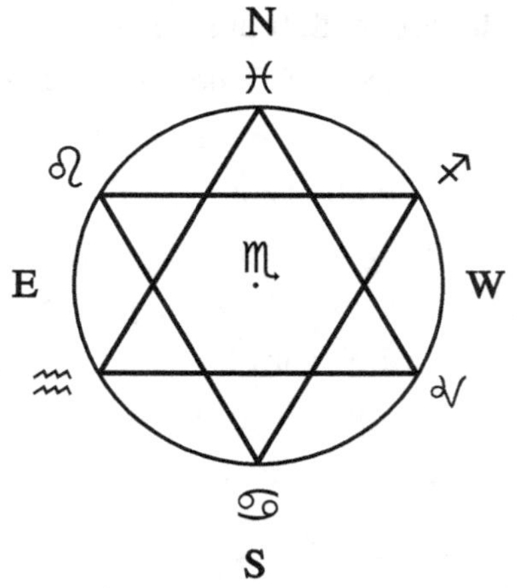


**Figure 23. The star of humanity**

The upward pointing triad are the signs governing the final stages of the evolutionary process, from Initiation in Capricorn to the Bodhisattva path in Aquarius, and finally, for those upon the path of earth service, the role of the Avatar in Pisces.

The downward pointing triad consists of Cancer in the southern position, signifying imprisonment in one's personality attributes and repetitious (clinging, emotional) experiences in the Waters of sensation. Next is the Leonine position. It signifies the development of self-centredness, pride and the self-consciousness

37 Ibid., 178-79.

that will eventually allow the empirical mind to dominate the fields of experience. Finally, Sagittarius signifies the manifestation of selfish ambition to gain personality wants and desires at any cost to the general environment. The Archer eventually appears, who fires arrows of aspiration to worthy causes, and finally upwards towards enlightenment. The archer thereby enacts sacrificial acts to serve others.

The eastern direction of this hexagon relates to development in the field of consciousness – from self-centredness to group awareness (Leo). There is also the Aquarian transformation from superficial, shallow, selfish concerns to the universal consciousness of the Initiate.

The western direction signifies the processes of the Sagittarian directives needed to master the sum of the hardships and materialism of incarnate life. This is the material domain (ruled by Capricorn). Once that materialism is fully experienced, then there is the possibility to climb the steep, rocky mount of Initiation.

Scorpio governs the downpour of the energies from the cosmic astral plane that conditions the environment during all stages of human evolution. Scorpio eventually rules the testings that each disciple must undergo (specifically associated with the Watery astral domain) that will allow the Archer to fire the arrows of the will to master those testings as the path up the mountainside is trod.

The remaining five signs also play important roles in the human story, but their role is more subjective, providing the conditioning environment wherein the human drama plays out. (It has already been shown above, for instance, how Gemini and Libra condition human experiences.)

Aries, Taurus and Gemini represent the stages of descent into manifestation of the subjective conditionings and qualities that govern human experiences. Virgo is the Mother's department, signifying the *devas* that embody the substance of all that is, within which the human play is enacted. Libra is the point of balance between all experiences. It governs the turning of the wheel of incarnation, of repetitive experiences and the manifestation of the law of *karma,* according to the proclivities of human activity. It therefore sets the stage for all that must be.

## The zodiac during the Atlantean epoch proper

In D.K.'s description below, which concerns the zodiac that appeared during Atlantis, he posits that Leo-Virgo were united in one sign to produce the sign of the Sphinx. What happened was that during the final epoch of that ancient history, so many Lemurians became Atlantean that the accounting of the zodiac with two different Tau crosses was largely irrelevant. The two Taus were therefore incorporated into one sign. Also, the energies from their polar opposites, Aquarius and Pisces, had to now be incorporated into the account. The influence of Libra (the sign of meditative awareness, the turning of the wheel, and the governance of *karma)* then manifested in two ways:

a. As far as human perception went, the effect of Libra was practically non-existent. Very few Atlanteans had any proclivities to meditate. The balance in consciousness that would produce the resolution of the sex instinct, for instance, was yet far into the future.
b. The subtle effects of the turning of the wheel of the zodiac and of the manifestation of the law of *karma* were universal in their effect.

The combination of these points meant that Libra was the central point of what in reality was another ten-signed zodiac. This was needed because the Atlantean focus was to develop the potency of the 'abdominal brain', the Watery qualities of the ten petals of the Solar Plexus centre. This centre governs and synthesises the *prāṇas* from the Inner Round of minor *chakras.*

D.K. states:

In the days before Leo-Virgo were divided into two signs, Libra was literally the midway point. The situation was then as follows:

| | | | | |
|---|---|---|---|---|
| Aries. | Taurus. | Gemini. | Cancer. | Leo-Virgo. |
| | | LIBRA | | |
| Scorpio. | Sagittarius. | Capricorn. | Aquarius. | Pisces. |

And in this round of the zodiac (as far as humanity is concerned) you have depicted the entire history of the race.[38]

This involves:

*Aries* – its mental beginnings (the will to manifest) and the start of the outgoing life.

*Taurus* – its directed desire, producing manifestation.

*Gemini* – then emerges its dual consciousness or the Soul-body realisation.

*Cancer* – the process of its physical incarnation goes forward here, followed by:

*Leo-Virgo* – the dual development of the Soul-body or the subjective and objective consciousness, and the God-man.

*Libra* – wherein the point of balance is eventually reached between spiritual man

38 Ibid., 230.

and personal man and the stage is laid for the final five-fold process which is, in reality, the subjective correspondence to the outer externalisation upon the Path of Outgoing and which is carried forward upon the Path of Ingoing, or the Path of return.

Thus in:

*Scorpio* – takes place the reversal of the wheel and the beginning of the new orientation and of discipleship.

*Sagittarius* – the directed and controlled life of the disciple.

*Capricorn* – initiation.

*Aquarius* – followed by service.

*Pisces* – the work of a world saviour and final liberation.[39]

Libra effectively marks the distinction between the ordinary wheel of Life and the reversed wheel. It is the hub of the wheel, conveying Airy *prāṇas* from *buddhi* to influence the remaining ten signs in accordance with the progress of the equinoxes. Because its influence works through all of the signs simultaneously, according to their capacity to handle the influx of *buddhic* energies, so it stands at the centre of the *maṇḍala*.

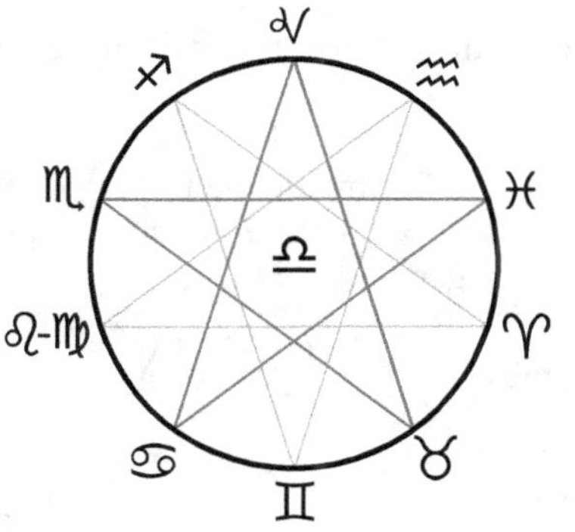


**Figure 24. The Atlantean ten-signed zodiac**

By this time, the Atlantean consciousness had grown considerably in sophistication compared to the Lemurian pentads. As before, there are two main pentads of concern, one pointed upwards whose head is Capricorn and the other inverted with the head being Gemini. The other pentads can also be considered, but in relation to the function of the signs that are their heads. Because the emotions were now well developed, so the upward and downwards pointed 'hands' of the

39 The section above uses D.K.'s words from *Esoteric Astrology,* page 230. I have rearranged the passage given in order to turn the signs dealt with into a list.

*prāṇas* associated with the Solar Plexus centre also need to be assessed.[40] The five *prāṇas* (hence Elements) are conveyed by the five fingers of each hand, each finger projecting a different *prāṇa*. The main expression of these *prāṇas* was then concerned with the projection of the Watery energies – to grasp, control and to manipulate the objects of desire, and of emotional attachment to material things.

The thumb, with its ambidexterity, conveys Watery *prāṇas*. The forefinger, by means of which one points to objects, conveys Fiery *prāṇas*. The middle finger, which is the most extended, conveys Earthy *prāṇas*. The ring finger conveys Airy *prāṇas* and the little finger, Aetheric *prāṇas*. (To which the Atlanteans had no receptivity, hence its energies were akin to somewhat intensified Fiery *prāṇas*.)

The pairs of signs in the *east-west direction* are also of major significance. Because the Atlanteans were psychically awakened, so the *siddhis* associated with the ten petals came into predominance. Therefore, taking all of this into account, the energies influencing this ten-sided zodiac are somewhat complex. The attributes of the Atlanteans can also be thought of as being categorised in terms of the functions of the *chakras*, viewed upon a planetary scale instead of in terms of a person. The focus of their evolution was the expression of the energies of the Solar Plexus centre. (For the Lemurians, at first it was the Base of Spine, Sacral and Splenic centres, and the related minor centre of the Inner Round.)

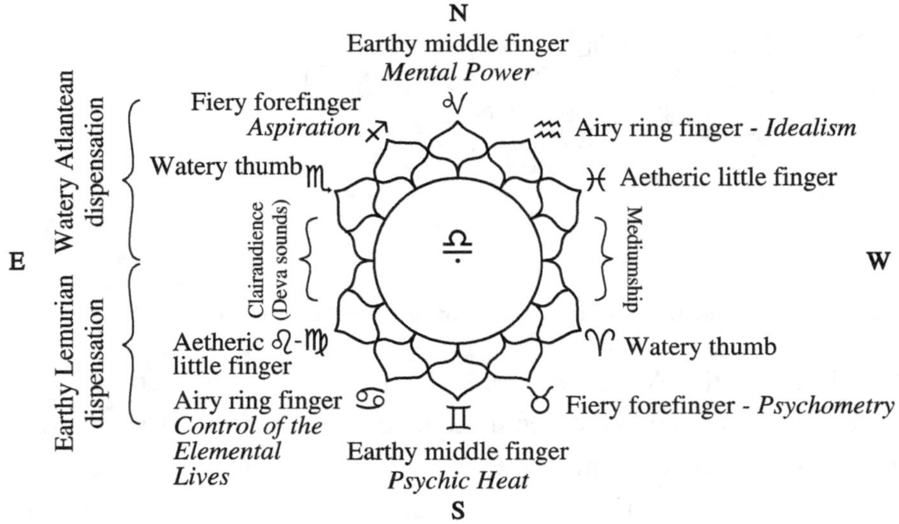


**Figure 25. The Atlantean Solar Plexus centre**

40 See Figure 11 and accompanying text of my book *The Esoteric Exposition of the Bardo Thödol,* Part A, for an explanation of the functioning of the 'hands'. Pages 306-07 of that book explain the *siddhis* that are a product of the awakening of this *chakra*.

In the above figure of the Solar Plexus centre, one can see two groups of five main petals, which are here considered as 'hands' of petals. The upper 'hand' mainly projects *prāṇas* to the *chakras* above the diaphragm, whilst the lower 'hand' projects *prāṇas* to the major *chakras* below the diaphragm and to the minor (Inner Round) series of *chakras*. The main petals are here viewed as projecting the *prāṇas* of the fingers and thumb of the right and left hands.

The *upward pointed pentad* consists of the signs Capricorn (head), Pisces and Taurus (the left hand and foot), Scorpio and Cancer (the right hand and foot). They specifically relate to the field of consciousness developed by the Atlanteans, the focus being magical incantations to control the forces of Nature. (Predominantly of the Watery psychic domain). This pentad therefore concerns the attributes purely developed by the Atlanteans.

The *downward pointed pentad* consists of the signs Gemini (the head), Leo-Virgo and Sagittarius (the right hand and foot), Aquarius and Aries (the left foot and hand). It is concerned with activities focussed upon the earth sphere. This pentad therefore incorporates both the Atlantean and Lemurian dispositions, producing the concept of Atlantean-Lemurians (which the sign of the Sphinx refers to). The Leonine part concerns the Atlantean consciousness and the Virgoan part relates to what is developed by the Lemurians. The attributes of the two Tau crosses have therefore been incorporated into the symbolism of the Sphinx.

Within the context of the expression of these two 'hands', the information concerning the pentads of expression of the Lemurio-Atlanteans also needs to be incorporated. The pentads of expression for each of the signs of the zodiac depicted in Figure 25 must be similarly incorporated. There is therefore a complex potpourri of energies to consider. One must also conceive of a vast time period, wherein various characteristics associated with each of the pentads slowly evolved. The zodiac depicted in Figure 25 can be understood to govern the last five thousand years of Atlantean development.

Concerning the expression of the ten petals of this Atlantean Solar Plexus centre, the signs Aquarius, Sagittarius, Cancer and Taurus have a special interrelationship. They relate to the flow of the *iḍā* and *piṇgalā nāḍīs* for the then humanity.[41]

Aquarius the water bearer projected the *iḍā nāḍī prāṇas* to the then relatively embryonic Throat centre of humanity. The functioning of this centre was at first

---

41 The information provided on Figures 11 and 12 (pages 289 and 307) of my book *The Esoteric Exposition of the Bardo Thödol*, Part A, is incorporated here. The reader needs to refer to that book for detail.

almost non-existent. The Watery-Fiery dispensation (the *manasic* flow that was then contacted) helped produce the relative superficiality, selfishness and shallow thoughts typical of the average Aquarian. The gain was the massed covetousness that maligned that epoch. The Atlanteans slowly became more mental, thus their use of the Throat centre produced incrementally more powerful mantric invocations which were directed to obtaining the possessions they desired. This became the basis of their later black magical practices. For those that discovered the right hand path, the increased *manasic* receptivity produced an idealism directed to learning the attributes of Nature, human psychology, and how to use mantras to heal, to protect people from harm and to build via magical means.

The aspirants of the time needed to temper the Fiery *iḍā* flow (that produced the desire-mind, because of the Atlantean Watery proclivity) through contact with Airy *prāṇas* from the higher ethers. This produced a bonding ('ring finger' activity) with others that possessed like-minded attitudes. The gain was an Aquarian idealism, which was the basis for the founding of the Schools of learning from which many Atlanteans benefitted. Modern day scientific enquiry had its true foundation here.

Sagittarius directed *piṇgalā prāṇas* to the Heart centre, which at this stage was the relatively embryonic Hierarchy. Via these *prāṇas,* Hierarchy could project (utilising the Sagittarian impulse) the needed energies to help stimulate the ideals of family life, aspiration to higher ideals and group living. Aspirational zeal was fanned to rightly develop the needed Fiery attributes and thought-form building that would allow the aspirants of the time to eventually attain their third Initiations. The energies of the Fiery forefinger were pointed upwards to the higher domains in order to try to transform the inherent Watery dispensation that came via the *piṇgalā* flow.

The average Atlantean, however, utilised these energies to foster cupidity (their desire to possess vast material possessions). In Sagittarius, such personality ambition became increasingly one-pointed and selfish and it focussed the will by magical means to obtain what was desired.

Taurus generates *iḍā prāṇas* in the Sacral centre. When projected downwards, the sexual and desire thought-form building aspects of humanity were highly stimulated. The strong sexuality of the Lemurians was converted to the sex magic that became rampant in Atlantean times. Downward projection towards the Base of Spine centre produced the awakening of psychometry, which was a widespread natural phenomenon. Knowledge of the psychic composition and evolution of the elements and the forms of Nature was significantly perverted by the magicians of those days for selfish gain. They built strong avaricious thought-forms to attract to them what they desired. Fiery *iḍā prāṇas* were projected (effectively via the pointed forefinger) as their intellects slowly evolved. The result became reflected in their residences: opulent palaces of beautiful and precious things. This set the stage for later black magical practices, when acquisitive desire became uncontrolled and rampant.

Cancer controlled the complete expression of the major Watery dispensation of the Atlanteans massed consciousness. The average people created desire forms and thought constructs that cumulatively became astral heaven and hells. The potency of the created astral images were fundamental to their lives, for their natural clairvoyance made this so. Most lived in a visual field of hallucinatory images. (Most of humanity since then have further developed and refined these heaven and hell states of livingness, because they are still Atlantean in their disposition.)

Cancer regulated the *piṇgalā prāṇas* from humanity's combined Sacral centre, which intensified the Watery proclivity of the Atlantean epoch. Massed Atlantean sexual *prāṇas* and desire images were created, absorbed and organised by the magicians of the time. Fearsome images were created whereby to attack others.

This Cancerian petal of the Solar Plexus centre facilitated the ability of the Atlanteans to control the Elemental Lives that constituted the substance of things. (The function of the Airy ring finger governing this petal allowed the Atlantean magicians to wield the subtlest, most powerful of the astral energies available to dominate these Lives.) Many earth-bound Nature Spirits were thereby controlled and manipulated into the grotesque shapes that embodied the objects of desire of people.

Atlantean proclivity for black magic attracted dark brotherhood entities from beyond the solar system, for which Cancer represented the open door to incarnation. These beings then controlled the evolving Watery Atlantean forms of magic. The resultant sorcerers and witches manipulated the emotional consciousness of the masses of humanity. Their desire-emotions could easily be controlled by those who possessed the will to do so.

Combined Taurean and Cancerian energies (linked as they were to Sacral energies) helped produce the Earthy-Watery psychic beasts of predatory activity that were controlled by the sex magicians. Vast were the resultant sexual derangements and proclivities in those days. This also produced the manifestation of a huge population explosion.

The southernmost position ruled by Gemini governs the general *prāṇas* flowing to the Inner Round *chakras,* but at that time the main flow was to the planetary dual Splenic centre.[42] These centres are concerned with rejected *prāṇas* from the entire *prāṇic* circulation. This was the body of vitality that energised the Atlantean activities. The higher Splenic centre redirects viable *prāṇas* back into the system. The lower (superimposed Splenic centre) projects waste *prāṇas* down to the Sacral centre and eventually out of the body altogether. The combined Splenic centre therefore exemplifies the Gemini duality. This centre was consequently quite inflamed with desire-thoughts at that time.

The basest energies from the Atlanteans flowed from the superimposed Splenic centre to the Sacral centre. These waste *prāṇas* empowered the grossest sexual depravity that the Atlanteans were capable of. The yoga of the psychic Heat *(tum mo)* was also developed, which facilitated their 'earth-magic' abilities (signified by the function of the 'middle finger') to work with the Lemurian Magicians to levitate and 'mould' stones. It is not possible to properly explain the nature of the intensity of the *kuṇḍalinī* Fires available to the Atlanteans. They flowed towards the head of the upright pentad (Capricorn), which assisted in the development of potent black magic. The hard, rocky, cruel materialism of the Capricornian mind controlling these psychic Fires manifested on a mass scale. This is one of the reasons that necessitated the sinking of the continent at the time when Capricornian influence was dominant. (This happened at the then correspondence to the ending of our present Aryan cycle.)

Capricorn represents the mountain of mind/Mind. It signifies the highest and the lowest aspects the mind is capable of. Here the sign represented the cruel, separative, one-pointed, wilful mentalistic form of sorcery that gained precedence in latter Atlantean days. The mystery of Makara (the fifth creative Hierarchy, the *devas* embodying the substance of mind) also comes to the fore here. The forceful manipulation of these *devas* to cause the precipitation of the desired forms into physical objectivity (the psychic use of the 'forefinger') was the basis of the then sorcery. Vast was the evil that came into being through the development of mind. This included the influx of cosmic evil, the doors to which were opened by appropriate mass magical activity in Atlantis. The opening of the pathways of mind when Capricorn was in the ascendency also offered opportunities for

---

42 The Splenic centre is a dual centre, with one larger wheel of twelve petals (Splenic centre I) superimposed upon a smaller one of eight petals (Splenic centre II). See my book, *A Treatise on Mind,* Vol. 3, 163.

aspirants to climb up the craggy slopes of the mountain towards the attainment of the abstract reasoning that facilitated the taking of the third Initiation.

It is interesting to note that in those days it was the extension of the Earthy finger from Gemini to Capricorn (rather than from Cancer to Capricorn, as presently exists in the twelve-signed zodiac) that represented the *suṣumṇā* path of the awakening of *kuṇḍalinī*. The Earth Element had then to be fully mastered, whereas nowadays it is the Watery attributes signified by Cancer. (Cancer being the store of the *karma* of the Watery Atlantean dispensation.)

Scorpio and Leo-Virgo in the eastern direction manifested the energies of the Watery-Fiery-Earthy triplicity of the Elements governing the three planes of human livingness. This triplicity facilitated the natural Atlantean clairaudient abilities to hear the mantric sounds from the *deva* kingdom. They then abused this knowledge to control and to manipulate the *deva* lives upon the mental, astral and physical domains. The potency of control was primarily Watery, empowered by the Watery Scorpionic thumb. The Agnishvattas, Agnisuryans and Agnichaitans thereby came under domination of black magicians.[43]

Scorpio also provided the power to visualise astral images, which obviously relates to the lower psyche, encouraging a propensity for sex magic. Leo-Virgo helped the Atlanteans to mentally control the developed thought-forms. Leo provides an egoistic, self-centred projective potency, whilst Virgo facilitated the ability to control the *devas* of the lower orders, the Elementals, to do the bidding of the person. The magicians' invocations could thereby be precipitated to produce physical plane phenomenon.

Scorpionic psychic power and the projection of its sting produced all of the heads of the Hydra (especially via sex magic) as an obvious consequence. The sorcery, however, was primarily associated with the feminine (with witchcraft), the expression of the influence of the Virgoan part of the Sphinx. Atlantis was thus largely matriarchal in nature and sex magic was a natural focus of activity. Scorpionic energies intensified the desire element empowering the Atlantean sex magical practices. The complete expression of all forms of desire produced the murky swamp wherein resides the Hydra and the sum of its qualities. Being the Atlantean Watery thumb, Scorpio represents the *piṅgalā* aspect of the dark brotherhood activity and the Capricornian mind represents the *iḍā nāḍī* aspect.

43 These *deva* orders are explained in Alice Bailey's *A Treatise on Cosmic Fire* and my earlier books.

Leo-Virgo's influence as the sign of the Sphinx was waning by the end of the Atlantean epoch (hence its attribution to the Aetheric little finger). With increasing mental capacity, Leonine attributes became more dominant, producing the self-assertion of the individual.[44] The related moon Chain *karma* was increasingly being expressed, coming under one pointed aspiration (for the object of desire) in the next sign, Sagittarius. This then intensified the wilful black magical propensities of the Atlanteans, producing increasing war-like ravaging right up to the time of the sinking of the Atlantean continent.

The western direction of Pisces and Aries concerns the development of mediumistic and clairvoyant abilities. These abilities were related to the various service arenas and thought-forms demonstrated by the more advanced Atlanteans. There was also the intensification of the ability to visually project thought-forms by members of the left hand path. The natural clairvoyance of the Atlanteans was the subjective correspondence to the images that are now materially projected via people's cell phones. In those days the Arian will was needed to formulate and to project the images. (Nowadays scientists and technicians have provided the means for people to do so.) This function became increasingly prevalent near the end of the Atlantean cycle, signified by the Watery thumb assigned to the sign Aries.

The will was developed via the awakening of the mind, but at first the impetus of strong desire manifested. The development of the personality will is the basis behind all true dark brotherhood activity. It was used to control the forces of Nature and the masses of people, in order to counter the evolutionary process and the service arenas of the white brotherhood. The will was the force behind the overpowering avarice and acquisitiveness they possessed that caused them to build their palaces of opulence and to fight their various psychic wars. The planetary Stomach centre was thereby developed. This centre (at the western direction of the Solar Plexus) is the store of the blacker, more violent *iḍā nāḍī* emanations of humanity, such as anger, hatred and spite. The eastern direction of the Solar Plexus centre developed the more benign, but negative attributes of the Liver centre, the greyish *prāṇas* of humanity associated with their general desires and selfishness.

---

44 One can therefore postulate that by the time of the erection of the great Sphinx at Giza (at the advent of the sign Leo) the Sphinx had a lion's head. This would be consistent with that sign appearing on the horizon, where the Sphinx's gaze was directed at the vernal equinox at that time. This was symbolic of the appearance of the fifth (Aryan) Root Race. The attributes of Leo would dominate human evolution from that time to our present epoch.

Before such wilful development, Piscean mediumistic and psychism of all kinds dominated, as possessed by the masses of Atlanteans. Such massed psychicsm of the then humanity ruled for far the greater part of the Atlantean epoch. As there was little or no *manasic* input for such expression, so Pisces is represented by the Aetheric little finger. This Element here signified the energies from the higher Mind projected by their Souls or by the overseeing *devas* that gently moulded their experiences. The witches (and the occasional sorcerer) easily manipulated the masses of mediumistic, psychic humanity. The witches (the manasic, wilful ones) rose to control and to manipulate all, and so to govern the various districts, zones of dark influence (similar to our nations today) of the Atlantean continent. These zones were carved out as the power bases through psychic projection (and also materialistic power) developed by the strongest of the witches.

Pisces represents the storehouse of past Watery karmic activity along these lines from the moon Chain, and which had to be somehow cleansed through such activity.

## The downward pointed pentagram

The downward pointed pentagram has Gemini as its head, Aquarius and Sagittarius as the left and right feet, Aries and Leo-Virgo as the left and right hands. This pentagram combines the two Lemurian Tau crosses via Leo-Virgo (the Sphinx), thus it mainly energises those who were Atlanteo-Lemurian. (This consisted of the bulk of the then humanity.) The upward turned pentagram, in contradistinction, conditioned the attributes of the elite who had some mental development and were well versed in the magical arts.

The consideration of this pentagram must also be incorporated with the functions of the lower hand. (It was also primarily Atlanteo-Lemurian in disposition.) Note the Elements attributed to the signs differed compared to what is now. This relates to what the Lemurians had to develop in the respective signs. What was developed (within the overall Earthy development by the Lemurians) became the foundation for later conversion by the Atlanteans into the Elements of the associated signs that still influence us today. This is because the disposition of average humanity is still Atlantean.

Gemini governs the etheric body of the earth. Its energies are directed by Sagittarius (where the Earth is the esoteric ruler) whose disposition is Fiery because of the Sagittarian will and because it embodied the functions of the forefinger in those times. Through this inverted pentad the energies and *karma* of the moon

Chain[45] (veiled by Gemini) find their outward expression via Sagittarius (the right foot of this pentad). This was grounded via the Earthy disposition of Gemini. This *karma* had to manifest right into the sum of the physical constitution of the planet. The Sagittarius-Gemini interrelation was explained earlier with respect to the Lemurians. What was further developed during the Atlantean epoch concerned a more mental (Fiery) approach to awaken *kuṇḍalinī,* thereby directing its energies with greater ability to totally control the Earth Element.

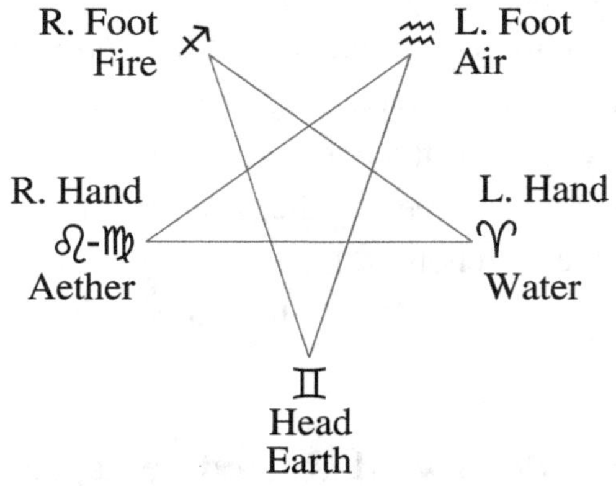


**Figure 26. The inverted pentagram**

Once the Atlanteans could convey Aquarian energies (the left foot of this pentad), this brought into manifestation Airy energies. These energies fanned what awakened via the psychic heat of the southernmost (Gemini) point. The effect was to gradually convert the Earthy focus of the Atlanteo-Lemurians in Gemini more towards the Airy dispensation, which governs Gemini today. The left foot function facilitated the Airy energies to be incorporated into the earth. There was thus a 'lifting up' of focus from Earthy levels (Gemini) to Airy levels (Aquarius). This facilitated the later ability of the Atlanteans to master the Air, hence to produce vehicles that could fly therein. With this development also came the ability to think more abstractly, hence to properly comprehend the nature of the astrological signs, and of other stars in the night sky. The science of (esoteric) astrology thus came to the fore.

The general purpose of this inverted pentagram was to awaken genuine self-consciousness and a more appropriate working relationship with *devas* – as veiled

---

45 Both the moon Chain and our present earth Chain are part of the present earth Scheme, which consists of seven such chains of globes. This subject would be explored in depth in a possible future volume of my series *The Astrological and Numerological Keys to the Secret Doctrine.*

by Leo-Virgo (the right hand of the pentad). Aries (the left hand of the pentad) provided the mental awakening and the will to use their minds for the then budding Hierarchy. It accomplished this via the general Watery domain they resided in. The Aetheric Element of Leo-Virgo was in fact the most refined Fiery-Earthy energies the Atlanteo-Lemurians could express. Sagittarius provided the Fiery Element *(manas)*. Aries also harboured its potency, whilst Aquarius fanned the flames.

For that early Hierarchy, this pentagram assisted in the right control of forces within the etheric body, which exemplified the close connection of the fourth Root Race to the plant Kingdom. The gain of this was increased understanding concerning the nature and function of the *chakras*. This activity (via Aquarian impetus) helped to transform somewhat the laborious Lemurian *hatha yoga* practices formerly needed to achieve their goals. A more ritualistic, fluid approach to Initiation manifested during the Atlantean epoch. For the Lemurians, the gain from rightly expressing the energies of Sagittarius and Aquarius produced the first degree Initiates (the Cyclopes), who were the high point of their evolution. In this way the early Atlantean Hierarchy gradually developed.

In the latter Atlantean epoch the black adepts (called 'Trees'[46]) and the witchcraft covens used the same energies to wage war against the vegetable kingdom, against anything living and vital. Adherents of the left hand path perceived the vegetable kingdom to be associated with the white Hierarchy (hence had to be eliminated). The entire continent consequently became denuded of trees. Atlantis became a blackened, scarred continent at its end. The black adepts little realised that in doing so they also destroyed their own capacity to survive on earth. This was a reason why the Atlanteans were later drowned by 'God' by means of 'the great flood'.

Much *karma* was accrued by the then exponents of the left hand path, however, many have since been converted to the right and are presently disciples. Many are consequently now ardently trying to save our environment, in the face of the present mass destruction of the world's forests. (In this higher fifth Root Race correspondence of the past fourth Root Race epoch.) In Atlantean times, the destruction was both by psychic and physical means. As a consequence, the *karma* will also necessitate cleansing of psychic misdeeds by the former miscreants.

---

46 The symbol was used because of the Atlantean affinity to the vegetable kingdom. The shade that trees manifested, the fact that their roots were anchored in the soil of the earth, and also that in jungles they often carried strangler vines (etc.), were qualities akin to the attributes that the black magicians manifested.

From the normal perspective, this pentagram consists of two Air signs (Gemini and Aquarius), three Fire signs (Aries, Sagittarius and Leo), and the Earthy sign Virgo. The Airy quality relates to the *prāṇas* governing the etheric double, which was the focus of the Atlanteo-Lemurians, allowing them to totally master the Earth Element. There was however (as stated) an increased *manasic* (Fiery) input from the three Fire signs. The empirical mind *(manas*[47]*)* was thus the onus of evolutionary development. (The implied dangers are explained with respect to the upwards-turned pentagram.) The wilful, self-focussed attributes of the personality were thereby intensified. The Arian and Sagittarian combination with Leo produced this result.

The upturned left and right feet (Aquarius and Sagittarius) received the toned down downpour of potent Shambhalic energy[48] that needed to be expressed onto the dense physical plane, so as to produce the *manasic* stimulation. The feet grounded the more astral qualities associated with the hands (with their ability to grasp and manipulate the substance of people's desires). Aquarius also represents the ring finger for this pentad, which channelled the Airy energies. For the Atlanteo-Lemurians, however, the influence of Aquarius was generally only at its shallowest, superficial level (impacting primarily upon the ethers), for the ability to process the *manasic* Fires was only very slowly developed.[49] What was utilised was mainly directed to battle the hardships of physical plane living or towards fostering cupidity.

The Fiery influence (the pointed forefinger of the magician) via Sagittarius (the upturned right foot) was potent, but made aberrant through incorporation of Watery *piṇgalā prāṇas.* This combination developed the desire-mind and intensified the yoga of the psychic heat that could be expressed via Gemini. This combination assisted in the control of physical plane substance in the form of Earth magic. This energy also intensified the selfish ambition of the self-willed personality.

Leo-Virgo (which acts as the right hand for the downwards pointing pentad) combines the attributes of both of the pentads, via their interrelation with Scorpio in the eastern direction of the Solar Plexus centre. This combination was powerful because it also combined the attributes of the two Tau crosses, the right hands

47 *Manas* technically relates to the Fires of the mind/Mind.

48 This principally happened via the Fire signs and the Aquarian impetus, whereby they developed a fluidic feeling-perception receptivity to *buddhic* impressions.

49 The Lord of the World released the Fiery potency in such a way as to try to mitigate as much as possible the effects of a certainty of massed dark brotherhood activity.

of which were the main implement to manipulate the expression of the Watery astral forces. This implies that the previously mentioned clairaudience (which became a major factor for the Atlantean dispensation) was also integrated with the mystery of the Sphinx. What was heard, and the resultant utterance of mantric sound, was a great factor in the manifestation of their magical incantations. The entire Atlantean history is therefore signified by the mysteries of sound. Mantras were needed to empower the visualisations and images they created, to produce the needed effects in their magical activity. The present Sphinx on the Giza plateau stands in mute testimony to this ancient time. It can accordingly be deduced that the lion may have had its mouth open, as it stared at the sky at Leo (specifically Regulus, the heart of the lion) when this constellation was ascending. The appearance of the age of Leo (the epoch of manasic propensity) signified the culmination of the Atlantean civilisation. Similarly, the polar opposite of Leo (Aquarius) now in the ascendency, signifies the ending of our present materialistic age (which was effectively birthed in that ancient epoch).

Scorpio and Leo-Virgo, therefore, signified an important triad of energies governing this period. This triad empowered the potency of the nine-headed Hydra, via the natural clairaudiance of the Atlanteans and the potency of their thought-form production. The Scorpionic energies could 'sting' the Sphinx—to bind the Elemental Lives (Virgo) into the convoluted and grotesque shapes of the thought-constructs that the Lion (the egotistic personality) used for his purpose. Present day magicians also know the nature and power of thought constructs, coupled with the emission of the right mantras. Conscientious disciples must, however, work to zap with light the dark, evil forces on the astral plane created by them and others in past lives, so as to cleanse their ancient psychic *karma*. This is needed if they are to pass their Initiation testings.

Aquarius and Leo-Virgo form another important coupling (being one arm of this pentacle) that empowered the activities of the grey hued *Anubis*. They are well known from the Egyptian religion, but their predecessors and ancient potency stem from the Atlantean epoch.[50] The Anubis are important entities existing in the astral plane. Their speciality concerns psychic deception and the cunning use of thought-forms and whispering lies into the ears of aspirants upon the path of Initiation. The Anubis know well the weaknesses of targeted disciples and project a barrage of subtle thoughts to capitalise upon their vulnerabilities.

---

50 See my book *The Constitution of Shambhala,* part A, 363-70, for further detail concerning the potency of the Anubis in human psychology.

The interrelation between Aries and Leo-Virgo intensified the wills of the Atlanteo-Lemurians. People's psychism became more intensified and focussed through the Arian impact via the influx of the energy of mind. The Atlantean clairvoyant faculty was significantly enhanced thereby and this facilitated the mantric work they manifested. The energies of the Sagittarian will flowing to Aries (the left hand of the pentagram) were similarly directed towards amplifying the personality will. This produced the true beginnings of sorcery, empowering the qualities of the downturned horns of the ram to batter other beings with. Self-serving groups of black magical endeavour countered the work of the young Hierarchy. This one-pointed magical focus (empowered by manasic development), coupled with the type of self-awareness associated with Leo-Virgo, was however a major factor in the genesis of the fifth (Aryan) Root Race.

All energies of this pentad converged upon Gemini (the Earthy 'finger', as well as head of the pentad), thus one needs to properly comprehend the significance of this sign. Gemini is the house of etheric energies, under whose auspices many temples of worship were established during Atlantean times. These temples were also halls of learning. Taught therein were the modes of constructing the architectural wonders of the Atlantean civilisation through control of the Airy Element in its Earthy connotation, via magical incantations. Airy *devas* were invoked to lift huge blocks of stone into the air, so that the blocks could be easily transported and put into place.

Airships (Vimanas, as testified by ancient Hindu sources) were built and flew through the atmosphere by controlling the Air *devas* through means of mantric sound. Cyclopean buildings and palaces of great grandeur were likewise built through knowledge of levitation. The Initiates of this period were master masons. Modern masonic practice has its ancient forebear in those times.

The Atlanteans could thus map the physical geography of the earth and spread their civilisation from continent to continent. Traces of this civilisation are thus found all over the earth. With their clairvoyance they could easily locate the sources of magnificent crystals and other minerals, such as gold, silver and the ores with which they fashioned the splendour of luxurious places of residence.

Material plane science and technology were also known to them, but such knowledge was a gift from the higher Initiates, as the average Atlanteans had too little mental development to comprehend the needed scientific formulae.

Aquarius, Sagittarius and Gemini formed an important triangle in relation to this, for the Aquarian and Gemini combination also invoked the Pleiadian dispensation. (The Matriarchal high Initiates that instructed in the then temples of Initiation.) Shambhala was then externalised, so these Initiates openly taught at special locales of learning for those few capable of receiving such instructions. However, as the Atlantean epoch reached its climax, many that were formerly upon the white path converted to witchcraft and black magic. The loss of so many who should have been the defenders of the right hand path spelt the inevitable doom of this civilisation.

The mortal brother (of Gemini) needed to aspire towards Sagittarius to learn to rightly handle forces upon the astral and physical planes. (These forces could then be grounded by means of the activity of the 'right foot'.) This produces the full experience of the energies in the Waters of Life (Aquarius). At first, such ability was atavistic, mediumistically expressed, thus not understood. (As stated, this was the general way of the Atlanteans; as the mind was still generally nascent, yet to be developed by the masses.) Therefore, those that had developed their minds were generally those in command of the masses, but normally the means of command was sorcery.

The development of perceptive experiences produced an elementary mental (though Watery) grasp in Aries, whilst final resolution of dualities in the mind of an Initiate were accomplished in Gemini. The activity of the immortal brother (the Soul) assisted the mortal brother to ascend the heights of awareness, to finally give birth to self-consciousness (Leo-Virgo). When enough people achieved this, then Leo-Virgo divided into two signs, producing the twelve-signed zodiac presently governing us.

Such was the objective of that epoch. The second Initiation, signifying the mastery of the Waters, was the goal, though at the stage represented by this pentagram the first Initiation was symbolised by the aspiration of the mortal brother in Gemini. Such activity concerned the beginning of the rectification of moon Chain *karma* by those who generated it upon that planetary Scheme. The most advanced Atlanteans began to do so, but real progress was stifled by so many who were prone to witchcraft.

Two more pentads could be analysed – one pointing in the eastern direction of inwards to the Heart of Life, and the other pointing in the western orientation of outwards to the field of service. They are much weaker than pentads of the north-south orientation because they relate to the path of discipleship, which was rare in those times.

The Master D.K. provided the following information in a private communication, concerning the *time of the actual sinking of Atlantis.* Astrologers can base their computations from this date to use in their calculations concerning earthly changes. He stated that:

> Poseidonis sank in 9,872 B.C. The 2,160 year astrological cycle is based on a mathematical error, an error of omission. 2,500 years is close enough to 2,400 years. Earth goes through cycles of slowing down and speeding up, therefore time *per se* can vary according to earth standards. The sinking was the result of a line up, a cacophony of signs, producing the emergence of the dry sign (Leo).[51]

## The upward pointed pentad

Capricorn and the associated upward pentad of Pisces, Scorpio, Taurus and Cancer manifest the dominant energies that influenced the Atlantean population. The focus of these energies is to awaken the attributes of the mind, which was the onus of Capricornian development. The more relatively refined Fiery-Watery *prāṇas* that were then developed were directed to Capricorn via the planetary Splenic centre I. This centre directs the coarser *prāṇas* from the circulation below the diaphragm to Splenic centre II, and the remainder upwards. Capricorn, the head of this pentad, also represents the middle Earthy finger, used to control the substance and entities of the dense physical domain. Through passing respective Initiation testings for those days the Initiates of both the dark and white brotherhoods utilised this manasic development to empower their forms of magic. Capricorn thereby greatly facilitated the selfish materialistic attitudes of the Atlanteans and their proclivity towards dark magical incantations. This was increasingly egged on by the dark forces that flooded into this civilisation from cosmic sources, because of the invocative appeal of Atlantean thought and desire for magical activity. It

---

51 Given by D.K. on 12/3/95. See also *Esoteric Astrology* page 344. Pisces was the starting point on the clockwise wheel at this time for the greater zodiacal wheel of approximately 25,000 years. Further information concerning the fifth Round, globe and Chain of the earth Scheme, especially regarding the *Judgement Day* in the fifth Round, can be found in Alice Bailey's *A Treatise on Cosmic Fire,* pages 389-93, 424-7, 492-3 and 705. The presented time compares well with the figure of approximately 9,600 B.C.E. given for the sudden melting of the glacial ice sheets that caused massive flooding and a 400 feet rise in the ocean level. The technical term for this advent is 'melt water pulse 1B' during the younger Dryas period. For detailed information see the works of Randall Carlson, Robert Schoch and Graham Hancock. They give somewhat different causes for the event, but nevertheless the results are the same, which they uniformly state caused the extinction of what was an advanced civilisation.

was the mount of selfish materialism that was thus overwhelmingly climbed, not that of aspiration to enlightenment. Black magic ran supreme.

The higher hand of the Solar Plexus centre (where Capricorn represented the central petal) is the focus of the upright pentad and was primarily Atlantean in disposition. Here the Elements and signs are the same to what is now.[52]

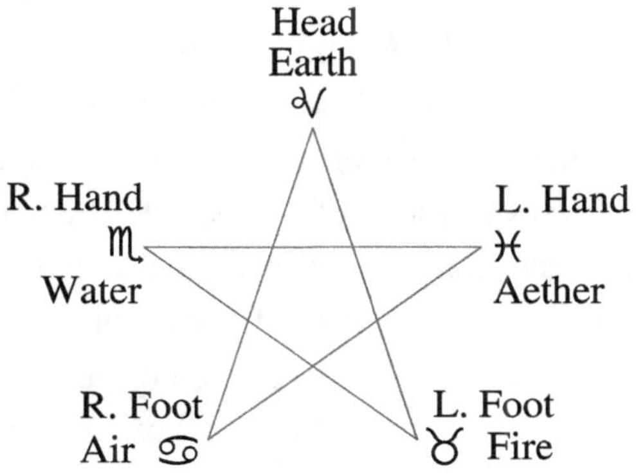


**Figure 27. The upright pentad**

Scorpio governed the right hand of this pentad. Scorpio's main function in those times drove the desire impulse and produced the various forms of sexual licentiousness. The *manasic* stimulation of the *prāṇas* pouring through Capricorn was distorted by Watery perversions. It however helped the Atlanteans to articulate clairaudience and clairvoyant vision, facilitating the projection of desire and emotional thought-forms to produce the wanted purpose.

Scorpio facilitated the manifestation of sex-magic and all of the attributes of the nine heads of the Hydra.[53] The then clairvoyance (which was a natural expression of the Atlantean psyche) was prostituted to the worship of psychic (astral) images of all types. Beautiful *deva* lives were grotesquely converted into psychic beasts used to attack other people by those that actively pursued the dominant form of magic, witchcraft. The Watery-Earthy energies of Taurus and Cancer (the legs of this pentagram) significantly assisted to build the desire-forms projected to, and attacking, others. Through utilising these energies, the Atlanteans could project powerful thought-forms into the dense world. Massed fear (ruled by Cancer) was generated by their means. The onrushing bull of desire rampaged, to build

---

52 Note that some information already presented will be occasionally repeated in a new format in the information below when the signs already dealt with are revisited.

53 They are explained in my book *The Constitution of Shambhala,* parts B and C.

'homesteads' of potent images, sexual pleasure, and to control the treasures from the earth. Taurean potency helped project the desire to psychically control the physical domain, by gaining magical impressions (through psychometry) that facilitated the manipulation of all psychic entities. Cancerian energies built Watery mantric shells of controlled Elemental Lives that did the bidding of the witches.

Taurus materially grounded the influences from the Pleiades (the Seven Sisters), to which it was the open gate. The Atlantean epoch was governed by them, from which the matriarchal Hierarchy (who largely ruled in the then Shambhala) drew its sustenance. Their feminine dispensation seeped right through the civilisation, but was perverted into multifarious forms of witchcraft. The major wars fought were by the most powerful witches that battled each other to gain supremacy over their respective territories. They desired to gain from all others the sum of what they possessed. Their covetousness was insatiable. There was thus complete projection (prostitution) of base Taurean energies (the 'cow' of cosmic and systemic desire) onto the material domain via the Watery triplicity (Cancer, Pisces and Scorpio) sustained by this pentad. This produced the consequent manifestation of the *karma* of rampant psychic and material desire, which was further concretised by Capricorn (the head of the pentad). The feet (Taurus and Cancer) thus represented major signs that governed the then dark brotherhood activity. It is thus now obvious how the entire pentad facilitated the rise of the left hand path.

Intensified desire (Taurus) moulding the fluid, Watery emotional nature (Cancer) of the masses eventually produced the basic power of the Hydra (Scorpio) and the personal power of the black magician (Capricorn). With the inpouring of the energy of mind into the material world (Capricorn), this desire energy was projected deep into the hearth of the earth (Taurus) to control the elementary forces of Nature (Cancer). They were the psychic 'beasts' of the astral field and of the ethers that incarnated into the sum of Nature's domain. The 'beasts' were attributes of Makara the Mystery (the fifth Creative Hierarchy), fused with the serpentine *kuṇḍalinī* Fire that was evoked. The period indicated is when black magic was at its height, with much Watery energy inundating the planet: cosmic Waters (Taurus), systemic Waters (Cancer), the astral waters of the human kingdom (Scorpio), and the Watery activity of past Logoic cycles (Pisces). All flooded into the Earthy domain (Taurus and Capricorn). This is also signified by the fact that the path of Initiation was activated, both for the black and the white Hierarchies. The corresponding Initiates then passed their grades of testing, either under the auspices of the past (left hand clairvoyance and mediumship, Pisces) or the then present (Scorpio). The brothers of the left hand path produced and intensified the qualities of the Hydra (Scorpio) whilst those of the right hand path battled the associated qualities, to produce the higher Capricornian attributes.

Scorpio is the sign governing humanity in general, thus it is fitting that here, in the domain of the Hydra, the battles between the adherents of the left and the right hand paths were most intense.

There was a process of conversion of energies taking place, from the time when the Airy 'index finger' was governed by Cancer, to when it became Watery. The focus of humanity then moved from the ethers to become much more astral in nature. As Cancer is the predominant Water sign, so this 'finger' exacerbates its Watery proclivity for the Atlanteans because the right foot stepped these energies down towards the material domain. The ability to control the Elemental Lives intensified when humanity could more consciously, knowingly, draw upon the Sacral centre's potency, to which the Cancerian right 'foot' trod. Consequently, Sacral centre magic (sex magic) became exceedingly potent.

The then Fiery Taurean potency stepped right down into the dense physical domain (via the left foot) to direct the gain of their impressions of what they desired in the earthy terrain. (This activity was empowered by their magical invocations.) The direct link of both Cancer and Taurus (of both feet) to Capricorn facilitated a down flow of manasic materialistic impetus to ground the potency of desire. The *iḍā* (more mentalistic) attributes of the Sacral centre were consequently potently awakened. The Taurean attributes then became decidedly Earthy.

The path of aspiration (for exponents of the right hand path) was stimulated by experiences in the fields of desire (Taurus) – for the developing mind produced disillusionment with the nature of the transient and impermanence of things. Nothing that one wanted to really possess lasted. Much was stolen by the cupidity of the black magicians and witches, and what they could not rapaciously steal was aggressively destroyed. Thus was produced the first perceptions of lighted thinking, the illumination which occurred in Taurus. This led to the various trials and tests for Initiation in Scorpio (specifically of the sensual and desire aspects of the Hydra). Eventually, the Soul-infused disciple rose out of the mass consciousness in Cancer and began to climb upwards to master the craggy rocks of desire-mind in Capricorn, to the Initiation that was the pinnacle attainment. The inevitable mastering of Cancerian attributes was the foundation for the taking of the second Initiation by the most advanced of the Atlanteans.

The members of the dark brotherhood utilised the growing mental powers to seriously intensify their destructive rampage against the environment (Capricorn), especially as the power of the Hydra (Scorpio) was by then fully developed.

The left hand of this pentad projected the potency of the Watery dispensation of the Atlanteans via Pisces. The Aetheric 'little finger' at that time mainly worked to project into the morass of human consciousness the darkened *saṃskāras* from moon Chain activities. However, as the Atlanteans developed increasingly Watery attributes, so the disposition of Pisces gradually became Watery (via its direct links to Cancer and Scorpio). Mediumistic tendencies were at first fostered, but later true clairvoyance became the norm. Plutonian Piscean attributes (reinforcing the personality will) consequently became the major conditionings governing the then humanity. These attitudes were moulded into the societal structure through the manipulative activities of the 'left hand', and associated magical practices. This was the genesis of the base condition associated with Pisces (of the lower 'fish' yoked to the Waters of sensation), explained by D.K.:

> (T)he unfoldment of the mass consciousness of all the kingdoms in nature into the group consciousness of the three highest kingdoms through the mediatorship of the human kingdom which, through its peculiar and specific type of awareness, can relate the higher and the lower expressions of divinity. It is here and in this connection that the sign Pisces is of much importance, as it is the sign of mediatorship. Mediumship in its true meaning is expressive of the mass consciousness—impressibility, negativity and receptivity. These points will become clearer as we study the signs and their many inter-relations. The thought I wish to convey to you here is that at this stage the influence of Pisces on the involutionary arc, and as the Sun retrogrades through the signs, is felt largely in the anima mundi and in the hidden, incarnated and imprisoned Christ; the germ of the Christ life is psychically impressed, becoming constantly more sensitive to these psychical impressions, swept by desire which ever changes, constantly aware of all impinging contacts, but unable as yet to interpret them correctly, for the mind has not been awakened adequately in Virgo. This hidden Christ is unable to free itself from "contact with the Water."[54]

The Capricornian pentad consisted of the three Water signs and two of the Earth signs, demonstrating the predominant predisposition of the Atlanteans. Libra in the centre, regulated the manifestation of the consequent *karma,* to try

54 *Esoteric Astrology,* 122.

to direct the magical flow towards a progressive conclusion. One can think of Libra here as the expression of the All-seeing Eye of the Logos. Via this Eye the zodiacal wheel could be turned by feeding appropriate energies through the zodiacal signs, when they were to play their roles. The hope was that the massed human consciousness would begin to rightly walk up the Capricornian mountainside towards Initiation. Testings could then be presented to those who were able to look upwards towards the Light. They could manifest a higher, far more powerful form of magic, one that projected forms of Light in a relatively selfless manner, rather than the prevalent, dark self-focussed magic. Those that were receptive to this path were appropriately energised via the Libran Eye. Obviously, this ideal manifested only for the comparatively few. The great majority chose the path of least resistance to the materialism, selfish concrete mindedness and cruelty associated with Capricorn. They chose black magical practices, and as a consequence the Atlantean continent was inevitably destroyed.

## The ten-signed zodiac of the future

The nature of zodiacal conditionings, like all else in *saṃsāra,* is not static. We have already seen that humanity were conditioned by an eight-signed zodiac in the past, then a ten-signed one, which eventually evolved into the twelve-signed one that conditions us today. The zodiacal rearrangements will continue in accordance with the changing conditionings in the mass human psyche. The twelve-signed zodiac will accordingly evolve into a ten-signed one in the future.

D.K. states:

> In this world period we have the division of the sign of the Sphinx into two signs (the Lion and the Virgin, Soul and form) because the state of human evolution and conscious realisation is that of a recognised duality; it is only at what is called the "final judgement" that another fusion will take place and Virgo-Libra will form one sign, for then man's sense of antagonistic dualism will be ended and the scales will have turned finally in favour of that which the Virgin Mother has hidden from expression for aeons.
>
> This final judgement, as far as the planetary cycle is concerned, will take place in the next great world cycle and by that time two-thirds of the human race will have unfolded the Christ principle in one or other of the various stages of unfoldment and be upon one of the final stages of the path of evolution: they will be either probationary or accepted disciples or upon the Path of Initiation. Eventually, in some mysterious way, there will be only ten signs of the zodiac

again; Aries and Pisces will form one sign, for the "end is at the beginning." This dual and blended sign is called in some of the ancient books "the sign of the Fish with the head of the Ram." We shall then have

1. Aries-Pisces
2. Taurus
3. Gemini
4. Cancer
5. Leo
6. Virgo-Libra
7. Scorpio
8. Sagittarius
9. Capricorn
10. Aquarius[55]

These signs can be put on to the zodiacal wheel thus:

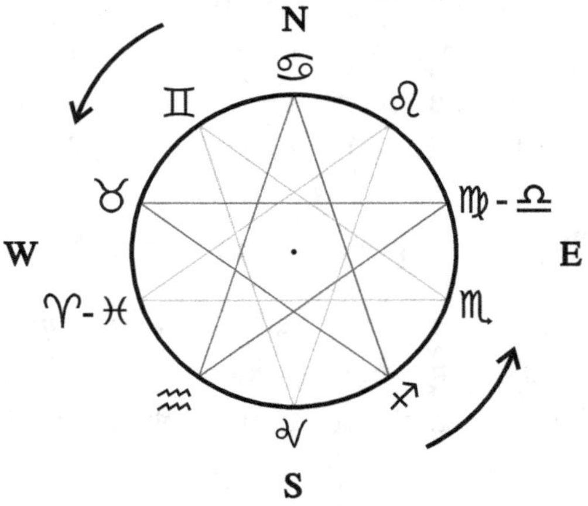


**Figure 28. The zodiac as it will be seen in the Aquarian age**

The ten-signed zodiac will have its genesis during the Aquarian age after a large proportion of humanity are upon the path of aspiration, or of probation for Initiation. By this time a new world government will have commenced under the auspices of the reformed United Nations, where Initiates will be in charge of many of its departments. It will be an epoch of planetary Initiation, when an increasing number of people will take their first and then higher Initiations. Hierarchy will then be fully externalised to assist humanity in this process. There will consequently be a large number of Initiates existing upon the planet. The analysis below of the pentads will be concerned with the process of Initiation undertaking immediately ahead of us, from the Aquarian to the Capricornian age. This will inaugurate the period of the fifth Round for humanity. This Round will concern the epoch of humanity's receptivity to the attributes of the abstract Mind.

55 *Esoteric Astrology,* 230-31.

The energies manifesting through the ten-signed zodiac will not just concern its revolution, but internally there will also be a process of spinning in a spiral-cyclic motion. Eventually there will be fourth dimensional motion. The time of the transition from the twelve-signed motion to the ten-signed one will produce chaotic events on the earth and will tie in with manifesting cataclysms.

Figure 28 shows a zodiacal wheel that has been inverted, to reflect the Initiated level of awareness now being interpreted. This zodiacal wheel starts from Cancer and moves downwards via Gemini. It expresses the mode of descent of the potent energies from the liberated domains to Capricorn (the mount of Initiation), wherein they are grounded in the Initiate's consciousness. This mount represents the mental plane (the cosmic dense physical), which is the base level for the interpretation of this zodiacal wheel.

The signs Sagittarius, Scorpio, Virgo-Libra and Leo represent the stages of ascent of the disciple from aspiration (Sagittarius), to pass through the fields of testing (Scorpio) towards the next Initiation to be attained. This necessitates overcoming the Leonine egotism and the Cancerian emotions. Finally, after many turnings of the wheel, the ability to tread the cosmic Paths via the Cancerian Door looms ahead for the Initiate.

The first sign upon the path of descent of the cosmic Waters is Gemini the twins, who projects these energies into the four cosmic ethers (the liberated planes of perception). They finally manifest into dense objectivity via Capricorn. (Seen here as the direct link between Gemini and Capricorn.) Gemini will integrate these energies with the sum of Hierarchical purpose. The new temples of Initiation that will be established will facilitate the process of working with these potent cosmic *prāṇas*. The energies will externalise into the four ethers of the physical plane, giving many people etheric vision. This will awaken them to subjective happenings.[56] (Some forms of hallucinogenic drugs also provide such vision, but this will be a more natural awakening.)

The temples of Initiation will mainly be dedicated to bringing down into conscious experience (thus to educate humanity) the nature of the Pleiadian perspective and purpose. During this period, Shambhala will manifest as a feminine dispensation, under the auspices of the Mother of the World and Her key advisors.

Taurus the bull will project the sum of the Pleiadian purpose into the field of service representing humanity. Taurus is one of the arms of the western direction

56 Some of the ramifications of this development will be explained below.

of this zodiac and also carries the Pleiades upon its shoulder (symbolically upon its back.) Taurean energies will therefore help ground the new Pleiadian dispensation into the civil structures of the forthcoming civilisation. Taurus will consequently assist the world disciple to build new forms within their 'homesteads' that relate to the development of wisdom. They will awaken the Eye (clairvoyant perception) that will allow working with *devas*. All of the Eyes—the right or wisdom eye, the left or manasic (intelligent) eye, and the central third Eye (Ājñā centre) will begin to properly be awakened. The nature of this feminine kingdom will begin to be comprehended, and rules of contact and cooperative endeavour established. This activity will be assisted via the rituals established in Gemini.

Aries-Pisces (the fish-tailed Ram) signifies the development of the Will (Plutonian and Uranian energies) that will help project the energies from the cosmic ethers into manifestation. The projected energies will transform planetary evolution in accordance with Logoic Purpose. Eventually, death to the limitations of formed life will happen (as a consequence of the Plutonian influence of Pisces). This will allow people to better perceive the nature of the attributes of enlightened perception and to facilitate their aspiration upwards to the higher domains.

Aquarius the water bearer signifies active service work in all arenas of Life, through demonstrating the Bodhisattva ideal in cooperation with all members of Hierarchy. The laws of group evolution (of which Aquarius is the custodian) then come to rule all aspects of human society. The attributes of the Aquarian age (that have already been provided elsewhere in my books) will then be in flower.

Capricorn the goat signifies the fact that once the service arena has been successfully accomplished by a disciple, then the next Initiation can be undertaken. (Once the required testings for the Initiation concerned have been passed.) Capricorn will also feed a better comprehension of things as they are regarding the world situation. Proper critical reasoning abilities and abstract thinking will come to the fore amongst the mass of humanity. This will supplant their present Watery Cancerian (Atlantean) disposition. Correct thinking will help people to overcome their present materialistic bias in favour of addressing the true causes of suffering for all in this world.

Sagittarius the archer signifies the driving forwards to greater Hierarchical and Shambhalic purpose for the Initiate concerned and their Ashram. There are many service oriented goals and higher aspirational ideals that the world's Archers will fire their arrows to. The constitution of the Hierarchy and the nature of the path to lighted perception will be discussed by many. Humanity as a whole will therefore begin to forego selfish ambitions to serve wider community oriented goals.

Scorpio the scorpion signifies the main focus of the service work to be accomplished by the world disciple. This will be to thoroughly cleanse the astral plane (humanity's major field of testings) of the attributes of the Hydra lurking therein. The down pouring cosmic Waters during this Aquarian epoch will be used to wash clean the murk of the Hydra's swamp. This necessitates washing away the grey and black emanations of the dark brotherhood, of all the evil thought and desire constructs that humanity has created through the ages.

Virgo-Libra (symbolised by a dragon holding the scales of justice in its mouth[57]) signifies the mode of the elimination of material *karma* created through the aeons of incarnate activity. An increasing number of people will be inspired by the new teachings concerning the *deva* kingdom and the virtues of a meditative lifestyle. The meditative Mind will automatically be developed as they contemplate all aspects of life in a way that karmic consequences for selfish actions are properly comprehended. The means to the rightful resolution of *karma* and the laws governing rebirth will have become widely known. The focus of people's lives therefore will move away from the (Earthy) material domain (Virgo) towards Airy Libran attributes. These two signs will consequently merge into one contemplative process. As large numbers of people develop meditative lifestyles, so this will produce an increasing downpour of the Fiery energies of cosmic Mind (Mahat). As humanity as a whole begins to properly bear this force, the process that produces the appearance of Masters of Wisdom will be accelerated. Larger numbers of Initiates will finalise the treading of the zodiacal wheel, allowing escape into cosmos when they have attained their sixth Initiations. Where before the path was one of individual attainment, in the future we will see group evolution of enlightened attributes and of liberation from formed space.

Leo the lion signifies the complete mastery of the material domain, of a cycle of planetary purpose, to produce a Chohan of a Ray. Many will contemplate the nature of the cosmic Paths that lead to Sirius, to the Heart of the lion (Regulus), and also to other cosmic shores. The consequent *nirvāṇees* become Lions of our solar evolution, demonstrating their prowess as they symbolically 'roar out' their cosmic mission.

For average humanity, the energies pouring through Leo in this future period will energise their Souls, which will then work to produce Soul-infused personalities. People will learn much about this kingdom, and also of Hierarchy. They will then strive towards taking their third Initiations, which will signify

---

57 The serpent (symbolised by the curved movement at the end of the glyph of Virgo) grows into a Dragon of Wisdom. (Another term signifying the appearance of a Master in time and space.)

the death of their mentalistic concepts of ego, of the self-focussed personality (a leonine attribute). The brilliant light and ageless wisdom of the Soul will then take the place of 'ego'.

Cancer the crab signifies the open gate to cosmic astral space. It is represented by the fifth Creative Hierarchy ('Mass Life', 'the Numbers') who straddle between the seventh cosmic astral sub-plane and *ādi* (the highest of our planes of perception). As each *nirvāṇee* passes through the gate of Cancer, so the claws of the crab lessen a little more of their hold of the 'jewel' of the substance that ties them to cosmic systemic space. (The seven planes of perception.) The fifth Creative Hierarchy will consequently (from its perspective) become liberated from incarnation when a sufficient number of *nirvāṇees* move into cosmos.

Average humanity will begin to comprehend the true nature of the pain inducing and glamour building effects of their Watery (emotional) proclivities. They will thus begin to seriously curb these detrimental effects upon their own psyche and upon society in general. The potency of the astral plane that conditions humanity's activities will therefore wane. An increasing number of people will consequently find themselves in higher domains (such as the mental sub-planes) in their afterlife.

The above is a brief synopsis of some of the main points concerning the manifestation of this ten-signed zodiac. Astute astrologically minded individuals will discern much more, such as the interrelation between the pairs of opposites, and the lines of relation between the arms of the pentagrams.

## The inverted pentad

There are two pentagrams shown in Figure 28. They do not relate to the Solar Plexus centre, as was the case in Atlantean times, but rather to the vitalisation of petals in the Head centre via pentads of *prāṇas*. The pentads depicted are also not static, but can also be considered to form a moving figure-eight (making the symbolic infinity sign). The zodiac also moves to accommodate this increasingly rapid moving motion. This is not easy to depict, or to explain, for the first Ray energies of the Will generated, through Sagittarius, Capricorn and other signs (such as Vulcan in Taurus and Pluto in Pisces), produce a detachment from substance, its etherealisation, as *pralaya* approaches. There is thus a sequence through time of increasing dematerialisation of matter as the incarnating Lives begin to move through the open Door of Cancer into cosmos. That Door becomes increasingly larger and consequently more cosmic energy pours through to further dematerialise the substance of things. The description of the pentads therefore provided only indicates their qualities for the period up to the next zodiacal sign (Capricorn) after the Aquarian age.

The inverted pentagram will consequently signify the path of the descent of cosmic energies. The upward pointing pentagram will govern the Initiation path leading towards liberation in cosmic space. Average humanity will move around the zodiac, as described above, but the pentads here described are pentads of enlightenment, which condition the Initiates of the higher degrees (the third Initiation and up). They also condition the planetary whole via Shambhalic impetus.

The inverted left and right feet signify the mode of reception of energies that pass through the lowest (most concreted) cosmic astral sub-plane to the cosmic dense physical plane.

There are a descent of energies from the Pleiades, where the left foot 'stands' upon the plane *ādi* (Gemini), the left hand (Aries-Pisces) wields *ātmic* energies, and the Capricornian Head empowers the mental plane. These are the planes signifying the descent of the energies of cosmic Mind. There is then an ascent via the second Ray line upon the right hand side to *buddhi* (Scorpio), signifying the energies providing the field of service. Leo, the right foot (standing in an inverted manner upon *anupādaka)* signifies a mode of descent of the potency of cosmic Love that has been sufficiently reified so that this energy can be appropriately utilised by the Initiates receiving it. The Logoi projecting the energies must carefully measure the intensity delivered to high Initiates that must receive them. These Initiates must re-transmit the energies to humanity who still manifest emotional proclivities. Mass emotionality must be carefully monitored, thus the projection of energies to those demonstrating mental-emotional conditionings must manifest in a toned-down fashion.

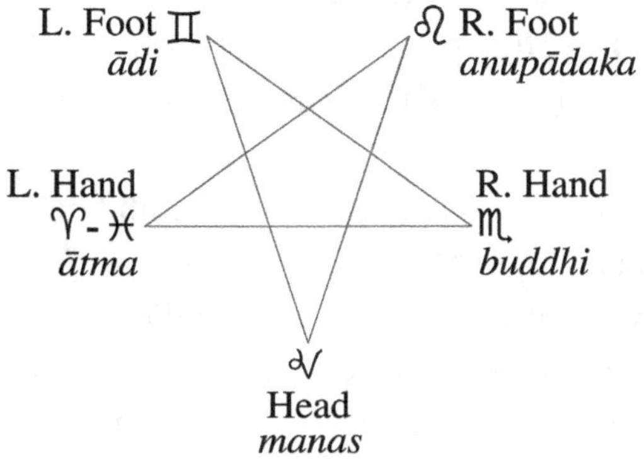


**Figure 29. The inverted pentagram**

The left hand of this pentagram will be governed by Aries-Pisces, the ram-fish. Aries signifies the power of the Will-to-Overcome all obstacles upon the path. The bonded self-focussed forms of Atlantean mediumship (and clairvoyance) under Pisces will consequently be transformed into vast fields of visioning. The zodiacal wheel will continue to turn, but the cycles of death (signified by Pisces) will cease. People will still obviously die, but human consciousness will overcome their fearful aspects of the concept of death. The Fiery Arian impetus will work to project human consciousness into the higher dimensions, thus the Watery Piscean disposition will consequently dry up. Many will develop the perceptions to see clairvoyantly and make the astral plane their field of service. The astral plane, as we now understand the term (with its heaven and hell realms), will consequently begin to dissipate.

The ram-fish will project the energies via the *ātmic* plane that the Pleiadians will utilise to help to cleanse the *kāma-manasic* (desire-mind) *karma* of humanity.[58] As this is accomplished, a large number of people will attain their second Initiations. Upon the path of descent, the cosmic Waters from Taurus impacting upon *ātma* via Aries-Pisces will work to abstract into the ethers the material forms that were originally created from the beginning of time.

Capricorn governs the Head of this pentad, to project the energies of Logoic Mind (Mahat) into the dense physical plane. The left foot of this inverted pentad (Gemini) channels energies from the Pleiades. The right foot (Leo) will channel the energies from Sirius into the planetary domain. Capricorn will be the representative of the potent Will energy from the Seven Rishis of the great Bear. These are the three main cosmic energies brought to bear upon the sum of the *maṇḍala* of the zodiac. The Pleiades, Sirius and the Seven Rishis will thus also energise the upright pentad, which manifests as a mirror-like image of the inverted one, as part of the spiral-cyclic nature of the energisations.

The most intense energies need to be brought to bear in order to transform and convert the substance of the dense physical plane via the transforming minds of those that abide in that substance. The empirical mind must be transformed into the enlightened Mind to do so. Mahatic Fire must be projected to the lowest level of the physical, to wed with the feminine *kuṇḍalinī*. The combined effect will consequently be raised to the Head centre, the highest expression of incarnate Life. The entire purpose of the *manvantara* will thereby be accomplished. The

---

58 The *karma* that governs the system emanates from *ātma* (Aries) and is eventually resolved (Pisces).

Head centre here, however, does not just bear this cosmic Mahatic energy from the Seven Rishis, but also the Pleiadian energies from the left foot, and the Sirian energies from the right foot of this pentagram. The sum of these energies are brought to bear upon the Head of the upright pentad, governed by Cancer.

Under Capricornian influence, Hierarchy will instigate the new curriculum for attaining the third Initiation, to manifest via groups of Initiates. The future disciples will learn the arts of Earth magic, where all aspects of this Element will be mastered. Such accomplishment will be facilitated through the scientific discoveries and investigation of the nature of the ethers, and the accompanying laws of Sound. Spiritual materialism will at first be at its zenith, with a consequent resurgence of the Lemurio-Atlantean forms of magic, though now with a far greater *manasic* capacity with which to comprehend. The focus will also concern the 'raising' of *kuṇḍalinī.* A problem will therefore arise concerning the widespread susceptibility of humanity to resort to sex magic and other forms of left hand practices. This advent will be further stimulated by the potency of the right hand of this pentad, ruled by Scorpio.

What will prevent the disasters of the Atlantean epoch, however, is that by now[59] the forces of the Christ will have externalised, and with them the second Ray epoch of Love-Wisdom. Proper teachings and a large number of spiritual instructors will exist to help steer humanity towards the white path, and to master Initiation testings. The new world religion and associated temples of Initiation will attract a very large audience. The nature of the *karma* of left hand practices will be quite evident to the seekers of the higher Mysteries, and much information will be available for disciples to study. The dark *karma* will therefore be cleansed through appropriate visualisation practices with mantric sound, projected through right knowledge.

The polar opposite of Taurus in the twelve-signed zodiac is Scorpio. In the ten-signed zodiac, Scorpio manifests a similar function. This implies that the Pleiadian Initiates will also oversee the Watery testings that will be undertaken by the world's disciples. This is especially so, since Gemini (also wielding Pleiadian purpose) is coupled to Scorpio on an arm of this pentagram. There will be some remnant predatory psychic *karma* that will be promulgated by those that still espouse dark brotherhood attitudes. These magicians, however, will now live in an environment wherein many disciples will be awakened to the light, which will then be psychically directed at them. Their darkness will be zapped away with

59 The sixth Root Race epoch.

light in the resultant psychic war. The power of the evil forces upon our planet will consequently rapidly diminish. There will be mass conversions from the dark side to the light, but this will mostly be an astral plane phenomenon.

Through Scorpio, buddhic energies will increasingly pour to our planet via the ethers, for now large numbers of disciples (manifesting in groups) will be able to bear this energy. The disciples will also be working to eradicate their tendencies to produce all forms of desire-attachment and selfish thought constructs. The entire massed thought-form constructions upon the astral plane since Atlantean times will begin to be properly deconstructed. The testings for the world disciple will thus concern the means whereby the astral murk of the Hydra's swamp can be eliminated. Eventually there will be 'no more sea'[60] —the astral plane conditionings, as we now understand them, will then no longer exist. The nature of this conversion will be much discussed and become the testing ground for a mass of aspirants and disciples.[61]

Leo, in the position of the upturned right foot, receives energies from Sirius, or from Regulus (the Heart of the constellation Leo), so as to project them into the planet via the group conscious disciple. Leonine energies therefore directly feed Hierarchy as a unit. The sun (which rules Leo on all three levels of expression) therefore signifies the modes of expression of the Hierarchical dispensation, now and well into the future. All of humanity and the world's disciples will be brilliantly illumined thereby. The methods of the service arena for the (Leonine) group conscious disciple will change somewhat in the New Age to take into account the changed conditions. Self-consciousness will be subordinated to directives from the Soul, and from Hierarchy. The selfish Leonine egoistic pursuits that so strongly characterise the activities of our present human society will largely be eliminated, to be replaced by humble, wise decision making.

The energies from *anupādaka* will manifest more intensely, producing an increasing number of Chohans that will be preparing to travel to their cosmic destinations. The nature of the local cosmos, and the attributes of the Logoi that inhabit it, will be much in the public imagination and discussed by esotericists. This will intrigue the then scientists to do the appropriate experiments to validate the new 'theories'. The new massed clairvoyance and demonstration of the reality and properties of the four ethers, will thus begin to be properly studied by scientists.

---

60 *Rev. 21:1.*

61 Little needs to be said here concerning these testings, as such information can be found in my book *Meditation and the Initiation Process,* and also in the books by Alice Bailey.

The logical extension of discerning the nature of the four cosmic ethers and their ramifications will therefore also be an object of scientific thinking.

## The upright pentagram

This upright pentad expresses the response of the then Initiates, as they aspire upwards to the liberated domains to receive the downpour of energies from cosmic sources. This pentad responds in a mirror-like fashion to the descending spiral-eight motion of the energies. The left and right hands and feet consequently change their position when compared to the zodiac shown in Figure 28. The altered positioning for these signs can be seen in the figure below.

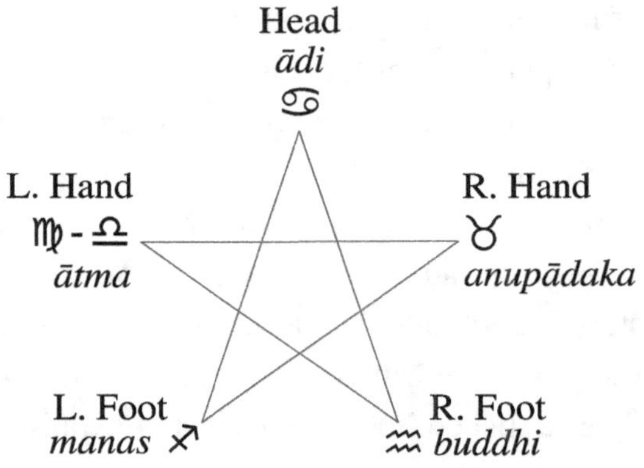


**Figure 30. The upright pentagram**

The right hand of this future dispensation will be occupied by Taurus, which will bring into manifestation the cleansing Waters of the cosmic astral plane. Taurus will thus project its cosmic Watery function (as the Womb of the Mother carrying the divine Child) rather than the Earthy Element presently attributed to it. (For Taurus governs the Waters in the Womb of Virgo.) This action will help wash away the drudge of the earth's astral murk with the energies from *anupādaka*. This eventuation will be a major purpose of the Pleiadian dispensation of the Mother of the World during this time. Shambhala will be constituted according to the *maṇḍalic* formation created by this feminine department. Taking into account that Taurus is considered an Earth sign, there will consequently be an Earthy-Watery mix associated with Taurus. The Pleiadian dispensation that builds the forms of what must come to be manifests via *ādi* (Electra's domain) and is fundamentally Earthy in nature. (This Creative function is also an expression of the Watery expression of Logic Desire.)

The Pleiadians will ground Taurean purpose to produce the manifestation of Wisdom in all beings. They will thereby assist people's ability to (clairvoyantly) vision via awakening their Ājñā centres, for Taurus also governs the awakening of this Eye. The Pleiadians will empower the Greater and Lesser Builders, who will help build the divine constructs needed for the New Age. They will also help cleanse the planetary astral plane from the effects of the former spells and magical constructs of the Atlantean witches. The Pleiadian high Initiates need to return to earth through karmic duty, for they were the Initiates that guided humanity through the disastrous Atlantean epoch. Many are the strands of *karma* that need weeding out at their roots by all of the actors and actresses that created them. Several rinses of the planet's Watery substance must be undertaken before this cesspool will be properly cleansed of its murk. (The impact of these karmic cleansing energies happens upon the *ātmic* plane under the auspices of the ram-fish.)

The right foot position of the pentagram of the Initiate is governed by the Aquarian attributes of being the world server. The Initiate will bring the free-flowing energies of the Aquarian epoch into manifestation upon the planetary dispensation via the etheric domain of the earth. The Aquarians will consequently ground the new Mystery Schools and their teachings. Universality of consciousness and religious expression will be espoused, riding on (and expanding upon) the service arena already established in former cycles of expression. The gain of the downturned pentagram's right hand's activities in Scorpio (concerning mastering the astral plane) will bear its fruit in Aquarius. Much that was formerly Watery in disposition will become Airy. Significant information has, however, already been given concerning this Aquarian epoch elsewhere, thus needs no repetition here.

The spiral motion of the energies between the two pentagrams will move from Gemini, and the plane *ādi* (bearing Pleiadian energies), to the left hand of the inverted pentagram (Aries-Pisces, the plane *ātma).* It will then be directed via the planetary Head centre to Taurus, the right hand of the upright pentagram. This will happen via the new temples of Initiation, whose activities will be assisted by Aquarius (the right foot of this pentad). The new Mystery Schools will then come into being. Therein, students will learn the teachings concerning the nature of the 'immortal brother' and of his relation to the 'mortal one'. The mode of how they are to join hands in service to each other and to humanity will be high on the curriculum.

The cycling of energies now moves to the left foot of this pentad, governed by Sagittarius, wielding Fiery energies. Here Sagittarius signifies firing the one-pointed arrows of the Will towards Shambhala, the planetary Head centre. The objective is to draw into the field of service the Shambhalic Potency. As the Initiate can increasingly do so, he/she becomes a Shambhalic recipient. The mechanism that will allow these arrows to be fired necessitates the development of the abstract Mind, thus of the third Ray aspect of Mathematically Exact Activity. Eventually, when there are enough Initiates that can draw upon the energies from the Mind of the planetary Logos, the Kingdom of 'God' (the New Jerusalem)[62] will externalise exoterically on to the physical plane. Sagittarius will draw the needed second Ray flux from *anupādaka* via Taurus (which forms an arm of this pentad with Sagittarius) to help impel its arrows. The Aquarian right foot dispensation moves more energies to Sagittarius, to help produce its points of tension.

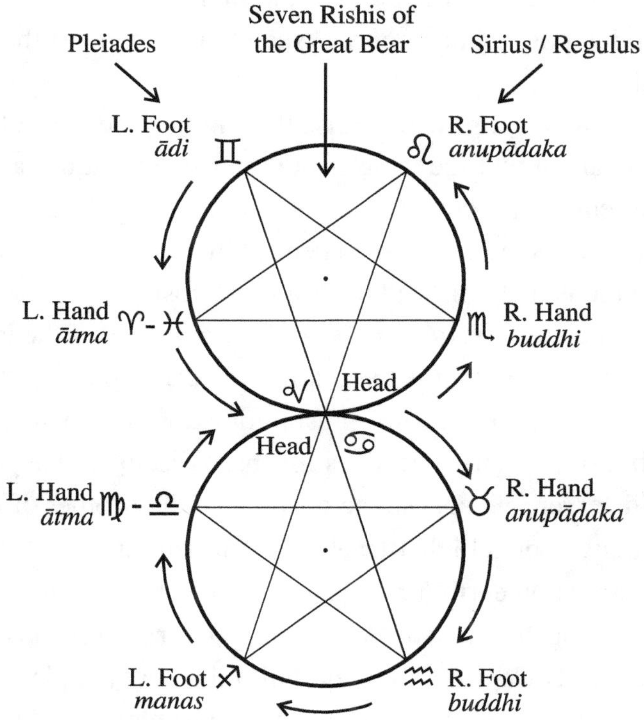


**Figure 31. The spiral-cycle of Hierarchical attainment**

Figure 31 shows that there is a direct line of relationship between Gemini and Aquarius. As Gemini rules the ethers in general, so Gemini will rule the manifestation of the etheric visioning that will be widespread amongst humanity.

62 *Rev. 21:2.* See my revised book, *The Revelation* for detail concerning this process.

Such visioning will be facilitated by an increased downpour of energies from *ādi* into the fourth cosmic ether *(buddhi),* which Aquarius will ground. The consequent intensification of buddhic energies working through the etheric body of humanity will produce an etherealisation of substance. Consequently, as stated, large numbers of humanity will see etherically. With this development the fear of death will go, as many will clearly see the transition of the deceased into the ethers. Nature's finer forces will be clearly visible to most. The violet *devas* of the shadows will be seen, and consciously worked with, to produce works of magic in the new temples of Initiation that will rival and supersede what the Ancient Lemurio-Atlantean Initiates accomplished. This advent will inaugurate the era of new scientific discoveries based upon such visualisation. Investigation upon such things as the *chakras* and *nāḍī* system will thus produce a new era of scientific productivity. Many theories, such as the origin of the universe, will be transformed.

The energies from Gemini will vitalise the adytum, the Holy of Holies, found within the inner sanctum of the temples built during the Aquarian epoch. Many of the mysteries concerning this star system, and also of Regulus (the Heart in the Body of That Logos) will be comprehended by the Initiates that are preparing to pass the Initiations that will lead to travel into cosmos.

The Leonine energies (via *anupādaka)* of the right foot of the inverted pentad will strongly impact upon Sagittarius. This will cause the Sagittarian disciple upon the mental plane to fire arrows of aspiration upwards to *anupādaka.* There will be a number of possible objectives for these disciples. They may aspire to become a world server to dispense the purpose of the Mother of the World (via Taurus). They may, upon a higher level of attainment, manifest the final stages of their service arena on earth (under the auspices of the cosmic Christ in Leo) preparatory to entering their cosmic Paths. The Sagittarian disciple may fire arrows of Revelation towards Capricorn to help build the new temples of Initiation in accordance with Manasic Shambhalic precepts. The ultimate objective will then be to externalise the New Jerusalem.

The left hand of the upright pentacle of the Initiate is governed by Virgo-Libra, the next sign to be energised. This hand consequently wields the sum of the attainment previously accomplished. This facilitates the attributes of the plane *ātma* to be mastered here, and consequently the appearance of Masters of Wisdom.

As an Initiate is continuously in a state of contemplation, or meditative absorption, so the influence of Libra becomes 'below the threshold of consciousness'. The Initiate then embodies the Libran attributes *in toto*. Much of the meditation concerns the factor of *karma* and its annulment. The Initiate is automatically the judge of everything that transpires in the three worlds of human livingness, thus making the correct decisions. Once this process is perfected, then a Master (in any of the sub-Ray lines) has arisen. Such activity is not so much for the Initiate's sake, but rather for the entire well being of the planet. Such Initiates must contemplate vast cycles of expression.

The appearing Masters will help aspirants to overcome the lower Piscean attributes and to correctly steer their wills. (Developed via the corresponding Arian impetus of the Aries-Pisces position of the inverted left hand.[63]) The manifestation of the will must be correctly lubricated by Love-Wisdom, otherwise left hand practices in the field of magic might ensue.

The Head of this upright pentad is governed by the Watery sign Cancer, the sign of mass incarnation. In this case the process has been reversed to make Cancer the sign of escape back to the cosmic sources wherein the liberated Monads *(nirvāṇees)* have connections.

Cancer is the polar opposite of Capricorn in the twelve-signed zodiac, but here both signs stand Head to Head. The imprisoned Lives from the sphere of attainment symbolised by the upright pentad can escape into the Waters of cosmic space by developing attributes of cosmic Intelligence (Mahat) wielded by Capricorn. This Intelligence (Shambhalic Potency) therefore directs the entire upright pentad via the Cancerian need to cleanse the systemic Waters from their impediments. The karmic causes of manifestation for the sum of the attachments to *saṃsāra* need thereby to be cleansed. (A function of the previous sign, Virgo-Libra.) Only then is it possible to enter the open gate of Cancer upon the path of cosmic return.

Through the Capricorn-Cancer interrelation, the Pleiadian Purpose from the upturned Gemini left foot becomes grounded in the Aquarian right foot. (This is a reason why the feminine Pleiadean dispensation will manifest during the Aquarian age.) There is a similar descent of Sirian energies from the upturned Leonine right foot to the Sagittarian left foot. This ensures that the Sagittarian manasic development is thoroughly Watered with the energies of Love-Wisdom. (The second Ray dispensation that governs our solar system as a whole.) The potent Will energies from the Seven Rishis of the Great Bear impacting upon the Heads of the *maṇḍala* (Capricorn-Cancer) are distributed in the needed

63 There will be an obviously strong interrelationship between the corresponding hands and feet of both the inverted and upright pentads.

gradients to the Initiates that are striving to be freed from the limitations of cosmic dense incarnation.

Via Cancerian energies *per se,* an Initiate works to cleanse the conditions of the world's astral murk, consisting of the myriad thought-forms created by humanity throughout the millennia. All of the fearsome phantasms of desire projections must be dissipated. Initiates will educate humanity concerning the nature of the effects of such thought constructs, of their illusionality and means of annulment. Inevitably, humanity learns the needed way to cleanse *karma,* so eventually producing freedom from the need for rebirth.

In the field of magic, the Cancer-Capricorn interrelationship is a symbiotic one. The focus of Capricorn is Earth magic, whilst that of Cancer is astral (Water) magic. Both streams stem from the ancient Atlantean cycle and earlier on from the moon Chain. The evil generated by the black magical activity from those ancient epochs needs to be cleansed by the Initiates and their disciples during the Aquarian age. This activity will be assisted by the impetus of Sagittarian mental directives. Thus, the activities of both left and right feet in this age will work to lift aspiring humanity from the ground (wherein they are presently focussed) into the higher domains. Symbolically, the feet step upwards upon the ladder of evolution to the higher domains of perception.

The moving spiral of energies continues from Cancer up to Scorpio, wherein those that have mastered attributes of Mind (in Virgo-Libra) gain the necessary experiences in the Scorpionic fields of the earth to become more Watery (Loving) in disposition. Thus, the spiral of Bodhisattvic activity moves towards Leo, and the plane *anupādaka.* Therein, Bodhisattvas are totally drenched with Sirian Purpose. The energisation increases – to the extent that they can move through the open gates of Cancer (once they have mastered the necessary Capricornian Mind) upon various cosmic Paths into the Waters of cosmic astral space.

# 6

# Further implications of the future Zodiac

This chapter shall provide further implications of the future ten-sided zodiac. This zodiac will manifest as a Solar Plexus centre[1] attuned to cosmic astral energies. These energies are to be mastered by the Mind. Receptivity to the attributes and energies of cosmic Mind *(dharmakāya)* will become the focus of all spiritual development as humanity enters the New Age. The mechanism thereto is based on the foundation of developed Love-Wisdom, via which greater aptitude to abstract esoteric reasoning can be developed. This brings into manifestation more green energy of the third Ray (of Mathematically Exact Activity). When coupled with the universal Mind of the second Ray of Love-Wisdom, the resultant blue-green Ray will work via the violet of ritualistic activity (the seventh Ray expressed by Uranus, the exoteric ruler of Aquarius). The Aquarian dispensation of the violet Ray will also draw an increased first Ray, crimson Will energy, into manifestation. This combination will activate the turning of the future ten-sided wheel when sufficient Initiates appear that can enable this process.

The crimson energy will destroy the foundation of the old wheel. The violet energy will set the new cycles, whilst the blue-green will manifest the consciousness-attributes that will sustain the activity of the new wheel.

By this time, the mediumistic tendencies associated with Pisces have been eliminated, allowing Pisces to properly assist in the downpour of cosmic astral

---

1 This centre is really the Solar Plexus in the Head centre. (The outermost tier of petals therein, which is explained in my book *The Esoteric Exposition of the Bardo Thödol,* Part A.)

energies (the Waters of Logoic Love). Pluto (the esoteric ruler of Pisces) now plays a commanding role to help end the conditionings of the 'underworld' (the astral plane). Many people will then be aware of the ancient thought structures that created this zone of human experience. They will consequently comprehend the need to deconstruct these astral fields of illusion. (This will happen through the effect of Plutonian first Ray energy.) The thought structures will no longer serve the roles that generations of humanity experienced. People will now aspire to experience the higher domains of perception. The astral phenomenon needs to be dissipated as they aspire upwards. Watery astral *karma* will begin to be replaced with the Fire-Airy energies that will be the Aquarian leitmotif.[2]

Aries anchors the incoming energies into the domain of the abstract Mind, which will then turn the new wheel of zodiacal activity. The combination of Mind with Love in Buddhism is called *bodhicitta,* which acts as a force that empowers the Bodhisattva ideal.[3] This is therefore the wheel that governs the realm of enlightened Being (the higher echelons of Hierarchy and the Lords of Shambhala). *Bodhicitta* is a compound Sanskrit word, where the *bodhi* part signifies the force of enlightenment and *citta* is the substance of the mind/Mind that is the vehicle of this enlightenment. The sign Aries-Pisces will manifest this function in the future zodiac, where Aries provides the substance of the higher Mind that drives the path to enlightenment as the zodiacal wheel is turned. Pisces provides the impetus of the liberation from the realms of form *(bodhi),* allowing eventual escape into cosmic space.

The ten-signed zodiac can also be considered as a pair of hands, and the organisation and functioning of the petals manifest in a similar way to that which is presented in Figure 11 of *An Esoteric Exposition of the Bardo Thödol,* Part A.[4] (Though now there are cosmological inferences.) In the early period of the Aquarian epoch, the field of service involves the retrogressing twelve-signed wheel (the progression of the equinoxes) that governs human activities. At first there will thus be a pull of many forces affecting humanity, until they develop more loving, compassionate attributes.

---

2 The Waters poured by the Water Bearer are actually cosmically Kāma-Manas, which manifest via the systemic ethers as a Fire-Airy quality.

3 See my book *The Buddha Womb and the Way to Liberation,* 124-37 for an explanation of the Bodhisattva *bhūmis* and the zodiac. See also my explanation therein of the zodiac and the Heart centre as part of the elaboration of the Tantra: 'The Samādhi, "Great Gate of Diamond Liberation"', 45.

4 Page 289.

With respect to the ten-signed zodiac, there will be two versions to consider. The motion between these wheels moves like yin-yang (or in spiral-eights), concerned with disseminating the appropriate energies to humanity. The first will govern the activities of Hierarchy. (Thus concerning the manifestation of the world-Bodhisattva.) This wheel posits Cancer in the northern direction and Capricorn south, as shown in Figure 33. The second of the wheels directly relates to the reception of cosmic energies and activities of the Lords of Shambhala. It will manifest with Capricorn in the northern direction, to receive the Potency from cosmic Mind.

With respect to the Virgo-Libra combination, the nurturing function of the Mother is no longer needed. She has given birth and the child has grown up. This process concerned Libra consuming the *karma* of materialistic activities associated with the Mother. The rule of matter thereby wanes.

Aries-Pisces is united in one sign because the ending is the beginning, because the Watery astral substance of objective manifestation (Pisces) has been totally subjugated by the liberated ones that have developed the attributes of Mind (Aries). Pisces then manifests as the Avatar who utilises Logoic Will to produce the needed changes in manifestation.

These two wheels will be explained in further detail below. Before delving into them, the nature of the development of the *siddhis* (psychic powers) via the Solar Plexus centre should be contemplated by the reader. The mode of expression of this *chakra* changes somewhat as a person becomes enlightened. This is explained in my book *An Esoteric Exposition of the Bardo Thödol.* The nature of the *prāṇas* directed via the five fingers of each 'hand' of the Solar Plexus centre must be comprehended, plus the association with the manifestation of the eight-fold cross of direction in space *(aṣṭadiśas).*

In that book I state:

> Here we see that in relation to the mastery of the Liver and Stomach centres the major orientation of the (minor) *siddhis* is east-west. The focus is then clairvoyance and clairaudience, to which the other *siddhis* (apart from *dharmatā)* generate the fundamental support. Later the orientation shifts from below the diaphragm to above, in which case *dharmatā* becomes the base for the awakened Vision and Powers of the combined Head centres.
>
> In this arrangement of petals we have an awakened eight-petalled lotus, to which the orientations of the eight-armed cross of direction in space apply. The east-west petals work to direct the *kuṇḍalinī* flow to all of the minor *chakras.* The energies then vitalise Splenic centre II with *kuṇḍalinī* so that the sum of the Inner Round *chakras* can be awakened with the Fire and the remaining

*saṃskāric* obscurations burnt up. *Kuṇḍalinī* moves from an initial south-north line to east-west, manifesting thereby in the form of a fixed cross of steadfast liberating activity. The *iḍā* flow going west and the *piṅgalā* flow to the east. All *chakras* are thus included in one integral fusion of Fiery bliss. *Kuṇḍalinī* is the conclusion of the successful work of one's own mind integrated with the work of all the Peaceful and Wrathful Deities. Tum mo is a name for *kuṇḍalinī* that has awakened to vitalise elements of the form with its Fiery warmth.

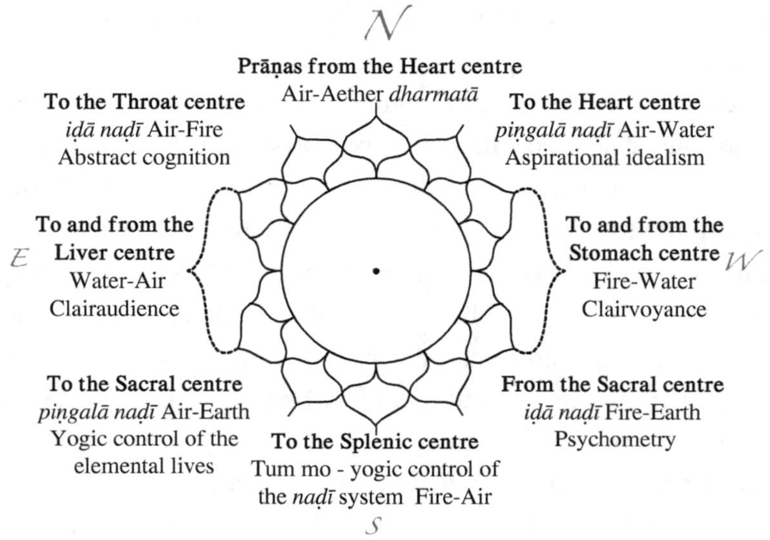


**Figure 32. The *maṇipūra chakra* and the *siddhis***

As well as manifesting as an eight-armed cross and thereby aligning with the functions of the Diaphragm centre, the east-west direction of *prāṇic* flow literally incorporates the Liver and Stomach centres as major petals of the Solar Plexus centre. These two major petals (energy streams) can be added to the ten to make the twelve that align with the Heart centre. Effectively the Solar Plexus centre then reflects the attributes of a Heart centre. When this occurs the energies of the Heart centre dominate the centres below the diaphragm so that *bodhicitta* can affect every expression of the three-fold personality.

Practitioners should take care, as the process leading to the development of such *siddhis* necessitate firstly the cultivation of *bodhicitta*. There can be no equivocation concerning this. If the will is evoked without prior rightful cleansing and transformation of the *prāṇas* and *saṃskāras* concerned, as explained above, then the gravest dangers of falling into the dark path will manifest. The Wrathful Deities exist to try to protect practitioners from falling into egoistic and desire-ridden traps (because they still possess unrefined unruly *manas*) when awakening the *siddhis*. These Deities help protect the unwise from the dire consequences of any such premature eventuation. Otherwise the possibility of myriad violent, disease-engendering and pain-causing serpents will course through the *nāḍīs*.

A properly qualified preceptor; a master of meditation of the white *dharma*, must be sought and found that will truly reveal the illumined path that awakens the *siddhis*. Let the seeker also beware, as the charlatans professing to be enlightened gurus are myriad. The true Master of the white *dharma* is rare and consequently most precious. Auspicious *karma* is needed for the most earnest and gifted seekers to find their teacher, such as Milarepa had when he sought and found Marpa. The *karma* must ripen to allow this, and only then the fruit of past life's beneficence may be plucked, not before. The enlightened teacher appears only when the time is right. Such teachers shun the limelight, material wealth, and do not have time for adoring crowds of students. Nor will they kowtow to the demands of the unready, and few indeed there are who can ride the cleansings of their *saṃskāras* through to enlightenment. In the meditation-Mind, however, the Master can always be found.

The mind must be rightly controlled through the development of the Will-to-Love, thence the generation of *bodhicitta* as the emotions come to be mastered.[5]

## The Hierarchical ten-signed zodiac

As earlier stated, the orientation of the zodiac in this Hierarchically oriented wheel has altered. Cancer now governs the northern Gate of the wheel and Capricorn the southern. Cancer represents the open Gate into the cosmic astral domain, via which the Buddhas (Chohans of the sixth degree and greater) pass when they enter their cosmic Paths. Cancer also assists in the downpour of cosmic Watery energies (Logoic Love) into manifestation. This Watery energy from the various stellar spheres and constellations then represents a major source of energisation for the members of Hierarchy. Cancer represents the Gate for the *prāṇas* coming from the cosmic Heart centre, which are collectivised under the term *dharmatā*. The cosmic Heart centre represents the great wheel of the turning zodiac of the constellations. The energies are, however, directed by the Will of the respective Logos of the seven Rishis of the Great Bear governing the manifestation of any particular cycle.[6] Some of these sources are indicated in the chapter entitled 'The Science of Triangles' in D.K.'s *Esoteric Astrology*.

5 Bodo Balsys, *An Esoteric Exposition of the Bardo Thödol,* Part A, 306-8.

6 It should be noted that this zodiacal arrangement will be but one way of interpreting the way that Hierarchy uses the zodiacal potencies during this epoch, for there are many factors to consider. They are all in dynamic mutability, depending upon the focus at any time, and also because Hierarchy itself is continually evolving.

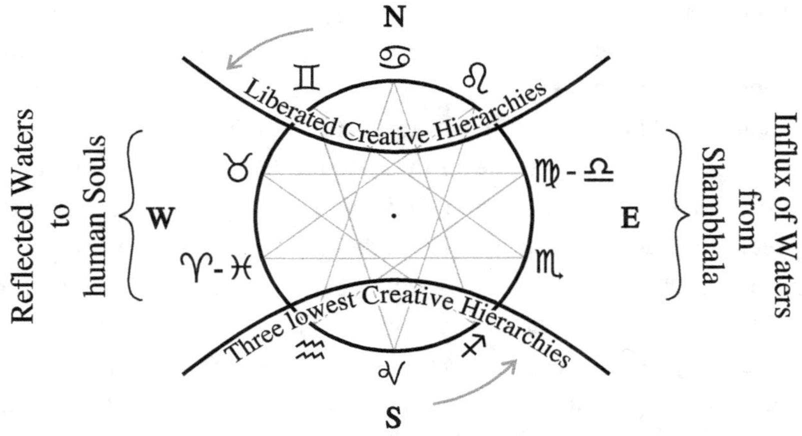


**Figure 33. The Hierarchical zodiac**

Capricorn (in the southern direction) represents the open Gate of energies directed downwards into the increasingly material domains of the three lowest planes of perception. (These planes are embodied by the substance of the three lowest Creative Hierarchies.) Capricorn thus manifests as the Gate wherein is generated *tum mo,* the psychic heat (an expression of *kuṇḍalinī)* that sustains the activity of the entire material domain *(saṃsāra).*

Effectively, the main expression of this zodiac is a cardinal cross (Cancer-Capricorn and the east-west interrelation). This is because an increasing demonstration of the first Ray will be the focus from now on. The mutable cross (Gemini-Sagittarius) for this wheel was fully expressed in the earlier cycle that resulted in the appearance of this ten-signed zodiac. The focus of these energies is to now work to fully cleanse the effects of all *saṃsāric* activities upon earth manifested by humanity.

Aquarian energies are the main energies pouring to the planet during this time (inundating all via the Shambhalic ten-signed zodiac). Thus what is seen in Figure 33 is the mechanism of the distribution of these energies via the sum of the *maṇḍala.* Aquarian purpose will impregnate the sum of what will be, for Hierarchy will see to this in their service arenas. The Aquarian gate depicted here indicates that these energies will now properly govern the substance of all forms within the planet.

One can also think of the east-west arm of the *maṇḍala* as representing the *potency of the fixed cross* for this zodiac, where its activity is now fully integrated with (or an expression of) the first Ray purpose. This arm consists of Scorpio (coupled with Virgo-Libra) in the east and Taurus (coupled with Aries-Pisces) in the west. We can see, therefore, that the effects of this arm will be exceedingly powerful during the Aquarian age, constituting the major field of activity for the bulk of the then disciples. The energies from this arm will help disciples to develop clairaudience and clairvoyance. These *siddhis* will attune them to Hierarchy and assist in the work to be accomplished. Here, clairaudience signifies the ability to listen to instructions from the Masters and *devas* (or the Pleiadians) that will help guide the disciples. Higher Initiates will listen to the mantric Commands stemming from the Lords governing the various constellations (specifically Sirius) that affect our earth. Clairvoyance will concern the developed vision that will allow disciples to see astral images, allowing them to work to dissipate much of the astral plane phenomena. Clairvoyance will also assist them to work with *devas* and to act under the impression of thought-forms projected by the Masters. Fully awakened *chakras* will assist the enlightened Ones to influence the sum of the evolving Lives in *saṃsāra*. The safe awakening of these psychic centres and their powers will become part of common discussion. Discovering the ramifications of the manifestation of the *chakras* governing all of Nature will be an object of scientific pursuit. Their externalised glandular secretions as a factor in healing will be investigated, and the relation between the Solar Plexus and Ājñā centres (as both are the main organs of clairvoyance) will be properly observed. Scientists will also look to study the effects of the *chakras* cosmologically.

Scorpio and Taurus represent the thumbs of the hands of this Hierarchical wheel. The thumbs are relatively ambidextrous, compared to the other fingers of the hand. They are the main conduits for cleansing and transmuting the Waters of the astral murk (of people's emotional proclivity) of this planet. Reified cosmic astral Watery energies via *buddhi* will be channelled for this purpose. Scorpio has a direct affinity to Sirius:

> *Scorpio* is under the influence or inflowing energy of Sirius. This is the great star of initiation because our Hierarchy (an expression of the second aspect of divinity) is under the supervision or spiritual magnetic control of the Hierarchy of Sirius. These are the major controlling influences whereby the cosmic Christ works upon the Christ principle in the solar system, in the planet, in man and in the lower forms of life expression. It is esoterically called the "brilliant star of sensitivity".[7]

Scorpio is therefore the dominant sign governing the expression of the eastern direction of this cross. Libra-Virgo regulates the cycles of expression for the

7 *Esoteric Astrology,* 197.

projection of Sirian energies to humanity (the western direction) according to the nature of the planetary testings (wielded via Scorpio). The energies move from Scorpio to Taurus (they are polar opposites), which then utilise the Arian Will (Aries-Pisces) to impel the changes to be implemented within the matrix of human civilisation. Aries-Pisces will work to end humanity's cycles of materialistic *(saṃsāric)* activity.

Leo and Aquarius are the other two signs of this fixed cross. Their energies are conveyed as the matrix of this great wheel. This matrix incorporates all of the energies of the wheel, whose Purpose manifests as the attributes of Abstract Cognition. This Cognition is an expression of the Energies from the Logoic Soul, directed by Leo via Regulus in the Heart of the Lion. Regulus bathes all manifestation with this Mind substance to clarify the Purpose of what must Be. The overall mode of the cyclic expression (or Impulse) of it all is directed via Polaris, the pole star.[8] This star provides right direction (or orientation) for the expression into manifest space of the Logoic Personality. (Whose objective the turning of this great wheel accomplishes.) The combined interrelated energies are then fed into the planet via Aquarius during the Aquarian epoch. Divine psychometry (occult touch) is thereby expressed into the field of the planetary evolution. The matrix of substance that is accordingly ordered also comes under the direction of the Pleiades. This happens specifically via Alcyone, who governs the etheric form of the planetary manifestation. (Alcyone has a direct affinity to our earth humanity.) The Pleiades working through the constellation Taurus then condition the expression of the appearing forms.

The above information is but an elaboration of the statement given by D.K.:

> There are four of the zodiacal signs which are mysteriously concerned with what one might call the "personality expression" (if such an unsuitable term can be used in default of better) of the solar Logos Himself, or with the Divine Quaternary, the fourfold manifestation of Deity.
>
> These four signs are Aries - Leo - Scorpio - Aquarius, and they involve the expression of the energy of one Cardinal sign and of three signs which form part of the Fixed Cross of the heavens. We could express this truth in another manner: God the Father, the Will to manifest, initiates the creative process which is worked out through the activity of God the Son, the cosmic Christ, crucified upon the Fixed Cross in the heavens. The activity of God the Holy Spirit, implicit in the Mutable Cross, is closely allied to the previous solar system, and the energy of

---

8 This pole star is currently manifesting, but this will change in the future.

that divine aspect is practically entirely occupied with manipulating the forces inherited from that system and inherent in the very nature of substance itself. This divine aspect is to the whole general divine manifestation what the lower nature (form life or personality in the three worlds of human evolution) is to the soul where an individual human being is concerned...[9]

The four signs - Aries, Leo, Scorpio and Aquarius - are related to the following stars which are not numbered in the twelve signs of the zodiac; they constitute another field of relationships:

- Aries to one of the two stars, found in the constellation, the Great Bear, which are called the two Pointers.
- Leo to Polaris, the Pole Star, found in the Little Bear.
- Scorpio to Sirius, the Dog Star.
- Aquarius to Alcyone, one of the seven Pleiades.[10]

During the Aquarian epoch, the projection of the energies of the third Ray (Abstract Cognition) on earth will principally manifest via the Mahāchohan's department. The second Ray department will provide the overall matrix of the consciousness principle via Scorpio. The first Ray department works via Aries. The sum of this triple expression is coordinated by Leo, working via Polaris, the pole star.

## The hands and tridents of the Hierarchical zodiac

As stated, for the *downward pointed hand* Scorpio represents the thumb that deals mainly with the projection of cosmic Watery energies from Sirius. The focus of these energies is humanity. These Waters condition the battlefields of their tests of Initiation. The energies then swing straight to Taurus to activate the All-Seeing Eye, or else to rectify aspects of the field of desire and glamour that have not been properly cleansed. (This allows those still ensconced in the normal twelve-signed wheel to turn via a rectified fashion – from Taurus, to Gemini, Cancer, Leo and Libra-Virgo. They can then move on to this ten-signed zodiac.)

What is effectively established is the motion of the yin-yang, or of the moving swastika. The focus is now upon the esoteric and Hierarchical planetary rulers. Because the phenomena of *saṃsāra* is on the wane, so the exoteric rulers are no longer active in the process that will eventually lead to *pralaya* for humanity.

9 Ibid., 193-4.

10 Ibid., 194.

The *downward projected trident* that energises the Lives of the three lower kingdoms (or Creative Hierarchies[11]) in Nature that are ensconced in *saṃsāra* are represented by the signs Sagittarius, Capricorn and Aquarius.

There a change in function between Sagittarius and Aquarius develops. Normally Sagittarius would represent the Fiery forefinger, following the thumb of Scorpio (of the downward projecting 'hand' of energies, when taking this pentad as a Solar Plexus centre). The Sagittarian impulse would then empower the evolutionary development of the animal kingdom. Capricorn would represent the middle Earthy finger, that projects crystallised Fire towards the dense material domain. Aquarius then becomes the ring finger that projects the vitality that will encourage the growth of the plant kingdom. However, in relation to the change in function between Sagittarius and Aquarius, D.K. states that Sagittarius comes between Capricorn and Aquarius in the presented chart of the Creative Hierarchies:

> This is a temporary emphasis and will change in another world cycle. This is one of the mysteries revealed at Initiation.[12]

From this perspective, Capricorn vitalises the mental plane (Fire *per se)* and the tenth Creative Hierarchy (Makara the mystery). Being the middle finger, Capricorn therefore manifests this function, projecting the Fiery purpose right into the mineral kingdom. (In the form of planetary psychic heat—*tum mo.)* These *manasic prāṇas* from the middle finger will work to control the Earthy Fires that govern the manifestation of terrestrial events. Hierarchy works with these *prāṇas* to govern the appearance of phenomena.

Utilising Sagittarian energy, Hierarchy projects the Watery potency into manifestation via the forefinger to control the Lunar Pitris. Via them will manifest the inevitable precipitation of the Elemental Lives into dense forms. The Airy Watery energies from Aquarius, directed by Hierarchy, can then 'psychometrise' the mass movement of the Elemental Lives (the Baskets of Nourishment), which thus symbolically manifest via the ring finger. Aquarius projects the principle of Logoic Love that sustains the flow of the energies into the etheric body of the earth. The Elemental Lives are thereby automatically moulded into the required forms that people experience.

---

11 These are: for Capricorn—Makara the mystery, for Sagittarius—the Lunar Lords (Sacrificial Fires), and for Aquarius—the Elemental Lives (Baskets of Nourishment). All of the Creative Hierarchies are explained in detail in chapter 7, but are introduced in this chapter out of necessity.

12 Ibid., 35.

The little finger (Pisces-Aries), that channels the energies from *ātma,* is part of the western direction (or spoke) of this wheel. This spoke directs energies from the cosmic astral towards the kingdom of Souls. The Masters of Wisdom are responsible for directing this energy flow via their Ashrams. Human Souls thereby receive impressions concerning the collective mode of sequencing for the reincarnations of their personalities. Everything comes under the auspices of group law, and the associated *karma*. The various categories of the flow of human civilisation are thereby directed, according to the Hierarchical Plan. This Plan is instigated via the polar opposite sign (Libra-Virgo) in the eastern direction. The combined Hierarchical meditations in the 'east' produce the broad brushstrokes for the entire panorama of all aspects of civilisation (based also upon dictates from Shambhala). Such meditation mainly manifests via the Hierarchical ruler of Libra (Saturn) that directs planetary *karma*. Libra then turns the wheel of the Law in accordance with Shambhalic diktat. The Masters respond (in accordance with their Ray lines) to what must be. They appropriately modify the directives so as to accommodate the needs of the kingdom of Souls. The evolutionary plan can thereby be accomplished.

The *trident pointing upwards* is towards the open gate of Cancer and the five liberated Creative Hierarchies. They channel the energies from the twelve signs of the zodiac as a unit, which are the twelve petals of the Heart centre of That Logos. The seven Rishis of the Great Bear direct the overall Purpose of these energies to our solar system via the pole star (Polaris). The energies are triune. First there is the expression of *dharmatā* manifesting via Cancer. Abstract Cognition is expressed via Regulus in Leo. Aspirational Idealism is the generalised energy coming from all the star systems. (This energy manifests via Gemini, who governs the expression of the *nāḍī* system of our planet). These terms (*dharmatā,* Abstract Cognition and Aspirational Idealism) must be interpreted in terms of what the Masters are aspiring to fully develop. They can then project these qualities into manifestation and so direct the sum of evolutionary space in accordance with the evolutionary Plan. These qualities are the first, second and third sub-Ray aspects of Divine Will, where that Will is but an expression of the Cosmic Love of our solar Logos. The sum of these energies is borne by the cosmic Christ into the planetary dispensation during this Aquarian epoch.

The direct first Ray Divine Will-of-Love *(dharmatā)* manifests via the fifth of the liberated Creative Hierarchies (Cancer). This energy then impacts upon the plane *ādi,* wherein exists the first of the seven manifested Creative Hierarchies, the Divine Flames ('the Divine Man'). This first Ray energy is borne in the form of the attributes of Amoghasiddhi's All-accomplishing Wisdom.[13] This aspect is conditioned by the Law of Economy,[14] which governs the mode of manifestation of the cosmic dense physical plane. All of the Lives evolving through the spirals and spirillae of the Logoic physical permanent atom are thereby directed.[15] Capricornian Purpose is then expressed, being the polar opposite of Cancer.[16]

The second Ray aspect of the Divine Will-of-Love (Abstract Cognition) manifests via Leo, which conditions the *anima mundi* of our planetary life. The impact is via the plane *anupādaka* and the second of the manifest Creative Hierarchies, the Greater Builders. It manifests in the form of the Waters poured fourth by Aquarius. The Equalising Wisdom of Ratnasambhava then appropriately disseminates these energies. Leo here (via its polar opposite, Aquarius) specifically wields the energies of the Law of Attraction. (Directed from the fourth of the liberated Hierarchies, 'the Builders' who manifest the 'Desire for Duality'). This Law concerns the mode of attracting to Hierarchy and thence to Shambhala, the sum of the Lives evolving in *saṃsāra*.

The third Ray aspect of the Divine Will-of-Love (Aspirational Idealism) manifests via Gemini. It impacts upon the plane *ātma* and via the third of the manifest Creative Hierarchies, the Lesser Builders. Amitābha's Discriminating Inner Wisdom processes this energy and it impacts via the tenth Creative Hierarchy, Makara. Therefore Makara bears the impact of the cosmic Law of *karma* as it organises the sum of manifest space. The potency of these energies is then directed via Sagittarius into our planetary Hierarchy (the Christ's department – the 'immortal brother'). Their specific focus is to control the Lunar Lords that embody the sum of the Watery astral condition of humanity and of manifestation in general (which represents the 'mortal brother'). The mastery of the Waters is accordingly the onus of our planetary evolution.

In general, all energies streaming to Hierarchy come via Sirius the Dog Star, who rules all Hierarchical activities. Leo has a direct alignment to Sirius, and

---

13 The first five volumes of my *A Treatise on Mind* delve into detail on the attributes of the five Dhyāni Buddhas. Their qualities are summarised in Volume 5A.

14 The five cosmic Laws are explained from page 378 onwards in my book *Meditation and the Initiation Process*.

15 See my book *Esoteric Cosmology and Modern Physics* for a detailed explanation of this permanent atom.

16 Cancer is the Gate for the downpour of all cosmic energies from the liberated Creative Hierarchies.

Gemini to the Pleiades (who wield their Creative potency via the four cosmic ethers, which Gemini controls). As stated, the direct flow of Sirian energies manifest via the eastern direction of this wheel, which concerns Hierarchy's alignment with Shambhala and its planetary directives. This Sirian Purpose is reflected into manifestation via Akṣobhya's Mirror-like Wisdom, which projects the Law of Synthesis in order to control the sum of the planetary dispensation (via Shambhala).

In the *upward pointed hand,* Taurus manifests the attributes of the thumb, which directs the main flow of cosmic Watery energies to humanity via the combined Wisdom of Hierarchy in accordance with their overall planning. Gemini manifests as the Fiery forefinger, which projects Hierarchy's Idealistic purpose via the one-pointed potency of Sagittarius. Cancer (on the cardinal cross) also bears the stream of Purpose from the seven Rishis of the Great Bear. The Earthy finger is Cancer, which concretises, or materialises cosmic directives, so that they can be wielded via Capricorn into the substrate of the Logoic form. Leo is the Airy ring finger, which projects the Law of Love to condition the world Soul via the outpourings of Aquarius. This energy will then help bring into manifestation the New Age. Libra-Virgo manifests as the little finger, projecting energies from *dharmakāya* into awakened Minds, to assist them to wield the purpose of the cosmic Law that conditions the cycles of the expression of systemic *karma.* Vairocana's Dharmadhātu wisdom is invoked to distribute the sum of these energies into manifestation. All cycles (internal and external) must be coordinated, so that the mechanism of the grand Clock of the Heavens manifests with effortless efficiency. The cosmic Law of Identity then incorporates the whole into unity.

## The Shambhalic zodiac

Shambhala manifests as the Head centre for our planetary system. From a cosmological point of view, however, it is a Solar Plexus centre, for its function is to respond to the energies of the cosmic Waters. Shambhala receives directives from cosmos and appropriately projects them into manifestation via the Logoic Will. Shambhalic Purpose is specifically empowered by energies (diktats) from the seven Rishis of the Great Bear.

In the Aquarian epoch, the zodiacal wheel for Shambhala will have Capricorn at the top. The constitution of Shambhala will change from what now exists and will simplify. This is because planetary evil will have largely been defeated. The problematic moon Chain *karma* will have been sufficiently dealt with so that it no longer poses a threat to our planetary stability. The Lords of Life will have gained the upper hand and Hierarchy will have externalised, to serve the planetary need. Sanat Kumāra (the Lord of the World), also called the Youth of endless Summers, the Silent Watcher, will then no longer need to keep His long vigil on earth and will leave. With Him will also leave a number of other great Ones, for their purpose here will likewise terminate.

The epoch of the feminine dispensation of the Mother of the World will replace what was. This concerns the higher correspondence of the Matriarchate that ruled Atlantis. She will represent the Aquarian gate for the new planetary dispensation, for the entire Aquarian dispensation will flow through Her Mind via Her cosmic contacts. With Her will come a number of great feminine entities to help administer the new dispensation. There will be three representatives from Venus, Lords of Flame that have still to work out ancient *karma* with our earth and with their former relationship to the moon. Emissaries from the seven Pleiades will also manifest to play their roles. They will be the rulers of the seven planes of perception.

The three Venusians (Gemini, Leo and Cancer in Figure 34) will also represent the higher triad of another zodiac, which will incorporate the regents of the seven Pleiades as the other points, plus two other emissaries from feminine stars. They will thereby form a twelve-signed zodiac, out of whose substance unenlightened humanity will form the thought constructs that keep exoteric astrology (concerning the precession of the equinoxes) sustained for a while yet.

Many of the Chohans from Hierarchy will also progress to their cosmic journey, leaving a needed few who will continue on with their earth Service. They will include the Christ, Jesus, Master *R*, Serapis and the new Mahāchohan. The Avatar of Synthesis will stay, to assist in the further generation of the first Ray upon our planetary evolution, and also to help introduce His needed cosmic contacts. The influence of Sanat Kumāra will still remain as the centre of the Shambhalic *maṇḍala* established, for He is the Logos of the earth Chain (of which our planetary evolution is only a part).

The new Mahāchohan is an ancient cosmic traveller, symbolised by the Arthurian legend of the Green Knight. He is a time Lord of ancient antiquity from the green Ray that harks from Saturn's hoary past. His history is unique in Hierarchy, thus He is also styled 'the Non-Such'. He was in charge of the feminine dispensation of the moon-Chain evolution at the time of the catastrophic events that caused the destruction of the planet. Wrong decisions were made to try to hasten the exceedingly long evolutionary process that was governed by the third Ray methodology of the past solar system. First Ray Souls were prematurely released, the consequence of which was the intensification of first Ray energies on the planet, which the humanity thereon were ill-equipped to handle. This immensely facilitated the development of the aberrant wills of the dark brotherhood. Sorcery and rampant cruel forms of sex magic rapidly gained dominance over the planet. The planet's evolution became an unredeemable disaster and was prematurely destroyed as a living organism. The moon that exists now is a dead skeleton (possessing many anomalous mysteries that still baffle scientists) of what once was alive.

The great majority of this dark humanity from the moon-Chain were directed to earth during the Atlantean epoch. They contributed significantly to the problems on earth from then on. The future new Mahāchohan followed them to Atlantis. As part of His karmic adjudication (or resolve) he buried Himself in the matrix of earth humanity (and its subsequent civilisations) as the penultimate Bodhisattva.[17] (He thereby significantly postponed His own spiritual evolution in cosmos for many millennia.) His karmic responsibility demanded the conversion of the dark ones from the moon, and this sacrificial activity was the method chosen. This is a long-time chore and will involve more than just this earth evolution to accomplish.

Only now, with the advent of the happenings that will produce the New Age and the earth becoming a sacred planet, can He rise from the murk and trappings of *saṃsāra* and its *karma*. He can thus begin to assume His rightful spiritual age and responsibilities. This means a rapid rise up through the Initiation levels, allowing His Logoic 'Head' to return to His shoulders, where it belongs. This is the triumphant Song of a successful retribution for an ancient miscalculation that has cost Him dearly. His Sagittarian Will can now assist in the projection of the Crimson Tide upon earth in conjunction with the blue crystalline liquid of cosmic Love that will inundate the planet during the Aquarian age. The emanation of red, indigo-blue, emerald green and violet via the golden energy will produce the forthcoming epoch of Mind on earth. This is His objective.[18]

---

17 In Atlantis He was styled the 'green *yogin*', who struggled to psychically protect the civilisation from the dark emanations of the evil ones as much as possible. At a certain stage, when the prophecy related to the fate of the Watery fourth Root Race was to be fulfilled, there was a pre-programmed removal of His protection. *Karma* in the new *manvantara* was needed, and He chose an appropriate path with humanity. The wall of protection from Shambhala broke, the old green *yogin* became covered by the strangling vines *(antaḥkaraṇas)* of the new dispensation, and the ocean flooded the Atlantean continent.

18 See the statement from Sanat Kumāra concerning this One. He states 'he is my Son, the seventh. He is my grand master of ritual...' in my book *The Constitution of Shambhala,* Part C, 350.

As with the zodiac governing Hierarchy, the Shambhalic zodiac is effectively divided into three groupings. The top group of Capricorn, Aquarius and Sagittarius represent the three highest planetary executives. They possess direct links to the stars and constellations of the cosmic astral plane. They express the energies of Logoic Mind in its three aspects. Capricorn is the position occupied by the Avatar of Synthesis, who embodies the Logoic Will-of-Mind that sets the entire zodiac into motion and sustains its activity. He is the Mount of the Mind of cosmic Purpose in the New Era.

Aquarius signifies the position held by the Mother of the World, who will embody the function of the Logoic abstract Mind in the New Age. She will bear the energy of the third Ray of Mathematically Exact Activity into manifestation (specifically via the *deva* Hierarchy). She will help direct the energies through the Aquarian epoch that will assist humanity to think abstractly (thus to take their third Initiations). She will also be the Water Bearer pouring the seventh Ray dispensation to our planet. These Waters will pour through *anupādaka* and will also thereby convey the energies of cosmic Love.

One can see here the very close symbiosis between the New Mahāchohan and the Mother of the World. He is an agent of Her feminine department and His Sagittarian purpose transfers Her *deva* potencies into modes of expression woven into the fabric of human *karma* that will ultimately produce the liberation of all.

Aquarius incorporates the assimilated energies of the general field of expression of all the stars and constellations in the Body of THAT Logos. One can consider here the various Logoic Sounds (communications between the stellar Brethren, of which the regulated expression cyclically pours into Shambhala). This multifarious energisation is symbolised by the wavy lines for the glyph of Aquarius. Aquarius's polar opposite (Leo) projects the energies that impact upon Hierarchy via Regulus in order to produce right group evolution. Leo purposely impels the group Laws that bind the evolutionary development of Hierarchy and all upon the planet via the *anima mundi* and the kingdom of Souls.

The new Mahāchohan (the green Christ) will bear the needed fifth Ray of the Scientific Mode (reinforced by the third Ray of the Mother) for the world's disciples in order to help them think properly. This will be according to esoteric verities that will allow them to comprehend the Logoic Plan. He will embody the Logoic Empirical Mind (Mahat) for the planet via the ātmic plane.[19] Hence He

---

19 This manifests as a red-orange spiral of energy that must find a point of application via the third Ray Purpose of this new epoch.

wields the function of the Lord of *karma* and directly rules via mantric Sound and the activity of the *devas*.

When Sanat Kumāra leaves for greater duties, the green Christ is destined to occupy His vacated Seat as the Silent Watcher and the One Initiator. This is the consequence of being the 'seventh Son' of Sanat Kumāra and 'the grand master of ritual' – that which will govern the Aquarian Age. He will be the embodied Son aspect of the triune Logos. The Avatar of Synthesis will manifest as the Father aspect of this new dispensation and the Mother of the World remains the (Deva) Mother of all that is.

The 'seventh Son' has risen out of the murky sphere of *saṃsāra,* as the rest of humanity must also. He knows their problems and so has the full capacity to fire the Sagittarian arrows towards all of the trouble spots in human evolution. The purpose concerns rectifying planetary ailments via the compassionate Purpose of the energies of the triune Logos in the form of the seventh Ray dispensation. He is the embodiment of the Logoic Mind that will see the evolutionary Plan through to humanity gaining their third Initiation upon a planetary scale. The energy of Mahat that He wields will enable Him to Initiate them into full Hierarchical activity.

Concerning this One's future role, it can be stated in the symbolic language of the Masters of Wisdom that:

> Saturn must still run rings around the sons of men.
> So His role is clear.
> The blue-green Rays of His Crown fill the earth,
> and the Seven Sisters will rise again
> to feed the masses their celestial milk.
> He is bound to Earth Service as the ox is bound to the plow
> and every step of His mighty hooves furrows a mountain.[20]
> The followers must return,
> but who can follow such a One as He?
> We can!
> The pronouncements of His Voice soften.
> His Throat stills.
> His Voice rustles not His garment,
> and the true Being can be seen by those in Shambhala,
> and those few disciples brave enough

---

20 This statement refers to the making of high Initiates ('mountains') out of the soil of the earth.

to breech His Voice of Silence.

The Wheels are moving.

What are directed to Hierarchy via the combined energies of the new Mahāchohan and the Mother of the World are Instructions from the domain of cosmic Mind (plus those related to the expression of cosmic Love via Aquarius). This combination of Mind and Love constitutes Logoic Kāma-Manas, which is the direct potency of the Sirian Lore[21] that is recognised on earth as Love-Wisdom. This Lore allows Hierarchy to comprehend how to navigate cosmic astral space when the Chohans are to enter upon their cosmic Paths. It will help the Masters to perceive star Lore, the mode of expression of the various Logoi that are incarnate in cosmic astral space.

The central *east-west direction* of the new Shambhalic zodiac constitutes a Throne of four of the highest representatives of the present Hierarchy. Of them, the Christ (Pisces-Aries) and Serapis (Taurus) occupy the *eastern* direction of this zodiac. The Christ will obviously bear the second Ray of Love-Wisdom for the planetary dispensation, which He projects via Pisces-Aries to start and so to impregnate the entire zodiacal wheel with its purpose. The Christ is the 'alpha' (Aries) and the 'omega' (Pisces) of the new dispensation as far as humanity's consciousness evolution goes.[22] Serapis, governing the fourth Ray of Harmony overcoming Strife, will work to fully integrate the Pleiadian dispensation (via Taurus) into the planetary matrix. He will act as a central hub of interrelationships between humanity (the field of strife), Hierarchy (bearing the energy that overcomes strife) and the new feminine dispensation (bearing the 'harmony' via the Pleiades).

Jesus (Scorpio) and Master ℛ (Libra-Virgo) will occupy the *western* direction. Jesus will continue his role in helping to cleanse the world's astral murk. He works via the sixth Ray of Devotion-Aspiration, His close interrelation with the Christ and via his Scorpionic seat of Power. Master ℛ will dispense the seventh Ray Aquarian impetus from the Mother into the planetary matrix through the correct ritual pulsations according to karmic Law, as wielded via Libra. He will also directly work via the *deva* kingdom to foster the objectives of the Mother's department via his connection to Virgo.

---

21 One could also use the term Law here.

22 See *The Revelation of St. John,* 1:7-8. Forever bound is the Christ to earth Chain humanity, therefore He will occupy the Seat of Sanat Kumāra after the One who's responsibilities are mainly to the moon Chain humanity vacates it.

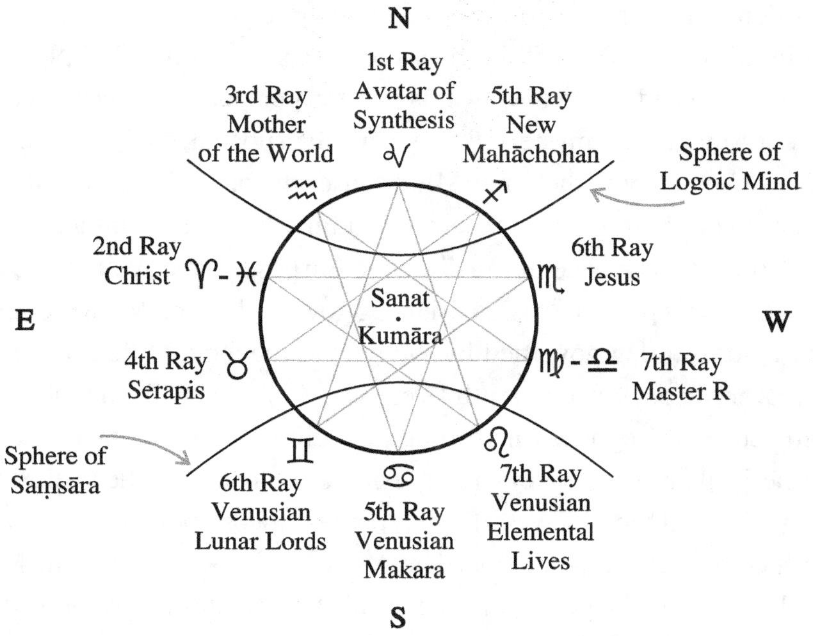


**Figure 34. The Shambhalic zodiac for the New Age**

The three *Venusians* that will have come to our planetary dispensation are direct empowerments of the *deva* Hierarchy. They will directly embody the three lowest Creative Hierarchies, for their activities and energies must reflect the fact that the earth will now be a sacred planet. The *devas* that formerly inhabited the planetary space must be replaced with new ones that better reflect the new planetary energy fields, and also the seventh Ray Aquarian dispensation. These *Venusians* will embody the functions of the signs Gemini, Cancer, and Leo. These three signs are also the polar opposites of the signs governed by the three planetary executives. They provide their input so as to help transform the addiction that humanity possesses to these elemental Lives. Higher quality *devas,* more akin to the energy of Love-Wisdom, must replace those that presently occupy the human habitation.

Gemini (the right foot of the upwards-pointed pentad headed by Capricorn) is the Temple of the Lord and will mainly deal with the conversion of the Lunar Lords. (The Watery Lives that are presently the main nemesis of humanity's spiritual growth.) Gemini is also a focal point of two arms of this pentacle – Aries-Pisces (the blue Christ) and Scorpio (Jesus). The planetary Avatar (the new Mahāchohan) is the polar opposite of this Gemini position. The base irascible emotions, avarice and selfish desires of humanity have to be transformed into

Love-Wisdom. The very potent forces of these three great Ones are thus focussed to assist in this conversion within the sacred precincts of this Temple.

Cancer is the head of the downwards pointed pentacle. Its energies control the activities of Makara the mystery that govern the substance of the mental plane. This fifth Ray potency of the mind/Mind causes the precipitation of all the forms that appear upon the physical domain, including that of the human personality. Cancer is the polar opposite of the directive Purpose of the Avatar of Synthesis. The two legs of this pentad (the Aquarian leg governed by the Mother of the World and the Sagittarian leg governed by the new Mahāchohan) directly bear upon Makara. Every aspect of this tenth Creative Hierarchy will now be controlled by the attributes of Logoic Mind through the direct focus of this triune Logos.

Leo (the Soul or Sun of Life) will govern the emanation of the twelfth Creative Hierarchy, the Elemental Lives. They represent the embodied substance of all forms that come into manifestation. The Aquarian dispensation of the Mother of the World represents the polar opposite of this left leg of the upright pentad. This ensures that the seventh Ray will govern the manifestation of all substance that appears in the Aquarian epoch. The Avatar of Synthesis and the Christ signify the other two main lines of energisation for this substance. The Avatar will ensure that the sum of the substance of this planet comes under the Will of the Logos. The Christ will ensure that this substance will be governed by the second Ray energy that is needed for the earth to be a sacred planet.

Another way of looking at this new dispensation concerns the form of a Sagittarian arrow pointing downwards into the planetary dispensation. The Sagittarian arrows are fired to produce the objectives of the Logoic Thought processes. The shaft of the arrow will be the line of the Avatar of Synthesis, the Mother of the World and the new Mahāchohan (who now manifests the role of the externalised planetary Logos). He will also manifest the tension of the 'bowstring' that projects the arrow unerringly towards fulfilling its Purpose. As stated, this triune Logos manifest the first, third and fifth Rays of the Logoic Mind. The 'arrowhead' will consist of the integrated fourth, sixth and seventh Ray purpose of Serapis, Jesus and Master *R*(who will embody the function of its piercing tip). The second Ray energies of the Christ will embody the substance of the arrowhead that will eventuate the New Era, so that Love becomes all. All planetary and zodiacal wheels will move to bring this eventuation about.

New *deva* hosts will emerge to coalesce around the energy projections of the then planetary Heart, for this 'great simplification' of the New Age will cause all parts to unify into one direction. The great cosmic arrow that is fired will draw the myriad little Lives forwards to convert the solidity of form into a sea of Flame. New streams of Lives will thus come forward, and other streams will recede, and all Lives will obey the Fiery dictates of the three Logoic planetary Executives. The Lives listening will Hear the Heartbeats of the Logoi bringing all to the Christ's table.

# 7

# The nature of the twelve Creative Hierarchies

## General considerations

As stated previously, astrologers have done much to popularise exoteric accounts of the nature of the twelve signs of the zodiac, but little is understood concerning their true functions. These signs are constellations of embodied Lives whose energies influence our solar Logos as He esoterically courses round the cosmic Heart centre. The twelve signs of the zodiac are twelve great gates of energy expression that are the twelve main petals of the Heart Centre of THAT Logos.[1] The Body of Manifestation of THAT Logos incorporates the sum of the 88 visible constellations, plus a number of etheric ones. Each constellation absorbs *prāṇas* from the *chakra* and *nāḍī* system of THAT Logos and processes them in the manner explained in my book *An Esoteric Exposition of the Bardo Thödol*. As such, the energy interrelations between the constellations are great. The true attributes of these energies are incomprehensible to the unenlightened mind. They are veiled by such terms as Fohat, Mahat, the Spirit, Life and the Will. Such are the factors sustaining Life, the underlying purpose behind every evolving Being. They concern the creation, sustaining and ultimate resolution into *pralaya* of all Lives within the Bodies of manifestation of the solar and planetary Lords. These Lives can be categorised

1 These signs more specifically embody the functions of the Heart in the Head centre, integrated within the twelve main petals of the Head lotus. For a description of this interrelation, see my book *An Esoteric Exposition of the Bardo Thödol*, Part A, from page 377. The Heart centre is but a lower, simplified version of these twelve main petals. This centre expresses the base energies that are conveyed to the Heart in the Head centre.

in the form of twelve Creative Hierarchies, which can be viewed from different levels of perception.

The energies emanating from the twelve constellations are received by our planetary Head centre (Shambhala) and are focussed into the planetary Heart centre (the Hierarchy of Light), then into the kingdom of Souls. The energies are then finally projected (in a toned down, qualified form) into *saṃsāra* and the human personality. This represents the *piṅgalā nāḍī* stream for our planetary Logos. Another mechanism of focus for the Lords at Shambhala are the human Monads, for their forms constitute the base substance of the Eye of the planetary Logos. The *iḍā nāḍī* stream of our planetary Logos are the *devas*, who embody the substance of all that is.

Within the domains of the human personality, these energies become clashing forces that impel the evolving emotions and mental patterns of an individual. They also manifest upon a massed scale. The integrated energies of the ideas are then conceptualised under the patterns of the signs. Over time, the massed mental-emotional thought-forms created by humanity have produced the attributes of the signs of the zodiac that average humans are conditioned by. (These influences are upon those that are immersed in *saṃsāra* and attached to its conditionings.) In this way they delineate the ideas and conditionings dealt with by orthodox astrologers.

Upon the path of return, the Initiate is learning to consciously master *saṃsāra* and is also coming to terms with the energies coming from cosmos. These energies are transformative potencies that convert base substance into exalted forms of Light. As Initiates come under the sway of cosmic energisations, they must increasingly develop the first Ray of Will. Once Initiates have freed themselves from *saṃsāra,* then they are also liberated from the influence of the substance of the conditioning orthodox zodiacal signs. The variegations of Light that are encountered and developed upon the higher way are the Rays streaming from Ray Lords (the planetary Logoi). Only those that have undertaken the higher Initiations (those that function in their Causal bodies, in their spiritual triads, or Monadic forms) can consciously respond to the extra-solar forces without distorting them in any way. They are freed from the great illusion, thus can perceive the realms of Reality normally veiled by the chimera of transience associated with *saṃsāra*. The signs of the zodiac no longer have any hold upon them, but rather they are conditioned by the energies of the Rays, constellations, and of the twelve Creative Hierarchies, via which everything comes into being. The Initiates have had the necessary training, developed the understanding and possess the needed sensitivity to subjective energy impacts (via Love-Wisdom) to rightly handle and express the destroyer and regenerator (the first Ray of Will) aspects associated with the constellations. This is possible because the Initiates are an integral part of the Hierarchy of Light and Love and sup directly upon group energies. Within the agency of group consciousness, the twelve Creative Hierarchies can become an experiential fact, for all such groups are patterned after the paradigm of the cosmic Heart or Head centre.

The twelve Creative Hierarchies are streams of conscious Lives; they are the guardians of the gates of the petals of the Heart or Head Lotus of the respective Logoi of whose Bodies they are a component part. The Hierarchies are mediators, the Sons of evolutionary purpose, translated into terms of Light and Love. (As will be explained in detail later.)

Initiates of the fourth or higher degrees respond to cosmic energies, seen as variegations of the Will (of a Logos). Initiates that have not yet attained the fourth Initiation respond to the energies from the Soul – to the force of Love from intra-solar (planetary) sources that affect them as Soul groups. These groups are organised according to the seven Ray and forty-nine sub-Ray energies that vitalise the Ashrams of the Masters of Wisdom. The Masters evolve via these sub-Rays as a consequence of cyclic purpose.

General humanity (and the world disciple) are still centred in their threefold personality vehicles, thus they respond primarily to the various planetary energies along the line of active Intelligence (which they normally express emotionally). They must yet learn to use substance constructively. Humanity finds its scope for evolution within the Womb of the earth, conditioned by the factor of inherent sentience, which plays in and through substance. They mould it according to the patterning of a divine archetype, which has its source in cosmic Love. Because there are twelve main petals to the Logoic Head and Heart centres, there are therefore twelve conditioning factors (or gates) for incoming energies. These energies are the expressions of Consciousness. They manifest as twelve differing streams of Lives (the Creative Hierarchies) that are self-conscious (or who are in the process of developing self-consciousness) and shape the patterns of all that IS. Their representatives on the earth embody the substance of all forms in the phenomenal world. D.K. states that these Hierarchies are 'interlocking energies which play through, traverse, return, stimulate and energise every part of our solar system'.[2]

---

2 *Esoteric Astrology*, 32.

Each Hierarchy transmits the energies emanating from a particular zodiacal sign to which it is energetically aligned. These energies are then woven into (or as) the corporeal substance of our various sheaths. The ordinary (orthodox) astrologer computes his/her charts upon the effects of the resultant energy impacts, but has no understanding of them, being little aware of how the great illusion is effectively delineated.

Five of the Creative Hierarchies are said to have gained their liberation from the substance of the cosmic dense physical plane (the seven planes of perception), though the fifth is, as D.K. states: 'on the verge of liberation'.[3] The remaining seven are the Builders of the solar system and are incarnated in systemic space. They are intermediaries between spirit and matter in varying degrees, as is the human Soul. Each of the Hierarchies sacrifice something of themselves to help the lower Lives. They can thus be considered as various levels of the 'fallen angels' mentioned in the Bible. Humanity is the fourth Creative Hierarchy, embodying the qualities of the sign Scorpio (the Hierarchical ruler of which is Mercury). The lowest three Creative Hierarchies must yet attain self-consciousness, hence their evolutionary development is controlled by the three highest of the seven manifest Creative Hierarchies.

| Hierarchy | Sign | Name and Energy | Law and Dhyāni Buddha | Ray | Chakra |
|---|---|---|---|---|---|
| 1 or 12 | ♓ or ♍ | The Essences: Intelligent Substance | Law of Identity Vairocana | 3 | |
| 2 or 11 | ♈ or ♎ | The Flames: Unity thro' Effort | Law of Synthesis Akṣobhya | 4 | |
| 3 or 10 | ♉ or ♏ | The Elements: Light thro' Knowledge | Law of Karma Amitābha | 5 | Throat in the Head Centre |
| 4 or 9 | ♊ or ♐ | The Builders: Desire for Duality | Law of Attraction Ratnasambhava | 6 | Heart in the Head Centre |
| 5 or 8 | ♋ or ♌ | The Numbers: Mass Life Veiling the Christ | Law of Economy Amoghasiddhi | 7 | Solar Plexus in the Head Centre |

**Table 7. The five liberated Creative Hierarchies**

3 Ibid., 34.

In tables 7 and 8, the names, types of energy, and numerical correspondences of the Creative Hierarchies are given.[4] Note that D.K. states that Sagittarius coming before Aquarius here is a 'temporary emphasis and will change in another world cycle'.[5]

The terms 'The Essences', 'The Flames', 'The Elements', 'The Builders' and 'The Numbers' (etc.) for the Creative Hierarchies are derived from Stanza 4:3 of Blavatsky's *The Secret Doctrine,* which states:

> From the effulgency of Light – the Ray of the ever-Darkness – sprung in Space the re-awakened energies *(Dhyan Chohans):* the One from the Egg, the six and the five; then the three, the one, the four, the one, the five – the twice seven, the sum total. And these are: the Essences, the Flames, the Elements, the Builders, the Numbers, the arupa *(formless)*, the rupa *(with bodies)*, and the Force or Divine Man – the sum total. And from the Divine Man emanated the Forms, the Sparks, the sacred Animals, and the Messengers of the sacred Fathers *(the Pitris)* within the Holy Four.[6]

This stanza is explained in my book *The Astrological and Numerological Keys to The Secret Doctrine,* Vol. 2, to which the reader must refer for explanation.

In table 8, of the seven Hierarchies that are incarnate within the seven sub-planes of the cosmic physical plane, the fourth (the human) mediates between the three lesser and the three greater Hierarchies. (Therefore, they are the correspondence to the *antaḥkaraṇa.)* The lowest three Hierarchies are still immersed in the substance of the past solar system, whilst the higher three are aloof from dense physical incarnation. Such substance is what must still be properly converted from the third Ray conditioning (of the past solar system) to the second Ray attributes that condition this solar system. As they do so they gain the attributes that will allow them to Individualise into a human kingdom. The key agency for this conversion is the fourth kingdom in Nature (the fourth Creative Hierarchy – humanity).

---

4 These figures are taken from pages 35 and 46 of my book *The Astrological and Numerological Keys to the Secret Doctrine,* Vol. 2. The information was adapted from *Esoteric Astrology,* 34-35.

5 *Esoteric Astrology,* 35.

6 H. P. Blavatsky, *The Secret Doctrine,* (Theosophical Publishing House, Adyar, 1888), Vol. 1, 88-89.

| Hierarchy | Sign | Names | Dhyāni Buddha Ray and Plane | Chakra |
|---|---|---|---|---|
| 6 or 7 | ♌ or ♒ | The Divine Man:<br>Divine Flames<br>Divine Lives | Amoghasiddhi<br>Ray 1<br>Ādi | Ājñā Centre |
| 7 or 6 | ♍ or ♊ | The Holy Four:<br>Greater (Divine) Builders<br>Burning Sons of Desire | Ratnasambhava<br>Ray 2<br>Anupādaka | Heart Centre |
| 8 or 5 | ♎ or ♈ | Sacred Fathers:<br>Lesser Builders<br>The Triple Flowers | Amitābha<br>Ray 3<br>Ātma | Throat Centre |
| 9 or 4 | ♏ or ♉ | The Messengers:<br>Human Hierarchy<br>The Initiates<br>Lords of Sacrifice | Akṣobhya<br>Ray 4<br>Buddhi | Solar Plexus Centre |
| 10 or 3 | ♑ or ♀ | The Sacred Animals:<br>Makara, the Mystery<br>The Crocodiles<br>Human Personality | Vairocana<br>Ray 5<br>Mental | Sacral - Base of Spine Centre |
| 11 or 2 | ♐ or ♂ | The Sparks:<br>Lunar Lords<br>Sacrificial Fires | N/A<br>Ray 6<br>Astral | Substance of Splenic Centre I |
| 12 or 1 | ♒ or ☽ | The Forms:<br>Elemental Lives<br>The Baskets of Nourishment | N/A<br>Ray 7<br>Physical | Reject substance of Splenic Centre II |

**Table 8. The seven manifest Creative Hierarchies**

## The five liberated Creative Hierarchies

One can also look at the interpretation of the astrological symbols. The glyph for Pisces, for instance, is normally pictured thus – ♓, but it can, as stated, also be turned on its side, producing a different meaning that has a direct reference to the qualities of the first Creative Hierarchy.

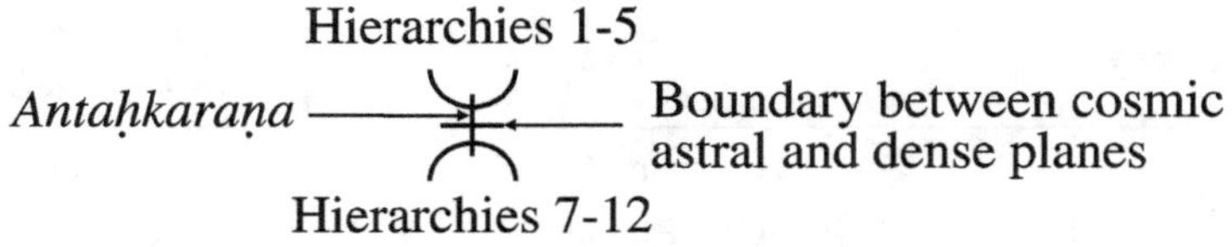


**Figure 35. Pisces and the Creative Hierarchies**

The first liberated Creative Hierarchy embodies the sum of the qualities of all of the others. It is the alpha and omega of their expression in the manifested realms. In my book *The Astrological and Numerological Keys to the Secret Doctrine,* Vol. 2 (where the Creative Hierarchies are explained in detail), this Creative Hierarchy is also termed 'the Essences', to add to the descriptive phrase ('Intelligent Substance') that D.K. gives for them. They manifest the attributes of the law of Identity that emanates from the third cosmic mental sub-plane to impact upon the third cosmic astral plane, thence into cosmic dense manifestation via the plane *ādi*. This 'Identity' holds the ring-pass-not of a cosmic Incarnation into a coherent form and propels the construct onwards to produce the *manvantaric* Purpose.

The *maṇḍala* of the Creative Hierarchies can also be viewed in terms of a reinterpretation of their astrological symbols, from which more clues concerning evolution will be found. Hierarchies one to five can be viewed as Hierarchies constituting the Dragon (of Fiery Life), whilst six to twelve can be viewed as Hierarchies of the Serpent (of wisdom). Within the patterning of their existence, the dark brotherhood aspect of development can also be found in manifestation. The Creative Hierarchies can also be considered as dualities, trinities, quaternaries, etc.

The Hierarchies are principally the Builders or Intelligences that use the Rays as their vehicles of manifestation. They are: 'the primordial forms of certain lives who carry in their hearts all the seeds of form'[7] as their means of expression. The Rays veil the Hierarchies, and the quality of a Ray is dependent upon the quality of the Hierarchy embodying it. The planes of perception are also said to have an analogous function to certain Hierarchies (similar to the relationship of a Monad's sheaths to itself). The planes act as agents to distribute the forces of the Hierarchies, through which the Hierarchies can express their evolutionary purpose. The incarnate Hierarchies (that together are a Logoic Serpent of Wisdom) form an intricate multihued diamond pattern on its back that is the result of the interblending of the colours of the Hierarchies, Rays, and planes.[8]

---

7 *A Treatise on Cosmic Fire,* 1195.

8 See *Letters on Occult Meditation,* 212.

The Hierarchies are said to principally express the Desire for manifested Life by the solar Logos. As stated by D.K.:

> They receive their primary impulse from the cosmic astral plane. They are also the expression of a vibration emanating from the second row of petals in the logoic Lotus on the cosmic mental plane.
>
> They are, therefore, one and all an expression of His love nature, and it is for this reason that buddhi is found at the heart of the tiniest atom, or what we call in this system, electric fire. For the positive central life of every form is but an expression of cosmic buddhi, and the downpouring of a love, which has its source in the Heart of the Solar Logos; this is itself an emanating principle from the ONE ABOVE OUR LOGOS, HE OF WHOM NAUGHT MAY BE SAID.[9]

Here we see that the entire subject of the Hierarchies is very abstruse. Little more can be done than to reiterate and elaborate upon certain statements made by D.K. about them, from which further esoteric knowledge can be derived. The *buddhic* energisation stems originally from the fourth cosmic astral sub-plane, and the second of the liberated Hierarchies. (The Flames, who embody the quality 'Unity thro' effort'.) They project the cosmic law of Synthesis into manifestation. This law integrates all atomic Lives into a coherent whole, allowing the incarnating Logos to control the evolutionary Purpose of all that is to manifest.

Because the solar Logos is polarised on the cosmic astral plane, so we can deduce that His level of Consciousness must be a transmuted correspondent analogue to that obtained by the fifth Atlantean sub-Race. (The intellect was then first developed.) The evolutionary goal for the last solar system was the attainment of the cosmic Intellect *(Mahat),* when the five liberated Hierarchies were in dense physical incarnation. The objective of this current Incarnation of the solar Logos is the attainment of cosmic Love, as expressed through the cosmic astral plane. For our solar system, this energy comes from the star Sirius, then to the second tier of petals in the solar Causal form, and are reflected eventually in our Causal forms (the ninth Creative Hierarchy, counting from above down). The energies will then mould the evolutions of the tenth, eleventh and twelfth Creative Hierarchies. Upon the cosmic astral sub-planes, the solar and planetary Logoi also interrelate with their Peers, the sum of the stars and constellations that are also found thereon. Much is obviously gained by the Logos through Conversation with them.

9 *A Treatise on Cosmic Fire,* 1225-6.

The fourth, fifth and sixth cosmic astral sub-planes (counting from above down), associated with the liberated Hierarchies Aries, Taurus and Gemini, are wherein our planetary Logos is polarised. These Hierarchies, as a unit, vitalise the cosmic physical plane through the fifth liberated Creative Hierarchy (Cancer). The Waters of space, poured forth through Cancer, form the substance of the planes of perception from which the planetary system is formed.

The five liberated Hierarchies embody the pentagram, the corporeality of Brahmā – the 'five senses' through which the solar Logos can meet His outer obligations as the solar system evolves. As they express their various qualities, so the Logos demonstrates His[10] Personality aspects within the greater cosmic whole. The seven lesser Hierarchies constitute His inner constitution, the psychic equipment of response. They qualify the impressions received from the external cosmic world and modify them according to their inherent qualities. They produce His internal 'Moods' and express the consciousness and sentience of what must be, according to the state of evolution of the myriads of lesser evolving Lives. By manifesting the five astral senses, the liberated Hierarchies regulate the course of this inner activity, for they qualify the type of 'Food' that must be digested by the Logos. (This process then thereby energises the lesser Lives.) They monitor the impressions received by contact with other solar Personalities that they have karmic interrelations with, thus projecting the cosmic direction for the solar system. These senses manifest the Logoic Discriminatory Capacity that is the higher correspondence of our intelligence.

Concerning *the first Creative Hierarchy* (veiled by the sign Pisces) D.K. states:

> Pisces is seen at the head of the list of the zodiacal signs, because it is governing the present great astrological world cycle of 25,000 years. It was also one of the dominant signs, influencing our planet at the time of individualisation when the human kingdom came into being. It is basically related to the first or highest Creative Hierarchy, which is in its turn, related to the third Ray of Active Intelligence. It was the product of the first solar system. The development of illumination through an awakened intelligence is the first goal of humanity.[11]

The (cosmic) Sense that can be attributed to the first Hierarchy is *smell,* allowing it to contact potent energies from the cosmic mental and *ātmic* planes, to which the solar Logos aspires.

---

10 Though I use the masculine pronoun conventionally for our planetary Logos, our planet is actually feminine in constitution.

11 *Esoteric Astrology,* 37.

The five liberated Hierarchies have an analogous function to the five Kumāras in our system, as shown in Figure 35. The middle three of the liberated Creative Hierarchies are, firstly, 'the Flames' ('Unity thro' Effort'), manifesting as 'Life Itself' (Aries) empowering the law of Synthesis. Next, 'the Elements', manifesting the divine Power of evolution, signified by Taurus. Finally, we have 'the Builders', who wield the law of Attraction, via Gemini. These three Creative Hierarchies manifest as a cosmic triangle. (The first Creative Hierarchy exists as the central point of Light within that triangle.) Via this mechanism, these three Hierarchies direct the cosmic *karma* (here a Taurean function) that vivifies the systemic planes with the needed Light (Aries), Love (Taurus) and Vitality (Gemini) to progress the sum of evolutionary space. The solar Logos projects this potency via the fifth Creative Hierarchy (Cancer) in the form of the law of Economy. This law governs the incarnation and evolution of the massed Lives that aspire upwards as they evolve in the cosmic dense physical domain. This Creative Hierarchy thereby embodies the substance of the pentagram of the Kumāras. This pentad expresses the energy wielded by the cosmic Lord of Fire, Agni.

D.K. states:

> Agni is the sumtotal of that portion of the logoic Ego which is reflected down into His physical vehicle; He is the life of the logoic Personality, with all that is included in that expression. He is to the solar Logos on His own plane what the coherent personality of a human being is to his Ego in the causal body.[12]

D.K. further states:

> In the ninth, tenth and eleventh Hierarchies lie the clue to the nature of Agni, Lord of fire, the sum total of systemic vitality. He who understands the significance of these figures, and their relation to each other as *the triple division of a Unity in time and space* will have discovered one of the keys which will unlock a door hitherto fast closed. They are the numbers of achievement, of potentiality brought into full activity and of innate capacity demonstrating in perfect fruition. All potentiality lies in the vitalising, energising power of Agni, and in His ability to stimulate. He is life itself, and the driving force of evolution, of psychic development and of consciousness. This fact is hidden in these figures, and not the evolution of substance, which is but a result, emanating from psychic causes. These three numbers are the basis of the cyclic calculations which concern the

12 *A Treatise on Cosmic Fire,* 603. Note that D.K. uses the term 'Ego' here and 'egoic cycles' in the subsequent quote as referring to the Causal form of the Soul.

egoic cycles, and the cycles of Vishnu, as distinguished from the cycles dealing with the third aspect. [13]

## Numerical interrelationships

Much concerning the Hierarchies can be intuited if the relationship and meanings of the numbers associated with them are analysed. The number *nine,* for instance, is the number of major petals in the three tiers of petals of the Soul form. It symbolises the unfoldment (awakening of the petals) of this lotus – of its psychic development via its many personality incarnations. The number nine is thus one of the numbers governing humanity. Humans are the ninth Creative Hierarchy when counting from above down or fourth from the bottom up (9, IV, 4). This number is the number of Initiation and its permutations indicate the respective Initiation level undertaken. Thus 2 x 9 relates to the second Initiation, and 9 x 9 indicates the number of Initiations that must be undergone before one can evolve to become a Heavenly Man (a planetary Logos). This is the higher correspondence of the nine months of prenatal life. One of the appellations given to humanity is 'the Initiates', for good reason, for they must consciously walk the path of Initiation into the mysteries of Life.

The figure below shows that the Creative Hierarchies manifest in the form of three triads of expression that stem from one Watery sign (Pisces). The attributes of the highest triad are reflected into the lower ones by the two other Water signs (Cancer and Scorpio). A direct relationship can be seen between Cancer ('Mass Life') and Scorpio ('Humanity') as both can be viewed as bridges or 'links' between the triads. They are therefore intermediaries that channel the Waters from the cosmic astral plane (the energies of cosmic Love) into manifestation. This happens in an increasingly reified manner as we progress down the planes of perception. The inevitable result is to produce the transformation of base mineral plane substance into consciousness attributes. The Waters make fluid what is otherwise hard, rocky and unyielding. These liberated Hierarchies therefore manifest the cosmic pull to elevate the Elemental Lives upward towards the human domain. They project the solvent of Life, the energies of the Mercurial substance in the Divine retort, to help produce Alchemical gold.

Cancer and Scorpio are the bridges between the store of the Lives and energies of those that stand aloof from incarnation, and the Lives that form the substance

13 Ibid., 605-6.

of the appearing forms. In the case of Cancer, the bridge is between cosmic astral space and incarnation into the substance of the cosmic physical plane. In the case of Scorpio, the bridge is between the various Builders upon cosmic etheric space and the Lives that embody the substance of the cosmic *dense* physical plane.

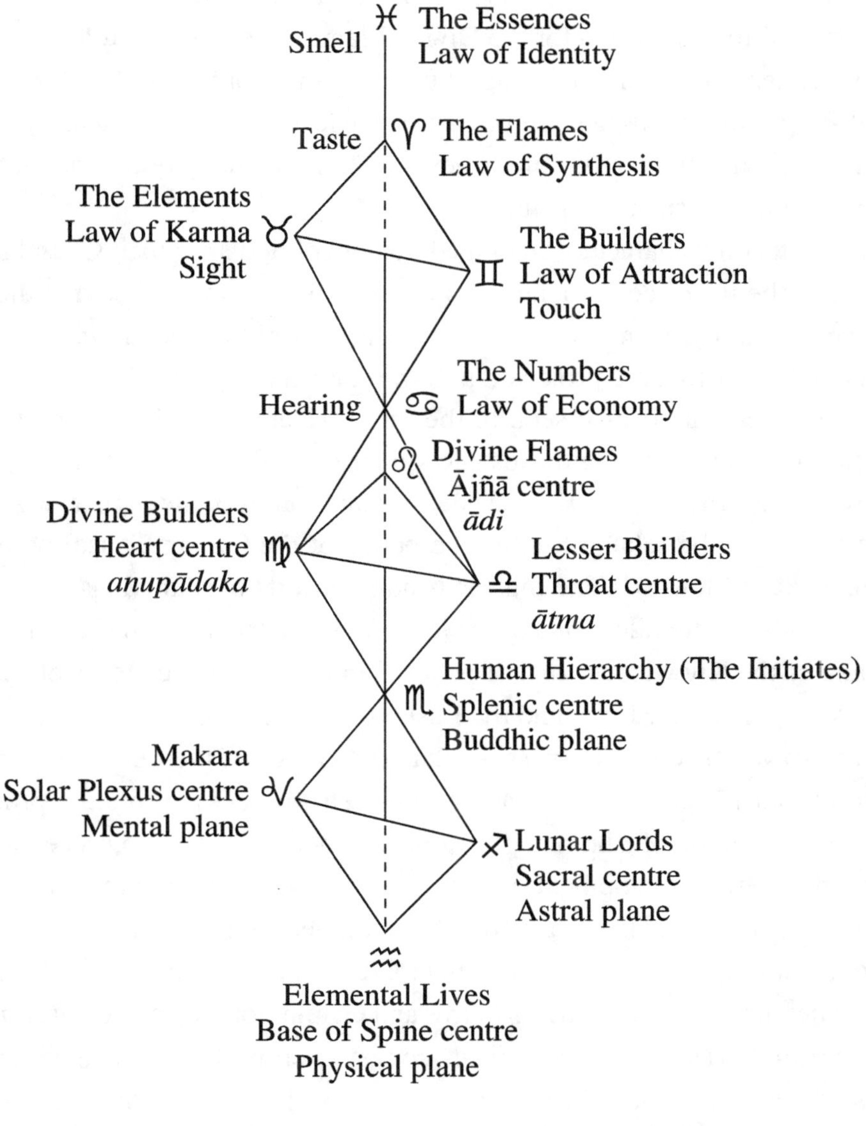


**Figure 36. The Creative Hierarchies as triads**

The kingdom of Souls (the fourth Creative Hierarchy) manifest as the containment of the cosmic Waters, whilst the human incarnation process is a methodology whereby the Waters will eventually produce the alchemical purpose.

The human astral plane is inevitably formed, through human emotional (Watery) volitions, wherein various alchemical transmutations must eventually take place via the Fiery impetus of the transforming Mind. (For ultimately the potency of Agni, the Lord of Fire, must rule all.) The fifth Creative Hierarchy (Cancer) is the point of influx into the sum of cosmic dense space for the cosmic Waters. Fiery-Water manifests a similar function for the Divine Flames, the Divine Builders and the Lesser Builders. All such forces impact upon the kingdom of Souls. They project reified Fiery-Watery energies in order to transform the cosmic dense physical substance into that which the human personality perpetually reincarnates. Fiery-Water is the transformative agent.

The outstanding characteristic of the kingdom of Souls are their Causal forms, whereas in the list of correspondences in the above figure we see that the fifth Creative Hierarchy (Cancer) incorporates the Causal bodies *(anima mundi)* of the Massed Lives that are projected into the solar Incarnation.

The number nine is also seen in the three triads shown in the figure. The lowest triad (Capricorn, Sagittarius and Aquarius) is the shadow, being the field of substance for the interplay of the energies and forces of the higher two triads. These triads can be related to the nine petals of the human Causal body (the Sambhogakāya Flower).[14] The highest triad manifests the functions of the Will triad of petals, the middle group of the Love-Wisdom triad of petals and the final grouping of the Knowledge triad of petals. This final group consists of Makara the Mystery, the Lunar Pitris and the Baskets of Nourishment. They are worked upon to evolve self-consciousness, so that knowledge of their environment and how to master its qualities become possible. This process eventually produces the Individualisation of a human kingdom. The onus of evolution proceeds from intelligence to the development of Love-Wisdom. Such development inevitably produces the process of liberation from the trammels of dense physical form. The development of the qualities of the higher Creative Hierarchies is then possible.

The Hierarchies denoted Aries, Taurus and Gemini form an analogous function to the spiritual Triad in humanity. They convey energies from the higher cosmic planes into manifestation. This Triad is responsible for vivifying the systemic planes with the necessary Light, Love and Vitality that the Logoic Personality needs in order to achieve its aims. (For it aspires to gain liberation from affiliation with the cosmic dense form and so travel to its Ineffable Source.)

---

14 For an in-depth explanation of the Sambhogakāya Flower, see my book *The Buddha-Womb and the Way to Liberation.*

In further consideration of the *number nine* (and the Initiation process), we see that Initiation is here regulated by the cosmic sense of Touch (Gemini, the ninth Creative Hierarchy), through which contact with what is external to the organism can be made known. Touch helps to produce the birth of the Divine Child, whose evolution can then become an accomplished fact. This sense is an expression of the sixth cosmic astral sub-plane, which 'Touches' the systemic astral plane. An effect is to intensify humanity's problems concerning their (in) ability to master the Waters. Despite this, the manifestation of cosmic Touch also helps awaken the Love-Wisdom petals of the Causal form and then its extension in a person's Head lotus.

This 'Touch' extends from 'the Builders' (Gemini) upon the sixth cosmic astral plane to the Greater Builders (Virgo) upon the plane *anupādaka*. (Who also manifest as the systemic Heart centre.) The Greater Builders represent the great Lords at Shambhala, who work via the human Monads and the Life aspect of this planet. This 'Touch' then moves via Scorpio (humanity) to Sagittarius (the Lunar Lords), upon whom it is 'grounded'.

Here the Logos eventually Touches the object of Desire. The effect of the cosmic law of Attraction is thus impelled upon the human Watery domain, which produces the relationship of the Beloved to the Lover. There is a consequent intense energy impacting upon the Lunar Lords. When humanity adds the intensity of their desire upon this *deva* order, there is a propensity of these Watery Lives to run amok. Wisdom will inevitably be gained by human consciousness as a consequence of the lessons learned regarding what not to be attached to – for their interactions with the Lunar Lords have produced many disasters and may continue to do so because of the dangers of psychically 'drowning' by the Waters. This has happened before upon a mass scale, as in Atlantean times. Learning to master the sense of touch on all levels of perception constitutes passing the Initiation testings that progress one into the cosmic astral domains as a *nirvāṇee*. The Chohans thereby pass through the cosmic gate in Cancer under the auspices of the cosmic law of Attraction.

Through the sense of Touch, Gemini also projects the energies of the cosmic Christ into the manifesting Logoic form. Gemini is responsible for the psychic development of the incarnated Lives as they struggle to overcome the hindrances of Watery perturbations. By 'psychic development' here is meant the ability to develop higher spiritual awareness, to reach upwards so as to 'touch' the higher dimensions of perception (the planes of liberation). Through the sense of touch, one contacts (or gains comprehension of) what is thereby experienced. This is the only way to really Know something. Accordingly, Gemini stands as the Temple wherein the Mysteries of Being/non-being can be fully experienced.

The *number ten* symbolises the perfection of consciousness, of the purpose for the evolution of the ten planetary Schemes within the Body of the solar Logos. The 10 of perfection can be subdivided into the 7 + 3, relating to the Logoic *chakras*. The *chakras* are organs of vision – of the cosmic sense of Sight that is wielded by Taurus, the third liberated Creative Hierarchy. (This Creative Hierarchy is signified by the numbers 3 and 10, counting from below up and from above down.) Taurus embodies the cosmic Ājñā centre (via Aldebaran, as earlier mentioned). Sight allows things to be seen in perspective and therefore to be made known. The fifth (mental) cosmic astral sub-plane is related to this sense, from whence emanates cosmic *karma,* as directed by the Logoic Third Eye. Energy is projected and the whole Body moves wherever the Eye directs. The Eye projects the lines of Reasoning that interrelate the One to the other. Note the direct relationship between Sight and Touch (Taurus-Gemini), for Touch is greatly facilitated by the ability to See.

This activity unfolds the Knowledge petals of the Logoic Head Centre, producing the Divine Power of Evolution. The Eye of Knowledge (Mahat) that directs the entire *manvantara* of a Logoic Incarnation is therefore opened. The line of descent of Mahat manifests from Taurus to the Lesser Builders upon the ātmic plane, then to impact upon Makara the Mystery (Capricorn) that wields the substance of the systemic mental pane. The Lesser Builders represent the *deva* Hierarchies that are impelled to act under the directives from the Pleiades, who are part of the constellation of Taurus. Accordingly, they work under Capricornian conditionings (the tenth sign in the zodiac).

The *number eleven* (10 + 1) symbolises the resolution of all into a synthesis (e.g., the ten Planetary Schemes becoming the unity of a solar Logos) and the expression outwards and onwards of the Power of that Synthesis as a law via the Fiery Will. The eleventh (or the second counted from the top) Creative Hierarchy ('the Flames') under the auspices of Aries wields this law for the sum of a Logoic *manvantara.* Eleven is the number, therefore, of an Entity who has gained mastery. It also concerns relationships, relating the One to the other, the lesser to the higher, the personality to the Soul, and the Soul to the Spirit. This thus concerns the development and projection of the *sūtrātma* or *antaḥkaraṇa* and the way of escape from the limitations of form. (The number is symbolised by the lightning flash.) It is the One extending itself outwards from the centre to the periphery of any body of manifestation (to make the perfected 10). This extension esoterically builds the *nāḍī* system. The Flames (denoted by the numbers 2, 11) utilise the law of Synthesis to reflect the Divine Thought into manifestation by means of the Logoic Will. (Or by means of the Sacrifice triad of petals of the Logoic Causal form.)

The attribute wielded by this second Creative Hierarchy is 'Life Itself' – that directs the Life principle of all that must be and which awakens a Logoic Head lotus. The Sacrifice triad of petals therefore empowers the Mind of Sanat Kumāra on earth. (Thus He is also called 'The Great Sacrifice'.)

The associated cosmic sense is that of Taste, which here manifests via the fourth cosmic astral sub-plane. This is the plane of reflection of what might be considered the Triune Essence of Life (the Father-Son-Mother aspects to a Logos, veiled by the first Creative Hierarchy, Pisces) into the attributes of the form—the Divine Personality. From this perspective, the third, fourth and fifth Creative Hierarchies manifest as an abstracting trinity that projects the attributes of this Triune Essence into the septenary of the form—the seven Creative Hierarchies incarnate in systemic space. This then produces the abovementioned 3 + 7 interrelation that signifies 'perfection'. Taste thus concerns the utilisation of abstract discriminative abilities that allow the Logos to utilise subtle cosmic discernments of impressions from the higher cosmic realms. They are needed to appropriately build the needed Logoic constructs and to direct units of Life throughout the manifesting form of a *manvantara.*

When added together, the numbers 9, 10 and 11 make the *number 30* (3 x 10), which relates to the perfected activity of any entity. Here it governs the Mathematically Exact Activity within the ring-pass-not of the spiritual Triad of the liberated Hierarchies that stand aloof from cosmic Incarnation. They focus the directive potency of the cosmic Waters upon the fifth of the liberated Hierarchies, denoted as 'the Numbers', or 'Mass Life'. This Hierarchy is not yet fully liberated, hence they straddle the cosmic Waters and the cosmic physical domain.[15] Their number is also the eighth (counting from below upwards). Here, the eight signifies a spiral-cyclic motion, where the attributes of the Spiritual Triad are reflected into the triad of Hierarchies established on the abstracted planes of our solar system – the Divine Flames, the Divine Builders and the Lesser Builders.

The cosmic sense attributed to the eighth Creative Hierarchy (Cancer) is that of Hearing. This means that this Hierarchy listens to the mantric Commands from the liberated Hierarchies and directs their purpose into cosmic manifestation.

15 Between the seventh cosmic astral sub-plane and *ādi.*

They consequently direct the *devas* that build the forms of the Massed Lives that manifest in the cosmic dense sub-planes. The mantric Sounds (Songs and Stanzas) produce the first Outpouring of what-is-to-Be. These mantras are the music of the spheres that bathe the creative *deva* Builders with the Commands they listen to. (Thus causing the appearance of the sum of the phenomena manifesting in our solar sphere.)

The five liberated Creative Hierarchies manifest the attributes of the five major tiers of petals of a Logoic Head centre.[16] The seven Hierarchies manifesting into cosmic dense space embody the functions of seven major *chakras*. These Hierarchies can also be considered dual in their constitution – associated with the consciousness-aspect and the substance of the forms wherein that consciousness incarnates. One can therefore also consider the manifestation of seven great departments of the physical form of a Grand Heavenly Man. Thus can be seen:

- The Divine Flames (Leo) upon *ādi* manifest attributes of the Head/ Ājñā centre of this Man (shared with Cancer), as well as the head and brain.
- The Divine Builders (Virgo) upon *anupādaka* manifest attributes of the Heart centre of this Man, as well as the heart, lymphatic and glandular systems.
- The Lesser Builders (Libra) upon *ātma* manifest attributes of the Throat centre of this Man, as well as the throat, vocal cords and lungs.
- Humanity (Scorpio) in the form of the Hierarchy upon *buddhi,* also manifest the attributes of the Heart centre, whilst common humanity manifest the function of the Splenic centres and the three lower *chakras* (incorporating the related Hierarchies) of this Man, and the liver, kidneys and eliminative system.
- The human Personality (Makara—Capricorn) upon the mental plane manifest attributes of the Solar Plexus centre of this Man, as well as the digestive system.
- The astral Lunar Lords (Sagittarius) manifest attributes of the Sacral centre of this Man, as well as the reproductive system.
- The Elemental Lives (Aquarius) manifest attributes of the Base of Spine centre of this Man, as well as the bones and muscular system. They embody the appearing forms upon the dense physical plane.

The abovementioned physical organs of the grand Heavenly Man are embodied by the Hierarchies of the *devas* that build the substance of the forms incarnate

---

16 These tiers of petals are explained in detail in my book *An Esoteric Exposition of the Bardo Thödol,* Part A.

in *saṃsāra*. I will not discuss this subject here because of its vastness, and because it lies outside the scope of this astrological text, but it is included here for completeness. The fourth Hierarchy, humanity, shares the function of the liver, kidneys and eliminative system with the Hierarchy below them (Makara), with whom they form a symbiotic relationship.

The numbers 9, 10 and 11 can also be multiplied by three to produce the attributes of the Trinity: Father-Son-Mother. The number 9 multiplied by three makes the *number 27,* the number of the laws of Fire that are the attributes of the Logoic Mind (Mahat). As an attribute of Agni (the Rāja Lord governing this Element) this Fire underlies all Life. It is the primary energy of manifestation, the gain of the former solar incarnation. The widespread dissemination of the Fiery Element indicates that all is inherently intelligent.

Fire is the basic energy governing the *devas* that build the forms throughout Nature. Cosmic Fire is the energy specifically conveyed by the tenth Creative Hierarchy (Taurus). Its purpose is projected via the ninth Creative Hierarchy, 'the Builders', whose attribute (under Gemini) is 'Desire for Duality'. The basic dualities governed by Gemini are comprehended by the Intelligence principle as what must BE to incorporate the Lives with their evolving forms. Inevitably, this Duality relates to the reflection of the attributes of subjective space into the manifestation of the solar form in such a way that the principle of Love-Wisdom dominates solar evolution. (This is the foundation of the Law of Attraction.) This attractive energy then manifests through to the Greater Builders (the seventh Creative Hierarchy) working via Virgo, the Mother of Forms.

The number 10 multiplied by 3 produces the *number 30,* which also represents the perfected Activity whereby the Laws of Fire (in the form of regulatory *karma*) can be projected throughout time and space. Such Activity is a function of the tenth Creative Hierarchy ('Light thro' Knowledge'), who wield cosmic Desire (via the attributes of the sign Taurus) to activate the *karma* of cosmic form building.

The number 11 multiplied by 3 produces the *number 33,* representing the Creative Intelligences that will disseminate the energies of Logoic Fire (as the effect of the Arian Will) throughout the incarnate form. This produces all the Laws of manifestation that the lesser Lives are controlled by. Thus the eleventh Creative Hierarchy ('the Flames') projects the Fiery *antaḥkaraṇas* of Life to the sum of manifest Being. This Creative Hierarchy thereby projects into manifestation (via the esoteric Triad of which it is a part) the triads of Creative Intelligences, the 33 *crore* (330,000,000) of Deities mentioned in the Hindu cosmogony. They are the *deva* Potencies that embody all manifested Life. This eleventh Creative Hierarchy therefore sets the entire cosmic landscape into activity, awakening the solar *manvantara* from a former *pralaya* condition. The subsequent evolutionary process is then rightly directed throughout that *manvantara,* which D.K. depicts as 'Unity thro' Effort'.

The eighth Creative Hierarchy (or fifth from above down) then projects this massed Life into manifestation through the emanation of the Creative Words.

When added, the numbers 27, 30 and 33 produce the *number 90,* signifying the perfected Initiation process – of all the factors that concern the appearance of a planetary Logos. A Logos comes into being when an Initiate attains the ninth Initiation.

The attributes of the ninth, tenth and eleventh (liberated) Creative Hierarchies are also reflected into:

1. The ninth Creative Hierarchy, Humanity (Scorpio), whose esoteric domain is the buddhic plane. They work as the Logoic Splenic centre, the organ of *prāṇic* cleansing and vitality. This is for the attributes that they develop as a consequence of interrelating with and incarnating into the substance of the three lower Creative Hierarchies. This work consists of transforming and properly integrating into our solar constitution the rejected substance from the former solar system. Humanity wields the cosmic law of Attraction for these Elemental Lives. Thus humanity draws them to the higher domains through working to transform their substance, which manifests as the human periodic sheaths.
2. The tenth Creative Hierarchy, Makara (Capricorn), the goat-like God of the Waters. They embody the substance of the mental plane and also of the Logoic Solar Plexus Centre. They are concerned with the development of the empirical minds of humanity. The cosmic law of *karma* manifests via the substance they wield, for *karma* is an expression of the wilful volitions that stem from the mind.
3. The eleventh Creative Hierarchy, the Lunar Lords (Sagittarius), who embody the substance of the astral plane, the fluid Watery energies expressing the creative activity of objectivised thoughts. They are the crystallising forces within the Logoic Splenic to the Sacral centre. The cosmic law of Synthesis works via them in order to produce the integrated forms (embodied by the Elemental Lives) of all that comes into manifestation.

These three Hierarchies distribute the vitality in the cosmic dense sub-planes wherein our threefold personalities reside and interrelate with the material world.

The *number 12* and its permutations govern the cycles concerning the awakening of the Heart of Life, where each of these twelve Creative Hierarchies play their roles in one or other of the twelve petals of that centre.

## The cosmic triangle

The major sources of energies to our solar system come from the cosmic triangle in the Heavens, delineated by the constellations:

1. The Great Bear, the source of cosmic Will – the Father.
2. Sirius, the source of cosmic Love – the Son.
3. The Pleiades, the source of cosmic Intelligence – the Mother.[17]

They transmit these cardinal energies to a constellation of seven solar systems (of which ours is one) that constitute a *chakra* in the Body of a great cosmic Lord.

The Mahatic energies from the Great Bear (the central Spiritual Sun) first play through the first and second Creative Hierarchies, 'the Essences' (Pisces) and then 'the Flames' (Aries), via the fourth cosmic astral sub-plane. This is the higher correspondence to the systemic *buddhic* plane. These energies stimulate the Intuitive and archetypal mental faculties of all the incarnate Logoi, to produce an integrated harmony of action, conditioned by the cosmic law of Synthesis. All their activities are thereby but emanations of the One Purpose. This Purpose becomes the primal source of the Will to all Lives within our solar system, and is the Life that vitalises the *nāḍīs* of all lesser Lives. This Synthesis then impacts upon the third Creative Hierarchy, 'the Elements' (Light thro' Knowledge) upon the fifth cosmic astral sub-plane wherein cosmic *karma* is activated. Logoic Purpose then manifests through the entire Spiritual Triad (shown in Figure 38) and organises all Lives into activity. The Logoic Thought-Form of what is to Be has thereby been formulated and projected into manifestation. The building of this Thought-Form manifests the golden Egg *(hiraṇyagarbha)* within which the Lives evolve. The sense of Sight is utilised to build the forms that must come into being.

The energies of the seven solar systems are borne by the third liberated Creative Hierarchy that is polarised upon the fifth cosmic astral sub-plane. This is the higher correspondence of the systemic mental plane. (The realm of our Causal forms.) Here we expect to find the externalisation of the divine Logoic Eye, the Body of Mahat, via which 'Life Itself' (Aries) can See into the realms of form.

17 See Tabulation III of *Esoteric Astrology,* 50.

(Similar to the function of the Causal form of the Soul.) The third Hierarchy projects the energies from the Will petals of the Logoic Soul. The Logoic sense utilised is therefore that of Sight. The Logoic Personality must be seen if it is to be properly formed and vitalised. All are projected upon the cyclic journeying of the Logos through the cosmos via the fifth cosmic astral sub-plane (for the body goes where the Eye directs). Where the Eye directs its Power, so the visualised Plan comes to BE. All crystallised structures of the past shatter and are consumed by the Fiery Light of that Eye. The related Lives are then dispersed and drawn back into the Heart, the store of Consciousness. They are to be Breathed out in the present cyclic opportunity.

This Eye then activates the next (fourth) Creative Hierarchy, 'the Builders', who express the 'Desire for duality', thus to produce the appearance of phenomenal form. This is produced by means of the energies from the sixth[18] cosmic astral sub-plane, via which the energies from the Love-Wisdom petals of the Logoic Causal body manifest the 'Divine Power of Evolution'. This 'Divine Power' is the potency of Love that emanates from Sirius, here manifesting as transmuted Logoic Solar Plexus energy. Cosmic Desire concerns the interrelation of all forms into a working harmony, producing, therefore, the driving impetus behind all manifest Life. This prompts the (psychic) development of the evolving Lives towards Light and Love.

The cosmic sense projected is that of Touch, which allows the building of the cosmic form. The Duality expressed is symbolised by the sign Gemini, who wields the function of the cosmic Christ. The 'immortal Brother' associated with this sign embodies the qualities of the three Creative Hierarchies constituting the Spiritual Triad. They remain aloof from cosmic manifestation. The 'mortal Brother' manifests via the next (fifth) Creative Hierarchy, signified by the constellation Cancer and the manifestation of Mass Life, via the seven Creative Hierarchies that consequently empower the seven systemic planes. The 'immortal Brother' (the cosmic Christ) then wields the law of Attraction, that at the appointed cycles pulls towards cosmos everything that emanates from the 'mortal Brother'. The substance of the various sheaths of the Logos must be Touched to be experienced, to be adequately controlled and moulded into the forms Desired. The sense of Touch underlies the evolutionary urge of eventual union, or fusion with, that which is the polar opposite on all levels of expression. This is the underlying foundation for the sex expression found throughout Nature.

---

18 Note that the sixth plane or principle is that of desire, or of crystallising power.

The Love-Wisdom petals of the Logoic Souls empower the second Ray of Love-Wisdom (the energy of the cosmic Christ), making Touch the major sense governing solar evolution. The qualities that are Touched and expressed become precipitated into the systemic planes (the Womb of Being) via the open gate of the next Hierarchy, denoted by the sign Cancer. In the present incarnation of the solar Logos (which is upon the Love-Wisdom line), such gaining of knowledge through Touch is essentially astral in nature, for we learn what we *desire* to know.

At the sixth cosmic astral sub-plane level of 'the Builders', there would also be an integration of the qualities of the seven Logoi of a constellation. They can then coordinate and project the 'Power of Evolution' to mould the attributes of the appearing forms via the crystallising forces of the cosmic Waters. They thereby project Logoic Purpose upon the cosmic dense realms via Touch. This Power wields the five types of *prāṇas* (or energies) conveyed by the Logoi. It allows them to direct all Lives within the seven systemic planes with Logoic Purpose. This is projected via the polar opposite of Gemini – Sagittarius the archer. The Archer fires the arrows of Logoic Purpose via the next Creative Hierarchy to mould the prima matrix of cosmic dense evolution.

All that is seen can then become known. The past can be resolved into the present to make the future, and all the forces and factors that decorate and make splendid the Temple of the Lord (Gemini) can be organised and interrelated so that incarnate Purpose can be achieved. As a consequence, the whole Body can be filled with the Light of Love.

The fifth Creative Hierarchy has a relationship to the four and twenty Elders that sit round the Throne of God, as mentioned in *Rev. 4:4.* The fourth Creative Hierarchy (Gemini) relates to the Seven Spirits before the Throne, the third Creative Hierarchy (Taurus) to the four 'Beasts' supporting the Throne (who are therefore the Lipika, the Lords of *karma*). Finally, the One who sits upon the Throne is signified by the attributes of the second Creative Hierarchy (Aries), who veils the Will of the One above all (Pisces).

The energies of the *Pleiades* express the qualities of the third Ray of Mathematically Exact Activity (cosmic Intelligence), which is responsible for the creative expression of the entire Form nature of any incarnate Logos. This energy finds outlet via the fifth Creative Hierarchy (Cancer), 'the Numbers', that project the Massed Lives into incarnation. They 'awaken' the 'slumbering ones' in *pralaya,* and so project into them the Commands of the new *manvantara.* Thereby all 'thrill' with the new evolutionary momentum.

The blending of the second Ray quality with that of the third Ray, and their projection downwards into the realms of form, is also an aspect of the 'Desire for Duality' of the previous Hierarchy (Gemini). The second Ray is related to the 'immortal Brother', and the third Ray to the 'mortal Brother'.

The fifth Creative Hierarchy (Cancer) wields the law of Economy, to help build the forms that appear upon the cosmic dense physical plane. This Hierarchy is signified by the numbers 5 and 8, where the number 8[19] is symbolised by the reflection of the higher triad of Hierarchies into the lower triad. This triad is the Divine Flames, Divine Builders and Lesser Builders, to whom the energies are projected into, and which they then mould into the Life of the various evolving forms. These forms are the vehicles of the 'Mass Life' of this incarnation of the solar Logos. The solar Logos is a 'Son' in incarnation. As the fifth Creative Hierarchy have not yet gained their liberation from dense form, so they are still attached to the etheric sub-planes of the cosmic dense physical. (The three highest sub-planes of the plane *ādi.*)

The associated sense is that of Hearing, which relates to the ability to Hear and to utter the Pleiadian commands (mantras). They regulate the activities of the *devas* that are to build the forms that are and will be ensconced in the cosmic dense physical plane.

The triad of the Divine Flames, Divine Builders and Lesser Builders reflect the energies of the triune groupings of petals of the Logoic Soul into the substratum of the solar form. Hence they are principally vitalised by Sirian energy (the energies of that Soul as a unit) and are consequently 'Touched' thereby. The energies of the Sacrifice petals however are 'grounded' within the Divine Flames, those from the Love-Wisdom within the Divine Builders, and the Instructions from the Knowledge petals manifest within the Lesser Builders.

## Further numerological implications

As stated, the five liberated Hierarchies can be viewed as expressions of the five tiers of petals of the Logoic Head Centre (the *sahasrāra padma).* There are many ways of analysing this centre and the subdivision of its tiers of petals. There are three major tiers (relating to the Father-Son-Mother aspects of Deity), whilst the

---

19 In considering the number 8, we see that it is primarily the number of the expanding Christ-consciousness by means of spiral-cyclic motion, until eventually the limitations of incarnate form are transcended. (Such motion incorporates the various powers of the number 8, such as the number 96.) The number 8 is a form of the infinity sign.

innermost tier is dual (producing the five tiers). They relate to the projection of the five major *prāṇas* or Powers of Deity, the five aspects of Logoic Mind.

The whorls of petals are ordered according to the mathematics of the number 12. One of the ways that the 12 petals can be arranged is in terms of the 5 + 7 subdivision of the twelve Creative Hierarchies. The innermost tier of the Head centre is dual and is governed by the first and second Creative Hierarchies (Pisces - Aries).

This is followed by the third tier, a grouping of 96 petals signifying the Throat centre in the Head, which is governed by the functions of the third Creative Hierarchy (Taurus) existing on the mental sub-plane of the cosmic astral.

The number 96 (12 x 8) plus the twelve of the overall petals makes 108, the sacred number of the Hindu and Buddhist philosophies. This number denotes the number of the 105 Lords of Flame that came to the earth Scheme at the time of Individualisation of animal-man, plus the three of the abstract triune Logos of the planetary Scheme. The number 108 represents the innermost major tier of petals of the Head Lotus. They allow the influx of the cosmic energies that express the energies of the Heart centre of The One about Whom Naught can be Said. (This arrangement is signified by the twelve signs of the zodiac.) These petals express the qualifications of Logoic Will or Power that manifest the Plan for the entire body of manifestation. The rest of the petals of the Head lotus are then empowered via eight groupings of twelve petals associated with this Throat in the Head tier. The eight directions of space are thereby vitalised. Via these directions, the Logoic Commands can govern the rest of the body of manifestation to produce their Purpose.[20]

The next (fourth) tier is constituted of 192 (12 x 16, 24 x 8) petals. These petals are governed by the functions of the fourth of the liberated Creative Hierarchies, signified by the sign Gemini. This is the Love-Wisdom tier of petals (the Heart in the Head) of the Logoic Head lotus. This tier wields the cosmic Law of Attraction by way of the manifestation of the powers of the Logoic Heart centre. From one perspective, the 192 petals of this Heart within the Head tier can be viewed in terms of one grouping of 96 (12 x 8) petals focussed inwards, to project Logoic *prāṇas* towards the Logoic Soul, and a similar grouping directed outwards. This allows them to relay the Commands from the Throat in the Head tier of petals to the rest of the *maṇḍala* of the Logoic Body of Manifestation. This outwards focussed grouping receives the *prāṇas* coming from the majority of the petals of

20 Much detail concerning the functioning of this tier of petals of a Head centre, and of all the others, are provided in my book *An Esoteric Exposition of the Bardo Thödol,* part A.

the Head lotus from the outermost (third) major tier of petals (the Solar Plexus in the Head). These *prāṇas* are along the line of Love-Wisdom that need to be processed by the Heart in the Head tier. The *prāṇas* relate to the highest qualities of Consciousness developed by the evolving Lives. (Here of the seven Creative Hierarchies incarnate in the cosmic dense physical sub-planes.) A vast amount of study is hinted at here for a future esoteric scientist, concerning the mode of activity of the Lords of Shambhala, when the information in Volume 5A of my *A Treatise on Mind* is properly integrated here. The activities of the three Creative Hierarchies embodying the second triangle of Figure 36 now comes into consideration.

The final (outermost, fifth) tier of the Logoic Head centre (the *Solar Plexus in the Head)* relates to the development of Knowledgeable attributes. This is the active Intelligence developed by the entire Body of manifestation of the incarnate Logoic Personality. This tier of petals is composed of 768 (96 x 8, 12 x 8 x 8) petals, governed by the fifth Creative Hierarchy and the law of Economy. The lowest four incarnate Creative Hierarchies (from humanity downwards) generate the *prāṇas* processed by this outermost tier. The most refined of these *prāṇas* are directed upwards by the eighth Creative Hierarchy (the Sacred Fathers, the Lesser Builders). This Creative Hierarchy is represented on earth by the upper echelons of the Hierarchy of Light and Love, plus their *deva* complements.

The significance of these numbers is great and will not be apparent to the casual reader. When the numbers of petals are added together, the number 1068 (12 + 24 + 72 + 192 + 768) is produced. The numbers of petals (or their derivatives) are also the basis for the precessional cycles utilised by the ancients for the computation of time.[21] These numbers are also found integrated into the mathematics of the sacred geometry underlying the construction of most ancient temples.

If the twelve innermost petals are subtracted from the 1068, then the number 1056 (66 x 16, 33 x 32, 11 x 96) is obtained. There are 8 x 96 (768) petals for the outer, Activity tier, 2 x 96 (192) petals for the middle, Love-Wisdom tier, and 1 x 96 petals for the inner, Will tier. There are thus eleven tiers of 96 petals or flowers altogether. These numbers are central to the understanding of the Creative Hierarchies.

---

21 The *kali yuga,* for instance, contains 432,000 years, whilst a *manvantara* contains 4,320,000 years. The number 432,000 when divided by 768 produces 562.5, when divided by 192 produces 2,250, when divided by 72 produces 6,000, divided by 96 produces 4,500, when divided by 108 produces 4,000 and by 120 produces 3,600. See Vol. 2 of my books *The Astrological and Numerological Keys to the Secret Doctrine* and *Esoteric Cosmology and Modern Physics* for further information on this subject.

As well as what was previously considered, the *number 11* is the number of adeptship. It is the perfected expression of energies (10), plus the extension of their amalgamated expression or purpose (1) outwards through and to the conceived goal or objective for manifestation. The extension therefore is an implied central point to the periphery of any sphere of attainment, as well as the resolution of what has been attained back into the One. This movement signifies the possibilities of the expression of the *antaḥkaraṇa* of any enlightened Being. Implicit in it is the fusion of the extension of Will and of Love-Wisdom. The number 11 thus signifies the wise projection of the energies of the focussed Eye throughout the sum of the *nāḍī* system. It is the Will that interrelates the petals into a unity, and causes the overall movement of the spheres, the turning of the greater Wheels. There are also twelve modes, or gates of energy projection *(antaḥkaraṇas),* stemming from the central twelve petals that move outwards to the sum of the 1056 petals constituting the Head centre.

The *number 96* (12 x 8) is also of great significance, for it implies the evocation of myriad cycles of spiral motion, where cycles of eight are superimposed upon each other to make the substance of the spirillae of the permanent atoms. All is ordered according to the sequence of the pattern of the twelve great zodiacal and Hierarchical gates. The twelve gates are multiplied by the number 11, to eventually produce complete and perfected mastery of the related cycles – the interrelation of lesser spirals into the embrace of the arcs of the greater spirals of evolutionary Purpose. Also hinted at in the number 12 x 8 are the attributes of the eighth sign of the zodiac (Scorpio the scorpion), thus all the cycles concerning the testings of discipleship before eventually attaining Initiation in Capricorn. The significance of the 96 petals of the Ājñā centre can also be included in this discussion, for this combination of petals allows this Eye to 'see into', or experience, all of the spiral eights incorporated in the Head lotus.

The *number 108* (9 x 12) then signifies Sagittarius, which stands between Scorpio and Capricorn. Sagittarius the archer fires arrows of aspiration to the heights of the mountain (Capricorn). The number 11 is here symbolised by the arrows that signify the projection of *antaḥkaraṇas* from 'here' to 'there'.

The tenth sign in the zodiac (Capricorn) signifies the completed Head centre—the *number 120* (the 12 petals x 10). The number 10 represents the complete, perfected awakening of all the petals of the Head lotus, which is the goal of evolutionary striving. The number 120 is but a form of the number 1,200 (12 x 10 x 10) explained below.

When the number 12, associated with the overall pattern of the Head centre as a unit, is added to the number 1068, then the number 1080 is obtained. (Which esoterically is a version of the number 108.) Also, technically, the first Creative Hierarchy (Pisces) governs the general empowerment of the twelve petals as a whole, whilst the second Creative Hierarchy (Aries) governs the inner functioning of all of the groupings of twelve petals. These petals are the dynamic gates for the energies from the reservoir of Life that emanate from cosmic sources, and which move from grouping to grouping. Aries and Pisces therefore complete the circle of the ring-pass-not of the sphere of activity of the Head centre. (The Womb of Being within which all other factors have their embrace.) They are the 'alpha and omega, the first and the last',[22] as far as the evolutionary purpose of a solar system is concerned. Each petal of the Head centre becomes an embodied Being that overshadows groups of lesser Lives (thus groupings of petals). The petal thus becomes a factor projecting the unfolding purpose of the overall system.

The numbers 1056 (1000 + 7 x 8), 1068 (1000 + 17 x 4), and 1080 (1000 + 8 x 10), representing the petals of the Head centre (viewed from different perspectives), are symbolised by the 1,000 petals that are normally ascribed to this centre. One can also consider the symbolism veiled by the numbers:

a. The evocation of spiral-cyclic/*kuṇḍalinī* energies (the number 7 x 8) on all seven levels of expression that manifest the mode of unfoldment of all groups of petals of the Head lotus. This concerns the turning and spiralling of all the lesser wheels from left to right within the embrace of the one great Wheel of the Head lotus unfolding. This brings into manifestation all of the laws and cycles that govern evolutionary purpose.

b. The energies responsible for building a Logoic seat of Power (17 x 4). The number 17 relates to the attributes of deity. When multiplied by 4 it signifies the quaternary, which represents the sum of the form nature. (The dense physical, etheric, astral and lower mental bodies. There are also the four Elements and four quadrants or pillars upholding the universe in most creation myths.) Here the quaternary signifies the Seat of Power of any Logos, or the principle of consciousness.

c. That concerning the enthronement (or awakening) of the powers *(prāṇas,* the number 5) of a Christ (the number 16), producing the compassionate spiral-

---

22 *Rev. 1:8, 11* and *22:13.*

cyclic undertaking (8 x 10) of such a being. Such compassion manifests the Word in the active flower of its expression.[23]

When the 96 petals associated with the Ājñā centre, plus the 48 petals (that are the number of main petals of the major *chakras* below the Head centre)[24] are added to the number 1056, then the number 1200 is obtained. It can be inferred that this number signifies the Way of unfoldment of the twelve major petals of the Head lotus (12 x 100). The twelve petals therefore manifest as a Heart centre that distributes the sum of the energies and attributes governing Life. These petals are thereby aligned to everything that embodies the principle of Love-Wisdom in our local cosmos. They thus express the mode of distributing the twelve major zodiacal and Hierarchical energies throughout the form. This manifests as the Great Perfection (Mahāmūdra) of Buddhist philosophy.

When twelve conditional organisational petals from the Logoic Soul (or of the twelve constellations) are added, then the number 1212 (1200 + 12) is obtained, which is but a form of the abovementioned Pisces-Aries interrelationship. This provides a hint also as to the nature of fourth dimensional motion.

A deeper understanding of the mysteries of esoteric numerology in relation to the Hierarchies has now been provided than was possible at the time of D.K. One must, however, not utilise the empirical mind to concretise the information concerning numbers with respect to the Hierarchies. What is described is a dynamic, living, ever-changing process. It is one of constant mutability, interblending and rearranging order when seen from the broader perspective of the eternal Now. The numbers depicted concern specifically the arrangement of the inner Councils governing the expression of each of the Hierarchies. The number of actual beings composing each Hierarchy is greater. It is interesting to note that the last two numbers of the descriptions in D.K.'s *Esoteric Astrology* concerning each of the *five liberated Hierarchies* all add to 15 (for example, Cancer = VII + 8 = 15). This indicates that they are already perfectly endowed with the Manasic principle (Mahat), cosmically speaking. (The number 5 being the number of the

23 A proper explanation of the science of esoteric numerology is provided in the two volumes of my book *The Astrological and Numerological Keys to the Secret Doctrine,* which should be referred to here to comprehend this fascinating subject. This book analyses in depth the Cosmogenesis section of Blavatsky's monumental work, which concerns the subject of the genesis of a cosmos (or more specifically of a solar sphere).

24 Four for the Base of Spine centre, six for the Sacral centre, ten for the Solar Plexus centre, twelve for the Heart centre, and sixteen for the Throat centre.

mind, an attribute of the fifth plane of perception, and the number 3 relates to activity.) The members of these Hierarchies are Kumāras, Mind-born sons of Brahmā (the great Mother of time and space). They are the flower of the former solar system where Mind was the evolutionary objective, whilst for this solar system the Love-Wisdom (Christ) principle will flower.

Much sacred lore will be gained when esoteric numerological considerations are thoroughly contemplated. Such lore will unravel the Mysteries of divine geometry and of the Kingdom of 'God'.

## The glyphs of the liberated Creative Hierarchies

The liberated Creative Hierarchies are the embodiments of the functions of the five major tiers of petals of the Head centre of a Logos upon the cosmic astral domain. The attributes developed by the seven incarnate Creative Hierarchies are accordingly processed by the petals of this centre. In meditating upon this subject, however, one must think in terms of the processes involved with the evolution and movement of liberated beings *(nirvāṇees)* that travel to various stellar destinations. (Rather than in terms of *prāṇas* and *saṃskāras.)* The incarnate Creative Hierarchies, however, do function as the petals of the major *chakras* below the Head centre, counting the Splenic centre amongst them.[25] In the list below, [26] the Roman numerals indicate the Rays governing the respective Hierarchies. The Ray qualities act as the vehicles through which the Hierarchies manifest, qualifying their actions and attributes.

- The sixth Creative Hierarchy, 6, I, 7, the Divine Flames (Leo) embody aspects of the outermost tier of petals of the Logoic Head centre. They (along with the fifth Creative Hierarchy, and the seventh and eighth Creative Hierarchies to a lesser extent) are the mediators between the Head centre and the rest of the body of manifestation.
- Hierarchy 7, II, 6, the Divine Builders (Virgo), embody the qualities of the Logoic Ājñā centre.
- Hierarchy 8, III, 5, the Lesser Builders (Libra), embody the qualities of the Logoic Throat centre.
- Hierarchy 9, IV, 4, the Human Hierarchy (Scorpio), embody the qualities of the Logoic Heart and Splenic centres.

---

25 In fact, the sum of the body of manifestation comes under their impress, but the major *chakras* are the controlling factors for the appearance of things.

26 See *Esoteric Astrology*, 34-35, for the source of the numbers.

- Hierarchy 10, V, 3, the Crocodiles (Capricorn), embody the qualities of the Logoic Solar Plexus centre.
- Hierarchy 11, VI, 2, the Lunar Lords (Sagittarius), embody the qualities of the Logoic Sacral centre.
- Hierarchy 12, VII, 1, the Elemental Lives (Aquarius), embody the qualities of the Logoic Base of Spine centre.

Together, these Hierarchies can be viewed to be an evolving solar Christ, because the potency of the organisation of the petals of the Heart in the Head governs their general *modus operandi*. The energies *(jīva)* of the Heart centre are also indicated by the fact that the last two of the numbers given in the list above for each Hierarchy add to 8. Thus the numbers of the Divine Flames = 6, I, 7 (where 1 + 7 = 8), and those of the Divine Builders = 7, II, 6 (where 2 + 6 = 8). This implies that spiral-cyclic motion and the consequent evolution of consciousness is what links the highest to the lowest. A major clue is thereby provided as to the nature of their evolutionary characteristics. They must unitedly become the solar Christ by means of unfolding spiral-cyclic motion.

The seven major *chakras* via which the incarnate Creative Hierarchies express themselves, or are incorporated into, come under the umbrella of the fifth (i.e., the eighth, counting from below upwards) Creative Hierarchy, ruled by Cancer. This Hierarchy integrates the *prāṇas* from the seven major *chakras* that feed the 8 x 96 petals of the outermost tier of the Head lotus (the Solar Plexus in the Head). The *prāṇic* attributes then produce consequent energy qualifications in the Logoic Head centre. The spiral-eight motions[27] of the incoming attributes of consciousness continuously produce an expansion of Consciousness of the Mind of the planetary (or solar) Logos. This allows Him to send the needed directives to the Lords of the *chakras* at the right time of the appropriate turning of each lesser wheel. Thus the objectives of cyclic Incarnation for each incarnate Being can be accomplished.

D.K. states:

> In connection with the etheric centres, we should note the fact that the major head

---

27 One needs to think here in terms of the energies of the seven *chakras* integrating with petals in the Head lotus, to complete the cycling of the spiral motion. The Logoic response then moves downwards to instruct the seven with the next evolutionary directive. The process continuously repeats itself and so is driving the entire *maṇḍala* of the Creative Hierarchies forwards to evolutionary perfection.

centre is twofold in structure, and consists of a lotus of ninety-six petals between the eyebrows, and a twelve-petalled lotus at the top of the head, with ninety-six petals in a subsidiary whorl. The significance of these figures is profound. In every case the figure twelve is met with, showing a definite relation to the basic psychic lotuses on egoic levels. Twelve multiplied by eight stands for the twelve petals in each case, while in the figure eight lies hidden the idea of duality:

a. The four of the quaternary,
b. The four of the egoic auric egg (the three aspects, and the ring-pass-not.)

We must note also, that the idea of twelve in connection with the centres is found in three of them:

a. The higher head centre,
b. The secondary head centre
c. The heart centre.

If the student studies this condition, and links up the idea of the three tiers of petals in the twelve-petalled lotus, he may find illumination. More it is not possible to give at this stage.

It is only when the etheric centres—the two head centres and the heart centre—are fully active with their twelve petals completely unfolded that the central circle of petals in the egoic lotus (the fourth or inner circle) unfolds. The significance of the four circles in the egoic lotus, and the eight circles of twelve petals each in the etheric lotuses on the mental plane is of great importance.

The centres with which man has to deal are necessarily five at this stage.[28]

In terms of *solar evolution,* the constituency of the various liberated Creative Hierarchies can relate to the levels shown below. As they are Hierarchies, there is a gradation of the entities concerned. One can, however, presume that they can be basically viewed from two levels of perception. (Similar to the fifth Creative Hierarchy, and the fourth, where concerning the liberated beings, we have Shambhala and Hierarchy.) All have members in one or other of the three

---

28 *A Treatise on Cosmic Fire,* 859-60. The term 'egoic lotus' refers to the Soul, the Sambhogakāya Flower. This lotus also manifests in the form of an 'auric egg'. The second of the Head centres that D.K. mentions here is the Ājñā centre, which also manifests according to a twelve-petalled arrangement. The five centres that people have to deal with 'at this stage' can be thought of in Buddhist terms, where the Head and Ājñā centres are counted as a unity, as well as the Base of Spine and Sacral centres. The Splenic centre is discounted. This leaves the Throat, Heart and Solar Plexus centres to complete the pentad.

synthesising Schemes, but the major distribution of their populations is indicated below. The information is based upon the constitution of a Head centre. The first level is that related to members of the three synthesising Schemes (Uranus I, Neptune II and Saturn III that are explained in *A Treatise on Cosmic Fire).* The second level will bring our vision to the rest of the body of manifestation of the solar system – the remaining planetary Schemes (the major *chakras)* and the Inner Round of minor *chakras.* As this subject is highly abstruse, thus the information provided is an outline (an idea) only of the nature of the internal esoteric dynamics of a solar system.

1. The *first Creative Hierarchy* ('the Essences', Pisces) are the members of the inner Council of the solar Logos, drawn from the three *synthesising Schemes.* One could consider that five members come from Uranus I, four from Neptune II, three from Saturn III, making the necessary number twelve. This also makes the 3-4-5 triangle that is the basis of the *maṇḍalic* foundation for the geometry of space-time and of the Initiation process that leads from one dimension of perception to a higher one. This number represents the archetype of the number of petals to the Heart centre that governs all Life, and from which everything is derived. The entire evolutionary pattern is bathed in Love, an emanation of the cosmic Love of a divine Bodhisattva that reincarnates for the purpose of salvaging all beings still karmically trapped within the realms of cosmic woe.
2. The *second Creative Hierarchy* ('the Flames', Aries) can be considered to be drawn from the members of the inner Council of the Logoi of the seven sacred planets, plus the higher triad of the superimposed Logoic Splenic centre. This produces eight planets, which when multiplied by the number three of their central triads make the necessary number 24. This Creative Hierarchy acts as a mirror, reflecting the pattern of the divine Archetype into the corporeal, Logoic etheric space. The archetype thus becomes the scaffolding upon which all is built.

   The glyph for this Creative Hierarchy is:

**Figure 37. The second Creative Hierarchy**

The first grouping of twelve Entities (spiralling from right to left) deals with the involutionary projection of energies into space. The second group (spiralling from left to right) deals with the resultant evolution of Consciousness back towards cosmic space. The point of application is via the respective petals in the Eye associated with the third Creative Hierarchy and thence into objectivity.

The number of Entities presented for the Creative Hierarchies only relates to the members of these Hierarchies that are outwardly focussed during any cycle, in order to energise the embodied form of the solar Logos. There will be others concerned with other tasks (hence those who are inwardly or upwardly focussed).

3. The *third Creative Hierarchy* ('the Elements', Taurus) can be considered to represent the inner Council of twelve members of each of the Logoi of the five non-sacred planets, plus for the forthcoming future Saturn globe of the earth Scheme. Though one can think of the evolution of great Beings through time, members of this Creative Hierarchy also presently function as part of Saturn III Scheme. One must also add the Entities that embody the zodiacal gates that delineate the Womb of space-time. Within that Womb, human units evolve by passing their testings. This concerns the mode of the transmutation of base reject substance from the past solar system. This third Hierarchy extends the Logoic 'blueprint' to incorporate the fine detail associated with the cladding that is to be placed upon the framework in the 4 x 24 directions that emanate the swastikas of space-time. What is signified here is a Seat of Power for a Logos that can project Mahat into the four directions of space. This is via lesser Beings that further disseminate this cosmic Fire via the twelve major petals of the Head centres of various Logoi. Through this dissemination of the zodiacal variegations of Fire, they project the *karma* of what is to be into the forms that come into manifestation. Each group of 24 acts in a similar manner as the 2 x 12 members of the second Creative Hierarchy. This grouping represents the Eye that directs the forces and energies pertaining to the appearance of a *manvantara*.

The glyph for the third Creative Hierarchy is:

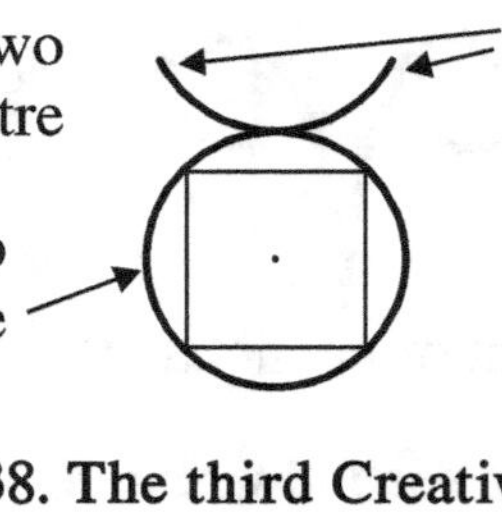


**Figure 38. The third Creative Hierarchy**

4. The *fourth Creative Hierarchy* ('the Builders', Gemini) concern the inner Council of the Logoi of the planetary spheres, large asteroids and some comets that constitute the Inner Round of the solar system (not counting the Splenic centre). There are twenty-two such minor *chakras,* and if the dual Splenic centre is counted then we have the number 24.[29] These 24 minor centres are foci of attention of the directing Eye of the third Creative Hierarchy. The fourth Creative Hierarchy infuses the *nāḍī* systems of the planetary spheres with *prāṇic* substance, the vitality of the Lives that will stream into manifestation via the minor centres. The doors of expression for all of these *prāṇas* are the major centres that in the solar system are the planetary Regents. There are ten of these, plus the Moon and the Sun[30] (which symbolise the *iḍā* and *piṇgalā nāḍīs).* Together, the links *(nāḍīs)* between the major petals of all of these *chakras* produce the *nāḍī* system of the solar system. The numbers 12 (for the planetary Regents) plus 24 make the number 36 (numerologically signifying Gemini, the third sign of the zodiac). When the number 36 is multiplied by three (to incorporate the energies of the *iḍā, piṇgalā* and *suṣumṇā nāḍīs,* or of the Father-Son-Mother attributes of Being), then the sacred number 108 is obtained.

The sum of the activity of the energies manifesting through the *nāḍī* system will manifest in accordance with the law of Love, which is but the expression of the law of Attraction wielded by this Creative Hierarchy. This Hierarchy thus have their representatives in all of the planets in the solar system, for all must interrelate with the Inner Round.

The two uprights of the sign Gemini represent the pillars of the Temple of Being, which houses the inner sanctum wherein can be found the sum total of the Creative *prāṇic* energies producing the Purpose for evolutionary space. In this symbol the dome of the sky contains the great Beings that embody the constellations. They are the 'immortal Brother' projecting the energies of

29 There are two centres at the feet, two at the knees, two at the hands, two gonad centres. There are also the Stomach and Liver centres, the Diaphragm centre, two centres at the breasts, one between the shoulder blades, one at the mouth, two eye centres, two ear centres, the Alta Major centre, and minor centres for the pituitary and pineal glands. One can also count the dual Splenic centre. The planetary bodies mentioned are but physical plane anchors for subjective Beings.

30 The earth Scheme is of interest here because it will manifest a trinity of planetary spheres that have or will contain a human evolution. They are the former moon Chain, the earth and the future Saturn globe. If this function is taken into account, then from this perspective, the ancient moon and the future globe can substitute for the Sun and Moon in this listing.

the cosmic Christ. The 'mortal Brother' then manifests as the incarnate solar form and the Lives evolving therein. They are energised by the cosmic *prāṇas* flowing via the twelve great gates of the zodiac. The Builders therefore convey these energies downwards into the solar form, according to the ritualised cycles for their expression. The 'duality' associated with this sign then relates to this wider cosmic landscape, as incorporated into the 'mortal Brother'.

The glyph for the fourth Creative Hierarchy is:

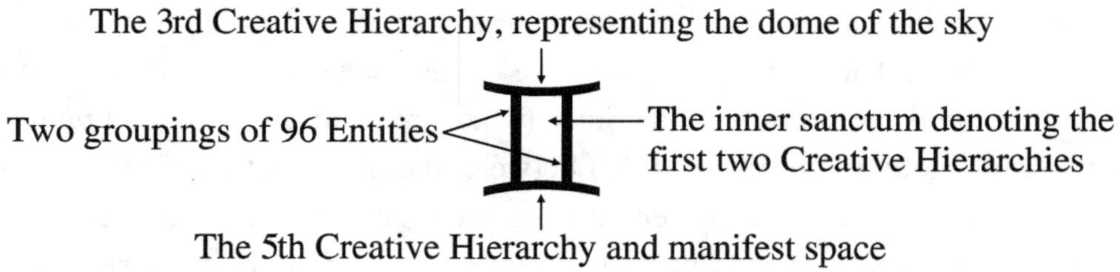


**Figure 39. The fourth Creative Hierarchy**

The abovementioned number 24 is the number of the four and twenty Elders that sit round the Throne of God.[31] They embody the Wisdom aspect, or awakened Eye, of any embodied Logos, as associated with the functions of Taurus, the second sign of the zodiac. (The number 24 therefore numerologically symbolises this sign.) When this number is multiplied by eight, then the number 192 (4 x 48) is produced. As well as signifying the spiral-cyclic motion that is the basis to the evolution of consciousness, the number 8 also represents the eight arms of the compass that manifest the directions in space: north, south, east and west, and the intermediate positions. (As these positions have been thoroughly elaborated throughout my books, I need not elaborate here.) The number eight signifies subsidiary Entities associated with any of these *chakras*.

The number 192 (4 x 48) can be viewed in terms of a Seat of Power (the number 4) that is constituted of, or supported by, four groups of 48 (4 x 12) Entities. Each group of twelve is a subdivision of a Creative Hierarchy that supports one leg of a Seat of Power. This Seat of Power is the square or platform, the Throne of 'God', upon which such a One sits.[32] He is an embodiment of the 96 + 12 Entities constituting the first three Creative

31 See *The Revelation of St. John,* chapter 4.

32 *Rev. 4:4.*

Hierarchies. They represent the Father, Son and Mother aspect of the triune Deity, the triple Word that is One.

This constitutes the *maṇḍala* associated with the *swastika*. It is the foundation of the *nāḍī* system underlying all manifested space,[33] which is veiled by the qualities of the sign Gemini the twins. Gemini here takes the attributes of the abovementioned superimposed Splenic centre. This centre is wherein the *prāṇas* and entities associated with the *eighth sphere* of the Logos are cleansed. From one perspective, this is the major purpose for solar evolution. The basic outline of this multidimensional Throne can be viewed thus:

**Figure 40. The geometry of a Seat of Power**

The number 192 can also be thought of in terms of a fundamental triad (of the representatives of the triple Deity), pointing towards any of the directions in space. The focal point of their activity, in terms of *manvantara,* would be downwards into manifestation. This then leaves 189 = 7 x 3 x 9 Entities that provide seven groups of triads that are responsible for the direction of the seven Ray energies (or Ray Lives) whose energies impact upon the three highest sub-planes of the cosmic dense physical. They convey potencies from the nine petals of the Logoic Causal body into manifestation. This vitalises or organises the activities of the greater *deva* Builders, called Triads. It produces the triadial interrelations of all that is.

In relation to this, human Monads, for instance, exist in three groups of seven, answering to the three fundamental Rays (Will, Love-Wisdom and Mathematically Exact Activity) and seven sub-Ray groupings for each of these Rays. The kingdom of Souls contains nine major whorls of petals each.

33 This highly esoteric subject is detailed in my book *Esoteric Cosmology and Modern Physics*. See, for instance, Figure 17, page 261.

This kingdom is also divided into seven Ray and 49 sub-Ray categories. (The sum total are organised into twelve groups, answerable to the energies of the zodiac.) This entire schema is energised from the sixth cosmic astral plane via the activity of the fourth Creative Hierarchy (Gemini) thereon.

5. The *fifth Creative Hierarchy* ('Mass Life', Cancer) are constituted of the Creative Intelligences drawn from the Activity petals (the Solar Plexus in the Head) of the Head centres of the various planets, plus those of the Inner Round. There are 768 (8 x 96) petals of the Logoic Head centre of this Activity tier. The number 8 x 96 can be viewed as basic groups of 96 petals projected into the eight directions of the compass. Through these 8 x 96 petals this fifth Creative Hierarchy continues the work of projecting the attributes of Mahat coming from the 96 petals of the third Creative Hierarchy (Taurus). By the number five (that delineates this Hierarchy), it can be seen that all of the five *prāṇas (vayus)* or Elements associated with Logoic Mind[34] concerned with the vivification and enlightenment of all manifest Life can now find full expression. This completes the purpose and manifestation of the swastikas that move quaternaries of energies throughout the *nāḍī* system.

The *iḍā* and *piṇgalā* attributes of the four Creative Hierarchies preceding the fifth are incorporated into the *maṇḍala* of what is to be, by being projected via the eight directions of space. Their energies thereby vivify the sum of the manifestation of the Lives embodying the cosmic dense physical plane. This is accomplished by means of spiral-cyclic motion. From this perspective, the potency of this *maṇḍala* is vitalised via the third Creative Hierarchy. The first two Creative Hierarchies (Pisces and Aries) then represent the abstracted potencies that direct the movement of what passes through the swastikas embodied by the fifth Creative Hierarchy. This fifth Hierarchy then grounds the manifestation of what must be, via its 8 x 96 petals of the Solar Plexus in the Head.

The third Creative Hierarchy, with 96 petals, can be considered as the Father aspect of the system (signifying inherent Unity). The fourth Creative Hierarchy, with 2 x 96 petals, can be considered as the Son aspect (an inherent Duality). The fifth Creative Hierarchy, with 8 x 96 petals, can be considered as the Mother (as inherent Activity).

---

34 Prāṇa, Samāna, Apāna, Udāna and Vyāna. See the revised version of my book *The Revelation* for a detailed explanation of the *vayus.*

The petals to the Logoic Head centre occupied by the liberated Creative Hierarchies are thus:

| | |
|---|---|
| 12 petals | first Creative Hierarchy (Pisces) |
| 24 petals | second Creative Hierarchy (Aries) |
| 96 petals | third Creative Hierarchy (Taurus) |
| 2 x 96 petals | fourth Creative Hierarchy (Gemini) |
| 8 x 96 petals | fifth Creative Hierarchy (Cancer) |

The first two Creative Hierarchies can be viewed as abstracted, whilst the third through to the fifth are responsible for the manifestation of the cosmic dense physical plane and the Lives that evolve through it. They reflect energies from the cosmic mental and astral planes into systemic space. Here can clearly be seen the numerical affinity of the third, fourth and fifth Creative Hierarchies, and that the third reflects the subjective work of the first (the number 12) into manifestation via spiral-cyclic motion:

| | | |
|---|---|---|
| 8 x 1 x 12 | Taurus | third Creative Hierarchy |
| 8 x 2 x 12 | Gemini | fourth Creative Hierarchy |
| 8 x 8 x 12 | Cancer | fifth Creative Hierarchy |

The fourth reflects the work of the second (the number 24), and the fifth has a similar function regarding the third. These three Hierarchies delineate the qualities of the 3-4-5 or right-angled triangle, the triangle of Initiation. As abovementioned, the 96 + 192 + 768 petals = 1056 (11 x 96) petals of the fully vivified Head centre *(sahasrāra padma).* When the number 24 of the second Creative Hierarchy is added, then the sacred number 1080 is obtained, whilst the 12 petals of the first Creative Hierarchy represent the over-all patterning of the Head lotus.

When the numbers of the third and fourth Creative Hierarchies are added together, then the number 288 (144 x 2, 6 x 48 or 12 x 12 x 2) is obtained.[35] The number 12 x 12 (144) is of considerable significance. For instance, it refers to the 'hundred and forty and four thousand of all the tribes of the children of Israel' that had 'the seal of the living God'.[36] This number effectively relates to the complete expression of all twelve Creative Hierarchies, or of the movement of the zodiacal

35 Similarly, if the number 768 is subtracted from the number 1056 of the petals of the Head centre, then the number 288 is the gain.

36 *Rev. 7:3-17.*

signs around the zodiac. When multiplied by two, then this number signifies the reflected expression of the energies of these Creative Hierarchies into manifested space. This is accomplished via the fifth Creative Hierarchy and the eight gates (or directions) that it wields.

Note that there are 3,000 cycles of 144 years to make the 432,000 years attributed to the *kali yuga*. When the number 144 is divided into the 311,040,000,000,000 earth days of a divine year of 360 days for an age of Brahmā (or one hundred years of His divine years), then we get the number 2,160,000,000,000. This is one great month of such a year of Brahmā. (The number 2,160 relates to the duration of the number of years of one zodiacal sign during the precession of the equinoxes. One great zodiacal year on earth is therefore 25,920 years. There are 12,000,000,000 such great years in one year of Brahmā.)

The glyph veiling the fifth Creative Hierarchy is:

**Figure 41. The glyph for Cancer**

The glyph for Cancer represents the claws of the crab (Logoic Desire) holding the jewel of manifestation firmly in their grasp. The non-liberated and liberated portions of this fifth Hierarchy form the seed germ for the yin-yang concept, the masculine-feminine polarity associated with all of manifested space. The interrelation sustains evolutionary Being via the sex-drive in its esoteric connotations. This Creative Hierarchy works to resolve all dualities.

In further analysing the number 288, or 6 x 48 (6 x 6 x 8), we see that it concerns the *maṇḍala* of the hexagram, the Womb of formed space, through which consciousness may arise. The number 6 x 6 is a way of numerologically writing 66, or 666, signifying a material body of manifestation. The number 8 implicates the spiral-cyclic motion that will eventually convert substance, the hexagrams of formed space (6 x 6), into consciousness-attributes.

The groupings of 6 x 48 Entities form a *maṇḍala* of the hexagram (a symbol of the angelic kingdom). They embody the substance of all forms in their entirety.

The number 6 x 48 can also be viewed as a trinity of Entities manifesting through the systemic planes. Each group of 48 can be considered to be dual, where one group of 24 Entities is inwardly focussed, and the other group of 24 is outwardly focussed into objectivity. Therefore, 144 members of the third and fourth Creative Hierarchies will be positively engaged in sending energies to the Lives incarnated in systemic space. The focus of these Entities is via those members of the fifth Creative Hierarchy that are externalised, thus who have not yet gained their liberation.

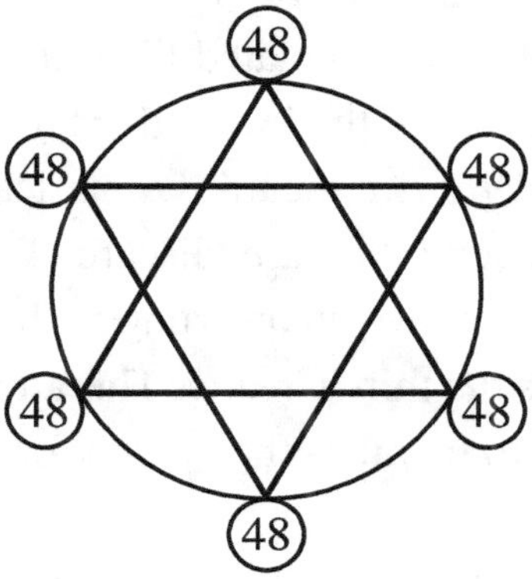


**Figure 42. The Logoic hexagram**

- The energies from the first group of 3 x 48 (12 x 12) Entities (the upward pointing triad) manifest via (or impel) the first group of the fifth Creative Hierarchy that are externalised in the first cosmic dense sub-plane *(ādi)*. They manifest in conjunction with the sixth Creative Hierarchy, the Divine Flames (Leo). The main focus of the Divine Flames, therefore, is upwards towards cosmic astral space.
- The energies from the second group of 2 x 48 (8 x 12) Entities (of the downward pointing triad) manifest via the second group of the fifth Creative Hierarchy that manifests upon the second sub-plane *(anupādaka)*. They manifest in conjunction with the seventh Creative Hierarchy (Virgo), the Divine Builders.
- The energies from the third group of 48 (4 x 12) Entities manifest via the third group of the fifth Creative Hierarchy. They are externalised in the third sub-plane *(ātma)*. This energy conditions the four lower planes of perception via the work of the eighth Creative Hierarchy (Libra), the Lesser Builders. The conditionings wherein humanity finds scope for evolutionary attainment are thereby created.

The interrelationship between the Divine and Lesser Builders principally concerns building the groundwork for the evolutionary process that produces the Individualisation of animal-man. (Consequently awakening the fourth kingdom in Nature.) Humanity can then walk the way of Initiation, eventually to ascend out of the ranks of the fourth Creative Hierarchy. As they do this, they manifest the process that also liberates the fifth Creative Hierarchy. Their need to be incarnate in cosmic dense space consequently evaporates.

Interestingly, there is also an associated liberation, or driving into full self-consciousness, of the members of the lower, third (or tenth) Creative Hierarchy (Makara). To help produce *pralaya,* the third esoterically merges with the fourth Hierarchy, the lowest two Hierarchies are 'discarded' (to be recycled), whilst the remaining nine move on. All move up one rung of the 'ladder of evolution', thus the merged fourth becomes the third Creative Hierarchy. One Hierarchy (Pisces) is abstracted, leaving eight to manifest the motion for seeding the activity for the next great manvantaric cycle.

The upward pointing triangle can be considered to consist of 3 x 24 (72) members of the fifth Creative Hierarchy, who dance in a spiral-eight fashion with a similar number of the sixth Creative Hierarchy (the Divine Flames). As they do so, the spiral motion simultaneously weaves the energies of the third Creative Hierarchy into the planetary structure by 'en-Flaming' the Divine Flames with Logoic Purpose. The number 72 (6 x 12) relates to the sign Virgo, the great Mother, who embodies the matrix of substance that is the Womb of time and space. The number 3 x 24 allows the passing of energies and information (mantric Sounds) between the subjective Head centre existing in cosmic astral substance (of the five liberated Creative Hierarchies), with its correspondence[37] existing in cosmic dense physical space. The interrelated groups of 72 Entities produce the number 144, with the esoteric significance already outlined above. The indicated trinity (of 24 petals) concerns the ability to process or project the needed triune Fiery (Mahatic) energies of Father-Son-Mother.

The downward pointing triangle can be considered to consist of two groupings. Firstly, 2 x 24 (48) members of the fifth Creative Hierarchy that form the Ājñā centre, integrated with a similar number of the seventh Creative Hierarchy (the

37 The innermost tier of petals of the Shambhalic Head centre consists of twenty-four petals. There are also 2 x 12 outermost petals. The permutations of the number 24 largely govern the manifestation of the Head lotus. For instance, the number 1056 when divided by 24 gives the number 44.

Divine Builders). This also happens via a spiral-eight motion upon the plane *anupādaka* that integrates the two Hierarchies in a dance of information and energies. As they do so, the spiral motion simultaneously weaves the energies of cosmic Love from the fourth Creative Hierarchy into the planetary structure.

The Ājñā centre (the third Eye) possesses two lobes of 48 petals each, related to the conveyance of *iḍā* and *piṅgalā nāḍīs* to and from the manifest form. The spiral-eight 'dance' thus also relates to the movement of energies between these two lobes and the interrelated Creative Hierarchies that occupy the associated petals.[38] The arrangement is not as simple as one Hierarchy occupying one lobe and another the other, but rather in the manner shown in Figure 17 (page 354) of my book *An Esoteric Exposition of the Bardo Thödol,* Part A. The *iḍā* petal will contain a majority of the members of the seventh Creative Hierarchy, whilst the *piṅgalā* petal will mainly consist of members of the fifth Creative Hierarchy. This integrated arrangement allows a Logos to Peer into and rightly direct all manifest space, organising correctly the constituency of the Womb of space-time. These forces or factors that condition this Womb play upon and through *saṃsāra*. This centre is thus concerned with directing the Life principle in manifestation. By virtue of its petals, the Ājñā centre is also uniquely adapted for someone within the Logoic Body of manifestation to see through into cosmic space at will.

The third grouping of 48 petals of this downward pointing triangle consists of 24 members of the fifth Creative Hierarchy, who form spiral-eight motions with the major centres below the head. As they do so, they also draw the energies of the cosmic law of Attraction via a spiral-cyclic dance with a similar number of members of the fourth Creative Hierarchy. The function of this dance of energies is to help draw the positively generated *prāṇas* upwards towards the Head centre (Shambhala) for appropriate processing. They also appropriately govern and process the expression of the associated evolving Lives, according to the directives of the law of Economy wielded by the fifth Creative Hierarchy.

The distribution of the members of this Hierarchy can be considered as four for the four main petals of the Throat centre, seven for the seven sacred petals of the Heart centre. There are five members for the upward pointing hand of the Solar Plexus centre, as well as three for the upward pointing triad of petals of the Sacral

---

38 The upwards and downwards motion of the eights, plus the lateral motion between the two lobes of the Ājñā centre form *viśvavajras*, which allow an awakened being to possess multidimensional visioning. (See my book *An Esoteric Exposition of the Bardo Thödol, Part A*, 58, *ff.*, for an explanation of these.)

centre. There are two for the north-south axis of the Base of Spine centre, and three for the upwards pointing triad of petals of the twelve-petalled Splenic centre I.

The 72, 48 and 24 members of the fifth Creative Hierarchy who are still incarnate in cosmic physical space make the number 144. One can deduce that the number 12 x 12 also helps in the integration of the needed astrological attributes upon our planet as the earth cycles through its course in the heavens. These Beings anchor and fix in space the energies from the zodiacal constellations as the earth continues to do so.

As the reader can by now deduce, it is not easy to do more than provide a general outline as to the dynamic moving functions of these Lords of Life. (Distortions in perception thus can easily happen.) The true picture is not simple, because the sixth, seventh and eighth Creative Hierarchies also manifest functions as part of the three main tiers of the Head centre of our planetary Logos (Shambhala). Thus there is a Throat in the Head centre function (the sixth Creative Hierarchy), a Heart in the Head centre function (the seventh Creative Hierarchy) and a Solar Plexus in the Head centre function (the eighth Creative Hierarchy). This relates to our planetary system (a non-sacred planet), rather than of the solar Logos. There is consequently a spiral-eight between the cosmic astral centres occupied by the liberated Hierarchies and their correspondences upon the seven systemic planes of perception. Interrelated with this Head centre function are the attributes associated with the other main centres in the body. The attributes that *concern the main centres* in the body of the planetary Logos are the topic of discussion here.

When relating to the Creative Hierarchies, the principal concern is with building the forms through which consciousness can evolve. For most of evolutionary time, the Lesser Builders (mostly in the form of angelic Triads) rule manifest space.

The energies of the third of the liberated Creative Hierarchies are 'grounded' in the Divine Flames. Those of the fourth liberated Creative Hierarchy are 'grounded' in the activities of the Greater Builders. Similarly, those of the fifth liberated Creative Hierarchy are 'grounded' in the Lesser Builders.

When the 48 petals of the major *chakras* below the Head centre are added to the number 2 x 48 petals of the Ājñā centre then 3 x 48 main petals are produced for the overall schema. They are therefore directly receptive to (or expressions of) the guiding impulses of the energies from the downward pointing hexagram of Figure 42.

The significance of the number 4 x 12, which numerologically symbolises Cancer (the fourth sign of the zodiac) is by now plainly evident. This is especially so when considering the fact that Cancer is designated as the sign of birthing into incarnation. This therefore hints at some of the factors underlying a planetary evolutionary process. The significance of the number 48 here concerns the organisation of the Lesser Builders (the wielders of the karmic dispensation upon the plane *ātma)* into creative activity. As the fifth Creative Hierarchy has to yet gain liberation from cosmic dense space, so members of this Hierarchy are able to produce the above interrelationships. Because their *antaḥkaraṇas* are projected into the Mother's Womb, so *manvantara* is possible. The fifth Hierarchy therefore acts as a mirror, whereby the qualities of the Hierarchies upon the lowest three of the cosmic astral sub-planes can be projected into dense form to impact upon the plane *ātma*. This plane thereby bears the imprint of cosmic *karma* as wielded by the Lesser Builders. From them comes the substance of the petals of the various *chakras* in the body of the planetary Logos that remains, after that which is embodied by the fifth Creative Hierarchy has been accounted for. The purpose of the activity of the Lesser Builders is to seed the evolving Lives with the factor of mind. This activity is mainly upon the Inner Round sequence of *chakras,* in order to eventually help produce the appearance of a human kingdom (Individualisation). They then also help fan the flames of mind in humanity.

Together there are 48 main petals to the minor centres:

- There are 16 main petals of the Throat centre, deriving energies from the *ātmic* plane (the Lesser Builders).
- There are 12 main petals to the Heart centre, relating to the *buddhic* plane (the Human Hierarchy).
- There are 10 main petals to the Solar Plexus centre, relating to the mental plane, and the tenth Creative Hierarchy, Makara the Mystery.
- There are 6 main petals to the Sacral centre, relating to the etheric plane and the eleventh Creative Hierarchy, the Lunar Lords.
- There are 4 main petals to the Base of Spine centre, relating to the dense physical plane and the last of the Creative Hierarchies, the Elemental Lives.

When analysing the petals of the major *chakras* governed by the Lesser Builders, then two groups of *chakras* and their accompanying *prāṇas* must be counted. The first group consists of the Throat, Heart, Solar Plexus and Sacral centres. The second grouping consists of the Base of Spine and Splenic centres.

After the four major petals occupied by the fifth Creative Hierarchy have been subtracted from the sixteen petals of the Throat centre, then twelve petals remain. These twelve petals are mainly concerned with the reception of energies from the zodiacal gates that must be disseminated as a *manasic* impetus into the planetary body via the Inner Round *chakras*. Because the sacred petals of the Heart centre are governed by the fifth Creative Hierarchy, so the remaining five petals are governed by the Lesser Builders. These non-sacred petals project a qualified pentad of *prāṇas* upwards to the Head centre. The five petalled downward-pointed hand of the Solar Plexus centre governed by the Lesser Builders is mainly concerned with projecting their manasic impetus into the Inner Round. Similarly, the three downward pointing petals of the Sacral centre are mainly concerned with the generation of *iḍā, piṇgalā* and *suṣumṇā nāḍīs,* which will later be projected upwards to sustain the entire *nāḍī* system. These petals are also anchors for the zodiacal potencies from the Throat centre. (These potencies therefore manifest as triads from the Sacral centre.) The zodiacal energies that manifest at any time must be infused into the *nāḍīs* so that the entire body of manifestation can be vitalised by their effects.

Taking all of the petals governed by the Lesser Builders into account, there are therefore 25 petals distributing five pentads (25 = 5 x 5) of *prāṇas.* With respect to this, the twelve zodiacal gates of the Throat centre manifest as a pair of petals at any one time (of the zodiacal potency that is then manifesting, plus its polar opposite). Its energies are then channelled into the planetary *nāḍī* system via the available triad of petals of the Sacral centre. (This centre always relates to the process of the vitalisation of any activity.) The combination of the pair of petals with the triad from the Sacral centre provides the needed pentad that allow the projection of the *vayus.* (The five types of *prāṇas.*)

When considering the second group of *chakras,* one must firstly consider the downward pointing triad of Splenic centre I, sending *prāṇas* via Splenic centre II to the east-west petals of the Base of Spine centre. This centre then processes these *prāṇas* in accordance with its connections to the Inner Round, or sends the qualified results upwards. Together with the abovementioned 25 petals, this makes a hexagon of 30 petals (6 x 5). There is also an incoming stream of *prāṇas* coming from the Inner Round to be processed either in an east or west direction by a triad of petals of Splenic centre I and one axis of Splenic centre II. (It is an eight-petalled lotus.) These *prāṇas* are of an Earthy nature. This produces a septenary of petals (35 = 7 x 5) that can process the Ray attributes of the manasic

Earthy-Watery *prāṇas* concerned. (The Solar Plexus centre mainly processes the Watery *prāṇas* developed by the human kingdom.) The petals occupied by members of the fifth Creative Hierarchy process the Fiery *prāṇas* developed by humanity, plus those of the two higher Elements.

The 768 petals (Beings) associated with the *fifth Creative Hierarchy* (Cancer) also vitalise the outer Knowledge tier of petals of the nine petalled lotus of the Logoic Soul. This number can relate to the associated triad of petals.

**48 (4 x 12) petals (0.5 x 96)**

They relate to *the Father,* the Knowledge-Will petal of the Egoic Lotus of the planetary Logos. These 48 petals from the Head centre manifest as a quaternary associated with the Throne of 'God'. They manifest as four groups of 12 petals each, where each group empowers one or other of the four cosmic ethers. They manifest as a Base of Spine centre for the sum of manifestation. Here one can think of the attributes of the four and twenty Elders reflecting the energies of the twelve signs of the zodiac to condition the Mother's Womb via the twelve-fold ordering of all the main petals of the Head centre. The energies from the Throat in the Head are directed to this Knowledge-Will petal.

**144 (12 x 12) petals (1.5 x 96)**

They relate to *the Son,* or Knowledge-Love-Wisdom petal of the Egoic Lotus of the planetary Logos. They imply the inherent duality of the Son or Consciousness principle as He prepares to abstract Himself into the Father, whilst supporting the activities of the Mother. The Son organises the *prāṇas* of the twelve main petals of the Head lotus towards the inner tiers of petals of this centre. This happens in accordance with the Son's receptivity to zodiacal and Hierarchical attributes. The energies from the Heart in the Head are directed to this Knowledge-Love-Wisdom petal.

**576 (4 x 144, 12 x 48) petals (6 x 96)**

They relate to *the Mother* or Knowledge-Knowledge petal that becomes the *maṇḍalic* matrix to dispense the attributes of the six Creative Hierarchies above the fourth (humanity). They are directly concerned with the active processes of the evolution of a *manvantara.* These Creative Hierarchies incorporate the third liberated Creative Hierarchy (the Elements) down to the eighth (the Lesser Builders). They bear the energies or Purpose of Logoic Mind (Mahat) into manifestation. These energies vitalise all of the *chakras* of the Logoic Personality so that they conform to Logoic Purpose via the activities of the Mother. The number 12 x 48 indicates that the Mother is conditioned by twelve groups of petals. This allows the qualities of all of the twelve Creative Hierarchies to be expressed in the manifest form. (Each manifests in a similar fashion as the number 48 of the Father petal of the Egoic lotus.) The number 4 x 144 signifies the ability to manifest as a quaternary (a Seat of Power) that disseminates the zodiacal potencies into the sum of the formed realms. The number 12 x 48 represents the extensions of the twelve zodiacal gates that open and close according to the turning of the great wheel.

From the above perspective, the first of the seven manifest Creative Hierarchies (the Divine Flames) can simply be said to be composed of twelve petals or entities. From another perspective, this Hierarchy represents the sum of the Head lotus, synthesising all the qualities of the Hierarchies that are below it. Their title 'the Divine Flames' indicates that they en-Flame with the energies of cosmic Mind the sum of the manifesting Purpose of the Logoic Head lotus. The seven manifest Creative Hierarchies are thereby viewed in terms of the seven major *chakras*. When taking the Head lotus into account, the number of Directing Entities to be counted for a solar system can be deduced to be:

| | |
|---|---|
| The inner 12 that govern the entire schema | = 12 |
| The inner 108 of the three Synthesising centres | = 324 |
| The inner 48 of the seven sacred planets | = 336 |
| The inner 24 of the five non-sacred planets | = 120 |
| The inner 12 of the 22 members of the Inner Round | = 264 |
| | 1056 |

The inner 12 petals of the Head centre are attuned to the major 12 petals of the outermost tier of petals, thereby integrating the entire structure of the inner and outer form. This pentad of expression can be considered to relate to the projection into manifestation of the 'five Elements' as viewed from the perspective of a solar Logos.

This list can be divided into two groups. First, the grand governing Council, related to the Synthesising centres (Uranus I, Neptune II and Saturn III). This consists of 324 + 12 = 336 great Beings. They are the overall governing Body under the auspices of the solar Logos. The number 336 = 7 x 48, where the number 7 relates to the mode of dissemination of the seven Rays to govern the sum of manifest space via the many permutations of the number 48 discussed above. The permutations of the number 12 in the four directions of space relate to the dissemination of the energies of Love-Wisdom via the Heart centre, which is the objective of this solar Incarnation.

The three remaining groups represent the mode of Activity for the energies and Directives of this great Inner Council. Together there are 720 great Beings. The number 720 = 15 x 48, as well as 5 x 144. The numbers 5 and 15 represent the attributes of MIND (Mahat), the cosmic *prāṇas* that are accordingly disseminated throughout the entire solar form. This MIND is the gain of the past solar Incarnation, but which is now directed via the turning of the petals of the Heart centre in the modes of the 4 x 12 and 12 x 12 Entities discussed above. Other permutations of this great Council are obviously possible, such as would produce the numbers 1068, 1080 and 1,200.

## The Womb of *saṃsāra*

The vision so far was from above down, but now the conditionings within the Womb of space-time must be analysed. The focus is upon humanity, the fourth Creative Hierarchy (counting from below up), for they are the apex or purpose of attainment within that Womb. This kingdom is the great transmutative agent in the scheme of things. The failures from past aeons of evolution, the dark brotherhood (the former reject substance) thus again have opportunity to achieve their evolutionary purpose. The three upcoming Hierarchies can also be tried in the crucible of experience, seeded with the agency of mind and watered with the principle of Love. They thereby also must evolve into a human kingdom, so that enlightened Minds can eventually awaken that can free themselves from the conditionings of that Womb.

When the fourth Creative Hierarchy came into existence (as the kingdom of Souls under Scorpionic influence) they created a whorl of forces upon *buddhic* levels. The bud petals of the Logoic Heart awakened. As humanity developed the necessary qualities through the appearance of the Hierarchy of enlightened Being, so that Logoic Heart centre began to blossom. Members of the human kingdom thereby arose that could take over the functions of governing the lower *chakras* of our planetary Logos, to eventually supplant the members of the second and third Creative Hierarchies (the Greater and Lesser Builders) that formerly ruled manifest space. This is the consequence of the process of liberation from the woe of *saṃsāric* conditionings for all of these Hierarchies. This process will also supplant the functioning of the fifth Creative Hierarchy (Cancer) as petals of the Logoic *chakras* and so assist this Hierarchy to gain their emancipation from cosmic physical substance. The process also necessitates the moving upwards of the tenth Creative Hierarchy (Capricorn) into self-consciousness.

The 768 (8 x 8 x 12) groupings of petals, for the outermost Solar Plexus tier of expression of the Head lotus of the planetary Logos, are mainly concerned with processing the Watery *prāṇas* that are the mainstay of human evolution.[39] As stated, the number 8 x 8 refers to the invocation of spiral-cyclic motion via the superimposed levels of the eight points of the compass that delineate the directions in space. These directions represent the pathways via which the potencies of any Creative Hierarchy (the number twelve) can manifest. As also stated, this activity is governed by the pattern of the general spiral-cyclic motion of the 768 petals associated with the fifth Creative Hierarchy. The overall evolution of the major petals in the Head centres of humanity (or of a planetary Logos) come to the fore here.

The expression of this number also concerns the way that the Heart centre influences the Solar Plexus activity of humanity. Thus, if the number 768 is divided by 12 (the major petals to the Heart centre) then 12 x 8 x 8 is obtained. This number relates to the mode of spiral-cyclic motion of the activities of the Heart on all levels of expression.

The Throat centre also has a direct relation to the number 768, for if the number 768 is divided by 16, then 16 groups of 48 (4 + 12) petals are obtained. Thus here is seen the mode of vitalisation of the Throat centre, which governs the assimilation and projection of the Fires of Mind (or of intelligence) by a human unit. This is seen by the fact that as each of the 12 signs of the zodiac turn, wherein that sign manifests its purpose, so the four main petals of this centre are directly energised by it. The zodiacal input, plus the four responses (e.g., of the four Elements, or of the energies from the four lower kingdoms in Nature, or of the energies from the four cosmic ethers), make the number 5, wherein Mahat or *manas* can be expressed. The number 16 x 48 can also be considered as 16 x 12 petals projected towards the four directions in space (making thus the Seat of Power of Mind in manifestation), allowing complete control of the four Elements.[40]

The 16 main petals of the Throat centre can also be subdivided into the three levels of expression relating to the triune abstract Deity, when viewed from their own integral level of expression. In this consideration, the number 48 here relates to the possible energy flows, along either an *iḍā* or *piṅgalā* nature, that can flow from the 96 innermost petals of this *chakra*.[41]

---

39 See my book *An Esoteric Exposition of the Bardo Thödol,* part A, 428.

40 See Ibid., 424, for further information concerning the number 16 x 12.

41 For the mode of expression of the Throat centre, see my book *An Esoteric Exposition of the Bardo Thödol,* part B, 22-39. Note that the main petals of all of the major *chakras,* except for

The relation of the petals of the Throat centre to the Solar Plexus in the Head centre can be seen as:

| | | |
|---|---|---|
| 1 x 48 | = | the Father aspect, oriented north. |
| 3 x 48 | = | the Son aspect, where one or other of the three remaining directions are taken into account by the remaining major petals. |
| 12 x 48 | = | the Mother aspect, where the twelve subsidiary petals wield zodiacal energies (or from the twelve petals of the Heart centre) via any grouping of 48 innermost petals. |

The four major petals become the inner Throne or Seat of Power that turns or empowers the outer twelve (3 x 4). Together they also present an arrangement of four groups of four whereby the square of manifestation (depicted in Figure 40) may also function. The Throat can thereby emanate the Words of Power *(mantras)* that cause the entire material universe to come into manifestation, in accordance with the orientation of the qualities of any of the four directions in space.

The number 16 also equals 2 x 8, implying the basic spiral-cyclic motion – the interrelation of positive and negative (yin-yang) polarities that is the mainstay of evolutionary progression.

The Heart and Throat centres absorb the *prāṇas* developed from the centres below the diaphragm, plus from the Inner Round minor centres. The general *iḍā nāḍī prāṇas* are anchored in the Throat centre, and the *piṇgalā nāḍī prāṇas* are anchored in the Heart centre. After being processed in these two centres they move upwards to the Head centre via the Ājñā centre. The *iḍā nāḍī* stream moves via the left lobe and the *piṇgalā nāḍī* stream moves via the right lobe of the Ājñā centre. This centre overlaps some of the petals of the Head centre, thus together they form a functioning unity. The *iḍā* and *piṇgalā prāṇas* from the 2 x 48 petals of the Ājñā centre thereby circulate and awaken the 1056 petals of the Head centre. From this perspective we see how in every way possible the Ājñā centre becomes the All-seeing Eye – the directive Eye of 'God' and of the enlightened human unit wishing to Peer into all aspects of cosmic space.

By now it will be obvious how much is hid in numbers. We saw, for instance, that the number 72 (6 x 12) symbolises the qualities of the sixth sign of the zodiac (Virgo). Virgo embodies the Womb of space-time, within which the Christ-Child (the consciousness aspect) grows and matures. Virgo also governs the sixth Creative Hierarchy (the Divine Builders) counting from below up, who hold the substance

---

the two Head centres, are derived from an inner tier of 96 minor petals.

of that Womb in their embrace.[42] These Builders are responsible for overseeing the building of the forms (the Causal bodies of our Souls) that can bear human consciousness. The next Creative Hierarchy (the fifth counting from below up), the Lesser Builders, sacrifice themselves to be the substance of human Causal bodies. Others of their ranks are also builders of the forms of all Life incarnate in the three realms of human livingness. The Builders are the *devas* that embody the forms of the Life that evolve within the confines of our solar sphere.

Collectively, the Lesser Builders are the great Mother. She is concerned with projecting the four main Elements from the four cosmic ethers to govern the planes of Causation. These Elements are the underlying substance of manifestation and with them the *karma* of what must be is incorporated into the substance of things. The Elements condition the 'Waters' of the Womb. Therein She further modifies and qualifies Logoic Purpose while the Divine Child grows in space through time. The Love of the Son (the awakening human Hierarchy) assists the activity of the Mother when humanity becomes increasingly conscious and then compassionately receptive to Her energies. The various tiers of petals of the Head centre are thereby awakened, whilst the path of Initiation is trod, whereby eventually the fourth Initiation is attained. Liberation from the conditionings of *saṃsāra* is thereby attained, and so the Hierarchy of Love and Light evolve. The Lesser Builders that embodied the substance of the Causal form are also thereby liberated, and so gain their own next level of Initiation attainment.

---

42 Note the relationship of the number 72 here to the number 720 = 72 x 10 mentioned above, which links a ten-signed to a twelve-signed zodiac.

# 8

# The Tablets of Revelation

These tablets (which I painted in 1979) are intended as aids in visualisation for the qualities of each of the signs of the zodiac. On each card the rulers and qualities associated with that sign are presented from three angles of perception (levels of interpretation). They are the exoteric (or normal) rulers, the esoteric rulers that govern the life of the disciple, and the Hierarchical rulers, governing the activities of the higher Initiates. The colours presented in the Tablets are meant to convey information of a symbolic nature. They but imitate the colourings they are intended to portray, as it is impossible to depict the intensely vibrant hues of the subtle realms by means of paint. Accordingly, colours must be considered to veil the real, a view from the angle of perception of one incarnate in dense form. Turquoise, for instance, is the colour I have sometimes utilised to indicate the quality of the sixth Ray that manifests through the astral plane in a way that affects the human kingdom. It relates to the energies of aspiration and the creative imagination. However, the sixth Ray can also be depicted by pink, where it specifically relates to devotion and a more Watery (emotional) aspiration. Astral colourings specifically can change entirely from one type of emotional perception to another. This is seen in the colourings normally attributed to a person's aura. Turquoise refines into a sky blue when aspirational perception becomes the intuition.

The colour images of the respective tablets are presented on the inside covers of this book. This chapter will contain some information that has already been presented earlier, for some repetition is needed to explain the symbolism of the cards. Much new information concerning the signs they treat will also be presented.

**Plate 1. Aries**

## Aries

The central figure in *Aries* symbolises a Logos, because the first Ray energy of the Will (which is disseminated by Aries) is directed by such a Being. This sign is concerned with all beginnings, stemming from the Mind of 'God', which initiates all cycles and sustains Being. Sanat Kumāra is the Logos for our planetary sphere. He is the One Initiator, the Ancient of Days, the 'first and the last', the One Who sits on the Throne (of 'God').[1] In the Bible, this Being is termed Melchisedek.[2]

*The blood-red robe* is the energy of the principle of Life that sustains manifest Being. This wine energy emanates from the sixth cosmic astral sub-plane and manifests in the form of the combined sixth and seventh Ray energies on earth. It is the energy of:

> 'the great winepress of the wrath of God. And the winepress was trodden without the city, and blood came out of the winepress'.[3]

The force of the energy turning this 'winepress' can be considered to come from Aries. Aries turns the zodiacal wheel from epoch to epoch until eventually the 'Blood' of compassionate undertaking is evolved by humanity.

The *aura* radiating from the figure is an even more intense red than that of the robe, directly pertaining to the energy of the Will conveyed by Aries.

The Logos is coloured *blue,* the colour of the Love-Wisdom. This is the fundamental hue or radiation of the present solar evolution. The first and second Ray energies work together as a unity.

The *golden ornaments*, crown, etc., symbolise His enlightenment, the fully awakened Head lotus (for the planet), producing spiritual prosperity for all. Gold is the most noble metal, symbolic of the philosopher's stone. This indicates that the Logos has completely mastered the transmutative aspects associated with divine Alchemy for our planetary sphere.

Directly facing us are three major points to the *crown.* They relate to the Will, Love-Wisdom and Divine Activity (the extended crown) of Deity. In the next tier down, there are also five points to the extended crown that relate to the attributes of the five Dhyāni Buddhas. These five points signify the mode of projection of Logoic Mind (Mahat) into the sum of manifestation. They also imply that there are five more points to consider, to make ten points altogether. This relates to the ten-petalled zodiac. There are also ten petals governing a Solar Plexus centre.

Together, the five plus three points symbolise the eight directions of space. These directions are also part of the twelve-petalled lotus, signifying the powers of the Logoic Heart manifesting in the eight directions of space. From one perspective, the Logoic Heart centre is veiled by the six main points to the crown, if the back

1 See *The Revelation of St. John,* chapters 1:8 and 4:2.

2 *Heb. 7:1-4.*

3 *Rev: 14:19-20.*

three points are added (for the number six is half of twelve). The *maṇḍala* of the hexagram, however, is directly implicated, which as earlier stated, governs the manifestation of the sum of *saṃsāra*.

The bottom circle of the crown has six jewels upon it. When extended around the crown, they signify the twelve main petals to the Head centre and the turning of the twelve signs of the zodiac. With the other two tiers, the bottom circle of the crown symbolises the major triplicity to the Head centre. This triplicity relates to the Logoic Throat in the Head, Heart in the Head and Solar Plexus in the Head. Here, the Heart in the Head is symbolised by the band with the gems, and sits closest – directly upon the head of the Logos. (For the energies of the Heart are what must govern all.) The Throat in the Head is symbolised by the ten-pointed tier, which signifies the conveyance of Mahat into manifestation. The Solar Plexus in the Head is signified by the six-pointed crown, which implicates the Sacral centre energies of Logoic Desire. This Desire governs the manifest activity of the 768 petals of the outer tier of the Head centre. This Sacral activity has the capacity to integrate the Watery *prāṇas* from the cosmic astral plane into the planetary manifestation. As it does so, then the response produces Nature's Solar Plexus centre activity. Together there are six plus ten points to this crown, just as there are six plus ten petals to the combined Sacral and Solar Plexus centres.

The *dark blue sword* – of the *dharmakāya* (Manjushri's sword), signifies the first and second Ray qualities (the Divine Will that cuts and pierces and the blue of Love-Wisdom) needed to liberate the Life embodying the form nature. (The generation of the qualities to sever all ties with *saṃsāra*.) The sword symbolises Fiery aspiration, the means to cut away illusions at their roots, as well as the *antaḥkaraṇa* that can project energies to where needed. It also signifies the energies from the central channel in the spinal column *(suṣumṇa nāḍī).*

The *emerald throne* and aura behind the head signify the gain of the evolution of the past solar system (thus it forms the basis to this one). It is the third Ray of Mathematically Exact Activity that underlies their initiating Wills, which is therefore embodied by all planetary Logoi. This Ray allows them to wield the cosmic law of *karma* via the ātmic plane (the fifth plane of perception) in order to govern *saṃsāra*. These karmic Lords can thereby instigate the beginning and ending of things. With the central deep blue, this Ray signifies the colour of Logoic Compassion. This emanates (as an attribute of the Mind) the Sacrificial Fire that becomes the Flame of the Throne and of the Sword. The *throne* is symbolic of the material universe (the Base of Spine centre) upon which the Logos sits.

*Orange and yellow Fires* signify the Fires of the Mind admixed with *buddhi* – that is needed to create or destroy the manifestation of all-Being. Aries signifies initial mental beginnings, which this Fire implicates, but what is also seen is that the underlying Mind directing the Fire is Green.

Of the *gold and white radiations* of the aura, white relates to absolute purity, and the gold is explained above. Here the white also relates to the *iḍā* and the gold to the *piṇgalā* emanations. They are aspects of the presented Divine Will of the Logos.

The *indigo sky* relates to the second Ray of Love-Wisdom quality of our solar Logos that bathes all with its Presence. The *light blue* in the distance indicates the approach of the dawn of time and manifest being – of any new cycle of expression, which Aries initiates.

The indigo blue *book of Life* held in the right hand by the Logos contains all wisdom. It has seven seals[4] that symbolise the seven *chakras,* planes of perception (etc.). They are arranged in the division 5 + 2. The number 5 relates to the constitution of Brahmā, the five Rays, planes of perception and Elements. All are associated with the development of the enlightened (abstract) Mind – with the perfection of humanity as such. The number 2 here symbolises what is beyond Mind: the highest two Rays (Will and Love-Wisdom) and planes of perception.

The colours of the five main seals: red, indigo blue, green, gold and violet relate to the Rays that are responsible for the forthcoming Aquarian dispensation. The two subsidiary colours (pink and orange) are the two Rays (the sixth and fifth) that are now mostly going out of manifestation because their energies have become too aberrant in the present cycle.

Note also that in interpreting left from right, one must view from the position of the seated figure.

The *violet-purple colouring* of the (ram's) horns is the basic seventh Ray colouring of etheric space via which all energies must manifest. They take the form of trumpets blown by two serpents. Their esoteric meanings are explained in my book: *The Buddha Womb and the Way to Liberation.* Therein the ram's horns are explained in relation to Figure 4.

The involution and evolution of the entire evolutionary process is indicated here, which the Ram drives onwards. Specifically, however, it is concerned with the initial impetus and then the abstraction process back to the source.

---

4 See *The Revelation of St. John,* chapter 5.

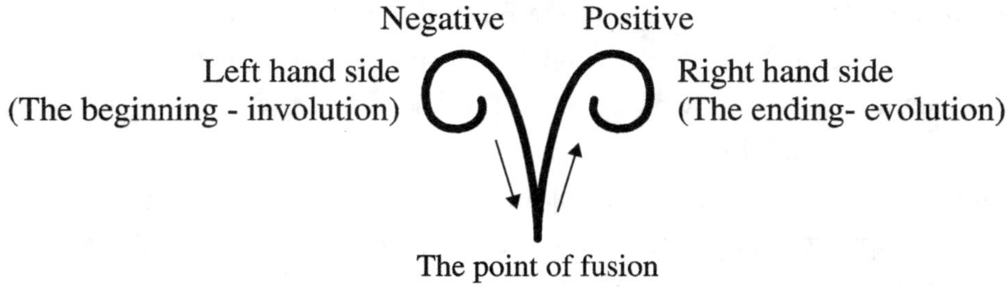


**Figure 43. The Ram's horns**

The *trumpets* announce the Sounds or mantras that command the emanation of substance – the word of 'God', of creation, manifesting in the form of spirals symbolising the paths of evolution. They also sound the mantric dispensation for the new Aquarian epoch. The right spiral indicates the evolutionary path taken by the human kingdom and the white magician (or white *dharma).* The left spiral indicates the path taken by the path of descent into matter, and also of the black magician that fights against the evolutionary direction.

The *yellow and blue serpents* here symbolise the right and left psychic channels, *piṅgalā* (blue) and *iḍā* (yellow) *nāḍīs.* The central column is the *suṣumṇa nāḍī,* through which *kuṇḍalinī* is said to flow so as to liberate the disciple. It also takes the form of a male sperm (when related to the trumpets, but they can also symbolise the ovaries). The complex symbol associated with these three *nāḍīs* indicates the imminent potential of the creation of an entirely new universe, wherein the Christ-Child can be born and evolve.

The *sandals* of the Logos are oriented to the *piṅgalā nāḍī* because the evolution of consciousness (and consequently of Love-Wisdom) is the objective of the evolutionary cycle. The sandals are golden and show the trinity underlying the manifestation of all forms and of divinity. They are united by an *antaḥkaraṇa,* which must be developed as one treads the path on earth. The *antaḥkaraṇa* uniting the three golden straps also forms a fixed cross pattern, which symbolises the evolution of consciousness to eventually become a crucified Christ on this cross.

The underlying geometric symbols epitomise the three aspects of divinity, the triune abstract forces that together constitute the liberating *kuṇḍalinī* energy. (There is also an interrelated geometry between this and the other cards, which is too complicated to explain here.)

The entire compound symbol of the ram's horns also indicates the qualities associated with the Alta Major centre at the base of the skull, which supports the 1,000 petalled lotus *(sahasrāra padma)* at the crown of the head. (This is symbolised by the *maṇḍala* associated with the seated figure.)

Together, the entwined serpents also hint at the caduceus symbol, the staff wielded by Mercury. He is the messenger of the Gods (the intuition), which is the esoteric ruler of Aries. Mars, the orthodox ruler of Aries, is symbolised by the Fiery sword. Uranus, the Hierarchical ruler of Aries, is the embodiment of esoteric knowledge, as symbolised by the book held in the right hand and by the seventh Ray colouring of the horns.

The *white lamb* symbolises the purity of thought, the word, deed, etc., needed to eventually attain the qualities of the Deity in the Throne. The lamb is the symbol of the Christ energy, connoting tranquillity, peace, gentleness and harmlessness. It is part of the 'flock of the Lord' that possesses definite first Ray qualities. (Spiritual Will and one-pointed determination.)

The *green background* signifies the colour of the general tone of Nature, of the third Ray of Activity, the plane *atmā.* It represents the *karma* of the past, which the Ram impels into manifestation. This activity represents the background qualities needed to help build the present.

The *grassy fields* indicate that the Arian empirical mind is relatively uncluttered with *saṃsāric* impressions and sensual images. Forceful determination, impetuosity, and all of the more reified expressions of mind exist for the average Arian, instead of what the seated Logos (here the emperor of the Mind) manifests. Nevertheless, everything needed to allow the lamb (the meditative Mind) to grow and mature is found in the Arian personality's environment.

The *first* keynote for Aries (the higher esoteric implication) is *The Divine Will.* This is the Will of an enlightened or liberated Being that holds the Book of Life. This Will relates to the Spirit aspect and concerns the mode of attaining the higher Initiations.

The *second* keynote (signifying the attributes of the aspirant to the mysteries of Being, of wisdom and enlightenment) is *The Lamb of God.* Here the Book of Wisdom is opened and the attributes of the Soul are aspired to. The normal esoteric implications of this keynote are related to the undertaking of the first three Initiations.

The *third* keynote (signifying attributes of the average person) is *The Fiery Warrior.* The book here is that of the appearing transient form, of manifest life – everything concerning *saṃsāra* (the fleeting phenomenal world of the senses). The determined 'warrior' travels the path of worldly concern (with a forceful impetus) in order to master all of its travails. This produces eventual aspiration to pass the tests for Initiation into the Mysteries of the nature of Being. To eventually master *saṃsāra* necessitates the development of the Fiery Will.

**Plate 2. Taurus**

## Taurus

In *Taurus* the *emerald Eye* in a triangle is the All-seeing Eye of the planetary Logos (Sanat Kumāra, the One Initiator, the most High). The fourth degree Initiate can see 'eye to Eye' with[5] this One within a triangle of Light. It is the third Eye (Ājñā centre), that of Shiva, which 'fills the whole body with light'.[6] Much that concerns Taurus involves illumination – the opening of the 'third Eye' that allows the entry of all forms of Light (enlightenment). The power to visualise the three times (past, present and future) is at the command of the possessor of the Eye. The Eye sees in all directions in time and space. As stated, the emerald colouring was the evolutionary achievement of the past solar system, therefore was the base colouring to start the present one.

The dark *indigo blue* of the second Ray of Love-Wisdom surrounding the Eye is that of the *dharmakāya*, the fundamental Source of all Being and non-being. The second Ray is the primary energy conditioning the present solar system. This colouring is found within and without the central triangle, which indicates the essential Identity between inner and outer space.

The *triangle* symbolises the three fundamental aspects of Deity, or of Being: the first Ray of Will (the Father, pure energy), the second Ray of Love-Wisdom (the Son, consciousness) and the third Ray of Mathematically Exact Activity (the Mother, the form nature). It is surrounded by the *white light* associated with enlightenment, the blending into one of the primary colourings of all of the Rays. The triangle also implies the totality of the symbolism associated with the great Pyramid (which is said to have been built during the Taurean era, three or so millennia B.C.).

The *radiating rose colour* emanating from the white here implies the cosmic astral plane (which is governed by Taurus). It hints at the energy of cosmic Love. From this plane emanates the magnetic energies productive of form building (producing the appearance of the cosmic dense physical plane).[7] The radiations emanating from the triangle signify the energy body of deity (of inherent duality, *iḍā* and *piṇgalā*, male and female, human and *deva)* that governs the expression of all forms in Nature.

The surrounding *rings of seven colours* represent those of the seven Creative Hierarchies still incarnate in cosmic dense substance (of which the human Hierarchy is the fourth). As earlier stated, they constitute the substance of the consciousness principle and the Lives evolving through this incarnation of the

---

5 Alice Bailey, *The Rays and the Initiations,* 176.

6 *Matt. 6:22.*

7 This work is esoterically a function of the seven Pleiades, who are carried on the shoulder of the constellation Taurus the bull.

solar Logos. The Creative Hierarchies incorporate the substance of the Womb of time and space.

The *outer violet* indicates the seventh Ray energy that causes the precipitation of the form nature – the result of (cosmic) Desire. The pink colouration within the rings of colour and the violet therefore also signify the systemic astral plane (whose fundamental energy here is of devotion-aspiration) and of the etheric double. The sum of the dense physical plane precipitates from them. Taurus therefore represents the expression of the field of the Desire to bring into manifestation the habitation of an incarnate Logos. There is also the desire of a human Soul to incarnate into a form. The onrushing Bull of cosmic Desire is the Will-to-Achieve that drives the entire wheel of the zodiac onwards to produce the fruition of its purpose. This fruition is the gestation of the divine Child within the Womb, as signified by the Creative Hierarchies. The cosmic Womb is reflected into the larger terrestrial sphere wherein we find the environment for the Christ-Child to grow.

Emanating from the Eye is a central band of *gold and silver,* which implicates the transmuted qualities of the right and left *nāḍīs* associated with the treading of the higher Way of cosmic Identification. (The attainment of the *dharmakāya* Mind of Buddha.) Otherwise it represents the stream of Logoic Thought that empowers the Desire to create what must be. The stream passes over the *square,* which symbolises the quaternary, or the form nature associated with manifestation. This square also represents the four lesser Rays – of Harmony overcoming Conflict, the Scientific Mode, Devotion-Aspiration, and finally of Ceremonial Activity and of material Power. The square is black in colour because it also represents the primal matter or matrix that is the base substance of the Womb of Mother Nature, via which everything evolved. This Womb is impregnated with the seed Idea of Life by the Bull's 'sperm' – the instigating Logoic Thought. The central band of white signifies the *suṣumṇā* that is the integration of the two *nāḍīs.*

The two *'bulls'* associated with the square are an earthy colour, because of their relationship to dense corporeality. In reality (though not depicted), one is a cow (of the left) and the other (of the right) is a bull, signifying the male-female duality that causes the appearance of all phenomenal things. This duality also runs throughout the card, with the *nāḍīs* from the Eye and the stream effectively uniting to divide the sphere into two portions. Taurus is also the second sign of the zodiac, hence signifying the primal duality of Father-Mother. Together the cow and bull possess four horns, also signifying the quaternary that conditions the form. The animals complete a 'square' with the rectangle that signifies the Womb and form a trinity with it. They represent the evolving animal form within that Womb. This is the principle of desire that must eventually master the substance of dark space *(saṃsāra)* through the transformation of desire into aspiration and illumination by a human kingdom. They must thereby eventually find the stream of Life flowing through them as a mechanism to travel to the triangle that signifies the three higher principles of the human condition. By this means they learn to awaken the Eye. This awakening conveys the illumination that is a major aspect of Taurus.[8]

The quaternary and the triangle above it then represent the septenary of Nature, of all the septenaries that condition the manifest form:

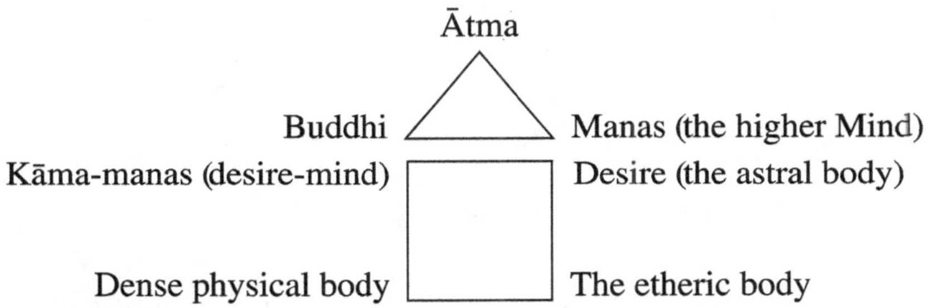


**Figure 44. The septenary of manifestation**

The triangle is separate from the square because the dense form is an illusional body of activity and has no substantiality of its own. It is a thought-form built by the mind/Mind of the meditating entity, projected via the Eye into time and space to serve a specific purpose. It has a phenomenal life for the duration sustained by the Will of the Entity concerned. The triangle, however, is the symbol of the Real, the eternal, the archetype of the form (the spiritual Triad). The triangle and square are in fact interwoven in the form of a hexagram. This interrelation involves the geometry of causation.[9]

The *bull* and/or *cow* signify the nature of thought-form building. The cow sustains the form with her life-giving milk, and symbolises the various cow Gods and Goddesses developed during the Taurean dispensation. Such are Hathor, Isis, the Mithraic Bull, the Akkadian Te (the 'Bull of Light'), and the sacred cow in India. The pair face in two directions, symbolising the innate duality assigned to this sign.

8 See *Esoteric Astrology,* 374.

9 See Chapter 7 ('The Spiral of Consciousness, the Geometric View') of my book *Esoteric Cosmology and Modern Physics.*

Taurus is the sign of the Divine Hermaphrodite, of the second stage of Creation (the fertilisation of the Mundane, or world-Egg). This signifies the projection of the Thought-Form of Deity into the Womb of matter. It is the golden egg, Hiraṇyagarbha (another name of Brahmā), the world egg of the Hindus, and the Seb (the 'great cackler') – the goose that laid the world Egg of the Egyptian mythology.

The symbol for this stage is: ⦶. This process is symbolised by the central stream that divides the bottom sphere (the world sphere) of the card into two.

Together, the two sets of circles depicted on this card constitute a form of the orthodox glyph for Taurus, thus:

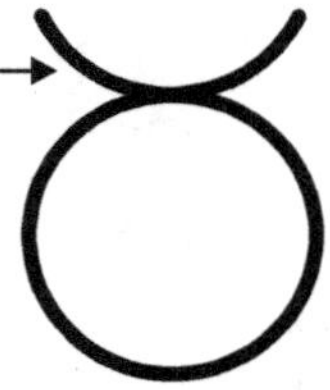


**Figure 45. Taurus as a cosmic Egg**

The *cosmic Egg* (symbolised by the sphere) is the universal primeval matrix. Taken by itself, the circle represents the abstract Spirit, but when divided, to produce the symbol ⦶, it signifies the process of fertilisation (of coming into generation). The central line is that of the masculine principle of the Will that projects the Thought into the primal matrix to create the universe of forms that must be in any *manvantara*.

The *bull's horns* represent the crescent moon. They are a symbol of duality emerging from unity, of the psychic nature and of the forces that sustain and also arise from the form. The horns are therefore turned towards the spiritual domains. The horns represent an arc, an incomplete circle, implying limitation. They can also symbolise the form nature subjugating the spiritual. Later (on the rectified wheel), as is the case here, they are the symbol of the Soul rising out of the confining cycles of the form and the material world. (If the symbolism associated with the glyph is reversed, then the two main *nāḍīs* emanating from the Spirit are implicated.)

The bottom circle is divided into two halves by the central flowing *turquoise blue stream*. This and the colour pink are colours that signify the astral realm. The turquoise also signifies the creative imagination and aspiration needed to tread the path to illumination. It is calmly meandering through the scenery that represents the mundane world, reminiscent of the serene mind to be developed by an aspirant if illumination is to be gained. This allows the undertaking of the second Initiation (the Baptism), mastery of which is the onus of the Taurean to achieve. The true purpose of the astral plane is thereby revealed.[10] This stream represents the stream of Life and of the *dhyāna* (the meditation Mind) that indicates a placid serenity that effortlessly brings one from the alpha to achieve the omega of manifest Being. The stream flows as the *suṣumṇā* path that divides the two portions of the greenery of the landscape.

From another perspective, the stream takes the guise of the *piṅgalā* channel leading to the Solar Plexus centre. Here this *nāḍī* absorbs all of the attributes developed by the person in the green scenery. The Solar Plexus centre is the 'abdominal brain', the reservoir of the Watery astral environment. It is the outlet for astral plane perceptions, thus is the organ of clairvoyance (which Taurus governs). It integrates the entire lower person and his/her psychic centres. The right and left fields imply the qualities of the right (*piṅgalā,* represented by the houses that house the consciousness aspect) and left (*iḍā,* represented by the sheep that graze in the fields of activity) *nāḍīs*.

Everywhere there are *fields,* coloured in different hues of green, arranged in a scattered rectangular patterning. This has the same basic meaning as the square explained above, but the symbolism is more particularly related to human consciousness. The fields represent the work of the human mind and hands, as influenced by the Venusian quality (the fifth Ray) of ordered beauty and mental activity (thinking scientifically). Venus is the orthodox ruler of Taurus. From the field of the earth (the Element said to govern this sign) the Taurean has to master the Watery Element. The fields then represent the fields of striving to the higher domains, signified by the symbolism of what supports the bull and cow in cosmos. The Bull of the will (transformed desire) then manifests to overcome all impediments of desire-attachment to the phenomenal world.

The various *shades of green* indicate the totality of the hues associated with Mother Nature (signified by Venus), of the third Ray of Mathematically Exact Activity and of *ātmic* perception. (Which makes one fully realised, a Master of Wisdom.) This represents the high attainment gained through incarnation into *saṃsāric* phenomena. Grey green is the predominant hue in the human aura, signifying the self-focused adaptability that allows people to master the allurements of the world. There are also the colours of compassion (light green), and the ability to teach the *dharma* (bluish green). Light bluish-yellow green signifies healing,

10 See *Esoteric Astrology,* 388.

whilst the various more earthy shades relate to the activity aspect of the third Ray associated with average humans.[11] Taureans manifest a fondness for the home life, tending to the fields of their own personalities, plus the sensual allurements that need to be overcome if illumination is to be attained.

The *jungle* (or forest) in the background indicates the wild, animal-like passions that need to be subdued in Taurus (or in its polar opposite, Scorpio).

In the left hand side of the stream (the *iḍā nāḍī),* the *three animals* on three fields symbolise the basic animal nature associated with our three-fold personality. They represent the elements of the desire-mind and the sensuality of the bull that must be tamed if people are to tread the Path. They also symbolise the *deva* Triads that govern the animal kingdom as a unit. The animals and the paddocks they are on form a symbolic hexagram, indicating the general qualities of manifestation as well as the angelic kingdom (Venus). As the paddocks are basically square, so also the triangle upon the square is again implicated, of the 'fall of the three into four'.

The right hand side of the stream (the *piṇgalā nāḍī)* signifies those elements directly associated with humanity. The shape of the *home* (humanity's personality nature) has fused the symbol (a) together with (b), which in turn, makes an implied pentagram (c). This is symbolic of what a human being represents, indicating the complete realisation of the attributes of the mind.

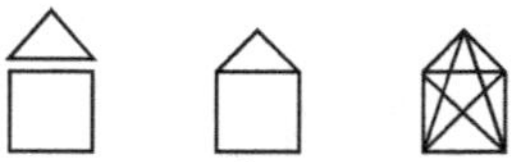

a b c

*Smoke* gently rises from the chimney, which introduces the Element Fire (again implied, for it is hidden within the house, or the personality). This implies the ability to utilise the mind, which distinguishes the human from the animal kingdom. The mind is able to create, make, mould or transform the elements of the earth. It also produces the smoke – the pollution, illusions and glamour associated with human thinking. This is another of the problems that definitely concern the Taurean subject.

In the background there are *four volcanoes* billowing Fire. They at first indicate the Fires of the desire-mind; everything associated with the personality and the rocky materialism (the Earth Element) that often confront the Taurean. (The number four relates to the quaternary that is the personality vehicle.) More specifically, however, the volcanoes indicate the qualities of the esoteric and

11 For more about auric colourings, see the revised *The Revelation,* chapter 6.

hierarchical ruler of this sign – Vulcan, the God of the transmutative Fire, hidden deep within the bowels of the earth. This is the cause of the first Ray destructive potency associated with earthquakes and volcanoes. Vulcan wields or forges the powers of the Gods and represents the nuclear energy that sustains the potency of the sun. It is the hidden dynamo illumining the Eye of the Bull. The symbolism of the arising of *kuṇḍalinī* is also implicit here.

The volcanoes rise into a normal *light blue* sky – here the colour of illumination (the light of day) which allows the Taurean to vision clearly what he/she aspires to or desires. The faint *orange* bordering indicates the impending mental development characterised by the undeveloped Taurean (and which gains its full ascendancy in Virgo, the next Earth sign). This colour also refers to the primeval evolutionary period, which Taurus governs.

The large circle is divided into three main spheres of activity.

1. The blue sky *(buddhi)* via which the illumination governing the Taurean is derived.
2. The *mountainous volcanic terrain* (the mental domain). Here this terrain governs the first Ray power that awakens the All-seeing Eye that facilitates the Initiated Taurean to see deeply into subjective space.
3. The relatively gentle fields and homestead (the physical domain), the world of the senses that becomes the fields of desire for the average Taurean native. There is also the central stream running through the Taurean landscape, indicating the astral plane and its illusional incentives that are glamour forming, as well as relating to psychic receptivity. This astral subjectivity is always the underlying conditioning affecting the Taurean subject until the path to enlightenment is trod. In many ways, Taurus projects this astral proclivity into manifestation.

## Gemini

The central figure of the *third card,* denoted *Gemini* the twins, shows a twelve-petalled lotus, golden-yellow in colour. The twelve petals symbolise the Heart centre, but this lotus specifically organises the 1,056 petals of the Head centre. The twelve petals also relate to the twelve Creative Hierarchies, the twelve zodiacal and planetary energies, and the twelve principal groupings of human Egos (Souls) on the higher mental realm. These petals can be viewed as an iris of the 'Eye of God' (explained in the previous card), with the central black disc as the pupil that is opened to emit and receive Light of varying degrees of potency.

**Plate 3. Gemini**

The central sphere for the Head centre is the *brahmarandhra* (the hole of Brahman), the place of entry or exit of incarnation or disincarnation.[12] It also symbolises the place of the transference of consciousness into multidimensional space for one in profound meditation *(dhyāna)*. Its colour is that of the deep indigo-blue of the *dharmakāya* (the fount of all-Being). It is also the colour of the

12 This is so for Initiates, but for average humanity the Centre between the Shoulder Blades serves this purpose.

external universe (in the early morning), replete with the stars and galaxies that indicate the countless sentient beings and world systems that together constitute cosmic manifestation. Gemini exemplifies the nature of the etheric body (space *per se)* of a human or of 'God' and its myriads of inherent and actualised dualities. Gemini is the sign of duality and its resolution into unity.

The colour of the *innermost sphere* indicates the three primary Rays (red, indigo-blue and green). This is the seed point *(bindu),* the focal point of all creative activity, the central concentrated point of dynamic energy that allows the Logos to manifest a *maṇḍala* of all-things. The *bindu* can be considered the point of actualisation from subjective to manifest space. The retina, the focal point in the eye that allows us to perceive all visual images, is a physiological homologue to function.

From this *bindu* twenty-four streams of Light emanate. They express the energies of the 'four and twenty elders' of chapter four of the *Book of Revelation* that 'sit round' the throne of 'God'.

The twelve petals are circumscribed by a *halo of seven colours:* yellow, rose, orange, indigo, green, blue and violet. They represent the colourings of the seven sub-planes of the *mental plane.* Yellow, rose and orange are those of the abstract sub-planes, and the rest are the colourings of the four concrete sub-planes. The relation between the higher and the lower mental plane is an important factor for the consideration of this sign. The higher Mind is the doorway between inner and outer space, between the world of form and the non-manifest, abstract, archetypal domains. All forms of phenomena are contained within the mind/Mind, where the mind is the basis of the way to liberation. The intuitive Mind (integrated with *buddhi)* represents the potency of the fluid, mercurial attributes symbolised by the orthodox ruler of this sign, Mercury. With this higher Mind, Mercury tends to create beautiful forms and images of all types that actualise the archetypal. The esoteric ruler (Venus) rules the sum of the mind/Mind. Venus manifests the creative potential that actualises all forms, producing the beauty of the feminine demonstration of Nature. Mercury and Venus together constitute the divine hermaphrodite that was central to the consideration of the previous sign (Taurus), whereas for Gemini the inherent duality is separated into male and female forces, as symbolised by the two human figures.

The being on top of the central glyph is sitting in a lotus position *(padmāsāna)* and wears a meditation band, indicating that he has gained mastery of the qualities associated with the Head centre by means of dedicated meditation (which has become his integral being). Above his head is a five-pointed star of Life, the star of Initiation. It expresses the Potency of the planetary Logos. From this perspective, the pentagram indicates that this being is a Master of Wisdom, an Initiate of the fifth degree. Only such a one (or one greater) has fully mastered the qualities associated with the Head centre and can measure the temple of the Lord in its entirety. His outstretched hands that touch the ends of the two pillars indicate this. An Initiate of the sixth degree (a Buddha or Dhyān Chohan) is able to create the temple in its entirety, to thereby become a planetary Christ.

The *two pillars,* golden in colour, represent the temple, which is also the Causal body of the Soul. This is symbolically depicted in the diagram by the pearly colouring of the outer sphere, which attempts to depict the colouring (and therefore qualities) of that exalted form that exists on the higher mental plane. The Soul is the intermediary between the Divine (the Spirit) and the dense form, and therefore expresses one of the major esoteric qualities attributed to Gemini. The pillars seem to be burning with blue, yellow, golden, etc., flames. This indicates the 'gold tried in the fire' *(Rev. 3:18)* associated with the alchemical process and the formation of the philosopher's stone. (As was already mentioned in the sign Aries.) It symbolises the wisdom that must be developed by one wishing to enter the portals of the temple. The pillars make the square of the Base of Spine centre *(mūlādhāra chakra)*[13] from where emanates the *kuṇḍalinī* Fire that sustains the entirety of the edifice of the temple. The emanation of *kuṇḍalinī* is here symbolised by the Rays streaming from the central Eye.

From a higher perspective, the temple indicates the nature of the City of the Lord – Shambhala, wherein resides the great King, the planetary Logos. The entity measuring the distance between the pillars can also be considered as what is known in the Masonic terminology as the Grand Architect of the Universe (G.A.O.T.U.). He is the grand Geometrician, the Scribe or Lipika that circumscribes a sphere of attainment – the ring-pass-not that a Logos builds for an entire *manvantara,* within which He stays for the duration of that entire evolutionary epoch. The pink colouration of his figure and around him here relates to the energies of the cosmic astral plane, the expression of cosmic Desire that causes a Logos to bring forth the appearance of a *manvantara.*

The Lipika resides both within and without that sphere, for He interrelates the internal *karma* within with the integrated *karma* of the universal whole. The five-pointed star then relates to the attributes of the five liberated Creative

---

13 Depicted here in the form of a square.

Hierarchies, and the qualities of the five Dhyāni Buddhas. They are viewed as the embodiments of the Mind (Mahat) of the cosmic Logos that builds the etheric structure of all that must come to Be. This is impelled via the central Eye, which also functions as the Adytum, the Holy of Holies of the Temple. Everything manifests according to mathematically precise activity, as indicated by the geometry seen in the temple construct. We have the three main tiers of the Eye structure: the central sphere, the indigo-blue iris, and the outer sphere within which the twelve-petalled lotus is enclosed. All of this is circumscribed within the sub-planes of mind/Mind as the expression moves multi-dimensionally from the subtlest planes outwards into physical manifestation (signified by the two pillars). Squaring the circles (which here are ten in number, the number of perfection) are a blue triangle and a square (shown in black outline), which signify 'the fall of the three into the four' associated with dense manifestation. They also depict the inherent septenaries governing the manifestation of all forms. (The functions also of the seven manifest Creative Hierarchies.) The apex of the triangle emanates from the Base of Spine centre of the seated figure, signifying that the entire expression is an emanation of the lowest centre of this Being – that which expresses material incarnation.

This interrelation also symbolises two groups of great liberated Beings:

a. The *Contemplatives* – that meditate upon the future, via universal (zodiacal) energies, and direct those energies to Shambhala.[14] They represent the square or Throne of the manifesting Logos, from the higher perspective of the inward focussed Eye. The Grand Architect sits upon them, allowing them to peer upwards through His Base *chakra* into the sum of His Body of Manifestation and to cosmos. From a lower perspective, this square represents the four-fold Lipika that govern the demonstration of the *karma* of the four worlds of manifestation *(buddhi* and the three lower planes).

b. The *Buddhas of Activity* that radiate these energies to the sentient beings within the ring-pass-not of a planetary or solar sphere, as planetary or Hierarchical energies. They thereby cause all that presently is. Each of the Buddhas embody the evolution of one or other of the kingdoms below the human, whilst the Grand Architect (now viewed as the planetary Logos, Sanat Kumāra) governs human evolution.

---

14 Their function is described in Alice Bailey's *Discipleship in the New Age,* Vol. 2.

The twelve wavy and twelve straight lines indicate the duality between feminine and masculine forces.

In the Bible, *the pillars* are called Jachin (the right pillar) and Boaz[15] (the left pillar). As well as supporting the temple, they stand as portals guarding the door to the entry of the mysteries therein. When externalised on the earth this temple will take the form of the New Jerusalem, or the New Age temples that will then be established. The right pillar signifies the *piṅgalā nāḍī* and the left pillar the *iḍā nāḍī*.[16] This is important because Gemini rules the etheric bodies of all things, as well as the blood circulation and the nervous system. The etheric plane underlies the dense physical form, being the mould via which the dense form is built. The four cosmic ethers *(buddhi* and the higher planes of perception) play a similar function for the cosmic dense physical plane. The ethers are a body of energy containing the *chakras* (psychic centres) and the *nāḍīs* (energy channels) that interrelate every aspect of the form. Gemini is principally concerned with these energy interrelations. This constitutes the relationships between the twins (the positive and negative elements in the body), yogically understood. The radiating streams of energy also symbolise this. Much could be further stated here in relation to the subject of meditative unfoldment from an energy viewpoint.

The geometry associated with the central symbol (of the triangle superimposed upon a square within the circle) is also the template associated with the Head centre. This geometry represents the Divinity that emanates from the physical form within the ring-pass-not of any incarnating entity. (The geometry found in most of the other cards are interrelated or derived from it.)

There are *four* series of concentric circles. First, that of the central *bindu,* next the indigo disc, then that of the twelve-petalled lotus of the Head centre and the symbolism of the sub-planes of the mental plane that it processes. Finally, there is the surrounding halo and the outer circle that symbolise the Causal body (aura) of the Soul.[17] The four circles also represent the fourth-dimensional perception that is the *upādhi* or basis to inner or outer space: the four ethers (the higher planes of perception) that are responsible for the formation of manifest space.

---

15 *I Kings 7:21.*

16 Here left and right are viewed from the orthodox perspective (from the point of view of the perceiver).

17 Five tiers could be viewed if one divides the central *bindu* into an inherent duality, or twelve if the seven mental sub-plane circles are counted separately and added to these five.

From the central dot emanates *a path or rainbow bridge (antaḥkaraṇa)* composed of seven colours, which are the Ray colourings that together qualify all manifest being. The *antaḥkaraṇa* must be constructed (through meditation and service work) by those (here the dancing couple) that wish to enter the portals of the sacred Temple.

These Rays are divided into two groups of three, indicating again the basic dualities associated with this sign. The right hand group signifies the *piṇgalā nāḍī* (here also represented by the dancing male).

- Red—Ray I of Will or Power, emanating from the plane *ādi.*
- Indigo-blue—Ray II of Love-Wisdom, emanating from *anupādaka.*
- Green—Ray III of Mathematically Exact Activity, emanating from *ātma.*

Gold—Ray IV of Beautifying Harmony overcoming Strife is represented by the golden hued clothing of the dancing figures. They are members of humanity (that is itself governed by this Ray). This Ray also exemplifies the middle path of the *antaḥkaraṇa* that must be developed by those awakening the Eye to see and so enter the portal of the temple.

The central blue band is the colour of the night sky and signifies the unifying Love that is the fundamental energy to be conveyed by the twins:

> It is the constellation Gemini and its inherent second ray influence which control every one of the pairs of opposites in the Great Wheel. Gemini, therefore, forms with each of the pairs of opposites in the Zodiac a third factor, powerfully influencing the other two constellations, and thus forms, with them, certain great zodiacal triangles. These only become of importance when considering the horoscopes of advanced human beings or esoteric groups.[18]

The left hand group signifies the *iḍā nāḍī* (here also represented by the dancing female).

- Orange—Ray V of the Scientific Mode, governing the mental plane.
- Turquoise—Ray VI of Devotion and Aspiration, governing the astral plane.
- Violet—Ray VII of Ceremonial Magic and Materialising Power, governing the etheric body, hence dense physical manifestation.

Everyone must incarnate many times under the auspiciousness of each of the Rays before becoming sufficiently adept in their qualities to be able to

18 *Esoteric Astrology,* 346-7. See also page 349, where it is stated that 'Gemini—forms a point of entrance for cosmic energy from Sirius'.

appropriately tread the rainbow bridge (the *antaḥkaraṇa)* to enlightened Being.

Normally, Gemini the twins are symbolised by a mortal brother (associated with the evolving form) who is corruptible and an immortal brother (the Christ principle) who is incorruptible. The symbolism of 'the brothers' is here replaced by that of a dancing couple. They signify the inherent duality of Life, the polarity of male-female, the objective of which in this sign is to resolve into a unity. The couple therefore hold hands as they dance into the temple of Life. The dancing pair signify humanity's spiritual attainment, hence they also circumscribe the outermost sphere (of their own Souls). This indicates their ability to Measure – or to gain comprehension of – the Mysteries of Initiation. (Thus inevitably revealing the nature of the Kingdom of 'God'.) All of this happens upon our terrestrial sphere (the earth), which is also the Hierarchical ruler of Gemini.

From another perspective, the couple are dancing or travelling onwards *from* the *maṇḍala* that represents the Head centre and the Causal body to the unknown (abstract space). In this case, they represent enlightened beings that are holding hands as they dance with the energies that animate them. This indicates that only by being focussed upon group-service, thus united consciously to the all (in love and service to humanity), can one travel the path to liberation and enter through the gate of Initiation. The Initiated lovers inevitably find themselves in cosmic space, in the immeasurable universe.

Their hands in embrace form a symbolic arrow[19] (with the path) that points either to the past or to the future. With respect to the past, it is the door through which they have already travelled. This indicates the totality of the qualities and esoteric understanding gained that allowed them to travel the path. The symbolism also instantaneously indicates the future, of travelling in consciousness towards the vast domain of space via the Head centre. One can also interpret the dancing couple to be travelling towards the Head centre of the planetary Logos (Shambhala), governing the Temple they are in the process of entering. They have left the vicissitudes of *saṃsāra* behind.

Together, their other *hands* touch or measure the outer form of the Causal body, the qualities and constitution of which they know through aeonic involvement. This also indicates their ability to measure the context of the city of the Lord, which they will come to know from the third Initiation onwards. The process that will enable them to eventually thus 'measure' is what will make them Masters of Wisdom (fifth degree Initiates).

---

19 Hinted at here is the symbolism of a function of the arrow wielded by Sagittarius, the polar opposite of Gemini.

With the seated figure on top of the *maṇḍala,* they constitute the qualities of the Trinity (Father-Son-Mother) associated with the manifestation of all Being. The *yellow-white* clothing that they wear symbolises the purity that is to be developed upon the rainbow path, and which synthesises all the Rays. As Initiates, they will have the ability to express any of the Rays at appropriate times.

In the upper right and left hand corners there are two glyphs that symbolise the qualities of the right and left hand *nāḍīs; the sun* (the pentagram in the circle, *piṅgalā nāḍī),* and *the moon* (the hexagon within the sphere for the symbol of the moon, the *iḍā nāḍī).* The pentagram and hexagram are associated with human and angelic (or *deva*) development (also indicated by the two dancing figures), of the evolution of the material universe, and the consciousness-engendering factor. The pentagram relates to the development of human consciousness (inbreathing), and the hexagram to the manifestation of the formed realms, as wielded by the *deva* kingdom (breathing out). The two symbols thus remind us that esoterically this sign is also concerned with the right control of the breath *(prāṇayāma),* of the positive and negative energy channels (*nāḍīs*) within the body, and also of the Body of 'God'.

D.K. states, in relation to the fact that the seventh Ray influence is missing in Gemini, 'accounting for the instability and fluidity of the Gemini subject', that:

> Six forces meet in Gemini and, for this reason, the double triangle or King Solomon's seal is one of the subjective symbols of this sign, linking it again with the Masonic tradition and indicating also again the essential dualism of this sign.[20]

## Cancer

The complicated compound symbol in the *fourth card (Cancer)* depicts the central theme of Cancer's symbolism – incarnation into dense physical activity. Aries was concerned with the initial mental conception, Taurus with building the details of the thought construct, and Gemini with the etheric framework, the energy field that underlies the form. Cancer is then concerned with the actual incarnation, symbolised by the 'house' that the crab carries on its back.

The complete implications of this glyph cannot be explained here because of the complex metaphysical and occult subtleties associated with the geometry that it is based on. Cancer is also upon the cardinal cross, hence betokens of the nature of the manifestation of cosmic Will, producing a difficult level of cosmic weave to rightly comprehend. The basic symbolism is, however, provided below.

20 *Esoteric Astrology,* 364.

**Plate 4. Cancer**

The *crescent Moon* (with the horns pointing down on the upper part of the symbol) represents the gateway into incarnation. The Moon (the exoteric ruler of Cancer) is the symbol of the psychic nature, of the material form, of one's personality and all the forces that animate it. This is particularly so for the Watery emotional qualities that inundate most people. The *silvery-white colouring* is that of the *mirror* that reflects all things and forces (divinity) into manifestation. In a similar sense, the moon (or a human unit, the personality) illumines the night by reflecting light from the (spiritual) sun.

The circle of the Moon contains two lesser circles, each of which enclose interrelated hexagrams. This compound geometric symbol represents the Sacral centre *(svādiṣṭhāna chakra),* which expresses the sexual, animal, or physically vital forces in humanity. The two lesser circles represent the two minor Gonad (or Ovary) centres associated with the building of the manifest forms that must come to be. They embody the male *(piṅgalā)* and female *(iḍā)* sexual energies that, together with the Sacral and the Base of Spine centres, form a functioning unity.[21] From this grouping of *chakras,* therefore, manifests the entire creative function of a Logos, the Creative Intelligences, or of human activity. Therefore, from them come a downward projection of energies, symbolised by the Rays that emanate from their combination.

The Sacral centre is the agent for the distribution of the various *prāṇas* in the body. This function corresponds to that of the physical sun in the solar system. This symbolism 'is concerned primarily with the gestation period prior to birth and in its right understanding can be traced and expanded the whole story of conception'.[22] Through it, by means of impersonality, 'the whole problem of dualism must be solved'.[23] The Sacral centre is directly related to the Ājñā centre (the third Eye) in that the Sacral and the Base of Spine centres form a functionally overlapped unity, in a similar way that the Ājñā centre and the Head lotus are interrelated. Together, they form a synthetic duality, the alpha and omega of Life controlling the sum total of the energies that make a personality.

The Base of Spine centre *(mūlādhāra* centre) is implied in the *orange-red serpent* that spirals around the compound symbol of the *chakras*. Its head appears under the crescent moon. The serpent represents the arousal of *kuṇḍalinī,* the procreative energy of the world Mother that causes all manifest things to come into being. When fully liberated by a *yogin, kuṇḍalinī* produces the complete awakening of the Head centre. Orange-red is the colouring attributed to the *mūlādhāra chakra*, and signifies the evocation of the mental principle (orange) by the Desire of the Logos (red) so as to procreate. The entire creative process produces the arousal of *kuṇḍalinī. Kuṇḍalinī* is the effect of the Fiery force of the Mental energy (Mahat) of the Creative Logos that binds the elementary Fires of primal substance into a unified form. *Kuṇḍalinī* is the combination of the fused product.

21 In the Buddhist meditation system these two centres are also viewed as a unity.

22 Alice Bailey, *Esoteric Healing,* 176

23 Ibid., 177.

The spiralling serpent also represents what Babbitt calls 'the thermo spirals' that surround the atom, occultly (etherically) understood.[24] The subject is explained in detail in my book *Esoteric Cosmology and Modern Physics*. Esoterically, the atom is considered to underlie all manifested being. When incarnate, all entities (be they a solar or planetary Logos, the Creative Hierarchies, or a human being) can be considered as such, for the atom is the focal point of the Eye of the creative Entity. It conveys the spirals of energies and cycles of manifest expression. Here one must also consider the permanent atoms through which the Soul is able to incarnate into the material world from life to life. The permanent atoms are retained by the Soul throughout its incarnations (one atom for each sheath) and are the repositories of *karma* and the *saṃskāras* developed for each particular incarnation.[25] (In a similar sense, the genes are repositories of the physiological characteristics of any being.)

From the interrelated spheres stream five Rays of Light. They signify the five different types of *prāṇa* that animate five lines of energies *(nāḍīs)*. They are accordingly related to the five Elements, the Wisdoms of the five Dhyāni Buddhas (Buddhas of meditation), the five instincts, and in yoga philosophy the five stages of liberation by means of *prāṇayāma*. (The science of the control and right direction of breath.) These *prāṇas* are collectively termed the *vayūs,* and are:

- *Prāṇa* – the inbreathing of Life, the assimilation of the external Life force for internal usage. This concerns the control of the *nāḍī* from nose to the heart. *Prāṇa* therefore involves the right relationship between a person and the surrounding environment.
- *Samāna* – the control of the *nāḍī* from the heart to the solar plexus, which concerns the integral inner assimilation or digestion of all elements of Life.
- *Apāna* – the control of the *nāḍī* from the solar plexus to the feet, which involves the right handling of one's external impact to the environment.
- *Udāna* – the control of the *nāḍī* from the nose to the top of the head, thus the coordination of the various *prāṇas,* the at-onement of breath and Mind.
- *Vyāna* – the unimpeded circulation of all aspects of Life in the body, thus the sum total of the *prāṇic* energy as it is distributed evenly throughout the body.[26]

---

24 See *Principle of Light and Colour* (The College of Fine Forces, New Jersey, 2nd Ed., 1896) by Edwin Babbitt and *Occult Chemistry* by A. Besant and C.W. Leadbeater (Theosophical Publishing House, Adyar, Madras, 1951).

25 See Bailey's *A Treatise on Cosmic Fire* for detail.

26 The subject of the *vayūs* is explained in detail in the revised edition of my book *The Revelation*.

The *vayūs* and the five Elements represent the sum total of manifest being, via which the *karma* of the three worlds (the dense physical, astral and mental) can manifest. The colours as provided: yellow, rose, blue, green and violet, are some of the Rays governing the mental sub-planes. They symbolically represent the five Rays that may be in incarnation at any one time. The colourings of this plane have been used because the Mind is the Source of all Being. It is what sustains manifestation and resolves it back to its Source at the appointed time.

The geometry associated with the bottom circle that delineates the body of the crab signifies the geometric basis to understanding the nature of the Head centre. This is based on the superimposed, interrelated *maṇḍalas* associated with the pentagram and the hexagram, that when fully developed express the totality of manifest space.

The five *nāḍīs* depicted also form central concentric circles, implying that they have turned at right angles from their original direction. This indicates a transposition of consciousness from one dimension of perception to the next. The symbolism is compound, because it also indicates a downward expression of energies from Logoic sources to eventually awaken the Head centres of what has come into manifestation. Such is the objective of a human kingdom that eventually aspires upwards to gain Initiation in Capricorn, the polar opposite sign of Cancer.

From this centre radiate three arrows pointing downwards, manifesting as a form of Neptune's trident, the esoteric ruler of this sign. Neptune rules the Watery Element (the cosmic and systemic astral plane) and governs the sixth Ray of Devotion or Aspiration when related to human development. In the process of causation it is the driving energy that produces the crystallisation of form from out of the Waters.

Neptune governs the qualities that allow people to control their emotions and desires and so to undertake the second Initiation (the Baptism). During the Atlantean era, Neptune manifested as the incarnate Christ. The triple pronged trident of spiritual energy indicates what wields power over the entire three-fold personality nature, the life of the form residing in the Waters of *saṃsāra.* The prongs represent the three-fold channel *(iḍā, piṅgalā* and *suṣumṇā)* from whence the entire *nāḍī* system of an incarnate individual emanates. Upon the path of return they are the means to liberation from the throttlehold of the phenomenal universe.

The Moon is the exoteric ruler of Cancer and governs the psychic disposition of the Watery aspects of a human unit. The Moon can therefore be considered to veil the attributes of Neptune with regard to the way that Neptune's energies are utilised by the vicissitudes of the every-changing form, its shadowy interplay with divinity. The Moon and Neptune together make Cancerians the most mediumistic of the natives of all the signs (except maybe Pisces with Cancer rising).

Part of the symbolism associated with the crab (and Cancerians) is extreme tenacity. The crab would rather lose a claw than let go of what is desired. Tenacity is here indicated by the crab's claws that hold the *white lens* close to its body. This lens and the claws are part of the geometric foundation of this sign. The lens is colourless, allowing the clear white Light emanating from the Soul or spiritual Sun to be differentiated into the hues of the seven Rays, so that they can be utilised by the manifesting form. The lens can also be considered the lens in the eye, which allows light to be focussed upon the retina, to be transmitted to the brain in the form of electromagnetic *(prānic)* impulses, thus to be decoded and analysed. What is shown is effectively a side-on view of the *brahmarandrha vidhara,* the 'opening' on the top of the head (as explained in the consideration of Gemini).

The *diamond* (or prism) inside the body of the crab represents an actuality in etheric matter. Within the head is a three-dimensional triangulation of energy between the pineal gland, the pituitary gland[27] and the Alta Major centre. When expanded to include the major centres in the head and fully vitalised with energies, then this interrelation is the basis for equating an enlightened being's awareness with a diamond. The geometrical lines of relation between these centres, the Ājñā centre and the Head lotus, have become ablaze with Fiery light. Thus there are such Sanskrit words as *vajra, ciṇtāmaṇī* and *tri-ratna*[28] associated with the diamond-like qualities of the enlightened Mind. This diamond refracts the light from the inner domains so that it can be utilised by consciousness. Similarly, once the rough stone of its ore is correctly faceted, the resultant diamond sparkles with scintillating brilliance in the sun.

A basic duality associated with human existence, of the conflict of various forces within and without the system (whose resolution drives one on to fulfilment by developing the higher creative function), is depicted in the diamond's two highly refined colours:

a. The left hand side, seen as a light transparent green, is related to the (transmuted) energies associated with the Solar Plexus centre, thus to the lower half of the person (the centres below the diaphragm). The Solar Plexus is the 'abdominal brain' that synthesises all of the energies of the minor (Inner Round) *chakras.*

---

27 These glands also manifest as minor *chakras.*

28 The *vajra* is sometimes translated as 'diamond sceptre', *ciṇtāmaṇī* is the diamond-like consciousness (the 'philosopher's stone') and *tri-ratna* means the 'triple gem'.

b. The right hand side, in a transparent golden-yellow, is related to the *prānas* emanating from the Heart centre, the source of Life. This *chakra* synthesises the energies from the higher centres, directing them upwards to the Head centre.

The general colouration of the mind is orange, signified by the colour of the central rectangle and the claws of the crab. All of the mental sub-planes manifest the hues of this fundamental orange colouring. One can also think of Makara, the fifth Creative Hierarchy that governs or embodies the substance of the mental plane. They are also termed the Agnishvattas and are the order of *devas* that work to build the forms of those that incarnate into dense physical space. The process of manifestation (that Cancer is concerned with) emanates from the domain of the mind.

The *indigo-blue* (which is the basic colouring of the body of the crab) signifies the principle of Love-Wisdom, which governs solar evolution. It is the overriding energy, therefore, that is rayed into manifest space (via the *six legs* of the crab). These legs represent the major pathways of descent (the six planes below *ādi)* for the streams of Life (the Creative Hierarchies) that come into manifestation during *manvantara.* The plane *ādi* signifies the domain of the Grand Council (the Divine Flames) that regulate the building activities of the Creative Intelligences as well as the movements of the lesser Lives that obey the evolutionary call. These legs also symbolise the potency of the hexagram in the incarnation process. The hexagram represents the totality of the incarnate form nature (with which Cancer is primarily concerned).

The *green* square signifies the cosmic Door into incarnation via the third plane of perception *(ātma)* that governs the *karma* of what is to be. It signifies the general colouring of Nature and its third Ray attributes, which therefore govern the major forms of activity on earth. As well as being the Doorway of incarnation, the square signifies the sum of the personality attributes, formed space, the four Elements and the quaternary of attributes that undergo evolutionary journeying.

The surrounding *turquoise-blue* is directly related to the astral plane (and the *lunar pitris)* – to that energy that causes the precipitation of Thought-Forms of a human, a Soul or a Logos.

The crab is moving downwards and backwards (as they are apt to do in Nature). This movement symbolises the descent of the Divine energies in the process of incarnation. It also relates to the fact that the signs of the zodiac retrogress as the earth travels around the sun while it pursues its course in the heavens. This is the great wheel of illusion *(māyā),* for all beings that travel upon it, life after life, do so because they are firmly yoked to *saṃsāra.*

The colours of the background sky (from turquoise to the various shades of violet, then yellow) basically represent the colourings of the four etheric sub-planes, from the astral plane (turquoise) to the light of day (the colouring signifying the physical day – yellow). They represent the subtle conditionings of the vital body through which each being must descend before incarnating. This produces the dawning, esoterically understood.

The *blues* and *greens* of the ocean represent the emotional (astral) and *saṃsāric* conditionings. These Waters are often troubled, full of turmoil, much agitated and in ceaseless movements of varying kinds (as indicated by waves). Also implied are violent emotions (the breaking of waves on the rocks), or forceful birthing into *saṃsāra*. The *rocks* upon which the waves break symbolise the dense physical plane – concrete, rocky, materialism, unyielding selfishness, etc. We have the embodied form and its allurements, through which the liberation process must be accomplished.

Everywhere on the beach (the Earth Element) there are signs of decay and death, the ceaseless struggle and scurrying that is so much a part of life in the material world. There are the spiral forms of the seashells that remind us that all is energy. They also indicate the basic spiral-cyclic motion that underlies the activities of all beings, of the incarnation process itself. Spirals are so fundamental that it is even imbued into the calcification (densification) process associated with evolving life and its remains. The Fibonacci series and the Golden Spiral associated with the mathematical concept of *pi* can also be noted here.

The *fish bones*, with their serrated edges, exemplify the nature of our present fifth Race (Aryan) era, wherein the mind is the dominant factor. It causes all types of divisions, strife, warfare and materialistic death-like turmoil. Ego-centred separateness in many ways is the keynote of the past and the present era, implicating the basic nature of being incarnate in a form.

The *scurrying crabs* that carry their homes on their backs remind us of the more mundane qualities associated with this sign, which can be found described in any astrological text-book.

The *vegetation* in the foreground indicates that life in *saṃsāra* is much concerned with group activity, with the interrelationships of myriads of entities. It shows that Cancer is the sign of mass incarnation, of psychic sensitivity and reaction associated with the sea of consciousness in which we are all involved. The *ocean* also symbolises this (implicating the myriads of Lives contained within it). It represents the Waters of the Womb (of Mother Nature) from which all Life evolved, according to the tenets of both modern science and the world's mythological systems. Cancer governs the nutritive, maternal nature of the Mother, the forces protecting the Watery womb (from which the crab symbolically emerges).

Brown, grey, green, etc., are the colours of the earth and of manifest Life in the material domain.

**Plate 5. Leo**

## Leo

The central picture in the *Leo* card is that of a nine-petalled lotus. This blossom represents the Causal body of the Soul (the Sambhogakāya Flower).[29] The colourings depicted in the card are a reification of the subtle hues explained in *A Treatise on Cosmic Fire*.[30] The three tiers of the Causal body are arranged thus:

1. The outer Knowledge triad (coloured orange)
2. The middle Love-Wisdom triad (coloured rose)
3. The innermost Sacrificial triad (coloured yellow)

The pearly colouring surrounding and interpenetrating the petals signifies the auric egg that constitutes the resplendent radiance of the Causal body. It manifests as the highest hue or quality that any form in *saṃsāra* can sustain. The Soul exists on the higher mental plane, the highest of the planes of *saṃsāra*. Its hues are the colourings of the three abstract sub-planes of the higher mental plane. The hues of the petals express the general colours of the mental plane. They also veil the energies from the higher planes of perception, which are reflected into manifestation via the Soul. The colours of the outer halo are the reverse, signifying qualities that are expressed into manifest space. They represent the four hues of the lower mental plane mentioned in relation to the Gemini card. They should be considered as sub-hues of the fundamental orange that colours the mental plane, but ordinary rendition of physical paint makes such subtle discernment of hues impossible. The violet colouration moves into the darker shades depicted that endeavour to show the generalised hues of the sub-planes associated with the manifest form. (The astral and dense sheaths of a human unit.) They are domains of darkness *(saṃsāra)* compared to the radiant luminescence of the Soul form.

The entire symbolism of the Soul takes the form of an Eye. The Eye is central to metaphysical and spiritual philosophy, both eastern and western, for as Jesus stated: 'The light of the body is the eye: therefore when thine eye is single, thy whole body also is full of light'.[31] The implications of the Eye are profoundly esoteric, as indicated by these cards. The pupil of the Eye (here the central dot of the discs of light) is coloured *indigo-blue*, relating to the Love-Wisdom manifesting

---

29 The Soul is well described in Alice Bailey's *A Treatise on Cosmic Fire,* 816 *ff.,* whilst the Sambhogakāya Flower is explained in Vol. 3 of my *A Treatise on Mind* series.

30 See *A Treatise on Cosmic Fire,* 822, for detail of these hues.

31 *Luke 11:34.*

via the *buddhic* plane (the fourth cosmic ether). This energy underlies the Causal form on the mental plane (the cosmic dense physical realm).

The pupil of the topmost (Monadic) sphere constitutes a gate through which everything can manifest to influence the central attributes of the kingdom of Souls. This brings to perspective one of the major aspects of the symbolism associated with Leo – that of Individualisation. Individualisation concerns the formation of a new human kingdom (human Souls) from out of the ranks of an animal kingdom that have evolved the needed characteristics to do so. This process is described in the Anthropogenesis section of *The Secret Doctrine* by Blavatsky and detailed in Bailey's *A Treatise on Cosmic Fire*. D.K. states that the sun was in Leo when Individualisation took place as a result of the potent stimulation of energies, and that:

> Several major triangles of force were active when individualisation took place and the "Lions, the divine and tawny orange Flames" came into being, and thus humanity arrived on the planet'.[32]

These 'tawny Lions' represent the qualities of the human Soul during the early formative stage of human evolution.

The yellow-orange-gold colour of the *lions* (as well as of the background) indicates *manas* (the Fires of the mind/Mind). This colour is also the general hue of *prāṇa*. The intelligent empirical mind and self-conscious evolution is a fundamental attribute associated with the general orange fifth Ray of the Scientific Mode indicated here. This concerns everything associated with humanity's egoistic sense, the 'I am' attribute of the mental faculty that enables one to know oneself. This is a fundamental attribute of the human persona, both from an esoteric and an exoteric viewpoint. Therefore, the throne or seat upon which the *yogin* sits is inscribed with the famous injunction of the Delphic oracle: 'Man, know thyself'. Despite its platitudinous nature, this statement is still pregnant with meaning, for it is something that humanity must learn to properly comprehend.

The lion is the regent ruling the Fiery domain and all the elements and forces in it. Much concerning its symbolism is given in orthodox astrology books that need not be repeated here. An important aspect of the lion's symbolism is its direct relationship with the *sun,* which is the source of *prāṇa,* of the natural strength of the lion, and of all evolutionary growth. This affinity with *prāṇa,* for instance,

32 *Esoteric Astrology,* 301. D.K. then proceeds to analyse one such triangle, that being the sun, Jupiter and Venus.

makes the Leonine subject magnanimous, full of vitality and of healing powers, the natural leader in his/her group or society.

D.K. states that: 'The energy of Leo is focussed through the Sun, and is distributed through to our planet via the Sun and the two planets which it veils'.[33] These veiled planets are Neptune and Uranus. The Sun is the orthodox, esoteric and Hierarchical ruler of this sign. Esoterically, the Sun must be viewed from three levels of perception:

a. The central Spiritual Sun, symbolised here by the topmost solar disc. This Sun is the central animating Source of Life in our solar system. It stimulates humanity's spiritual Will, and is the powerhouse that animates the Monad, our Spirit-Self. This energy is governed by Uranus and manifests via the cardinal cross.
b. The Heart of the Sun, symbolised by the central solar disc. It is the central animating dynamo associated with the Soul of all manifest Life and of the twelve Creative Hierarchies. This energy is governed by Neptune and manifests via the fixed cross.
c. The physical sun, symbolised by the central white sphere in the flower held in the hand of the *yogin*. It governs the mutable cross of incarnate life, which stimulates the personality (the third aspect of Deity) and his/her body nature by means of light, warmth and *prāṇa*.

In their totality these Suns govern the essence of a 'human', be it a human personality or that of a planetary or solar Logos.

The solar discs are interrelated by a *white line,* which represents the *sūtrātma* (Life-line), or upon the path of return, the *antaḥkaraṇa*. It is the cord that unites the personality and higher Self, making the process of incarnation possible.

Leo is the principal Fire sign, as indicated by the general colouring of the background. This also symbolises the general harshness of *saṃsāra,* the environment of the lion (here the incarnate personality). This Fiery nature is also indicated by the flames that come out of the mouths of the two lions (that aspire upwards to the Soul). The flames take the shape of a *bird* winging upwards. They signify the aspirational energy from the animal kingdom that allows the process of Individualisation to eventuate. Individualisation relates to the attainment of the self-consciousness governed by Leo, and the formation of a Soul upon the

33 Ibid., 297.

higher mental plane. The Fiery bird also symbolises the thought-form making tendencies of intellectual humanity.

The *throne or seat* upon which the *yogin* sits represents the Base of Spine centre *(mūlādhāra chakra)* and the earthly material nature (the body made of the 'clay of the earth'), which is the basis to all subsequent human development.

The *yogin* is sitting in a lotus posture, indicative of the means that must be utilised to eventually 'know himself' when the mind is fully developed. His right hand is in the earth-witnessing *mudra (bhūmisparsa)* that touches a *radiant gem,* the philosopher's stone *(cintāmaṇī,* described previously), which is the result esoterically of earthly realisation. The gem is the most refined, sparkling, exalted, light-bestowing result of meditative awareness. It is the symbol of humanity's diamond-like attitudes that allow them to conquer time and space.

A *seven-leafed plant (saptaparṇa)* is held in the left hand of the *yogin.* These leaves relate to the seven subtle sheaths that constitute our being. They are expressions of the substance of the seven planes of perception. Humans are considered as Monadic 'plants' that are sown in the fertile ground of the second plane of perception *(anupādaka),* where they can be adequately nourished with the cosmic Waters. These 'plants' grow downwards, where the main 'flower' is the Soul. Subsidiary flowers become the seven main *chakras* in the human body. Each of these *chakras* expresses the awareness and energies of one or other of the dimensions of perception. They grow from the Base centre relating to Earthy experience, to the Head centre wherein *ātmic* perception can be realised (and which can ultimately awaken the potency of the Monad). The higher dimensions are accessed by means of constructing the *antaḥkaraṇa,* allowing multidimensional perception. This is symbolised here by the line of light from the head of the *yogin* to the Eye of the Soul and is then extended to the Monadic sphere.

The *twelve-petals* of the flower held by the *yogin* relate to the Heart centre which is normally golden in colour, but here the colouring is violet. This is the hue of the seventh Ray of Ceremonial or Cyclic Activity and Spiritual Power that will govern the Aquarian age through Uranus. (The exoteric planetary ruler of Aquarius.) The *yogin* is therefore contemplating the attributes that humanity will develop during this epoch and of the service arenas needed in order to serve them. Through such contemplation the twelve main petals of the Head centre can be awakened, the attributes of the Soul (veiling the Heart of the Sun) developed, and finally the Monad (veiling the Central Spiritual Sun) experienced.

The guru or Master is said to reside in the Heart, for therein the Voice of the Silence can be heard that gives esoteric instructions to those wishing to travel from this to That. The Heart is the Source of Life. The other *chakras* indicated here (the Throat, Ājñā and the Head centres) are associated with the higher Way that provides Hierarchical and Monadic impression. The attributes of the centres below the diaphragm are strictly controlled by the yogic posture, and so are hidden, as they play no direct involvement in this higher aspiration. (Other than the Base centre.) There is a direct line of interrelation between the Jewel that is touched (which here can also symbolise the Base of Spine centre), through to the plant and upwards to the Monad. This shows that all are linked and directly related in the meditation process, for the highest must be brought to the lowest and *vice versa*.

There is a pentagram taking the position of the Head centre. The meaning of the *pentagram* has been explained previously. Here it takes the position of the Teacher (or tutelary Deity above the Head, the seat of consciousness), as well as signifying the importance of Leo being the fifth sign in the zodiac.

The *green colouring* of the leaves of the plant relate to the third Ray of Mathematically Exact Activity, which must be fully expressed in order to properly master the attributes of mind/Mind.

The general *yellow* colouration of the landscape and the lions relates to the fourth Ray of Harmony overcoming Strife. This Ray is a conduit for the energies from the Heart of the Sun, which Leo expresses in many ways. This Ray energy acts as the mediator between the higher planes of perception and *saṃsāra*. Mastering the energies of harmony to overcome the strife of *saṃsāra* allows building the links to the various sheaths that facilitate the meditation process and the mastering of all life's challenges. Meditation is effectively a third and second Ray function that produces the perfected twelve-petalled flower of group activity (another main aspect of the Leonine), and the ability to eventually respond to the energies of the central Spiritual Sun.

Though not directly depicted here, this Sun is esoterically Regulus (the Heart of the Lion), which pours the energies feeding the Heart of Life to our planet. Sirius can also be considered, which channels its version of this energy (mixed with the cosmic Waters). Specifically, these energies are contacted by Hierarchy during the Leo full moon in August.

The fourth Creative Hierarchy (consisting of Hierarchy and the Human Souls), who are esoterically termed 'Initiates, Lords of Compassion and Sacrifice', are also generally governed by the fourth Ray. They mediate between the three abstract Hierarchies – The Divine Flames, the Greater and Lesser Builders, and the three lower ones that are the Life of the three lower kingdoms of Nature.

The colours of the *serpents* on top of the diagram (that are arranged in a five plus two grouping) represent sub-Rays of the mental plane, with the orange serpent being central. The colourings, however, can take other hues if a higher view of the serpents is taken. They can convey the energies from the central Spiritual Sun. Taken from a planetary, solar or cosmic (Monadic) viewpoint, they can symbolise the seven Rays and planetary Regents. One can also think in terms of the interrelated *kuṇḍalinī* energy that needs to be liberated by the seated *yogin*. When done so, *kuṇḍalinī* awakens the Fiery Leonine prowess that will enable the *yogin* to Know through direct yogic perception.

The meaning of the Rays radiating from the Causal Body was explained previously in the sign Gemini, and there is a link between the central glyphs of both these cards. When superimposed, a compound meaning is shown by them.

Leo signifies the 'I Am' principle of an embodied Logos that allows such a One to be differentiated from all other Logoi in cosmos.

## Virgo

The sixth card is denoted *Virgo*. Virgo is the sign of the developing Christ-Consciousness, the birth of the enlightenment Mind (Intuition) within the cave of the Heart of the individual aspirant. It is therefore also the sign where the intellectual nature (its discriminatory, analytical, separative qualities) is most developed. For this reason, the central figure in this card is a woman, representing Mother Nature[34] (the sum of the angelic kingdom). She holds in Her Womb the Divine Child, the seed of the future. Throughout Nature we see the effect of this analytical, separateness producing the multitudinous diversifications seen all around.

The colour of the Mother's clothing is the green of the third Ray of Mathematically Exact Activity, indicating that Her direct empathy with Nature is governed by this third Ray function. She stands with Her back upon one of the pillars depicted in the sign Gemini. She is thereby identified with the substance associated with that pillar (the *iḍā* path to the Temple) – with what is material. Behind Her is also a portion of the geometry associated with the pillar. First seen is a circle with an

34 This divine Mother can also be considered to be the Mother of the World.

inscribed form of the hexagram, which manifests as the door to incarnation (as associated with the sign Cancer). As it stands behind Her, so it indicates what Cancer aspires to, which is the gain of the incarnation process. Cancer and Virgo are directly related in this respect, because Virgo gives birth to what Cancer seeds.

**Plate 6. Virgo**

This *circle* is also part of four interrelated circles that together depict the process associated with the formation of the world-Egg, or divine Child. This is the central sphere she holds in Her hands. In this sphere there are two figures, the first is a being forming a circle (indicating Spirit-Being) with his head and feet touching and facing outwards. This symbolises the evolutionary direction (of a planetary Logos) during any particular incarnation. The second being (in the centre) is in the form of a child (inwardly focussed), which represents the gain of that particular planetary or world incarnation – the Christ-Child. The colours of this central sphere are:

1. Red *ādi*
2. Indigo *anupādaka*
3. Green *ātmic* plane
4. Yellow buddhic plane
5. Orange mental plane
6. Rose representing the devotion needed to build the forms. (The meaning of the turquoise or light blue also attributed to this plane was explained previously.)
7. Violet the four ethers, of which lavender-rose is the subtlest.

These colours indicate the substance of the planes of perception rather than of the Rays.

The circles also inscribe the *lingam* and *yoni* (male and female sexual organs) that are central to the Hindu Tantric meditative system. They manifest in the form of a *vesica piscis* constituting Her womb. The goddess *kuṇḍalinī* (the serpent energy) is often found wound around statues of the *lingam* in Hindu temples. The *lingam* is pointing downwards (implying fertility, involvement with dense material forms), and the *yoni* encloses the world-sphere (which therefore takes the form of the head of a child emerging from the womb of the great Mother). She holds this sphere, which indicates that Nature is responsible for the *karma* of the evolution associated with all forms governed by the material world, to which the Mother gives birth.

The pillar takes the form of an upright *lingam* (of Shiva, the Father or first Ray aspect of Deity). This indicates the procreative and also sublimated sexual energies that support the edifice of the temple of the Lord, of the entire material foundation of the universe. When interrelated with the geometry associated with the *lingam,* it is the realm of ceaseless mutable activity associated with the Lives in manifestation. The arrow is composed of two right-angled triangles constituting half a square. (The implied quaternary as described in the sign Taurus.) It represents the cornerstone of the temple of the Lord. The right angle is one of the principal symbols of the Masons. It is used to determine what is straight and true. The 3-4-5 triangle symbolises the path of Initiation from one dimension of perception to the next.

Also implied is part of the fixed cross of the heavens associated with the evolution of the Christ-consciousness, to which Virgo gives birth. Virgo therefore governs the transposition from the mutable cross (of activity in the world of forms) to the fixed cross (of life in the realm of enlightened Being).

Seen from the above, therefore, Virgo is a sign where the various energies in Nature (male and female) are actively expressed and divinely interrelated, producing its various effects in the world and in the realm of enlightened Being. Everywhere in the background is seen the superabundance of Nature's kingdoms, the wealth of foliage and forms that are in constant activity, the ever-bountiful harvest of Life's earthly toils.

The *orange wheat* (the general colour of *prāṇa* and of mental unfoldment) stands for the mental body that must be used to sow and harvest the seeds of plenty and prosperity. The wheat is also a symbol of Ceres, the Goddess of the harvest and of Nature in general. (She is generally depicted holding stalks of wheat.)

Dancing amongst the wheat are three *butterflies* (blue in colour), representing the qualities associated with the higher Mind and the spiritual Triad via *buddhi*. (The association of the butterflies with the air, the freedom of the Mind to move unhindered in space.)

The violet *five pointed flowers* symbolise the etheric body and the *nāḍī* system therein, which is based on the qualities associated with the pentagram.

The *white lilies* in the foreground represent the purified astral (or emotional) body, as well as the *iḍā nāḍī* (feminine energy of the *devas).* The feminine has always symbolised the qualities to be obtained by those wishing clairvoyant or psychic perception (of white magical practises). These powers are especially associated with the Solar Plexus centre *(maṇipūra chakra).*

The *red roses* in the foreground symbolise the *piṅgalā nāḍī* (masculine energies of humanity) associated with the evolution of consciousness. The red colour symbolises generating the Will to awaken the Mind (via the perceptions of the Heart), producing wisdom and enlightenment. This colour also signifies the Blood of the Christ shed for the salvation of the world, whilst the roses also symbolise the powers and perception associated with the unfoldment or blossoming of the higher psychic centres. The roses and lilies are the most advanced representatives of the two classes of plants found in Nature: monocotyledons and dicotyledons.

They therefore symbolise the dual paths found throughout the realms of Being. The violet-lavender flowers symbolise the etheric double via which the phenomenal world comes into being.

Directly behind the lilies and roses sits a *boy* (symbolising the evolving Christ-consciousness) who is in the process of plucking a white rose, the symbol of divine wisdom. Virgo's responsibility is to nurture that child until he has grown 'and waxed strong in spirit, filled with wisdom; and the grace of God was upon him'.[35] When he is able to 'do his Father's business',[36] then the influence of Virgo, the Mother, recedes.

The child is also toying with the *sphinx,* possessing a lion's body and a woman's head. This indicates that Virgo and Leo (the principle of self-consciousness) veil the attributes of the mystery of the sphinx, the relation between the Soul (signified by the lion) and the ephemeral form. To solve this mystery one must utilise the keen, fluid, intuitive Mind of Mercury, which is the orthodox ruler of Virgo. The path undertaken in solving this riddle will develop wisdom. This necessitates the ability to completely know oneself.

In this arrangement, the boy (in relation to the lilies and roses below him) takes the qualities of the *suṣumṇā nāḍī* in the central spinal column.

In the background to the left of the woman there is a *red serpent* wound round a tree (indicating the *kuṇḍalinī* energy, or the Desire of the Logos), which brings to mind the imagery associated with the temptation of Eve in the 'garden of Eden'. She was to pluck the forbidden fruit that was to make humanity 'as Gods, knowing good and evil...wise...with eyes that were opened',[37] which is the central esoteric theme of this sign.

In the background there is the *cosmos* with its countless stars, spiralling galaxies and nebula. They indicate that Virgo governs the immense duration of space-time associated with cyclic manifestation, and all of its ramifications. The cosmos can figuratively also be said to be born in Her Womb. In relation to this, it can be noted that the heart of the local group of galaxies (of which ours is one) is said by astronomers to lie in the constellation Virgo. There is also a swastika formed of stars, indicating that Virgo's attributes govern the movement of the mutable cross (of which she is a member, along with Pisces, Gemini and Sagittarius).

---

35 *Luke 2:40.*

36 *Luke 2:49.*

37 *Gen. 3:5-7.*

**Plate 7. Libra**

## Libra

The seventh card is denoted *Libra*. The central symbol is the balance, or scales, governing the wheel of the law *(dharma)* and of *saṁsāra*. The balance stands on top of the geometry associated with a pillar of the temple (Gemini). Libra can stand upon either pillar, depending upon whether the attributes of the *iḍā* or *piṅgalā nāḍī* are to manifest as the governing cycle. Mostly, however, the balance stands upon the central part of the pillar, signifying the *suṣumṇā* path that determines the expression of the law (the adjudicator of all of Life's attributes), for Libra is one of the arms of the cardinal cross. From this perspective, the lotus upon which the balance sits can also be considered as the four-petalled lotus of the Base of Spine centre (though not depicted here). This is because this centre is the support or foundation of all manifest Life. It is the foundational support of the Law of 'God', which sustains all Life and causes the manifestation of the cycles of activity pertaining to it. These cycles govern the sum of the manifestation of *saṁsāra,* where the lawgiver adjudicates all aspects of the associated *karma.* (Directed by Saturn, the Hierarchical ruler of Libra).

Vast is the undertaking of the four *yugas* and their subsidiary periods within the course of *manvantara,* of a great year of Brahmā.[38] As the great Wheel turns, so accordingly humanity (and all Life on earth) becomes conditioned by the determining influences of that epoch.

The colour of the pillar is gold tempered with red, where the red signifies the first Ray energy of the Will that the ruler must evoke to adjudicate the Law. The gold signifies the basic hue of humanity, whose evolutionary development Libra specifically develops. The Lawgiver rules all of the vicissitudes of Life metered out to humanity, in accordance with the *karma* they have sown and in relation to the zodiacal or racial cycle they are manifesting through.

Libra is the sign of equilibrium, the forces associated with meditation, the balance between all extremes (governing therefore the Buddha's Middle Way), the adjudicator between all positive and negative energies. Libra balances the field of desire, of the entire sexual expression, the male-female interrelation. This sign literally governs the interlude between all of Life's forces – the process of *dhyāna,* of meditative concentration or contemplation, wherein all of the attributes of a subject are carefully discerned. It stands between Spirit and matter, or between Soul and form, allowing the meditative one to integrate the two. Libra therefore represents the middle between extremes, hence can act wisely as the adjudicator. As D.K. states, it is the 'place of judgement'.[39] This is a major reason why the Creative Hierarchies are specifically depicted in relation to this sign. They represent the Soul-aspect of all manifested Life in the solar system. (The Soul is the mediator between Spirit and matter.) Via the mediating, adjudicating agency of Libra, and the governance of the cycles of Life (the turning of the great Wheel), the Hierarchies come into manifestation at their appointed cycles to play their roles.

---

38 *3,110,400,000,000 years.*

39 *Esoteric Astrology,* 229.

The geometric basis to the construction of the central glyph is too detailed to be fully explained here. There are *six spokes* to the great Wheel, relating to the hexagram, which is the symbol of manifest space. The Buddhist philosophy, for example, illustrates this by the six Realms it denotes as the constitution of their Wheel of Life: the heavenly realm, the realm of titans *(asuras),* the human world, that of tantalised ghosts *(pretas),* the animal world, and the realm of hell.[40] The *maṇḍala* of this Wheel is outlined in the light electric-blue colour of *buddhi,* to signify the energies of the cosmic *nāḍī* system via which the energies of Libra manifest. As the Wheel cycles, so the *prāṇas* of the *nāḍīs* move in and out of etheric space.

The indigo blue in the background symbolises the *dharmakāya,* the source of all Being and non-being, the eternal fount or body *(kāya)* of the Law *(dharma).* The colour also signifies the fundamental second Ray of Love-Wisdom, which governs present solar evolution. Consequently, the law that Libra adjudicates is that of Love-Wisdom, though the mode of the adjudication is via the emerald green of the third Ray of Mathematically Exact Activity. Blue-green therefore is the nature of the mode of the manifestation of *karma* governing us all.

Within the great Wheel is a band of seven colours, and twelve interrelated spheres, seven of which are depicted. The twelve spheres represent the spheres of influence associated with the twelve Creative Hierarchies. They convey zodiacal energies to our solar system. As mentioned in chapter seven, four of the Hierarchies are said to be liberated, with one on the verge of liberation from cosmic dense incarnation. Hence seven are incarnate in the cosmic dense realm. They govern the streams of Lives incarnate in the seven systemic planes.[41]

The colourings of the Hierarchies depicted are:

- Orange – (Leo) the first Creative Hierarchy, the Divine Flames.
- Blue – (Virgo) the second Creative Hierarchy, the Greater Builders.
- Green – (Libra) the third Creative Hierarchy, the Lesser Builders.
- Yellow – (Scorpio) the fourth Creative Hierarchy.
- Indigo – (Capricorn) the fifth Creative Hierarchy, Makara.
- Red – (Sagittarius) the sixth Creative Hierarchy, the Lunar Lords.
- Violet – (Aquarius) the seventh Creative Hierarchy, the Elemental Lives.[42]

---

40 See my book *The Esoteric Exposition of the Bardo Thödol,* Part A, 146-63, for detail.

41 This information is briefly given in Bailey's *Esoteric Astrology* and *A Treatise on Cosmic Fire.* They are also detailed in the two volumes of my book *The Astrological and Numerological Keys to the Secret Doctrine.*

42 The colours depicted are indications only. Colours veil the Real, they are vehicles for the Life principle, and can be interpreted from different perspectives. It is impossible to depict the intense,

The band of seven colours also represents the seven layers of *kuṇḍalinī* energy that move from one Creative Hierarchy to another, integrating them into unity.

The *left hand pan* holds a sphere with two pentagrams.[43] In contradistinction to the present twelve-signed zodiac, it is part of the zodiac based on ten signs (as given in Figure 24 for the Atlantean dispensation). This represents the *past,* an aspect of the involutionary process that created the material universe. In the centre is the sign for Libra that signifies the karmic law governing the turning of the entire Wheel. In the card, this position corresponds to the third Creative Hierarchy, the Lesser Builders ('the Triads' of Life). They confer form to all that comes into manifestation (everything concerning *saṃsāra)* and yet this Hierarchy stands aloof from dense physical incarnation. This indicates that this Hierarchy represented the Lords of Life during the Atlantean dispensation. Their representatives manifested as the Lords of Flame that ruled from the then Shambhala under the auspices of Sanat Kumāra.

In the centre there is another sphere formed by the interrelationship associated with the past and future. It thus represents the present, the focus of the weighing in the pans. This sphere is governed by the present twelve-signed zodiac and is represented by a *hexagram.* The material form here dominates, with the Spirit endeavouring to rise from it. The upward pointing triangle points towards the domains of light and Life, and the downward triad to material involvement in *saṃsāra.* This central sphere serves as a battleground where the higher energies developed by humanity may battle with the substance of the past in order to produce the domain of the future. Scorpio, governing the fourth Creative Hierarchy (humanity, the Lords of Sacrifice), governs this transformative process. Humanity are signified here by the outward focussed child that is 'crucified' upon the glyph. This Hierarchy perfectly blend Spirit and matter in their constitution. Thus their esoteric home is the *buddhic* realm (the fourth plane of perception). They are the active participants in the battleground of *saṃsāra* in order to transform its base attributes into those that pertain to liberation. This is an esoteric reason for the pain, struggle and suffering humanity has upon earth.

---

vibrant luminosity and radiance of the colours of the higher dimensions with mere paint. The subject is quite esoteric. For a better understanding, readers need to read the section on the use of colour and sound in Alice Bailey's *Letters on Occult Meditation,* (Lucis Trust), 1950.

43 Concerning directions: I normally think in terms of the way it is for the being concerned or in this case of the card, rather than the way that people normally view things from their perspective. (Which presents a mirror image.) In this case, the mirror image of the great illusion *(saṃsāra)* is presented. (Involution is from right to left and evolution is from left to right.)

The Greater Builders upon the plane *anupādaka* oversee the activities of this middle sphere. With respect to humanity, they work via their Monads.

The *right hand pan* holds a sphere of pentagrams as depicted in Figure 28. It stands for the future. Cosmic energies focus upon Capricorn the goat, to transform the fifth Creative Hierarchy – the Crocodiles (Makara the mystery). They govern the realm of the empirical mind, incorporated by the human unit. From mind comes the evolution of Mind that allows one to master the sum of *saṃsāra*. Everything associated with the mastery of the material form, of climbing up the mount of Initiation (governed by Capricorn) comes to the fore here. This future sphere signifies the (previously explained) ten-signed zodiac that will govern the New Age. The Divine Flames (the sixth Creative Hierarchy) upon the plane *ādi* govern the transmutative energies that integrate the tenth Creative Hierarchy with the ninth (humanity). This process will inevitably produce the etherealisation of substance that leads to *pralaya*.

The threefold spinal column constituting the path of liberation in humanity (signifying the arousal of *suṣumṇā*) is symbolised by the central spoke of the Wheel that manifests as the fulcrum. The *iḍā* and *piṇgalā nāḍīs* are symbolised by the left and right hand pans.

The central spheres (outlined in light blue) forming the mechanism of the fulcrum that holds the pans are but outlines of the central Eye depicted in the Gemini card. As the Wheel of Life turns, so accordingly the energies from the various Creative Hierarchies and associated signs of the zodiac pour into the pans to energise the unfolding activities within them.

## Scorpio

The eighth card is denoted *Scorpio* the scorpion. Scorpio is concerned with the various struggles, trials and tests of the aspirant for enlightenment, of Initiation into the mysteries of the Kingdom of 'God'. The central symbol of the card depicts the world disciple, Hercules (who, because of his labours, personifies the disciple in this sign) battling the nine-headed Hydra (or serpent of desire). The heads of the Hydra embody the mental-emotional attributes that need to be mastered by the disciple. It is said that if one head was destroyed two more would take its place. Hercules needed deep humility, wise discrimination, patience, effort and labour to overcome the Hydra. He was eventually brought to his knees. In that position he lifted the Hydra up in the air, thus away from contact with its lair (the darkness and filth of the earth) which he realised was the source of its strength.

He could not battle the monster on its own ground and hope to win. Thus it is with all disciples in this sign, if they continue to intoxicate their senses and cloud their vision with the pursuits and habits that have always kept them tied down to the mud of *saṃsāra*. This battle therefore constitutes their particular problems, or torment.

**Plate 8. Scorpio**

An astrological sign is depicted on each of the Hydra's heads, indicating the nature of the test associated with that sign. These the aspirant must overcome, both within themselves and also in relation to the external world. From life to life the disciple progresses from one sign to the next, iteratively gaining the ability to overcome the sum of the testings. The tests are triune and concern the purification and transmutation of the base qualities associated with one's threefold body nature (and the related Element). These tests were explained in detail earlier, thus they will be only briefly explained here.

1. The tests (governed by *Scorpio* overall) concern the control of attributes associated with the physical body and its concerns. The Element is Earth. The ramifications of the related three heads of the Hydra therefore manifest throughout the other tests, for everything upon the Initiation path must be mastered whilst incarnate. The physical form also includes the *nāḍīs,* the body of energies that influences the advancing disciple who increasingly refines the substance of the sheaths and the organs of reception *(chakras).* Mastery of this triad of heads produces the attainment of the first Initiation.
    a. Scorpio and the tests concerning *sex,* the conflict between all opposing energies and of the attraction to form. These energies are eventually transformed into service arenas via right human relations. This testing is fundamental to all of the others because the conflicting energies manifest via the *nāḍīs* and must eventually be dealt with yogically.
    b. Taurus and the tests that relate to the *desire* for material comforts. Desire needs to be transformed into desirelessness.
    c. Aquarius, where the tests concern *selfishness* (desire for money). Selfishness needs to be transformed into unselfishness.
2. The tests (generally governed by *Taurus*) concerning the purification and control of the desire nature, hence the Watery Element. The entire murky swamp (the astral plane) must now be fought. Hence the full ferocity of the Hydra is confronted, for all emotional proclivities need to be mastered. These tests awaken a disciple's psychic *karma,* of wrong magical and yogic practices in past lives. Disciples must therefore battle with and overcome the dark brotherhood, who embody the attributes of these heads. Eventually, the second Initiation is thereby attained.
    a. Cancer and the tests concerning *fear* of all types, gross or subtle. Fear needs to be transformed into fearlessness upon the path to the second Initiation. Fear is the basic energy of the astral plane.

b. Aries, where *hate* is to be transformed into loving-kindness. Disciples normally only have to overcome the subtler aspects of this attribute. These are its cousins – irritability, and a certain dislike or disdain for other philosophies, mental-emotional attributes possessed by others, etc. Compassion for all must be developed upon the road of gaining wisdom to help overcome erroneous perceptions. Hatred is a major quality of the dark brotherhood, and the disciple must learn to battle and to overcome their predations. The forces of evil must be overcome along the path of attaining the second Initiation.

c. In Sagittarius, *ambition* must be transformed into aspiration. Here the disciple must fire one-pointed arrows to the goal of gaining enlightenment, to serve the need in whatever form it appears.

3. The tests (generally governed by *Pisces)* that concern the control of the mind. Pisces is the sign of death, thereby the experiences associated with all the tests need to be consummated. The objective concerns attaining the third Initiation, wherein all subtle aspects of the former heads of the Hydra must now be completely mastered, as well as the subtler forms of all the mental-emotions. The attributes presented are qualities that primarily condition the followers of the left hand path. The battle with the evil forces rages psychically until they are made impotent.

The grounds of compassion *(bodhicitta)* manifest as the disciple ensures that any subtleties associated with all attributes of these heads no longer exist. Service work must also manifest to help overcome them in humanity.

a. Leo concerns *pride,* to be transformed into humbleness. Pride in the sense of accomplishment, or being the 'one in the centre', can often exist in the disciple.

b. Virgo concerns *separateness,* to be transformed into the sense of oneness. Lack of true group harmony and cohesion can manifest as the Virgoan head.

c. Capricorn concerns *cruelty,* to be transformed into harmlessness. Not listening to the subtle impressions from the inner Voice to rightly serve and teach others can manifest as a form of 'cruelty', for then those that should have been served will remain ignorant. They will continue manifesting activities that inevitably cause pain and suffering. To pass these testings, constant meditation upon the needed service work (compassionate activity) is needed to develop the sense of oneness, harmlessness and humbleness that allows one to symbolically climb up the Capricornian mountainside upon one's knees.

The geometry upon which the heads are based is part of the *maṇḍala* of the pentagram associated with the Head centre.

To battle the Hydra, he could rely only on his innate, inner resources, fundamental to his being. Thus Hercules is *naked,* as he has had to discard all of his external weapons, including the skin of the slain Nemean lion from his youth that was worn as a protective coat throughout most of his trials. The lion (the king of the jungle) symbolises pride, plus the ability to dominate the sum of the personality in *saṃsāra* (the 'jungle').

Hercules kneels on the head of the lion (the pride has then been conquered) to signify the complete subservience of his personality (or ego) to his higher self (the spiritual Will). His other foot is placed in the mire of the murky swamp that symbolises materialism *(saṃsāra* or *māyā),* which is part of the environment of the Hydra. As with the struggling aspirant, he must learn to fully extricate himself from this swamp as the battle progresses.

Hercules has a *bronze* or sunburnt colour to indicate that he has completely adapted to the open air and sunshine of the desert and the life therein.

The *desert* (the traditional home of the scorpion) is the symbol of life in our present materialistic world, with its harsh mental-emotional environment, its death-like qualities and those entities that need to emotionally sting, bite or poison. The concept of separateness is indicated throughout the desert scene. This symbolises people's empirical minds (the often selfish mental-emotions and the way they segregate and separate themselves from others in their societies). The competitiveness and forms of selfishness that many people think they need in order to survive are thereby produced. This is opposite to the group harmony and cooperative spirit leading to enlightenment that need to be followed. The tests for Initiation concern the transformation in consciousness from concepts of separateness to universality and Oneness.

The basic *red-red brown* (or rust) colours of the Hydra and of the desert are those of the lower nature: sex, desire, pride, etc. These need to be mastered through developing the energies of Love-Wisdom. The swamp also has a hint of the blue Ray, for all was originally seeded in Logoic Love, but has been made aberrant through mental-emotional distortions. This dark colouring indicates the 'outer darkness' that is the astral plane.

The *green* colouring scattered here and there is mainly of the self-focused adaptability (the most prominent colouring of the human aura) that most beings have to develop if they are to survive in the material world. (Emerald green is the colouring of the third Ray of Activity.) The *green cacti* thus indicate attributes of *saṃsāric* life, for even a desert has sources of nourishment, though they are difficult and often costly to obtain, involving many barbs of karmic repercussion through wrong actions in the past.

The *serpent* and *eagle* (or vulture) are ancient symbols of the qualities associated with Scorpio. The serpent contains poisonous venom (people's emotionality, exemplified as the Hydra's heads), but can also be the serpent of wisdom once the attributes of these heads have been transformed. The serpent then stands for the *kuṇḍalinī* Fire that can liberate. The serpent slides on its stomach over the rough terrain. People similarly use their Solar Plexus centres (governing the Watery emotions) in their interrelations with the material domain, and with incarnate personalities. The eagle hovers high in the sky and can see all with a far-sighted vision, thus symbolising the vision of the accomplished *yogin,* with the awakened All-seeing Eye (Ājñā centre). Such an enlightened One (a fourth degree Initiate) has mastered *saṃsāra* in its entirety. The eagle thus signifies 'God's third Eye'. Another version of the bird imagery related to Scorpio can be the vulture that is scavenging for carrion, the titbits of offal (information) possible to obtain in the harsh environment of *saṃsāra.*

The *light blue* of the geometry in the Hydra's head indicates the basic electric quality of the *nāḍīs* of the Hydra when the lower nature is transformed by the tests.

The Hydra's *eyes* are *violet,* symbolising the etheric body and the *chakra* system, which those undergoing the Scorpionic testings also need to master. The colour hints at the seventh Ray, and the ritualistic way that black magicians ride the power of the Hydra's heads to influence the sum of humanity.

The *yellow* colour signifies daylight visioning, as the tests must be mastered whilst in a physical body. It is the dawning of a new spiritual day, wherein all things are possible. The fourth Ray of Beautifying Harmony overcoming Conflict must also be utilised as the disciple masters the material domain, to enter the spiritual. This colour also symbolises the basic quality of the fourth Creative Hierarchy (humanity) that must pass through the testing ground.

The deep indigo blue of the night sky indicates the second Ray quality, which is the objective for the tests in Scorpio to awaken.

The *single star* represents *Sirius,* which governs the development of humanity and Hierarchy on earth. Scorpio has a direct relationship to this sign. From another viewpoint, this star can also be taken to represent the morning star (Venus), or else it represents the One Initiator.

The *violet* colour of the sky indicates the etheric body. The rose, orange and yellow indicate the dawning of the spiritual day that awakens as the disciple aspires upwards by battling the Hydra. They are the colours associated with the development of the higher Mind, of the three tiers of petals of the Soul. These energies manifest as the aspirant masters the tests. The indigo also indicates the nature of the intuitional perception, that when listened to, will allow the aspirant to gain the higher perceptions. Rose and orange also symbolise the colours of aspiration (rose) to undergo the testing process and the development of higher reasoning faculties (orange) that allow the disciple to see through the illusionality of *saṃsāra.*

There are *clouds* in the sky, indicating that the aspirants developing spiritual perception are still often clouded by glamour and illusion.

## Sagittarius

The ninth card designated *Sagittarius* is particularly concerned with the path of aspiration to the goal of enlightenment. For average people, the concern is with ambition for material things, or to satiate themselves with objects of desire. The card depicts the history of the symbolism associated with the sign. In early Atlantean times, Sagittarius was symbolised by the *centaur* (who was half man and half horse). The centaur implicates selfish thought-form making tendencies. Desires, various ambitions, incentives and lofty aspirations of the person were united to the animal aspect, which took him/her this way and that over the plains of the earth (the fields of *saṃsāra).* This Earthy focus is symbolised by the brown colouration of the horse part of the animal-man.

The control of material plane living was the task that confronted the centaur, but for a long time he was swayed by the instinctual reactions of the group or herd, of the masses of humanity and their passions. The main objective then was bodily nourishment and wellbeing. It took many tens of millennia for the indwelling Soul to work through and begin to overcome the limitations of this form. Later, in Aryan times, the mind was sufficiently developed to be in control of the animal nature. It could soar free from the instrument that grounded it to earthy considerations, for that instrument was becoming a purified and highly refined vehicle. Man and beast became separated, and so the symbol for Sagittarius became the *rider on the white horse,* who, with the bows and arrows of his thought-form making process, could fire the arrows in whatever direction wished. The goal could consequently be consummated. The rider was able to find sustenance and adequately nourish the form nature through intelligent aspiration.

**Plate 9. Sagittarius**

Nowadays, the archer, horse and centaur have been eliminated from the symbol, leaving only a fragment of the bow and arrow to remind us of the major incentive of the Sagittarian – aspiration and its direction by the intuition.

The centaur stands solidly on the ground upon four feet, which symbolise the quaternary of the personality: the empirical mind, astral and etheric bodies and the dense physical form. This quaternary needs to be mastered by the rider on the white horse as he sets to fire his arrows of aspiration to higher domains.

The symbol of the arrow represents the narrow, strait and pointed line that leads to liberation, for it can pierce all the veils of illusion and glamour. The arrow represents the one-pointed directive thought of the archer. It is quick, direct to the point and piercing. (These qualities are associated with the intuition.) The archer can penetrate the heart of any matter and thus quickly receive an understanding of the associated properties or qualities, or to rightly direct any meditation to produce the needed revelations. In Sagittarius, the person is inspired and carries out the practical result of former periods of contemplation (symbolised by the sign Libra), and the illumination that the tests conferred in the previous sign (Scorpio).

The white horse represents the purified material form, adequately trained by the rider and is upon two legs, to signify the aspiration of the animal form (or human personality) to the domain of mind, then to the higher planes of perception. The rider is the governing mind/Mind, which is one-pointedly focussed upon entering the domain of Hierarchy, signified by the seven targets (the Ray Ashrams) – or towards Shambhala, the central integrating sphere. This sphere is thus the Doorway leading to this City of 'God'. Its central colouring is that of the three major Rays: red, blue and green, surrounded by the gold (signifying enlightenment).

The archer is depicted firing his arrow at a *maṇḍala* of seven targets arranged around a central one. These targets represent the Ray Ashrams of the Masters of Wisdom that constitute the sum-total of the Hierarchy of enlightened Being. The aspirant or disciple aspires to consciously become an inclusive part of the organisation of that Hierarchy. The targets also represent the planetary spheres (Ray paths) to which an Initiate may aspire. The colours are:

| | | |
|---|---|---|
| • Red | Vulcan | Ray I of Will or Power |
| • Indigo-Blue | Jupiter | Ray II of Love–Wisdom |
| • Emerald Green | Saturn | Ray III of Activity |
| • Yellow | Mercury | Ray IV of Harmony overcoming Conflict |
| • Orange | Venus | Ray V of Science |
| • Rose | Mars | Ray VI of Devotion—Aspiration |
| • Violet | Uranus | Ray VII of Ceremonial Magic, spiritual Power |

The central target also represents the internal organisation associated with the form of the Hierarchy of enlightened Being. It consists of the twelve petals of the lotus of the Heart (and the Heart in the Head), which are responsive to the energies from the seven of the twelve Creative Hierarchies that are incarnate in systemic space.

The outer colours of the spheres represent the energies of the kingdom of Souls that can be considered the outer forms or embodiments of the Ashrams (depending upon the fundamental Ray qualities of the Souls concerned). The internal bands of colours, of emerald green moving to blood red, signify the energies of divine spiritual Activity that will eventually produce the Will that opens the Door to Shambhala. That Door is entered through the indigo blue of the central star, which is the fundamental Ray colouring of Love-Wisdom conditioning all of Hierarchy. Inevitably, the central red colouring of Divine Will must be developed to properly enter that Kingdom. The twelve points to the star, or the twelve outermost petals (of the Head lotus that is Shambhala), point the way to the twelve signs of the zodiac that condition all manifest activity.

An intense rose colour is given to the sixth Ray Ashram, which is the fundamental driving, crystallising or motivating energy causing all phenomenal or manifest life. Rose is the colouring of the second tier of petals of the Causal body (on the mental plane) and the sixth Ray Ashram is essentially concerned with precipitating those energies into the realm of form, with the goal of eventually awakening Love-Wisdom therein. Rose is the hue associated with devotion. (The alternate colourings are sky blue or turquoise, depending upon the nature of the astral energy evoked.)

The Ashrams are divided into a triad manifesting above a square (or rectangle), demonstrating the symbolism of 'the three falling into the four'. This statement provides the hint as to the entire process of manifestation.[44] The triad represents the mode of demonstrating spiritual Power to produce the manifestation of objective form. The first Ray of Will or Power (Vulcan) instigates the process that impels into manifestation Hierarchical thought constructs. The sixth and seventh Rays (Mars and Uranus) help materialise (externalise) Hierarchical Purpose onto the physical domain. They govern the astral plane of desire (Mars) and the etheric body (Uranus) via which the forms will appear.

---

44 See chapter seven ('The Spiral of Consciousness, the Energy View') of my book *Esoteric Cosmology and Modern Physics* for detail.

The qualifying mechanism is signified by the throne of Ashrams consisting of a *piṅgalā nāḍī* (the second and fourth Rays – Jupiter and Mercury) and an *iḍā nāḍī* aspect (the third and fifth Rays – Saturn and Venus). The directing Sagittarian Will is drawn upon for the process of thought-form projection (on whatever level it is directed).

The triad of Ashrams above the square represent the conduits for the energies from the cosmic astral sub-planes. The seventh Ray Ashram (Uranus) stands above the second Ray Ashram (Jupiter), as it externalises the energies of materialising Power from the seventh cosmic astral sub-plane. Love-Wisdom becomes the vehicle of expression for ritualistic manifest Power. The sixth Ray Ashram conveys the energies of Logoic Desire from the sixth cosmic astral sub-plane via Mars. This impacts upon the *ātmic* plane and the third Ray Ashram of Mathematically Exact Activity to express the *karma* governing manifestation via Saturn. This Activity governs the mode of expression of the driving energy of the Desire (the sixth Ray) to produce form. Together, the 7 + 2 and the 6 + 3 produce the number 9 of planetary Initiation via the *iḍā* and *piṅgalā nāḍīs.*[45] The first Ray Ashram conveys the potency of the Will energies of the Logoic Mind from the fifth astral sub-plane in order to direct the All with its Purpose via Vulcan. This triad of Vulcan, Uranus and Mars then signifies the evocation of *suṣumṇā.*

The violet triangle within the circle integrates the energies of the first, second and third Rays via ritualistic or cyclic activity. The green square within a circle integrates the activities of the four Rays of Mind (the fourth, fifth, sixth and seventh Rays) via the green of the Mother's department upon the ātmic plane. The violet energy also governs the manifestation of the energies governing the etheric sub-planes, whilst the green of Mathematically Exact Activity governs the activity of the three planes of the dense physical (the Fiery, Watery, and Earthy), for *karma* must govern all aspects of its expression.

The entire construct is encircled by the gold that governs the activities of Hierarchy in general. This signifies the energies emanating from the Heart centre that the Ashrams express, which is but a reflection of the gold of the Shambhalic Head centre.

The deep indigo-blue of the night sky signifies the *dharmakāya* (Mind), the attainment of which is the goal of the archer. The dawning (or sunset) of the day

---

45 Alternately, the sixth Ray could be placed above the second Ray, and the seventh above the third Ray in order to convey the nature of the expression of the second and third Ray lines of energisation.

signifies the intuition that is the tool utilised by the Sagittarian to obtain his/her spiritual goal.

The mountains in the background signify the heights to be scaled if one is to achieve the fruits of aspiration or ambition. This symbolism also relates Sagittarius to the next sign (Capricorn) where the mode of scaling the mountainside of the Initiation process is exemplified.

Everywhere in the foreground is seen the grassy greens and flowers of the plains that support the grazing activity (information gathering) of the animal nature in the material world. This allows the archer to train his steed and develop the qualities (the horsemanship, etc.) needed to fulfil his/her aspirations. The landscape is not cluttered by a multitude of objects, because the mind and emotions of a Sagittarian are relatively uncomplicated and uncluttered. He/she possesses a single-minded or one-pointed focus that allows the fulfilment of the tasks set out to be achieved.

The colours of the saddle represent the seven Rays of the rainbow-bridge or path *(antaḥkaraṇa)* that lead to liberation. Upon this path the archer travels to the highest attainments.

## Capricorn

The tenth card sign of the zodiac is *Capricorn* the goat. Its central theme is the mount of transfiguration and of initiation. Ten is the number of completion, of perfection. The mountain symbolises what is most material, hard, rocky and cruel in humanity. All such qualities must be mastered upon the mountaintop to attainment, the heights of material or spiritual achievement. Capricorn (via Saturn, its exoteric and esoteric ruler) signifies the mountain load of *karma* governing the three worlds of human livingness, of the various conditionings of the material world. The mountain implies the mode of termination of earthly *karma,* of every restriction to the limitations of the form nature. It signifies the completion of the tests associated with the sign Scorpio and is the objective of the aspiration manifested in Sagittarius.

The *goat-fish (Makara)* is an early symbol of Capricorn, reminiscent of Lemurio-Atlantean times when the qualities of Capricorn and Pisces were closely integrated in the western direction of the ten-signed zodiac.[46] The astral (Watery) receptivity (wherein the Piscean 'fish' swims) was slowly developed in

46 See Figure 19. Though not shown, Capricorn and Pisces were then one integrated sign.

the humanity of that epoch, until it became particularly prevalent during later Atlantean times. The *goat-fish* was concerned with the transition of the zodiac from that shown in Figures 19 to 24. Pisces was one of the two added signs to which the Atlanteans gained receptivity. (The other was the Airy sign, Aquarius.) In the earlier phases of that transition, emotional development was strongly influenced by the materialistic Capricornian aspects of the Lemurians. Sexual, fear based, strongly self-focussed and violent emotions often developed.

**Plate 10. Capricorn**

Makara also relates to the growing rulership of mind over the form, of the process associated with the precipitation of *manasic* substance via the Watery domain and its eventual crystallisation into objectivity. The entire mode of the procreation of the emotional mind is therefore veiled by the term 'Makara'. The zodiac that Capricorn ruled specifically concerned the evolution of the material domain, dominated by the creative activities of the *devas*. As the mind became increasingly developed, it facilitated a forceful control of *devas* by the then humanity. As a consequence, Watery forms of black magic evolved, focussed upon the manifestation of widespread witchcraft. The *goat-fish* signified the turning of the great wheel of that zodiac.

Makara is the tenth of the Creative Hierarchies (also called the Agnishvattas), but the precipitation process also involves galvanising the Agnisuryans (Lunar Lords) into activity. The integration of these two Creative Hierarchies (the tenth and eleventh) is veiled by the symbol of the crocodile that lives both in the water and on the land. This accounts for another late Atlantean term of the Capricornian development – 'the crocodiles'. They relate to the often vicious snapping, biting aspects of the emotions that were then developed, especially when the Watery aspect is reinforced by psychic power and mental awakening.

The esotericism and history relating to Makara is what made Capricorn a mysterious sign, because the left-hand attributes were unwise to elucidate. Many are the mysteries of physical plane creation that must be understood to properly unravel the significance of Capricorn. The higher recurrence of past forms of black magic in the New Age is a possible situation that Hierarchy would like to avoid. Necessary revelations, such as are elucidated in my books (which come under cyclic law) must be carefully provided.

The symbol of the *crocodile* (Sebec of the Egyptian mythology) has a similar meaning to that of Makara. It is a greedy, determined, voracious, and sometimes vicious animal that is able to take refuge both in the waters (of sensation, desire, etc.) and on the material realms. The mode of control of substance via the *devas* embodying the Waters of sensation must thereby be understood, which is obviously one of the secrets of the third Initiation.

The goat (the next symbol relating to Capricorn) is able to free itself from the Watery domain and so seek sustenance in the most rocky, barren and inhospitable terrain. As it can eat most anything therein, its evolving ambition and struggle to succeed thereby is virtually assured success. The rocks symbolise cleavages, fractures and friction – the hardness of the material world over which the goat can travel with sure footedness and determination. (This signifies the development of the mental principle in the Aryan epoch to master this domain.) It can move to higher, dizzier heights than any of its competitors. From pinnacle to pinnacle it can jump, until finally, when reaching the top, it is transfigured into the unicorn. This stately and courageous animal is sometimes represented with wings (of the Soul, or of the petals of the Head or Ājñā centre) with which it can fly to wherever it wills. (Signifying thereby the accomplishment of the third degree Initiate.) Its one horn (the symbol of the third Eye), strait and spear-like (the *antaḥkaraṇa),* allows it to pierce and conquer the various 'beasts' and illusions of the world. Even the lion, the king of the beasts, is killed by him. (The lion specifically signifies pride in material plane accomplishments.) This story is depicted by an old English folk-myth of the lion and the unicorn.

In medieval times the unicorn had been likened to the Christ, who raised a horn of salvation for humanity. Its horn was reputed to have wondrous properties, including the ability to cure the various sicknesses and ills that beset humanity. (Which is what enlightenment, the Initiation process confers.) Note the relation of this to the cornucopia—the horn of plenty, which is a goat's horn that overflows with flowers, fruit and food. The cornucopia thereby signifies the abundance of Nature's harvest that is bequeathed to the victor of the haughty mountainside.

The central compound symbol in this card is an adaptation of what is expressed concerning the seven Ray Ashrams explained in the sign Sagittarius. However, here the concern is with *saṃsāra* rather than aspiration to be liberated from it. The important aspect of the symbol is the associated pentagram, indicating the qualities associated with both black and white magic, which is definitely an attribute of Capricorn. The goat's head is frequently associated with the concept of the Devil, the dark brotherhood's 'god'—which they worship. This head manifests in the form of a pentagram, hence also signifying the five sense-consciousnesses, the five Elements, etc., that must be mastered in both the left and right hand paths, though for each the methodology and motives differ. This head is turned upwards, signifying white magic, but if downturned then the left hand path is indicated.

The head is wrapped, enclosed within the crocodiles, signifying the power base of the dark forms of magic, for Makara and the lesser Hierarchies of *devas* is what they work to dominate. They must manipulate the bestial aspects of Nature to make them subservient to their power, if black magic is to be wrought. Hence, the Mystery also concerns the war between black and white magic, of the differing modes of attaining control of the material domain.

The white magician leaves the Waters (the crocodiles, or *kāma-manas)* and materialism behind, in the form of the white goat steadfastly climbing the mount. The brother of the left, on the other hand is entwined with Makara-Crocodiles and cannot escape from the imprisonment of this form. The upturned goat's head indicates that eventually even the black magician must learn to look upwards towards the spiritual light.

The geometry of the pentagram indicated in this symbol is seen extended to encompass the space of the mental plane. This geometry signifies the nature of mind/Mind (hence the sum of the Head centre) that must be mastered on the path of magic, white or black. (Though only the white brother has complete mastery of all of its petals.) This geometry and its symbolism also underlies the building of the entire *nāḍī* system (and its *chakras).* The climbing goat must learn to master this as it travels upwards to the pinnacle of attainment.

The *colours surrounding the mount* are those of the mental plane, for both the positive and negative attributes of the mind are exemplified in this sign. The central point is the blue of the *dharmakāya,* surrounded by white Light.

The *turquoise blue stream* is the colouring of the astral plane, the Watery (emotional, desire) Element, hence signifying all of the conditionings associated with that plane of perception, the ideal home for the snapping, dangerous crocodile.

The brown-purple-yellow-orange of the crocodile symbolises the element Earth. It indicates also (in conjunction with the reptilian crocodile) the *kuṇḍalinī* Fire that sustains the material world, hence in its most elemental form. Some of the mystery of the symbolism associated with this sign concerns the rousing of this Fire.

The *crocodiles* thus symbolise the union of the Watery and Earthly Elements in relation to the manifestation of energy and its control. The crocodiles can also be interpreted to symbolise the midpoint between the two realms where the practical magician must stand if the magical work is to be accomplished. There are five crocodiles, symbolising the eventual complete mastery of the five *prāṇas,* Elements, etc., of the mind/Mind, through which the magician must work.

The *white goat* climbing up the rocky slope signifies the gradual climb of the (white) magician up the mount of transfiguration to the third Initiation. When attained then the control of the Earth Element becomes absolute. The magician then symbolically becomes the unicorn.

The white-yellow-brown of the shoreline signifies the qualities associated with life in the material world and the eventual development of intuitive perception by those who stand upon the 'shoreline' between *saṃsāra* and the Waters of the cosmic ethers.

The general *green* of Nature is also that of the Lord of Activity – Saturn (ruling the third Ray), and the *karma* whose expression is dominant in this sign. All aspects of *karma* must be mastered. They must be experienced as the fate that conditions the personality, because of mental-emotional activities in former lives. The goat climbing the mountain works to cleanse all aspects of material plane *karma*. Conversely, the lords of the dark path (and general humanity that are conditioned by selfish and self-centred activity) become continuously ensconced deeper in *karma's* retributional action. Vast is the three-fold *karma* that is created by the brother of dark face. It must eventually be cleansed when the horned one turns its head upwards to seek forage on the path to great light.

## Aquarius

The eleventh card is *Aquarius* the water bearer. Aquarius governs the general attributes of a person, being the sign of a man bearing a pitcher of water. This symbolises the totality of someone's energies and capabilities (exoteric, esoteric, latent or real and made objective) when integrated and aligned, after having gained the visions and awareness that the mountaintop experience affords.

The Aquarian sits in meditation, signifying the fluidly awakened Mind obtained in this sign. The pitcher that arises out of the geometry rests on his upward turned hands (the gesture of universality) and extends to his eyes, by means of which he sees what needs to be done. The area that is mapped out by the pitcher (and the related *chakras)* indicates the substance or energies composing the 'water pots of stone' [47] that form the receptacle for the vitality and consciousness of the Aquarian subject. A water pot symbolises the sum total of the Watery qualities (or energies) associated with a personality. These energies and qualities are what the Aquarian subject must master, for the Waters must eventually be turned Airy, thus freed from the constraints of the pot. (Aquarius is an Air sign.) The Water Bearer is the bringer of Life, quenching the thirst for knowledge, wisdom, love and the transcendental. For the undeveloped person, however, the Waters feed the sensual, selfish emotional volatility and transitory material aspects.

---

47 See *John 2:1 – 11.* Here there are six water pots mentioned, signifying the significance of the hexagon in relation to the process of manifestation. This section concerns the marriage 'in Cana of Galilee' that constituted the first of Jesus' miracles, the turning of water into wine. The symbolism relates to the attaining of the first Initiation by a disciple, which Aquarian energies will incur on a mass scale upon humanity during the coming Aquarian epoch.

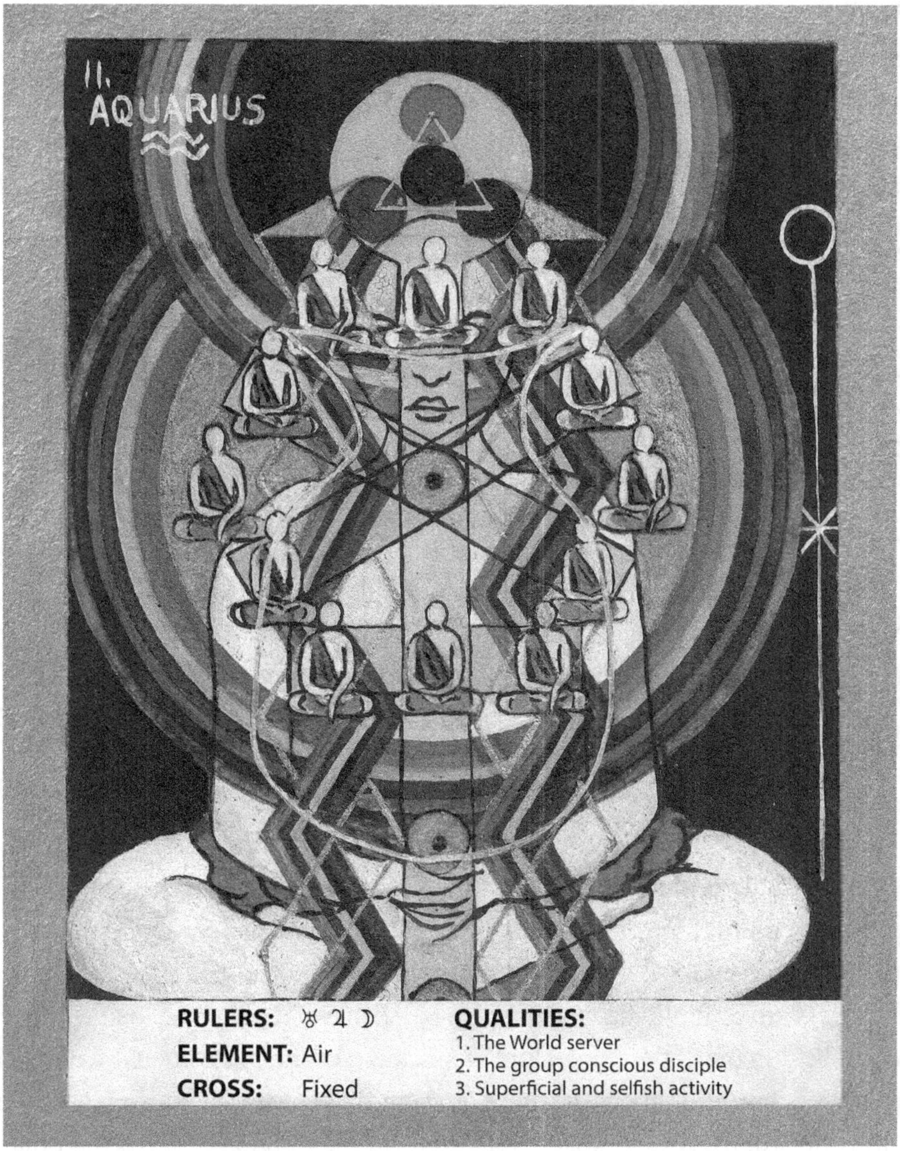


**Plate 11. Aquarius**

The vital energy contained by the vessel is symbolised by the *wavy lines* that stream down from the upper circles associated with abstract Deity (Father-Son-Mother). This is signified by the three primary Rays: red for the Will or Father aspect, blue for Love-Wisdom or the Son, and the emerald green for divine Activity or the Mother. The central blue sphere relates to the fact that the primary Ray of Love-Wisdom governs everything in our solar system. The surrounding yellow colour is that of the fourth Ray of Beautifying Harmony overcoming Strife, which the Bodhisattva utilises to help heal the problematic attitudes of humanity (the fourth Creative Hierarchy), who are also ruled by this Ray. This colour (as well as that of the cross at the throat of the meditating one) signifies the plane *buddhi* (the fourth cosmic ether) via which the Aquarian energies flow. They eventually impact upon the cosmic dense physical plane (our mental plane), and so affect the Lives in *saṃsāra*.

The symbol of this dual sign can be depicted thus:

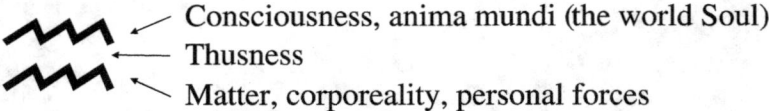

Consciousness, anima mundi (the world Soul)
Thusness
Matter, corporeality, personal forces

**Figure 46. Aquarius and Thusness**

This symbol indicates the mutual embrace of two parallel streams of energy. The upper band represents the higher Self: the human Soul, the source of all inspiration, high ideals and creative aspirations. It is the storehouse of all the knowledge gathered through many aeons of evolutionary growth and experience. This line can also symbolise Purusha of the Hindu's, the Heavenly Man that far outlasts the birth and death of the solar system. (Which is its physical manifestation.) One can also think in terms of the *anima mundi,* the world Soul.

These higher aesthetic qualities are paralleled by the energies of the material world: of sensual corporeality and selfishness, symbolised by the lower line. There is a vibratory mutual interplay, a balance of forces between Soul and matter. This has the ability to evoke the highest in humanity, the most visionary, constructive, artistic, or creative amplitude that a person is capable of. Otherwise, one will become fully involved in the superficial, fluid vicissitudes of the phenomenal world. Either way, the person will respond to the Aquarian influences via participation in the activities of groups, for the wavy lines indicate that one is open to the polarised influences from all energy sources. On a higher cycle, the two wavy lines symbolise the relation between Spirit and matter. From the Buddhist perspective, the junction between them is signified by *śūnyatā* (the Void, here denoted as Thusness).

The wavy lines on the card are directed downwards, indicating a direct flow of energy from the highest to the lowest realms. The colours of the bands are those of the seven Creative Hierarchies, because these orders of creative Lives in the solar system direct the highest spiritual energies into manifestation. They produce the appearance of all phenomena, and are also the embodiments of what manifests.

The central yellow band passing from the sphere above the head and through the meditating figures indicates that Thusness is experienced via meditative pursuits, by mastering all aspects of the yogic precepts. Such meditation is the keynote to the service work that is enacted in this sign after the Initiation process has been accomplished in the previous sign, Capricorn.

The geometry associated with this sign is a summation or extension of what was presented in the previous signs. Here, therefore, is represented a series of three solar discs, as explained in the sign Leo (the polar opposite) with which Aquarius is a member of the fixed cross of the crucified Christ. The central major sphere is here situated over the Throat centre (instead of the Heart), the organ of the creative Word (Aūṁ) that is utilised to help manifest the needed visualisations for one's service work. The Heart centre is, however, the predominant centre depicted, for Aquarius is the sign of the world-server and group-conscious being, who are produced by the active expression of the Heart centre. Therefore, projected outwards in an amplified manner of the Throat centre's influence (the creative mind/Mind), sits a *maṇḍala* of twelve meditative figures. This arrangement tries to express the nature of fourth dimensional consciousness, the added dimensional perception gained through awakening the attributes of the twelve petals of the Heart centre. (The twelve meditating figures thus signify pathways to experiencing the sum of the zodiacal energies.) They also represent the integrated mode of functioning of the members of the Hierarchy of enlightened Being. By integrating their combined energies, the Aquarian must learn to serve humanity. The awakening to Hierarchical awareness is the means to the full development of compassionate undertaking (enlightenment).

Both the Throat and the Heart centres must be active as an integrated unity in order to manifest the enlightened service arena. The *iḍā* (the Throat centre's focus) and *piṅgalā* (the Heart centre's focus) must therefore function appropriately to produce a fully awakened server.

The meditative being that sits at the man's forehead and on top of the vase represents the Ājñā centre (the third eye), the focal point of inner and outer visualisations. This also represents the 'guru', or essential Self, whose Consciousness (the Head centre) manifests as part of the uppermost sphere of energy. A trinity of meditating ones are expressed within this sphere, signifying the mode of channelling the attributes of the triune Deity, as well as the three main tiers of the Head lotus. (The Solar Plexus, Heart and Throat in the Head tiers of petals.)

The *golden aura* that surrounds the upper torso of the meditating figure indicates the energy of the awakened Heart centre that unites the twelve meditating ones in a common embrace of expression.

The *orange clothing* signifies the fully expressed mind/Mind through which the Intuition and the higher perceptions must be expressed. It is also the apparel of a monk that follows the yogic precepts needed to gain enlightenment.

The colours of the *top circles* are those of the seven Ray Ashrams of the Hierarchy of enlightened Being that the serving Aquarian contacts to work with. The Ashram within which the disciple is found colours the mode of activity of their service arena.

The colours of the *bottom circles* are those of the rainbow (as seen on the dense world) for the focus of the service work of the Aquarian is primarily to educate those ensconced upon the seventh (densest) plane of perception.

The central triangle in the upper sphere and the triangle in the central glyph of Taurus, as well as the two arcs of Taurus, are correlated with the two arcs of coloured energies in the Aquarian card. The central streams in Taurus can also be correlated with the central yellow band in the Aquarian card. There is thus a similarity in meaning, showing the deep interrelation between the two signs: the illumination generated in Taurus finds its complete expression in Aquarius. Both are members of the fixed cross.

The water pot is outlined in *buddhi* blue, which also colours the cross at the Throat centre. This indicates the intuition that is properly developed in this sign – that the 'pot' is the container for the energies of cosmic electricity conveyed to the intuitive and meditating ones.

Outside of the central figure is drawn in white a sphere (symbolising the Monad) and a line emanating from it that makes the eight-pointed star of direction in the centre. The strait line *(sūtrātma)* is what leads from the circle of abstract Deity to the material world. It also signifies the return journey of the consciousness link *(antaḥkaraṇa)* that the disciple consciously projects towards the realms of divinity. This line thus symbolically depicts the essence of the meditative technique that the Aquarian must esoterically master. This line effectively signifies the nature of the aspiring consciousness as it moves upwards from the transient point in space towards the sphere of the all (the *dharmakāya).* The cross represents the mode or qualities associated with the meditative development. The eight arms signify:

- North – upwards to the realms of divinity.
- Northeast – the attribute of unity.

- East – inwards to the Heart of Life.
- Southeast – the field of expression of the energies.
- South – downwards to serve the little ones in *saṃsāra.*
- Southwest – the domain of understanding as one learns to serve.
- West – the field of service to humanity in general.
- Northwest – the manifestation of goodwill and ascent into the liberated domains.

The central yellow and blue glyph also manifests a form of this cross, but broken into its main components:

Here the directions northeast, southeast, southwest and northwest manifest in the form of the mutable cross, whose activities are governed by the Throat centre. The cardinal directions, north, east, south and west, represent the attributes of the fixed cross, whose functions are governed by the awakened Heart centre.

This glyph is an extended form of the Egyptian *ankh,* the sign of Life.

The indigo-blue background is that of the *dharmakāya* and the second Ray of Love-Wisdom, which incorporates all Being. This is the Ray energy that bathes the awakened Aquarian. It is the energy that empowers their service arenas.

There are two other spheres implicated in the card. One is upon the top of the hand at the base of the water pot. This sphere signifies the Solar Plexus centre, which controls the general dispensation of the Watery Element, hence is the foundational basis to the service arena. This centre is held in the hands, signifying that the Solar Plexus must be appropriately mastered if the service arena is to properly manifest. There is another sphere at the feet of the meditating one, signifying the Sacral and Base of Spine centre combination, which is the foundation of all meditative activity. Altogether, therefore, the five main centres are represented:

- The Base of Spine-Sacral centre.
- The Solar Plexus centre.
- The Heart centre – the major centre implicated here, viewed as fully awakened via the twelve meditating monks.
- The Throat centre – also viewed as awakened by manifesting the creative potency of the blue Mutable cross.
- The Ājñā centre and Head centre combination – also awakened and energised by the energies from Hierarchy (and ultimately from Shambhala).

The above represents the energies that ideally manifest via the serving disciple and Initiate as a consequence of developing the ability to become a world server.

**Plate 12. Pisces**

## Pisces

The twelfth card is *Pisces* the fishes. Pisces is the sign of the world Saviour and of sacrifice and death. It is the last sign of the zodiac, thereby it signifies the completion (death) of one major cycle of experience. It produces the deep sleep state *(prayala)* before the commencement of a new cycle of evolution.[48] The death here is basically from the angle of the Soul (Sambhogakāya Flower) and of its evolution. This process can be viewed from two angles.

First, the Soul detaches itself from identification with the Spirit (Monad) and descends into the ocean of sensation, form, and matter. It becomes bonded or yoked to the life of the personality aspect by means of the silver cord and undergoes what the mutable cross has to offer. Humanity thereby comes under the general beneficence of the planetary Christ, under whom Love-Wisdom is evolved. Jupiter (governing the second Ray) is therefore the exoteric ruler of this sign. This bonding process is symbolised by the green and blue fishes that overlap to produce the central Buddha figure in the centre.

Because Pisces is the first sign on the reversed wheel after Aries, so here the personality exists in its most unevolved, negative, fluidly psychic and sensitive state. The Soul is bonded to the form and held captive to the experiences and sensations acquired by the person in the ocean of antagonistic forces (as well as beneficent forces) engendered by countless beings. Therein, deep within the turbulence of the oceans, the 'fish' (the Christ nature) swims. Jupiter brings the Soul into new and fresh relationships with all aspects of the form, from which the Soul-personality can glean the needed qualities. Cataclysms, civilisations and cycles come and go – yet this bond always exists.

Next, due to the evolutionary process, the Soul can eventually detach itself from the personality and strongly align itself to the Monad to produce the final death of the Soul-form at the fourth Initiation (the Crucifixion). The bond is then the higher one of the fully vivified *antaḥkaraṇa* between the Spirit and the form, and is composed of living conscious Light. All lesser attachments and unions have been severed. The detachment process manifests through the agency of Pluto[49], the esoteric as well as Hierarchical ruler of this sign. Pluto is the regent of death. He rules the first Ray of Will or Power that produces all of the various detachments, renunciations and deaths throughout the cycles of the personality life.

The geometry of the fishes depicted on the card is an extension of what is shown in Libra. In Libra there were pans, in Pisces there are the eyes of the fishes.

---

48 For human units, such *pralaya* signifies the after death state between rebirths. Similarly, the energies of Pisces terminates the turning of the great zodiacal wheel on earth (or any other planetary sphere) and conditions the places of sojourn for those that have been liberated from incarnation.

49 See *Esoteric Astrology,* 509 ('The upward pointing arrow is the astrological symbol of Pluto.')

The *green fish* represents that associated with the material world (governed by the third Ray of Mathematically Exact Activity), thus the *past.* The person in the eye of this fish is therefore turned inwards, representing the involutionary process producing *manvantara.* It also symbolises the inward-focussed type of meditation developed in the East.

The *violet fish* represents the future, the demonstration of the energies manifesting through the etheric body. In the Aquarian epoch, this activity will be governed by the seventh Ray of Ritualistic Power, to which this fish refers.

The figure in the eye of this fish is turned outward, symbolising the evolutionary forces, and the outward-focussed type of meditation developed in the West. This is based upon rational intellectual discernments, the systematic analysis of the external universe. (This symbol was also explained in the sign Virgo.)

The two interrelated fishes produce a central circle that forms the iris of a larger Eye, within which sits a Buddha whose hands are in the process of teaching the wheel of the Law (the *dharmacakra mūdra).* He represents the present and takes the guise of a world Saviour, as well as forming part of the *band* that unites the two fishes. He can also signify the potency of the Soul. The band is extended to form two arms of the mutable cross (卍) governing incarnate life. Its colourings are those of the seven manifest Creative Hierarchies.

The central *turquoise-blue* aura of the Buddha represents the transmuted radiation of the highest qualities that the emotional (astral) body can produce, with which the Saviour must endeavour to cleanse the massed glamour (etc.) of emotionally polarised humanity.

The halo around the Buddha's head is *violet,* signifying the purpose of the coming Avatar, who heralds the transition from Pisces to Aquarius and so will manifest the seventh Ray dispensation for the new Era. Here is the function of the coming appearance of Maitreya Buddha, thus this colour also circumscribes the central figure. New revelatory teachings will manifest that will integrate the green and the violet Rays, impelled by the red Seat of Power. Red signifies the first Ray quality of the Will that will also empower His actions. All disciples in the New Era must utilise the will to cut the bonds that limit and veil.

The forthcoming teachings will also empower the potency of the red and indigo-blue crosses as well as the golden aura.[50] The indigo-blue *mutable cross* (×) embodies the second Ray of Love-Wisdom, which will also be an important attribute of this great One. This Ray governs Jupiter, the orthodox ruler of Pisces,

50 Note that these colours are a transformed potency of what would normally be associated with these crosses.

but here it manifests via mutable activity. The red *fixed cross* (+) symbolises the first Ray quality of Pluto, the esoteric and Hierarchical ruler of Pisces. This represents an energy conditioning the forthcoming crucifixion of this Saviour, to herald the mass first and second Initiation testings needed for humanity. The red energy (in the form of a crimson tide) will flood into manifestation, directed by Sanat Kumāra, so that the appropriate changes can be produced.[51] The integration of these crosses forms the eight-armed cross of direction in space *(aṣṭadiśas).*

The *pink lotus* represents the purest expression of devotion (to the work that confronts humanity). This energy (of Jesus) will accordingly support the Avatar as part of the process concerning the phrase 'the Reappearance of the Christ'. Jesus will help to teach the New Age dispensation to the devotional masses. The response of humanity to these teachings will help produce their salvation from the Waters.

The *golden-yellow-white* aura is the colour of the light body of the Soul, of enlightenment consciousness, and is ultimately the Light that liberates. The colours surrounding this radiance are those that embody the petals of the Soul (the Sambhogakāya Flower).

The main arm of the mutable cross also signifies the downpour of Aquarian energies (the cosmic Waters) into manifestation (as conveyed by the Avatar). This represents the potency that will pierce the Causal form, causing the Death of the Sambhogakāya Flower at the attainment of the fourth Initiation for those that are ready to do so. Previously there occurred the death of the personality life, when it merges into the constitution of the Soul at the attainment of the third Initiation. This is an effect of the power of Plutonian first Ray energies, that help to eliminate the attachments associated with desires that disciples normally find hard to eliminate. There was also an earlier 'death', when the Initiate dies to Watery astral form. This death is denoted 'the second death' in the Bible, for the 'first death' concerns the process of normal physical death.[52]

The major arm of the mutable cross signifies the upward evolutionary motion into cosmos of all of the Creative Hierarchies. They move towards liberation as they 'die' to the trammels of their forms.

---

51 This tide will produce significant planetary convulsions. Much *karma* concerning the happenings upon the moon needs to be rectified by those that formerly created the conditionings for that planetary disaster. (This mystery can be somewhat comprehended by those that study with care the information presented concerning the moon in the two volumes of my book: *The Constitution of Shambhala.)*

52 For more information about these deaths, see chapter eight of my revised book *The Revelation.*

The outer silver-blue-white circle represents the colourings of the cosmic astral realm, of the Waters in which the Logoic 'Fishes' swim. They are bonded to the forms of their Bodies of Manifestation. (Logoic Spheres, such as the earth.) Each of these 'Fishes' is yoked to the form of a *manvantara* (a great year of Brahmā).

The circumscribing indigo-blue is that of the *dharmakāya,* from which all is expressed and into which all is resolved.

# Appendix

## The four spiritual festivals and their seven Ray subdivisions

Due to the ability of the moon to reflect the light that falls upon it, and because of the potencies that it veils, the time of each full moon is used with effectiveness by those that meditate. In doing so, they coordinate their meditative rhythm with that of the planetary Logos, who is said to pour the reflected light from associated constellations onto the earth during each full moon period. This happens via the medium of the Hierarchy of Enlightened Being. All people that are in any way sensitive to the call of their inner being become aware of the heightened meditativeness that then falls upon them, according to their ability to tap the energy currents during these periods.

This downpour of energy is particularly potent during the Wesak Festival at the first full moon in May. The Buddha previously appeared on the mental plane during each Taurus full moon. Owing to recent spiritual events, the Buddha has finally entered His complete *parinirvāṇa*. Thus He will no longer frequent the earth once a year. His work will be superseded during the Aquarian epoch by the energies of the Mother of the World, heralding the feminine cycle in this New Age. We all live within the great beneficence of Her nurturing embrace. All of Hierarchy are Her children and bow to Her as the embodiment of their Love. Another great Being, the Rider, now substitutes for the Buddha's former presence. Everything in *saṃsāra* is subject to change. Accordingly, the Bodhi tree that the Buddha earlier sat under, which manifested the form of the Initiation cycle that he heralded, will be supplanted, as this New Age brings into flower a new Initiation Tree.

The Christ, the Rider and the entire Hierarchy meet and energise the earth in rhythmic unison. They invoke the various energies needed for the cycles that will answer the massed needs of humanity and project the beneficent Plan forwards during the great astrological seasons. To do this, certain mantras are intoned, the most important of which is *The Great Invocation.*[1] Every meditative being should play their part with Hierarchy during these periods, especially regarding the invocation of this mantra. It is an avenue of approach that will facilitate the appearance of the Avatar bearing the energies of the cosmic Christ.

## The Festival of the Arising and the Living Christ

This happens in the first full moon in Aries. The originating energy comes from Sirius via *anupādaka* (the domain of the Monad). Overall, it is a second Ray dispensation, though manifesting via a first Ray impetus (as ruled by Aries), which is needed to project the qualities for all of the festivals throughout the year onto the dense physical plane. The general impact of this festival is upon the astral plane. The focus is the conversion of the astral miasma created by humanity into a domain of light.

The esoteric impact of this Festival is directly upon the planetary Heart in the Head centre,[2] then into humanity. The sub-Ray attributes are directed by the inner Council of Hierarchy to help produce the related purposes outlined below.

D.K. calls this 'The Festival of the Living Christ' and relates its dispensation to Hierarchy in his book *The Externalisation of the Hierarchy.* When looking at humanity in general, the festival is more appropriately the 'Festival of the Arising Christ', because the Christ aspect is still arising within them. This is the function of Hierarchy to achieve therein, hence D.K.'s assignment of Hierarchy to this festival.

### *The sub-Ray aspects of* the Festival of the Arising Christ

This festival is related to the direct work of Hierarchy, thus the general overtone of these seven statements is of the manifestation of the second Ray of Love-Wisdom.

---

1 For detail concerning this mantra, see my books *The Constitution of Shambhala,* Part A, 387-394, Part C, 465-68, plus Alice Bailey's *The Externalisation of the Hierarchy,* 488-91.

2 The terms 'Throat in the Head', 'Heart in the Head' and 'Solar Plexus in the Head' are explained in my book *An Esoteric Exposition of the Bardo Thödol,* Part A, in relation to the mode of functioning of a Head centre. Here the entire planetary dispensation can also be taken into account. The planetary Head centre is Shambhala.

The first three statements are along the second Ray line, followed by those of the Rays of Mind.

**The festival of Love itself** – manifesting via *anupādaka.* The second sub-Ray energy is projected, which is the Purpose of the festival to generate. 'Love itself' is a direct expression of the Christ energy. Here, the Love (of the Logos via Hierarchy) manifests in such a way that it moulds the consciousness stream of humanity into an integration with the All that is Love. Love is the guiding energy sustaining our solar system.

**The festival of Unions** – manifesting via *buddhi.* The fourth sub-Ray of Harmony Overcoming Conflict is expressed, producing the major integrations of the planetary Purpose. The series of 'unions' that are the effect of Love and developing wisdom produce group integration. They culminate upon the buddhic realm (the realm of at-onement). Here Hierarchy meet to organise their planning of what should be accomplished for that zodiacal year and thence well into the future. There are various unions, such as between people on the physical plane, attributes of consciousness, humanity and Hierarchy, and the various Ray Ashrams. There is inevitably the union between Hierarchy and Shambhala, and the union between *deva* and human Lives.

**The festival of Beggars** – manifesting via the astral plane. The sixth sub-Ray is utilised, which vitalises the astral plane. 'Beggars' can relate to human Souls, which at first 'beg' for reincarnation experiences. Later, as the Initiation process progresses, they 'beg' for energies from higher sources. More specifically, however, this is the humanity that are steeped in astral glamour, hence they must yet pass the tests productive of the second Initiation. They live in the 'outer darkness' of the astral miasmas, starving for light, love and wisdom. Thus they are 'beggars' for spiritual nourishment. It is Hierarchy's purpose to provide them with such nourishment via active loving service. (This story is well explained in my various books and those of Alice Bailey, hence needing no repetition here.)

**The festival of Sinners** – manifesting via the physical plane. The seventh sub-Ray is here represented, incorporating all the Ray lines via manifest activity. The 'sinners' relate to the human personality, which produces the *karma* that eventually educates on what not to do. The process of 'sinning' introduces the factor of desire *(kāma).* Such *kāma* is generally directed from the mind *(manas)* when united with desire-emotions. This is implicated by the term *kāma-manas.* This festival thus manifests the plans of how to mitigate the burden of *kāma-manas* that afflicts humanity. This energy works to rectify human *karma* in such a way that eventually there is a progressively positive outcome.

**The festival of Gratification** – manifesting via the mental plane. Expressed is the fifth sub-Ray, the mind's understanding of the nature of phenomena, and of its knowledge of 'things' related to human emotional conditionings. 'Gratification' concerns the expression of the senses, as directed by the mental-emotions, to obtain what is desired (mentally, emotionally or physically). There is subsequently spiritual gratification: thanksgiving for the energies received from Deity or Hierarchy. The mind must inevitably come to rightly dominate and rule the astral plane and its phenomena. Hierarchy must teach humanity how this is accomplished. The manifestation of selfish materialism is to be transformed into loving-kindness, and then aspiration to high ideals. Eventually *kāma-manas* must be superseded by Love. The mind must be used to create things of beauty, to master the emotions, and to develop the abstract reasoning that signifies the attainment of enlightenment.

**The festival of cyclic Endings and Beginnings** – manifesting via the ātmic plane. The third sub-Ray of Activity, mathematically exacted, governs the manifestation of the cycles of *karma* that come and go as each attribute of manifest life is mastered. 'Cyclic endings and beginnings' therefore here relates to the process of *manvantara* and *pralaya* – a continuous rebirthing *(manvantara)* of attributes needing mastery, thence their cessation *(pralaya)*. Once mastered, then another cycle of *karma* is to be cleansed upon the road to enlightenment. The cycles conditioning humanity (and the world disciple), and how they manifest, must be rightly regulated by Hierarchy in accordance with present need.

**The festival of sacrificial Life** – manifesting via the plane *ādi*. The first sub-Ray governs, empowering the reincarnating compassionate activity of the Bodhisattvas that appear amongst humanity. For them 'sacrificial Life' relates to dying to the blissful experiences on the enlightened domains in order to appear into our 'oh so wonderful' physical lives that need to be transformed upon the Initiation path. The Monads sacrifice themselves through the 777 incarnations. This festival therefore directs the course of such evolution towards the Initiation Path. Through this process, the highest energies possible can be brought upon our terrestrial sphere.

## The Wesak festival

This festival happens at the first full moon in Taurus. Overall, it is a first and second Ray dispensation – the directing of cosmic astral plane substance by the Eye of the Bull. The festival's energies impact upon the mental plane, being the focus of this festival to transform. This was signified by the wisdom religion founded by the Buddha, whose emphasis was the right understanding and control of the mind/Mind.

D.K. states that Shambhala directly empowers Wesak. That is true because Shambhala is the major open Door to cosmic sources through which the energies impacting Wesak flow. However, the major recipient of this energy flow is Hierarchy, who then distribute their purpose to humanity, according to the Desire of the Logos. The energies can come from any of the three major cosmic sources, plus also the constellation Leo (the present residence of the Buddha). The energies of cosmic Mind and Love are directed via the Throat in the planetary Head centre. Sirian Purpose is thus thereby wielded by Hierarchy (in conjunction with what else the Bull directs).

The Eye of the Bull focuses cosmic Desire through Shambhala to Hierarchy. Hierarchy then tone down the energies for humanity in order to help foster the energies of Love-Wisdom amongst them. The sub-Ray attributes to the Wesak festival relate to this. The overall impact of Wesak upon the mental plane is to stimulate the development of the Mind within humanity. From this plane also manifest the energies that condition all of the other kingdoms of Nature, via the *devas* that administer to them. The Eye of the Logos thus manifests in a three-fold manner during Wesak: upon Shambhala, Hierarchy and the kingdoms of Nature.

### *The sub-Ray aspects of this festival*

**The festival of the Buddha** – the fourth sub-Ray. This energy manifests via *buddhi* to demonstrate the wisdom of the Buddha's purpose in endeavouring to help dissipate the world's illusions. His was a fourth Ray dispensation, which is also the Ray governing humanity in general. The importance of the Buddha's teachings on earth and the subsequent development of Buddhism are well known. Yet, to properly flower in the New Age, the religion must still grow in wisdom, so that its outstanding errors are eliminated. The true nature of the abstract Mind and of the *dharmakāya* must yet be revealed to the Buddhist world. Thus the consequent epoch of Maitreya will produce further spiritual revelations for the world, standing upon the shoulders of what the Buddha formerly established. Buddhism will grow thereby, signifying the import of this festival.

**The festival of the Sun** – the third sub-Ray. This relates to the plane *ātma*. Here, 'the sun' is viewed in terms of the physical sun,[3] of the Logos that rules the

---

3 The reference here is to the three suns esoterically considered. The physical sun, the Heart of the Sun (represented by Sirius), and the central Spiritual Sun (signified by the seven Rishis of the Great Bear).

sub-planes of the cosmic dense physical plane. This is the domain of the karmic interrelationships that govern all Lives in this solar *manvantara*. The sun is the active expression of the radiance of Love. This festival therefore concerns the way that the *karma* of material involvement of all that evolve on these planes can be annulled, so as to produce their liberation from substance. (In a similar manner to what the Buddha accomplished personally.)

The major objective here is to eventually propel the human kingdom, so as to master the transformative tests that will eventually allow them to become Masters of Wisdom. They can then become *nirvāṇees* and so travel through the gates of Shambhala into the cosmos as Buddhas (Chohans).

**The festival of the East** – the second sub-Ray. The east relates to the direction inwards to the Heart of Life. The related plane is *anupādaka*. These energies are naturally directed to the kingdom of Souls (the Sambhogakāya Flower). All of Hierarchy (the planetary Heart centre) work to help stimulate this kingdom, and thereby foster liberating energies from this domain. Human Souls are thereby greatly stimulated to assist the work to engender the principle of Love amongst human personalities. This process will inevitably produce the externalisation of the Hierarchy, thus transforming human civilisation in a way that the earth becomes a sacred planet. The development of compassionate thoughts help to turn humanity's thought life inwards to Heart-centred attitudes.

**The festival of Life itself** – the first sub-Ray. This relates to the plane *ādi*. 'Life itself' relates to Monadic Life, as well as to the kingdom (Shambhala) that governs the manifestation of all streams of Life on this planet. This festival therefore aims to increase the level of contact between Shambhala and Hierarchy. The aim is to eventually dissipate the *māyavirūpa* of humanity's glamour-making tendencies. The astral plane must eventually cease to exist, and for this purpose the highest energies must be brought to bear, utilising the Fires of the Mind. This allows the Life principle to shine through what was formerly veiling substance. To do this, humanity's thought life needs to be empowered with clear logic to eliminate emotional and desire-based thinking. The purpose is to produce the conditionings that will eventually allow Shambhala to exoterically manifest on earth.

**The festival of Taurus, hence of Vision** – the fifth sub-Ray, relating to the mental plane. Vision necessitates using the energies of mind/Mind to visualise (via the third Eye). Thereby to use clear logic, abstract thinking, to reveal the truth that was obscured by the darkness of ignorance. Inevitably, the objective is to perceive the true nature of Logoic Desire (as governed by Taurus) that conditions the sum of the manifestation of cosmic astral and systemic space. Here, Hierarchy empowers the world's disciples to see clairvoyantly (astrally). They thus develop the inner vision. Hierarchy also projects images into the minds of the world's disciples and Initiates that assist their path to enlightenment. These are provided in their meditations and also manifest in the form of the intuition and through dreams. They often relate to future activities, and hint at the part of the overall Hierarchical Plan for world salvation that is to be played by the disciple. Such imagery is normally coloured by their religious affiliations.

**The festival of giving Life** – the sixth sub-Ray governing the astral plane. 'Giving Life' concerns the act of creative birthing and is always projected by the sixth Ray if it is to produce manifestation (the appearance of 'things'). This energy, moulded by the Buddha's wisdom, projects the purpose of the Wesak festival via humanity's (or the earth's) *nāḍī* system, to produce necessary changes in the physical domain. Societal and civil structures can thereby be influenced for the better. The focus is upon dissipating the world's Watery (emotional) substance. This will allow humanity to truly experience the nature of spiritual Life, rather than the blindness of glamour and illusions. The fogs and mists of astral plane substance eventually dissipate via the impact of the radiance of the Buddha's teachings, and by those that help to disseminate Love as a consequence of this festival. This allows the principle of Life to be liberated from the confining form.

**The festival of Time Began** – the seventh sub-Ray. Time only exists on the physical plane, thus it is cyclic. Hence time brings the energies and Wisdom of the Buddha (thus of Hierarchy) right down into physical plane manifestation via seventh Ray activity. The ritualistic activity of those who are responsive to Hierarchy's overtures will help ground His purpose throughout the cycles of time.

## The festival of the New Age Temple – of Good Will

This seventh Ray dispensation is ruled by Gemini. D.K. calls this the festival of Good Will. The ritual manifests via the *nāḍīs* and *chakras* within the etheric double of the earth. This festival is at the first full moon in Gemini. The general impact of this festival hence is upon the etheric plane, but it is then precipitated into the realm of forms. All magical activity is accomplished via the *chakras* and appropriately manifested ritual. The planetary Solar Plexus in the Head centre is here principally stimulated, governing the activities of general humanity. This work is primarily civilisational in its mode of expression, thus is done via the Mahāchohan's department.

### *The sub-Ray aspects of this festival*

**The festival of Serving, of Sharing** – the seventh sub-Ray. Service work involves sharing of energies via the active demonstration of the power of Love. The ritualistic function of the seventh Ray governs all of the Rays of Mind and conditions the world's disciples to manifest their various forms of service work upon the physical plane, according to Ray lines. From the group to the individual, the energies flow. Disciples consequently learn to build the new world communities wherein cooperative sharing and communal service work are keynotes.

**The festival of Loving Embrace** – the sixth sub-Ray. 'Loving Embrace' involves the transformation of desire (sixth Ray) and self-focus into Love as a consequence of the abovementioned process of learning to share. The energy is predominantly Watery (astral), precipitating its devotional and loving purpose on to the physical plane. The sixth Ray acts as the conduit for the downpour of energy from cosmic astral realms. The energy fosters high aspiration amongst the world's disciples. They learn to emulate the work done by the great Ones that have incarnated amongst humanity in past cycles, and so tread the path of Initiation that leads to Hierarchy's domains.

**The festival of Sleeper, awoken** – the fifth sub-Ray. The 'sleeper' (massed human consciousness) awakens through the process of becoming enlightened via development of the intellect and then gaining receptivity to the higher mental plane. This energy is directed to convert materialistic, empirical thinkers to look upwards to the higher dimensions of perception. Thus they learn to think more abstractly, universally and lovingly. The rituals manifest, therefore, in a way that helps empower human Souls to be able to more actively incarnate into people's minds. The objective of this festival is to help produce the third Initiation amongst humanity.

**The festival of Bleeding Heart** – the fourth sub-Ray. The fourth cosmic ether *(buddhi)* pours into manifestation the energies of the integrating, unifying Logoic Love through the work of the temple builders. The purpose of the associated ritual, therefore, is to draw the all into the embrace of the One. This 'Bleeding Heart' is the prime quality of all awakened Initiates. It Bleeds as a consequence of the vast amount of erroneous doctrines and opinions generated by human thinkers over the centuries. The needed thought-forms must be generated that inspire right human devotional and aspirational thinking, rather than the mundane empirical fare they are presently largely indoctrinated with in our materialistic societies. The Heart Bleeds for those that have been converted to dark brotherhood methodology as a consequence. The work is to try to mitigate and to eventually eliminate via sacrificial activity the hell states of humanity. The associated rituals manifest the shields of protection for humanity that will hopefully ward off massed dark manipulative thought projections. Cosmic energies from *buddhi* are used to help produce this work.

**The festival of ripened Harvest** – the third sub-Ray, and the ātmic plane. The 'ripened Harvest' is the consequence of the field of service, with the aspirant, disciple or Initiate learning to obey the dictates of the Soul or Monad. As groups of humanity increasingly walk the Initiation Path, so this 'harvest' ripens quickly, and consequently can be reaped by the One Initiator. The focus is upon those steeped in glamour (the great majority of humanity), with the priority being to guide them towards overcoming habitual emotional based thinking, and thus cleansing *karma* from former past actions. They must therefore learn to pass the tests for Initiation. Temples of Initiation are to be constructed wherein the 'harvest' can be reaped by Hierarchy. The concept of 'harvest' also implicates the function of the *deva* kingdom, who embody all of the attributes of Nature's kingdoms. They work to produce all of the harvests of Life. The New Age temples will integrate both types of 'harvests', those associated with humanity, and those governed by the *devas*. Their true mode of interrelation will become understood via the development of Mathematically Exact Thinking.

**The festival of golden Keel** – the second sub-Ray, drawing energies from the plane *anupādaka*. The 'golden Keel' here relates to the Argo. This is the ship of Hierarchy travelling upon cosmic etheric energies, utilising the energies of dynamic Love. (The 'Keel', being the lowest part of the boat, relates to the *nāḍī* system of the earth.) The myth of Jason (an incarnation of Morya, the first Ray Chohan) and the Argonauts relates to when Hierarchy as a whole travelled to Shambhala. Therein the present Chohans (sixth degree Initiates) took their third Initiations. It relates to the coming of age of Hierarchy, when they won over the Golden Fleece (the Hierarchical aura) from the sleeping dragon guarding it. Here the purpose of the temple ritual is to draw Hierarchical energies through into the *nāḍīs* of humanity, so that their 'ship' will eventually journey to the golden Sun that is Hierarchy. Similarly, Hierarchy must 'sail' to the precincts of Shambhala. Humanity must eventually learn the nature of the *chakras* and their functions via the temples of Initiation that are appropriately established to teach them. This festival also concerns the mode of interrelationship between the Ashrams of the Rays of Mind and those of Love-Wisdom. Thus this 'Keel' sails across the Waters of the ocean of Love.

**The festival of spun Wheel** – the first sub-Ray. The 'spun Wheel' relates to the sum total of Hierarchical activity, the Wheels of Love, Wisdom and Will constituting the Ashrams of the Masters of Wisdom.

The 'spun Wheel' can also relate to the turning of the great zodiacal Wheel. This concerns the process that will produce the externalisation of Hierarchy. Evoking the power to make this an accomplished fact in a way that humanity comprehends is thus the focus of this festival. Similarly, the 'city of God' (Shambhala) will also be later externalised. One can also consider the turning of the wheels of all the *chakras* to produce the reticulation of the sum of the *prāṇas* in the *nāḍīs*. These energies are spun into the fabric of Life.

## The Festival of the Great Mother

The third Ray dispensation, as ruled by Virgo, is the obvious Ray line of the Mother and the *deva* kingdom. This ritual is enacted in the Virgo new moon. The general impact of this festival is upon the physical plane, on whatever is deemed as the substance into which the Life principle incarnates. The *devas* build in each new moon the forms that are to be effectively made manifest in the full moon periods. This festival is only hinted at by D.K., as the time for the epoch of the Mother of the World was not then imminent. However, now much more can be revealed, especially as to the mode of the cooperation between *devas* and humanity. All magical work is accomplished by means of *devas,* and via loving ritual. Obviously, the sub-Ray statements of the festival of the New Age Temple and those of the Great Mother should be correlated to obtain a better picture of the nature of *deva* and human interrelations that will manifest in the New Age temples to be established. These festivals can also be correlated to the seven Pleiades that govern the attributes of the *deva* lives manifesting through the seven planes of perception. They are Electra, Maia, Celaena, Alcyone, Merope, Tayeta and Sterope.[4]

### *The sub-Ray aspects of this festival*

**The festival of *devas*** – the first sub-Ray. This concerns the development of the Will via the *deva* Initiation process that allows *devas* of Power to evolve. They are the Rāja Lords that govern the substance of manifestation in all of the sub-planes of the cosmic dense physical. The main flow of this substance is via the first

4 See my book *The Constitution of Shambhala,* Part B, for detail concerning the Pleiades. More information shall be presented in the last chapter of Volume two of the present work.

Outpouring from the ātmic plane.[5] What empowers the flow of the substance, however, are the Rāja Lords enthroned upon the highest sub-plane of each of the planes of perception. They take their overall purpose through this festival enacted upon the highest of the planes of perception. This festival resounds the mantric Sounds (the plucking of the strings of the Lyre) that are the Commands for the sum of the *deva* Lives.

Electra, governing the substance of the plane *ādi,* oversees this festival, pervading the all with her electrical vitality.

**The festival of Active Love** – the second sub-Ray. 'Active Love' fused with Divine Intelligence relates to the mode of Initiation for *devas*. The energies from the second cosmic ether *(anupādaka)* govern the manifestation of the related *deva* rituals. This Love also concerns the mode by which *devas* interrelate with humanity. It produces the betrothal, marriage and fusion at the latter stages of both human and *deva* evolution.

Their Love is fundamentally directed to build appropriate forms through which the streams of Life (the Creative Hierarchies) can incarnate, so that evolutionary perfection will be obtained. This Love sings out the music that is the harmony of the spheres of active Life. This festival is especially attuned to the four cosmic ethers.

Maia is the Pleiadian Sister that wields the substance of *anupādaka*.

**The festival of Femininity** – the third sub-Ray. Femininity obviously refers to the third Ray functions of the Mother, allowing Her to give birth to all things through Mathematically Exact Activity. Her purpose manifests via the ātmic plane but resounds upon the higher mental plane, which produces the path to the precipitation of all forms onto the dense physical. Upon the higher mental plane also exists the kingdom of Souls, the Christ-Child in the Mother's Womb. This 'femininity' therefore also relates to the mode of giving birth to this Child out of Her Womb. It nurtures all of the lesser streams of Lives that are evolving into the next Child to-be.

Celaena bears the Womb of the substance that all Lives utilise as their forms as they evolve through time and space. This Womb consists of the angelic Triads that build the forms of things, and which thereby govern the *karma* of what is to be.

**The festival of Beauty** – the fourth sub-Ray. This festival utilises the fourth Ray energy to spread Beauty and ordered Harmony throughout Nature. The ungainly

---

5 See my book *Meditation and the Initiation Process,* 277-84. The Outpourings are also explained in Volume two of *The Astrological and Numerological Keys to the Secret Doctrine*, and Volume two of the present work.

mental forms (the clashing sounds and din) created by humanity must eventually be turned into a harmony of Sound, with all the colourations beautified and sanctified. The Lives within the Womb are orchestrated by symphonies of melodious Sound from cosmos: from the zodiac and various other stars and constellations. The forms within the Womb are thereby conditioned by the integrated unity of the whole. Many are the Brothers and Sisters to our planetary Logos (and the liberated Lives therein) that sing the mantric Songs to help liberate the Lives within the planetary Womb. Alcyone, the fourth of the Pleiades, relays these Songs into a symphony of creative activity.

Alcyone wields the substance of the fourth cosmic ether *(buddhi)* to mediate between the harmonies of the above and the clashing sounds of the cosmic dense physical Lives. Eventually, the ungainly forms created by humanity (the fourth kingdom in Nature, who thereby have a direct affinity with Alcyone) will be transformed into ordered Beauty. Thus the flow of evolution proceeds.

**The festival of Above** – the fifth sub-Ray. The 'Above' here relates to the forces of Logoic Mind (Mahat). The *devas* draw Mahat down into manifestation in order to produce the sum of their building work. These forces are the zodiacal and planetary energies constituting the Womb of space-time for any manifesting Logos. *Devas* are inherently mind/Mind and use the fifth Ray quality of right intelligent activity to aspire and rise up the planes of perception. This festival therefore relates to the mode of attainment of their forms of Initiation. They thereby become increasingly potent *deva* 'cells' within the Mind of the Logos. The forte of the *deva* kingdom is the manifestation of the *iḍā* line: Rays 1-3-5-7. Nevertheless, this work also helps to produce the eventual transformation of the Watery astral plane into the divine paradigm upon the plane *anupādaka*. Upon *anupādaka,* the *deva* and human kingdoms appropriately merge in the divine marriage at the sixth Initiation.

Merope is the Mother who gives birth (via this fifth Ray dispensation) to the forms that must struggle through *saṃsāra's* mire. Thus they eventually gain receptivity to Mahat (the *dharmakāya).*

**The festival of Nourishment** – the sixth sub-Ray. 'Nourishment' relates to the journey of the Waters of Life (the sixth Ray energies) as the food for all struggling 'plants'. All of Nature is sustained thereby. The etheric bodies of all manifest Life are thereby nourished by the vibrant *prānas* conveyed by *devas* from the higher domains. Humanity are also described esoterically as 'man-plants', sown into the fertile ground of systemic space. The astral plane, to which this statement relates, does not exist *per se* for *devas*. They do not experience the astral heaven and hells that humans do, for they have not created its conditionings. They wield the substance thereof, but are dispassionately involved in the human activity struggling within the *māyā* of it all. Instead, *devas* wield the karmic effects that are projected, so as to eventually free humanity from this substance. For *devas,* the astral plane is but a body of energies, a field of nourishment that can vitalise the evolving Lives as they move along the evolutionary path.

'Nourishment' can also relate to the gentle bathing of the Watery Lives and humanity with the manasic principle. Therefore, the inherent sentience of the lesser kingdoms eventually develops the attributes of mind, and thus can Individualise into a human kingdom. For humanity, this manasic stimulation helps to properly develop their minds, and so to reason out right from wrong.

Taygeta is the Pleiade that rules the conditionings of the astral plane.

**The festival of Creation** – the seventh sub-Ray. Creation is ultimately the purpose of all *deva* activity within the Great Mother. This purpose involves dense physical manifestation via ritualised or cyclic activity (the seventh Ray). This festival relates to empowerment with the appropriate mantras to command the substance of the spheres or forms at the level of expression of the associated *devas*. Whatever is to be comes into existence via them. Sound bathes all *devas* with the Commands they obey. Inevitably, the *devas* will joyously build the forms of the new civilisation and Temples of Revelation, for the musical scores from the festival of Active Love will resonate downwards to this, the most material sphere. The highest Creative activities will then manifest, and this is the present import of this seventh sub-Ray festival as the Aquarian Age (which is also governed by the seventh Ray) rapidly approaches.

Similarly, humans are bathed in the light from the sun, which helps stimulate their minds to obtain the images via which they act out their *saṃsāric* roles. In contradistinction to humanity, *devas* hear colour and see sound. To learn to integrate both methodologies is part of the marriage process between the two kingdoms. Such will be part of the curriculum of the new Temples of Initiation.

Sterope is the Pleiade that rules the conditionings of the physical plane.

# Bibliography


Babbitt, Edwin D. *Principles of Light and Color,* The College of Fine Forces, New Jersey, 2nd Ed., 1896.

Bailey, Alice A. *A Treatise on Cosmic Fire.* New York: Lucis Publishing Company, 1977.

——. *A Treatise on White Magic*. NY: Lucis Publishing, 1991.

——. *Discipleship in the New Age, Volume 1.* NY: Lucis Publishing, 1991.

——. *Discipleship in the New Age, Volume 2.* NY: Lucis Publishing, 1991.

——. *Esoteric Astrology*. NY: Lucis Publishing, 1991.

——. *Esoteric Healing*. NY: Lucis Publishing, 1981.

——. *Esoteric Psychology I.* NY: Lucis Publishing, 1977.

——. *Glamour: A World Problem*. NY: Lucis Publishing, 1998.

——. *Letters on Occult Meditation*. NY: Lucis Publishing, 1950.

——. *The Destiny of the Nations*. NY: Lucis Publishing, 1977.

——. *The Externalisation of the Hierarchy*. NY: Lucis Publishing, 1981.

——. *The Labours of Hercules*. NY: Lucis Publishing, 2011.

——. *The Rays and the Initiations*. NY: Lucis Publishing, 1960.

Bauval, Robert & Gilbert, Adrian. *The Orion Mystery*. London: Heinemann, 1994.

Balsys, Bodo. *A Treatise on Mind, Volume 1: The 'Self' or 'Non-self' in Buddhism.* Sydney: Universal Dharma Publishing, 2016.

——. *A Treatise on Mind, Volume 2: Considerations of Mind – A Buddhist Enquiry*. Sydney: Universal Dharma Publishing, 2016.

——. *A Treatise on Mind, Volume 3: The Buddha-Womb and the Way to Liberation*. Sydney: Universal Dharma Publishing, 2016.

——. *A Treatise on Mind, Volume 4: Maṇḍalas – Their Nature and Development.* Sydney: Universal Dharma Publishing, 2015.

——. *A Treatise on Mind, Volume 5A: An Esoteric Exposition of the Bardo Thödol - Part A*. Sydney: Universal Dharma Publishing, 2015.

——. *A Treatise on Mind, Volume 5B: An Esoteric Exposition of the Bardo Thödol - Part B*. Sydney: Universal Dharma Publishing, 2015.
——. *A Treatise on Mind, Volume 6: Meditation and the Initiation Process*. Sydney: Universal Dharma Publishing, 2014.
——. *A Treatise on Mind, Volume 7A: The Constitution of Shambhala - Part A*. Sydney: Universal Dharma Publishing, 2017.
——. *A Treatise on Mind, Volume 7B&C: The Constitution of Shambhala - Part B&C*. Sydney: Universal Dharma Publishing, 2018.
——. *Esoteric Cosmology and Modern Physics*. Sydney: Universal Dharma Publishing, 2021.
——. *The Astrological and Numerological Keys to the Secret Doctrine, Volume 1*. Sydney: Universal Dharma Publishing, 2020.
——. *The Astrological and Numerological Keys to the Secret Doctrine, Volume 2*. Sydney: Universal Dharma Publishing, 2020.
——. *The Revelation: The Evolution of Transcendent Perception by Humanity*. Sydney: Universal Dharma Publishing, 2022.
Besant, Annie & C.W. Leadbeater. *Occult Chemistry*, third edition, editor, C. Jinarajadasa and E.W. Preston, Theosophical Publishing House, Adyar, Madras, India, 1951.
Bible, *King James Version*, London: Oxford University Press, 1922.
Blavatsky, H.P. *The Secret Doctrine. Vol. 1.* Adyar: Theosophical Publishing House, 1888, 2005.
——. *The Secret Doctrine, Volume 2.* Adyar: Theosophical Publishing House, [1888] 2005.
Cremo, Michael & Thompson, Richard. *Forbidden Archaeology*, LA: Bhaktivedanta Book Publishing, 1998.
Jones, Marc Edward. *Astrology: How and Why it Works*. Sante Fe: Aurora. 1993.
Oken, Alan. *Alan Oken's Complete Astrology*. Newburyport: Nicolas-Hays, Inc. 2006.

# Index


## A

Abdomen, 92
Adam & Eve, 234–235, 247
Adept. *See* Initiate/Initiation, 5th
Adytum, 300, 393
Age/Epoch
  Aquarian, 14, 45, 53, 75–76, 82, 90, 101, 107, 131, 172, 192, 311, 319, 322, 379–380, 409, 436, 447, 459
  Capricornian, 288
  New. *See* Age/Epoch, Aquarian
  Piscean, 76, 101
Agni, 329, 332, 336
Agnichaitans. *See* Creative Hierarchies (1st/12th)
Agnishvattas. *See* Creative Hierarchies (3rd/10th)
Agnisuryans. *See* Creative Hierarchies (2nd/11th)
Ākāśa, 16, 23–25, 87
Akṣobhya, 315, 327
Alcyone, 11, 310–311
Aldebaran, 6, 69, 338
Amitābha, 314, 327, 329
Amoghasiddhi, 314, 327, 329
Ancient of Days. *See* Sanat Kumāra
Angel of the Presence. *See* Soul(s)
Angels/Angelic. *See* Deva(s)/Devic
Anima mundi, 51, 166, 179, 286, 314, 318, 336
Ankh, 49, 69, 160, 441
Antaḥkaraṇa, 24, 39, 52, 60–61, 65, 149–152, 162, 164, 328, 338, 341, 349, 367, 378, 380, 395–396, 408–409, 431, 434, 440, 443
Anubis, 142, 279
Apāna, 400
Apollo, 16
Aquarius, 7–8, 14, 47, 71–72, 75–78, 81–82, 90–92, 96, 98, 101, 119, 130–131, 144, 155–156, 165–173, 176, 183–184, 188, 192, 200–201, 228–229, 237, 256, 262–267, 269–270, 275–281, 288, 290, 298–302, 308–322, 340, 353, 409, 418, 422, 436–442
Argo, 455
Ariel, 23
Aries, 47, 59–66, 78, 96, 113, 116, 119, 135–136, 138, 140, 144, 160–161, 176–177, 179, 182, 197, 202–204, 208–209, 237–239, 248–251, 265–266, 274–275, 277–278, 280, 290, 293–294, 304–305, 310–311, 320, 332–333, 336, 343, 350, 355, 360–361, 376–382, 397, 423, 448
Aryan civilisation. *See* Root Race
Ascendant (rising sign), 192, 194
Ashram, 117, 132, 150–151, 449, 455–456
Aspect(s), astrological, 205–206
Aspect(s) of Deity, 13, 17–19, 51, 80, 151, 346, 347, 350, 359, 372, 383
  1st (Father), 13, 16, 19, 63, 357, 369, 413, 437
  2nd (Son), 13, 16, 18–19, 33, 36, 62, 111
  3rd (Mother), 13, 16, 17, 18–19, 36, 93, 97–98, 108, 132, 157, 373. *See also* Mother
Aṣṭadiśas, 445
Astral. *See* Body/Bodies, Planes
Asuras, 418
Atlantis, 54, 258, 265, 277, 282, 316–317
Atlas, 11
Ātma, 24
Atom(s), 400
Atonement, 63
Aūṁ, 11, 24, 51, 52
Aura, 150, 375, 377–379, 394, 425, 440, 444–445
Avatar, 32, 76, 82, 101, 106–107, 180, 184, 199, 260, 264, 305, 316, 444–445, 448
  of Synthesis, 55, 150, 318–319, 322

## B


Beauty, 151, 152
Bindu, 391, 394
Black magician. *See* Dark brotherhood
Blood, 169–170
Bodhicitta, 74, 304–307
Bodhisattva(s), 74, 84, 263–264, 290, 302, 304–305, 317
Bodhi tree, 447
Body/Bodies
  Astral, 25, 41, 186, 252, 257–258
  Causal, 90, 95, 162, 240, 325, 331, 333–334, 336–337, 339, 344, 359, 374, 392, 394, 396, 406–407, 411, 429, 445
  Etheric, 26, 74, 76, 172, 243, 275, 277–278, 300, 384, 391, 393–395, 397, 414–415, 425–426, 428–430, 444
  Mental, 40, 107, 114, 204, 216
  of Deity/God, 36, 44
  Physical, 210, 240, 242, 252
  Subtle, 189
Book of Life, 379
Brahmā, 16–19, 37, 93, 332, 362, 379, 386, 417, 446
Brahmarandrha vidhara, 390, 402
Breasts, 92
Buddha(s), 392, 444. *See also* Maitreya
  Dhyāni, 377, 393, 400
  Middle Way, 417
  Mind, 384
  of Activity, 393


## C


Cancer, 47, 63–64, 80–85, 88, 93, 96–97, 99, 103, 108, 115, 119, 132, 139–142, 144, 146, 157, 159, 180, 182–186, 202–204, 213–214, 240, 246, 249–251, 262–264, 266, 271, 282–286, 289–290, 292, 301–302, 305, 307, 313, 315–316, 321–322, 332–336, 339, 345–346, 351–352, 360–361, 366, 371, 397–405
Canis Major, 3–4
Capricorn, 7–8, 47, 62–64, 66–68, 73, 76, 79, 82–83, 93, 96, 107–108, 112–113, 116, 118, 128–131, 141, 144–146, 152–164, 179, 183–184, 186–188, 195, 197, 202–203, 225–228, 237–238, 246, 249–251, 257, 263–264, 267, 272–273, 282–283, 285–287, 289–290, 292–295, 300–302, 307, 308, 312, 315, 318, 321, 336, 338, 340, 342, 349, 353, 371, 432–436
Castor, 72
Causal form. *See* Body, Causal
Central Spiritual Sun, 12, 30, 64, 87, 88, 170, 402, 408, 410–411
Centre(s). *See* Chakra(s)
Ceres, 92, 414
Chain
  Earth, 276, 282, 316
  Moon, 182, 259, 275, 276, 281, 315–317
  Planetary, 22–23
Chakra(s)/centres, 1, 9–11, 22–23, 26, 31–32, 74, 76–77, 93, 118, 120, 122, 127, 185, 189, 309, 394, 453
  Ājñā, 6, 39, 69, 71, 112, 117, 127, 144, 248, 329, 338, 349, 351, 352, 354, 365, 373, 383, 399, 402, 410, 425, 434, 439, 441
  Alta Major, 126, 357, 380, 402
  Base of Spine (mūlādhāra), 10, 159, 185, 329, 378, 392–393, 399, 409
  Diaphragm, 306, 357, 373
  Ear, 126, 357
  Eyes, 43, 126, 357
  Gonad, 123, 357, 399
  Hand, 122, 357
  Head (sahasrāra padma), 10, 18, 127, 144, 159, 324–329, 337, 347–356, 366, 369, 370, 377–378, 381, 389–392, 394, 396, 399, 401–403, 409–410, 429–430, 434–435, 441
  Heart, 12, 32, 36, 51, 87–88, 117, 124, 132, 137, 144, 150, 306, 324–329, 347–348, 351–353, 366–368, 372
  Knee, 121
  Liver, 123, 181, 274, 305, 306, 357
  Lung, 124
  Mouth, 125, 357
  Pineal, 357, 402
  Pituitary, 357, 402
  Sacral (svādiṣṭhāna), 6, 11, 121, 154, 186, 367, 378, 399, 441
  Solar Plexus (maṇipūra), 4–5, 41, 55, 80, 89, 122, 136–137, 139, 142, 182, 268–269, 271, 274, 303, 305–306, 309, 312, 315, 377–378, 387, 400, 402, 414, 425, 441
  Splenic, 5, 121, 125, 182, 272, 305, 329, 340–342, 357, 367–369
  Stomach, 80, 123, 306, 357
  Third Eye. *See* Chakra(s), Ājñā
  Throat, 3, 6, 12, 32, 125, 137, 144, 327, 329, 340, 347
Chohan. *See* Initiate/Initiation(s), 6th
Christ, 32–33, 36, 55, 57, 70, 75–76, 78, 83, 86, 88, 90–93, 169, 177–178, 314, 316, 320, 322, 381, 396, 401, 434, 445, 448–449
  Blue, 78
  Child, 57, 66, 67, 78, 92, 96, 112, 115, 133, 218, 373, 380, 384, 413, 457
  Consciousness, 36, 79, 174, 196, 346, 411, 414–415
  Cosmic, 22, 76, 309–310, 313, 337, 344–345
  Green, 78, 318–319

Light, 94, 98, 133, 141
Planetary, 54, 96, 174, 392, 443
Christianity, 33, 41
Chronus, 17
Cintāmaṇī, 409
Clairaudience, 175, 279, 283, 305, 309
Clairvoyance, 37, 93, 97, 125, 150, 175, 271, 274, 280, 283–284, 286, 290, 294, 296, 298, 453
Colours, 27, 37, 41, 375
Blue, 24, 35, 375, 377–380, 386, 389, 395, 403–404, 418, 420, 424, 428, 435, 437, 440
Blue-green, 41, 43, 303, 418
Crimson, 303, 445
Emerald, 378, 382–383, 418, 425, 428–429, 437
Gold, 377, 379–380, 384, 392, 395, 407, 417, 428, 430, 440, 445
Green, 36–37, 379, 381, 387, 395, 403, 404, 410, 413, 418, 425, 428–431, 436–437
Indigo, 379, 383, 390–391, 393–395, 403, 406, 413, 418, 426, 428–430
Orange, 27, 40–41, 379, 389, 391, 395, 399, 403, 406–407, 413–414, 418, 426, 428, 435, 440
Pink, 42–43, 375, 379, 384, 386, 392, 445
Red, 23, 27, 42, 377, 395, 399, 413–414, 428, 444
Rust, 424
Turquoise, 375, 386, 395, 403–404, 413, 429, 435, 444
Violet, 44, 303, 379, 384, 395, 409, 413–415, 418, 425–426, 428, 430, 444
Yellow, 37, 379–380, 406–407, 410, 413, 418, 425, 428, 437–438, 445
Complacency, 149
Consciousness, 8–9
Contemplatives, 393
Copper, 41
Cosmic Egg, 386
Covid-19, 123
Creative Hierarchy(ies), 6–8, 24, 81, 87, 100, 308, 324–374
1st/12th (Elementals), 26, 169–171, 312, 329, 332, 334–336, 348, 353, 367, 418
2nd/11th (Lunar Lords), 25–26, 112–113, 143, 154, 170–171, 312, 329, 333–334, 340, 342, 353, 367, 403, 418, 433
3rd /10th (Makara), 26, 37, 40, 90, 109, 127, 161–163, 186, 272, 284, 312, 314, 322, 329, 336, 338, 340–341, 342, 347, 364, 367, 371, 403, 418, 420, 431, 433–435
4th/9th (Humanity), 73–74, 90, 109, 112, 154, 163, 171, 264, 327–328, 333–334, 337–338, 340, 344, 348, 360–361, 363, 365, 369, 371, 418
5th/8th (Lesser Builders), 109, 328, 329, 332, 334–335, 340, 348, 363, 366–368, 374, 411, 418–419
6th/7th (Greater Builders), 60, 89, 180, 239, 314, 328, 332–333, 335–337, 340, 341–342, 352–353, 359, 363–366, 369, 411, 418
7th /6th (Divine Flames), 89, 313–314, 328, 332, 335–336, 339, 340, 341–342, 363–364, 366, 369, 403, 411, 418, 420
8th/5th Liberated (Numbers), 83, 313, 327–330, 332–336, 338, 339, 340, 342, 347, 351–354, 358, 360, 361–365, 367–369
9th/4th Liberated (Builders), 313, 325, 327–330, 332–335, 337, 339, 340, 341–342, 347, 351–352, 357–358, 361, 363–364, 369
10th/3rd Liberated (Elements), 65, 313, 327–330, 332–335, 338–339, 340, 341–342, 347, 351–352, 354, 356–357, 358–359, 363, 366, 369
11th/2nd Liberated (Flames), 313, 327–335, 338–339, 340, 341–343, 347, 351–352, 354–355, 358–359
12th/1st Liberated (Essences), 174, 313, 327–335, 339, 340, 343, 347, 351–352, 354–355, 358–359
Crocodile, 433–435. *See also* Creative Hierarchy(ies), (3rd/10th)
Cross(es), 80, 186, 196–198
Cardinal, 63–64, 150, 201–202, 237–238
Fixed, 64, 70, 185–186, 200, 308, 310
Mutable, 64, 78, 198–199, 238
Tau, 237, 243, 246–253, 259, 266, 269, 275, 278


## D


Dark brotherhood, 9, 32, 52, 54, 56–57, 101, 105–106, 119–127, 129, 138–141, 157, 160–161, 172, 179, 183–184, 186–187, 192, 249, 256–258, 260, 271, 273–275, 278, 282–286, 291, 330, 371, 422–424, 436
Darkness, 9, 68–70, 82, 92–93, 114, 119, 123–124, 133, 140–141, 163, 177, 257, 295
Dark ones. *See* Dark brotherhood
Death, 223, 231–232, 259, 404, 423–424, 438, 442–443, 445
Dependent Origination, 104
Desert, 424–425
Desire Mind. *See* Kāma-Manas
Desire(s), 41, 59
Deva(s)/Devic, 10, 14, 21, 31, 37, 94, 98, 126, 154, 238–240, 243, 248, 250, 261, 265, 273, 280, 290, 318, 337, 340–341, 346, 348, 359, 374, 449, 451, 456–459. *See also* Creative Hierarchy(ies)
Elemental(s), 7, 14, 19, 26, 112, 154, 170, 258, 271, 273, 279, 284–285, 312, 322

Kingdom. *See* Kingdoms, Deva
of the Shadows, 44, 171, 243, 300
Rāja Lord(s), 23–24
Dharma, 33, 108, 148, 416, 418
Dharmacakra mūdra, 444
Dharmakāya, 107, 303, 315, 378, 383–384, 390, 418, 430, 435, 440–441, 458
Dharmatā, 313
Dhyāna, 417
Dhyāni Buddhas. *See* Buddha(s), Dhyāni
Diana (goddess), 27
Diaphragm, 109, 269, 402. *See also* Chakra(s)
Dragon of Wisdom. *See* Initiate/Initiation(s), 5th
Duality, 120
Dweller on the threshold, 119, 141, 159

## E

Earth (astrologically), 22, 27, 49, 50, 153–154, 224–225
Eightfold Path, 56, 96–97, 116, 148, 219
Eighth sphere, 5, 54, 121, 181–186, 191–192, 204, 260, 359
Elementals. *See* Creative Hierarchy(ies), 1st/12th
Element(s), 71, 121, 350, 374
Aether, 23, 27, 237
Air(y), 72, 97, 117, 167, 237
Earth, 66–67, 94, 97, 157, 236, 388
Fire(y), 17, 40, 62–63, 78, 86, 151, 236
Water(y), 25–27, 41–42, 62, 79, 83–84, 91, 115, 186, 236, 315
Equinoxes, 104, 238, 267, 304, 316, 362
Esoteric, 28
Etheric Body/Double. *See* Body, Etheric
Exoteric, 28

## F

Father, 13, 33–34. *See also* Aspects of Deity (1st)
Feet, 173, 180
Festival(s), 182, 447
of the Great Mother, 456–459
of the Living Christ, 448–449
of the New Age Temple, 74, 75, 453–456
Wesak, 450–453
Findhorn community, 171
Fohat, 324
Form(s). *See* Body/Bodies
Four Noble Truths, 56

## G

Gabriel, 25, 26
Galadriel, 26
Garden of Eden. *See* Adam & Eve
Gemini, 47, 72–79, 82, 88, 91, 96, 107–108, 145, 150–151, 153–154, 178, 182, 185–186, 198–199, 202, 212–213, 238, 240–244, 245, 247, 249–251, 253–254, 260, 262–263, 265–267, 269, 272–273, 275–276, 278–279, 289, 293–295, 298–300, 315–316, 321, 332–333, 337–338, 341, 344–346, 357–358, 360–361, 390–397
Glamour, 133, 455
Goat, 420, 431–436
Grand Architect, 392–393
Grand Heavenly Man. *See* Logos, THAT
Great Bear, 14, 197

## H

Harmlessness, 129–130
Head (& Brain), 59. *See also* Chakra(s), Head
Heart. *See* Chakra(s), Heart
Heavenly Men. *See* Logos/Logoi(c)
Helios, 16
Hercules, 54, 86, 95, 114, 119, 420, 424
Hierarchy, 447–456
Hierarchy (of Enlightened Being), 6, 12, 36, 53, 54–56, 91, 150, 236, 241, 250, 254–257, 277, 284, 296, 304–305, 307–309, 314–316, 320–322
Externalisation of the, 75, 288, 448
Hips & Thighs, 145–146
Hiraṇyagarba, 386. *See also* Brahmā
Holy Ghost, 92
Houses (astrological), 189, 191, 196–197, 208
1st, 202, 204, 208–210
2nd, 200, 210–211
3rd, 198, 212–213
4th, 202, 204, 213–214
5th, 200–201, 204, 205, 208, 215–216
6th, 199, 217–219
7th, 202, 219–221
8th, 201, 204, 205, 221–224
9th, 199, 204, 224–225
10th, 202, 208, 225–228
11th, 201, 228–229
12th, 199, 230–232
Rulers, 198
Hydra, 54, 95, 114–115, 119–122, 124–126, 138, 144, 195, 204, 251, 257, 273, 279, 283, 284, 285, 420–426
Ambition, 119, 123–124, 126–129, 423
Cruelty, 113, 118, 125, 129–130, 157, 423
Fear, 122–123, 139–140, 422
Hatred, 124, 132, 135–136, 423
Money, 119, 121, 130–131
Physical/material comfort(s), 119, 121, 134, 422

Pride, 118, 120, 125–126, 133–134, 423–424
Selfishness, 130, 167, 422
Separative(ness), 118, 120, 123, 125–128, 132–133, 423
Sex, 112–114, 119, 121–122, 124, 422, 424

## I

I AM, 11, 62, 88, 91–92
Ignorance (avidya), 119–120, 126
Imperil. *See* Irritation
Individualisation, 90, 107, 235, 237, 239–243, 261, 407–408, 459
Initiate/Initiation(s), 47, 48, 62, 82, 87, 116, 189–190, 221, 301, 325, 334, 337, 342, 364, 375, 410, 445, 447, 449, 450, 454, 455
1st (Birth), 78, 178, 195, 219, 445
2nd (Baptism), 7, 71, 78, 84, 88, 138, 140, 195, 249–250, 445, 449
3rd (Transfiguration), 63, 78, 116, 129, 139, 159, 195, 202, 223, 250, 319, 434, 454
4th (Renunciation), 7, 20, 41, 60, 62, 69, 117, 200, 223, 250, 322, 374, 382–383, 425
5th (Revelation), 8, 150–151, 201, 227, 232, 250, 254–255, 259, 291, 300–301, 307, 309, 313, 316, 319–320, 322, 387, 392, 396, 410, 428, 456
6th (Ressurection), 7, 263, 291, 296, 307, 316, 320, 337, 392, 452, 455, 458
Intelligence, 249, 254, 258, 301
Intuited/Intuition, 105
Irritation, 136–137, 139
Ishvara (Īśvara), 15
Islam, 41
Israelites, 176–179

## J

Jesus, 33–34, 57, 75–76, 138, 177–178, 316, 320–322
Jewel in the Heart of the Lotus, 94, 104, 149, 200
Jewish People. *See* Israelites
Jīva, 353
Jupiter (Lord of second Ray), 15, 17, 24, 34, 38, 50, 87, 170, 174, 179, 224–225, 228, 428, 430, 443–444

## K

Kali yuga, 348, 362
Kāma-manas, 4, 41, 107, 114, 157, 187, 192, 294, 304, 320, 435, 449–450
Karma/Karmic, 21, 23–25, 27, 30, 36, 51, 53–54, 63, 101–103, 108–109, 112, 114–116, 135, 140, 148, 153–154, 158–159, 162–164, 183, 187, 189, 195, 211, 220, 223, 227, 266, 277, 279, 291, 294–295, 298, 301, 307, 313, 317, 378, 381, 392–393, 400–401, 403, 413, 417–418, 422, 430–431, 436, 445
Kingdom(s), 188, 393, 414
Angel(ic). *See* Kingdom(s), Deva (devic)
Animal, 19, 31, 188, 235, 312, 388, 407–408
Deva (devic), 7, 90, 161, 164, 188, 218, 248, 261, 273, 290–291, 320, 388, 397, 411, 455, 458
Human, 7, 19, 26, 31, 64, 68, 85, 90, 97, 188, 375, 380, 385, 401, 407, 452, 458. *See also* Creative Hierarchy, 4th/9th
Mineral, 19, 26, 30, 41, 66, 68, 157, 188, 312
of 'God', 28, 44, 54, 57, 75, 85, 103, 396, 420
of Nature, 21, 31, 84, 102, 451
of Souls, 10, 23–24, 26, 94, 107, 162, 313, 318, 407, 429, 452, 457
Plant (vegetable), 9, 19, 37, 188, 235, 277, 312
Kleśas, 204
Krishna (Kṛṣṇa), 35
Kuṇḍalinī, 17, 117, 122, 124, 126, 159–161, 179, 227, 308–309, 350, 380, 389, 392, 399, 413, 415, 419, 425, 435

## L

Lamb, 63, 202, 381
Law(s), 100, 102, 327
of Attraction, 333, 337, 341–342, 344, 347, 357, 365
of Economy, 333, 346, 348, 365
of Identity, 330
of Karma. *See* Karma/Karmic
of Life, 115
of Nature, 40
of Sacrifice, 32
of Synthesis, 331, 333, 338, 339, 342–343
of the Good, 127
Lemuria(ns). *See* Root Race(s), 3rd (Lemurian)
Leo, 38, 47, 62–64, 71, 78, 81, 84–92, 94, 99, 103, 115, 117–118, 133–134, 144, 146, 167, 170, 182, 197, 200–204, 215–216, 237, 241, 243, 245, 248–250, 254, 256, 261–267, 269, 273–275, 277–279, 281–282, 288, 289, 291, 293, 296, 300, 310–311, 313–314, 316, 318, 321–322, 340, 352, 363, 405–412
Libra, 47, 62–63, 72–73, 99–110, 113, 115–116, 131, 145, 155, 164, 197, 199, 202, 219–221, 238, 240, 245, 250, 260–263, 265, 266–267, 286, 289, 291, 300–301, 305, 308–309, 313, 320, 340, 352, 363, 416–421

Light, 9
Lingam, 413
Lipikas. *See* Lord(s), Lipika
Liver, 180. *See also* Chakra(s)/centres, Liver
Logos/Logoi(c), 2, 23, 48, 163, 323, 336–341, 350, 376, 391, 393, 399–400, 408, 411
  Active Intelligence, 4
  Body of Manifestation, 22, 117, 365
  Desire, 378, 392, 399, 415, 430, 451
  Head, 82, 378
  Heart, 8, 377
  Love, 304, 307, 312, 424
  Manas (Mind), 4, 377, 430
  Personality, 53, 310, 369
  Planetary, 8, 12, 21–22, 32–33, 321–323, 332–334, 342, 366–367, 369, 376–377, 381–382, 392–394, 396, 413, 447, 458
  Purpose, 9, 364, 369
  Solar, 6, 8, 10, 12, 15, 83, 89, 181, 310, 331–333, 338, 345–346, 355–356, 366, 370, 384, 451
  THAT, 2, 12, 14, 59, 65, 72, 80, 92, 111, 127, 318, 324, 331, 347
  Will, 33, 51, 67, 305, 379
  Word, 2
Lord(s)
  Lipika, 82, 345, 392–393
  Lunar. *See* Creative Hierarchy, 2nd/11th
  of dark face. *See* Dark Brotherhood
  of Flame, 90, 107, 239–240, 253–254, 316, 347, 419
  of karma, 102, 319, 345
  Rāja, 457
  Shambhalic, 240
Love-Wisdom, 4, 12, 21, 33–35, 41, 45, 50, 55, 80, 97, 155
Lower back, 99, 103
Lunar. *See also* Moon
  Lords. *See* Creative Hierarchy, 2nd/11th
  Orb, 46
Lungs, 72, 340
Lymphatic, 180, 340

## M

Mahāchohan, 36, 76, 78, 184, 311, 316–318, 320–322
Mahāmanvantara, 4, 10, 450, 452
Mahāmūdra, 351
Mahārājas, 82
Mahat, 3, 4, 11, 70, 127, 291, 294–295, 301, 318–320, 331, 338, 341, 343, 351, 356, 360, 369, 371, 377–378, 393, 399, 458
Maitreya, 444, 451
Makara. *See* Creative Hierarchies, 3rd/10th
Manas/Manasic. *See* mind/Mind
Manjushri, 378
Man-plants, 9, 409–410, 458. *See also* Creative Hierarchies, 8th/5th
Mantra/Mantric, 123, 125–126, 130, 253, 257, 259, 270, 273, 279–280, 284, 295, 339–340, 346, 364, 373
Manu, 31–32, 36, 183, 186–187
Manvantara, 13, 15, 75, 160, 174, 180, 182, 330, 338–339, 342, 345, 348, 386, 392, 403, 417, 444, 446
Marpa, 307
Mars (Lord of sixth Ray), 15, 26–27, 34, 36, 41–42, 46, 49–50, 61, 113–114, 135, 142, 154–155, 191, 192, 208, 221–222
Mary, 75, 92
Mass consciousness, 81
Master R, 316, 320, 322
Master(s) of Wisdom. *See* Initiate/Initiation(s), 5th
Māyā, 45, 403, 459
Māyavirūpa, 109, 452
Media (mass), 122–123, 130, 139, 168
Medium(ship), 46, 83, 174, 183, 231, 274–275, 281, 284, 286, 294
Medusa, 121, 125
Melchisedek, 377. *See also* Sanat Kumāra
Mercury (Lord of fourth Ray), 15, 24, 38, 45, 49, 61–62, 68, 73, 87, 95, 208–209, 212–213, 391, 415, 428, 430
Michael, 24
Milarepa, 307
mind/Mind, 45, 55, 115–116, 157, 162, 270, 278, 310, 379, 381, 384–388, 391, 393, 401–404, 407, 409–411, 414, 420, 423, 426, 428, 430, 433, 435–436, 440, 449–450, 452. *See also* Dharmakāya
  Cosmic. *See* Mahat
  Desire. *See* see: Kāma-manas
Monad(ic), 9–10, 12–13, 18, 34, 60, 63, 86, 90, 149, 160, 174–175, 181–182, 325, 330, 337, 359, 407–411, 420, 440, 443, 448, 450, 452, 455
Moon, 190, 192–194, 213–214, 242, 386, 397, 398, 399, 401–402, 410
  Chain, 259–260, 274–276
  Node(s), 26–27, 46, 67, 83, 88, 95, 193
Moses, 108, 176
Mother, 13, 16, 17, 19, 45, 261, 265, 305, 383, 413, 415, 430, 456–459. *See also* Aspects of Deity (3rd)
  Nature, 40, 92, 384, 387, 405, 411
  Of the World, 76, 289, 297, 300, 316, 318–320, 322, 399, 447
Mt. Olympus, 18
Mudra, 409, 444

Mystery(ies), 63, 295
of (enlightened) Being, 58, 90, 140, 159
of Makara. *See* Creative Hierarchies, 3rd/10th
of Sound, 279. *See also* Mantra/Mantric
of the Kingdom of God, 28, 156
of the Sphinx. *See* Sphinx
Schools, 298

## N

Nāḍī(s), 3, 10, 22, 76–77, 124, 151, 159, 339, 359, 378–380, 384, 386, 394, 400–401, 420, 453
iḍā, 74, 120–121, 159, 186–187, 325, 357, 365, 368, 373, 380, 383, 387–388, 394, 397, 399, 414, 416, 430, 458
piṇgalā, 5, 74, 120–121, 159, 186–187, 325, 357, 365, 368, 373, 380, 383, 387–388, 394–395, 397, 399, 414, 416, 430
suṣumṇā, 24, 120, 157, 159, 186, 357, 368, 378, 380, 387
Neck. *See also* Chakra(s), Throat
Neck & Throat, 65
Neptune (6th Ray), 24, 44, 83, 85, 88, 142, 179–180, 401–402, 408
New Age. *See* Age, Aquarian
New Group of World Servers, 56, 81–82
Nirvāṇa, 131, 176
Nirvāṇee, 7, 176, 291–292, 301, 337, 352, 452
Noah, 30

## O

One About Whom Naught Can Be Said. *See* Logos, THAT
Orion the hunter, 3, 5, 6, 11
Outpouring(s), 23–24, 457

## P

Padmāsāna, 391
Parinirvāṇa, 69, 447
Pharaoh, 178–179
Pillars, 392, 394
Pisces, 47, 78–79, 84, 94–97, 111, 116, 118, 125, 145, 150, 156, 163–165, 168, 173–187, 190, 197–200, 230–232, 237, 254, 256, 260, 264, 266–267, 269, 274–275, 282, 284, 286, 290, 293–294, 298, 301, 303, 305, 310, 313, 320, 334, 343, 355, 360–361, 364, 442–446
Plane(s), 6, 27, 116, 188, 234, 289, 329, 394, 403, 413, 418, 428
Ādi, 6, 23, 329, 340, 363, 403, 413, 420, 450, 452
Anupādaka, 4, 6–7, 19, 24, 27, 34, 180, 296–297, 302, 314, 318, 329, 337, 340, 363, 365, 420, 448–449, 452, 455, 457–458
Astral, 26, 41, 45–46, 78, 80, 122–123, 187, 233–235, 238, 257, 273, 279, 291–292, 294, 296, 298, 304, 309, 329–330, 331–332, 335, 337–340, 375, 377, 383–384, 386–387, 389, 392, 395, 401, 403–404, 406, 413, 414, 422, 424, 429–430, 435, 449, 453, 458–459
Ātma/ātmic, 6–7, 37, 40, 163, 186, 236–237, 294, 313–314, 329, 332, 338, 340, 363, 367, 378, 387, 403, 413, 430, 450–451, 455, 457
Buddhi(c), 6–7, 24, 34, 37–38, 41, 72, 76, 97, 117, 163, 167, 187, 236, 329, 340, 342, 391–393, 419, 449, 451, 455
Mental, 25, 27, 38, 40–41, 78, 85, 97, 125, 161–164, 180, 186, 192, 235–236, 240, 273, 289, 329, 332, 338, 340, 343, 391, 394–395, 401, 403–404, 407, 411, 429, 435, 438, 450
Physical, 45, 97, 159, 164, 180, 235, 240–243, 247–248, 255, 273, 278–282, 289, 294, 299, 314, 327–330, 335–336, 339, 346, 361, 383–384, 394–395, 403–404, 433, 438, 449, 453, 456
Planet(s)
Esoteric, 194, 197, 207
Etheric, 29
Exoteric, 194, 197, 207
Non-sacred, 28, 48, 57, 81, 181, 190–192, 197, 203–204, 214
Outer, 44
Rulers, 29, 47
Sacred, 47–48, 57, 81, 181, 190, 197, 317
Plan (the), 49, 50
Plant Kingdom. *See* Kingdom(s), Plant
Pleiades/Pleiadian(s), 4–6, 11, 13–14, 75, 196, 240, 253, 280, 284, 289–290, 294–295, 310–311, 316, 320, 338, 343, 345, 346, 456–459
Pluto (1st Ray), 26, 30, 44, 111, 125, 175–176, 178–179, 183, 185–186, 191–192, 204, 221–222, 232, 304, 443, 445
Polaris, 310–311, 313
Pollux, 72
Poseidonis, 282
Pralaya, 21, 173–174, 176, 192, 292, 324, 342, 345, 364, 420, 443, 450
Prāṇa(s), 26, 29, 42–44, 46, 61, 76, 87, 104, 109, 114, 120–121, 124, 152, 169, 171, 191, 211, 305–307, 312, 324, 342, 345, 347–348, 350, 352, 353, 357, 360, 365, 367–369, 371, 373, 378, 399–400, 407–408, 414, 418, 435
Prāṇayāma, 397, 400
Pretas, 418
Probationary Path, 191
Prometheus, 11

Psychic(s), 26, 44–45, 54, 64, 68, 74, 79, 82–83, 85, 93–94, 102, 120, 122–125, 140, 154, 157, 161, 174–175, 179, 186, 211, 213, 221, 227, 235, 257, 259–260, 268–279, 283–284, 286, 295–296, 332, 333
  Centres. *See* Chakra(s)/centres
  Heat (tum mo), 306, 308, 312
Pyramid(s), 5, 383

## R

Rainbow bridge. *See* Antaḥkaraṇa
Raphael, 25–26
Ratnasambhava, 314, 327, 329
Ray(s), 1, 2, 5, 6, 8–10, 14–15, 28, 47, 48
  1st, 3, 13, 15, 18, 20, 28–35, 43, 52, 55–56, 60, 66, 68, 72, 123, 138–139, 151, 175, 179, 193
  2nd, 13, 20, 24, 30, 33–35, 87, 179
  3rd, 13, 14, 24, 35–37, 51, 93
  4th, 24, 38–39, 45, 49, 62, 87, 88, 95, 171, 212–213
  5th, 25, 40, 51, 71
  6th, 14, 24, 26, 33, 41–43, 49–50, 88
  7th, 14, 26, 31, 43–45, 48, 50, 76, 88, 220
  esoteric, 190
  of Aspect, 36
  of Attribute, 36
  Paths, 9
  Soul, 209
Regulus, 91, 291, 296, 300, 310, 313, 318, 410
Resurrection, 33
Rider on the White Horse, 127, 147, 150, 239, 426, 428
Rishis of the Great Bear, 2–3, 6–7, 12–13, 307, 313, 315, 451
Rivendiel, 26
Root Race(s), 233, 234
  1st (Adamic), 235
  2nd (Hyperborean), 235
  3rd (Lemurian), 81, 154, 233–235, 237–238, 239, 240, 242–250, 256–258, 265, 267–270, 272, 275–278, 432
  4th (Atlantean), 30, 54, 81, 83, 89, 97, 146, 233, 236, 245–253, 256–260, 265–291, 277, 317, 401, 419, 426, 431–433
  5th (Aryan), 30–31, 33, 76, 86, 113, 115, 116, 147, 157, 233, 236, 277, 280, 404, 426, 434
  6th (Neptunian), 32–33, 76, 108, 233, 236
  7th, 237

## S

Sagittarius, 7–8, 47, 62, 77–79, 79, 86, 96, 116, 119, 127, 131, 141, 143–147, 150–155, 185–186, 188, 198–199, 204, 224–225, 237–243, 245, 247–249, 251, 261, 263–265, 270, 275–276, 277–278, 280, 288, 290, 292, 298–299, 312, 315, 317–319, 322, 336, 342, 349, 353, 423, 426–432
Samādhi, 150
Samāna, 400
Sambhogakāya Flower, 94, 116, 235, 336, 354, 406, 443, 445, 452
Saṃsāra(s), 28, 31, 42, 46, 60, 83, 97, 105, 114, 116, 126, 187, 197–198, 216, 223, 317, 319, 325, 371, 378, 381–382, 385, 396, 401, 403–404, 406, 408, 410, 419, 424–426, 434, 438
Saṃskāra(s), 119–120, 191–194, 204
Samuel, 26
Sanat Kumāra, 57, 184, 239, 255, 259, 316, 317, 319–320, 376, 382, 393, 419, 445
Satan, 54, 136
Saturn (Lord of third Ray), 14, 17, 24, 27, 34, 36, 38, 51, 153–155, 158–159, 162, 195, 203, 225, 226, 417, 428, 430–431, 436
Scheme(s), 338
  Earth, 176, 276, 282, 347, 356–357
  Mercury, 242
  Planetary, 23, 281
  Synthesising, 48, 51
  Sythesising, 355
  Venus, 107
Science of Triangles, 196
Scorpio, 47, 62, 70–71, 84, 86, 94, 96, 111–119, 121, 132, 134, 142–146, 152–159, 163, 186–188, 192, 195–196, 200–201, 203–204, 221–224, 240, 244, 246, 249, 251, 257, 261–262, 264, 265, 266, 269, 273, 282, 283, 284–286, 288, 291–292, 295–296, 302, 309–311, 320–321, 334, 340, 342, 349, 352, 371, 421–427
Seasons
  Autumn, 155
  Spring, 78
  Summer, 99
  Winter, 155
Septenary (of Nature), 385
Serapis, 316, 320, 322
Seven Rishis. *See* Rishis of the Great Bear
Seven Sisters. *See* Pleiades
Shakti (Śakti), 17
Shambhala, 7, 52, 55–57, 63, 85, 107, 156, 161, 187, 239, 241, 253, 257, 281, 284, 289, 297, 299, 304–305, 313–315, 317–319, 325, 337, 365, 392–393, 396, 419, 428–430, 441, 448–449, 451–452, 455–456
Sheaths, seven, 22
Shiva (Śiva), 16–19, 69, 383

Siddhis, 122, 244, 305–307
Sin of the mindless, 252
Sirius, 3–6, 12–14, 75, 107, 196, 197, 309, 311, 314, 331, 343–344, 448
Solar
  Angel, 240
  Fire, 87
  Logos. *See* Logos, Solar
  Plexus. *See* Chakra(s), Solar Plexus
Son, 12, 33. *See also* Aspects of Deity (2nd)
Sorcerer/Sorcery, 27, 120, 124, 157, 160, 186, 259–260, 271–273, 275, 280–281. *See* Dark Brotherhood
Soul(s), 60, 62, 64, 71, 86–87, 94, 97, 111, 116–117, 119, 141–142, 146, 154, 157, 161, 162, 166, 174–175, 196, 215–216, 231, 235, 449, 452, 454. *See also* Kingdom, of Souls
  777 incarnations of, 201
  Group, 21–22
  Purpose, 194
Sphinx, 89–90, 182–183, 237, 243, 249–250, 265, 269, 273, 274, 279, 287, 415
Spirit, 64, 94, 417
Sun, 38, 51, 87, 88, 99, 190, 215, 408–412. *See also* Central Spiritual Sun
  Sign, 194
Śūnyatā, 41, 104, 117, 438
Surya, 15
Sūtrātma, 60, 174, 237, 338, 408, 440

## T

Taurus, 11, 47, 65–72, 78, 82, 96, 99, 107–108, 111, 119, 122, 134, 144, 160–161, 176–179, 182, 186, 196, 200, 210–211, 240, 246, 248–249, 251, 253–254, 257, 261, 265–266, 270, 282, 284–285, 289–290, 294–295, 297–298, 300, 308–309, 320, 332–333, 336, 338, 341, 345, 347, 356, 358, 360–361, 382–389
Tension, 147–152
Trinity, 51, 397. *See also* Aspect(s) of Deity

## U

Udāna, 400
Unicorn, 164, 434–435
Upādhi, 394
Uranus (Lord of seventh Ray), 15, 23, 44–45, 62, 72, 88, 118, 170–172, 193, 215, 219–220, 228–229, 408–409, 430
Uriel, 24

## V

Vairocana, 315, 327, 329
Vaivisvata, 31
Varuna's trident, 25
Vayūs, 9, 400–401
Venusians, 316, 321
Venus (Lord of fifth Ray), 5, 15, 25, 27, 38, 40, 42, 51, 65, 69, 73, 107, 157, 162, 191, 210, 212, 219–220, 387–388, 391, 428, 430
Virgin, 92–93
Virgo, 47, 62, 66, 78–79, 89, 92–99, 105, 112, 115, 117–118, 132, 135, 144, 146, 149–150, 164, 165, 169, 182–183, 185–186, 195–199, 217–219, 237–238, 241, 242–243, 246–247, 248–250, 254, 256, 261, 263, 266, 269, 273–274, 277–281, 287, 288, 289, 291, 297, 300, 305, 308–309, 313, 320, 337, 340, 352, 363–364, 373, 412–416
Vishnu (Viṣṇu), 16–19, 35
Volcano(es), 388–389
Vulcan (Lord of first Ray), 17–18, 20, 23, 29, 42, 50, 68–69, 95–96, 190, 193, 210, 389, 428–430
Vyāna, 400

## W

Wheel(s), 13, 48, 63–64, 84, 86, 98, 104–106, 113. *See also* Zodiac
  of Life, 63, 67
  of the Law, 102, 108
  Reversed, 7, 96, 105, 115, 386
Will, 28–29, 33, 55, 61, 84, 96, 378, 381–382. *See also* Logos/Logoi(c), Will
  -to-Be, 60
  -to-Good, 52, 57
Wisdom, 27–28, 33–35, 37, 70, 75. *See also* Love-Wisdom
Witchcraft, 249, 260, 277, 281, 283, 284. *See also* Dark Brotherhood
Womb, 66, 89, 92, 97, 112, 242, 297, 326, 345, 350, 356, 362, 364–365, 367, 369, 371–372
Word, 51, 176
  of God, 35, 65, 129, 148
World egg, 66, 386
Wrathful Deities, 306

## Y

Yogin(is), 41, 399, 407–410, 425
Yoni, 413

## Z

Zachariel, 27
Zeus, 17
Zodiac, 59, 70, 105, 233–302, 320–321
  Reversed/Reversal, 46, 67, 69, 79, 82, 84, 86, 94, 104–105

# About the Author

BODO BALSYS is the founder of The School of Esoteric Sciences. He is an author of many books on subjects centred on Buddhism and the Esoteric Sciences, a meditation teacher, poet, artist, spiritual scientist and healer. He has studied extensively across multiple traditions including Esoteric Science, Buddhism, Christianity, Esoteric Healing, Western Science, Art, Politics and History. His advanced esoteric insights, gained through decades of meditative contemplation, enable him to provide a rich understanding of the spiritual pathway toward enlightenment, healing and service.

Bodo's teachings can be accessed via the School of Esoteric Science's website: https://universaldharma.com

For any other enquiries, please email
sangha@universaldharma.com

# About Universal Dharma Publishing

Universal Dharma Publishing is a not for profit publisher. Our aim is make innovative, original and esoteric spiritual teachings accessible to all who genuinely aspire to awaken and serve humanity. The books published aim in part to provide an esoteric interpretation of the meaning of Buddhist dharma with view of reformation of the way people perceive the meaning of the related teachings. Hopefully then Buddhism can more effectively serve its principal function as a vehicle for enlightenment, and further prosper into the future. A further aim is to provide the next level of exposition of the esoteric doctrines to be revealed to humanity following on the wisdom tradition pioneered by H.P. Blavatsky and A.A. Bailey.

www.ingramcontent.com/pod-product-compliance
Lightning Source LLC
Chambersburg PA
CBHW080120020526
44112CB00037B/2815
* 9 7 8 0 6 4 8 7 8 7 7 3 0 *